The Cinema
of Québec

The Cinema of Québec

Masters in Their Own House

Janis L. Pallister

Madison • Teaneck
Fairleigh Dickinson University Press
London: Associated University Presses

Associated University Presses
440 Forsgate Drive
Cranbury, NJ 08512

Associated University Presses
25 Sicilian Avenue
London WC1A 2QH, England

Associated University Presses
P.O. Box 338, Port Credit
Mississauga, Ontario
Canada L5G 4L8

The paper used in this publication meets the requirements
of the American National Standard for Permanence of Paper
for Printed Library Materials Z39.48-1984.

Library of Congress Cataloging-in-Publication Data

Pallister, Janis L.
    The cinema of Québec: masters in their own house/Janis L.
Pallister.
        p.   cm.
    Includes bibliographical references and index.
    ISBN 0-8386-3562-8 (alk. paper)
    1. Motion pictures — Québec (Province)   I. Title.
PN1993.5.C2P27   1995
791.43'09714 — dc20   94-43507
                                                                                            CIP

Printed in the United States of America

For Edith, Fanny, and Alice Buss

who still send sinuous laces and embroideries
forth from their dark shuttles, hoops,
and hooks.

and for Bea, too,

whom we loved.

Ma pensée est couleur de lumières lointaines
Du fond de quelque crypte aux vagues profondeurs.
  [My thought is the color of distant lights
  Issuing from the bottom of some crypt with shadowy depths.]
                                    —Nelligan (Sylvestre, 78)

"For me, the cinema is not just pictures. It is something great, mysterious, and sublime, for which one should not spare any effort and for which one should not fail to risk one's life if the need arise."

                            —Abel Gance (in Sinyard, 150)

Contents

Acknowledgments

This book was written with a Canadian Embassy Canadian Government Fellowship and a travel grant from the National Endowment for the Humanities. The author wishes to thank Dr. Ramona Cormier, Dr. Henry Garrity, Dr. Emile Talbot, Dr. Tom Conley, Dr. Lenita Locey, and Margaret Lanoue and others of the Canadian Film Distribution Center at SUNY (Plattsburgh). Profound appreciation is also extended to Cinémathèque Québecoise for stills, to the Bibliothèque de l'Université Laval for use of its collections; and to the National Film Board Center for information and for stills. To Dr. Joseph Donohoe (Michigan State University), my gratitude for permission to reproduce my essay on Léa Pool, and to Professor Bradley Hayden (Western Michigan University), who first published my essay on *Le Déclin* ..., sections of which appear in this book. Finally, to Bowling Green State University, and especially to its Department of Romance Languages, for significant material support of this study.

The Cinema
of Québec

1

Introduction and Orientation

La Petite Aurore

Il y a certainement quelqu'un
Qui m'a tuée
Puis s'en est allé
Sur la pointe des pieds ...
(Certainly someone is there who killed
   me and then went away on tiptoe ...)
               —Anne Hébert

Although there are already a few books about the *québécois* film
on the market, there is no recent study in English that accomplishes
the objectives I have in mind in writing this book. These are to
study the history and aesthetics of this particular cinematic field
from the perspective of an American, in a positive, albeit selective
light.

Almost consistently, the American critics, and often the Canadian
critics themselves, have been unsympathetic toward even the greatest
of *québécois* films, *Les Bons Débarras* being a good case in point. I
want to suggest some reasons why this should be, with an eye
toward obviating subsequent damaging critical biases, which may
well emanate from subconscious prejudices. Moreover, printed
comments on the differences between the cinematic art of the two
countries tend to be superficial and even nonsensical (e.g. Gerald
Pratley[1]); therefore, I would wish to draw some reasoned comparisons from time to time.

This book will, then, have a triple purpose: to function as a
hermeneutic exercise, to provide correctives, and to serve as the
first large-scale historical and critical introduction to the Québec
cinema ever offered in English. It is my intention to deal with all
three of these rubrics at once. In so doing, I shall speak briefly of

3

some films, and at length of others that the reader should consider
as prototypical.

Where does the English-speaking film buff go to find valid and
useful commentary on Québec film? A leading question, for the
field is more often than not severely underrated, especially by
Americans. For example, *The (Toledo) Blade* listed *Les Bons
Débarras* as a two-star film; Leonard Maltin seldom even deals
with *québécois* films, but of *Les Bons Débarras*, to which he
awards 2½ stars, he says, "Cogent but overlong and repetitious
drama about growing up, aided by a strong performance from
Tifo." In his 1991 guide, exactly the same appreciation follows a
brief statement about the plot.[2] Steven H. Scheuer's *Movies on
TV, 1986–7*, does not even mention the film. Who would bother
to watch this film under such guidance?

But, as if this were not bad enough, even among the Canadians
themselves one finds a tendency to undervalue Canadian film products. In *Canada Today/Canada Aujourd'hui* (published by the
Canadian Embassy) we find the following commentary regarding
the film industry in Québec from the 70s forward: "The censorship
that had afflicted the film industry for so long was lifted, and today
there are fewer restrictions on films shown in Quebec than anywhere
else in North America .... Particularly in Montreal, Québec's
urban heartland, with its cosmopolitan cluster of two million people
and its important English-speaking minority, the cultural diversity
is almost without parallel: American films are shown there at the
same time they appear in New York ... and French and European
films at the same time they are shown in Paris ...." Now, unless
we turn to another part of this same pamphlet, where there is a
brief discussion of "Canada's Young and Diversified Film Industry,"
in which Richard Gay mentions a few of the most recent of Québec
films (Denys Arcand's *Déclin* ...; his *Jésus de Montréal*; his earlier
Québec: Duplessis et après; Francis Mankiewicz's *Portes tournantes*
[not *Les Bons Débarras*!]; Léa Pool's *A corps perdu*, or *Straight to
the Heart*; Jacques Godbout's *Alias Will James*; the producer Rock
Demers's *Contes pour tous*; and Frédéric Back's *Crac*, as well as his
more recent *Homme qui plantait des arbres*)[3], such a description of
the movie scene as this pamphlet gives leaves the reader supposing
that there is no such thing actually being shown in Montréal as a
Canadian, much less a *québécois*, cinema in its own right.

For the American film critics, and apparently even for the French
critics, the Canadian, and more specifically the *québécois*, film is,
then, almost nonexistent. One will look in vain through most

"Histories" of film and through most encyclopedias and dictionaries of film for directors, actors, and titles of films from Québec. No such information can be found, for example, in Ephraim Katz's *The Film Encyclopedia*. And until recent times Québec film was seldom reviewed in journals, with the exception of such thorough-going periodicals as *Variety*. In Georges Sadoul's *Dictionnaire des cinéastes*[4] one finds only the most famous, the most commercially successful "Canadian" directors listed. Denys Arcand, Michel Brault, Gilles Carle, etc., are given their due; but none of the great women directors is to be found (no Léa Pool, no Mireille Dansereau, no Anne Claire Poirier). But then, neither are such European directors as Nelly Kaplan or Diane Kurys.

In the September 1990 issue of *Séquences* we read an explanation for the Americans' general neglect, on a distribution level, at least: Here Gilles Carle is quoted as saying: "Il faut dénoncer notre situation avec les Etats-Unis, car on y constate des quotas cachés. Ils n'acceptent pas des films sous-titrés, des films doublés. Alors vous êtes classé 'éthnie.' [One must denounce our situation with the U.S., for they establish hidden quotas there. They do not accept subtitled or dubbed films. So you are classified as ethnic.]."[5]

But the matter is somewhat more complex. In many cases the dubbing or the subtitling is poorly done. And besides, *most* (but not all) Americans are disinclined toward foreign films in foreign languages portraying foreign cultures; one might accuse them of the same insularity so often attributed to Quebeckers, in fact. Then, too, American films are made on huge budgets, and therefore tend to achieve a higher technical quality than the Canadians have up till now been able to achieve. The actual shooting for *Jacques et Novembre*, for instance, cost only $13,000 and the total budget, which the codirectors begged, borrowed, and "stole" from all conceivable sources, was only $225,000.[6] The beginning budget was $50,000.00.[7] *Bethune*, a rather recent anglophone production, is said to be the most expensive Canadian film ever made, at a cost of between $15,000,000 and $17,000,000 — hardly an unusual budget for an American film. These financial matters will often have an effect upon the technical quality of the film, and will therefore have an impact ultimately upon the aesthetic pleasure that an American, geared to the slick commercial films of his/her country, might derive from the viewing.

On a deeper level, there may well be a profound difference of taste, determined by cultural divergencies. Until recent times, with *Pouvoir intime*, *Un Zoo la nuit*, etc., rapid action and extreme violence were usually either lacking in the *québécois* film, or else

violence was very much understated. Then, too, the films from
Québec are often long and move very slowly; hence, Maltin's 1991
guide will write of *Les Bons Débarras*, as cited above, "Cogent but
overlong and repetitious drama ...." In fact, this body of film is
more like that of the French: it is inclined toward more introspection,
toward a more leisurely examination of psychological states and
relationships than is the case with most American films. Of course,
I am generalizing; there are notable exceptions to this sweeping
claim. But I would submit that something of what Joseph M.
Boggs has to say about the film as regards speed, or editing rhythm
(i.e., that Italian films average about fifteen seconds per running
shot, whereas American films average about five seconds per shot)[8]
would apply to the films of Québec, and for that matter to many
anglophone Canadian films as well. This difference of pacing is in
part cultural; but whatever the reason for the difference, the risk in
presenting a slow-moving film to the average American moviegoer
is, as Boggs says, that he/she is apt to become "terminally bored."

Sometimes, too, the setting may seem too "exotic," although
this should be a plus. The "Northern" nature of the "True North"—
the vastness of snowy expanses, and the like—may not seem
urbane, or cosmopolitan enough. (Even in an urban film like *La
Vie heureuse de Léopold Z.* the principal impression one may
be left with is the enormity of the problem of snow removal in
Montréal.) The candidacy of Québec for an "exotic" site may seem
peculiar to the sociologist or to the anthropologist. But its foreign
language, its Catholicism, its differences in matters of architecture
and cuisine, etc., make it almost as "foreign" to the average
American as is Mexico; the American just does not realize this.
It is no accident that the recent American film *Agnes of God*
(1985; 98 min.) was situated and filmed in Québec. Of course, John
Pielmeier's play preceded the film, and, of course, Norman Jewison is
an "expatriated" Canadian director. But in addition, and even
though the story is in large part a true one—something quite
similar happened not too many years ago to a nun living in the
Eastern part of the U.S., and was reported at length in *Ms.
Magazine*—, Québec is, sad to say, and as Jewison no doubt
surmised when he chose Montréal for its setting, seemingly a much
more believable site for a story about half-mad, hysterical nuns.[9]
And, too, Gratien Gélinas, whom we will encounter as an actor in
Les Tisserands du pouvoir and elsewhere, added to the foreign feel
of this curious film. This notion of exoticism is no doubt maintained
by distributors who by and large do not present films to Americans
when they think there is only limited interest.

Can it be, too, that there is often an unfortunate casting of prime Canadian stars in inferior films and in inferior roles? Marilyn Lightstone — who plays the mother in *Bonheur d'occasion* (or, *The Tin Flute*) — makes a dubious appearance along with Carole Laure (the star of the recent *Maria Chapdelaine*) in a very ugly film by Don Carmody, entitled *The Surrogate* (1984), a film that has aired and still airs on the premium channels of American television, and one that, incidentally, gets the same rating in Maltin's 1991 guide as does *Les Bons Débarras*! Geneviève Bujold, the star of *Anne of a Thousand Days* (d. Charles Jarrott, 1969), and of her husband Paul Almond's *Isabel*, as well as of Claude Jutra's *Kamouraska* (1973), was introduced to the world in René Bonnière's *Amanita Pestilens*, a 1963 film about the destruction of a family through its effort to achieve materialistic perfection (Pratley *TS* 1987, 176–7). Despite her many successes, she has had some very questionable roles, including one in the gruesome if well-rated Michael Crichton film *Coma* (1978). Less well regarded — and with reason — is the film *Un Autre Homme, une autre chance*, or *Another Man Another Chance*, a Western that she made in 1977 with Claude Lelouch, the French director born in Oran. Still, her performance in *Dead Ringers* redeemed her from the one in *Coma*, and perhaps the role in *Coma* even led to her being cast in the Cronenberg masterpiece. And her performance as Claire in Michel Brault's 1990 *Noces de papier* — Québec's version of Peter Weir's *Green Card* (also 1990) — was quite competent.

Those are some examples of casting problems; good, bad, and indifferent scripts seem to be on par when it comes to allocating roles to Canadian stars. (Donald Sutherland can be a similar example in the anglophone domain.) Add to this the fact that Canadian pride is sometimes counterpoised by an apparent inferiority complex: Pratley's work is significantly entitled "*Torn Sprockets*": i.e., something is missing or blemished. (He probably means sprocket-holes; but in any case he dwells upon the imperfections of the Canadian film industry. See, e.g., *TS* 1987, 145–50 ss.)

Leaving aside such celebrities as Geneviève Bujold or Carole Laure, the American is also unaware of the rich store of French-Canadian actors, so well known to any Québécois. (Incidentally, a French professor recently confessed to me believing that Bujold was French.) A sort of star system, in place in Québec — but probably not in the rest of Canada — , makes possible the seeing of Rémy Girard in three different places in one month: In the fall of 1989 he could be seen in one month in *Jésus de Montréal*, on stage in Robert Lepage's production of *Galileo*, and on the program *Un*

Signe de feu. But is that star system strong enough so that *foreign* awareness of Québec film is clearly growing? Not really, it seems; not even in France, where, in literature, at least, Marie Claire Blais's *Une Saison dans la vie d'Emmanuel* is considered more "*québécois*" than Hubert Aquin's stylish *Prochain épisode*, the latter being thought too "French." This lack of knowledge or appreciation can be proved out: after a reasonably careful reading, I find that Sadoul's *Dictionnaire des films*[10] — although it chooses 1300 films to figure in "a panorama of world cinema since its origins" — manages to list from French Canada only Pierre Perrault's *Pour la suite du monde* (w. Michel Brault, 1963), his *Voitures d'eau* (1969), his *L'Acadie, l'Acadie* (1972), his *Bête lumineuse* (1982), and nothing from anglophone Canada. (The bibliography suggests that Breton used only Houle's 1978 *Dictionnaire*[11] for all of Canada.)

So American (and sometimes even Canadian) film buffs and critics tend to belittle the *québécois* cinema; and unless the customer knows where to go, in many Canadian/Québec video stores it is quite difficult to rent even recent *québécois* films, let alone any classics. Rather, the stores are glutted with American films dubbed in French, and this may well reflect the tastes and preferences of the general Québec public itself. (Some Canadian professors have told me in person that it is difficult to interest their young students in Québec/Acadian literature and film.) Meanwhile, in the typical American video store, the accessibility to films from Québec — or, for that matter, any Canadian films — is even more restricted. Leaving aside films that are not even recognized to be Canadian (such as *Meatballs* or *Porky's*), *Le Déclin de l'empire américain*, *Jésus de Montréal*, *Pouvoir intime*, and *I've Heard the Mermaids Singing* may just about do it. Add to this the confusions with mainstream producers that often occur, so that in Tamarelle's 1990 catalogue of foreign films, *Pouvoir intime* was said to come from France and *The Grey Fox* from the U.S.A. The spelling of the word gray should alone tell us something different.

Then, when Canadian film *is* mentioned in print, it is more often than not the anglophone works that are stressed. A case in point is an article in the *Detroit Free Press* entitled "Study Thy Neighbor,"[12] which suggests five films that offer an "introduction to our northern neighbors" — two of which are about the Jewish community, while one is from francophone Québec. That one is *The Decline of the American Empire* (1986), said to show "sex styles of the bourgeois and academic, set in a summer house near Montreal." Yet, when in 1984 a survey of roughly one hundred international film critics and academics (80% Canadian, the remainder U.S. and European critics) was conducted, and that group selected the top twenty-seven films ever made in Canada, the best ever was deemed to be (francophone) *québécois* (*Mon oncle Antoine*), while of the ten top films, six were *québécois*, and of the twenty-seven, fourteen were *québécois*. Notably, several of the anglophone films in the list were also from Québec.[13] From this it would appear that, at least from the perspective of the critic, the Québécois produce more superior films than do the anglophone Canadians.

Nonetheless, a glance at the bibliography at the end of this book will show to the reader the quantity of books and articles that have been written by Canadians, mostly francophone, in the past decade. And although the present study may well be the first book-length treatment of the *québécois* film in English and by an American, certain breakthroughs are occurring in the American press, as is witnessed rather strikingly in a short article on *Jésus de Montréal* found in the *Christian Science Monitor*, an article notable not only for its very presence, but also for its praise, — despite reservations —, and, above all, for its conclusion that points out that the film "deserves credit for moments of great visual beauty, and for being one of the rare recent films with something more than simple comedy or melodrama on its mind. It's also a reminder that Canada has a thriving film industry, capable of turning out movies with a flavor unlike anything Hollywood normally gives us."[14] Even more remarkably, in David Robinson/Ann Lloyd's *Illustrated History of the Cinema* we read that "Québec cinema remains the most original and stimulating in North America today"[15] (and this was written in 1986 — even before *Le Déclin* ..., before *Les Bons Débarras*, before *Jésus de Montréal*, etc.!). Such an assessment hopefully heralds a new approach to the *québécois* cinema, which has traditionally had more content than has been generally recognized. Let us hope so; let us also hope that this book will serve to expedite a new approach.

So, in fact, that disrespect in which *québécois* film has historically been held by Americans may well be disappearing. I note that several museums around the U.S. have mounted festivals devoted to Québec's contemporary film. And two recent films of Arcand — *Le Déclin de l'empire américain* and *Jésus de Montréal* — have been widely shown in the U.S., and have received considerable attention; both have been nominated for the Academy Award for best foreign film, and though they did not make it, one day soon a *québécois* film seems bound to receive this award, if indeed to receive this award is a needed ratification. More and more, Arcand's films, and others, are reviewed in the American journals and newspapers (e.g., *The New York Times* and *The Christian Science Monitor*). And in Robinson/Lloyd we find a three and a half page passage devoted to the Canadian film, most of it dealing with Québec filmmakers.

Better marketing of the Arcand products may explain their American reception, although — to dip into the 1989 *québécois* offerings — , upon occasion it is a (Mapplethorpe-like) controversy about title and content that causes the film to be noticed. Such is the case, for example, with *Comment faire l'amour avec un Nègre sans se fatiguer* or *How to Make Love to a Negro without Getting Tired*, produced by Richard Sadler and directed by Jacques Wilbrod Benoît.[16] A "self-assigned media watchdog coalition [in Los Angeles] called for a boycott of this Montréal-based film," Julia Nunes writes.[17] Sadler contends in this same article that the humor of the film, which has many black actors, completely escaped the coalition's president; but the title was shortened to "*How to make love*" after complaints rolled in. Although a boycott of the film was called for in Los Angeles, the theaters did not respond. *Variety* wrote: "The small foreign film made almost as much of a media splash in New York as *Another 48 Hours*, even though its budget would hardly cover the fast food bill of Eddie Murphy's entourage." (Quoted by Nunes, who claims the film cost $3,000,000.)

One of the major purposes for writing this book is, then, to point up to American film lovers the large body of good to excellent movies they remain unaware of or unappreciative of. Of course, a film worthy of a viewer's time (and even many that are not necessarily excellent) stands as a key to the culture from which it originated. It can, and often does, convey both to the native and to the foreign viewer the socio-political structures of the society it is portraying. Films following the War Powers Act in Québec are obvious examples of this (e.g., *Les Ordres*); less obvious but just as revealing are the socio-political subtexts of films such as *Tit-Coq*, or *Mon oncle Antoine*, or *Le Déclin de l'empire américain*. Any and all of them will show to us things about *québécois* society we may never have realized existed: we will see the conflict between English- and French-speaking Canada; portraits of the family and its collapse; scenes that evoke the old agricultural values of the *habitant* and the fisherman; films that are concerned with women's issues, and other motifs. We will devote some attention to those aspects of *québécois* cinema. But beyond this, a good film is at once entertaining and aesthetically satisfying. A film deals with icons, to be sure; but it often captures, too, the sonic characteristics prevalent in a certain locality. In other words, a film is at once art and artifact. Therefore, as I go along I will be considering the cultural load, together with the visual beauties of certain films and the "universal" charge of the content.

One may not be able to easily distinguish, to mediate between film as cultural product and film as aesthetic, all human, universal product (between the Hegelian notion of the particular and the "general," as we might say). That is, I will be concerned here with what in various films is the ethnic (local, temporal), which presents a half-truth; and also with the elementary, or what in the film may present the eternal, general, or universal truth. Perhaps, in the final analysis, this is a needless distinction anyway. I will be concerned, too, with offering an acceptable interpretation of the given film, for interpretation is a necessary role of the informed viewer, and more often than not is a political act, willy-nilly. Film, like modern literature, is often polysemic, as its interpretation must then also be. (Postmodern issues are, of course, at stake here.) As regards the problem of novel to film, I believe that such polysemic interpretation as I just mentioned may sometimes result in a state of isotropy between a piece of literature and its film; but I hold firmly to the conviction that a good film is usually iconic: i.e., it uses images rather than words to convey its narrative. Who, then, is the storyteller and to whom is the story told?

For all this, I will not withhold exegetic commentary on themes, as well. And these recurrent themes may well be the most interesting material of my book for some readers: the Québécois as "true northerners"; Québec mythologies of hunting, and fishing; the Québécois as xenophobes; the absence of the father — and nowadays the mother; Canada as a place of salvation versus America as a place of corruption; the feminist movement in Québec; and so forth. This thematic material will be found woven into my text. As concerns Québec history (the Québécois in search of their roots), that too is a theme; but does the American reader know the history of Québec and of Canada? For the less initiated I have provided a short historical tableau (Appendix A).

Now, whatever the critical regard for Canadian film, both at home and abroad, we undertake this examination at a precarious moment in Canadian history. The Meech Lake Accord has failed (July 1990; see my App. A, under 1987), leaving the province of Québec dangling, and its language and culture still undefined and unprotected in the larger context of anglophone Canadian life. The situation raises many questions in one's mind. What will Canada be in a decade? Will Québec really achieve the state of sovereignty association it continually threatens, and even announces on political billboards slightly east of Montréal? Will Canada undergo the economic and cultural disasters predicted on Thursday, 31 May 1990? Marie-Josée Drouin, one of Canada's leading economists, stated then: "We could become irrelevant on the world field." ("In Search of Ourselves," on *The Journal*; CBC.) This intellectual and financial failure, often expressed by the Canadian intelligentsia, would of necessity embrace the collapse of an already underfunded cinematic field, one already perceived by many film critics to be irrelevant, if their silence on the subject, and if their underrating of the Canadian cinema can be taken as proof. More specifically, Québec, after all, is now not manifesting a post–revolutionary, post–referendum syndrome, but, rather, a post–Meech Lake Accord syndrome. Now more than ever it is drawn in upon itself to reconsider once again — as a result of Bourassa's wide-ranging commission, whose report (the Allaire report), given in February 1990, called for a great deal of power to be taken away from the federal government, and leaving separation from, or a possible "sovereignty association" with, the rest of Canada as a seeming inevitability. This is a political arrangement Québec has always ultimately feared; yet a new referendum, this time under Parizeau, and clearly on separation, is on the horizon. Nevertheless, it is an arrangement that is, as Heinz Weinmann[18] has suggested, fundamentally a contradiction in terms. It is a schizophrenic concept; but schizophrenia is somewhat implied by the curious bicultural, bilingual nature of Canada, by which remark I do not mean to overlook the reality of its *many* ethnicities and its resulting poly-cultural nature, frequently reflected in its films. But the stressful conflict between anglophone Canada and francophone Québec is long-standing and endemic; it is the major source of "racial" strife, as such a book as Pierre Vallières's *Les Nègres blancs d'Amérique* might attest.[19] The major source, but surely not the only one. As immigrants continue to flow into Canada, new conflicts arise; besides there are the permanent and presently exacerbated grievances of native peoples, such as the Mohawk branch of the Iroquois, who gave the whole of Canada, but especially the Québécois — who did little worrying about them in the Meech Lake Accord battle — a run for their money in the summer of 1990.

   In the long run I think this doomsday prediction of irrelevancy to the rest of the world is not or will not be the case, and it is therefore exactly that "universal" quality beyond the provincial content — a quality that has been present in recent *québécois* film, and that I expect to be present in forthcoming films — that I seek to isolate in the coming pages.

Historical Background: Some Archaeomorphs

The reader who is particularly interested in early manifestations of the cinema industry in Québec may find an excellent outline in English in David Clanfield (Ch. I: "From Origins to Grierson: 1896–1939").[20] The deeply interested, who have the skill of reading French, should make use of all works of history by Pierre Véronneau as well, and, in particular, his history of Québec cinema, recently published in three volumes.[21] Here, however, we shall, for the most part, recapitulate the work of Clanfield (1987, Ch. I) and Lever (*Hist.* 1988) on this subject, while bearing in mind that the ability to view these early efforts would probably require a trip on the part of the viewer to Ottawa, where the National Film Archives are found, or else to Cinémathèque in Montréal (or, for Tessier, the Cinémathèque in Trois-Rivières). A few clips can be appreciated in the videos *Has Anybody Here Seen Canada?* and *Dreamland.* Another documentary on the Canadian film that contains clips of films long since out of circulation is called *Cinéma Cinéma*, and is directed by Gilles Carle and Werner Nold. It classifies and tells the history of the French team at the Office National du Film (ONF) or, in English, the National Film Board (NFB), during its first twenty-five years. This is, of course, the government bureau that supports the Canadian film industry. It has been in existence for many years — in fact, since 1941, when the old Motion Picture Bureau became the Film Board, under the directorship of John Grierson. The headquarters were transferred from Ottawa to Montréal, a move planned by Arthur Irwin and completed in 1956 under Irwin's successor Albert Trueman. The intention was to show Canada to Canadians and to the rest of the world; but, as can be seen, it had precedents, and these are discussed by Clanfield. (See also the article on the National Film Board of Canada in *The Canadian Encyclopedia*, 3:1429.) Obviously, a film industry supported by its federal and/or provincial government has at once advantages and drawbacks, the latter often being in the form of interference if not outright censorship. I will cite some examples of this in my study.

According to Clanfield, the first film ever shown in Canada was on 27 June 1896; it was a demonstration of the famous French

Lumière brothers' Cinématographe, a combined camera-projector. (Lever [*Hist.* 1988] accords with this projection in Montréal.)[22] Throughout the early phases of film activity in Québec, films from France, and then from the United States, were shown, the latter often without any regard for a need for French intertitles. Among the films shown were Méliès's *Cauchemar* (1897), *Le Château hanté* (1897), *Jeanne d'Arc* (1900), *Le Voyage dans la lune* (1902); and works from Pathé, such as *Histoire d'un crime* (F. Zecca, 1901), *Les Victimes de l'alcoolisme* (F. Zecca, 1902); and, from America, *Life of an American Fireman* (E. S. Porter, 1903), and *The Great Train Robbery* (E. S. Porter, 1903).

One of the first persons from France to present film to the French Canadians was the Countess Marie Tréourret de Kerstrat (1841–1920), a Breton who, between 1897 and 1906, showed hundreds of films as she travelled about the province, usually assisted by her son, the Vicomte Henry de Grandsaignes d'Hauterives (1869–1929), projectionist and "bonimenteur" of the Historiographe, as they called their particular projector. The historical and religious nature of the films they showed (*La Passion; Epopée napoléonienne*) met with the approval of the clergy, so that, for the time being, cinema was allowed in the schools. Since the films were silent, the vicomte frequently provided the commentary.

The odyssey of this curious pair took them into rural Québec as well as into the cities, then to the Bermudas, and then to the U.S.A. Since they were nobles, they were really not interested in delivering to the needs of the bourgeoisie. But along the line the Québécois did see some American materials as well (*La Case de l'oncle Tom*; and *La Luciole* and *Le Baptême du Bébé* by Merrit and Pritchard).

As entertainment pure and simple, the French Canadians demonstrated a great taste for this new piece of magic, and many silents were shown in such places as Sohmer Parc.[23] But it was not so long before permanent theaters were installed for the purpose of viewing these films, and the name Léo-Ernest Ouimet (1877–1972) is especially connected with these theaters. He opened his first Ouimetoscope in 1906 (*Dreamland* says 1903!), and a few months later showed, with great financial success, *La Vie et la passion de Jésus-Christ*. In 1906 he showed *The San Francisco Earthquake*; *Lutte japonaise pratique*; *Chasse au forçat*; *Le Coffret du rajah*. In 1907 he built a luxurious 1200 seat "Ouimetoscope" in Montréal—the most luxurious in North America; and it was for francophones! Ouimet bought films in New York and translated the intertitles himself; he made his own newsreels and became the exclusive Canadian importer of Pathé. Indeed, as early as 1907 he realized the interest his public had in local "vues," and so he bought a camera and began to make his own works. He showed his first film, which was about a footrace, on 17 November 1906, and a week later he filmed *Une Scène d'intérieur*. He continued to expand his empire through the next several years.

Indeed, movies were a profitable commerce in the first decade of this century, profitable to the native Montréalais. So when Grand-saignes d'Hauterives got off the New York–Montréal train for the last time, in April, 1908, the young electrician who had worked for him in Sohmer Parc a few years earlier had by then become a millionaire. For a week, the vicomte showed *La Passion*, *Guerre au Maroc*; *Grand Steeple-Chase*; *Semaine sainte à Séville*. He then went back to New York. In *Le Canada* (18 April 1908) one read: "Holy Week being practically over, M. le vicomte d'Hauterives will, after this evening, stop showing us, in the form of artistic tableaus, the unforgettable scenes of *The Passion of Christ*. Each thing has its season."[24]

Ouimet went bankrupt in 1922.

At first film was seen as a possible vehicle for portraying (and preserving) traditions and values of Québec. In this respect, both the Church and the government saw film as a propaganda tool (and sometimes as a danger to Catholic morals). For quite some time the Church and the government (the Assemblée nationale of Québec and sometimes the federal bureaus in Ottawa, as well) worked hand in hand to control this powerful new medium; for three decades there ensued a ferocious struggle between the Québec clergy and the film industry (Lever *Hist.* 1988, 31). In some ways Monsignor Paul Bruchesi, Ouimet's worst enemy, literally led the clerical opposition, giving an order on the sanctity of Sunday, founded on the law of 1906, that forbade commercial transactions on Sundays. Indeed, back in 1899 the Bishop of Sainte-Hyacinthe had formulated a similar interdiction. In 1908, the city of Montréal passed a law forbidding Sunday screenings; the film industry fought this law and won, but they had great difficulty recovering from the blow. As Lever points out (*Hist.* 1988, 62), the Church's attitude toward cinema was little more than a transferral of suspicion in which theater was held for centuries. But its main goal was to "keep the Sabbath holy." Whether or not Pius XI's 1936 Encyclical, *Vigilanti Cura* (bearing only on cinema and concluding that whether cinema was good or bad depended on the use made of it), really ended the thirty–year war waged by the Québec clergy on the cinema, as Lever contends (*Hist.* 1988, 62), is truly moot. One can find lingering evidence of this effort at control well beyond 1936.

As with other aspects of life, such as birth control, these prohibitions and dictates weighed upon the populace until the upheavals of the Quiet Revolution, at which time Quebeckers left the institutional Church in droves—and, dare I say?—went instead to the movies.

The Catholic clergy, then, allied itself to the governmental legislation (and perhaps at times forced this legislation), for the cinema was regarded as a corrupting and denationalizing force. The struggle in particular was against the American cinema, as a destabilizing power and as a robber baron, too; for American companies— including the Famous Players Canadian, Corporation Limited, a filial of the American Famous Players (established in 1920 and ultimately owned by Gulf and Western, together with Paramount)— had a virtual monopoly on the Canadian market, which they could sustain to a considerable extent until the talkies appeared. Very rarely did these American silents—featuring Charlie Chaplin, Buster Keaton, Douglas Fairbanks (Zorro), Mary Pickford, Rudolph Valentino—offer bilingual intertitles, and even more rarely were they in French alone.

With the advent of talkies,[25] however, the American monopoly of *québécois* film audiences was seriously threatened. Thus, the francophone field, which had remained rather wide open until around 1929–31, was more amply addressed when Robert Hurel, another Frenchman, established his Compagnie cinématographique canadienne (CCC) in 1929 and Les Films des Editions Edouard Garand in 1931—both of which were merged in 1932 to become France–Film. Intending to market the French talkies, with films from France, and also with dubbed films, Hurel, along with Joseph Alexandre De Sève, formed a new monopoly that played on the nationalist agenda and on the campaigns being mounted for "speaking French well."

Hurel dominated the francophone film distribution for two decades. But meanwhile, De Sève had bought the Théâtre Saint– Denis, seized hold of France–Film, renamed it Franco–Canada films, and had thus secured the monopoly of the francophone market for himself. He entered into partnership with the Church: his "spiritual adviser" was l'Abbé Aloysius Vachet, who supported the efforts of Hurel and De Sève; for, by now, the clergy wanted moving pictures for their educational mission. In 1946 De Sève built studios on the Côte des Neiges Road in Montréal. He made heavy use of stereotypes in his films, such as rescue from icy waters, clips of which may be seen in *Has Anybody Here Seen Canada*? However, Paul L'Anglais (sometimes written Langlais), who had a much stronger sense of cinema, claimed that De Sève and Vachet were trying to sell Catholic films, and, as far as he was concerned, "you cannot sell Catholic films any more than you can sell Catholic shoes." According to the narration in *Has Anyone Here Seen Canada?*, L'Anglais was "the most ambitious filmmaker since the advent of talkies." His *La Forteresse* (1947; d. by the Russian-born Fédor Ozep), costing three-fourths of a million dollars, was double-shot, first in French, and then in English with the famous stars, Paul Lukas and Helmut Dantine. In English it was called *Whispering City*. Houle finds that the film was very American in style, some of the technicians and other crew members having been brought from Hollywood for the film, and that local atmosphere was provided by the usual standard shots of Québec City and of Montmorency Falls (v. Houle *Dict.* 1978, 221–22). *La Forteresse* failed at the American box office, and L'Anglais blamed this on his inability to control distribution of the English version. L'Anglais's success in Canada, however, is to be attributed to his use of Québec mythology, which is illustrated by such films as *Séraphin*.

Throughout the period of the silents and the early talkies, censorship continued to make its mark on the industry, in Canada at large, and in the province of Québec in particular. Fines were levied as a means of control. Ouimet, for one, had to pay fines for charging admission on Sunday, and other fines as well. As early as 1911 Québec had its first law intended to limit the cinematic product or else the audience. By 1912 it had created a Bureau of Censorship, having the duty to examine films and grant permission or else denial to show. This law became effective in May 1918 and was rewritten in 1928, at which time it was stated that children under sixteen might not attend films unless they were educational in nature; this law remained in effect for thirty-three years. (The laws were in part introduced after the Laurier theater fire, in which seventy-eight children died; but safety was no doubt not the sole motive of the legislators.) We are saying that, for better or for worse, Québécois children of the period had, as a consequence of these laws, a different childhood from that of most other North American children, whose imaginations were then being fed with films by Shirley Temple, with the *Wizard of Oz*, and the animations of Disney.

By now films might be shown on Sundays; but the censors reserved the right to modify or cut the film according to their lights. (Shades of *Cinema paradiso*! And we should also bear in mind that in the United States, the self–imposed Hollywood Hayes code was operative for many years, as well.) These laws were in effect from 1928–67. (Criteria for censorship are the subject of Lever's Appendix I, by the way.) As late as 20 February 1964, we find the diocese of Québec requesting the film industry to observe certain guidelines it lays down. In its *Mémoire du Comité de Civisme et de Moralité Publique au Gouvernement de la Province de Québec* (*proposant "La Régie du Cinéma du Québec"*), criteria for possible suppression of a film include (a) fear and anxiety; (b) violence; (c) crime; (d) ridicule or scorn of religion; (e) under-mining of prestige or authority of parents; (f) impropriety; (g) misrepresentation; (h and i) disrespect of social and civic sense; (j) excitation of sexuality. Unacceptable also are brutality and sadism; delinquency; terror; improper clothing; lascivious kisses; scorn of law, of authority, of morality, and of religion. Just how much the filmmakers paid attention to these guidelines at this late date would be a matter of interest to explore.

Until the local authorities came to a realization of the potential of cinema, both good and bad, there had been a good deal more showing than making (i.e., as Lever says, this is the period of "cinema *in* Québec, rather than cinema *of* Québec"); and even when it came to the showing there was an effort on the part of the authorities to "serve the goal of cultural survival through preser-vation of language, rural values, and traditional Catholic faith" (Clanfield 1987, 2). Thus, as we saw above, the traveling shows mounted by Grandsaignes d'Hauterives and his mother, the Countess Marie-Anne d'Hauterives, and by others, such as, Wilfrid Picard, the churchman Benjamin Paradis, etc., revolved around religious subjects. The d'Hauterives are especially notable; as we saw, they arrived in Montréal as early as November 1897 with a projector and tapes by the Lumière brothers, Méliès and Pathé, and with these works traveled throughout the province. More than others, the countess negotiated with the ecclesiastical powers to "sell her product" (Lever *Hist.* 1988, 28). Picard, another of these traveling salesmen, went all over Québec in all directions, from 1905 on, showing the best films, mostly films on religious subjects or else documentaries. Because he showed materials the clergy could approve of, he was even allowed to post his advertisements on church doors (Lever *Hist.* 1988, 29).

And people, especially the working class, thronged to the movies, as they continued to do throughout the first three or four decades of the century; they had the *désir de cinéma* that can be observed in other countries as well: we have only to read *The Tin Flute (Bonheur d'occasion)* of Gabrielle Roy (and to see the film of it) to become aware of the picture show as a rather novel, or at least important, means of entertainment, a treat a fellow might offer his girlfriend on a date. The film *Cinema paradiso* has most translated this love and even craving as people of that era experienced it, whatever their nationality. (In 1952 the Québécois made 58,761,000 *entrées* into the moving picture shows. If in the following two years there is a marked drop in ticket sales, this is due to the advent of television: by 1956, two-thirds of *québécois* households had screens; by 1962, 90.8%.[26])

It was inevitable that the Québécois people would come to evolve their own film products, given the moral objectives mentioned above, for these conservative Catholic values (almost Jansenistic) were scarcely the concerns of a Méliès or a D. W. Griffith. And no doubt prior to this the first silent films made in Canada were not necessarily *québécois* in nature either, nor did they serve the needs and purposes of the Québécois much better than the French or American products did. One should mention, however, that the first dramatic feature-length film made by Canadians was a story revolving around the 1755 Expulsion of the French Canadians from Acadia, and the subsequent French diaspora. I am speaking of *Evangeline*, of course, a story, or a "drame en images," immortalized — ironically — by an American poet (Longfellow). The movie version was filmed in Halifax, Nova Scotia, in 1913 by the Bioscope Company, established for the very purpose of shooting this film. Nothing remains of this film except a few stills (seen in *Dreamland*).[27] One reads of this film in all historical accounts of Canadian and/or *québécois* film.

As regards *québécois* production, specifically, one must look to the work of Léo-Ernest Ouimet (1877–1972), who, in addition to installing theaters in Québec (discussed above), turned also to the production of newsreels, these being, mostly of great news events of Canada: the Québec Bridge Disaster of 1907, for example, or the Trois-Rivières fire of 1908 (Clanfield 1987, 7). He filmed as well an electoral speech of Sir Wilfrid Laurier, the 1908 visit of the Prince of Wales to Québec for the tricentennial of the founding of that city, the eucharistic Congress of Montréal in 1910 (Houle *Dict.* 1978, 220–21). He also made films of his family from 1906 on. (One was entitled *Mes Espérances.*) The first to produce pictures from Québec, his work constitutes a genre of sorts, which Lever calls "actualités filmées." (One may see a 1908 example of this in *Dreamland.*) Some of his work anticipated the later documentary or "direct cinema" for which Canada became so well known. In 1922 Ouimet went to Hollywood, where he undertook the production of *Why Get Married?*, which came out in Montréal in 1924 at the Loews, but knew only a small amount of local success (Houle *Dict*. 1978, 221). Ouimet, who planned a production of *Maria Chapdelaine*, did not achieve this before the crash of his industry. Houle points out (*Dict*. 1978, 220) that Ouimet had some problems with the archbishop of Montréal regarding Sunday showings; this is of some interest in considering the role the Church (and censorship) played in the history of Québec cinema.

It is perhaps of interest to know, also, that Edison made eighty documentaries in Canada, registered with the Library of Congress in Washington.

Fiction films of specifically Québec production did exist; but of this very early work only three titles survive: they include Frank Crane's *Dollard Des Ormeaux* (or *The Battle of Long Sault*; 1913); and Larente-Homier's *Madeleine de Verchères* (1922), which Lever says is the first full-length fictional feature that might be called fully *québécois* by subject, conditions of production, artisans, and actors; it showed a heroine against the Indians, but, like *Evangeline*, nothing survives except a few stills (to be seen in *Dreamland*). This film — though made by a Québec company — got little distribution. The third film, also by Larente-Homier, was *La Drogue fatale* (1924); of it nothing remains either. Homier's son had to destroy his father's work upon the order of the Fire Bureau, for the film was nitrate-supported. Jean Arsin also produced three fictional films, of which no excerpt or copy remains.

It can be seen, then, that French Canadians did not *make* very many early films; but this did not save the French Canadians from having been manifestly *shown* on the screen, and especially the American screen. In an early film of D. W. Griffith (*A Woman's Way* [1908], a key segment of which is shown in *Dreamland*), we see the French-Canadian male as a sex-starved rapist. And indeed, in British or American cinematic representations of the Québécois, he is always scorned, almost always given a negative image; almost always he is a *coureur des bois*, an adventurer, a woodsman, or a guide. He is stupid, physically strong, a sexual maniac, and a wife-beater. In one of Laurence Olivier's earliest films, we see him in his plaid lumberjack portraying such a stereotype with an extremely ridiculous accent. It is one of his most unfortunate moments.

In Québec, there was growing resentment against these portrayals, especially the American ones. And it is interesting to note the rather long-lasting character of this resentment, for as censorship was introduced into the climate of World War II (which the Canadians participated in well before the Americans), anti-

Americanism was manifested in the fact that the first thing censored in Canada were scenes showing the American flag.

It seems that the Americans were the ones selecting the "icons," even those assumed to signify Canadians. As an ironic illustration of the American invasion into screen depictions of *québécois* culture (as Americans saw it), one might mention that although newsreels of the Dionne quintuplets were made in Canada, all the feature-length fictional portrayals of this world-renowned event were made by Americans. By 1922, *Nanook of the North* (sixty-nine minutes) — a classic and enduring documentary about the Canadian Arctic and the "Eskimo," or Inuit, and one that fed handily into the "myth" of Canada as a country of the "True North" — had been made by the Irish-American documentarian Robert Flaherty, financed by the French Paris-based fur trade company Revillon Frères. (According to Pratley [*TS* 1987, 38], Flaherty made a second version of the film after the first went up in flames in Toronto during the printing.) Though not a *québécois* film, and though still today a stunning piece of documentation or "film poetry" (just recently made available on video, as restored by David H. Shepard) that grippingly portrays the struggle of the "Eskimo" Nanook to survive the rigors of life in the Arctic, I mention it here not so much for the work itself (it is a masterpiece, named in 1989 as a film worthy of historical preservation) as for the fact that the subject and the theme have bearing on my considerations in some parts of this book, and show up the manner in which the Canadians — Québécois or otherwise — were handed an image of themselves and their environment by outsiders. It goes without saying that that image was also handed to the rest of the world, as well. Still later, a film of fiction set in the Canadian Wilderness in the 1670s continued the American trend of showing Canada to Canadians; I am speaking of *Hudson's Bay* (1940), featuring Paul Muni and Gene Tierny.

The name most associated with early Québec talkies is Albert Tessier (1895–1976), who was a historian and also a teacher at the Trois-Rivières Seminary. Over a period of thirty-five years, he is said to have made more than seventy films. Much if not most of his work celebrates in an early cinéma-vérité style those cultural characteristics we have already mentioned: the life of simple "farm people, child-rearing, spiritual values, and history, as the Church saw them" (Clanfield 1987, 16). Tessier used a single projector and no tripod; he wrote his own intertitles and worked at his own expense. Lever writes that for Father Tessier cinema was above all a means of exposing the beauty of the world and communicating values. He was a nationalist with a respect for the language, for the grandeur of peasant life, and for the discipline of well-done work. He stressed the importance of school, the wisdom of old people, etc. Tessier had made photographs as early as 1913 with his Brownie camera, and had done his first films on La Mauricie in 1925, followed by several films between 1927 and 1937, so that by 1939 he was a member of the "Committee of Initiative and of Censorship," having been nominated by the "Catholic Committee of the Council on Public Instruction, for the Formation of a Catholic Student 'Cinéthèque'." He was that committed to film as an instructional tool, and known to be so committed that early in his life.

René Bouchard has done the most important studies on Tessier.[28] His two-part article in *Cinéma Québec* portrays Tessier as one of the greatest precursors of Québec cinema, and, in particular, of the "direct" style that we will be encountering repeatedly throughout this study. We see Tessier as an artist, with his Eastman model K, his Bolex, and his Leica (which he facetiously called his "Leica Pectoral," referring to the pectoral cross worn by priests of certain orders) doing his editing in the long winter months, but we also see him as a humanist and a priest, concerned about the humiliations of the peasantry. We also see him as the first filmmaker-lecturer of Québec. Above all, both in Bouchard's writings, as in Tessier's interview with Bouchard (Part II of the article), we learn that Tessier's aim was always to bring out the beauty of the environs (especially with the films he made on the St. Maurice river and its forests — a region he himself named La Mauricie in 1934); to teach through image; to acquaint people with that beauty; to make them understand; and to glorify the (joyous) work ethic. Tessier states that he had the greatest pleasure in making his *Hommage à la paysannerie*, and that he suffered to see peasants treated as thick-headed and ignorant, and to see them disdained by city dwellers who were probably only once removed from the peasantry themselves. He recognizes, too, that while his first films about nature and the peasantry — which he did not intend to be polemical but merely a defense of the peasantry — and his films about the family (*Don Bosco*, *L'Ile aux Grues*, etc.) were more in the realistic line, his films on spiritual themes moved away from the documentary and became "much more apostolic." These included *Gloire à l'eau*, *Cantique de la création*, *Bénissez le Seigneur*, and *Cantique du soleil*. As I stated earlier, Tessier made roughly seventy-five films; one of his last was *Le Miracle du curé Chamberland* in 1952.

Yet another name associated with early Québec film was Maurice Proulx, born in 1902, who became a member of the faculty of the

Sainte-Anne de la Pocatière college in 1934. Between 1934 and 1961 he made around 37 films, some of them for the Québec government's film agency, Le Service de Ciné-Photographie. Like the work of Tessier, the documentary films of Father Proulx are concerned with rural life and traditional ideology; however, Clanfield finds them to "offer a more official version." Though dissent was already present in Québec society, Clanfield contends that the films of Proulx present no hint of growing societal difficulty. Rather, his films "promoted co-operative management and self-sufficiency, the importance of maintaining traditional crafts in a period of mechanization, and the intertwined institutions of family, church and school . . ." (Clanfield 1987, 15–16; 34). Proulx's work on the Abitibi settlement is, nevertheless, of importance; perhaps the best known of his films is *En pays neufs*, originally created without a sound track. It was inspired by Bernard Devlin's *Les Brûlés*, and, as both Lever and Clanfield point out, Perrault borrowed footage from Proulx in making his *Retour à la terre* (1976). Segments from this film may be seen in *Has Anybody Here Seen Canada?* Lever (*Hist.*, 1988, 52) writes that Proulx's films reflect the triumphant spirit of the Catholic Church at that time, and the Duplessist mystique of peasant grandeur.

The most important article on l'abbé Proulx is Pierre Demers's "La Leçon du cinéma 'nature': l'abbé Proulx et le cinématographe."[29] Demers emphasizes the fact that Proulx's work was in large part intended as an instrument in the instruction of agriculture, for he was, after all, for many years a professor of agronomy on the faculty of agriculture of Ste-Anne de la Pocatière (affiliated with Laval). In addition to *En pays neufs*, Demers lists several other films that "reveal the ideology of the 'Québec communautaire et agricole'" including *En pays pittoresques*, *Ste-Anne de Roquemaure*, *Le Lin au Canada*, *Les Ennemis de la pomme de terrre*, *Le Tabac jaune*, and *Jeunesse rurale*.

In both parts of his double article on Tessier, Bouchard stresses the role of priests in the early history of Québec cinema. Besides Tessier (Trois Rivières and La Mauricie) and Proulx (Sainte-Anne-de la Pocatière), he mentions (I:23 and II:32) l'abbé P. Cyr (Cabano); l'abbé Imbeau (Lac-Saint-Jean and the Saguenay); l'abbé Georges Côté (Saint-Charles de Bellechasse); Father Louis Lafleur (the Abitibi-Témiscamingue and the amerindians); Monsignor F. X. Saint-Arnault; Monsignor C.-E. Bourgeois; Father Venance; Brother Adrien; l'abbé Reynald Rivard, etc. Bouchard expresses his admiration for the extraordinary vitality of the cinematographic current then operative in Québec, and he states that these priests offered us the most lively panorama of Québec from the 30s to the 50s. He finds that "their films reflected life as it was in Québec during that period. Oriented toward values such as the Catholic religion, rural life, and French-Canadian culture and history, their filmic production appears in direct contact with the customs and with the everyday reality of those times . . . ." But Bouchard's most important thesis is that their work, analyzed in both a cinematographic and historic perspective, is the first expression of *québécois* national cinema, because it constitutes a homogenous corpus in which the characteristics peculiar to the Québécois are expressed. Their work forms a rich loam, in which the most distant roots of the "cinéma direct" are buried: they were — Tessier being a proof and an example — among the first to use the hand-carried camera, to find hitherto-unknown and ingenious techniques for filming and editing; to draw near people in order to penetrate more intimately into their daily lives, and, finally, their cinema is unpretentious, simple, stripped of any mannerism (Bouchard, I:23; my translations and paraphrase). Certainly, again and again in the interview that Tessier granted Bouchard only months before his death the pioneer priest-filmmaker stresses simplicity. And certainly when one examines the magnificent stills that accompany Bouchard's article, one senses a Tessier behind Perrault; one sees Alexis Tremblay and his wife Marie in Tessier's "*habitants*," or peasants. The reader of French might note that early ethnocinematographers, including Tessier, Proulx, other priests and nonpriests, are also discussed by Yvan Lamonde in "Indirectement le cinéma direct."[30]

Among the most important of the pioneers of the documentary is Herménégilde Lavoie (1908–73), a seminarian and not a priest, who is held to be very influential in the history of Québec documentary, along with the pioneers Maurice Proulx and Msgr. Albert Tessier. He first worked for the Office of Tourism and Publicity for the Province of Québec, where he made a series of documentaries called "Les beautés de mon pays." But he was dismissed by Duplessis in 1947, and started his own production firm, Documentaire Lavoie. He made industrial documentaries and documentaries about Acadia, and an unfinished piece on the Hurons of Lorette. His son Richard — who was his collaborator on such films as *Le Bon Pasteur à Québec* (1949); *Franciscaines missionaires de Marie* (1950); and *L'Ame d'une grande dame* (1954) — directed a documentary about his father in 1976. It was entitled *Herménégilde, vision d'un pionnier du cinéma québécois, 1908–73*.

There were also several other priests who were *cinéastes*: Josée
Beaudet used a number of their very interesting images for her
Film d'Ariane (discussed in my Chapter 3). Obviously, the role of
priests in the making of films is one way in which "censorship"
functioned as a determinant, not only of what would go into the
movies, but of what would stay out. Surely these decisions even
had considerable influence in defining the culture and its values.
But the Church also introduced and continued to promulgate arguments against the film, especially the imported film, as a corrupter,
from many perspectives: the theaters themselves are breeding
grounds of disease and of immodest acts; the cinema itself is
an enslavement, a drug — not to mention its contents; it is often
immoral by its attacks on faith, religion, morality, and the clergy.
The American film is an even worse corrupter because it poisons
the popular imagination, and brings on American acculturation —
imported culture, that is — , always feared by the Québécois, who
are almost as xenophobic as the French. Moreover, it presents
irreality (according to Cardinal Rodrigue Villeneuve, 1937). Many
of the decriers of this "grave situation" attributed the immorality
of the American film to the fact that the cinema "belongs mostly to
expatriated Jews, *sans foi ni loi* ..."; and thus the cinema became
one of the best battlefields of Catholic anti-Semitism.[31] And, not
surprisingly, the theme of the immigrant and, in particular, of
the Jew, as a threat to the Québécois *pure laine* is not absent
from Québec literature and film. We find it at play in *Les Portes
tournantes*, in *Le Matou*, and, to some extent, in *Un Zoo la nuit*. It
is a theme that Weinmann dwells upon in his study of the cinema
of Québec. It is the subject of Chapter 7 of this book.

As I said earlier, viewing the film (video) *Dreamland: A History
of Early Canadian Movies* (1895—1939) can give the person curious
about early Québec film a quick overview of its early history. The
film *Has Anybody Here Seen Canada?*, tracing the history of the
Canadian film from 1939—53, supplements both *Dreamland* and
Lever's *Histoire* .... According to these films, the documentary
gained strength under John Grierson, who came to Canada to
direct the NFB, which had been voted into existence by an act of
Parliament on 16 March 1939. During World War II, Mackenzie
King needed documentaries, and Grierson produced these for King.
(He sought the collaboration of Louis de Rochemont of Time/Life
in America, among others.) The attempt to recruit the Québécois,
who were not in sympathy with the war, and still harbored resent-
ments concerning the conscription laws of World War I, was a

difficult one, and Grierson used "soft-sell programs" to persuade these unenthusiastic people to join the war effort. On the other hand, he did not try to involve Québécois in film manufacture; as a matter of fact, he did not encourage fictional feature films at all, thinking it best to leave that to the British and the Americans. As I suggested earlier, the portrayal of the French Canadian in these foreign films can be called little more than ugly and stereotypical. It was in such a film — 49th Parallel, by the British director Michael Powell — that Laurence Olivier portrayed that rough-hewn Québécois complete with plaid jacket and an absurd accent that I mentioned above; and, as I also said, it is surely one of his most infelicitous moments. But it certainly epitomized the contemporary treatment of the French Canadian. Clips of this performance can be seen on the video Has Anybody Here Seen Canada? The 49th Parallel was also discussed at length in the recent documentary about Powell's films, featured on the Adrienne Clarkson show (27 June 1991), at which time Olivier's caricature was mercifully not excerpted.

Notwithstanding the fact that this offensive portrayal comes from the British, it should be pointed out that subsequent (Anglo-Canadian and/or American) productions have not always been innocent of presenting these kinds of stereotypes, either. In a film of more recent times — the prize-winning children's film My Side of the Mountain (1969; d. James B. Clark; Canadian-U.S.), set in the Laurentians, with beautiful location photography in play — the French Canadian is seen as a cruel killer. The film is occasionally aired on premium stations in the United States; it aired on TNT in September 1991.

Just one brief word regarding technology at this juncture. (I will be referring to technological matters in a more specific manner in my critiques of the various films.) The Canadian film industry is sometimes berated as one that has brought little to the art: yet, in the province of Québec, as elsewhere in the nation, the direct style (akin to cinéma vérité methods) and the unusual placement of documentary in general at the service of fictional or feature cinema are outstanding, to say the very least.[32] As long ago as 1903, the visit of the Prince of Wales to Québec was captured on film and was shown all over the world! (One may sample it in Dreamland.) By World War II, and following the establishment of the Canadian National Film Board, the Canadians were making documentaries that claimed the respect and admiration of the whole world. The person seeking proof of this assertion has only to view one superb example, September, 1939 (60 min.; 1961), a documentary of the

German Blitzkrieg launched against Poland, marking the start of World War II. (It was produced by Frederick Gavsie and narrated by Frank Willis.)

In the first several decades of the century Canadian filmmakers had suffered from considerable isolation and were forced to invent ways of solving their problems, which would have been more easily handled, had they been in contact with the industry at large. In the technological realm, the recent book of Gerald G. Graham[33] will demonstrate that Canada has made significant contributions, among which the most important is the IMAX 70-mm film system. But Graham stresses, too, the difficulty of filming remote, sometimes subzero, areas of Canada, in an effort to respond to the raison d'être of the Canadian Film Board; these handicaps, which often played havoc with the equipment — then heavy and hard to transport, besides — led to considerable inventiveness. David Suzuki has hosted a documentary — shown on *The Nature of Things* — that studies the four Canadians who developed the OMNIMAX film projection format, which completely envelops a viewer. One supposes that the initiation film at the Grand Canyon, which used this type of projection, has influenced the closing sequences of *Thelma and Louise*. It is certain that IMAX equipment was taken aboard the January 1992 Discovery space mission — along with the first Canadian woman to make a voyage in space.

As regards actual filmmaking in Québec, we have seen that the strong control of the Church and the State was applied to the film industry in an effort to reinforce traditional *québécois* values. In the 1940s l'abbé Proulx was one of the chief directors (and that speaks for itself). One of his best-known films was *En pays neufs*. Alexandre De Sève with his Côte des Neiges studios was also a prominent producer-distributor: in films sponsored by him we can observe such tried and true formulas as "rescue from the rushing northern waters" (a melodramatic situation well-known from D. W. Griffith's *Way Down East*, in which Lillian Gish is rescued as she floats down the river on an ice floe about to go over the falls). Of course, if the film had been shot in French, marketing was a problem, as it still can be. Nowadays, however, the French of France sometimes — but not always — show considerable interest in the film products of Québec. On the other hand, the filmmakers of Québec found themselves free of any particular need to compete with Hollywood and more or less went their own way. By 1946, however, L'Anglais double-shot his *La Forteresse* in both French and English; the latter featured the famous international stars Paul

Lukas and Helmut Dantine. The English version proved unsuccessful, however. The distribution blocks did not permit the film's reaching a sufficiently large audience. As we saw, L'Anglais tended to use Québec mythology to create "Northerners"; and it seems to me that the tendency to exploit a mythic Québec—sometimes in what is an intentionally subverted and/or subversive interpretation of the myth—still prevails in such modern films as *Un Zoo la nuit* and *Jésus de Montréal*, for example.

Two somewhat later, fictional films, *Tit-Coq* and *La Petite Aurore*, prolong the tendencies found in these earliest works, but, as we shall see, especially through a close examination of *La Petite Aurore*, the position of the Church in the eyes of the laity is beginning to crumble, while the role of Québec in the federation is likewise brought into question.

With *Tit-Coq* (1953) Gratien Gélinas and René Delacroix created one of the most important classics of *québécois* cinema. The *scénario* by Gélinas drew upon his already successful play to make a film that, as Weinmann claims, portrays the conflict of the orphaned Québec, abandoned by France and in rebellion against its "family," i.e., against the tradition of the *roman familial*. In somewhat the same vein, Christine Tremblay-Daviault finds that *Tit-Coq* demonstrates a theme common in *québécois* cinema—that of the tragedy of the homeless, counterpoised with the theme of the ideal family

Tit-Coq. (Courtesy Coll. Cinémathèque Québécoise.)

("of one's dreams").[34] It is also characterized by an implacable moralism. Added to this are the subsumed themes of the problem of identity and resistance to change.

Tit-Coq, returned from war, finds the woman he loved has been forced into marriage with a man she does not cherish. In the most powerful, and also the most famous scene of the film, Tit-Coq laces down a priest for "preaching" to him about divorce. His strong response is said to show the early rebellion of the Québécois against the Church, a rebellion that by the 60s will be in full force.

It is interesting to note, however, that in his chapter on *Tit-Coq* Weinmann takes the critical contre-pied, and finds that in the long run Tit-Coq must be viewed as influenced by religion, but not by the Church, the Padre being an army chaplain and therefore "outside the Church." The notion of the influence of Jesus outside the confines of the dogma and ritual of the Catholic Church will be a central theme in one of the most successful of all *québécois* films — the rather recent smash hit of Denys Arcand, *Jesus of Montreal*, coming almost forty years after *Tit-Coq*.[35]

LA PETITE AURORE L'ENFANT MARTYRE

A slightly earlier film that serves as an excellent touchstone for the illustration of this loss of faith in the clergy — and many other tendencies of the epoch — is the black-and-white film *La Petite Aurore l'enfant martyre* (1951–2).

Marie-Louise, a neighbor who is caring for the dying wife of the farmer Théodore and their child, having been given some medicine in case the wife has another attack, forces a big swig of the liquid down the sick woman's throat, as the little girl, Aurore, looks on, thus becoming witness to a murder. (The icons of traditional Québec ironically underline the sacred trust betrayed; a statue of the Sorrowful Mother is to be seen in the background.) Now Marie-Louise must fear the child's exposure of her crime.

In the following scene Théodore and the curé discuss Théodore's little daughter, whom he has temporarily sent to her aunt's. The priest urges the father to send the child to the village, where she can progress in her education. We learn from the priest's "Are you happy in your second marriage?" that Théodore and Marie-Louise are now "husband and wife" — a deadly combination in this particular setting.

Aurore, repeatedly placed in the attic, suffers from her terror of spider-webs and the claustrophobic atmosphere.

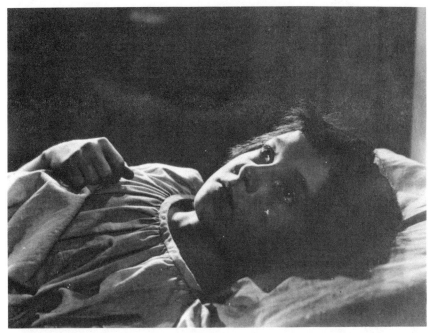

La Petite Aurore. (Courtesy Coll. Cinémathèque Québécoise.)

Maurice, Marie-Louise's son by a first marriage, finds Aurore in the attic, but she explains this by saying she has trapped herself there. Maurice is not fooled: "C'est maman, eh?" Théodore arrives. Marie-Louise tells him she found the two in the *grenier*, implying they were up to sexual acts. The father strikes Aurore with a large stick. "T'as fait ça?" She passes out; he then breaks the stick, and carries her to her room. "What's happened?" he asks; "Elle est toute brûlée [She's burned all over her body]." He then tells his wife never to beat her again.

Catherine, a neighbor, engaged to Abraham, comes into Marie-Louise's house. Aurore is in a bed in the corner, but Catherine pretends she has come for meat. Marie-Louise goes to get it. Catherine sees the burns. "How did you get these? How? Tell me!! No lies!" Aurore confesses, and tells her, "Papa believes everything that Marie-Louise says." Catherine is appalled: "It is not possible to go to church every Sunday and then 'massacrer un enfant comme ça'." Catherine reports all to the curé; she urges him to go to the legal authorities before the child dies.

Theodore returns; the curé arrives. Marie-Louise speaks of Aurore to the priest: "Elle n'est pas solide . . . c'est l'âge critique . . . je prends bien soin [She's not strong; she's at a critical age; I take

La Petite Aurore. (Courtesy Coll. Cinémathèque Québécoise.)

great care of her]." The curé asks Aurore if she would not want to confess; the child agrees. This means that Marie-Louise and Théodore must leave the room. She is told to tell the truth, and so she does. She exclaims, "O, m. le curé, sauvez-moi!' The curé: "Count on me, and on God." Then he calls the parents back, and tells the father that the child is "gravely ill."

The curé leaves; then Théodore. Marie-Louise screams at Aurore: "Tu as parlé [You've talked]." The child admits she has "told the truth." Marie-Louise burns her tongue and puts her in the attic. The next morning Marie-Louise goes to the attic. "Get up," she commands. She straps Aurore five or six times and then throws her down the stairs. When Théodore comes in, Marie-Louise pretends that Aurore fell. Théodore declares he is going for the curé because the child is dying.

Théodore returns with the curé and the doctor. Catherine shows up, and tells Marie-Louise to prepare for the priest's administration of the last sacrament. She then shows the doctor evidence on the steps; he goes to the attic, finds the strap and fresh blood. Catherine tells the curé about the burns; the doctor tells him of the attic scene.

In the closing scenes of this tragedy Théodore and Marie-Louise are in the courthouse. Says Marie-Louise, "I did all I could to bring her up well; she was hard-headed." But when the jury finds her guilty, the Judge condemns her to be hanged.

This graphic portrayal of child abuse at times takes on the aura of a documentary. More particularly, it shows a young child (Québec itself?) as the prey of human institutions, all of which fail her: family, friends, Church, and society. But even more importantly, this film has that universal charge we would stress as an unrecognized but not uncommon characteristic of the *québécois* cinema. Not only are we disturbed by this brutal and very direct documentation of a battered child, but we recognize the all-too-human fears portrayed in the film. It is a thorough-going study of fear: fear of exposure on the part of the Jungian terrible-mother figure (here the stepmother); fear of beating on the part of the child; fear of losing the new wife on the part of the husband; fear of a break-up on the part of the engaged couple (Catherine and Abraham); etc.

Moreover, *La Petite Aurore* shows us, sometimes too obviously, the wages of jealousy and of procrastination. Catherine procrastinates in telling the curé what is going on in Théodore's household; the curé as a representative of Holy Mother Church fails to act when Catherine finally tells him. (It should not be forgotten, either, that the curé is the one who urges Théo to bring Aurore back 'home,' at the point where she is staying with her aunt.) A remedy for Aurore's predicament and passion comes too late in the form of the hanging of the stepmother, Marie-Louise. (Interestingly enough, the fact that her unborn baby will die with her constitutes an unresolved ethical problem of the first magnitude.) On the deepest level we understand that this is, iconographically speaking, a depiction of true martyrdom: the innocent lamb sheds blood for the purification of the society. When the doctor finally detects the pools of blood in the attic, together with the instruments of torture, justice must prevail.

By and large the film is not exaggerated, though there may be a few somewhat too melodramatic scenes for modern taste. It reminds us of the D. W. Griffith classic *Broken Blossoms* (in French, *Lys brisé*; 1919),[36] in which the child — played by Lillian Gish — is abused and finally killed by her father (Donald Crisp), who in turn is killed by the Chinaman, who had befriended and protected her. A memorable scene in that film in which the child is shut into a closet, a kind of cell, is analogous to Aurore's attic prison. (Incidentally, Griffith's film, along with Germaine Dulac's *Fête espagnole*, is viewed as having elements suggestive of the documentary style, which is to be so important in the evolution of *Canadian* film.) But *La Petite Aurore* seems even more tragic than *Broken Blossoms*, though, like the child in that film, Aurore has her friend in Catherine. The portrayal of the abuse is more violent in *Aurore*; and, sadly enough, it also bears a very contemporary stamp, as we well know if we read our daily papers, or consider the recent celebrated case of the two professionals from New York — Joel Steinberg and Hedda Nussbaum — who tortured their adopted child to death.

Notably, Robinson and Lloyd term this film a failure. Not quite, I think. It is a watershed film, and one that, along with *Tit-Coq*, has historical as well as aesthetic importance when it comes to a consideration of French-Canadian filmmaking.

French-Canadian critical assessments of this film, its story, and its characters, vary considerably. For Weinmann, for example, Aurore is an *in-fans*; a nonprotesting masochistic Québec. He first studies *La Petite Aurore* in terms of the *refus global*, finding in the work the refusal of the Holy "family" icon. There is, he thinks, disproportion between the cruelty of the stepmother and the innocence of Aurore. And he believes that the tyranny, machiavellianism, and sadism of the stepmother are so exorbitant, enormous, and monstrous that they are discredited by their excess. (Still, real cases almost identical in their horror do exist!) The work, set in the 1920s, is melodramatic for him. Nevertheless, he finds parallels to the collapse of the family taking place in the society at the time. Aurore, for example, is the avatar of St. Jean Baptiste, the symbol of the child (Québec) abandoned by the parents, first France, then England. Aurore is the *bouc émissaire* — the scapegoat and the very psyche of French Canada. It is now the new era, that of Québec. Aurore first shows her *refus* when she will not call her stepmother "mother." The stepmother, on the other hand, seizes her power by force and becomes a despot. She is at once the *mère phallique* in this antifeminist film, and also stands for England. The film is, then, a study of a tyrannical totalitarian regime; it is the reign of terror, in which the stepmother (English Canada) suppresses the voice and human rights of the *in-fans*, the adopted child (Québec). The film for Weinmann has "antichild racist" overtones: the stepmother seeks to silence the child, to gag her; she uses work as an instrument of torture, puts Aurore into the uniform or work clothes that degrade, covers her with dirt; she eradicates her beauty, her resemblance to her own real mother (France), seeks to make her different, crowns her with thorns, cuts her hair, burns her with a curling iron, dirties her, and then cleans her up. The film is a portrayal of the clash of truth and lie, or dark (Marie-Louise) and light (Aurore), according to Weinmann. The Québec people identify with the film, with Aurore, who is born with her death, for the stepmother kills and cures the patient — above all, of the belief in family. She seeks to demolish the ideal, to cure the French Canadians of their masochistic nostalgia, which they exacerbated by regarding scenes of torture of their martyred saints. She is the orphan martyr, the witness to the truth of her faith, or else she is an antimartyr who dies for a truth she hides (the murder of her own mother by her "foreign" stepmother). That is to say, Weinmann proposes, the film may be a reaction to beatification and canonization of the martyred French-Canadian saints (the twenty).

Weinmann, who finds that there may be allusions to the Duplessis regime in this film, returns again to the story of St. John the Baptist, to link Théodore, Aurore's father, with the *bourreau aveugle* — the blind hangman — and Marie-Louise with Salomé. (Théodore, after all, hits Aurore on the head with his hatchet handle; but at first we believe there will be an actual decapitation, like that of St. John, suggested by the presence of the hatchet.)

Lever has an interesting, and, I would say, quite different assessment of *La Petite Aurore*: The itinerant projectionists must surely have shown this film, he supposes, in every village of Québec, not to mention its screenings in the big cities (*Hist.* 1988, 121). And the film can well have inaugurated a pessimism in the *québécois* film that has endured in the films of Jutra (but I might also add in those of Beaudin, and others). While Lever would not claim that *La Petite Aurore* is a cinematographic masterpiece, he recognizes that "on one level, it is not hard to understand why this film was the biggest success of the period: after all, the problem of battered children remains as current today as forty years ago. And, also on another level, it is one of the most explicit films of the period: the country is the site of the martyrdom of children, a place where there is no united family, in which marriage brings only unhappiness, and in which religion is completely ineffective. And this whole approach enters into an absolute contradiction with official ideology. The beautiful, compensatory little couple, the sympathetic doctor, the avenging judge do not suffice, today, to overturn the image" (Lever *Hist.* 1988, 105; my translation).

Contemporary Trends Summarized

The stage set by such films of the 50s as *Tit-Coq* (1953) and *La Petite Aurore* (1952) was followed by a generation of Québec filmmakers who display genius, originality, and world-class artistry. Claude Jutra brought forth his *A tout prendre* in 1963; it relied to a great extent upon the documentary traditions, and specifically those of "direct cinema," already well-established as the forte of *québécois* film. (This is a technique that has something in common with the *cinéma vérité* methods.) Jutra's film also showed the signs of kinship with the French *auteur* approach to cinema. But no doubt his masterpiece is *Mon oncle Antoine* (1971), which, among other things, revealed the exploitation that is ingrained in the most banal day-to-day activities, as Robinson and Lloyd say. It is much more, though: it is a story about love and death and about the burdens implicit in the assumption of adulthood. It will be one of the cornerstone films examined in this book.

Gilles Groulx is also a man of this generation. He began his career as a director of documentaries, among which is *Golden Gloves* (a twenty-eight minute black-and-white film made in 1961, produced by the ONF, with Fernand Dansereau and Victor Jobin). It concerns two unemployed black men, Ronald and Arthur Jones, as well as a French Canadian, George Thibault, all of whom aspire to win the Golden Gloves championship. But his best known work is no doubt *Le Chat dans le sac* (1964). It is a film that deals with the nationality problem and with political responsibility, and involves the appropriation of Québec's landscape. In it, a young couple, Claude, a French Canadian, and Barbara, an anglophone Canadian Jew, are about to break up. In the end, we have a dialogue between Claude and himself, "questioning the political reality of his environment and disturbed by his powerlessness to alter it" (Robinson and Lloyd, 398).

Gilles Carle has had an uneven career. Nevertheless, his *Vraie Nature de Bernadette* (1972–73) is regarded as something of a masterpiece, as is also his *Tête de Normande St-Onge* (1976). He is also known for *La Mort d'un bûcheron* (1973) and for the much earlier *Vie heureuse de Léopold Z.* (1965). In 1981 he directed the filming of *Les Plouffe*, giving us both the TV miniseries and an amended version. At present he may be best known for *Maria Chapdelaine* (1983–84), severely rejected by some critics, but found to be a fresh and lyrical masterpiece by others. We will be looking at several of these films in detail.

Jean Beaudin, too, will be the object of some scrutiny: His sometimes dark and often brooding pictures follow in the footsteps of Jutra: We will examine his *Cher Théo* (1975); his *Cordélia* (1979); *Mario* (1984); *Le Matou* (1985), and, above all, his splendid chef d'oeuvre, *J. A. Martin photographe* (1976). He is one of the greatest; his vision is sometimes feral and always electric. But do not bother to look for him in Sadoul's *Dictionnaire des cinéastes*. He is not there.

Another filmmaker of less importance, but known to some American viewers, is Arthur Lamothe, whose work on the Amerindian (e.g., *Mistashipu*) is said to contain fine balance and a lyrical quality. Lamothe is responsible for eight films of varying lengths that are known under the title *Images d'un doux éthnocide*, "passionnant travail sur la mémoire d'un peuple et sur la déculturation [a terrific piece of work on the memory of a people and on deculturation]," says Sadoul (*Dict. des cinéastes* 179). This film director is on Sadoul's list, perhaps because he was born in France and is an "immigré" to Québec. One cannot really know.

In the same generation, the work of Pierre Perrault (*Le Règne du jour*; *Pour la suite du monde*; *Wake up, mes bons amis*; etc.) and that of Michel Brault—both as director and photographer—stand out as monolithic tributes to the documentary and the docudrama. We will consider their work in detail.

Contemporary filmmakers on the Québec scene must include Jean Pierre Lefebvre (*Les Dernières Fiançailles* [1973]); Jacques Leduc (*On est loin du soleil* [1971]—a portrait of a kind of saint), and Denys Arcand, with his *On est au coton* (1971)—a full length documentary on labor problems—and the outstanding *Crime d'Ovide Plouffe* (1983), which is a two-hour excerpt from his six-hour television series. (These are follow-ups to the Gilles Carle work on *Les Plouffe*, mentioned above.) Arcand has also given two recent films that are perhaps the best known French-Canadian films outside French Canada: they are *Le Déclin de l'empire américain* (1986) and *Jésus de Montréal* (1989). Both of these films will be analyzed at length within the pages of this book. Francis Mankiewicz's work, in particular *Les Bons Débarras*, will be the object of lengthy commentary as well. And although in America there seems to be little attention paid to the films of the women directors of Canada, these women are producing some incisive and gripping work, both in the field of documentaries and in fictional film, often from a feminist perspective. Among them one might mention Anne Claire Poirier and Mireille Dansereau. But there are others; and their work has collectively merited a chapter in this book. I am concerned, of course, with how, in all the films, the cinema may mirror the political and social structures of the Québec people; but we will find that some do this more than others.

It follows that oftentimes my classification of a certain film under a certain genre or sociological rubric is somewhat artificial and may seem arbitrary; many films belong in two or more, even all, of the categories I have selected. I have simply tried to group these films in a manner that would allow discussion; there is usually nothing sacred about the genre classification, and it may well be that my readers will completely disagree with the characterization I give it by my classification. Genre placement of film seems a more precarious undertaking than of literature, even!

These, then, are the main issues and the main figures we will be considering. But we will look at many others in passing, and we will also speak, upon occasion, of the beautiful and highly original animation (for adults) coming from Québec; this is one of the filmic expressions at which the Canadians are expert, and their gift in this line has been vigorously supported by the Office National du Film. In a final chapter, I shall look at alterity as reflected in anglophone and other minority-based films coming out of Québec, before making some closing comments.

The fundamental thrust of this work will be to demonstrate that in the realm of filmmaking, the Québécois are "masters in their own house" — to play on the famous slogan of the late first minister of Québec, René Lévesque. Of course, he meant that the French Canadians were no longer to be "slaves" to the anglo(phone), or WASP, Canadian establishment (as Vallières had claimed to be the case in his *Nègres blancs d'Amérique*). In adopting this concept as theme and subtitle of my book, I obviously use the word "masters" in opposition to the word "slaves," but I also intend to convey the sense of "masters" of the technology and use of the seventh art to portray *québécois* society; master artists. It will also become evident that as the products of these men and women have evolved, Québec can hold its head high in the arena of world cinema as well.

A Word on Methodology

Leaving aside the above-mentioned subsuming of films under genre classifications which, it is conceded, they may often overflow, I deal with some *québécois* films only in passing. However, almost all films under discussion are presented with credits (Appendix B),

scénario (story, script), and a critique. The reader will note that
some films will be critiqued at much greater length than others,
due to their importance, either with respect to their period or to
their genre, or because of a major place I see them as occupying
within the spectrum of world cinema. Moreover, this study is
meant to be global, but not all-inclusive. It is not within my
expectation that all who use this book will entirely agree with the
choices, or with the wide-ranging lengths of treatment, anymore
than with the genre classifications. I avow that both have been
largely a matter of personal selection and decision. In any case,
with very few exceptions, I have actually viewed every film analyzed
within the course of this study (and some of them many times).
But because new films keep constantly appearing, I have found it
necessary to limit the films under scrutiny here mainly to those
made in or before 1990, while even so speaking, upon occasion, of
a more recent film. To continue after that date would obviously
have made of this a never-ending undertaking. This is essentially
only a postponement, no doubt. For at the end of the decade of
the 90s an update of this study will be in order, and it would
present an overview of the entire century of *québécois* cinema.
There is reason to believe that at that juncture the very definition
of the word *québécois* may be significantly altered. But maybe not.

2

A Search for Roots

"My people will sleep for one
hundred years. When they awake
it will be the artists that give them
back their spirit."

— Louis Riel

J'attends que tu viennes:
peut-être es-tu là déjà?
[I await your arrival; perhaps you are already
there?]

— Pierre Perrault

Documentaries (the "direct" method); Semi-Documentaries. History through fiction

One of the main things a national cinema usually undertakes is an investigation of its historical, political, and literary past. In this respect, the Québec industry has not been found wanting, and indeed, when one considers its associations with the National Film Board, which pushed the documentary and all film effort in the direction of a *Canadian* message for Canadians and for outsiders, one is not surprised to find that the documentary and the fictional feature film have greatly explored the Québec past, in search of an understanding of the Québécois' roots and identity. Such concerns led to the filming of a nineteen-part documentary on the province's history and on the society of today, called *Nostalgie*. Packaged in eight "episodes," it features films dealing with the recent past, including two on the "Region of Charlevoix" (*Terre de nos aïeux* and *Peintres populaires de Charlevoix*); a series on the "Professionnels des années 1950" (*Le Médecin du Nord, Monsieur le Maire*, and *Le Notaire de Trois-Pistoles*); another series called "Vie Monastique des années 1960" (*Les Petites Soeurs* and *Les Moines de Saint-Benoît*); yet another series entitled "La Coexistence pacifique"— concerned with anglophone and francophone relations in the 40s and 50s—(*Double Héritage, Entente cordiale*, and *Referendum*); a series called "Familles rurales au Québec et en Ontario" (*De Père en fils* and *Le Fils*); a series devoted to the "Mouvement coopératif et syndicalisme au Canada français" (*Caisses populaires Desjardins* and *Alfred J.*); and finally a series dealing with the "Théâtre et littérature au Québec" (*Alfred DesRoches, poète* and *Côté cour . . . côté jardin*). But of greater interest to us here are films, both documentary and feature length, that seek to recapture a time in Québec culture that is even more remote—the early twentieth century and before. This was, after all, one of the chief intentions of these films; and yet even in the films of the 40s and 50s forward, a social and political tension was already perceptible. As Michel Brûlé explains it in *Forces* (quoted in Lever *Hist.* 1988, 482–84), there was a desire to remain attached to the culture, especially to the language as the chief vehicle of that culture, at the same time that there was (already) a realization of an irreversible change (industrialization of a province historically dependent on agricultural pursuits). This tension is already shown as an "état de malaise social" in the short ONF films of the 1950s. It seems to me, then, that even as we examine films that seek to rediscover the *québécois* past, we must be on guard for social criticism, and for an examination of societal institutions.

PIERRE PERRAULT'S DIRECT DOCUMENTARY; *POUR LA SUITE DU MONDE*

In a kind of mystical documentary style, Pierre Perrault (b. 1927 [some say 1931] in Sainte-Famille on the île-d'Orléans, educated in history and law at the Université de Montréal; Université de Paris, and at Toronto University) has taken the lead in showing the rural past of Québec, as well as its traditional links to a maritime economy and its ties with the mother country, France. He follows in the great tradition of Robert Flaherty and Tom Daly, his teachers, or masters. He is not sentimental, not romantic, but sometimes elegaic. The philosophy of this ethnographer and poet is that the documentary should be "an album of essential images." Upon occasion he has dealt with the Acadian past, especially in *L'Acadie, l'Acadie*, which, stylistically speaking, is very similar to those films dealing with Québec per se, though Québec has been his principal concern. His film *Pour la suite du monde* is perhaps his best-known production in this domain; it, like many other films of his, enjoyed

Pour la suite du monde. (Courtesy Office National du Film.)

the cooperation of the great photographer, Michel Brault, whom one encounters repeatedly in any examination of Québec cinema.

POUR LA SUITE DU MONDE OR *THE MOONTRAP;* OR *SO THAT THE WORLD GOES ON* (1962; d. Pierre Perrault with Michel Brault)

The first Canadian film to compete at Cannes, voted Film of the Year at the Canadian Film Awards, winner of Seven International Awards, placed at tie for seventh position in the Critics' Choice (*Variety*, 8 August 1984; as noted in my Ch. 1), *Pour la suite du monde* chronicles the multigenerational Tremblay family and their neighbors, and their effort to reenact the ancestral ritual of hunting and trapping the Beluga whale (*marsouin*), which had endured up to 1924, by using a trap of tall, wooden staffs placed in the river shallows. (But note that according to Peter Morris, Jane Marsh had earlier directed an NFB film entitled *Alexis Tremblay, habitant* [1943; 30 min.]. It was a "picture of the life of a traditional French-Canadian family, headed by Alexis Tremblay," and followed "the family as they go about their normal tasks during the four seasons of the year.")[1]

Though some argue as to whether the French or the "*sauvages*" invented this method of catching Belugas, Alexis Tremblay proves from a book that in 1534, when Jacques Cartier stopped at an island on the lower St. Lawrence, and named it l'Ile-aux-Coudres (because he saw *coudres*, or hazelnut trees), he observed how the Indians caught the small white whales by setting a fence of saplings (*chicots*) into offshore mud. The method still works, as we see in this film, in which Old Tremblay attempts to tell the younger men about the need to follow the phases of the moon and the tides, and thus bespeaks the nobility of ancestral methods of dealing with nature. He preaches to them the need to keep absolute silence, and rants against science, showing the peasants' skepticism, as expressed in their doubts that there can be life or living on the moon. (Cf. Antonine Maillet's Gapi, husband of La Sagouine, who doubts that anyone ever went to the moon.) Alexis has a great reverence for the moon.

The film shows these moonlit scenes, with the shadows of the boats and with the saplings lined up vertically along the horizontal sea. It also shows other sociological (one might even say anthropological) rites and rituals of the people of the Ile-aux-Coudres, an island seventy miles downstream from the city of Québec. These include Lenten traditions: the mascarade (*couenne*), which has the ring of the most ancient of carnivals; the gathering of special water — pure and chaste — from a fast-running stream; sacred plants for the *aspereges* and Easter baptism; the auction sales for the benefit of souls in purgatory; attendance at mass; ethnic music and jigs; and other customs that go back to the very days of the discovery of Canada. In the snow scenes with their horse-drawn sleighs, in the spring scenes with the horse-drawn plough, in the rhythm of the traditional rocking chair, there seems to be a kind of peacefulness and continuity — a continuity that the younger Tremblays hope to preserve for posterity (*pour la suite du monde*). The scenes with the tall, wooden staffs used as traps are artistically composed and structurally ethereal. From a visual point of view the film is unforgettable; moreover, its subdued dialogue is in complete harmony with the iconography — as is the music. A somewhat eerie scene in an aquarium seems unforgettable: it is here that, as a pure white Beluga whale swims gracefully about the tank, the men discuss its nature, and how it communicates through its sounds. The photography here recalls Orson Welles's 1948 *Lady from Shanghai*, in which the camera is rightfully said to be the real star.

On another register are the discussions among the interlocutors about their forthcoming trip to New York to deliver the whale to a marineland, as are the accounts of the trip on return. America is seen as a place of glitz and a source of corruption. The theme is one we can observe in a number of *Canadian* literary and cinematic works (*Trente Arpents; Gapi et Sullivan; Ticket to Heaven; Videodrome*). And should the French Canadian decide to settle down in the United States, he is either victimized by or else bound to violence and materialistic ways (*Trente Arpents; Maria Chapdelaine; Les Tisserands du pouvoir*). And even in a rather shrill and overly-dramatic, if not melodramatic documentary/autobiography, *Le Grand Jack* (1987; d. Herménégilde Chiasson), we see Jack Kerouac — born in Lowell, Massachusetts of French-Canadian parentage, his father having come from Saint Hubert near Rivière du Loup — as a "canuck peasant" whose heart was broken by a materialistic, "industrialized, hardhearted, homogenized, money-grubbing" America that had/has "a disrespect of person." Conversely, Americans go to Canada as a place of protection, and refuge, as they have historically in the times of slavery (on the Freedom Trains), or to avoid the draft during the Vietnam war. Such motives are evident in *The Handmaid's Tale*, *The Grey Fox*, and Robin Spry's *Prologue*. In the bargain, the ugly American or ex-American (not necessarily Franco-American) is never far from the scene (*Kamouraska; Les Fous de Bassan; Les Plouffe; Les Tisserands du pouvoir; Night Zoo*, etc.).

Be that as it may, *Pour la suite du monde* has some of the most beautiful photography in all cinema, sometimes approaching oriental print, and not without appropriately poetic dialogue patterns subtending it (Conley's hieroglyphs[2]). Nevertheless, it is the reflection of a man's world, where women have little place, and say little, while they smile at the bickering of the men, remaining almost mute and always passive. A truly patriarchal system is fully functioning, though upon occasion Mme Alexis puts in a word. But can that word be important? She is not even given screen credit, as far as that is concerned.

In sum, the evocation of the past through Tremblay's quotes from Jacques Cartier and his as well as his wife's recollections of the old ways are nostalgic without being sentimental. And the use of nonactors adds to the effectiveness of the work. In fictional film this strategy gives "realism"; it has been practiced throughout the history of cinema, in such works as Pier Paolo Pasolini's *Gospel according to St. Matthew* (1966), or the recent Canadian film *Strangers in Good Company* (aka, *A Company of Strangers*, d.

Martha Scott [1990—1]). African film directors also often use nonprofessional actors.

Pour la suite du monde is, very simply put, a masterpiece. In 1969 Perrault remade this film under the title *Le Beau Plaisir* (*Beluga Days*).

LE RÈGNE DU JOUR (from 1965 to 1967; d. Pierre Perrault)

In *Le Règne du jour* the same man, Alexis Tremblay, after going to New York to visit Blanchon, the Beluga whale he and his relatives captured (in *Pour la suite du monde*), returns to the place of his ancestors in Brittany. Here the most remarkable kinds of cultural parallels are drawn, and, in particular, manners of scalding and butchering a pig, as well as how to make *andouille*. (One thinks of a more comical episode in *La Guerre, Yes Sir!*, where a pig is killed, butchered and prepared for the concoction of great quantities of *tourtières* to be served up at Corriveau's wake.) Tremblay is in France for thirty-two days, and while there he visits Saint-Malo, Normandel, La Rochelle; at Tourouvre he walks around the farm at Filonnière, which belonged to the first Tremblay of the family. Tremblay is accompanied by his wife, Marie, his son Léopold, and his daughter-in-law, Marie-Paule. A parish document is produced that shows the 1623 marriage of his ancestor Pierre Tremblay.

While in Paris, Tremblay treats his wife to the first trip she has ever made to the hairdresser. In this film women are less shadowy than in *Pour la suite* . . .; they have much more to say. Indeed, Marie Tremblay emerges as one of the distinct portraits of *Le Règne* . . . . But it is a portrait that cloys: this demure old lady with her cap around her hair, this "national treasure," spinning, knitting, praying. Her husband, Alexis Tremblay would be called a sexist by any modern standards: he rants against women wearing "le pantalon" (slacks), makes jokes about naked women, declares women have remained feminine in France, like his wife. And Mme T. agrees that she's not modern. Possessed of abundant *sagesse populaire*, Marie Tremblay observes that millionaires are not happy; and she goes on, "J'ai vécu . . . je vivais pour vivre ["I've lived a long time; and I've always lived my life in the intention of living (well and surviving)]."

In all, the male orientation of the Perrault film is in full force here; and here, as in all his work, it is something tenacious and overwhelming. It remains to be known whether this is in the nature of the particular kind of "direct" he is making, and thus reflects the culture. Still, Perrault and his crew made this choice of material, and these works, that for the most part reflect a man's world, are plainly manipulated. Thus in *Le Règne* ... the men do most of the conversing: they compare the old and the new, the ancient and the modern; it is Tremblay who has Carnac explained to *him* as a mysterious monument from 2500 B.C., while little girls sing a silly song about the dolmens and the menhirs. And men go to the hunt (*à l'épouvante*) with scores of hunting dogs — the images evoking *La Règle du jeu*. The men read aloud from the tombstones of fallen soldiers and recount their war experiences to one another. For the most part it is the men who speak about the differences of language (one Québécois says that the language of the Frenchmen is "plus sympathique que le nôtre") and about other differences of custom and lifestyle between the Québécois and the French. (But they are agreed that it is French blood that runs in all of them; and, as far as that is concerned, Tremblay emphatically declares that the French are "like our ancestors," and that French Canadians will not disappear, regardless of their conflict with the *anglais*.) Beneath the walls of the fortified city of Saint-Malo, on the seashore — in images that highlight the Breton origins of the prinicpals —, it is Tremblay who [as in *Pour la suite* ...] again recalls the adventures of his hero, Jacques Cartier.

The photography of this film is exceptionally beautiful, in particular the Québec snow scenes that are intercut with the scenes shot in Brittany.

Piers Handling makes some useful observations regarding this film. He speaks of the tensions that Perrault shows between past and present, and adds, "For him it is important to recognize the time-honoured myths and practices of yesterday."[3] This tension finds a correlative in the conflict between Alexis, the dreamer, and his wife, Marie, "who doesn't dream and for whom the present is an improvement on the past because it's not as hard." Handling goes on to quote Michèle Favreau from *La Presse*: "*Le règne du jour* expresses the reality of this country; it profoundly expresses the soul of its people and reaches the universal naturally and without premeditation." Handling also tells how Léo Bonneville in *Séquences* had pointed out that the image is subordinate to the word in Perrault, an idea I can not entirely subscribe to.

Pratley, like Handling, finds that *Le Règne* ... is filmed in the "*cinéma direct*" method and is less a motion picture than a filmed conversation. He adds that this film is "refreshing, often warmly funny," and "a look-in on family life." From a theoretical point of view he notes that "it raises once again the question of the validity of the *cinéma-vérité* technique as the last word in realism once it

becomes apparent that the people being photographed are aware
of the camera and modulate their behavior accordingly, or start to
act for the cameras" (*TS* 1987, 185). I would add that there are
even more problems regarding "realism" than that, as I will show
a bit further on.

LES VOITURES D'EAU (1968–70; d. Pierre Perrault)

Perrault's *Les Voitures d'eau* is the third part of the trilogy that
includes *Pour la suite* ... and *Le Règne* .... All three deal with
the Tremblay family, which lives on the island called Ile-aux-
Coudres, off the mainland, where an antiquated brand of French is
spoken. In this film, the concern is with problems of builders and
navigators of *goélettes de bois*, or wooden schooners. (Discussions
of ships were not foreign to the first two films of the trilogy, for
that matter.) In *Les Voitures* ..., the family and their friends build
a magnificent boat using exactly the same techniques as their
ancestors would have, just as in *Pour la suite* ... they use the
ancient way of trapping the Beluga whales.

Pratley finds this film "gentle, amusing, tender and kind." He
adds, "... this is a poetic film about rugged and independent
people, beautifully observed and a social document for all time"
(*TS* 1987, 193). Perhaps, but for all that, it does not have the
"poetry" — the visual vocabulary — of *Pour la suite du monde*.

The commentary on Pierre Perrault is seemingly endless, for, as
Dominique Noguez says, he, like Lefebvre and Groulx, renounces
the end of what for a long time characterized the *québécois* cinéma:
an "extremist realism."[4] As for *Les Voitures d'eau*, it constitutes
for Noguez the third "panel of the triptych" that had begun with
Pour la suite du monde and *Le Règne du jour* ; moreover, the three
films together amount to a "poetic act." Perrault is a poet, says
Noguez, because he has an ear, and his films are to be listened
to, while the images are there only to pull you by the sleeve and
tell you to be silent, for someone is speaking. This process is for
Noguez most evident in *Les Voitures d'eau*. The characters say
"everything." (Noguez, then, agrees with Handling and Pratley on
the predominance of speech over image in Perrault's films.) The
past is completely reconstructed here, says Noguez: the runaway
child in cheap boats; the school mistress with her penances; the
beautiful plump girl who comes and sits on your knees; the government who ignores you; the Saint-Laurent that "the others" (the
anglais) call the Saint-Lawrence. And all the archaisms, neologisms,

and Canadianisms of the navigators and fishermen of the Ile-aux-Coudres and of their *porte-parole*, Pierre Perrault, are there too (Noguez 1971, 200−201). The vessels are, as it were, possessed of speech; speech and act are here turned into a ritual frozen in immobility like the frescoes of the Valley of the Kings or the verses of Theocritus. Continuing the classical allusions, Noguez claims that Perrault shows us a carpenter or a navigator in the same way that Hesiod or Virgil showed us Greek peasants. And Noguez finds that Perrault is related to Virgil in another way: the world he fixes on film is a dying world. The protagonists in the film (Eloi, Laurent) long for retreat (withdrawal, retirement); the youth have the anxiety and bitterness of Melibea in the First Bucolic (Noguez 1971, 202).

Les Voitures d'eau, says Noguez (1971, 202), is the last stage of a moving and desperate procedure: to revivify, for art and through art, that which is in the jaws of death. The film, which took thirty-five hours shooting-time, does not consist of reconstructing but of producing a situation (Noguez 1971, 203).

UN PAYS SANS BON SENS!, OR *WAKE UP, MES BONS AMIS!*, OR *A RIDICULOUS KIND OF COUNTRY!* (1970; d. Pierre Perrault)

Through the interview process, Perrault has also looked at the past of the Québécois, and at the present problems of these "French-Canadian Catholic mice" who desire respect and independence, in a film entitled in French, *Un Pays sans bon sens!*. In the English version, furnished by a voice-over that translates from the French, it is called *Wake Up, mes bons amis!*, a title that bespeaks the sufferings endured by the French Canadian, as symbolized by loggers under the command of anglophone bosses: the colonized and the colonizers! The food was terrible, the quarters miserable, the lice huge and atrocious; and, above all, the fatigue, though enormous, could not be assuaged, for there was always the call of the foreman, "Wake Up, mes bons amis."

The film explores various levels of nationalism, by showing the sense of *dépaysement*, even embarrassment, of a French Canadian (Allan Dale) born and raised in the Canadian West, as well as the anger of the Bretons in France, who were fighting a fight similar to that of the Québécois at the time of the making of the film, and the sentiment of the Canadian "Indian" in the backwoods of Canada, for whom "happiness" is not possible. Many *métiers* are represented, including teaching, logging, farming, and fishing.

Early in the film we see the caribou moving across the vast snowy regions of northern Canada, and — as in *Pour la suite du monde* — we hear Jacques Cartier's account of all the birds he saw, and of the "savages," hardened to the cold. But the ice and snow and the mortality that came to his men in the first winter of their stay reduced their numbers greatly. The *récit* of Cartier, one of the first Bretons to arrive in Canada, sets the scene for this film, concerned with origins and destinies. The Bretons themselves also voice their anger at the treatment they receive at the hands of the French (and of their need to mask their Breton origins), while the Québécois find in this an echo of their own problems with greater Canada. It is, however, striking to hear the French Canadians trying to define the word *pays*: Many of them see themselves as Canadian, not Québécois; others see the word *pays* as referring to one's town, one's house, or the climate, and admit that it can even be a barricade. Woven in and out of the story is the testimony of the Tremblays of Ile-aux-Coudres, who return and who express their feeling of being "at home" in France. Marie, in her knit bonnet, gives a description of a typical *québécois* house, tells how it was painted, and recounts the poverty of her childhood and her hard work as a spinner at the textile mill (which is now "beautiful"). The Western French Canadian expresses his sense of alienation, even embarrassment at his mother's speaking French, the kind we read about in Gabrielle Roy's books about her life as a child; he tells how he feels comfortable only in Québec.

A political dimension is added to the film by the recollection of De Gaulle's motto "Vive le Québec libre" and more particularly by the use of footage of René Lévesque, in which he gives speeches advancing his platform of emancipation for the Québécois. French Canadians, he says, will not be a part of the melting-pot concept: they are not "immigrants." All the problems the Canadians have with communication (88% of them unable to speak the language of the other) and all the issues of separation vs. confederation are here aired in full.

This film, owing nothing to sentiment or nostalgia, adjures the viewer to forget the picturesque and look at the harsh realities of French-Canadian life and the unenviable situation in which the Québécois find themselves. Fundamental questions of nationhood and patriotism are asked in this film. The most fundamental of all is: "Who are the 'viable' people, whose 'maturity' permits them to be 'allowed' autonomy and territory? and conversely, what can a people call 'their country'?"[5]

As the credits roll at the end of the film, one hears the traditional Jew's-harp in the background.

While interesting enough, *Un pays* ... is far from the best of Perrault's work. Some critics find it to be without restraint.

L'ACADIE, L'ACADIE (1971; d. Pierre Perrault and Michel Brault)

One of Perrault's most political films, also photographed by Michel Brault, *L'Acadie, l'Acadie* concerns the uprising of the Acadian students of the University of Moncton, New Brunswick, in 1971, as they demand that education and services for themselves and for their people continue to be provided in French, and that their culture and language be respected by the anglophone majority. It is a fascinating piece of work, because it reflects through the Acadian experience the ongoing frustrations and aspirations of the Québécois vis-à-vis the anglophone powerblocks in *their* province, and the stonewalling, unsympathetic attitudes of Ottawa, and indeed of all the rest of Canada. So many measures taken to address this nationwide conflict have not worked, and the conflict, often taking on racist implications, a conflict that began when Wolfe defeated Montcalm, if not before, continues yet today.

L'Acadie, l'Acadie is a film to be seen; the students are magnificent and courageous, and the isolating and humiliating conditions of the older French-speaking people quite pathetic. But I do not know of an edition of this film that bears subtitles, and the spoken French is very difficult for many viewers.

Pratley, both in *Variety*[6] and in *Torn Sprockets*, calls the film "overlong, out-dated *cinéma-vérité* ..." He adds that "when the filmmakers talk to people in their daily life about their opinions this is fair comment; when public meetings are being filmed, bias is noticeable in the method of shooting and editing." He complains in his *Variety* article about the length and talkiness, but nevertheless concedes [both in the article and in his book (*TS* 1987, 198)] that it is a valuable and useful document for the future and, in the article, says it is a "fine example of the freedom which exists in Canada allowing dissidents to express themselves at public expense." (That is not the whole story, however, when one recalls the experiences of filmmakers in the times of the October, 1970, crisis, which will be discussed in Chapter 6.)

LA GRANDE ALLURE (1985; d. Pierre Perrault)

La Grande Allure is another, more recent documentary made by Perrault. In part one it deals with the trip of inhabitants of Saint-Malo to Québec on a ship named Le Blanchon, manned by a crew of Bretons and Québécois. It is again about Jacques Cartier (as it had been upon occasion in the trilogy and also in his 1983 *Les Voies bas et en travers*). This time, Perrault fabricates a crossing of the Atlantic in a sailship called "Le Blanchon," drawing his inspiration from Cartier's journal.

On the trip are Michel Garneau, the poet, and also the philosopher, Michel Serres; therefore the dialogue often becomes quite weighty as the men discuss the search for roots, and what constitutes the *"berceau"* (cradle) of the *québécois* nation. (In *Le Règne*, Alexis Tremblay had told the New Yorkers that he was going to France to see the *"berceau"* of his ancestors.) But these travelers, who are in quest of a country, come to wonder if "a country" really exists, and to what extent the quest is based on myth. This is at once the tale of a maritime epic and an interior adventure — the interior adventure of a crew in search of a country.

The second part of *La Grande Allure* deals to a large extent with the St. Lawrence River. It is *film-poème* on the musk ox of Québec's Great North. (Perrault elaborates on this theme in his newest film, *L'Oumigmag* [1993], the least characteristic of his works.) This part of the documentary "reinvents" the country that was sought after in Part I, and that country is at once real and mythical. Perrault concludes the odyssey by having those who spoke in his other films speak again. In the process, he also reconstructs images of an epoch now gone.

We should not wonder that Perrault's films seem at times (and are often said to be) like poetry; he himself is a poet, having published several volumes of poetry, which can be sampled in Guy Sylvestre's anthology.[7] This gift may explain why many commentators (Lever, Pratley, Noguez) insist upon the verbal and oral nature of his films, which then participate (like the novels of Antonine Maillet) in the oral (folklore) tradition of his country. But, on the other hand, the visual beauty of his films, the soft and luminous nature of many scenes, contradicts that insistence. And, interestingly enough, even Pierre Véronneau, writing of Perrault (in Coulombe 1991, 430) calls him a "cinéaste de la parole." Would it not be better to say that his work offers an uncommonly happy blend of the visual (or iconographic) and the oral, through both of which he collects the material and spiritual culture of a past age? (Not to mention the political turmoil of the late 60s and early 70s?, or the plight of the Amerindians in *Le Goût de la farine* of 1977—co-directed with B. Gosselin?) He is both poet and master of the "direct" film, which leans upon the visual; he is both personal and *engagé* (committed to a cause). Strangely enough, this former student of history and law, this seeker of the past, is often considered the pioneering force of *québécois* cinema: the one who set the tone and construct of that body of film, which for the most part retains the nature of the direct film, even in feature-length fictional films. A pioneer of the art form he used, who sought roots and traditions of his society in the common people around him, in their folksongs, in their words, their way of life, their beliefs.

Though Perrault's works are always classified as "direct cinema," or documentaries, Lever wants to underscore the fact that many of the scenes are staged. He shows this in his discussion of *L'Acadie, l'Acadie*, saying that "In spite of the reduction of the crew to a minimum, the suppleness and the dexterity of the operators, in spite of the discretion of the director, there is always a certain *mise en scène* [staging] (or *mise en place*—[placing]) of the participants, an organization of space and a choice of framings" (Lever *Hist.* 1988, 151). Lever again alludes to this planting or staging in his brief words about Perrault's *Pays de la terre sans arbre ou le Mouchouânipi*. "In documentaries," he writes, "there are often things planted, for the filmmakers to discover." (*Hist.* 1988, 224; my translations.)

Of course, it is especially when we discuss the works of Perrault and other similar directors that we also confront the problem of "realism" and "reality" in cinema. Without belaboring the point, since in this book we are not primarily concerned with theory, we should nevertheless bear in mind some of the issues that arise when we presume to think we have anything approaching reality in film representation. Barthes, Derrida, Bazin, and others have dealt at length with these questions, and their views are cogently analyzed in Peter Brunette and David Wills. At the very least, let us remember that the image is not reality, but appears as reality by virtue of being so close to that reality in terms of resemblance. And also let us bear in mind that in film reality is framed, and therefore cannot be complete. Besides, reality does not equal truth or there would, obviously, be no need of a camera. And, just as important, in every film we look at, be it documentary or fiction, or something halfway between the two, the process of editing has altered any even theoretical "reality." There are, also, alterations of "reality" that come through lighting, and so on. Therefore, realism in Perrault, or in any film creation, is a figment of our imagination, a part of the illusion.[8]

Réal LaRochelle (in Coulombe, 1991, 74–75) finds two major faults that characterize most of *québécois* direct films: ethnocentrism of the themes and political radicalism. These are attributed to Maurice Bulbulian, whose works make cutting criticism of social and economic inequalities, of political brutality, and of man's violence to man. Bulbulian did work with the Inuit and the Amerindians in such films as *Ameshkuatan — Les Sorties du castor* (1978, coprod. with M. Hébert); *Debout sur leur terre* (1982); and *Dancing Around the Table* (1988). But Noguez points out that through his films, Perrault gives to *québécois* culture one of its great myths, *without falling into "folklorization"* (1971, 204). Following his example, and that of Groulx, of Lefebvre, or of the Jutra of *Wow*, the Québécois filmmakers of the 70s will avoid this pitfall of "folklorization," and indeed may go in the opposite direction, exhibiting an attention to everything that exists in Québec (especially its youth), while looking sometimes upon this changing society with a lack of nostalgia or indulgence, with sarcasm even, with blasphemy, with violent criticism. And, like Perrault, the younger filmmakers will make of Québec the fundamental subject of their film (1971, 206).

Whatever else we may say, the fact remains that Perrault and Brault, representing a new kind of ethno-historian, recognized early on the role the camera could play in the telling of Québec history. As Yvan Lamonde writes, "To go into the ever-present past, to go out into the world in order to come to know it, it was obviously necessary to release the camera, to grasp all it was capable of. It was necessary to live out in and with the world. Brault, Perrault did that. They went 'directly,' to catch the gesture, to catch the word and language [of the people]." Lamonde goes on to speak of Marius Barbeau, who in the 1920s had gone out to record 'directly' the stories, songs, and legends of Charlevoix on Edison cylinders. He mentions other great documentarians of the past — Tessier, Proulx, and others. The trick for ethnographers was to put a picture with the sound, and then, later, to put sound to the picture. (An intermediary stage of ethnography came with the radio, but absence of picture and the tendency of the voices to become 'golden voices,' or idols, removed from ordinary people, lessened its force.) The trick was to make talking pictures, and to have the camera "participate" in ethnography. "In Québec's *cinéma direct* with Perrault and Brault, the thematic and ethnographic content was ... traditional .... But in addition ... the modalities proper to the camera, the very technological innovations of picture-taking and of capturing sound made a new medium of this technique of having the camera participate synchronically ...." And, finally, "... with the technology of direct cinema, with the participating synchronic camera, the ordinary world became a 'star'. The ordinary world could look at itself, hear itself .... And that seems ... to be the cultural innovation of *québécois* direct cinema. In it, a technology remains with the ordinary world, directly, intentionally. And in doing this, ... one passed from the ancestral Ile-aux-Coudres (by way of *Les Voitures d'eau*) directly to Moncton with *L'Acadie, l'Acadie*, and then indirectly to *Les Ordres*, by Michel Brault." Lamonde then shows us how the tradition of the *cinéma direct* "is no longer"; how we now have *cinéma indirect*, a cinema of transposition, in films we will be looking at in the course of this study: *Réjeanne Padovani* ("indirectement du vécu"); then *Bingo*; and *Les Ordres* (transpositions of the October crisis). Thus he traces the passage from the ethnographic direct cinema to an indirect political cinema. (Lamonde "Indir ..." 1974, 22–4; my translations and paraphrases.)

But in the evocation of Québec's past (as a source of present political and social problems) Perrault and Brault were not the only ones to create important "documentaries." For so did Denys Arcand, who was destined to become one of Québec's most renowned *cinéastes*. As an example of his early work, we will look at his *Champlain*. He has also made documentaries about the history of Montréal, which have important connections with his recent fiction film, *Jésus de Montréal* (Chapter 6).

CHAMPLAIN (1964; d. Denys Arcand)

This splendid piece of early work by Arcand, entitled *Champlain* (1964),[9] is especially notable not only for its intention to find roots in the history of Québec, but also for what it tells us about Arcand in his early days, and how these connect with his present work (discussed in Chapters 5 and 6). Known for his interest in history, and his desire to tell history on film, Arcand in this short piece not only tells the history of Champlain, the founder of Québec, and of the early Quebeckers, but sets the story in a global context. As is understandable, it was important to Arcand that he incorporate an account of what was going on in Europe while the province was being settled. But just how is one to do this in a "documentary," where color is desirable and motion is a necessity, yet that color

and especially that motion are not "documented"? Often reenactment is the solution to this problem, but not here to any great
extent. Rather, Arcand enlisted the services of Frédéric Back,
later to become one of the world's most distinguished animators,
who provided superb contemporary color drawings. Of course,
Arcand adds old prints and paintings (as stills). And he shoots
a great deal of scenery from the rocky ocean coastline of the East,
and of the Saint Lawrence river. As the camera moves from scene
to scene and drawing to drawing, we have a female voice-over
giving us the narrative. He adds some "dialogue," or what we might
call "narration dialoguée," as we learn of Champlain's encounters
with the Iroquois — during which he was wounded — and of his
interaction with the Algonquins. Some readings from the writings
of Champlain are also included. The task was to show not only the
life of Champlain (1603–35), but the major historical events that
occurred during his lifetime and impacted on the settlement of the
province. Arcand succeeded admirably at the task; so much so that
this film took prizes in Montréal and Toronto.

Most effectively, Arcand provides shots that evoke the time and
bespeak a humanist's sensitivity to the most daily of things; such is
the image of the socks hanging on a clothesline; such are the faces
of women — Indian women, in particular. To bring his work to
closure, he humorously gives a series of quick shots of places and
businesses bearing the name of Champlain, including one called
the "Hôtel Champlain," run by one C. R. Arcand! These shots are
accompanied by jazz music. Such strategic photos function as icons
of the material and spiritual culture of Québec, and foretell Arcand's
lifelong preoccupation with history and the solutions he has arrived
at in overcoming the problems of "filming history." But the history
he tells here cannot fall back on archival footage, nor is Arcand
able to take his camera into the scenes that "made history." And,
surely, too, he interprets the story of Champlain from his own
perspectives, mythologizing as much as Perrault, perhaps.

In other words, the direct style is not always so direct! Certainly,
"memory never lacks imagination," as Perrault himself has said
(Lever *Hist.* 1988, 18), and when it comes to the making of a highly
subjective and poetic "documentary" (dare we call it that?), Jean
Chabot's recent *Voyage en Amérique avec un cheval emprunté* may
well take all prizes. With a rather strong flavor of antiAmericanism,
Chabot takes a trip through Yankeeland, in part *through a desire
to come to understand his ancestors*; and on his return, he hears
"his wife" telling him that "*roots are not sought but invented.*"

VOYAGE AN AMÉRIQUE AVEC UN CHEVAL EMPRUNTÉ. (1987; d. Jean Chabot)

This is a meditation on the continent. This is partly personal autobiography and — since inseparable — also an historic evocation of the continent, showing, among other things, the ironic contrasts between the Mohawk past, the Iroquois present, and the white man's way of pollution and restlessness. It also shows contrasts between the American and the *québécois* way of life. It traces roots through the *coureurs des bois*, Nouvelle France, Québec, and contrasts the loyalists of Prescott, Ontario, with the citizens of a New England town celebrating the Fourth of July.

The Indians evoking Wounded Knee add to the nostalgia, as they chant of "expatriation; extermination." The sad blues in the background also contribute to the haunting tone of this work.

Chabot, about to be a father at the end of a millenium, wonders what will be left to the new generation: pollution, noise, acid rain. As for the memories of his childhood, very little will remain, for "this world no longer exists, it has disappeared without a trace." He lists the sufferings of his ancestors; he recalls his visits to the blacksmith, which now is destroyed.

At nightfall Chabot looks for silence and at first cannot find it in this brash, loud America. Later he falls asleep and dreams he is traveling the continent on a great white horse — whence the title. Because the horse (as transportation) is of the past and of dream, and loosely tied to the memories of the blacksmith's shop, it is a powerful sign in the film.

By day two of his journey, he is haunted by the notion of the terrestrial paradise we imagine America to be. He observes that all over the planet there is hatred of America and of Americans, this "... drôle de peuple ... le plus libre et le plus dangereux; riche et entêté, etc. [... strange people ... the freest and the most dangerous; rich and stubborn, etc.]." America crushes all in its path. Then comes a litany of the names of big American companies, meant to evoke its capitalist economy.

His thoughts return to his native country, which is being erased. He thinks of the Québécois who are yet to come. How will they seem? What will they look like? Will they have something distinctive about them?

He returns to Montréal, significantly between 11 p.m. and midnight; the return is as if from and to a foreign land. The city seems to have been built during his absence. "This people, from whom I come, are in risk of disappearing," he laments. (Read: of being swallowed up by the giant to the South ... no sleeping giant at that!)

The voice of a woman speaks of the birth of his child. Here we have a collective autobiography of the Québécois, threatened with extinction and with disappearing from the face of the earth. *Disparaître*: the verbal leitmotif of this unusual film.

Yet curiously enough, the evocations of a purer, more innocent, less stressful childhood — a time of horses and clean air — must touch the heart of any American of a certain age, as well. When I was a small child, the iceman delivered ice (for iceboxes; no one in our neighborhood had an electric refrigerator) by horse and wagon, and as he cut off chunks of ice, we would grab small pieces that scattered, and eat them with great pleasure. Who had heard of an ice cube then? And the mailman brought our mail, unencumbered by dozens of catalogues, charity pleas, and other "junk mail," directly to our houses twice a day. Candy could be bought with a now never-seen Indian penny. And, most ironically, the scenes of the blacksmith vividly restored to me scenes of my own childhood when I would visit my uncle's blacksmith shop in Owatonna, Minnesota. His face, hands, and arms black from his work, he would warn me not to get too close to the fire; he would take me and my brothers and sister out to farms, where we would watch him shoe the skittish horses. That shop too is long since converted to something else, perhaps destroyed. Americans too must be victims of "Americanization"!

In *Voyage* ... the search for roots and meaning is rather personal; in Carrière's *St-Denis dans le temps* we have an effort to "document" through film an important historical event.

ST-DENIS DANS LE TEMPS (1969; d. Marcel Carrière)

St-Denis dans le temps uses old footage, old photographs, reconstructions, flashbacks, etc., to evoke the French Canadian uprising of 25 November 1837, which took place in and around the town — or agricultural parish — of St-Denis (sur) Rivière Richelieu, 30 km. north of St.-Hyacinthe, and to portray the enormous festivals that surround the event, especially those that were held on the occasion of its centennial in 1937. This was of course only one of several skirmishes of the period brought about by the insurrections of the French-Canadian nationalists, organized through the Parti Canadien (led by Speaker of the Assembly Louis-Joseph Papineau), and then through the Patriot Party, after 1826.

Particularly effective are the enactments of the battles, in which the heavily armed English, having come from Sorel, approach the village on 23 November 1837, hungry for their breakfast and bent upon putting down these patriots, whose militant Montréalais representatives were known as the Fils de la Liberté, and who, in St.-Denis, were led by Dr. Wolfred Nelson. The English, who have come in two detachments led by Col. Charles Wetherall and Lt-Col. Francis Gore, also want a cup of tea, almost more than anything, of course. While the English under Gore are at first forced to beat a retreat, the insurrection, or rebellion, is ultimately supressed by Wetherall at St.-Charles; Gore returns to St.-Denis on 30 November, but the town surrenders and is sacked. Fifty houses of the village are burned and, in the end, in 1838 the guilty Québécois are rounded up, emprisoned, and condemned to be hanged and to be buried in unconsecrated land, having meanwhile been excommunicated, which only goes to show that the archconservative Canadian Catholic Church of the time was in complete accord with the English government and with the Governor General of what was then called "Lower Canada." Lord Gosford was Governor from 1835 to 1838.[10]

Woven throughout are the thoughts of Marie-Claire, a descendant of one of these soldiers, an actress who has come to St.-Denis to attend the festivities. But of greatest importance is the dialogue between Marie-Claire, a revolutionary idealist, and her friend Gilles (a bourgeois pragmatist) who accuses her of being — as most women are — *apolitisée*. Filmed in 1967−69, the work has definite contemporaneous applications to the separatist revolution then stirring in Québec, which culminated in the crisis of October, 1970 (studied through several films in Chapter 6 of this book), and which is, in fact, still fomenting through the failure of the Meech Lake Accord and the reports of the Allaire Commission.

While this film offers an account of a key event in French Canadian history and suggests an analogue we readily apprehend as we view it, I have seen this work without subtitles, and am convinced that the average English-speaking person would understand very little of the dialogue, cast largely in Joual or else expressed through a French that is heavily French Canadian in nature. This linguistic stance would be an integral part of the still-applicable political statements buried in the film, but limits the kind of audience outside French Canada that might otherwise view the film with profit.

As an addendum to *Saint-Denis* ..., one should note the full-length fictional film *Quelques Arpents de neige* (1973; d., Denis

Héroux). It, too, renders the 1837 Rebellions. (Denis Héroux, with an M.A. in history, had special interest in such a subject.) Briefly recapitulated, Simon returns to his family home, which has been confiscated and then resold by the English administrators of Québec. Simon refuses to side with the revolutionaries, however, and instead falls in love with his neighbor, who happens to be engaged to a young lawyer. Nevertheless, she reciprocates, and the two try to flee the rebellion and its woes, but are unable. The dénouement finds our hero escaping to the border, with his mistress dead. The film caused some controversy for its portrayal of the English as oppressors who desecrate a Catholic church. It was branded "political pornography" in Toronto. But in any case there are splendid scenes of the icebound St. Lawrence river. The beauty of the country is underlined, especially the snow scenes (v. title). In one rather exciting scene, the rebels ambush the English, and cut the ice out from under them. In *Variety* one reads: "The loosely-knit plot and lack of dramatic tension reduce substantially this film's potential." Criticized there, too, are the overuse of interior scenes and the confusing rendition of the period: "The story-line jumps from political plotting to groundless romance, all the while supposing that the spectator understands the historical background. To those not familiar with this period in Quebec, the picture will be confusing."[11]

We have seen that by tradition most makers of Québec film have as a preeminent goal the capture by camera of an essential if mythic Québec. First, in documentary, Perrault dug into the cultural past of the province. This tradition has been perpetuated in such a film as Jean-Daniel Lafond's 1987 *Voyage au bout de la route*, half-documentary, half-poetry. It has particular bearing on my understanding of *Le Matou* (discussed in my Ch. 4); nevertheless we shall look at it here as an excellent documentary piece that verges upon poetry.

Recent Documentaries

LE VOYAGE AU BOUT DE LA ROUTE, OU LA BALLADE DU PAYS QUI ATTEND (1987, d. Jean-Daniel Lafond)

Perrault's magisterial work aside, the Québec film industry, supported by the National Film Board, has produced other excellent documentaries, not the least of which is *Voyage au bout . . .*, a film that illustrates the contribution of popular music in the troubadour style in a very beautiful format, as the work of Douai, the French singer, is studied along with local Québec iluminaries such as Felix Leclerc, Gilles Vigneault, and even several fine Amerindian "singers," all of them giving us a sense of the impact on the society of various ways of singing. The two most striking things here are the portrayal of young Indians who sing in their language and yet betray the Indian style per se, and, above all, the melding of glorious shots of the Québec landscape with the music, as the Frenchman travels about in quest of the ultimate *québécois* "song." Among other things the generally unseen narrator conducts "interviews" that reveal his biases and the opinions of the Québécois themselves, and in particular of the Indian minorities, who refuse to play the role of "touristic" stereotypical Indians. The dialogue is in French, without benefit of subtitles.

In this beautiful film the French minstrel Jacques Douai travels through remote regions of La Côte-Nord, visiting such places as Baie Comeau, Port Cartier, Sept-Iles, Maliotenam, Rivière-au-Tonnerre, and Havre Saint-Pierre in his effort to come to understand exactly what Québec means to its inhabitants. We see segments from the *Terre promise*, from Perrault, who is acknowledged in the credits. We see majestic scenes of the mythic figure known as the *maître draveur* (master logger). We hear the testimonies of poets and singers, such as Claude Léveillée, Lawrence Lepage, Bernard Cimon, and, especially, of Jean Gagné, who tells how the song "L'amour de moi" has given him an appreciation of his culture and its possibilities for the future. We see Félix Leclerc in his January 1986 appearance at the Théâtre du Grand Dérangement and hear him declaring that only the language can, so to speak, define a country (*un pays*).

In sum, this film validates the use of song as a method of securing one's liberty, as Québécois have often done (e.g., in the folksong whose refrain says "Et merde à la reine d'angleterre"). It also utilizes the most important declarations of the poet Gaston Miron, from whom the following lines are quoted:

> Je n'ai jamais voyagé
> vers d'autres pays
> que toi mon pays.

The film features the poet Roland Jomphe, who speaks of the evolution of Québec culture and reads from his poem "Laisse-le s'en aller," sung by Jacques Douai. In Jomphe's most complex

Pays. (Courtesy Office National du Film.)

sentence lies the secret not only of *québécois* literature and film, but of the very psychology and motto of the people of Québec. He writes, as quoted in the film:

> "le réve d'hier portera l'avenir au bout du souvenir."
> [the dream of yesterday will carry the future to the end of memory.]
> This must be the end of the road that the title of the film bespeaks.

Another documentary in a similar vein that deals with the language conflicts experienced by all Canadian francophones is *J'ai pas dit mon dernier mot* (NFB).

In discussing the "search for roots," we should not overlook the recent attention to (sometimes expatriated) French Canadian "culture heroes" found in certain documentaries and fictionalized "docudramas." Will James is one such hero.

ALIAS WILL JAMES (1988; d. Jacques Godbout)

Alias Will James is in many respects the most fascinating of this group of films pertaining to roots and heroes. It was directed by Jacques Godbout, one of the most renowned of Québec's direc-

La Gammick. (Courtesy Office National du Film.)

tors. He has produced many films, both documentaries — e.g., *En dernier recours* — and fictional features, including a thriller, *La Gammick*, which attempts to be a popular *québécois* transposition of a film noir. It has a sociological thesis in the bargain (i.e., that "even in *la pègre* [the mob] French Canadians think small and lack confidence" [Lever *Hist.* 1988, 231]). It may well strike one as a parody of the genre: whether it is or not is for each viewer to decide. Godbout has also done a musical comedy entitled *IXE-13* [1972], a cynical film based on the 1950s *romans-feuilletons* of Pierre Saurel (Pierre Daineault), about a comic strip super-spy, with music by François Dompierre, with the chanteuse Louise Forestier, and the actors André Dubois, Carole Laure, and Luce Guilbeault. Unfortunately for them, *IXE−13* quickly became dated, as is confirmed by Lever (*Hist.* 1988, 230). The film examined Québec culture, which is Godbout's main interest, especially culture as reflected through information-gathering techniques. In fact, Lever contends that his films go beyond journalistic reportage to reach the status of the essay. Godbout is, incidentally, also one of Canada's most famous authors (*L'Aquarium; Le Couteau sur la table; L'Amour, P.Q.; L'Isle au dragon; Salut Galarneau!; Têtes à Papineau*).

Alias Will James tells the story of Will James, a famous novelist whose works provided Hollywood with many a cowboy film. (Clips from the film versions of James's *Sand* [1949], and *Smoky* [1933; 1946; 1966], produced by 20th Century Fox, are intercut from time to time in *Alias* . . . .) Godbout's film, which alternates facts about James's life and career as an artist, novelist, actor, and even cowboy, with scenes interviewing modern-day French Canadians who have exiled themselves from their *pays* and their people for the mythic "romance" of the (rodeo) cowboy (Bénard; David), i.e, that kind of man who must be a cowboy in spite of himself and everyone else ("It's like a vaccination; a drug"). But the most surprising discovery we make in this very well-done piece is that the celebrated Western novelist, artist ("he drew horses better than Russell"), and actor, Will James, was in reality a Québécois named Ernest Dufault (or Defaulx), who was born in Saint-Nazaire d'Acton, and not in Alberta/Montana, as he has claimed in his "autobiography" (*Lone Cowboy*).[12] We learn how as a boy of fifteen (in 1907), he left his home in Québec, after having seen the circus of rough riders, featuring Buffalo Bill and Sitting Bull. He took a train to the Far West ("I had to go to the Far West"). He started his cowboy career at Cypress Hills, near Val Marie, on the border of Saskatchewan and Alberta, and may have served a prison term for his involvement in a cattle-rustling scam. Upon coming out of prison Dufault officially became Will James.

James had a thirst to ride broncos, and had several accidents relating to this occupation. But he always drew bucking horses, even on the walls or wherever he could. He tried at first to sell pictures in San Francisco, but failed; meanwhile, he worked in the movies as a stuntman and an extra in the early Westerns. He was not successful in the first few years of his life. It was in the American West that he "invented his life," saying, as he does in *Lone Cowboy*, that he was born in Alberta. From several sources, including interviews with James's descendants in America, and with descendants of his close relatives in Québec, the story of his life unfolds. His father was Jean Dufault, "marchand général," from Québec, his mother a Baillargeon from Trois Rivières. He confessed at one juncture that people would have laughed at him if they had learned that he was born in Saint-Nazaire d'Acton and that every morning he served at mass before taking care of the cows. Still, he points out, those who read him thought him sincere, and "I was sincere." Curiously enough, Godbout asserts that even though American readers would take Will James for a full-blooded, died-in-the-wool cowboy of the Great American West—so well did he learn the English language (almost completely forgetting his French; e.g., "dis-elle," says he in a letter, meaning, "tell her");

and so well did he carry off the subterfuge — nevertheless, his writings bear the marks of his childhood, and in his books one can find themes that recall the contemporaries he left behind (Ringuet, Germaine Guèvremont, Félix-Antoine Savard). Incidentally, the story of Will James is somewhat reminiscent of the "Grey Owl" hoax perpetrated by the Englishman, Archie Belaney, who became Canada's most celebrated "native Indian."

In the course of this revelation, so many myths about cowboys are debunked as to give those who deal with cowboy lore considerable pause. (Especially discredited is the idea that the cowboy is always "mighty dangerous.") Yet what *most* comes through in the film are James's fear of being discovered and called an imposter, and the sense of loneliness and exile experienced by him and others in his "boots." Towards the end of his life, in particular, he became obsessed with the idea that, as his films came to be shown in Québec (Eugène Forde's *Smoky* featured Victor Jory, Irene Bentley, and Will James "as himself"), someone would recognize him as Ernest Dufault. His legendary nature is illustrated by the songs about him that Ian sings: "His heroes were his horses/and he drew them clear and true/on every page they'd come alive/and jump straight out at you," and again: "Whiskey was his mistress/ his true love was the West, etc." James became quite wealthy as a star, artist, and writer. He bought "un coin de paradis," near Prior, Montana: 8000 acres of land, with a handsome ranchhouse. He strove to live in a purist fashion, "*au naturel*," and refused the modern way of life — he refused to have smooth roads, or running water. (His wife, Alice Conrad, ten years his junior, and a beauty queen from Nevada — whom James sketched and painted over and over — would have a bath in the hotel when they went to Billings. He would have a drink, and see to his publishing tasks.)

Despite his great fame, not only as a novelist and film "star," but also as a "documentarian and an ecologist," and even though he received offers to go to Yale University and elsewhere, James always preferred to stay in Montana. Towards the end of his life, he began to disappear from time to time; he would be found after drinking bouts in hospitals or in post hotels. He separated from his wife in 1935. He died 3 September 1942 of cirrhosis, in a Hollywood hospital, disillusioned in part by the disappearance of the "Far West" — the gold mines were exhausted and closed, space was closing in, and only the memory of the former grandeur remained.

This strange man, who willed all his belongings to Ernest Dufault, "to whom he owed everything," had requested to be cremated. His ashes were scattered over Billings, Montana. But Godbout's film ends with the idea that in reality it was Dufault who died; Will James is still very much remembered. At the Will James High School, children are asked who Will James was: They are able to show his complexity in their answers, for various individuals respond variously, saying he was an artist, a pioneer, a poet, and a cowboy.

This striking work is studied by Jean Larose.[13] He sees in James's final fall from glory a prolongation, rather than a contradiction, of his youthful flight from his country of origin. Larose also sees in Québec's Survenant — whose name one never comes to know — a response to James's adventure.

I would add that James's life is a success story, albeit ending in tragedy, that may illustrate what America meant to turn-of-the-century French Canadians, turned Franco-American. *Les Tisserands du pouvoir* will show the downside of this immigration into the United States. For some, then, the *déplacement* transported them to Eden; for others it was a living hell of alienation, nostalgia, and hard labor. It will be remembered that the last episode of Ringuet's novel, *Thirty Acres*, is on this theme as well.

What also emerges from *Alias Will James* is the interest it might have not only for American lovers of the Western film, but also for Québécois audiences who feel drawn to America and especially to famous French Canadians who have been "successful" in America. It will be recalled that another such person (perhaps as tragic as James, in the end) was Jack Kerouac, about whom Herménégilde Chiasson made a film (1987; 54 min. 39 sec). By virtue of the fact that Kerouac is an American-born French Canadian of Breton descent whose story is told by Chiasson, an Acadian, this film will not be discussed in detail in this book. But my readers might note that there is a still from Chiasson's *Le Grand Jack* reproduced in these pages.[14] This film is, by the way, one of the few French Canadian works readily available through American video suppliers; it exists with English dialogue.

FROM DOCUMENTARY TO FICTIONALIZED FILM (Documentary Style)

A less well-known application of documentary style to "write history" — even contemporary history — is Robin Spry's now somewhat dated anglophone *fiction* film from Québec, called *Prologue*, an anglophone film made in 1969. In it an American, David, joins a commune in Massawippi, in southern Québec — on a lake near the New York border, not far from Lac Magog, and quite close to Sherbrooke — while Jessie, a Québécois, participates in the demonstrations outside the Conrad Hilton on Michigan Avenue that took place during the 1968 Chicago Democratic convention. The film depicts the conflicts young people faced during the Vietnam era, through the experiences of this young Montréal journalist and the American draft evader, and of their mutual friend, a renegade Jewess, who questions the motives of both, as she searches for her own identity through association with them. The fundamental problem posed — whether to practice an active or a passive resistance to perceived wrongs — seems to rise out of an existential frame, and, from that angle, certainly has relevancy yet today. But in any case, effects of documentary realism are gained in this film through the use of a great deal of newsreel footage, including scenes of the huge demonstration that occurred in Chicago during the 1968 Democratic convention. Thus the theme of relations between Québec and America in the troubled 60s is recaptured, almost as the encounters happen, in this particular "fictionalized documentary."

Indeed, this documentary style very often prevails in the fictional cinema of Québec, as in Canadian fictional film in general. This characteristic, perhaps a legacy of the National Film Board's early intentions to portray Canada to the Canadians and to the rest of the world, emerges as a strong trait of the films of the 60s. In the national arena, one of the best examples of this style carried over into feature films is *Nobody Waved Goodbye*. But there are good examples of it in *québécois* film as well. In addition to *Les Ordres*, mentioned above, we might single out, in particular, such an excellent film as *La Vie heureuse de Léopold Z. (The Merry World of Leopold Z.)*. It portrays Léopold's family life, work, and problems in a very realistic fashion; and the snow that it is his job to remove "documents" the conditions of living through a winter in Montréal in a way perhaps not demonstrated so vividly in any other *québécois* movie.

Yet another fictional film that relies heavily on the documentary style is *Jacques et Novembre* directed by Jean Beaudry and François Bouvier. As will later be seen in detail (Chapter 5), this striking short film presents a commentary on the *désir de cinéma* and, in the process, an anatomy of death. In fact, whenever we speak of the Canadian film, it is difficult not to include this "direct," or documentary, style in one's considerations; it permeates the field. Such a film as *Dear Theo* (Chapter 5) depends so much upon the contrasts between the neo-realism of the hospital milieu and the deeply spiritual kinship that is evolving between two roommates, that to dismiss the debt to the cinéma vérité and/or direct methods would be to distort the force that drives the film. And when it comes to discussing women directors' films, we will again have to divide their work between the documentary and the fictional, or feature, films; but in both cases this trend in Canadian film will be apparent. Among some of the great fictional films that, at the same time, may upon occasion set up a kind of reenactment of the events being examined, or even include excerpts from other real or simulated documentaries, one must especially note the work of Anne Claire Poirier, e.g., her *Filles du Roy* or *Mourir à tue-tête*, both of which are powerful and troubling films. It is little wonder, then, that documentary style should be heavily enlisted in films where roots are at issue.

Fictional Films with Historical Settings

It is, then, not only through documentaries and semi-documentaries that the heritage of Québec and its unique culture are explored and given filmic representation. Often a director will opt for a "docudrama" to portray some historical event or personality from Québec's (or Canada's) past. Or, as we have intimated above, s/he may even seek a mimetic evocation of the past through a purely fictional narrative.

The first fictional film we will consider for its documentary style and its look at early French Canadian history is *Etienne Brûlé*.

ETIENNE BRÛLÉ, GIBIER DE POTENCE OR, *E. B., THE IMMORTAL SCOUNDREL* (1951–1952; d. Melburn Turner)

This first full-length Canadian fictional film in color[15] is one that exploits French-Canadian history, portraying the adventures of Etienne Brûlé, an early explorer and protégé of Champlain, among the Indians. It was filmed in Montréal, first in 16 mm kodachrome and then transferred to 35 mm color. The lead actor, Paul Dupuis (b. Montréal, 1916), was a war correspondent in England, and there familiarized himself with the cinema milieus. He made a dozen films in English, and—in France and in Québec—a number of less-important films in French (Coulombe 1991, 171). Véronneau characterizes *Etienne Brûlé* as a *québécois* Western, set in the times of Nouvelle-France. He summarizes the film as follows: Having arrived in Nouvelle-France with Champlain in 1608, Brûlé quickly got involved with the Hurons, whose language and customs he rapidly learned. Champlain's agent of confidence when it came to the Indians, Brûlé took charge in 1615 of recruiting five hundred of them to help the French in military matters. A few years later, Champlain again sends him to the Hurons. This time, Brûlé decides to stay among them longer, motivated mainly by monetary potential, but also by the lustful life that he can lead with them, and also by the joys of alcohol. (His dissolute way of life among the Indians is shown in a still in Véronneau *Cin* ... 1979, 102.) Brûlé even goes so far as to betray his own people in favor of the British Admiral Kirke. Because of Brûlé, the French and their allies suffer losses at the hands of the English and of the Iroquois. Pursued by the French, Brûlé believes he can take refuge among the Hurons. But they, shocked by his immorality and the betrayals of which he has been guilty, give him an appropriate reception: they torture him and put him to death at the stake. (*Cin* ... 1979, 99; my paraphrase and translation.)

Marcotte writes "Its real originality is to have directly approached — and with success, often, for many of the shots do not lack strength — the Canadian landscape. With *Etienne Brûlé*, the French Canadian cinema for the first time breathes the open air of the country: it makes the link between man and nature, between the documentary and total cinema. It is our first (lucky) stab at authenticity." (From *Le Devoir* [22–9–52]; cited by Véronneau *Cin* ... 1979, 103; my translation.)[16]

The recent 1991 *Black Robe*, starring Lothaire Bluteau, deals with quite another aspect of these relations between Iroquois, Hurons, and white men (this time the Jesuits).

Another rather remarkable example of a "reconstruction" of a historical event, and one that bears traces of this tension, is found in *Les Brûlés*, or *La Terre promise*. This film is also oriented toward the documentary style. Nevertheless, it is a narrative film. The actors are Félix Leclerc, Jean Lajeunesse, and J.-Léo Gagnon.

LA TERRE PROMISE; ALSO CALLED *LES BRÛLÉS.* IN ENGLISH, *THE PROMISED LAND.* (1958, d. Bernard Devlin)

The Promised Land, based on a novel (*Nuages sur les brûlés* — in English *Clouds over the Clearing* — by Hervé Biron), might have been studied in my chapter on "Literature into Film," but its nature and style seemed to demand discussion here. It is strongly oriented toward the "search for roots," in that it looks back to the times of the settling of the northern Québec colony of Saint-Antoine (or, of the Abitibi). In the first several frames, we see a group of men travelling by train and boat. The narrator explains that it is the time of the depression (1934). As these men travel along, Félix Leclerc, who plays Dubé, entertains them with folk music, which he sings while accompanying himself on a guitar. (This is arguably the best thing in the film!) Among the men is the curé, Father Armand, who will figure heavily in the action. "Behind them lie the idle factories," says the narrator. "Ahead of them Québec's vast northwest, 'The Promised Land.'"

The men arrive at the site and set up temporary camp. There follow scenes of great toil and hardship (to be revisited in the recent filming of *Maria Chapdelaine*); the men clear the land, felling the great evergreens by hand, and pulling up the stumps. They are not without their compensations, however: plenty of beer is available, it seems. One of the important scenes is the early raising of the cross: the action bespeaks the pious devotion of these men (who are no sissies). In a larger sense, this cross is an icon of Québec Catholicism (and of all Catholicism). It will be seen in film after film.

Soon thereafter, a barge arrives, bearing women and children. The women—especially Bernadette, the wife of Ernest—and her daughter, Armande, are taken aback by the conditions, the isolation, and the primitive, unsettled nature of the site and of the crude log cabin they are to live in. The film focuses particularly upon the difficult romance of Armande and Freddie, whose father is a boozer and a very selfish man. Winter goes by and spring arrives. Bonfires are used to get rid of the stumps and waste timber.

One outstanding scene takes us into Langlois's "cooperative" store. All the accoutrements of the general store are present: such a place functioned as a central gathering place in colonies and small villages, as we will see in *Mon oncle Antoine*. Here, however, it is a matter of picturing the corruption of the chief merchant of the settlement.

In an action-filled sequence, we experience the Québec of the old times, French Canada True North. The scene shifts back to the bonfires. The wind is "getting up." The fire is out of control. There is a desperate effort to stop it. A terrible gale moves over the lake, which has grown very rough. Several of the men are attempting to reach the island. They cannot control their boat. They hit a rock and the boat begins to take in water. A rope is tied around the waist of Dubé (Félix Leclerc); he will attempt to swim to shore, to reach the island. Cut.

The storm has ended; there is peace again. The birds sing. But the men, lined up in a row, take off their hats, as a horse carrying a man's body (Dubé's) is led in procession past them, followed by the priest and some others. Then requiem prayers in Latin are said in the open air for Dubé. It is interesting to note that one of the men gives responses to the priest in Latin. (Cf., *Mon oncle Antoine*, set in the 1940s; Benoît gives automatic responses in Latin to the priest's prayers.)

An argument ensues between Armande and Freddie. Freddie feels he must go to work in the mine; he cannot let his family starve. Armande threatens him: "If you go now don't ever come back." But he must go, duty requires it. So he bids farewell and leaves. Armande turns to her mother Bernadette. She weeps and protests significantly: "You can't get anywhere in this miserable country."

In the next scene, many of the men are gathered discussing the situation; there is a call for the "acceptance" of Simard's resignation.

The curé, at table with Lajoie, contends that the people *want* the collapse of the cooperative. Cooperatives are not needed that much. What they *need* is women. "We're short of them. We've got to get women." Lajoie wants to know how? Advertise? Who would come? The curé answers, "No, not that. I'll go and choose them myself at once."

Shortly thereafter, Lajoie receives a letter from the absent curé: grants for construction of houses, etc. have been approved; four carloads of supplies will soon arrive. Five charming girls will also arrive. Fade-out.

The curé is then seen, returning with his "teachers." Lajoie protests that they cannot pay for five teachers, but the priest reassures him, saying: "They'll all be engaged within a month."

The men have built a chapel during the priest's absence — rough-hewn, but nonetheless a chapel. They drive him up to it in horse and buggy. Inside, the furnishings are explained to him: "La Tulipe carved the cross; the wives did the decorating; the accordion will serve as an organ." The curé is very moved. Once outside the chapel, he explains to the gathering, "I don't have a speech. All I can say is many thanks, with all my heart."

It is party-time now. Couples are seen dancing a reel; there is a lot of drinking. But the bachelors are not dancing. So the curate takes them outside; he teaches them how to ask for a dance and how to dance. The scene shifts to the inside of a cabin: the curate tends the babies while his parishioners dance. He sings to a baby who is crying. (Is this a *fais-do-do*?)

In a later sequence, Simard has a gun and is keeping people from the mill, situated on his land but belonging to the government.

The curé intervenes: "This violence has got to end!" He approaches Simard, to whom he says: "We'll have no more violence. We found La Tulipe dead in his shack. He committed suicide. Haven't we had enough misery?" The priest tells Simard off. He then commands him to give up his land, as he promised. "I will not." Says the curate, "We'll see about that .... We'll write a letter to the minister of colonization telling him what Simard has done ...."

Meanwhile, Freddie has returned to Saint-Antoine. He is chopping wood. Armande passes. They speak, at first haltingly. Then they embrace. Fade-out.

A few years later.

Church bells are ringing. The people face the church, and approaching the priest, they sing. Speeches are given. It is St. Jean Baptiste's feastday. (St. John the Baptist is patron saint of Québec; his feastday, 24 June, is a holiday [holy day], having considerable significance for the Québécois, especially in the past, but even yet today for many of them. It is, after all, a more appropriate holiday to a Catholic people who speak a Romance tongue than ceremonies concerning the Queen, with whom they have never identified. Weinmann builds considerable portions of his argumentation around this saint and this holiday.)

As is customary with Catholic people when they celebrate a holy day, the people are having a procession. In this case it reflects their past, their long struggle to settle the site. Dubé is remembered: the face and voice of Leclerc are given us in a flashback. The curé is asked, "If you had it to do again, would you?" He answers, "I doubt it. We were pretty young at the time ..."

The people continue with their procession, moving into the distance.

This film is far from a technical triumph. And in some ways it might be called generic. The photography is very straightforward, with lengthy fade-outs resulting in unpleasant black pauses between the scenes. No clever editing here; no dissolves and only one flashback, as the people remember Dubé and his music. It is without nuances, all told. One must, however, grant that the images are well lit, but that is about all one can say. Nothing new or innovative. Moreover, the characters are virtually stock types, most of whom we meet again and again in Québec film: the good curé; the *habitant*; the *coureur des bois*, *défricheur de bois* (clearer of woods; woodsman); the Québécois *pure laine* (died-in-the-wool); the hard-working woman; and the *marginaux* (marginalized people) — immigrants, crooked merchants, alcoholics, and so forth.

The men are characteristically taciturn. The women are generally strong. And in a memorable scene one of the men (La Tulipe) sits before his tent carving a figure; it is the corpus for a crucifix. A scene from the old times, to be sure: woodcarving was one of the main activities of many early Quebeckers—and there was lots of wood to carve. Some of the *églises classées* along the Gaspé side of the Saint Lawrence contain the finest examples of this craft, pushed to a high art. And as late as the forties and fifties, their roadside stands, stocked with carvings of *habitants* and what-not [handmade bedspreads and warm bread spread with maple butter], awaited the tourists. They are a rare sight today, for we travel more by turnpikes and superhighways than by those sideroads.

But for all its faults, *La Terre promise* does offer the viewer a very good notion of pioneer life in the far north, and of rural *québécois* society as it might have been in the 1930s. And it does often "feel" like a documentary. Peter Morris concludes that "This dramatized reconstruction of an important part of Québec history is always interesting despite didactic qualities in the dramatic structure. The whole, however, never lives up to the promise of the harsh poetry in the opening episode."[17]

On the other hand, the story of the métis (half-Indian, half-French hunter of the Prairies) Louis Riel, who was intertwined with the history of the Northwest Territories—and indeed led a revolt and was ultimately hanged for his trouble, is an especially outstanding example of the use of "docudrama" to paint almost epic canvasses dealing with past events.

RIEL (1978–9; d. George Bloomfield)

Flmed in a "documentary style," *Riel* is quite engrossing in spite of its length. The director, George Bloomfield, who may not be thought of by some as Québécois, being an anglophone actor and filmmaker and a man of the theater, was born in Montréal in 1930. He has portrayed this French Canadian subject through rather romanticized eyes. In the making, he used internationally known stars (e.g., William Shatner). But many other stars of Canadian nationality, including Christopher Plummer, Raymond Cloutier ("excellent in the title-role" one reads in Coulombe 1991, 115), and the celebrated filmmaker and actor Claude Jutra, figured in this memorable film. It has been characterized as "a fairly accurate version of Riel, a mystic visionary," and one might add that it is not lacking in epic sweep. I include it here for its description of the life of a French-Canadian culture hero, who led an 1868 revolt against appropriation of the Western territories by the Canadian government. He was "one of Canada's most debatable historical figures" (Pratley *TS* 1987, 238).

The story is told by General Gabriel Dumont to Taylor, a Toronto newspaperman (played by the well-known American actor Arthur Hill) who is eager to get a story. In a group of flashbacks we get the entire story of how Riel conceived of the métis as a "nation," and even became secretary general of a provisional government established through the Council of the Northwest. He was at first backed by the Montréal bishop Bourget; but he ultimately found it politically expedient to back off. Riel was thus betrayed.

Meanwhile, the prime minister of Canada, Sir John MacDonald, was eager for a union, a confederation. He pushed for the completion of the railroad as a binding force, and sent his troops to fight Riel and his men (Cree and Blackfoot Indians and métis), in the hopes of acquiring the Northwest Territories. The battle scenes are gripping. Twice the métis and Indians manage to drive off the green Canadian troops; but finally the Canadian forces prove to be too many and too powerful for them. The Canadian soldiers (some in the bright red coats that will be associated with the Royal Canadian Mounted Police) demolish the métis, gain the upper hand, arrest Riel, and throw him into jail. He is then tried in Regina on treason. But one problem is that he has meanwhile become an American citizen. Besides, the French look on him as one of them, and, with an election pending, it is possible to alienate the Québécois, while if they let him go free this will alienate the English. Either way the disposition of the case will tear the country apart.

Nonetheless, Riel is tried, and the court scene shows the prosecutor as claiming that the native peoples are not to blame for the "treason," but, rather, the personal ambition and colossal vanity of the man on trial.

Meanwhile, the dying bishop changes colors once again and proclaims that Riel must be saved. "If 'they' can extinguish the French voice in the wilderness, it will be snuffed out throughout the country. I once dreamt of a Catholic New France in the West, and so did Riel. Two dreamers, one foolish dream." He then dies.

Back in court, the attorney, Lemieux, wants to say that Riel is not guilty by reason of insanity, but Riel objects. A priest counsels him in jail to be like Galileo (who recanted and lived, so we remember his life) and not like Saint Thomas More (who chose to die, so we remember his death). But Riel is determined to speak in his own defense. In his summation he states that this trial has neglected the real issues: the métis turned to him because the Catholic Church neglected their suffering at the hands of the government. He tells how he was asked to return to Canada from the United States and adds that abusive government should not be surprised when people finally rise up against it. The métis, he claims, need a place to call their own, and he adds that he still believes he has a "holy mission"; he dreams of a Canada where people may live in peace with their god. "Yet I stand before you asking for my life. I ask for the liberty and dignity of the métis; if this is treason I am guilty."

Eloquent though the speech is, Riel is found guilty and sentenced to be executed by hanging. (He was executed on 16 November 1885.) The priest is shown giving him extreme unction. We then have the scene of the hanging (Raymond Cloutier will "die" in the same way again in *Cordélia*), and we are indeed reminded of St. Thomas More, for Riel says to the priest, "Courage, Steven"; then the sack goes over Riel's head and he falls through the scaffolding.

In the final scene we return to the frame, and Gabriel says to the newsman, "I have not told you whether he was a saint or sinner; a madman or sane; right or wrong; but I still believe in Louis Riel."

Although one of my students, a British Columbian, claimed after viewing the film that this was not the way Riel had been viewed in *her* history classes, the historical tale has been told here so as to have a very contemporary ring. Even today such differences split Canada apart and threaten the confederation. (Such, for example, was the effect of the events surrounding the Meech Lake accord and its ultimate failure.) The film has MacDonald saying, "I do pray that one day we may mature." And the present-day viewer finds the prayer still relevant.

Riel is an engrossing film in which we see present-day Canada reflected in a past historical event. We also see that for the Québécois the story involves the martyrdom of a culture hero who was at once a French-speaking Catholic, though born on the Red River Settlement in Manitoba (22 October 1844), and even a Christ-like mystic. Québécois know him also as a former seminarian who studied in Québec's Collège de Montréal, who had visions and heard God telling him to pursue his plan and establish a government for everyone, and to lead his people. He was also in some senses a scapegoat, yet he stood for "separatism" and against the threat to his religion and his culture by the increasing power of the English-speaking protestant expansionists and imperialists, even "capitalists," soon to become the crushing establishment. Riel's efforts were at once both in vain and an example for future "revolutionaries," as we readily see through Bloomfield's account of Riel's life. And far from being the first portrayal of Riel, many books have been written about him, both in French and in English. The Canadian composer Harry Somer has written a very moving opera about him too; it was commissioned by the Canadian Opera Company, written in 1967, and performed on CBC a few years ago.

George F. G. Stanley sums up Riel's career as follows: "Politically and philosophically, Riel's execution has had a lasting effect on Canadian history. In the West, the immediate result was to depress the lot of the Métis. In central Canada, French Canadian Nationalism was strengthened and Honoré Mercier came to power in Québec in 1886. In the longer term, Québec voters moved from their traditional support of the Conservative Party to the Liberal Party led by Wilfrid Laurier. Even after a century, Riel and his fate excite political debate, particularly in Québec and Manitoba. Riel's execution has remained a contentious issue even today and demands have been made for a retroactive pardon" (*Can. Ency.* 3:1871).

In the realm of pure fiction, the Canadian past has been amply re-created in the megafilm *Maria Chapdelaine* (1983), which featured the international stars Carole Laure (Canadian, but nonetheless international) as Maria, and Nick Mancuso as François Paradis. It was directed by Gilles Carle, whose film career has been a very uneven one indeed, but whose works often look at the past, not always too objectively, as is the case in *Cinéma, Cinéma*, or in *La Vie heureuse de Léopold Z.* Even where it may not be a matter of history, myth is often involved, as in *La Mort d'un bûcheron* (1973), a film with Carole Laure as a young village girl named Marie (Chapdelaine; some write Chapelaine), who comes to Montréal looking for her long-lost lumberjack-father, and becomes a topless dancer in a country-western bar. Here, as in many of Carle's films, the subject is the exploitation of women. And also presenting a theme of predilection is *La Vraie Nature de Bernadette*, in which the myths of pastoral life are deflected.

LA VRAIE NATURE DE BERNADETTE (1972; d. Gilles Carle)

Carle, who began his career as a documentarian, has not worked with the direct style for many years; nor does he always use historical material as the base of his story. After he broke with the ONF, he became a director of *auteur* films. This evolution from ONF director to *auteur* (not only in Carle, but also in Arcand, Leduc, Dion, etc.) is of some interest; and one might add parenthetically that the idea of the ONF's sponsoring an *auteur* film has been questioned by some (esp. François Macerola, quoted in Lever *Hist.* 1988, 362), for in the opinion of many, the State should not support "oeuvres," i.e., not the works of individuals.

In *La Vraie Nature de Bernadette* (1972) Carle shows a young wife (also mother), who leaves her city home and family to find freedom and purity in the fresh clean air of country life, another myth; she gives sexual gratification to many of the men who live nearby the farm she has taken over. She also "works a miracle cure" by persuading a young mute to speak, and draws on a crowd of handicapped people demanding equal assistance. Pratley (*TS* 1987, 204) says that Carle in this film gets away with subject matter that only Buñuel has treated successful.

One might point out that while Carle intended to ridicule the myths surrounding the "return to nature" and to denounce Bernadette's illusions, to confront her idyllic vision of "Nature" with the concrete realities of rural life (meanwhile satirizing her naiveté in believing that socially embedded attitudes could be changed by one's example), the film was, ironically, received against its own grain. Critics and public appreciated instead its verdure, its generosity, Bernadette's charm. It was the joyous amorality and the irreverence of her behavior that seduced audiences. Although Carle tried in numerous interviews to explain his critical intentions, it seems that he did not succeed in putting viewers "on track." Rather, each one of the scenes spoke a language and conveyed a message to the audience that was in opposition to the sense of the whole film. (Paraphrased and translated from Houle 1978, 304).

The True Nature of Bernadette has been described as a film that anticipates the romanticism of *An Unmarried Woman* and *Alice Doesn't Live Here Anymore*, and as a feminist satire. Bernadette herself has been compared to Buñuel's Viridiana, in that she is exploited by those she favors.

Lucien Fortin discusses the films of Gilles Carle most cogently in his article "Les expériences de Gilles Carle." He stresses the notion that Carle's protagonists are often people with abnormal behaviors in relation to society's established norms. This is true of *Red* (in which Red, a métis, steals cars, and while seeking refuge with the Indians is rejected, and thus alienated by both societies); of *La Vraie Nature de Bernadette* (Bernadette has a double nature, but both facets come from the same wellspring of generosity and availability: she is at once saint and prostitute); of *Le Viol d'une jeune fille douce* (in which Julie, a free-wheeling, modern woman is brought back to the straight and narrow by her three brothers); in *La Mort d'un bûcheron* (in which Marie is a topless singer of country-western music in search of her father); of *La Tête de Normande St-Onge* (in which Normande is in perpetual conflict with herself and with the people around her). The characters are, as one can see, excluded, marginal, and have difficulty expressing themselves, or even living freely. But it is society that designates these people as abnormal or immoral, and not a desire of the author to present them so.[18] Fortin finds, furthermore, that Carle mixes the two techniques of *cinéma direct* and fiction film in most of his work. This was already evident in *Solange dans nos campagnes*, where he "perverted" the documentary and almost ridiculed it, while borrowing fictional elements from American cinema. Likewise, in *La Vie heureuse de Léopold Z.* Carle fused the documentary elements of snow removal with the fictional plan, giving the film astonishing unity. Sometimes this fusion results in equivocation, or ambiguity, as in *Le Viol d'une jeune fille douce* and in *L'Ange et la femme* (Fortin 1988, 36). Leaning on Dominique Noguez's article on Carle ("Le pôle expérimental," *Revue d'Esthétique* [Toulouse, 1984]), Fortin then proceeds to analyze the poetic function of Carle's work. By poetic function Fortin and Noguez mean non-narrativity; and Fortin finds that in his films Carle does not always associate himself with traditional classical narrativity (Fortin 1988, 36): rather, his narrativity is often broken, or chopped up (Fortin, 1988, 37). Both Noguez and Fortin point out the rapidity with which the tale is told (Fortin 1988, 37). But, of course, this analysis does not deal with *Maria Chapdelaine*, which may not quite fit the mold that Noguez and Fortin have cast in their articles on Gilles Carle, especially as regards "rapidity of narrative." One will not find much of the "cinéma direct" in *Maria Chapdelaine* either. And yet, although a work based on a literary classic by a Frenchman, it is particularly *Maria Chapdelaine* that addresses the theme of the search for roots.

Now, authorities severely criticized *Maria Chapdelaine*, that long, long film, which also ran as a four-hour miniseries on CBC television in a dubbed version — one of the best pieces of dubbing I have ever seen — and then was edited down to a two-hour version shown on television and released as such on video. And incidentally, this severe editing harmed the film's integrity and coherence, while making it more useful for the classroom, and the like.

The film was looked at, of course, from the perspective of the Louis Hémon novel, and I will have reason to speak about this film again in Chapter 4, where I look at literature turned into film. It was compared to the early French version, which starred Jean Gabin and it was viewed as having too many "unauthentic" accents, etc. Still, the portrait of the life of the *défricheur* and that of the lumberjack as well are unforgettable. The film has moments of considerable drama; and if Maria seems a bit frail for the tasks she is shown performing, the conflicts that came to the family from the never-ending aspirations of the father and his restlessness are for all intents and purposes real. In any event, the impractical, "absent" male is a constant in French Canadian literature, and he will be encountered again in *Mills of Power* as well as in *The Tin Flute* (both novel and film). In fact these failures, even the impotence, of the Québécois male are at the base of one of Québec's great novels concerning the (Quiet) Revolution — *Prochain Episode*, by Hubert Aquin. It has never been turned into film, though an adaptation by Pierre Turgeon is, at this writing, in the planning stages.

In addition, the quality of life in the remote parts of Canada in those early days seems vividly conveyed here in *Maria Chapdelaine*: the importance of having a record player and a couple of records; the meaning of an orange in the midst of the bitter winter; the role of the Catholic religion in these people's lives; the strong loving ties of the family, that highlight the traditional values of the Québec people. We should note, too, the role of the priest from France in this film — his Breton blood gives him an affinity with his French Canadian flock.

The film is, in fact, a study of the religious foundations of these peasants. Maria's recitation of one hundred rosaries on Christmas eve to get her wish that François will return has all the elements of superstition, humor, and, finally, irony that such beliefs can muster in such a situation; but it also shows the touch of the *auteur*, as we realize when we read in Carle's 1976 account of his own childhood: "Mon père disait: 'A cheval pour le chapelet.' Nous, les petits enfants, nous récitions donc le rosaire au galop, apprenant qu'au Québec les rêves les plus contradictoires sont permis. [My father used to say, 'Everyone to horse, for the [recitation of the] rosary.' We children would therefore recite the rosary at a gallop, learning that in the province of Québec, the most contradictory dreams are allowed]." (Quoted in Lever *Hist.* 1988, 490.)

Moreover, humor is far from lacking in the film, as when the priest hears the confession of the whole family in their home, at the urging of the strong mother; or when he must have a tooth pulled, and the crippled village telegraph operator must play the organ to distract him. (The operator, madly in love with François Paradis, is played by Marie Tifo, one of Québec's most accomplished actresses [v. *Les Bons Débarras*].) Pierre Curzi as the awkward but sincere Eutrope Gagnon also provides us with a smile or two. Maria's return by boat from her visit to her aunt's, with her gramophone — one of the period — in tow opens the film, and is of consummate charm. (Humor is one of Carle's trademarks.) That same opening gave us simultaneously some of the most beautiful shots of the Lac Saint-Jean region ever made; the beauty of the scenery prevails throughout the film.

On a different level, everything seems to combine in this film to give us the sense of anguish involved in the clearing and settling of the land, but also to provide us with a notion of Québec types: the strong, long-suffering, and devout mother figure; the restless, dreaming, impractical male, Chapdelaine (played by Yoland Guérard), who always moves deeper into the wilderness, where his woman (played by Amulette Garneau) must follow. The sweetness of maple syrup poured over the snow to make a taffy takes on an iconic reality here; it is a custom we frequently read of. Wolves howl in a repeated montage that shows their shadows against the cold full moon and the skeletons of trees at night along a frozen, winter-locked lake. The film may be a manifest example of the cultural load implied in the expression "True North." Doubtless the portrayal is that of a mythical Canada, but at least the stereotypes are for the most part more positive than those of the French Canadian seen in the early American film. As we saw in Chapter 1, D. W. Griffith portrayed him as half-civilized and beastly, a rapist even; and in what may have been the lowest point in his acting career, Laurence Olivier, in Michael Powell's *49th Parallel* (British, 1941), impersonated the halting language and the crude manners of a rustic Québécois, complete in his lumberjack shirt — an insult to these people, especially given the period in which the picture was made.

Instead, Québec icons, or metaphors, of various sorts seem to be the strength of *Maria Chapdelaine*. Sugar maple, stump clearing, imported oranges for Christmas (for French Canadians always an enormous treat in earlier days; v. *Bonheur d'occasion* and the testimony of Suzanne Jacob, the author of *Laura Laur*), blueberrying, wolves, ice, snow, blizzards, fur trapping, lumbercamps and the dangers of that job — everything that bespeaks the Québec past seems to be included, and to be guaranteed to produce a bit of nostalgia.

Nevertheless, the film was poorly received by many. Lever sees it as a vehicle for Carole Laure, pure and simple, while Pratley lambastes the work mercilessly. He finds that Carle, "in spite of several clever directorial devices, fails to bring the events to life, or indeed, to give any life to the whole or to create any emotional depth to the characters, especially the young lovers played by Carole Laure and Nick Mancuso, who look too old for their parts. The settings are not convincing, the period feels wrong. It seems that Carle, afraid of being called 'old-fashioned' for taking an 'old-fashioned' book to the screen, has no fashion at all, resulting in a film without style or spirit" (*TS* 1987, 150−1). Elsewhere he writes: "Louis Hemon's romantic and sentimental story of pioneer life in Québec, first published in 1913, is here miscast, misconceived, and misbecoming—a subject for which Carle seems to have little sympathy or understanding. It has no sense of history, style or unity" (*TS* 1987, 256).

In an interview with Léo Bonneville, Carle presents his thinking on his most recent films. He speaks of *La Corriveau*, which, as he says, did not work because people preferred seeing an anglo-saxon protestant hero, Bethune, to a little Catholic Québécoise. At the time of that interview he was just making a film called *La Postière*, set in the 1930s, starring Chloé Sainte-Marie, alongside François-Nicolas Rives, and also featuring Steve Gendron and Michèle Richard. Again, the woman is central. Portrayed is a village in disorder, with "everyone wanting to leave chaos behind, but at the same time stay within it. Disorder," says Carle, "is freedom *à la québécoise*." (Carle also states that he wished to render homage to the Québécoise, who was eliminated from Canadian History in general and from *québécoise* history in particular.) Again, then, as with *Maria Chapdelaine*, Carle seeks to capture a pre-World War era, to show a moment in Québec history when just about everyone was happier.[19]

Cordélia (1979), by the director Jean Beaudin (who also made *J. A. Martin photographe*, as well as *Le Matou* [1985], *Mario* [1984], and *Cher Théo*), is yet another film that looks at the *québécois* past, but, as it too is based on literature, we will examine it in Chapter 4. And *J. A. Martin photographe* itself, as well as such a film as *Kamouraska*—one of the most expensive *québécois* movies ever made, and one that did not bring back returns—seek to portray the *québécois* society of early times. *Kamouraska*, based on the novel of Anne Hébert, will, like *Cordélia*, be looked at in Chapter 4. But as the perfect example of the evocation of the eminently collectible past of Québec, unencumbered by debts to a literary masterpiece with which it would have to be compared, one should focus on Beaudin's "historical film," *J. A. Martin photographe*.

J. A. MARTIN PHOTOGRAPHE (1976; Jean Beaudin)

If there is one word to describe *J. A. Martin photographe*, that word is "beautiful." From the story-line, to the dialogue, to the photography, this film is virtually flawless. Of it, Lever says: "An interpretation abounding in nuances, a well-constructed script, camerawork of a plastic beauty, a very modern subject [a woman's independence], and an intimate atmosphere make this film very convincing" (*Hist.* 1988, 242; my trans.). *J. A. Martin* ... was the winner of seven Canadian awards, including Best Picture, and for her performance in it Monique Mercure won the Grand Prix d'interprétation at Cannes (1976–7). One may contend that it is a film that recaptures all the atmosphere of nineteenth-century, or turn-of-the-century Québec, and also a film that captures the stunning beauty of the Laurentian landscape in all its grandeur. Indeed, for some critics the voluptuous fertility and vibrant color of the natural environment have been the catalyst of marital renewal present at the end of the movie. But at the same time it achieves the portrait of an early feminist. And one may also say that it is a feminist film, though directed by a male. (That is the contention, at least of Michel Houle, in *Dictionnaire du cinéma québécois*.) But this feminist independence is not, as Lever with considerable macho bravado contends (*Hist.* 1988, 350), more effectively drawn here; the portrait is not *"plus attachant"* than in any film any Québécoise has done. For the portraits of women in the works of Léa Pool are, at least for many women, as memorable and as arresting, and their evolutions more expensive and painful.

J. A. Martin photographe, whose fundamental tenderness is in stark contrast with the sadism and misogyny in gestures and words to be found in the more recent film *Un Zoo la nuit*, offers the nostalgic evocation of an era (which, as we will later see, is one of the themes of *Un Zoo* ... as well). Rose-Aimée Martin, having grown tired of her stay-at-home, wash-the-clothes, and feed-the-children routine, decides that for once she is going to accompany her husband, "J. A." (for Josephe-Arthur), an itinerant photographer, as he makes his rounds through the countryside, shooting weddings and group pictures of workers. Though he is very evidently a sensitive man, he is extremely taciturn, and his work in the dark room as well as his trips into the field add to his already uncommunicative nature. Indeed, his nature seems hereditary, or else of the nature of the male Quebecker; early on in the film Rose-Aimée states that her son, R. A., is, like his father, untalkative.

Her decision, of course, is an early example of woman's revolt against household drudgery, boisterous children, and the neglect of her husband, as well as against the stagnation and lack of communication that have set into her marriage of fifteen years. (A similar revolt in modern terms can be seen in the French film *Jument Vapeur* [*Dirty Dishes*], a 1978 release directed by Joyce Buñuel, and one that Maltin calls "an obvious feminist comedy"! [Maltin 1991 ed., 294].) The effort to rekindle the marriage, which is the fundamental drive of the protagonists of this lyrical work, does in fact have a successful outcome.

En route, in their ramshackle, horse-drawn buggy (a sort of "covered wagon" in which they also sleep), their conversation, especially at first, is stilted. As she undergoes a miscarriage in the wagon (during which a crucifix is dimly seen in the background), he stands at a distance; he is speechless and helpless. One empathizes with him. Without saying a word, he goes up to the wagon, picks up his shovel and the shapeless bundle that is the fetus, and goes to bury it. All this beside pink rock and a beautiful lake.

At the wedding her husband has gone to photograph Mme Martin is something to behold, as her long pent up natural gaiety comes springing forth. The next day she will suffer a terrible hangover. Her husband says little about it at first, but gives her a fast ride. She recognizes, however, that she has made a fool of herself. Finally, he offers her a jug in which she will find a remedial hair of the dog; he commands her to take it, saying simply, "Bois [Drink]." But then he too takes a sip: an excellent device for showing his silent forgiveness and their growing "togetherness."

After all these experiences — in a hotel room where a prostitute is being humped by a traveler in the room next to her, while her husband is downstairs shooting pool; at the wedding where she dances and sings; at a home where she tends a dying woman; at Uncle Joseph's farmhouse where she is clearly the object of the son Adhémar's unspoken desire — she and her husband arrive home. Now, after this five-week odyssey, after each has realized that it is possible and desirable to "help" one another, she appreciates her house and her family as never before. And what joy to be reunited with the children, who have been tended by her aunt! (The situation, by the way, is watched and commented upon, both at the point of

J. A. Martin photographe. (Courtesy Office National du Film.)

departure and at the return, by their neighbors, Hormidas and his wife, through their window — a motif of public opinion, even scandal, echoed by the comments of the women at the wedding.)

On the evening of the return, Rose-Aimée climbs up the stairs with her lamp. Once in bed with her husband, they embrace. We then see only a crucifix. The baby weeps; but the mother, intent now upon her husband, says, "Let her be ... she'll go to sleep." Five weeks in the blush of spring have brought on their renewal.

A feminist film? It is to be noted that the film does not portray a "rejection" of her fate by Rose-Aimée, as some contend, but, rather, a reevaluation. She returns to her role as housewife, but with a new attitude, for her husband will likely communicate better, and this has been her greatest problem.

The picture has political dimensions as well. There is an opportunity to tie in the tension over historical, or long-standing, ethnic differences (inequalities) and bilingualism in this film. Surveying the Wilson's sumptuous home and its surroundings, she says, "I'd like to live in that house." Says he, "You'd have to speak English." Additionally (as in *Les Tisserands du pouvoir*, or in *Mon oncle Antoine*) we see the condition of the French workers and their tension vis-à-vis their anglo boss. This film also touches upon the question of child labor. And the fundamental tenderness of Josephe-Arthur Martin surfaces very effectively when he insists that the small boy Julien, who has been sacked, be included in the picture. Having one's picture taken was an event of certain proportions in those prepolaroid days, both for the rural or small-town Canadian and for any American child as well. The temporary adoption of this young Tremblay, whom they decide to take to his home, only to find the mother dying when they finally arrive there, affords additional opportunity to witness in mimesis the simple lifestyle of the early Quebecker (through the depiction of the Tremblay house, which contrasts greatly with the book on Versailles, with its mirrors, gilt furniture, and the book on the king of France, which Rose-Aimée reads to the children). This not to mention our participation in the gradual drawing together of the couple.

In her sociological study of this first-rate film, Ginette Major[20] shows how the bipolarized solitudes of the couple collide. Indeed, she finds that this film mounts a portrait of three troubled families; in all three there is an almost total lack of communication. This is especially illustrated by the meals eaten in solitude. She insists unduly, however, on the role of J. A.'s mother in the film; it is in reality very minor. Major's study includes an examination of the partitioning of masculine and feminine universes, and the portrayal of the traditional morality with respect to the couple afforded by Beaudin. I personally find quite farfetched her interpretations that seek to establish adultery and pardon symbolized by certain scenes (such as the scene between Adhémar and Rose-Aimée, which is viewed as adultery, with the subsequent scene of the miscarriage and burial of the fetus as rejection of fruit and pardon of the husband). But her view that Adhémar symbolizes the flight into alcohol that has been and is a problem in Québec society is correct. Major also points out the portrayal of labor, and especially of child labor, noted above in my synopsis.

Most useful in Major's analysis are the passages in which she shows how the sounds of nature come to interrupt the hereditary silence of J. A. and his mother that Rose-Aimée has had to endure for so many years. (The break comes, too, through the feast that the landscape offers to her eyes.) Major's remarks about the editing and the lighting are also of interest. She points out one notably effective piece of editing in the overlapping of the scene of Julien's

mother's death with sounds of the wedding, heard before the scene
dissolves (i.e., life continues). Finally, Major finds that the most
outstanding technical feature of the film may be its lighting, which
contrasts the chiaroscuro interiors in which Rose-Aimée lives her
drab life and the luminosity of the exteriors that she experiences
on her self-willed voyage. I would prefer to say that all aspects of
J. A. Martin photographe — story, characterization, and technical
savoir-faire — work in concert to make an indelible impression
on us.

LE VIEUX PAYS OÙ RIMBAUD EST MORT (1977; d. Jean Pierre Lefebvre)

Le Vieux Pays où Rimbaud est mort is a narrative film in which
the picaresque character Abel (the only Québécois in the film)
goes to France to find his own identity. Made in 1977, it is of the
same period as *J. A. Martin photographe*, though it does not
represent a historical search for roots, but, rather, a contemporaneous one. And it is a quest for connections not with the traditions
of Québec, but with France as a motherland ... a quest that one
might justifiably characterize as failed.

Episodic in nature, this film — shot in eighteen days on location
in Paris, Charleville, and Marseille — opens with Abel (a Québécois
between 35 and 40) in a Parisian room where he is staying and
where he is trying to write his impressions of the "old country" on
a chalkboard. Subsequently he meets a guitarist on a street corner,
then enters the Chez Charles bistro where he tries to compose
a letter to his father. He has his portrait painted, then he pays
a visit to some old colonial friends, M. and Mme de Cassant. To
Abel's annoyance, the French cannot place his accent: is it Algerian?
Cambodian? Belgian? As his quest continues, he meets vendors in
the park and a policeman; later, armed with a huge bouquet of
flowers, he pays a visit to Jeanne, with whom he appears to be
having a relationship. (Jeanne is in charge of her sister Viviane and
her delinquent brother Yves.)

When Jeanne receives news of her mother's suicide, Abel accompanies her and the brother and sister to Charleville, where
Jeanne confides her sad past to Abel. Outside a café, Abel then
confides something of his own past to Yves. His mother is dead;
his father lives in Brazil, and he has come to France "to see if there
are still any Frenchmen," and if they resemble him.

Abel next leaves Charleville and goes to Cassis. There he meets
Anne, Yves's probation officer. They go to visit her mother; when
the phone rings he is told to answer it. It is Jeanne, who is calling

to consult with Anne about Yves. At the end of the film, Abel is having an affair with Anne (a character very much criticized by the French critics, according to Lefebvre[21]), but he intimates to her that he will (soon?) be going back to Québec.

Abel is the same taciturn Québécois we met in *J. A. Martin ...*, but here the reason for his lack of loquaciousness is that he is in France "to listen and learn." And although Lefebvre eschews the *style direct* (which he nonetheless never discouraged in such directors as Gilles Groulx and Michel Brault), many of the scenes in *The Old Country Where Rimbaud Died* come off as interviews. Lefebvre in this film may not use direct cinema but he does use a "direct address" shooting style, in which the actor/character looks directly into the camera while speaking. It is a technique that defies the general rule that one does not look into the camera, a technique that has been practiced by Jean-Luc Godard in his efforts to dissipate the illusion of fiction. In Lefebvre, but not in Godard, the effect is to involve the audience more completely than would otherwise be the case. Like Godard, Lefebvre also uses many scenes that are, as Peter Rist says, "filmed in single long takes."[22] The influence of the documentary we so often note in Canadian film is therefore present in this film.

Rist claims that "Shots of [Abel] are intercut with those of two men playing cards at another table and of various stock French characters standing at a bar (which may or may not be in the same location). An establishing shot of the interior which would link the card players, the other 'customers,' and Abel is never provided, so that the spectator cannot be sure if the spaces of the various shots are contiguous. Rather than provide a narrative spatial continuity in the 'classical' Hollywood manner, the shots of the other characters provide illustrations for Abel's letter which together present mostly a comical and negative image of French culture. In one shot, for example, three soldiers raise their glasses. The first toasts France, the second himself, and the third utters an obscenity. By contrast, the scene ends with a cut to another location, an art gallery, presenting a more positive view of French culture. The last shot in Chez Charles is of the card players and the first in the gallery is of a framed Paul Cézanne landscape. Later, a wider angle of view reveals two other Cézanne paintings, on either side, one of which is almost identical in composition to the film framing of the card players. Thus, through juxtaposition the conventional 'glory' of France can be seen against a contemporary rudeness."[23] Rist goes on to discuss the static frames, long takes, and other technical features; he draws comparisons with Godard and Renoir, and finds that stylistic decisions in the film were quite deliberate.[24] Lefebvre's use of geometric figures (called the "graphic intention") relates to my upcoming discussion of the films of Léa Pool; for, according to Rist, Lefebvre claims the triangle to be the major figure for *The Old Country Where Rimbaud Died*. Rist shows how the triangle is used in this film (as well as the manipulation of colors), but since his discussion is in English and is readily available, there is no need to reproduce it here.

Leaving aside Rist's claims, Lefebvre himself states that this film is structured "like a Cézanne painting, in the sense that Cézanne gave as much attention to each detail ... as he did to the entire work. It's a mosaic kind of painting" (Harcourt 1981, 147–8). He also points out in this conversation with Harcourt that the love for Cézanne was Mireille Amiel's, while his was for Rimbaud, and "so they put their loves together." He confesses in the same place to an affinity with and influence from Brecht, whom, he believes, most do not understand and who is above all a playwright, and could not succeed at making films.

The Old Country Where Rimbaud Died tells us, then, that a Québécois is not a Frenchman, and vice versa. This we always knew. But here the question is studied with great finesse; the characters are complex and contradictory. And while "the treatment of modern France, and particularly of the French themselves, is clearly critical, ... it is also multifaceted."[25] Parenthetically, I would point out that the relationship of Québécois to France and to the French has always been ambivalent and ambiguous, going from a sense of the motherland's historic rejection to unswerving love and loyalty (e.g., Assuréus' love of France in Roy's *Tin Flute*) to outright rejection and dislike. (In the forties I heard the French characterized by one Québécoise as "des sales cochons [dirty pigs].") But De Gaulle may well have done something to cement relations when, in the midst of the great turmoils of the late sixties he visited Québec (in 1967, to be precise), and, at that time, uttered his famous slogan: "Vive le Québec libre!" from the balcony of the Montréal City Hall. The "arrogant visit" — as Pratley puts it — is recorded in *Les Années de rêve* (*Years of Dreams and Revolt*) and also in the "documentary" *La Visite du général de Gaulle au Québec* by Jean-Claude Labrecque, which Lever suggests may be "the best film for showing how editing can become political discourse" (Lever *Hist*. 1988, 169). Sentiments also boil over into outright hatred of the anglo community, to which French Canadians have seldom related socially, linguistically, or politically (having

Le Vieux Pays où Rimbaud est mort. (Courtesy Coll. Cinémathèque Québécoise.)

seen nothing in the Queen that had anything to do with them).
This hatred, as typified in Vallières's virulent but true and timely
White Niggers of America, is transmuted sometimes to at least
a linguistic and cultural identification with the French, as in Claude
Jasmin's *Rimbaud, mon beau salaud*. Jasmin's reclamation of his
French heritage is, in reality, a response to the anglo-Canadian
community; the "ils"; the "eux"; the Other. Says he: "Notre histoire
est plus longue qu'ils le disaient ... ils faisaient de nous de tristes
orphelins et on imaginait souvent ... que nous étions nous-mêmes
peaux-rouges arrosés de baptême ... [Our history is longer than
they said it was ... they made pathetic orphans of us, and people
often imagined that we ourselves were redskins watered down by
baptism ...]."[26] France, with "the richest heritage in the world,"
is viewed as the cradle of the French Canadian people, upon
whom Jasmin — *l'enfant terrible* of Québec letters and author of *La
Sablière*, on which the film *Mario* is based — calls for a revival of
relationships between France and Québec.

Le Vieux Pays ... was part of a trilogy, introduced, as I said
above, by the film *Il ne faut pas mourir pour ça* (1966). The latter
took the Prix de la critique québécoise in 1967, the Grand Prix
du festival du cinéma canadien in 1967, and the Grand Prix du
meilleur film étranger at the Festival de Hyères in 1968. It told of
the initiation into reality of Abel — a naive and generous adult-

child, tender and slightly *"farfelu."* In a single day the dusts of childhood, of dream, of love, and of death suspended in his universe crystallize suddenly, and create the prism of a true conscience. And if at first Abel had hoped to be able to change the course of things, he was ultimately obliged to notice that it was instead the course of things that acted on him. This became abundantly clear to him after the death of his beloved mother.

So, as *Le Vieux Pays* ... opens, Abel has been being transformed for eight years by the course of things. And although he has evolved, he has even so remained deeply preoccupied with his past, his present, and his future. This is why he has taken the notion that he must find himself, and this search must be conducted in France. As Abel says in *Le Vieux Pays*, "Because France came to our country several centuries ago, and then forgot us there ... I came to France to see if there are still some Frenchmen here, if they still resemble those who came to our country ... And if I resemble them." A fundamental question at the time the film was made.[27] This is perhaps the same question Alexis Tremblay is asking in *Le Règne du jour*, when with other participants of the film he talks about France's "betrayal" of her rich colony and draws comparisons between the French and the Québécois.

Lefebvre himself explains that although the film is not about the life of Rimbaud, some of the sequences were shot in Charleville, Rimbaud's native city, others in Paris, where he led a tumultuous life, others in Marseille, where he died. The film's title is an indirect homage to the poet, but it also means that the internal message, social and political, of Rimbaud, was not really understood and assimilated.[28] Rimbaud, then, becomes a symbol of the marginalized figure in society (e.g., the Québécois, perhaps, vis-à-vis the French).

Le Vieux Pays ..., despite the critical acclaim it has enjoyed, is not unanimously admired. Pratley, for one, says, "It is really much too slight, but nonetheless the intent and the illusion are there" (*TS* 1987, 234). Is this not damning with faint praise?

Defensively, Harcourt laments the neglect this film has received, despite the fact that it is "Lefebvre's most accessible film." Harcourt goes on to say, "It is full of beautiful locations and extraordinarily crafted effects. Furthermore, within its more conventional narrative, there are many interesting characters all played by actors who give splendid performances. That this film has not done well either in Québec or in France is more a comment on the myopic policies of the two exhibition systems than on the film itself. And of course, except for an occasional festival screening, it has not been seen in English Canada at all" (Harcourt 1981, 77).

Lever explains this indifference in quite another way: Abel is "un personnage anachronique [qui] ne suscite guère d'intérêt [an anachronistic character who stimulates hardly any interest]" (*Hist.*, 1988, 75). He finds that Lefebvre's work has "tics godardiens," especially in *Jusqu'au coeur*, made in 1968, when the young generation recognized in Godard their porte-parole. He also finds *Le Vieux Pays* ... inferior to *Les Dernières Fiançailles* (*Hist.* 1988, 456), made in 1973, and dealing with the death of a couple in their seventies. This constitutes a good closure to our discussion of a search for roots, for *The Last Betrothal* is a film that points up the beauty and happiness of an ordinary life, lived in the dignity of the "simple acts of working, eating, sleeping," as Pratley puts it (*TS* 1987, 213). The "tender, evocative, and entirely beautiful study" of this couple (made by much the same crew as *Le Vieux Pays* ... and played by Marthe Nadeau and J. Léo Gagnon) is "conveyed by Lefebrve's style of long takes, slow panning shots, and a remarkable observance of real time" (Pratley *TS* 1987, 213). The counterpart of *J. A. Martin photographe*? It is a film that, at least, was also on the critics' minds when the survey was conducted by Toronto's Festival of Festivals, in which it was ranked twentieth out of thirty. (As previously stated, this survey was analyzed in *Variety*, 8 August 1984.)

The sequel to *Le Vieux Pays* ... was to be *La Mort du père prodigue* (slated to be filmed in 1978). According to my records, it does not appear to have been realized. Instead, two years after *Le Vieux Pays* ... Lefebvre made *Avoir 16 ans*, a critique of Québec education and "the autopsy of a civilization," as Harcourt calls it (1981, 177).

Roots Through Animation

In an important piece of animation, *Crac* (1981), Frédéric Back, a francophone Belgian who has lived and worked in Québec for quite some time (indeed, the artist who contributed to Arcand's *Champlain*, discussed earlier in this chapter), has managed to encapsulate in a fifteen-minute black-and-white piece the history and many aspects of the culture of Québec.

The beginning of the work shows a lumberjack cutting down a tree. Next we have the sawmill to which the tree is sent, to be made into lumber, and then a chair is made. It is painted green and presides at an old-time wedding with traditional violin music. Spooning and heeling are heard in the background of some of these folk songs. Early scenes alternate between sweet pastoral scenes and frolicking festivities, such as this marriage celebration. Babies arrive, and, as a lullaby is sung, the chair serves to rock them to sleep. At this point the chair is red. It is used for games; at times a child's fantasy makes of it a boat, at times a horse, at times a car. It becomes blue. With the advent of the auto it is still around; it becomes yellow. With the introduction of the plane the chair is chucked on a dump. The age of industry is upon us; the nuclear age as well. The chair is rescued from the dump, taken to a museum, and painted many colors, then finally yellow. Sometimes the museum guard rocks in it, and all the children who visit the museum get in the chair to rock in it, as it is a curiosity at this point. At night the rocking chair remembers its joyous past.

Without dialogue, the animation speaks for itself. The "humanized" chair's expression changes with its successive experiences, for it has a little round face etched on the frame, and the smile on the face comes and goes. The face smiles, becomes sad when the baby cries, and smiles again when the baby stops crying.

The film, which won an Oscar in 1982, manages to tell the allegory-history of Québec through the chair as a societal icon. It does so quite nostalgically. It has been characterized as a charming portrayal of French Canadian family life of former years; an affectionate visit to a happy past, and a gentle commentary on the rapid pace of modern life, as well as a masterpiece of humor.[29] I agree!

Conclusion to Chapter 2

The recovery of the rather distant past, and even of a less distant one (as in *Les Plouffe*, directed by Gilles Carle, or in *Bonheur d'occasion*, directed by Claude Fournier) — a recovery seen in so many novels and films of Québec — should not surprise one. Not only must this be a continuation in some sense of the lessons of l'abbé Groulx (whose obligatory history manual in the collèges was entitled *Notre maître le passé* [*Our Master, the Past*], according to Lever [*Hist.*, 1988, 182]), as well as of the documentary tradition established early on by the ONF, but it is, as well, part and parcel of the nationalist inclinations of many, if not most, of the Québécois people, and especially of its artists. Indeed, if Lever is right, there may be a desire here to forget the history per se, in order to be able to reappropriate myth (*Hist.* 1988, 182). For, after all, colonized peoples always learn sooner or later to reevaluate, and either reaffirm or reject consciously their traditional values. Such a process entails the discovery of their own authentic myth (history, to some), as a part of their coming to consciousness about their identity and their own dignity. This labor of recovery is the route often taken by the ex-slave, the African, the Amerindian, and by the world's women — in this, case, as we shall see in the next chapter, that of the Québécoises. "*Qui a tiré sur nos histoires [d'amour]?*" (lit.: *who has drawn on — taken aim at — our stories [of love]?*"), asks Louise Carré; and the title of her film is perhaps the most provocative thing about it. (In English, it is merely called *A Question of Loving.*)

An anamnesis, the search for a history, for a past and an acceptable future, for roots, for an identity separate from, distinct from the majority anglo-saxon population of most of Canada; the desire to preserve the New World French language, to be *enraciné*; and the sense that this is a fundamental human right (as Simone Weil insists in her *Enracinement*): these are the underlying themes of many of Québec's films; and yet in many others the assumptions of such ardent nationalism and of such a closing-off to other peoples, to the Other, to alterity are criticized.

3

Women's Cinema

je me sens femme et vallée lointaine et nuit à venir ...
Des femmes n'en finissent plus de coudre des hommes
et des hommes de se verser à boire ...
  [I feel I am woman, distant valley, and night coming
  on ....
  Women never stop sewing men
  and men never stop their drinking ...]
  —Marie Uguay in *Canadian Forum* (Dec. '84: 22–24)

"Le cinéma québécois n'a pas été particulièrement accueillant pour les femmes [The Québec cinema has not been particularly hospitable to women]," we read in a special issue of *La Châtelaine* devoted to women's cinema.[1] Still, while the sentence refers negatively both to the image of women projected by film, and to the role of women in the manufacture of film, several Québécoises (i.e., women) directors have been working for nearly two decades to correct that situation. One might add that for women in Québec, as in the United States, the problematics of cinema have been the subject of much critical and scholarly writing. In Bill Nichols's *Movies and Methods*, for example, there are several excellent essays on the subject. Also writing on woman in film are Hélène Cixous; Denise Warren (in her *Simone de Beauvoir*); Beauvoir herself (in her 1959 essay on the B.B. phenomenon, or the "Brigitte Bardot and the Lolita Syndrome"); Suzanne Lamy (and others) in the review *Spirale*; and many others on an international level.

Minou Petrowski says to her interviewer, Diane Poitras, the filmmaker (*La Perle rare, Pense à ton désir, Comptines*): "How do you expect there to be great roles for women, if the media will not recognize the work of actresses?"[2] Thérèse Lamartine, on the other hand, studies what she calls *cinématographie gynile* from the beginnings of moving pictures on, and, as she rereads the history

93

of world film *au féminin*, she includes consideration of what I, but apparently not everyone, would consider well-known work by such women as Alice Guy (Blaché), Yannick Bellon, Dorothy Arzner, Lotte Reiniger, and the controversial Leni Riefenstahl, whom Anthony Slide has told me in a personal conversation he considers to be the greatest of women directors. (Her shame was to be so closely associated with the rise of the Nazi party.) To shed light on women *cinéastes* (or what she calls "Lumière sur mes soeurs," punning, it seems, on the name of the brothers Lumière), Lamartine ultimately turns to later figures, including Liliana Cavani, Marguerite Duras, and the Québécoises Diane Létourneau and Anne Claire Poirier. All are, she contends, *terra incognita*. Most interesting here is Lamartine's idea of the "emergency aesthetics" that many of the contemporary women filmmakers practice.[3]

However, as Lever shows (*Hist*. 1988, 309), in Canada the situation for women directors did begin to take a radical change in 1971 when the ONF introduced a new program "En tant que femmes" within the cadre of "New Society." (Historical events preceding this include the establishment in 1968 of a small "Groupe de recherches sociales," headed by Robert Forget and Fernand Dansereau, who intended to be the French-speaking equivalent of Challenge For Change, which was the program of the English team. In 1969 the program continued under Forget, and took the name of Société Nouvelle or "New Society" [Lever *Hist*. 1988, 235–6].) Feminist pressure groups, desirous of using the tools of animation in order to prepare for the 1975 International Year of the Woman, arose. This ONF program engendered six films covering various aspects of woman's life, and also "was a veritable school of cinema, in the course of which several women were able to master various technical trades, as well as management of the production, direction of films, and so forth" (Lever *Hist*. 1988, 309). Under this program we saw the appearance of *Quelques Féministes américaines* (*A Few American Feminists*) by Luce Guilbeault and Nicole Brossard; *Fuir* (*Flight*) and *La P'tite Violence* (*The Small Violence*), by Hélène Girard; *Madame, vous avez rien* (*Mrs., you don't have anything*) by Dagmar Gueissaz Teufel; *Une Guerre dans mon jardin* (*A War in My Garden*) by Diane Létourneau; *Sonia* by Paule Baillargeon; and so forth. In the anglophone Canadian community, Studio D complements this *québécois* phenomenon. (On "En tant que femmes" and on Studio D, readers of French should consult Louise Carrière.[4]) It is the fact that a school of women *cinéastes* (making documentaries and feature films that deal with women's problems and bear a woman's orientation) should arise and flourish in Canada that in part justifies my devoting an entire chapter in this book to women (Québécoises) directors. Not all of them are connected with the ONF or with the ONF program "En tant que femmes," however. But whether associated with the ONF or not, Canadian women directors are quite numerous. Thus, Léa Pool thinks it not surprising that there should be a number of successful women filmmakers in Québec, where "there has always been a very strong feminist activity; feminism was a movement lived in a more intense manner than elsewhere, and that movement continues."[5]

Among the most prominent of Québécoises directors are Anne Claire Poirier, Léa Pool, Dorothy Todd Hénaut, and Sylvie Groulx, whose works we will here single out in particular. The films to be treated are often documentaries or docudramas on the history of women in Québec (*Les Filles du Roy*; *Le Film d'Ariane*), on women's problems in Québec — or in Western, even, broadly speaking, human — society (*La Quarantaine*, *Mourir à tue-tête* [*Scream from Silence*]), and even on the portrayal of women in film (*Il y a longtemps que je t'aime*). But there are also several excellent feature length films depicting women's subjects and women's situations in the society (*Anne Trister*; *La Femme de l'hôtel*; *Qui a tiré* ...; *Ça ne peut pas être* ...). Upon occasion, a man may well direct a film that shows the predicament of a woman in a given situation. *Valérie* (1969) by Denis Héroux was a film that invited woman to free herself; through it Danielle Ouimet became the "number one star of Québec." Lever (*Hist.* 1986, 281) gives us a startling still photograph taken from this rather famous work of Héroux; for *Valérie* belongs to the "movement," or campaign, in which the aim was "to undress the Québécoise" or, in short, to get rid of Catholic (*québécois*) prudery. Such a film as the political anti-porno film of Jean-Pierre Lefebvre, *Q-Bec my love* (1970), fell into the dialogue, but took a different tack. And often, too, men directors studied a woman's character *au fond*. In such films they often see their character as trapped and victimized by a repressive society (*Kamouraska*; *J. A. Martin photographe*; *Cordélia*). But these latter are treated under other rubrics in this book. In this chapter we will be concerned only with films made by women directors — *les femmes derrière la caméra*, as Lever puts it (*Hist.* 1988, 307–312) — and in particular with what can be called feminist issues in *québécois* cinema.

Documentaries and Docudramas

Feminist issues are indeed the proper domain of a great many documentaries. Showing up the relationship between American and Québécoises women is a 1977 work by Luce Guilbeault et al. Guilbeault has an illustrious record both as a stage and film actress and as a director. She has had roles in Denys Arcand's *Maudite Galette* (1971); Jacques Godbout's *IXE−13* (1971); Francis Mankiewicz's *Le Temps d'une chasse* (1972); Jean Beaudin's *J. A. Martin photographe* (1976); and many other movies, including several feminist films. With Paule Baillargeon she was a protagonist in *Le Temps de l'avant* (1975; d. Anne Claire Poirier; about abortion), in *Mourir à tue-tête* (1979; d. Poirier; about rape), and again in *La Quarantaine* (1982; d. Poirier). Her acting is characterized by its credibility, its chameleon-like character, and its naturalness. (Lever makes a point of the fact that Québécois actors of talent, including Guilbeault, are for the most part not 'spectacular' superstars, like those of Hollywood and France [*Hist.* 1988, 333].)

Turning to directing, Guilbeault has made *Denyse Benoît comédienne* (1975); *D'abord ménagères* (1978) and, of course, *Some American Feminists* (1977; 56 min.), which latter she directed with Nicole Brossard and Margaret Wescott. Highlighted in this documentary — which is not meant to offer a definition of feminism, but rather a document on the experiences, feelings, and theories of a select group of feminists — are such porte-paroles of American feminism as Bella Abzug (the American congresswoman, a vigorous proponent of women's rights and a pacifist, who helped found the Women's Strike for Peace in 1961); Rita Mae Brown (author and poet); Margo Jefferson (writer and critic); Kate Millett (author and sculptor); Lila Karp (writer and professor); Ti-Grace Atkinson (feminist theoretician and activist); and Betty Friedan (author). The film (produced at the ONF) is described by Michel Euvrard as "a gallery of portraits and an anthology of feminist discourse . . .; as an attentive film, which gets one's attention . . . because the people are presented 'in action.'" Euvrard also finds that "there is more fantasy, good humor, atmosphere and warmth here than in *D'abord ménagères* (also about American women), because, in order to track this invisible work, the camera had to go into houses and penetrate into the heart of daily life." Euvrard concludes that "a feminine complicity gives the film the best qualities of the *québécois* direct documentary, in which the directing team is on a level with the protagonists" (Coulombe 1991, 249; my paraphrases and translation).

One of the most brilliant docudramas in the field of feminist film is *Les Terribles Vivantes*, or *Firewords*. Its purpose is to portray the work and the inner nature of three renowned women (feminist) writers of Québec: Louky Bersianik, Jovette Marchessault, and Nicole Brossard, the latter of whom was one of the directors of *Some American Feminists*.

LES TERRIBLES VIVANTES (1986; d. Dorothy Todd Hénaut)
(1. LOUKY BERSIANIK)

Cutouts—illustrations for Louky Bersianik's *L'Euguélionne*—form the background for the reading of segments from this work, recited by Pol Pelletier. The Euguélionne is an extraplanetary woman; she is from the Planet negative, and has taken an acid bath. Since then, she seeks her positive planet—"le mâle de mon espèce." The earth is the planet of men. ("La terre ne nous appartient pas [Earth does not belong to us women].") The Euguélionne wants an answer to the question, "What is a man?"

Bersianik reads passages from *The Euguélionne* and speaks of woman's condition. Among women are "les terribles vivantes," the "géantes"; the woman who is becoming visible. But historically the noble role of women has been to clean up the shit—everyone's—that "sublime substance." Women were once thought to be goddesses until men found out the connection between intercourse and birth, she claims. Now the men have the power; women are vases. But, she exhorts, women must not lose their autonomy.

Bersianik explains how she invents words: language is political, she says, and the French language has mostly pejorative meanings for the feminine versions of roles (e.g.; *garçon* versus *garce*, etc.). Bersianik next reads some passages from *Ancyl*. (Ironically I find that this evokes, evidently unintentionally, the word Ancilla!). "Ma ralentie ... jouissance" is one of the chief readings. The passages are then sung by Judith Chevalier and Richard Seguin.

(2. JOVETTE MARCHESSAULT)

The passage dealing with the works of Jovette Marchessault is truly splendid. As she speaks of her grandmother and their strolls through the forest, where they hear the frogs, and so forth, the visual background is composed of reenactments of this all-important relationship of the child to her grandmother. It was from her, she claims, that she acquired a feeling for what is "vegetal and telluric."

Her grandmother taught her how to draw. (Her grandmother bought books as well.)

As Marchessault tells us this, we are treated to animated drawings that melt into photos of real hens and geese. Marchessault is next seen moving about on her farm, tending her plants, transplanting, winding skeins, etc. At the death of her grandmother she went into a deep depression that lasted for months: she became boulemic. She ate and ate; she came to weigh two hundred pounds.

Marchessault then decided to become an artist (painter) and a writer, but as a writer she found that she wrote only clichés at first. At this juncture, she worked as a *femme de ménage* at night. One night she went into a room where she saw a Chagall and then one of her own things. She resolved to stop her work as a cleaning woman and to "take charge of her life." She became *une écrivaine:* "je suis le scribe; j'invente; je transcris ... [I am the scribe, I invent, I transcribe"]; I am the bird who hears ("l'oiseau qui ouit")]." She recites, the chickens peck about, the geese wander around the farmyard, she builds and flies a kite. We see her cats, then her powerful sculptures of "telluric women," made from discarded objects reclaimed from Montréal garbage ("for women, taken, can be and are discarded in our society"). She talks about the spiral as the principle of life for her: it is a "living female sign." She tells of her ventures into theater, which is the "plaisir des autres," a collective. The actress Andrée Lachapelle speaks of Marchessault's *Anaïs dans la queue de la comète*; and we have stills from the play. But the most gripping and memorable scene from this entire documentary is the segment in which a passage from "Night Cows" (found in Marchessault's play entitled *Lesbian triptych*) is dramatized by Pol Pelletier. "Ma mère est une vache; avec moi ça fait deux. [My mother is a cow; that makes two of us.]" She is transformed "... belle ... une beauté." "Nous allons vers la tundra réveiller les corneilles ... [Together we go into the tundra to wake up the crows ...]." Pelletier uses a cow's skull and horns as a mask and a cow's hide as a costume. A magnificent moment on screen. A powerful moment.

We return to Jovette Marchessault's own witness: she distinguishes between *isolement*, or isolation (which is *douloureux,* or painful), and solitude (in which one is not suffering). She has animals all around out in the country, where she lives. "In the city," she says, "it is easy to find a lesbian community; in Montréal this community is everywhere." Marchessault's essential point is that as a lesbian, her love for women is not purely physical; men, she finds, are violent. It follows she is more comfortable with women.

(3. NICOLE BROSSARD)

The third segment of this film deals with the work of Nicole Brossard, which is less well transported to the visual plane. We are treated to any number of stereotypical talking heads, emblem of the patriarchal or male photographic approach to the documentary. Brossard is a wordier person than Marchessault, it seems; that is conveyed by the film.

The Brossard segment opens with her claiming that the two good environments for her are urban and the seashore: these are linked to writing, and that in turn to reading, reflection, and meditation. She, like Marchessault, wants to "take stock": this self-realization will be located, she says, somewhere between fiction and reality. Writing is a political act: she comes, through it, to a political pact with other women (for the personal is political). ("Je parle ... acte politique ... avec d'autres femmes ....")

Brossard tells quite a bit about the personal, in fact. Being a mother, she says, has forced her to reexamine her condition as a woman, and highlighted for her the importance of touch and sight, present in her writing. Here a very effective set of drawings is used. Brossard speaks of the *corps de mère* — mother's body (from *L'Amèr*, whose title puns on "the mother" and "the bitter one"); she is "writing the womb," she says. As for her lesbianism, she maintains she is expressing her love for all women through the love of one woman.

At this point a reclining odalisque provides a background for selected readings from *La Lettre aérienne*: It is less than a happy choice of "illustrations."

Brossard then talks of her love of wordplay. This material is shown unimaginatively by rearrangements of letters on the screen, as Brossard states that "each word explodes" (i.e., all words are firewords) and unfolds. Nevertheless, the image of the hologram, an "ideal image," is engaging.

Parenthetically, let me add that Brossard's interview with V. Tennant on the May 26, 1991, CBC Sunday Arts Show was a direct and clearcut statement of her intentions as a feminist writer, and conveniently supplemented the observations in *Firewords*. "Language," she said, "shapes the person and shapes the mind. The act of writing is one in which we discover certain realities not otherwise evident." Most interestingly, she declared that "men have dominated nature and women, and both [nature and women] are now saying 'that's enough!'"

Firewords, or *Les Terribles Vivantes*, is a documentary not to be overlooked. Speaking from a visual perspective, its value lies in particular in the segment on Marchessault.

UNE HISTOIRE DE FEMMES (1980; d. Sophie Bissonnette)

Sophie Bissonnette's *Une Histoire de femmes*, like *Les Terribles Vivantes*, is a documentary restricted to special concerns. It specifically treats the wives of strikers who put in question their traditional support role at the time of the 1978 INCO of Sudbury (Ontario) strike that involved the copper and nickel mines, foundries, and refineries. Bissonnette has written an essay about making this film entitled "Exploration féministe du documentaire" (Carrière *Auj.* 1982, 255–261).

Une Histoire de femmes studies the remarkable evolution of these ordinary francophone and anglophone women who rallied to support their husbands through an organization or committee. These steps were quite radical for these women. Through testimonials, we learn how they collected money and clothing, and how the men shared household work and child care. The women gathered in the cold around a bonfire to sing their song of "solidarity forever."

The women speak of their anguishes and insecurities, and tell how the strike was a community affair. They admit, in fact, that their participation was feminist or women-libbers' behavior on their part, "only don't say that."

We also witness arguments between the men and women as to who should be boss. One man claims that the man should be the boss — that the man is number one. But the women have learned to see their own value; they even go so far as to take a collective stand on how their husbands should vote about a possible settlement (7 May 1979). The wives oppose the offer and want their husbands to hold out for a better contract. And their opposition has an effect.

What especially remains with the viewer of this "documentary" is that the women have had a raising of consciousness. "We are not the ladies' auxiliary, making sandwiches. We have minds of our own, but the men don't realize this." Although the women go back to the housework and the men to the foundries and mines, the women will now get out of the house more. Many of these women, then, find their identity through their participation in the cooperative.

The film is honest, direct, and of considerable social interest. It was followed by the "militant" Bissonnette's 1985, eighty-one-

minute documentary *Quel Numéro?* or, *What Number?*, in which she
explored the condition of women who must work with computers —
everywhere present in this modern world — but feel they are controlled by these machines.

Une Histoire de femmes is in the tradition of the *cinéma direct*.
Bissonnette states that this is a *"cinéma d'intervention."*[6] But it
lacks the profundity and electricity of *Les Terribles vivantes* or
Les Filles du Roy. It also lacks the touching quality of Diane
Létourneau's *Les Servantes du Bon Dieu* (1978; 90 minutes), made
in the same years as the strike, and offering a portrait of nuns
formed to serve priests and living according to social and religious
traditions inherent in the Québec historical heritage, while — unlike
Antonine Maillet's Acadian, Jeanne de Valois — they remain
altogether impervious to the upheavals of recent years. And if
these are the characteristics we are looking for in a study of women's
experiences, of their history, of their exploitation and enslavement, of their sorrows and their *jouissances*, we will find them, and
more besides, fully explored in the works of Anne Claire Poirier.

LES FILLES DU ROY (1974; d. Anne Claire Poirier)

Though Anne Claire Poirier's work goes back as far as the 1960s
with a film focusing on pregnancy and motherhood (*De mère en
fille*; 1967), her *Les Filles du Roy* is also one of her earliest and
best known films. It is moreover one of her most poetic works; it
is a film à la Duras that translates the state of *attente* (or patient
waiting) in which women, like the black race, must find themselves;
it seems their opportunity for true participation in humanity's
"history" is forever projected into the future.

In the early frames of the work, we see how man and woman
have drifted apart — the man departing for adventure and the
woman dwelling on love. We sense how loneliness and isolation
have resulted from this rift. But the film then focuses on the specific
space in question: we have at hand the evolution of Québec society
seen through the optic of the female experience in that society
(behind the scenes).

The arrival of the *filles du roy* over the wide waters is invoked.
(These were the strong French women the king sent in 1760 for the
settlers, "robustes, courageuses, de bonnes moeurs.") The voice
speaks of the birth and death of children, of the interior life of
the women. Life was one long *attente*: they knitted, cooked their
tourtières.

Dramatically and in contrasts that bespeak a kind of purity and a kind of martyrdom, five nuns are shown lying in the form of crosses, their black habits vivid against the snow. For they too came across the sea to help with the settlements. (They are a reappearing montage.)

We learn of the criminal, the thirty-year old widow La Corriveau condemned in 1763 to be hanged as a witch; condemned "in a language she didn't understand."[7] From here the film moves to the condition of women prisoners today. "For," says the narrator, "women prisoners are still tried in English, do their time in English." Strikingly enough, this section is presented in English.

Old footage is again used to show soldiers off to war. It is the woman's role in this, says the narrator, to bear the loss. Some truly gruesome pictures of war and of the wounded are woven into this sequence, in which women are also shown in weapons factories.

The birth of a baby contrasts vividly with scenes in the cemeteries. Then in a litany that accompanies a series of old photos the narrator recites: "mon fils médecin; mon fils avocat; mon fils ministre; mon fils prêtre; mon fils juge; mon fils ingénieur, mon fils chirurgien, mon fils poète"; then, most ironically, "mon fils chômeur, mon fils drogué [my unemployed son; my drug-addict son]."

The group of women filmmakers discuss their relations with their women relatives. They speak of the women in their families who died so young, giving birth to many children. (This was considered to be their role, and was taught to them by the Church as their function — a teaching we encounter again in *Maria Chapdelaine*, *Bonheur d'occasion*, *Les Plouffe*, in which works the woman seems to take on the yoke, while not much liking it.)

We then see women at their household tasks, with no dialogue and only piano music for the sound track. The theme of *attente*, of patience and waiting is reintroduced. A voice says, "je nourris, je soigne, je rassure, je prie, etc.," and then "j'attends, j'ai le temps ..." and then, "je suis une femme qui ne travaille pas [I nourish, I care for, I reassure, I pray ... I wait, I have the time ... I am a woman who does not work.]"!! Equivocation is present, then, in the word "work." A man "works"; yet no one has ever labored any harder than the housewives of North America. And let us remember that they also had little say in government or politics; the Québécoises only got the vote some fifty years ago.

The *filles du roy* return to the screen in black, in the snow. Then the modern work force is introduced: "je suis sortie de la maison [I came out of the house]." So modern women are shown working in a clothing factory, as secretaries, as nurses, as bartenders, as seamstresses.

Ads are read aloud that list job opportunities: ads for key punch operators, for women to take dictation, for secretaries, stenographers, and waitresses, and in all these ads it is a requirement that the woman be bilingual. The age-old Canadian issue of bilingualism is thus raised here. The iconography of hands is also presented. The litany is resumed: " mon fils médecin, avocat, ministre, ingénieur." That is to say, the good jobs will go to the men; the women are doing the cleaning, they are picking up after the men, waiting on the men. We have dissolves. Then it is 1760 again, the time when the French king sent the healthy French peasant girls to the French Canadian *habitants* and loggers. We see the waters over which they came.

This, then, is the largely unwritten history of the Québécoise: from *fille du roy* (healthy, courageous, moral) to nun or to farm wife (housebound, bound to isolation and long winters), from farm wife (who knew of the country only through her husband's descriptions) to war widow [WWI and WWII], from worker in the war plant to housewife (the motif of the hands recurs), to modern working woman; bartender; secretary; nurse; cleaning woman; waitress; entertainer . . . always with her body as an object. Each personal history is the history of Québec, and that is the point.

Suddenly the scene shifts abruptly to a night club, showing a topless dancer, whom no one is even looking at; then to a stripteaser, who says "I'm not always sure of being a woman, a real woman, whom one marries; for men don't know the stripteaser, the call girl, [when they are] in front of their wives."

The image of hands is important to the film: hands are raised, and these extensions of the woman's body are the key to a woman's service . . . hands that feed, that nurture; hands that give care; hands that weave, that sew, that knit; hands that warm another; hands that pray; hands old and young.

Next, one sees the "statue" of a woman being wrapped like a mummy. Woman *should* be wrapped, for, according to traditional doctrine [indoctrinaction, I might say], she is *luxure, péché, tentation* (lust, sin, temptation). "It is true they have always spoken badly of me," says the narrator. Then a woman is unwrapping the statue, "freeing" it from this *suaire*, or winding cloth. "They had to unwrap me," the narrator says, "to see that my body was not rotten beneath. (But then) they used my body for advertising, for scandal, for money, for scorn." This unwrapping is a type of striptease;

a real woman is emerging, beneath the winding cloth. "Je m'appelle Valérie!" The allusion is of course to Denis Héroux's famous film *Valérie*, which here is called "*Valérie 1er film déshabillé.*" "So now you finally have the revelation, the uncensored *corps de la Québécoise toute nue [completely naked body of the Québécoise]* ... No more lies." "But," says the voice, "Valérie does not exist. I'm like all women. "Stop making up a dream about me; stop dreaming of what I am, I am here, take me as I am, my body. Look at the signs. You should recognize them; it is me. And I want you to love my body and know my feelings."

The voice supplicates the male: "We must speak to each other" .... of love?

But in the end the men are walking along the streets, and there are no women. Again the male and the female are separated, as at the beginning. Then there is a return to the domestic scenes, to birth, to the vast icy waters. For the time being, at least, no progress has been made; the thrust of the ending is quite pessimistic.

Les Filles du Roy was made without actors; the people appearing were real workers, real nuns, and so forth. Modern women are linked to the historic *filles du roy*, who are used to show the general enslavement of women. The device brings to mind Karen Anderson's *Chain Her by One Foot* (1990), a book of social history in which the argument runs that the subjugation of women in seventeenth-century New France was inextricably linked with the brutal colonization of native Indian populations.

Although as a producer at the ONF Anne Claire Poirier invited other women to direct certain films (e.g., Mireille Dansereau, in the film *J'me marie; j'me marie pas* [1973], in which four women artists seek to reconcile their careers with their family life), Poirier herself is especially outstanding among women directors for her strong portrayal of serious leprosies in the society. She was one of the first women directors at the ONF, and prefigured the feminist movement with such films as her *De mère en fille* (1967). The treatment of the problem of abortion came early in her career (*Le Temps de l'avant*; 1975) and caused a good deal of controversy. With Dominique Sicotte, she has more recently done an eighty-eight minute film-montage on the image of woman in the Québec film, *Il y a longtemps que je t'aime*, which we will look at momentarily. Meanwhile, let us note that something of the same question is raised by Mireille Dansereau in her docudrama-feature film *La Vie rêvée*, or *Dream(ed) Life*, although Dansereau is more concerned with women in advertising than in film. Moreover,

stereotypes from the beauty shop to the billiard hall are the subject
of another documentary, *Le Grand Remue-ménage* by Sylvie Groulx
and Francine Allaire. It is a "fierce expedition" into the question
of stereotypes as projected by media and by other forces rampant
in a preconditioned society. Before considering other films by
Poirier, let us look at Groulx's piece; this will observe chronology
and also pave the way for "*Il y a longtemps ...*"

LE GRAND REMUE-MÉNAGE. (1978; d. Sylvie Groulx and Francine
Allaire)

Jean-Pierre Tadros has cited the directors of *Le Grand Remue-
ménage* as intending to present a film in which men are recognized
as victims; they claim that their intention was in fact to affirm that
we are *all* victims, through our social conditioning. Not only men,
then, but women also, are shown in the film to be victims. "They
are alienated by their body, by the myth of the great love, of
marriage, and all that. And children too, because very quickly
and very soon little boys are like that and little girls like this and
there's no changing that." And Tadros himself finds this film to be
"un des films les plus intelligemment féministes qu'il nous ait été
donné de voir [one of the most intelligently feminist films that we
have been given]."[8] Tadros states that for Sylvie Groulx and Francine
Allaire it is not a question of making accusations, but of demon-
strating the social mechanisms that make man what he is and make
woman a creature of desire or the mother of a family. In *Le Devoir*
Tadros has claimed that this film gets you in the gut, both because it is well made and also because it touches you "sans vous
agresser."[9]
But is the film so objective as Tadros claims? It appears to me
that the images flashed before our eyes and the testimonials of the
interviewees are a trifle biased toward women. The film opens with
a woman introducing dolls, people who live in a city. It is night,
"Les femmes meurent étoufées dans leurs jacquettes [Women die
stifled in their straightjackets]," while men leave their cars with
their briefcases in hand. There is a witch among these people, an
hysteric, abandoned by her husband and children; all fear her; she
haunts them all. (The woman as witch is not uncommon in Québec
literature; Anne Hébert may be the most prominent among authors
including "witches" in their plots; La Corriveau, for example, was
found to be one.)
Commentaries by André Delorne and Madeleine Gagnon—the
celebrated Québécoise feminist who has worked with the conti-

nentals — are woven in and out of the film. In one such section, the transformations, the liberating forces that have occurred among women are explained. First, they had been taught to be "reines du foyer [queens of the hearth and home]," but now they work outside. Second, contraception has freed them from the burden of many children.

Many men pass before our eyes. They play billiards, they fulfill our "expectations" of them, they box and the boxing is brutal. An image of The Big Hulk is presented, a sign as to how to be a billionaire. War toys are shown at length. The meaning? Lever cites the directors Sylvie Groulx and Francine Allaire as consciously responding to such a "macho" film as Francis Mankiewicz's *Le Temps d'une chasse* by illustrating critically in their *Grand Remue-ménage* that (*québécois*) "masculinity is in crisis without even realizing it" (*Hist.* 1988, 351).

After being presented with a vignette in which a woman interlocutor discourses on the capitalist system, which according to her is supported by the concept of the monogamous, stable couple and the concept of *le grand amour*, an overly long passage presents shots of women learning the art of using cosmetics.

The interviews show us stereotypical ideas. A young man contends that feelings aren't so strong in men; women are more emotional, women have changed and are more liberated. Formerly if a woman had slept with a man, no one wanted her; but today promiscuity is common. He adds that laws are made by man. Man is stronger; he must dominate. Nature would have it thus.

Next comes a *scénario* in which an actress posing as "Linda" talks of losing her Steve; she has been jilted. This section, written and recited by Valérie Letarte, is one of the best segments in this early documentary. The use of a small boy and a small girl to show early socialization processes is no doubt effective, but without subtitles their language is truly a challenge to the American viewer!

"Dénonciation féroce et humoristique des rôles que tiennent implacablement les hommes et les femmes dans notre société. Un film coup de poing . . . et la grande révélation de La Semaine du cinéma québécois 1978 [A fierce and humorous denunciation of the roles that men and women implacably have in our society. A film with a punch . . . and the big revelation of the 1978 Semaine du cinéma québécois]."[10]

SONIA (1986; d. Paule Baillargeon)

With *Sonia*, Paule Baillargeon, who is also the outstanding actress of *I've Heard the Mermaids Singing* and of Léa Pool's *Femme de l'hôtel*, joins the ranks of directors of the "disease-or-illness-of-the-week films." But when it comes to portraying death and dying, this work is perhaps not in the same league as that small jewel *Jacques et Novembre* or Jean Beaudin's *Cher Théo* (both discussed in Ch. 5). Still, women and disease may be a subject of predilection among women directors, as illustrated in *Children of a Lesser God* by Randa Haines; *Tell Me a Riddle* by Lee Grant; *Cléo de 5 à 7* by Agnès Varda, the French-Greek director — though this last is a layered film that really deals with the transformation, under the threat of cancer, of an extremely unpleasant and narcissistic "star" into a full-fledged woman, finally capable of loving others. Here with *Sonia* it is a matter of Alzheimer's disease.

Baillergon's recent *Sexe des étoiles* (1993) is receiving a great deal of attention. The story of a man whose daughter grapples with his sex change, it has been invited to participate in the international competition at the FFM (Festival des Films du Monde).

Sonia, on the other hand, was excerpted in *Il y a longtemps que je t'aime*.

IL Y A LONGTEMPS QUE JE T'AIME (1989; d. Poirier and Sicotte)

Il y a longtemps que je t'aime is an extraordinary amalgam of scenes from many Québec films. It might be hard to follow for one who is not familiar with the cinema of Québec, but the narrator warns us not to try to identify films, for that is not the point. Nevertheless, I will point out that included here are shots from *J. A. Martin photographe*; *Le Déclin* . . .; *Le Temps d'une chasse*; *Alias Will James*; *J'me marie, j'me marie pas*; *Sonia*; *Trois Fois Passera*; *L'Amour à quel prix?*; *Voyage en Amérique* . . .; sequences from several of Perrault's films (*Pour la suite du monde, La Grande Allure, La Bête lumineuse, Le Règne du jour, Le Beau Plaisir*); from *La Peau et les os* (a film about anoerexia by Johanne Prégent[11]); from *L'Homme renversé* of Yves Dion, etc.; and from several of Poirier's own films, including her highly poetic *Filles du Roy, De mère en fille* (concerning pregnancy and motherhood; 1967), *Le Temps de l'avant* (concerning abortion; 1975), and *Mourir à tue-tête* (concerning rape; 1979).

Done under the auspices of the ONF (Programme: Regards des femmes), this work offers a very accurate picture of woman and woman's life. Drawing from old newsreels, women at war and women at beauty contests are depicted. We hear the opinions of men on physicality vs. femininity in women; we see the socialization processes coming in the early primer (reader), where Guy likes sports, while Yvette helps in the house, and always pleases her parents. We see shots of beer-bellied men gaping at dancers and stripteasers, and hear the tearful confessions of these women, offered through their distress. We see scenes of mothering: the disciplining mother of *J. A. Martin photographe*, for example, and the modern mother with the same problems. A segment from *Mon oncle Antoine* shows the clerk and the aunt doing the accounts and singing together. From *Le Temps d'une chasse*, the woman is seen as representing the object of the hunt, and a lesser one than the animal at that: "No woman however beautiful could make me stay away from the hunt ... There is the fraternity of the hunt; the hunt is the woman." Woman is seen giving birth; discussing her eating disorders. In short, *Il y a longtemps que je t'aime* (which in fact makes use of that song and of several other outstanding musical numbers, such as Félix Leclerc's "Moi, mes souliers" and Bernard Montanegro's "Petites filles") contains one hundred excerpts from sixty films, all intertwined. And surely among the most stunning scenes are those drawn from certain animated films, including *Universe* by Colin Low; *Premiers Jours* (*Beginnings*), by Clorinda Warny, Suzanne Gervais and Lina Gagnon; *Climats* by Suzanne Gervais; *Ah vous dirais-je maman* by Francine Desbiens; *Les Femmes parmi nous* by Evelyn Lambart; and, especially, *Cycle* by Suzanne Gervais. Most memorable are the excerpts from *Premiers Jours*, or *Beginnings*, a dreamy animated film (8 min. 2 sec.) in which "abstract landscapes evolve into strange, godlike figures, whose images revert into landscapes."[12]

This portrayal of woman in film appears, in the long run, to provide a history of Québec film in general. The excerpts are taken from ONF productions covering a span of fifty years (1940–88).

As I indicated previously, Poirier has also presented *La Quarantaine* (produced by the ONF) and *Le Temps de l'avant* (1975), as well as *De mère en fille*. These films are treated in the April, 1990, issue of *La Châtelaine* mentioned at the beginning of this chapter. But here we will devote our attention to her "docudrama," *Mourir à tue-tête*.

MOURIR À TUE-TÊTE (1979; d. Anne Claire Poirier)

No film of Poirier's can compare to her graphic and troubling work on the subject of rape, *Mourir à tue-tête* or *Scream from Silence*. The director has de-eroticized and universalized rape in this film, which oscillates between documentary and fiction. "Editorials" interrupt the story, and panning, tracking, and freeze-frame are used most effectively; the ultimate realization of the viewer, who sees the entire rape from Suzanne's point of view, and thus is forced into the position of identifying with her, is, in a sense, that the rapist can be anyone, as can the victim. It is a highly political film that criticizes the society and its institutions for victimizing, even criminalizing, the victim.

As a frame to *Mourir à tue-tête* — which contains several levels of diegesis — Anne Claire Poirier has used the concept of two women making a documentary on rape. At various junctures they do playbacks and discuss what has just been seen. The documentary within the "docudrama" therefore opens with a group of women saying "It's him," while many male faces are projected. They serve to reflect all professions, all ethnicities, all kinds of relationships. The film then focuses on Suzanne, a nurse (played by Julie Vincent), who is going home from her night shift — a classic opportunity for the rapist. Throughout the rape scene, which occurs in a van, the rapist drinks beer, urinates on the woman, and talks a steady stream. Through his monologue we learn that he is a failure and that for him this is a power trip. What makes the scene especially frightening and ferocious is that the rapist faces the viewer ... it is the viewer who is urinated upon, disparaged, humiliated, and raped. Then the director of the documentary explains to her colleague that the rapist and his victim must not be shown together, for "rape forms no couple." And interestingly enough, though this is never articulated, we do not see the rapist again through the rest of the film. He is anonymous; he comes and goes in the night, disappearing into the streets from which he issued; and he escapes prosecution.

But Suzanne's story continues; we are presented with the dreadful aftermath of the rape, which constitutes a series of mental rapes. As the nurse arrives home, bruised and shaken, she finally bursts into tears. Then she calls her boyfriend. "Philip, come quickly," she says. As she attempts to scream out her anguish, an intercut sequence unfolds; she is joined in her screams by the exploited women of Vietnam and the violated females of Bangladesh. (Clearly, rape is the universal experience of women, and the rape is not always

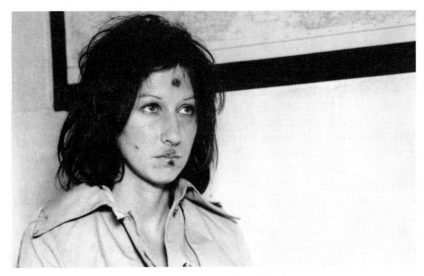

Mourir à tue-tête. (Courtesy Office National du Film.)

physical; but in any event these sequences generalize Suzanne's experience.)

Philip gets Suzanne to a hospital, where a doctor objectively takes smears and examines her. He has pictures taken of her physical condition, "for proof of violence." Again, a sequence unfolds. This time it is a violent portrayal of what is called "clitorodectomy" in the credits; the scenes are taken from Alain de Benoist's *Mouvement terre des hommes.* In reality we have a graphic and this time authentic documentary within a "documentary" within a fictional work that seems almost a documentary, and it deals with *excision,* or removal of the clitoris and of the labia — major and minor. This passage in the film depicts ritual "rape" and deprivation of the female's control over her biological destiny, as well as the elimination of any capacity on her part for pleasure or *jouissance.*

The camera shifts abruptly back to the nurse's bruised face. She is now being "interviewed" by a policeman. Philip is with her. This provokes the policeman to see in the nurse a moral derelict begging for rape. "You live with her?" he asks Philip. There follow a number of such "leading" questions. As is always the case with excellent film work, one must notice the details of the scenes. Here there is a notice pinned to the wall of the police station announcing a "Réunion de la fraternité" on Tuesday. The word fraternity bonds all policemen to one another, and perhaps the policemen to rapists.

Suzanne's tangled hair triggers further scenes that generalize the victimization of women. In still further documentaries within the documentary being made by the two women, we are shown war, and the cutting of hair and shaving of heads in war camps; we are presented with scenes of concentration camps. In other words, the holocaust of the Jews is tied to a universal holocaust of women, and we are given to understand that racism and sexism are one and the same thing. (Some view these passages as referring to the shaving of female heads in France after World War II, when it was believed that the women had collaborated or had "slept with the enemy.")

As the scene shifts to an interview between the moviemaker and the raped woman, we are given the illusion that the "documentary" being made is based on a "real" event.

"Fear," says the victim, "was my foremost emotion ... The worst thing was his contempt; it was not a sexual thing—there was no desire; rather, he managed an erection through contempt." She reiterates her shame, fear and guilt. "Now I'm afraid all the time. They examined me for any disease I might have caught from him; I didn't catch a disease; I caught fear." She compares the rape and its aftermath to a nightmare. "You want to cry out but you can't."

This concept of the silent scream, from which the English version takes its title, is a leitmotif throughout the film. But at this juncture the scene shifts to a group of blindfolded women who are being questioned by the authoritarian and unsympathetic judge. A series of "silent rapes" are suggested: these come between husband and wife, between boss and secretary, between director and actress, between psychiatrist and patient. In other words, it is a matter of domination. The judge, deaf to their arguments, reads the penal code of Canada regarding rape to them. (With rapes, he says, there are two truths: man's and woman's.) The woman is regarded as the guilty one. The confrontation of the women and the judge brings home the message that there is no hope for justice when it comes to rape. We now return to the documentary-in-progress. The victim has become listless, idle. Philip arrives; we see that his patience is growing thin. He tells her, "You must pull yourself together. It's been two months now. You must help yourself; I can't do it for you." But Suzanne's pose alone conveys to us her abject indifference. She tells Philip he cannot understand; he suggests a therapist, but this is not acceptable to her. The couple goes to bed; Philip would like to make love, but she cannot respond. She assumes a fetal position. Then a scene of vomiting ensues.

Suzanne looks in the mirror. She wants to scream but cannot. Philip leaves her ... we assume for good.

In the next scene Suzanne puts on a white nightgown — symbol of her own purity, but also of the nonnuptial cadre in which she finds herself. She takes many pills; suicide is implied. Then the two filmmakers discuss the scene. The director's colleague says, "The end is terrible." Says the director: "Rape is terrible." "But," she adds, "she did not kill herself; the rape killed her. Rape is a death gesture; she was already dead before she committed suicide." And the director then emphasizes that this is not an imaginary piece of fiction. In the interior "docudrama" — the documentary the director is making — Suzanne represents Francine, a real life woman who killed herself after being raped!

In the conclusion, we are presented with scenes of places where rape might occur. And if and when it does, there is a wall of unmovable silence that comes up around it. All women need whistles, therefore. In the end, there are no people, just shots of empty streets and alleys: a city lying in dark, lying in wait. Peter Rist, in discussing this film, sees the many whistles being blown at the end as "signs of hope."[13] But they more likely mean that rape comes from so many directions that whistles would have to be blown from almost every spot conceivable, and also constantly.

Mourir à tue-tête is a film to be seen by all people of all countries, men and women alike. Once seen it will not be forgotten. It is not like any other film on rape. It is a masterpiece of the (gyne) "documentary" genre — a work of fiction, scripted and acted, yet very much resembling a documentary or docudrama. The film is minutely analyzed by Denise Pérusse in *Le Cinéma aujourd'hui*.[14]

LE FILM D'ARIANE (1985; d. Josée Beaudet)

Ariadne's Movie is like *Les Filles du Roy* and to some extent like *Il y a longtemps que je t'aime*, in that it is a work that successfully portrays the history of Québec's women (1925–80), but this time through the story of one woman, Ariadne.

Early scenes in the film show a rapid history of the Québécoise, including nuns baling hay; Ariadne begins her tale. Born in 1910, she attended boarding school as a young woman. Her photo album provides visual iconography of her youth, and her voice tells us of her early life, a "mission of love" (1925–45). Against some very effective background music, she reminisces. As a child in Abitibi, she was happy; she did field work, and at sixteen she joined the Enfants de Marie. Indeed, the strong role the Church played in the lives of the women of her generation is emphasized in this segment of the film. Girls were expected to obey, not enjoy: exhortations were given to "beware automobiles," which were "driven to isolated areas" and "used for carnal desires"; girls were told to be wary of modern dances and the evils of fashions, and to beware also of promiscuity on the beaches. Ariadne explains that in those days women were also told not to mix into politics; the Church was against women's suffrage.

When she reached the age of twenty she could not become an artist as she might have wished to do, for there were really only three choices for women: teacher, nun, or wife. As she says, "most of us were potential nuns." *A la rigueur*, she adds, one might also consider being a nurse.

In the second part of this film, we learn that Ariadne is not interested in being a nun or a nurse; she is interested in being a wife and a mother, for she has met Pierre. Ariadne informs us that women "in those days" got married and then did as they were told. A man's voice — that of Ariadne's husband — explains that "in those days there was no divorcing."

In the following segments Ariadne tells of the war and how it brought on marriages. (We are here reminded of the consequences of the war as portrayed by Gabrielle Roy in *Bonheur d'occasion* [*The Tin Flute*].) Ariadne goes on to tell how the Royal Canadian Air Force called for women "to join"; but the French Canadians did not accept this idea of women in the service, for they thought that the women joined merely to serve men sexually. In any event, by 1943 Ariadne already had four children, and she thought that her husband, Pierre, would be safe.

An eternal question raised by many societies, including the French Canadian, has been whether women should work outside the home. It would seem that the answer to this question came with the war: as *Ariadne's Movie* shows, women became "soldats de l'industrie." Between the two wars, then, came the exodus of women from the home and into the work force.

The third section of *Le Film d'Ariane* deals with chairs. We are presented with an iconographic juxtaposition of rocker and secretarial chair, as a phenomenon of the period between 1945 and 1965. During this period, we are informed, men were no longer innocent, thanks to the war; but women still were. At thirty-eight, says Ariadne, she had had eight children within ten years. Every sexual encounter was high-risk. Yet, when she told the priest she had denied her husband sex just after her baby was born, the priest told her, "I'm going to excommunicate you."

There were other blatant prejudices against women. As concerned the family allowance check, for example, in Québec the government sought to issue it to men — heads of the household — although in other provinces it was given directly to women. In this instance, the women struggled and did get the check. That was in 1949. Ariadne concedes that this was but a small thing, and the amount of money was small; still it was something, and gave women a newfound independence.

Other items of significance to Ariadne were the union parade and the confrontation of Duplessis and Madeleine Parent. (She upheld the right to strike; Duplessis contended that these demonstrators were communists, and sent Parent to jail.) The acquisition of their first TV set and their interest in *Les Plouffe*, a highly-popular serialized version of Lemelin's epic, were also important.

Ariadne continues her story. She sent her eldest daughter to the nuns' boarding school, where she had gone before her. The leitmotif of fourteen years with the nuns, with constant stress upon chastity and virginity, is punctuated with scenes of communion, *Tantum Ergo* playing in the background. The girls are shown putting on a play, in which they are cast as "bees of God." In this play, which reflects the profound socialization processes to which the Québécoise was subjected before the Quiet Revolution, the girls illustrate the "truth" of their real purpose in life: to dust, to work, to shine. Still, Ariadne's eldest daughter wanted to study law and her next daughter wanted to learn home economics. Ariadne's daughters appear to have surmounted the obstacles; her third daughter even aspired to be a doctor, and indeed did become one.

The final segment of this fascinating documentary deals with the "generation of change," the period from 1965 to 1980, when women achieved more freedom. We see Mayor Drapeau opening Expo and scenes of Québec liberation. Ariadne is sixty. New things have come along to free women — the pill, for example. People have commenced to talk about everything quite freely; men have begun to fear that their wives will leave them; divorce has become more common; nuns are leaving the convents; children are appearing by choice; natural childbirth is the order of the day. Ariadne's first grandchild Isabelle is born. We see René Lévesque; a parade for abortion. Ariadne tells us she is interested in what women do, proud to be a woman. Placards appear: they have mottos in defense of lesbianism — "je suis votre vieille tante; votre femme; votre professeur; on est partout [I am your old aunt; your wife; your teacher; we are everywhere]." There are messages such as "un emploi, ou un revenu [give us a job]."

Well, concludes Ariadne, men may not still completely respect women; but, now, at seventy-five, she can say that she is happy.

JOURNAL INACHEVÉ OR, *UNFINISHED JOURNAL* (*UNFINISHED DIARY*) (1982–83; d. Marilú Mallet)

Marilú Mallet (born in Santiago, Chile, in 1944) cofounded, with Dominque Pinel, les Films de l'Atalante, in 1980. One of the most outstanding productions of this company was Mallet's own *Journal inachevé* (1982–83; 55 min.), a film that portrays the life of a young Chilean filmmaker who lives in exile in Montréal. Her perceptions of her lived reality and the films she works on — both documentary and feature fiction — become blurred together, as, in fact, they also nourish each other. Unlike *Ariadne's Movie*, *Journal inachevé* scrutinizes Québec society from the perspective of the alienated immigrant. It also examines the coup d'état of Chile, as recounted by the filmmaker's friend, Isabel Allende, during their brief encounter. Perhaps most importantly, we have in this work the clash of the filmmaker and her husband, also a filmmaker, and their conflicting value systems. As it says in *Cinéma au Féminin*, "In a moving self-portrait, realism gives way to intense emotion ... private life becomes political ... (and there is a) sudden awakening to the necessity of keeping one's identity and the attempt to discover what lies deep inside oneself — a Journal ... Unfinished."[15]

Richard Martineau states that this is a film "that walks the tightrope that separates the spoken from the unspoken, idea from emotion. It forges a new cinematographic language, original and very personal, which proceeds with hesitation, fear, and boldness. The camera becomes somehow the porte-parole of a "je" [I]: "je"-woman, "je"-immigrant; "je"-creator. The politics of daily events and what is everyday in politics. Impressive!"[16]

Carrière's study of this film is important. But Mallet also gets ample treatment by Michel Euvrard (Coulombe 1991, 359–60), where we read that *Journal inachevé* is a more directly personal film than her first major effort — *Les 'Borges'* (1978) — in which she documented a family of Portuguese immigrants in Montréal. Because of a language barrier, the father of this family cannot communicate with his coworkers and therefore feels exiled; he dreams of returning to die in his little house in Portugal. The more realistic mother, on the other hand, is attached to Montréal through her children and grandchildren. It is interesting to note that in this family one of the sons has become an anglophone, the other a francophone; and it is the latter who offers the explanations, information, and commentaries on the family, while "the camera is both familiar and respectful."

Journal inachevé — neither documentary nor fiction (though in Coulombe [1991, 574] it is called "fiction") — partakes of private correspondence, an intimate journal, memories. It consists of seizing hold of and repeating a series of images summoned up by deprivation, desire, and the need to reconstruct a life still balancing between childhood and adolescence in Chile, the years of Popular Unity — a past that is still present in Montréal, in the person and in the engravings of the mother and Chilean friends who have no visa and are harassed by immigration — and also by the problems of present-day life: a weak marriage, a difficult child, the problematic integration into *québécois* society. The three languages — the Spanish of the mother, the English of the marriage, and the French of the child and of the workplace — are used. Several series of images alternate and fuse: still photos and engravings (that is, images of the past in black and white); images of certain interiors (intimate space, closed, warm, protected); images of exteriors (vast cold and empty spaces such as streets and roads); images of intermediate places that are the links of social integration. The images make up an autobiographical fiction that collects what a conventional linear narration or a documentary approach would have excluded.

The 1992–3 catalogue of Women Make Movies quotes Julian Burton [of U.C. Santa Cruz] as saying: "The displacements and disjunctions of exile have never been more poignantly conveyed. Mallet uses her domestic space as mirror of the self struggling to find a place to call home. A compelling, resolutely tentative exploration of female subjectivity."[17]

In 1986 Mallet made *Mémoires d'une enfant des Andes*, about a Peruvian village seen through the eyes of a little girl who is handicapped. It is more directly a documentary than any other work of hers. More importantly for our concerns, Mallet in 1988 worked on a documentary for the ONF series "Parler d'Amérique" dealing with the meeting of a Québécoise with a "neo-Québécoise" of Portuguese origins. (Euvrard in Coulombe 1991, 360; my paraphrase and translation.)

Mallet has also written two collections of novellas — *Les Compagnons de l'horloge-pointeuse* and *Miami Trip*.

Another well-known documentary filmmaker is Diane Létourneau, who to some degree showcases political and societal realities we will pick up again as reflected in mainstream Québec cinema (Chs. 5 and 6). Such, for example is her *La Vie de couple* (1980), about the life of a married couple.

Having been a nurse, Létourneau's preoccupations are often concerned with health and with issues of death and dying. She began her career with two or three documentaries codirected with Georges Dufaux (*A votre santé* [1964]; *Les Jardins d'hiver* [1976]; and *Au bout de mon âge* [1975]). In 1979 she made *Les Servantes du Bon Dieu*, which dealt with the members of a religious community, women who had sacrificed their lives to serve priests. She does not seek to show them in any ironic light, but with honesty and respect. (Cf. the anglophone Canadian documentary *Behind the Veil*, by Margaret Wescott [1984; 130 min.].)

At ONF, Létourneau made *La Passion de danser* and *En scène*; but in 1985 she directed one of her most important works, *Une Guerre dans mon jardin*, where she studies the situation of members of a family following the accidental death of a man. They relive the tragic event, occurring in 1980 as a result of a military *obus* being tossed into the flames of a fire on the feast day of Saint John the Baptist, historically Québec's most important holiday. The resulting work is pacifistic in tone. The film took a prize for the best short work in that year. In 1987 Létourneau used her medical knowledge to look at the question of euthanasia in a somewhat fictional cadre (*A force de mourir* . . .). Twins are the subject of a 1988 work, entitled *Comme deux gouttes d'eau*. (Some information translated and paraphrased from Marcel Jean [in Coulombe 1991, 344–45].)

It is certainly safe to say, as the above discussions demonstrate, that the documentaries and docudramas by and regarding women coming from Québec are powerful, original, and worthwhile. They offer one of the best indices into the society, both in its past and in its present state. We must hope that the high quality of the documentary product offered by these women filmmakers will continue to appear, and indeed we have reason to believe that it will; for among recent feminist shorts from Studio D (the National Film Board's women's studio) is a notable work entitled *Petit Drame dans la vie d'une femme*, by actress-writer Andrée Pelletier. (She was the social worker in Tom Shandel's fact-based 1984 film entitled *Walls*, which told of a prison hostage-taking and a subsequent death.) *Petit Drame* . . . is a fable about a thirteen-year-old girl who has locked herself in the bathroom and refuses to become a woman. (Echoes of *Tin Drum* and even of *Plaza Suite*.) The film was issued in June, 1990, along with several works by anglophone Canadian women directors (e.g., *We're Talking Vulva*, d. Shawna Dempsey).[18]

Feature Films

LA VIE RÊVÉE (1972; d. Mireille Dansereau)

Kaye Sullivan, in her *Films for, by, and about Women*,[19] claims that in *La Vie rêvée* "the filmmaker wants to show that great friendships exist between women, so that for a time, at least, they don't need men." She also postulates that there is interest here in how the individual subconscious relates to the conscious mind. It seems to me, though, that the core meaning conveyed here is that the Dream life is representative both of the nightmare and of the "ideal" imposed upon the female psyche by advertising and by socialization processes, including dreams of incest and extermination. To be free, the dream must be dissipated. The nightmare content of these dreams is a trope reiterated by images of barbed wire, clothes strung on clotheslines, etc.

The two girls in the film (Isabelle, of wealthy parents — that is, of a very constrained background — and Virginia, of a middle class, less affluent family whose freedom is envied by Isabelle) are in advertising. They, like the viewer, are barraged with images. Some of the products alluded to — seemingly largely American — include 7-Up; Coca-Cola; Coffeemate; Heinz tomato ketchup; Pepto-Bismol. And in the course of this film the two enter the "real life," free of fantasy and, at the end, are delirious over their liberation.

The film is not as simplistic as Sullivan suggests. Great stress is put upon the viewer to follow not only the plot but to assimilate the many images flashed on the screen, and, ultimately to assess their purposes. Some of the specters raised through these images and scenes are incest, adultery, lesbianism, and some of the apparent endorsements include sisterhood, freedom of choice, and so forth. Criticism of certain social forces is also present, as for example, the control of the Church via a scene in which a priest conveys to Isabelle in one of her "bad dreams" a sense of shame; strong control through Nazi figures; and a firing squad. The firing squad recurs in another bad dream in which Isabelle tells Virginia that she dreamt she was condemned to death by a firing squad, when in prison(!), and that her father came to see her in prison, since he wanted to thank her.

Above all, the dream images, though initially suggesting odious forms of paternalism, sometimes portray the oedipal inclinations of the father-daughter relationship, going back into the archaeological beginnings of this powerful taboo, unspoken by Isabelle, but almost lived out in the dream sequences, where the mother — shown as very jealous—is linked to the wife whose husband George Isabelle lusts for. Once she finally gets to bed with this imagined superman we find that he is impotent. The dream is dissipated, even exploded; her dream was a fantasy; George was a phoney; now she is free. Now all the images can be torn to shreds and, for the time being, the women will go their own way, or at least no longer endorse the role they have been handed by society. Even more important, they are aware of their socialization. They are less interested now in the dream (Virginia had early on claimed that it is fun to dream); they are more confident (Isabelle had early on stated "I'm not talented"). The self is liberated from images, fantasies, paranoia, self-doubt, and guilt. They will no doubt refuse to be objects any longer (one of them having served earlier as her superior's ashtray). We are now in the realm of full color: the sepia recalls are dissipated. In Virginia's "bad dream" a dragon appears, evidently an image recalled from the back of her dressing gown and reintegrated as a threat. The exactitude concerning the manner in which images operate in our lives and in our dreams is one of the positive qualities of this film.

Sound is important, too. At one juncture, the music from *A Man and a Woman* is heard in the background. It seems to be sour, moreover. By its presence we are compelled to think about love and its "failure." An allusion to *Le Bonheur* of Agnès Varda provides, for those who know this film, an additional question mark concerning "love" and marriage, a convention the girls eschew. Other reversals occur, as well: in this film the man (Adam) splits an apple in two and gives it to the two women (Eve).

As we so often see to be the case with cinema from Québec, whether directed and/or produced by men or women, there is a documentary feel to this movie. But Agathe Martin-Thériault is quite right when she says that certain of the sequences (the realistic ones, more so than the ones devoted to dreams) seem to lack cohesion, and sometimes, as with the swim, in which children participate, even seem to be gratuitous. She adds that some of the editing is not always too fortunate. Still, she finds that the message of the film comes through quite clearly: denunciation of the traditional concept of woman as an unpaid workhorse (as in a marriage); satire of a patriarchal world; criticism of the use of woman as a commercial object; criticism of the commercial exploitation of feeling and of "beatific" imagery. But at the same time, Martin-Thériault suspects (justifiably, I think) that sometimes Dansereau's ideological objectives may have forced her to conceive and add scenes that were not necessary to the film. Thus, one has the feeling that the film is not well knit (*l'impression de décousu*).[20]

Louise Carrière (*Femmes* ... 1983, 164−5) claims that *La Vie rêvée* is inspired by sociological reflections on youth and the contradictions of *québécois* society. She finds that it also makes use of the manifestations of the counter culture, and that it explores new fronts: feminist movements; ecological movements; sexual liberation; problems of exploitation; economic questions. Social space in terms of center and periphery and repression constitute additional themes. For her the central tone of this film is euphoria.

What annoys Carrière with respect to this work is that throughout the film the author vacillates between criticism of mythical images and her desire to transform that which is common day into a game.

On the other hand, what redeems the work for Carrière is that, made in 1972, it was, for all intents and purposes, the first full-length fictionalized film by a woman in private (film) industry. At a time when other filmmakers were choosing to do direct testimonial or witness-type films on the working class world, Mireille Dansereau went against the current: she chose to make a fiction on the fantasies of two women, a rather slight and intimist subject. Her film thus takes into account the early films of women directors: they are often intimist, autobiographical, descriptive, rather than didactic.

Mireille Dansereau is for Carrière one of the first to attack the imaginary world and the imagination of women, a world that is, or was, often *imposed* upon them. But she hypothesizes that today we may see the film as naive: the girls are more childlike than autonomous. (It is interesting to note that, shortly after the appearance of *La Vie rêvée*, *Variety* stated that the film provoked varying reactions among the audience, and that it had already opened and closed in Montréal after a month's run. The author of the article predicts: "If there is a further commercial career for it, it will probably be among young audiences, in festivals, and wherever women's lib exerts influence." It goes on to say that the themes are not provincial, and that the film may even do better with English audiences than in Québec, to judge by its reception in Toronto.[21])

Commenting on the technical features of *The Dream(ed) Life*, Carrière points out that Mireille Dansereau, using slow motion, long shots, and pastel tones to denounce and to visualize the women's fantasies, makes her film somewhat blurry. The question is therefore raised as to what exactly she intends? What is intended by showing the two kinds of families from which the girls come? (The intention of these juxtapositions is not clear: new values for

Isabelle, or what?) Finally, Carrière finds that this, like many early feminist films, proceeds by psychological tableaus that are not developed. Young women are at odds with their immediate environment, struggling for autonomy. This environment is usually restricted to one social milieu and to one age group, although in the Dansereau film we find a contrast in the girls' socioeconomic backgrounds.

Dansereau has also made *J'me marie, j'me marie pas* (1973); *Famille et variations* (1977); *L'Arrache-coeur* (1979); *Le Sourd dans la ville* (q.v., Ch. 4).

LÉA POOL'S GYNEFILMS[22]

Léa Pool's films (*La Femme de l'hôtel*; *Anne Trister*) are outstanding as works whose visual structures and ideological, albeit minimal, stories fuse to present gynepathetic themes, sometimes in terms of a specific geometry. These films are not culturally based or bound, as *Mon oncle Antoine* or *Les Bons Débarras* might be said to be. Of course, since Pool is of Swiss origins, her use of Québec cultural materials is in a sense slight, even though the skyline of Montréal and other views of the city serve as a backdrop in her works. The symbolism and the geometry of her films reflect Jewish and feminist concerns, not social or political concerns pertaining uniquely to Canada or to any of its regions. Already in 1980 with her *Strass Café* she was seen to be more in debt to the French art-house style of Alain Resnais or Jean Cayrol than to any Québec artist. In this film, which bears the mark of Marguerite Duras's work, "disembodied voices, recounting fragments of the lives of two enigmatic nightclub performers, are heard over extended stills of urban landscapes" (Clanfield 1987, 82). But, as we shall see, this preoccupation with Jewish questions and feminist concerns is particularly notable in her film *Anne Trister*. Neither is Léa Pool making an ethical statement in her films, as *Le Déclin de l'empire américain* can be shown to be doing; nor are they presenting a predetermined narrative, as *Les Fous de Bassan* halfway intends.[23] Her pictures are not subverting the violent American crime story, as *Pouvoir intime* may in part be attempting. Pool is doing none of these things in quite the same way as other directors working in Québec, if she is doing them at all.[24]

Rather, one may contend that Pool's work clearly marks the entrance of the Québec cinema into worldwide feminist cinematic iconography. But Pool seems, among women filmmakers, to have an uncommon gift. Even so, her accomplishments to date will, like those of other women directors, probably not reach mass audiences; the analytical nature of her art will cause it to remain somewhat special. Of course, many new Canadian talents are presently coming to the fore in this field: and that is surely a true index of the extent to which Québec cinema will forge ahead in new and different patterns.

Mireille Dansereau was, as we have seen, something of a pioneer in women's films; Louise Carré and Anne Claire Poirier followed her, but Léa Pool carves out new terrain. She comes closer than most other Canadian women directors (excepting perhaps Patricia Rozema or Cynthia Scott in the anglophone domain) to a complete understanding of the medium and its own unique characteristics.

LA FEMME DE L'HÔTEL (1984; d. Léa Pool)

Like most feminist works of art, Pool's films present the woman's cosmos; men are characteristically marginal to the story line or to the visual preoccupations of the work. (The role of men in *Anne Trister* can, however, be said to be more ambiguous than is the case in *La Femme de l'hôtel*.) *La Femme de l'hôtel* captivates the viewer more for its atmosphere than for its photographic impact, though this is certainly not negligible. It is a gynefilm concerned with the haunting of one woman by another (not an uncommon *scénario* in feminist films, after all). But just as importantly, it is devoted to speculation on the art of film. This film, like Fellini's *8 1/2*, concerns the making of a film; the problems of making a film; the emotional involvement of the director in making a film — here a woman's film, moreover.[25]

Simply stated, in *La Femme* ..., the woman filmmaker meets a woman who might have been the heroine of the story she's filming. But *Anne Trister* (1986), even more than the earlier *La Femme* ... (1984), emerges as a highly compact and a highly visual film. Interestingly enough, in *Anne Trister* Pool uses, again, the talents of Louise Marleau, who had appeared — along with Paule Baillargeon (Andrea) — as Estelle or La Femme in *La Femme de l'hôtel*. Baillargeon will be the spectacular "Curator" in Patricia Rozema's excellent, prize-winning anglophone feminist film *I've Heard the Mermaids Singing* (1987).[26] And it may be of some interest to reiterate here the fact that Louise Marleau had in 1980 starred in Mireille Dansereau's *L'Arrache-coeur*, another film by a woman director in which fantasy and relationships between women are studied. In it, a young married woman tries to escape the domination of her mother.

LA FEMME DE L'HÔTEL: WANDERING AND THE PRISON OF THE SELF

But it remains to be seen whether *La Femme* ... is really a fantasy, as has sometimes been asserted; it certainly is not built upon a "subversion," as feminist critics seem bent on proving. Nor is Estelle, the elusive and mysterious woman who haunts Andrea the filmmaker, an allusion to *la femme fatale* portrayed in *film noir*, as has also been contended.[27] On the contrary, Andrea's desire for the mysterious woman, whom she "needs," whom she desires and loves, is a reappropriation, it seems to me, of the Garbo type, reflected through a reconfiguration of stereotypical symbols, just as the triangle used in *Anne Trister* might be thought to be standard or conventional in its signification, although in both cases the symbol is unexpectedly applied, and with considerable freshness, to the homoerotic experience.

In *La Femme* ... (so aptly called *Woman in Transit* in English), Pool introduces many scenes that reflect transition, restlessness, homelessness, and alienation, especially as it applies to the "Wandering Jew," a concept that will be heavily at play in *Anne Trister*. Andrea imagines the main character in the film she is making: "a foreign woman, a stranger, in a hotel, [which is] a temporary dwelling place." Suddenly she applies all this to her own situation: "je ne suis pas chez moi, pas plus ici qu'ailleurs [I am not at home; no more here than elsewhere"]. "Here" may be Montréal, or Québec City. But the floating geography, and especially the interchangeability of "here" and "elsewhere" or "there" ("là-bas; ailleurs") are insisted upon throughout the film, whether that vagueness of place applies to the situation of Andrea, to that of Andrea's character, or to that of Estelle — Estelle, who is the woman in transit, a "star" who dreams of the sea, of walking on the esplanades, of escaping, of "closing up" (the theater; life), of stopping doing what others want, but who, also, as her name suggests, thinks as she examines the empty theater of the *lumière douce* (soft light), which, in her melancholy, is imagined as being suffused with rain. She, perhaps an actress — a star — of the theater, comes to be not only the actress Andrea sought, for her film, but also the very woman who is her obsession, her love object ("Je vous cherchais," [I was looking for you]"). Estelle David — Star of

David — is, moreover the Jewish alter ego whom Andrea knows as a *landsmann*.

Estelle is, in fact, such a love object as Andrea could not recognize in her previous male lover, with whom she is separating at the beginning of the film, for, she tells him, she realizes "it" is impossible, (it = bisexual, heterosexual love?; the accomplishment of her film?). To this he responds angrily by saying that they were merely ships that passed in the night, anyway ("on s'est croisé seulement"). In *Anne Trister*, we will see the main female character also dismissing her male lover, this time clearly in favor of a woman. But ironically (and also as in *Anne Trister*), the relationship with Estelle, the woman, is, like the episode with her male lover ("man" as he is called in the credits), transitory; for Estelle, like Andrea, is fundamentally homeless, and restless. Her first appearance in the film shows her starting to catch a train — to go from East to West, in fact — then changing her mind, and taking a taxi to "a hotel"; the last scene in the film shows her this time really catching that train, which in both instances is Westbound. This East-West trajectory will be repeated, along with many of the other symbols of *La Femme de l'hôtel*, in *Anne Trister*. In conjunction with this, we should note, also, that in *La Femme de l'hôtel* we have endless symbols of this transitoriness and wandering: train stations, hotels, airports, one-way tickets, highways with traffic coming and going, subway trains, taxis, automobiles, etc. The theme of departure is echoed in Andrea's film, the film within the film, where an older woman (a mother) reads from Marie-Claire Blais's *David Stern* to a younger woman who is about to "leave." The passage restates Estelle's voiced longing for the sea. These symbols of homelessness and separation, along with the airport as a key locus for scenes of good-bye, will recur in *Anne Trister*. In *La Femme* ... we also have the introduction of allusions to the desert, the wasteland, which one also only "crosses," or passes through; the desert, too, will reappear in *Anne Trister*.

In *La Femme de l'hôtel* the key visual image, as important as those scenes evoking voyage, is that of rails, doors, and windows. Rails on the bedsteads, and bars on the windows are used in quite conventional ways to suggest that Estelle, like the main character in the film being made, is trapped, or in a prison. Curiously enough, the characters nonetheless pass back and forth through doors, often with glass and/or grill work attached, or go up and down stairs. The aimlessness of this constant coming and going forces one to conclude that even though doors ought to provide an "exit," in this case the very exit itself is part of the pattern in which these three women—Estelle, Andrea, and her film character—are trapped. Andrea's film character is, incidentally, a *comédienne-chanteuse*, who is imagined as "someone fragile, who wanders about without knowing who she is, half-dead, half-mad." While each of these three women is an individual, in a very real sense, and through a process of *dédoublement* common to Pool's strategies—as we shall again observe in *Anne Trister*—all three women can also be said to represent one woman.[28] (Cf. Bergman's *Persona*.)

Moreover, even though Pool is known for her unusual photography of Montréal, these compositions are basically little more than establishing shots; for she is, in truth, fixed on (urban) interiors. The characters go in and out of doors: yet, the prime space of these women—reflecting the habitual space of women—is indoors. They may walk in the streets, but more often they are looking through the windows out into those streets; more often they are looking through glass on doors, on restaurant windows, or through blinds onto a world they seem unable to enter; more often they are seen in bedrooms, studios, editing rooms, restaurants, bars, theaters. They are trapped by their space, as they are trapped by their restlessness, for the space is only appropriated. None of it really belongs to them. (Andrea even bunks with her homosexual brother, Simon, who tends to watch Italian films on TV, the clips of these affording yet another allusion to [art] film, as well as to director and spectator. And, as we have seen, the presence of Fellini is felt elsewhere in *La Femme* . . . .)

Even more tellingly, in Andrea's film the *chanteuse* is placed in an asylum. As Andrea explains to the actress portraying the *chanteuse*, the *chanteuse* finally gets out of the asylum. But Andrea then reforms her idea, saying that the *chanteuse* does not really get out—for part of the experience of being mad and of being in a madhouse will always go with her. The notion of "no exit"—here, from eternal exit(ing)—pervades this film, as perhaps also *Anne Trister*. Thus, like the characters in *Waiting for Godot*, these women are forever "exiting" their trap; but they make no exit, and therefore perpetually begin the journey over again. This must be the reverse of Tristan and Iseut, whose love story was typified by Cocteau as "*L'Eternel Retour*." Here we have the converse, the story of "l'éternel départ." Hence, it is not easy to understand why it has been said that the two women in *La Femme* . . . are "better off" for their encounter: Estelle has, after all, resumed her travels—as will Anne Trister—while Andrea, although she has made the film, weeps and searches for Estelle. Andrea says, at the end, that the meeting has *perhaps* made everything "possible" again, which takes us back to the beginning, where she has told her male lover that "it" is impossible. But, though the statement regarding possiblity may apply to her film, it does not readily apply to Estelle, that other nonartistic part of Andrea.

The claustrophobia experienced by the Poolian character gives her kinship with the women of Anne Hébert's novels (and therefore of the film *Kamouraska*, brought to the screen by Claude Jutra). This kind of entrapment also occurs in Marguerite Duras's novels and films. Indeed, Pool's films have been said to be "Durasian." But this is as if to glorify them, when in point of fact the films of Pool stand on their own, and, besides, have little other than the theme of entrapment in common with the Durasian world. Though Pool's films may have an application far beyond Québec — in a sense we shall later see — her characters are fighting a set of battles unknown to the Durasian character. In Pool, the problems of art and full-fledged lesbianism spring to the fore in ways unknown to the field of concerns found in Duras. Moreover, Pool's motion pictures are much more cinematic than those of Duras.

If alienation and homelessness, if marginality as woman and as Jew are the lot of Pool's women characters,[29] even so the major theme of the *La Femme de l'hôtel* is none of those, really. It is, rather, the making and the viewing of film. Therefore, the creativity and the suffering of the artist are subconsiderations here, as they also will be in *Anne Trister*. The focus, it seems to me, is on the glance: *le regard*. While in the traditional film the spectator looks upon the woman through the eyes of the hero, in a sort of scopophilia, here the spectator looks upon the mysterious woman through the eyes of a woman. Thus, Estelle's role does not represent a subversion of the *femme fatale*, sometimes found in *film noir*, and, for that matter in many films, but, rather, an *invasion of the myth of the mysterious woman* — the unknowable woman characterized by exoticism and having an unmatchable mystique — who was in part created by the film industry. For Estelle is Garbo-like in her dark-clothed glamour. (And for what it is worth, Garbo has been a cult figure to a couple of generations of lesbians; Marlene Dietrich as well.) Estelle is also to some extent androgynous, as is also the viewer, Andrea. Estelle is the dark lady of the sonnets. Still, the more Andrea observes Estelle, the closer she comes to understanding her character, and, in the final scenes, herself. Andrea reformulates Garbo's famous line, as she explains to the actress how to portray the *chanteuse* in the film they are making. Says Andrea to the actress, but in French: "She needs solitude, as others need air. It is not that she wants to be alone, but that she wants to be left alone" ("... qu'on la laisse seule ..."). Then Andrea translates into English: "I want to be left alone." The shifting of pronouns is a whole other question; it involves the assumption of one personhood by another, and the fusion of author and character.

Filmmaker, actor, and spectator are interlocked here. Andrea and Estelle reset the Garbo-Stiller combination; the famous couple was sometimes referred to as "Pygmalion and Galatea." To the extent that Estelle is the embodiment of the woman Andrea seeks for her film, her model, her dream woman and her alter ego, Estelle (the elusive woman "star" — reminiscent of the stellar Greta Garbo or the androgynous Marlene Dietrich —) is not only a *refashioning* (rather than a subversion) of a *stereotype*, with its accompanying myth and mystique, but also the *restatement*, the reinstatement, of a prototype, this time with a woman director and a woman spectator. And as director-editor, Andrea (not André; not Andrée; but Andrea [Eng., fem.; It., masc.!], the Andr-ogynous) has the power to undo her art, or modify it, just as Anne Trister will be seen to do. Moreover, the use of the television reinforces these ideas: upon two occasions we find Andrea so drowned in her obsessive preoccupations that time for viewing the picture has literally run out; the television screen projects nothing but snow in the late, dark night.

This *regard* and its role inevitably remind us of the formulations of Foucault, both on glance (in *Birth of the Clinic*) and on picture or icon, about which he says (in particular in *Madness and Civilization*) that the image remains in our minds, and ultimately presents only an enigmatic face, so that its power is no longer to teach but to fascinate. If we were speaking of emblematic art and literature, we might, then, assert that our impression upon first viewing the *res pictura* could linger and lose its connection with the *inscriptio* or *subscriptio*. My application of that formula here substitutes film for *pictura* and dialogue for *inscriptio* and *subscriptio*, so that the atmosphere provided by the shape and shadow of Estelle along with the imagery of the doors and windows will be the lasting impressions carried away from our viewing. Similarly, from *Anne Trister* we will retain above all the image of the obsessional triangle and its symbolism. Within its meditation on film, *La Femme* ... is predominantly concerned with the glance, and indeed, in a more specific sense, with the professional filmmaker's *regard*, which Andrea casts about her, just as the clinician or physician does in his or her own way. The important text from the French poet René

Char given at the start of the film tells us through its extraordinary use of synesthesia that: "Les yeux seuls sont encore capables de pousser un cri [The eyes alone are still able to utter a cry]." The quote is not to be overlooked!

Gerald Pratley aptly says of *La Femme de l'hôtel*: "A film of frosty beauty and introspective despair concerning a filmmaker and her encounter with an older woman" (*TS* 1987, 264). Despair that is echoed in *Anne Trister*, despair that frustrates, indeed prevents, the achievement of *jouïssance*, said by modern feminist critics (Annie Leclerc, et al.) to have been denied to women — to lovers, readers, spectators and so forth — for eons, a denial that was (is) expressly intended by the patriarchal structures of civilization. *La Femme de l'hôtel*: a gynefilm, centered on woman's experience, on essential longings: "Touch me; touch me" cries the pivotal song of the film and of the film-within-the-film; a film that does not, however, promise bliss in the fact of the castrated or absent male; a film whose world is very different from that of Marleen Gorris's *Question of Silence*, than Chantal Akerman's *Jeanne Dielman* . . ., than Dusan Makavejev's *Sweet Movie*; a film about homosexual problems, to which Pool will return in *Anne Trister*.

ANNE TRISTER (1986; d. Léa Pool)

Now, *Anne Trister*'s (homosexual) story line is as thin as that of *La Femme* . . .; but, in addition, *Anne Trister* provides a feminist meditation on triangle; on the letter **A** as **A**lpha, **A**nne, **A**lix, **A**rt; on the Wandering Jew — marginalized, **A**lienated, **O**rphaned (the **O**mega). Almost beyond the reach of language, this film has little to do with the theories promulgated by the European structuralists, deconstructionists, postmodernists, and the like. I will not, therefore, be concerned in my analysis of *Anne Trister* with "reconstructing the object in such a way as to manifest the rules of its functioning," for the film is not an object, strictly speaking, and it does not "function by rules." And although I recognize this work to be, like *La Femme* . . ., an authentic gynefilm, one should reject jargon-landen descriptors, and eschew such nonsensical claims as that Léa Pool's films "privilege the inscription of the feminine."[30] Inscription is not a word that applies very well to [Pool's] films, anyway.

It is, however, appropriate to analyze recurrent tropes in this film, with an eye to seeing how certain visual structures and how the portrayal of certain relationships (friend to friend, mother to daughter, man to woman, woman to woman, daughter to father) reinforce Pool's themes of alienation and artistic failure, or of art *per se*, threatened by contemporary concepts of "progress." The Alpha is Amour and Art; the Omega is Oneirism and the Oblivion and Obliteration of the person and the creator, Outcast and levelled, by Western civilization at least, if not even on a cosmic scale. The journey of the protagonist is one from Israel to the West and back again; it is the quest for another — a(m)other — country, a quest that fails in the end. Even though we read in *Maclean's* that Léa Pool's *Anne Trister* created a sensation at the Berlin film festival due to the fact that Pool announced herself as "telling stories more powerfully"[31] (the comparative is incomplete!), this "story" is not "told," but portrayed, and therein lies the essence of Pool's power.

The video catalogue (from Polyglot, to be specific) describes the film *Anne Trister* as telling the "story" of a young woman whose father has just died. The text concludes with the statement that: "She leaves her male lover to go the Québec, where she wants to become an artist, and where she falls in love with Alix."

But this is to say little, because the very point is not that the young woman falls in love with Alix, a female psychologist, nor that she wants to become an artist — "wanting" is not the issue anyway, since she already is an artist — but that the quest, which is a quest for another, for a(m)other country, for acceptance of one's art, and for absolute love, appears to fail. The onset of the quest is not so much stimulated by the father's death as by desire; departure is the Alpha, the beginning of the film; return after failure is the Omega, or, in one sense, the end. But the Omega is also representative of an eternal search, of a search reinitiated; thus the return to Israel may not be so much that of the prodigal daughter to the original motherland, as it is repositioning prior to new departures we cannot know of, since we are really only privy to a small segment of infinity.

The trajectory of the film — from Israel to Canada to Israel — is told in terms of a *battery of triangles and triangular motifs*. We must bear in mind that the triangle has infinite variations; and also that the circle implicit in the Omega is infinite, as the search is infinite. This is the visual geometry of the film, as well as the pattern of the protagonist's social and sexual relationships, and the triangle does not allow for artistic and sexual resolution.

A text in *Spirales* published at the time of Suzanne Lamy's death and replicating a conversation in which Lamy declared to her friend Andrée Yanacopoulo that they would never be "comme ça" (not like Anne Trister) tells us still more: resolution, like death and burial in the Portuguese Jewish cemetery on the Côte Sainte-Catherine in Montréal, would end the quest, of course. But failure at art and love also ends the quest.[32] Or was Lamy referring to the nature of her relationship to Andrée Yanacopoulo? In the context of this conversation between Lamy and friend, the expression "comme ça" is ambiguous, to say the least. We know its double meaning. But Lamy's statement confirms Pool's own assertion, in her *Rencontre* with Patrick Leboutte, that Anne Trister is "a Jewish name ... I saw on a tomb, in a Jewish cemetery ...," the female Jewish characters of Estelle David and Anne Trister being part of the questioning of one's identity.[33]

In order to see how these triangles function, let us first speak of the relationships in the film, perceived as shifting sands of the desert, ever changing their pattern, but always in a triangular mode.

At the beginning of the film, just after her father's funeral, which is portrayed without dialogue but which emphasizes the shifting sand that falls into his tomb in that desert locale, Anne embarks for North America. She must depart, following the trauma and devastation of her father's death; she must also depart, as she explains to her lover, because she feels "blocked by frames," by all that is standard, or "square." In one of the earliest scenes of the film, she is in the Tel Aviv airport with her boyfriend, Pierre, who has refused to accompany her, claiming he cannot just up and leave his job. After her departure, Pierre and Anne's mother take a drink together, and Anne's mother confesses she has never given Anne the love that she expected of her. A revelation for us, too.

Arriving in Montréal, Anne looks up an old friend of the family, Simon Levy, a Jewish bistro proprietor, who helps her to find her studio and to get established in this new environment. He appears to be a father replacement for her. But more importantly, she soon contacts Alix, a psychiatrist, who is also clearly symbolic of the rescuer, the healer, and the mother whom Anne seeks. We readily see that the first major triangle of the play involves Anne, Alix, and Anne's male lover in Israel, with whom she remains in contact, and who is later to arrive in Montréal for a brief and failed visit. However, Alix herself has an Italian lover—Thomas. This, then, is, the second major triangle of the film. Lesbian love is as a consequence pitted against heterosexual love, and one is curious to know which can win out, if either. Adding to the complexities, Alix has a difficult patient, a young girl named Sarah; she is a source

Anne Trister. (Courtesy Office National du Film.)

of some unexpressed jealousy for Anne, establishing therefore a third triangular relationship.

But there are greater complexities than this, as I have hinted at above. Anne, who embodies the theme of the Wandering Jew, has to relate to two fathers: her own dead one and the friendly Montréal barman. She must relate to two mothers, too: her own and Alix. She must relate to two strong macho men: Alix's lover, Thomas — who seems interested in Alix predominantly as a sex object — and her own male lover, Pierre, who, when he arrives in Montréal, is informed by Anne that she loves Alix now, even though Alix cannot love her in the same way. (After this confession, Pierre returns to Israel completely baffled and crushed.) Moreover, Anne must relate to her own childhood, which is represented by Sarah, the difficult, rebellious, and troubled patient of Alix. Sarah, too, is in search of the mother.

The interfacing relationships are, then, convoluted indeed. Nevertheless, I will insist that a triangular (not binary) configuration of the relationships is the dominant theme of the film, and is reinforced more powerfully by its visual content than by any amount of dialogue.

Let us approach our analysis of the visual content of *Anne Trister* by considering the names of the principals: both Alix and

Anne have names that begin with A, a letter that contains a triangle. Our heroine, becoming more and more obsessed with Alix as mother-figure in another land, another motherland, and as a potential lover besides, commences to paint endless designs on the walls of the studio; it becomes her chief Artistic preoccupation. We cannot help but notice that these designs revolve around the letter A. Moreover, these A's seem to be conjoined, to be a sort of constellation that figures and even consummates — vicariously — Anne's desire for Alix.

Prior to this, however, we have a scene in which Anne and Alix are preparing a model of the studio. The two women are seated on the floor, in the living room of the Apartment that Anne and Alix are sharing. Behind them, in the background, is Thomas, watching a game on television. The composition of the scene is very telling! It forms a perfect triangle, in fact, if not also the letter A.

Within this scene two important things occur, one visual, one aural. In preparing the above mentioned model of her studio, Anne is using a large triangle; she also makes the observation to Alix that they are like two little girls playing with their doll house. The statement is rife with significance. It highlights the mother-daughter relationship, the maternal drives of Alix, the subtheme of Sarah and Alix, who together act out Sarah's longings for maternal sponsorship, and so forth.

In the next several scenes showing Anne working in her studio, we have a multiplication of these triangular patterns, borne out by the scaffolding and the ladders she is using, and a straight chair whose rungs play in the conceptualization of the designs she is putting on the walls of her studio, the studio itself having become both an *objet d'art* and a space wherein other art works are to be realized. Shadows on the walls and on the floor carry out the triangles. The ladder of the scaffolding, for example, throws off a shadow that reiterates the image.

Anne, obsessed with her desire for Alix, draws large, merging A's against the moresco background on one wall of the studio. Lying on her back, while, like Michelangelo, she paints on the ceiling, the scaffolding and her back — propped by a triangular device — join together to make still another triangle.

Ultimately beside herself, Anne makes advances toward Alix, who can give maternal responses (by making Anne some eggs, giving her a grapefruit, bringing her pizza and wine, wrapping her in a towel, comforting her over her lost art), but not sexual ones. Frustrated and in despair, Anne, in the gesture of an editor, smears white paint over the conjoined A's, but is interrupted by Simon, who arrives to tell her that an artist cannot make judgments about a work that is being produced, as to whether it is good or bad. The overlapping of life and art in the scene go unnoticed by Simon, of course. Anne, Alix, and Art, all three—another triangle—are obliterated, at least momentarily, by Anne's gesture. Still, a few scenes later we will find that she has restored the two conjoining letter A's.

Now, echoes of the triangular patterns are to be found in almost every scene in the body of the film. One may notice them in the V-neck shirts, the collars of sweaters and jackets, and in the scenes depicting the struggle between Alix and her seemingly one and only patient, Sarah (the *dédoublement* of Anne). For example, one scene in Alix's interview room shows Alix and Sarah with a tripod in the background, the function of which is not openly stated.[34] It is to be noted, moreover, that the composition of the scene presents the same kind of arrangement we had with Alix and Anne preparing the studio model.

And in yet another scene on the wall surface between and behind Sarah and Alix, a child's drawing of a rabbit with sharp triangular ears and a sharp triangular mouth occupies the central plane of the frame.

When the camera shifts once more to her studio, we find Anne has restored the A's on the wall, and is continuing her work. In still another scene, she has gone to sleep, and a dove, who has gotten trapped in the studio, flies frantically about and then comes to rest on the paint-pot: the symbolism is clear, and the oneiric content begins to penetrate the film at this point. In subsequent scenes we may again pick up the triangular patterns in the bend of a leg or the arch of a knee, but they are especially evident in a car scene in which the two women struggle with their attraction for one another, while the ladder and triangle motifs are carried out behind their heads by the *traversins*, or headrests, that loom large, while through the rear window one catches a glimpse of Montréal. (The make of the automobile may well be a Volvo.)

The triangle, then, already announced as an earthly trinity, a three-in-one fusion of film star, director-artist, and the incarnate object of the glance—or the *regard*—in *La Femme de l'hôtel*, has by now become the subject of an intense meditation by Léa Pool in this film about love and art. So much so is this the case that we are inevitably reminded of the fine Canadian animated short entitled *Notes on a Triangle*, and after having reviewed this brief but elegant piece, we inevitably recall that the square, too, leads to the triangle when intersected. Can we conclude that in the scene where Thomas and Alix argue about Anne, the background, made up entirely of squares, conveys the message that the heterosexual love for which he argues is extremely "square?" One must leave this in the realm of speculation. Still, it is certainly of significance that all triangles and squares disappear into the background, as the two women decide to return to their male mates. Perhaps they do not have the strength to love beyond their fear. That Alix is not prepared to commit herself to a lesbian way of life, she makes clear to Anne. That Anne settles for compromise and the Omega (the final stance — failed art, failed love, and return, perhaps to errancy, certainly to circular patterns) is also clear.

Let us briefly explore that return. In the course of her stay in Montréal, Anne has been receiving tapes from Pierre. On one of them he tells the story of Tom Thumb, who, he says, moves back to his mother's womb through the ruins he makes. The story is, of course, assimilated to the story of Sarah, a type of Anne-as-child, who finally opts for a whole teddy bear, and to Anne herself, whose return to Israel, to the desert, follows an accident in which she falls and is hospitalized. (The fall itself can be taken on a symbolic level: already in *La Femme de l'hôtel* we encountered a strange piece of dialogue in which Andrea said, "You have the strength to fall; to live despair like the only hope that is still possible.") Does Anne have this kind of strength? this kind of despair? She is dismissed from the hospital, only to return to her studio, which has been destroyed and is to be replaced by condominiums, as a hallmark of urban progress and of the whole of Western civilization's triumph over personal, and especially women's, art. Devastated at the loss of this work, Anne is comforted by Alix, who for once appears to respond to Anne's hungers and even to her eroticism. Yet Anne decides to leave Montréal and Alix. In some ways, we might contend that the question of lesbianism remains unresolved here, just as it does in *La Femme de l'hôtel*, as well as in *I've Heard the Mermaids Singing* and even in *Desert Hearts*. This lack of resolution might, it seems, be regarded as a hesitancy on the part of the woman director; but more likely it is simply a matter of mimesis, ambivalence in such sexual conflicts often being characteristic of true-life experiences.[35]

Anne's return to Israel — to the Orient and to Pierre, who during his short visit to Montréal has been temporarily discouraged by Anne's confession of her love for Alix — suggests that her search for a mother, as for another (a mother) land has either been completed or else has failed. The latter is the more likely: the odds have been against her, both as an artist and as a would-be lesbian lover. More fundamentally, her return to Israel is, like Tom Thumb's, a return to the "mother's womb"—to the place of birth, to an earlier mother and to an earlier love (Pierre), and, it would seem, to a place where the sands and suns of the desert may heal the wintery landscape of Montréal. She is now filled with a relentless depression following these failures. The father's death has been accepted, the search for feminine affection somewhat satisfied, or at least adjourned. Or is it ? She remains in contact with Alix, and sends back off-center films of herself, and a bag of sand from the desert, which Alix has named as something she loves and craves. The desert is the new space of their understanding, no doubt. While the sexual square is reintroduced, a new, an ultimate triangle is nevertheless established, with the desert stretching between two motherlands—the desert, a space to be crossed, a place of healing, but also a place of sterility and loss. Will our heroine resume her search and her traveling? Has she already? For even though she smiles from the frame, suggesting that she has successfully passed over the desert and has· adjusted to her homelessness and despair, she is nonetheless now blocked by the frame—locked in the frame she abhorred and which was at least temporarily subverted by the triangle. She seems now to be the trapped dove of an earlier sequence, that dove being a type of the trapped madwoman we saw through the *chanteuse* of *La Femme de l'hôtel*, who in the film-within-the-film mirrors the equally caged existence of Estelle.

Besides, we do not know who is taking those pictures sent back to Alix, nor where they originated. We do not know whose *regard* or glance is fixed upon her; we do not know who the spectator is. We do not know if Anne has conquered her longings for the mother figure, the mother substitute, "the older woman," Alix—but we must assume not. Certainly in *La Femme de l'hôtel* her counterpart, Andrea, does not forget "the older woman" Estelle, perhaps her alter ego, perhaps a mother figure, but, if so, one she conversely seeks to nurture at times (e.g., "Have you eaten?" she asks her). Role-playing and role reversals abound in these two films.

This is the note upon which the film ends: the Orphaned, Alienated, ever-wandering, unappreciated woman Artist and the mother-hunter has reached Omega, which is circular, never ending, womb-shaped, ever reinitiated, and which ironically is, as it were, also Alpha—the Alpha and the Omega being, in the final reckoning, undifferentiated because they are indistinguishable. Anne Trister, ever Triste, Anne artiste, Anne Triste erre (ever errs or wanders), Anne Triste, Femme errante .... Juive errante.[36]

Still, this departure on my part into ludic linguistic fields is not legitimate, for I established at the outset of my segment on *Anne Trister* that the film was above all a visual work. I will abide by that assertion here.

La Femme de l'hôtel, a film about the making of a film, shows us not only how the myth has invaded the sign, a danger to the art film, according to Claire Johnston,[37] but also how the icon, or the sign, invades the myth and even becomes preeminent, just as it does also, and even more forcefully, in *Anne Trister*. And Pool's films are no more innocent of the workings of myth than are the films of Agnès Varda, though Johnston, in her fine article on Lois Weber and Dorothy Arzner, has mistakenly claimed that Varda's films — especially *Sans toit ni loi* — are indeed innocent.[38] In both *La Femme ...* and *Anne Trister* the narrative and its incarnation through the characters (i.e., the mythic content) are less important in and of themselves than the far more singular fact that woman, not man, is the visual center, as well as the mythic center of the film's universe. In both films the love object, as well as the lover-spectator, also is (a) woman. The substitution of woman as spectator reshapes all stereotypes, and infuses them with new and creative energy. Both films insist, then, on woman's centrality; and both show the traces of the *auteur(e)*, or director-marked, director-controlled tradition. One supposes both films are based on personal experience, perhaps the same experience, that provided the same thin plot and the same portrayal of an almost solipsistic despair present in the two films. Both are heavily gender-marked. Both are what Johnston calls "countercinemas." Both are films manipulated by a woman who has considered stereotpyes and rejects them. Above all, Andrea, like Pool, is in the position of power: she may prohibit the camera from freezing woman in stereotypical images; or she may instead explore the prototype and exploit the stereotype of the mysterious, unknown and unknowable woman ("Qui es-tu; d'où viens-tu?" asks Andrea; and she might have switched the pronoun, and asked: "Qui Est(-)elle?" or even asked: "Est(-)elle comme moi? — juive? lesbienne? seule?"). Andrea, like Pool, might introduce the fixed symbols of train, door and triangle, but arrange them or apply them in unfamiliar ways that have undergone reshaping, or, better, *redirection*, rather than, as some would say, subversion. (Pool does not, in my opinion, admit to "subversion," when she merely says that *La Femme ...* is constructed like a detective story[39] [except that where one expects to find action, one finds emotion]. Nor does this make of Estelle the woman of the *film noir*.)

The conclusion of *La Femme* ... postulates the proposition that reality is stronger than the imagination. Estelle, the woman Andrea meets in the hotel, is the embodiment of her creative efforts ("Elle est ce que j'ai voulu montrer"). And for Estelle, Andrea's assumption of her most intimate person by and into Andrea's creativity constitutes a theft. But what a blessed theft! — at least for Andrea, who has managed to centralize what elsewhere and otherwise is marginalized.

A Corps perdu (Straight to the Heart) (1988) is Pool's third film, and is "for adults only." Here again, it is a question of an artist, this time a photographer-reporter who, after doing a stint in Nicaragua, returns to Montréal, where he decides to visually incorporate his own city in the film. Upon his return, he finds that his two lovers (David and Sarah) have abandoned him. Gnawed by and in the very grips of violent jealousy, he begins following them and photographing them. This is one of the most visually-oriented films I have ever seen; the photography is at times luminous, and Pool's fame as a photographer of Montréal is truly deserved, particularly if *A Corps perdu* is the example. The suffering of Pierre Kurenwal is translated through closeups of his face and accompanied by the beauty of early classical music.

LA DEMOISELLE SAUVAGE (1991; d. Léa Pool, w/ Laurent Gagliardi and Michel Langlois) (Swiss/Québécois)

In this film, Pool chooses a nurse as her protagonist. Again the dialogue is at a minimum, indeed is reduced to such an extent that the characters speak less than in any other work of Pool's. Here she insists even more than ever on the iconographic power of cinema. And the camera work of Georges Dufaux, called "sublime" by Jeanne Deslandes, took a prize for best artistic contribution at the World Festival of Films. It is small wonder.

La Demoiselle sauvage opens with the flight of a young woman after she has committed a murder. In desperation she has attempted to commit suicide, but having failed, only finds herself all the more lonely and impoverished. She takes refuge in the magnificence and immensity of the Swiss landscape. There she confronts an enormous dam, which cuts off her escape route. And she also meets a man, Elysée, who will change her life by coming to her assistance and by "taming" this "wild girl." Their ways of dealing with the past are, however, at odds: he wants to dig into the past as a form of understanding and knowing; she wants to forget the past. Her sole desire is to live in the present. Toward the end, it seems she will face the law. However, she commits suicide instead, thus extinguishing the past — just as she had earlier killed her lover.

Jeanne Deslandes writes of this film that it is "highly symbolic [and] draws much of the meaning from shots of the hydraulic dam." She adds that the encounter with the dam marks a break between two sequences (like a new chapter in a novel). But also, the dam takes on the quality of a character, seen in two different ways by two different people (Elysée and Marianne), one seeing it as a place of passage, the other as an unscalable wall. Through the dam, Pool captures the dichotomy between culture and nature and shows two possible views of the rendering of justice: from the interior it seems equitable (Elysée's viewpoint), from the outside it sometimes seems insurmountable (Marianne's viewpoint). Her fear of the judicial system provokes in her not only resistance to order but also an incipient madness.[40]

The centrality of woman in Pool's art world and the internal criticism of, as well as the refashioning of, stereotypical states and symbols are fundamental ingredients of her superb (but not necessarily entertaining) gynefilms — films for, by, and about women; films that reach beyond the scene of Québec to strike a chord of recognition in women everywhere. With her portrayal of the intimate through script and through camera, she will remain in the vanguard of international feminist filmmakers for some time to come.[41]

In 1990 Pool released an NFB documentary, *Hotel Chronicles*, which formed part of the collection on "*L'Américanité*." It was Maurice Elia's opinion that the film had been fashioned upon the (preconceived) image of the subject treated. "She showed the incapacity, the moral disturbance which locks in heads and sexual organs, and made [the film] under cover of a vague love story told off . . . ." Still, the film, in his opinion, did not push the viewer to reacting (i.e., was not sufficiently subversive).[42]

Other Québécoises Women Directors

ÇA PEUT PAS ÊTRE L'HIVER, ON A MÊME PAS EU D'ÉTÉ (IT CAN'T BE WINTER; WE HAVEN'T HAD SUMMER YET.) (1980; d. Louise Carré)

"A splendid and touching performance from Charlotte Boisjoli," says Pratley (*TS* 1987, 246). But despite the prizes this film has taken, and despite Pratley's praise, *Ça peut pas . . .* seems to me to be inferior even to *Qui a tiré . . .* (discussed below). Adèle Marquis, a woman of 57, finds herself alone when her husband Albert dies. She decides to take stock, and in so doing, she decides she has been done a great injustice. She has served a selfish husband and these eight children for forty years. Near to a severe depression, she resists, and instead opens up to the world. She finds friendship, digs into her past for explanations, and discovers a meaning for her existence and her frustrations. Strengthened by this self-discovery, she defies her family to bring one of her dreams into reality: she will break away, take a long trip, and, thus undistracted by the people in her life, will look into the human soul and contemplate the mysteries of her own existence. The most pleasing part of this film is that she does not succumb to marriage to the roomer she has taken in, as we would have suspected!

Murray Maltais said in *Le Droit*: "I have rarely seen at the cinema so much *pudeur* and delicacy in the feelings"; while Luc Perreault wrote in *La Presse*: "A cinema which reconciles the young with the old, women with men, economy of means with an abundance of heart." In *Plexus* one reads, "The film will serve as inspiration to any woman who has perhaps felt that it was too late to change." And Dave Chenoweth, in *The Gazette*, said: "This is a small film in design, yet it has a quality of honesty, insight, and grace that shames the biggest commercial epics."[43]

In the dubbed version, the characters have English-type names: thus Adèle Marquis is Adèle MacNeil; her roomer's name becomes Jimmy Sandford (Jacques Galipeau); and so forth.

The long title makes us think of a title of a Lina Wertmuller film. But Lina Wertmuller this is not. Notably, Louise Carrière says little about this film; she mentions it in passing, however (*Femmes . . .* 1983; 113, 180, 120). She may have good reason not to dwell upon the subject!

QUI A TIRÉ SUR NOS HISTOIRES D'AMOUR? OR *A QUESTION OF LOVING* (1986; d. Louise Carré) may not be substantially superior to *Ça peut pas . . . .*

The story deals with the relationship between a mother (Monique Mercure), who is a sophisticated director of radio, TV, and film, and her daughter. The daughter, Renée, has come to look upon her mother—who is full of life and enthusiasm—with humor, tenderness, and irony. She has become for the young woman a model of passion and courage, which is not wholly lacking in hesitation, nevertheless. The two women spend one last summer together in a small, provincial town (Sorel). They come to appreciate each other and to discover their love is indestructible and invaluable.

While Louise Carrière is silent on this one, one of my students characterized it as suitable material for the afternoon movie on the Lifetime Channel. This seems to me to be quite on the money. Among other things, this is a sad use of such a great star as Monique Mercure—sadder even than the cameo appearance in *Mon oncle Antoine*, in which she bared her breasts for the potentially interested spectator.

RIEN QU'UN JEU (JUST A GAME) (1983; d. Brigitte Sauriol)

Lever claims that Sauriol has been one of the best subsidized of Québécois directors—and *Rien qu'un jeu* may well demonstrate that claim. It was made with the financial participation of L'Institut Québécois du Cinéma; Ciné II (1982); La Société du Développement de l'Industrie Cinématographique Canadienne; and Famous Players. Even so, says Lever, with these heavily subsidized directors there is always "un petit côté inachevé ... [some small detail that is left unfinished]" (*Hist.* 1988, 292; 301). This is not my reaction. Dealing with the problem of incest, this is a film of considerable sensitivity and unusual frankness. In my opinion it ranks with, or may even be superior to, another highly regarded Canadian film on the same subject, *Loyalties* (Anne Wheeler). Pratley finds *Rien qu'un jeu* to be "remarkably observed, understated and eloquent ..." (*TS* 1987, 257), and with this I fully agree, while emphasizing that there is a lot more at stake than that.

Perhaps because this work is filmed and scripted by women, the importance of power structures and manipulation in the unfolding of this "psychological drama" are not to be underrated. André Vézina, whose marriage to Mychelle is sadly wanting on many levels—it having been forced by Mychelle's pregnancy fifteen years earlier—is shown in the beginning as a man enlisting his authority role to force his daughter Catherine to have sexual relations with him. (One scene is especially lurid and graphic.)

"J'ai le droit; je suis ton père," he claims. And besides, he adds, "C'est pas grave. C'est rien qu'un jeu. [I have the right; I am your father; and besides, it is nothing serious; it's just a game.]" He warns her not to tell; he bribes her with gifts, as is characteristic of the child molester. (His long suit is, in fact, offering gifts to his daughters and to his wife.) But as Catherine becomes more and more resistant, he turns to her younger sister Julie. (Says Julie to Catherine: "Daddy says I'm nicer; that you're always in a bad mood.") The mother, who is intolerant, abusive, and not understanding, finally sees her husband with Julie, and this forces a turn of tables. When Mychelle confronts him, he breaks down, weeping and saying that he just can't help himself; it's bigger than him, and so forth. But she seems to pardon him, telling him he is not sick, and that it is just a matter of not touching his daughters any longer. This extraordinary scene ends with her calming him down, while he sucks at her breast.

Then in subsequent scenes we see that these acts — even if they are to stop — have destroyed the very fabric of the family. While the mother begs the older daughter to think of the episodes as "a bad memory," and adjures her "not to talk about it any more," and to consider that "her father is [just?] a man," the girl no longer has any trust and, for that matter, is submerged in the abyss of depression and shame that incest is said to foster even in the victim.

In another scene, near the end, we have an impressive traveling shot that takes in gulls, sea, and rocks off the coast of Percé on the Gaspé. (Some scenes were shot on the Ile Bonaventure.) The girl is clearly contemplating committing suicide by leaping from the high cliffs; and for those who have seen the more recent *Fous de Bassan*, the photography and the situation evoke the suicide of Irène in the latter film. I would have been willing to accept a suicide as one final turn of events in this sad tragedy. Instead, she does not commit suicide, but in the next sequence is seen coming out of school, and while her friend Maude and others tease her — not quite understanding why she is so quiet, so morose, and so withdrawn — we have a freeze-frame, with a cracked-glass effect coming over her face. We know there can be no good future for her; and, of course, that is another way in which the "shattering" experience of incest leaves its mark — one can scarcely say unravels itself.

It is understandable that Pratley should have said that this film, "while somewhat awkward in places . . ., rings entirely true" (*TS* 1987, 257–58). He is also right to point out that the film reflects a social reality wherein the children pay the price for their emotional suffering, while the fathers rarely are brought to trial. But one ought to add that the makers of this film have shown the role that alcohol plays in such a troubled household, and the mother's frequent abdication of duty when the cancer is brought to the fore: she, being weak and unhappy in her marriage, nevertheless seems to forgive the husband and to blame her daughters. "C'est toi qui l'as commencé [You began it]," she says to Catherine. Since the father has been taking her since she was ten, this seems a bit farfetched. But the psychology is quite believable. The mother is no doubt shocked by the incestuous relationship between the father and her daughter(s). She may also be somewhat jealous that her husband has preferred his daughters to her. ("Tu n'es pas une femme, [You are not a wife/woman]," he has told her as part of his excuse.) Thus she will rationalize to say it is the daughters' fault that these acts have occurred. No doubt this seems the easier way to handle the situation; but the film makes obvious that it will not work.

Brigitte Sauriol has more recently directed *Laura Laur*, a film that lacks the power of *Rien qu'un jeu*. Indeed, for me, *Laura Laur* is a greater failure than Micheline Lanctôt's *Sonatine*, which shares with both of the Sauriol films a taste for psychological exploration, but which has known a certain amount of critical rejection. Still, Joseph I. Donohoe, Jr. has devoted some time and energy to rehabilitating this "neglected" film, which he finds superior to *Le Crime d'Ovide Plouffe* and *Le Matou*.[44]

SONATINE (1983; d. Micheline Lanctôt)

Set against the background of an impending public strike, this three-part story concerns two adolescent girls—Chantal and Louisette—who are convinced that the world is full of nothing but aloof and indifferent people. They try to escape from the indifference they encounter in their daily lives by "discovering" Montréal—Chantal with a bus driver whose route she always takes, until he gets transferred, and Louisette with a Bulgarian sailor as a stowaway, until he exposes her. But, thanks to him, she experiences a fleeting moment of tenderness. The third part shows the two girls joining forces to try to get the world to prevent their suicide.

Sonatine was a failure of sorts, according to most critics, including Chabot. Lanctôt, who began her film as an animator and then as an actress (*La Vraie Nature de Bernadette*), first made *L'Homme à tout faire* (1980), where "her homage to the low-key wit and human warmth of the Czech movies of the sixties followed the travels of a somewhat tentative young handyman with a weakness for the ladies, who always seem to take amorous advantage of him" (Clanfield 1987, 81). Though Lanctôt's work has often been compared to that of Woody Allen, Robert Bresson, Lina Wertmuller, and to recent French comedies, *Sonatine* certainly obviated such analogies. Lanctôt has said of it that it is first of all a voice that is personal to her and that she took time discovering, a voice which does not want to be listened to for what it says but for the things it keeps silent about. Lever (*Hist.* 1988, 430) protests that, after all, the critic has difficulty in acquiescing to this invitation to consider the intentions, however admirable, of the director, rather than her film. That *is* a critical problem. Donohoe, on the other hand, compares the structure of the film to three movements in a musical piece, with Chantal as movement one, Louisette as movement two, and Chantal/Louisette plus coda as movement three. He also finds debts to Antonioni's *Deserto Rosso* in the second movement, and sees the third movement as reminiscent of Truffaut's *Quatre Cents Coups*. Above all, he sees the suicide of the two adolescents in the metro as attributable to the fact that the girls are given no moral sustenance in a society that has arrived at considerable technological sophistication and material prosperity.[45]

Sonatine was one of seven Canadian films shown at the International Freedom Festival in the Renaissance Center in Detroit, Michigan, in late June 1987. (The others were *My American Cousin*; *La Guerre des Tuques*; *90 Days*; *Sitting in Limbo*; *Decline of the American Empire*; and *Mario*. All the *québécois* entries are discussed in these pages.) But why does the Québécois flee such films? Part of the answer is provided by Lever, who sees the film as one in which "the tone was right, the treatment original but *déroutant*, and the mirror that it offered to young people unbearable in its raw truth" (Lever *Hist.* 1988, 446). Further on, he contends that the failure of the film was due to the fact that no adolescent girls who are of this age bracket and who have the Walkman culture and problems of communication as well as dreams of suicidal heroines want to see such a film, admirable though it may be, because the portrait is too close to reality and too realistically pessimistic. It goes without saying that the parents of adolescents do not like to see their failure flashed in their face either, he goes on to say. Then he adds, "paradoxically, for a cinema which intends to be profoundly inscribed in reality, one might wonder if a drop-in Martian viewer, however good an analyst he were, would learn anything about the four seasons, the principal cultural realities, the disparities of social groups, pluralism of beliefs and life-styles, the great ideological stakes, etc." (Lever *Hist*. 1988, 464). Donohoe goes even further, contending that the "average *québécois* film viewer remains ... unaware of the voice 'off camera,' so to speak, which continues *sotto voce* to remind him of other times and other values, and this is apparently the way he wants it. The inability to cut one's self off completely from the collective past is one matter, the willingness to make emotionally loaded choices when the past openly confronts the present is quite another ..."[46] Donohoe goes on to tell that on *Sonatine*'s release in 1983, Montréal's *La Presse* trivialized its 'gloom and doom' mentality and "this single-minded assessment rippled quickly through the provincial media." Yet, he stresses, *Sonatine* was awarded the 'Silver Lion' at the 1984 Venice Film Festival, where it placed second to Jean-Luc Godard's *Prénom Carmen*. (I can only add that with such competition it might well have been first!)

Lanctôt, who, as I said, is also an accomplished actress — she played the lead female role in *The Apprenticeship of Duddy Kravitz* (d. Ted Kotcheff, 1974) — continues to produce films. In 1987, for example, she made *La Poursuite du bonheur* for the ONF series *L'Américanité*, mentioned above in connection with Léa Pool. This latter effort was also put under a critical cloud: Marcel Jean finds that in this work she approached the question of happiness in a consumer society "without displaying the sensitivity or rigorous approach that characterize her fictional films" (Coulombe 1991, 309). She has also made a television film, *Onzième Spéciale* (1988), based on a *scénario* by Louise Roy and Marie Perreault, in which a woman painter, in her thirties, examines the failure her life seems to be (Jean, in Coulombe 1991, 309).

Marie s'en va-t-en ville is a film of fiction that, unlike *Sonatine*, received considerable recognition, but which in my opinion may not be among the greatest products of the Québécoises filmmakers.

MARIE S'EN VA-T-EN VILLE OR, *MARIE IN THE CITY* (1987; d. Marquise Lepage)

Having been assaulted by her older brother, Marie, still an adolescent, leaves their home in rural Québec and departs for the city, where she meets an aging and disillusioned prostitute named Sarah. Marie would like to move into Sarah's apartment and insinuate herself into Sarah's life, but Sarah is not interested in Marie's affection and not touched by her admiration. However,

Marie's naiveté and tenderness finally penetrate Sarah's hard surface, and the two women bond.

As one reads in *CopieZéro*, "This film tells the story of a short
friendship between two of life's 'dropouts'—both yearning for
affection—who, in spite of everything, try to cling to each other
... and to life."[47]
Women's cinema of Québec continues to flourish and to exhibit
the same vigor we have noticed in this chapter, as younger generations take the helm. To cite but one example, Johanne Prégent
(b. in Saint-Lambert in 1950), whom I mentioned earlier for her
film *La Peau et les os* (1988; a documentary on eating disorders),
directed *On a marché sur la lune* in 1990. Based on a script by
Josée Fréchette, it dealt with adolescence. (It took the Normande-
Juneau prize.) And she has quite recently presented a full-length
film of fiction, *Les Amoureuses* (1992). The story involves the
intersecting actions of two couples—David-Léa and Nino-Marianne
—the first in its decline, the second embryonic. As the title suggests,
the two women bond. Janick Beaulieu contends that those who
have thought to see in the first couple an allusion to "The Two
Solitudes" (Québec-Anglophone Canada) are off base: "The film
does not allow such an interpretation. Here it is a question of
love alone, and all the rest is nothing but literary extrapolation."[48]
Beaulieu finds that the film asks questions about fear of commitment,
the risk of loving and the future of the couple; indeed, he claims to
have '*fallen in love*' with this movie.

Concluding Remarks to Chapter 3

Interviewed on CNN News (28 November 1990) in the light of
her new film (on divorce), the French director Diane Kurys made
plain she is not interested in being classified as a "woman director,"
or in attending a festival of films by women directors. She claimed
she would be inclined to participate at the point where there were
also such a festival devoted exclusively to men directors. It really
does seem she misses the point. Although a woman director would
naturally wish in general to be judged by the same standards as
a man director, until the most recent times this could hardly have
happened anywhere in the film industry; and in Québec, though
women are and have been outspoken in their demands for equality
for twenty years and more, they have a long way to go before their
society is any better than the French or American on this most
important issue. We had only to listen to the young Québécoises

women on *Man Alive* (aired on 27 November 1990), as they discussed the 6 December 1989 massacre at the Ecole Polytechnique to realize how sad but true this is. And, incidentally, a videotape made by Gerry Rogers, entitled *After the Montreal Massacre* (27 min.) has been devoted to the subject. (It is available from Women Make Movies, Inc.)

The confrontation between the masculine universe and the feminine universe, together with the difficulty of making contact with one another, is the subject of an article by Denise Pérusse (in Chabot); she, too, sees these irreconcilable differences as confirmed by the reality of the mass murders at the Ecole Polytechnique de Montréal. It is hard to see a better kind of world depicted in the films by the male directors, either: the sex comedies of Forcier, for example, would drive a feminist, even a womanist, wild; his film *Une Histoire inventée*, whose American premiere I attended in Chicago in November 1990, while rather funny, nevertheless shows the sexes ever at odds. [Not surprisingly, a recent film by Guy Simoneau, *Est-ce ainsi que les hommes vivent?* (1992), intends to show how so many images of them are presented by society that men cannot find a balance: shall they be tender, shall they be macho? The film, which, like *Trois Pommes à côté du sommeil* (d. Jacques Leduc) and *Les Matins infidèles* (d. Jean Beaudry and François Bouvier), is concerned with masculine identity, gives a rather profound picture of contemporary man's inner torment.]

This canyon between the sexes, which is the source of considerable *désarroi*, is but one of the many we can observe in Québec—or Western—society; other kinds are reflected in the films we will examine especially closely in Chapters 5, 6, and 7.

4

Literature into Film[1]

Film and literature do more than share the distinction of
being storytelling arts; both come to this propensity naturally
. . . . The camera of course, has a very rare and special ability to
do so . . . and film is indisputably the most extra-ordinary
means man has yet discovered for reproducing his perceptions
of nature and for re-creating the world in its own image.
— Joy Gould Boyum in *Double Exposure* (31)

The transfer of literature to film is always done at risk, for
those trained in literature will decry any deviation from the story
line. But the medium may well demand such deviation, and upon
occasion the director's alteration of events or of sequences of
events may well mark an improvement. This was the case with
Gilles Carle's filming of *Maria Chapdelaine*, in which, as I said in
Chapter 2, many *québécois* icons were effectively used: the visual
impression of maple syrup taffying over snow here, as in *Bonheur
d'occasion*, can scarcely be equalled by descriptions. But more
importantly, Carle rearranged the crucial deaths of François Paradis
and Madame Chapdelaine, so that the loss of the mother is followed
by the even more devastating loss of the lover. The effect is much
more dramatic. And, of course, the very categorizing of films by
their "sources" will be misleading, except as we can see overlaps
with films already discussed or to be discussed in forthcoming
chapters of this book. It is primarily the film's use of icons of
nature and of the *québécois* society that interest us here. These we
find to some extent in *Mario*, and to a greater extent in *Maria
Chapdelaine*, in *Bonheur d'occasion*, in *Le Matou*, in *Les Fous de
Bassan*, etc.

* * * *

The Québec filmmakers saw practically from the beginning that they had a distinct mythology and a "national" literature that might be brought to film. As I demonstrated in Chapter 1, in its infancy this body of cinema saw some frightening exaltations of the "state religion" and some blatant examples of film used for exploitative and didactic purposes. Nevertheless, both Grignon's *Un Homme et son péché* (1948; Paul Gury Le Gouriadec) — which dealt with the story of the great love of Alexis Labranche for the beautiful Donalda, who is married to a miser, Séraphin Poudrier, and which fed the sequel *Séraphin* (1949; d. Jean Boisvert) — as well as Gratien Gélinas's favored *Tit-Coq* (1954; d. Gélinas and René Delacroix) were two outstanding early examples of Québec literary material brought to the screen. Unlike the early versions of *Maria Chapdelaine*, which, after all, was written by a Frenchman (1913; Louis Hémon) and filmed by a Frenchman (1934; d. Julien Duvivier; starring Jean Gabin and Madeleine Renaud), and again by a Swiss *cinéaste* (1949–50; d. Marc Allegret; starring Michele Morgan and Philippe Lemaire), *Tit-Coq* was a truly Québec product. Tit-Coq's confrontation with a priest on the question of divorce is one of the striking scenes of the film, and in my opinion affords a meaningful precedent for the rebellions we will witness in the times of the Quiet Revolution. Heinz Weinmann, on the other hand, believes that for the most part Tit-Coq submits to the authority of the padre who, however, is a chaplain, administering outside the Church, and provides an early example of the operations of the Holy Spirit in a nonritualistic and nonhierarchical context of the sort to come in *Jesus of Montreal*. Nevertheless, *Tit-Coq* shows the protagonist to be manifestly in disagreement with, if not in disrespect of, the padre's point of view. In any event, *Tit-Coq* is a film that clearly draws upon Québec literature for filmic material about Québec.

Yet another Québec novel that provided the story for a film was *Poussière sur la ville* (1968; d. Arthur Lamothe). The novel was written in 1953 by André Langevin. This is the story of the small-town doctor, Alain Dubois, and his bored and unfaithful wife, Madeleine. As he is sober and solitary, whereas she is sensual and loves social life ("la vie mondaine"), she takes a lover — Richard Hétu. All this scandalizes the small provincial town. The doctor takes to drinking, and confesses his agnosticism to his friend Dr. Lafleur. He also has conversations with the local curate on religion. The curé succeeds in separating Richard and Madeleine; Madeleine tries to kill her lover, fails, and then commits suicide. On the surface this seems to be a *québécois* version of *Madame Bovary*; but in fact the introspective Langevin's preoccupations are more along the existential line, dealing with the insoluble problems and the profound solitude of modern man. The novel is set in Macklin — a small mining town.[2]

This trend of exploiting Québec literature for a movie plot will continue down to the present.

Ringuet's *roman du terroir*, which, unlike the earlier examples from such writers as Félix-Antoine Savard, incorporates the threat that the city poses, will come to the screen through his novella, *L'Héritage*. And the works of Gabrielle Roy, both those that depict the western provinces and those that show the effects of urbanization (*The Tin Flute*), have also been filmed. *Les Plouffe* as well falls into this domain. As a general rule, these films fail to equal and they certainly seldom surpass their literary models. Still, they sometimes have merits of their own that make them worth considering. And besides, the films, when viewed, may succeed in making the authors better known to American audiences, who in general are not very conversant with *québécois* francophone literature. (This stituation seems to be improving, however.)

In our discussion of this genre — literature to film as it receives expression through the Québécois *cinéastes* — we shall see not only how the film may compare with the literary work behind it, but also how it portrays both Québec culture, and, in the larger sense, emotions that are the common lot of all human beings, such as love and hatred, attitudes toward family life, rebellion against authority, the thirst for power, the scourge of ambition; in short, the full range of feelings and urges associated with human existence.

One of the most often portrayed and absorbing of human conflicts is the love triangle. We observed this theme in women's films, especially in Léa Pool's original films, not to mention her 1988 *A Corps perdu* (*Straight to the Heart*). Yves Navarre's novel, *Kurwenal*, provided inspiration for this Canada-Swiss coproduction dealing not only with the lovers' triangle, but also with sexual ambiguity, solitude, madness, childhood, and creation. We can observe the theme again in films taken from *québécois* novels built on such an intrigue. One of Quebec's best known films, *Kamouraska* (1970), based on Anne Hébert's widely read novel, gives us the triangle plot. It is set largely in the Eastern cantons and Gaspésie, and involves witchcraft, murder, and death vs. eros, a theme Weinmann has found present in many Québec films, including *La Petite Aurore*, *Mon oncle Antoine*, and so forth. *Cordélia*, based on a novel drawn from a real *fait divers*, is a suspenseful tale in which the triangle is only presumed to exist, so that the question of justice is equally egregious.

CORDÉLIA (1979 [1980, acc. to Pratley]; d. Jean Beaudin)

In some ways a docudrama like *Riel* and in some ways not, the film *Cordélia* tells a story that (like that of *Kamouraska*) was drawn from a news story of its time. It has the dark and brooding mark of its director, Jean Beaudin, upon it. It is as dark as his *Mario*, and largely not so accomplished as his earlier (1976) film, *J. A. Martin photographe*. The story is taken from the novel *La Lampe dans la fenêtre* by Pauline Cadieux, and, like *Kamouraska*, deals with adultery and murder. But in *Cordélia*, the heroine might not be guilty, indeed probably is not, and so problems of judge, judgment, and justice arise here. We will see similar problems in *Les Ordres* and in *Jésus de Montréal*.

As the film tells the story, fun-loving Cordélia Poirier, née Viau, who reminds us of Mme Martin (*J. A. Martin photographe*), was afflicted with *rife/rifle* (eczema; exanthema) over her entire body, except for her face. This affliction kept her from doing domestic work. She was the church organist and a music teacher, but she also loved to play popular music and to dance. During the time that her husband was in California, she received men, and lived in a certain "*débauche*." She was accused of having conspired and collaborated with her supposed lover, Samuel Parson, in the murder of her husband—following his return to Saint-Canu—and a false confession, upon which the prosecution based its case, was wrenched from her.

Although the accusation and the second trial, held at Saint-Scholastique, end in a verdict of guilty and a gruesome hanging, one is not at all sure that Parson was Cordélia's lover, or that either of them killed her husband. Dominique Leduc, for one, stands up for her; he believes that someone powerful is being protected. And the judge—who functions like Meursault's prosecutors in Camus's *The Stranger*—uses *ad hominem* arguments: "Seeing her husband's corpse she did not sob or make an exclamation." Her silence condemns her. In addition, Joseph Fortier is convinced she has done it, and does all that is possible to witness against her. "Taking his [Joe's] testimony, all confusion disappears," says the judge, who is confident of "an honest and secure verdict." But Joe is perhaps motivated by Cordélia's sexual rebuff during her husband's absence. Indeed, could he not even be the murderer, and have plotted to pin the evidence on her as a form of revenge?

The prison scenes that depict Cordélia's growing madness are very impressive, and the visits of the mother tender and filled with pathos. The depiction of Cordélia's and Samuel's double execution is exceptionally graphic. (We might recall that Canada abolished capital punishment only during the term of Pierre Elliott Trudeau; still, it could come back again as it did in the U.S.) Prior to the hangings, attended by two hundred (adult male only) spectators — as if the event were some kind of circus — the anglophone hangman has bragged that he will use only one pulley and one rope, with Cordélia on one end and Samuel on the other, so that when he pulls the lever and the trap door opens, they will go up and down and hang each other, given that they are not of the same size. "They will shit their pants," he repeats; "all men and women shit their pants when hanged; that's one thing we have in common."

The story forces one to contemplate the horrors of capital punishment, especially in the face of a possible mistake in the conviction process. The film disturbs us at the deepest level. It is both like and unlike the situation in *Kamouraska*; unlike because we know that Elisabeth is guilty. A quite different moral issue is under scrutiny in *Cordélia*. As Lever points out (*Hist.* 1988, 291), it also

Cordélia. (Courtesy Office National du Film.)

has a theme that is very similar to that of *L'Affaire Coffin*, a film by Jean-Claude Labrecque that appeared in the same year and unleashed an enormous discussion on judicial error. (An excellent anglophone Canadian film of great importance on that same theme is *Justice Denied*, which deals with an aboriginal who is falsely accused of murder.)

The musical backgrounds of this film are very effective: a religious setting at the beginning of the film—Christmas mass, with the congregation receiving Holy Communion and the carol *Les Anges dans la campagne* being sung—is sharply contrasted during and after the hanging with the chanting of *in extremis* prayers by the priest and with the singing, apparently by nuns, of the hymn "O vierge, o princesse, Jésus votre fils ... O sainte voix, je veux vivre et mourir .... etc."

That the role of Cordélia was demanding is shown in the remarks of Louise Portal: "Of all the roles that I've played in cinema, the one that most revealed myself to me was Cordélia .... It was in playing her life that I became a woman. It was she who allowed me to explode internally for the first time, and to let the music I have in myself speak. When one embodies someone who has already lived ... one receives vibrations from that life. Cordélia Viau really existed. She was an exceptional woman whom people speak of ... she who knew a tragic destiny. She was certainly gifted with great strength and by demanding the same strength of me she made me grow ...."[3] Portal goes on to tell us how Beaudin even saw a physical resemblance between a photo of Cordélia and Portal, and also how she sought to use a spiritual approach to the filming of *Cordélia*. (How different her role in *Le Déclin* ...!)

Cordélia was a considerable step forward for Beaudin, who, in *Stop* (1971; 85 min.) gave us a very slight film like *Stop the World, I Want to Get Off*, about a racecar driver and his women, indeed people "destroying themselves in the human jungle for materialistic purposes and unable to commit themselves to each other or to communicate, all heavily laced with solemn sex both real and imagined. It should have been stopped before it began" (Pratley *TS* 1987, 199).[4]

L'HÉRITAGE

Early *québécois* films chose to bring to the screen stories dealing with the settling of the land. As we saw in an earlier chapter, one of the most notable of these films was *La Terre promise*, based on a novel by Hervé Biron (*Nuages sur les brûlés*); it portrayed the colonization of northern Québec during the 1930s Depression, and relived the hardships and the conflicts of the pioneer. But it was not only the novel that came to the Québec screen in the 1950s. Certain short stories, too, provided materials for screen adaptation, and these short films are excellent both as an introduction to French-Canadian literature and to early Québec society. *L'Héritage*, for example, is an adaptation of a story by Ringuet, and concerns an out-of-work young man, who inherits a farm, but is unable to overcome the obstacles and difficulties of a great drought. He finally returns to the city.

L'HÉRITAGE (1960; d. Bernard Devlin)

The narrator provides us with the setting: Grands-Pins, where the soil is so poor that only *tabac jaune* can be grown. People as poor as the soil settled here. As these opening lines are read, a young man (Albert Langellier) comes down the road; he stops to inquire at a farm as to the whereabouts of Jean-Baptiste Langellier and is told he died in February. The young man indicates that he knows that but he is looking for Langellier's land. He is given directions, along with the provision of a landmark ("Il y a un calvaire là-bas."). The young man arrives at the Langellier farmhouse and enters. The little resident dog begins to befriend him. He examines the house. It is obviously the home of a pious *habitant*; there is a crucifix on the wall next to a clock he resets. Over the bed is a Madonna with Jesus and St. John the Baptist (Langellier's namesake, and patron saint of Québec); there are also two photos. The narrator asks: "Was this his father ... who gave him life and this 'héritage inattendu [unexpected inheritance]' of the farm?"

Langeois, a neighbor, arrives. He asks Albert if he is going to grow tobacco, to which Albert replies "yes." Later, as he dries his dog, who has gone bathing with him, a young woman draws near. "I'm La Poune. I did Langellier's housework; he paid me 2 *pièces* a month. ... My real name is Marie St.-Onge; but they call me La Poune." Albert arranges for her to keep house for him and to help him raise tobacco.

A shift to the general store. We have encountered this before and will encounter it again in other films, this hub of the canton, this gathering place and "newsstand." Langeois and others are gossiping.

But soon the narrator's voice tells us of the failing crops; on the screen we see the fine tobacco leaves flourishing and then wilting. Next, Jacques, as he is going past the barn, spies La Poune; he goes after her, and she objects strenuously to his advances. (Maybe he rapes her, off camera.)

Albert talks to Marie, but she doesn't answer. He then notices she is bruised, and asks her if she has fallen. "No I didn't fall; c'est Jean-Jacques ... on s'est chamoillé; c'est lui qui m'a challé [we argued; he reprimanded me, because I wouldn't let him kiss me. I just want to be left alone. He said terrible things to me, called me names]."

Back in the general store, the client-habitués are listening to the weather forecast on the radio, and discussing their plight. Suddenly, Albert enters. He puts in an order for sugar, butter, and bread and turns to the men, asking for help for tomorrow. He is refused. As he closes the door after him, one of the men utters a proverb, very angrily: "They say that bearers of bad luck don't cast a shadow."

In the next sequence, Albert sits on his porch and reads a letter, in which he is being threatened with repossession of his land. La Poune announces to him that she'll not come any more. "After some stalling, she explains: 'Everyone says you bring bad luck; you brought it to us, to this country.'"

Albert sits down in his wooden rocking chair, the standard piece of French-Canadian furniture we see in film after film (*Pour la suite du monde*; *Crac*; *Le Chandail*, etc.). The narrator tells us of Albert's disgust and *impuissance*.

Albert then packs his carpet bag, closes the shutters, calls his dog, and takes up his ax. He will destroy this faithful friend before he leaves. As he moves to the exterior, we see him leave the house. He passes by La Poune's house; she joins him and they go down the road together.

The narrator has the last word: "And he left, taking with him the only thing that was not strange to him. Then from the thick clouds the heavy beneficial rains fell upon Grands-Pins."

L'Héritage, a film that illustrates the fatalism of Ringuet (real name: Philippe Panneton) as well as his favorite theme—city life as a threat to country life and its values—might well supplement a reading of *Trente Arpents*, a superlative *roman de la terre* that to my knowledge has never been brought to the screen, although, as one of my students observed, it should be.

In this category also is *La Dernière Neige*, an NFB French-language film (1973; d. André Théberge; produced by Jacques Bobet). It shows us the "slow agony of a family in northwestern Québec, undergoing the tragedies of poverty and madness." It is based on Jacques Ferron's short story, "Retour à Val d'Or." One would have thought, too, that *Menaud, maître draveur* would long since have been brought to the screen; and, indeed, in Lever (*Hist.* 1988, 327) one reads that it was "en cours de scénarisation" at the time of Lever's writing in 1988. Its director is Iolande Rossignol. (So far I have seen no reviews nor sign of it.) And also not unlike Ringuet's novel is a 1972 film by Raymond Garceau, entitled *Et du fils.* In this film an old man and his adult son live on a lovely farm, on the rural Ile-aux-Grues in the middle of the St. Lawrence River. The farm has been passed on from father to son. But the son lacks the pride his father has in farming, family, and nation. The son therefore agrees to sell his interests to Americans, who will convert the farm into a private hunting club. The father prefers to burn his home, which he does. The son's conflict between city and country, the agressiveness of American interests and their seeming desire to buy Québec out, the financial problems of the farmer and the inability of a father and son to understand each other, constitute the basic themes of this film, which seems to have not only a Ringuetian, but also a Marcusan stamp on it (civilization and barbarism; progress and suffering; ontogenesis versus phylogenesis, etc.).[5]

GABRIELLE ROY: SHORT STORIES AND NOVELS

An NFB release, *The Old Man and the Child* (1985; d. Claude Grenier; prod. René Piché; 51 min. 17 sec.) is, like *Tramp at the Door*, based on the writings of Gabrielle Roy. In *The Old Man and the Child*, taken from *The Road Past Altamont* (*La Route d'Altamont*, first pub. 1966), a little girl, Christine, meets a lonely old man in his garden; he longs to see Lake Winnipeg before he dies, and so the little girl and the old man take a train ride together. This short film has been released in both an English version and a French original. In my opinion, it is not so well done as *Tramp at the Door*, which, although made by a Manitoban director, deserves discussion here, because it had the collaboration of many French Canadians, and because of its close relation to the subject at hand.

TRAMP AT THE DOOR (1985; d. Allan Kroeker)

Dedicated to the memory of Gabrielle Roy, who had died two years earlier in Québec City, *Tramp* ... is faithful to her tone, and done in a style that is warm, moving, and certain. Based on the short story "Un vagabonde frappe à notre porte," which first appeared in 1946 in *Amérique française* and then in the collection

Un Jardin au bout du monde (Beauchemin, 1975), it is an award-winning work that was shown at the Venice Film Festival.

A Manitoba family, and in particular the mother (Madeleine), is skeptical when an elderly man, poor but dignified, arrives at their door and claims to be their long-lost cousin Gustave from Québec. He brings them news for which these "exiled" Quebeckers are starved. Before long, he is working as the hired man and is entertaining them with colorful yarns about their kinfolk. He wins over the mother, finally, by talking to her about and showing her pictures of St. Joseph's Oratory. He claims to have seen "saint" André and witnessed his miraculous cures. Through this he finds "grace" in Madeleine's eyes. This section of the film has special resonances, since Frère André and St. Joseph's Oratory in Montréal have importance to French Canadians who are religiously oriented. It is with bitterness that Maillet's La Sagouine points out that she has never been there — though she might well dream of going there, as also to Halifax. Frère André is the subject of a tasteful film that will be discussed later on in this book; the Oratory is also the major location of *Jesus of Montreal*.

One day the tramp disappears; he sends postcards from places where he is visiting other "relatives". Then one day he reappears, sick unto death. The family cares for him, and, when he is cured, he again leaves. But his rantings during his fever have returned them to the same doubt about him that they had first had at the beginning of their relationship with him.

The film is beautifully acted, with Ed McNamara and Monique Mercure (who, according to Coulombe, has made a number of films in English, including this one) giving memorable performances. Then, too, the photography is excellent; it has fine textures and captures the grandeur and desolation of the Manitoba scenery. It yields as well scenes that depict the beauty of wheat fields and of animals in motion [horses; white ducks floating on shiny water; a friendly dog, who has an important role in the film]. Equally excellent are the musical settings. Everything about this film is pleasing.

I have always thought that Gabrielle Roy may have concocted this fiction in order to use up odds and ends, or fragments, of stories she had in mind. But, on a more profound level, the written work and the film both make exciting statements about narrative. The orality of the old man's stories is complemented by a scene in which the family is listening to a story on the radio, and, in losing the signal, cannot know how the story ends. So the end of a story may dissolve, or remain "unfinished."

In addition, the story and the film are both a depiction of the techniques of fraud, imposture, and prevarication. More significantly, however, they are both a profound reflection on the art of conversation and, above all, of evocative and contagious storytelling. The plot is hung on the need to believe the story; the desire, or need, to hear a story; the need, too, of having a name. Yet the work also yields a window on the nostalgia of the displaced Western-Canadian francophone and his/her memories of Québec as a spiritual *patrie* .... or *matrie*. The homelessness of the tramp is, then, analogous to the loss of Québec for these displaced persons, who, as the narrator puts it, find themselves in "the middle of the continent," and can return to Québec only through the "magic of stories and dreams."

Tramp ... can therefore be seen as representative of the rural and western *matière* in Gabrielle Roy's oeuvre, *Bonheur d'occasion* as a filmic version of her urban, *québécois* concerns.

BONHEUR D'OCCASION, OR THE TIN FLUTE (1983; d. Claude Fournier)

In *Bonheur* ... Roy's portrayal of the sordidness of the 1930s and the early 1940s dime-store atmosphere and the general rundown nature of the dwelling-places of the Ducasse family, living through the Great Depression, the Second World War,[6] unemployment, and unwanted pregnancies, and still coming out on top — if only through the father's ultimate abdication of his position and his atonement for his failure to meet his responsibilities, as well as through Florentine's clever manipulations — is, for the most part, quite well replicated. A scene in which one of the children pursues a large mouse through the kitchen tends to sum up the situation. And the hospital sequences in which little Danny "falls in love" with the English-speaking Jenny and then dies are extremely poignant. They also fix the strong alienation that the Mother (Québec?) feels, when, after taking her small son to the "sugaring" at St. Denis)[7] — where her country relatives are shocked by the emaciation of her children, he falls ill and then shifts his love to a protestant anglo nurse named Jenny. (Charlotte Laurier as Danny's religious sister, bent upon being a nun, is as strong in the film as the great Marilyn Lightstone, who plays the Mother.)

However, chief among criticisms one might make regarding the transposition of this novel into film is that certain scenes are vastly more graphic than their equivalent description in the novel. Especially, on the down side, the portrayal of sexual intercourse between Florentine & Jean Lévesque takes on the quality of a rape, while in the novel the episode is discreet, amounting to one small paragraph or so. On the positive side, however, the scene in which the Mother gives birth is an instance of true coenesthesia (you suffer as you watch the scene). The collision of birth and death, so powerful in the novel (*T. F.* 1982, 359), is approximated by the juxtaposition of this scene to the one directly following, in which the father, Azarius, and his children bury little Danny in his "small coffin, white and narrow . . ." (*T. F.* 1982, 359).

Themes of war are, of course, common to both the novel and the film. Azarius's love of France (*T. F.* 1982, 297) is played off against federal conscription. For, what could conscription mean to a French Canadian—compelled as a Canadian citizen to support the English, whom they hardly recognized? A rather mediocre anti-World War feature film that shows the dislike the Québécois had of conscription is *Partis pour la gloire* (1975; d. Clément Perron). Similar themes occur in the novel of Roch Carrier, *La Guerre, Yes Sir!*, and have been incorporated into such films as *The Jewel in the Crown*; *For King and Country*; *His Worship, Mr. Montreal*, and *Le Devoir Pt. I* (*Do What You Must*).[8] But perhaps nowhere do we get a greater treatment of the financial meaning of this war to poverty-striken Quebeckers than in Roy's masterpiece. The film in its way replicates this treatment. Azarius, the stereotypical defeated Québécois (Father)—irresponsible, lazy, a dreamer (*T. F.* 1982, 295), yet not at all a mean man—may join the army, and in this way become the "absent" Father (another stereotype). Thus, Rose-Anna, the stereotypical (Québécoise) Mother, a strong woman with many children (cf. *Maria Chapdelaine, Une Saison dans la vie d'Emmanuel*, etc.), may be "rid of him" and at the same time get steady monthly income from his absence. And their son, Eugène, who joins the army—though promising his mother she will now have a steady income—will have all the cigarette and date money he wants, and shows himself to be on the road to irresponsibility, like the Father. Emmanuel, a soldier, too, can, by the fact that he is to return to active duty, become a likely husband, indeed dupe, and a lucrative one at that (and even a savior: God among us, as his name implies), a "second-hand choice, but an opportunity" for the sensual Florentine when she finds herself pregnant by Jean Lévesque, who in turn has jilted her in order to continue to realize his ambitions (or opportunities).

The portrayal of all these characters in the film does not deviate greatly from one's conception of them in reading the novel. Still, Florentine surely is much too plump to fit Roy's repeated reference to her as "thin," even as showing signs of anemia (*T. F.* 1982, 80; 186). The hunger portrayed in this film is such as we see in novels of Zola or Galdós. It does not seem present in the fullness of Florentine's figure, or the round cheeks of Danny, meant to look fever-flushed, but appearing instead to be rosy. Besides this, the script allows the mother, Rose-Anna, a bit too much complaining and certainly a much too-whining attitude to conform completely to the book, where she is strong, forbearing, and truly put upon. Philip Stratford, in the introduction to his translation of *Bonheur* ..., writes of her that "Her tenderness, her courage, her long-suffering as she tried to keep her family together against heavy odds, made her one of the great *mater dolorosa* figures of Québec fiction" (*T. F.* 1982, n.p.). Her courage (*T. F.* 1982, 257) is the glue, the cohesive force, the "lighthouse" of the family (which nevertheless seems to be falling apart). Though each of these characters is relatively true to the novel, the gulf that lies between them and the immense solitude of each and every one of them (Rose-Anna, Azarius, Florentine, Emmanuel, Jean Lévesque) do not come through in the film. This is especially apparent in the novel, both as Florentine finds herself pregnant, afraid, and bitter (*T. F.* 1982, 250–51; 267) and as Emmanuel takes his night walk through the great urban metropolis, which he comes to look down upon from the Westmount Lookout (*T. F.* 1982, 320–1). This kind of loneliness is seen in Euchariste of *Trente Arpents* when he finds himself in a hostile urban setting; a similar loneliness is felt by the narrator of *Prochain Épisode*.

Yet, inevitably, the symbol of the toy flute that arrives too late (a second-hand, borrowed, accidental happiness) comes through, as does that of the orange—a rare, imported, and therefore very special fruit to the Quebecker of the early depression-ridden decades of this century. (Such would be as true for American children raised during the depression.) An orange was a borrowed taste treat, for special occasions, such as Christmas. Blueberries and apples were more standard fruits. The pious little sister, Yvonne, has brought her hospitalized and dying brother a package containing "a row of little men, an orange." And Roy writes:

> "In the hospital they'd often given him a glass of juice that tasted like orange. But an orange wasn't juice, it was a fruit you got at Christmas-time. You found it in your sock on Christmas morning, and you ate it, quarter by quarter, making it last. An orange was like a new coat, or a shining flute; you wanted it so much you kept asking for it, and when at last you held it in your hand you had no use for it .... It wasn't winter and it wasn't Christmas, and there he was with a fine orange in his hand, round and soft and full .... But he had no appetite. He let it fall and turned so he could peek at Yvonne" (*T. F.* 1982, 354–5).

Following a very moving recitation of the *Our Father* by the two children, and a poignant discussion of who will be in Heaven and how Heaven will be, Danny closes his eyes, and Yvonne, "so as not to burst into sobs in front of him ... *put the orange into his hands* and fled, a puny figure in her skimpy dress which flapped about her slender legs as she ran" (*T. F.* 1982, 356.)

This orange, these prayers, function semiotically in the film version of the novel, and again in the film *Maria Chapdelaine*.

The city of Montréal is of great importance in the novel, too. The evocation of this great metropolis in an earlier period (less sophisticated; in the throes of the great depression) is, in fact, one of the focal subjects of Roy's novel, and she delights in dwelling upon all its sights and sounds and smells, many of them spelling out the dinginess and sordidness of poverty. Thus, the description of the sights, sounds, and smells of the dime-store lunch counter where Florentine works, with its "overpowering smell of caramel," somehow always returns when one thinks of the novel. (See *T. F.* 1982, 13).

The odors, of course, could not be caught in the film (nor could they in the novel, except by reference). But the sounds of the working-class neighborhood of Saint-Henri—e.g., the sound of the train passing close by the apartment that the Mother had gotten at such low rent after Azarius had lost yet another job—are certainly present. (See *T. F.* 1982, 281).

And the sounds of jazz music, which can only be described and not lived in the novel (for example *T. F.* 1982, 255—56), are in the film quite effective in setting the mood and in fixing the period. Especially memorable is the song, "Touch me . . . ," which becomes a kind of theme song in the film.

In all, the cinematic portrayal of Montréal in an earlier time has been well done, I think; and a similar effort to show an even earlier period has been mounted in a recent film about the life of Emile Nelligan, *L'Ange noir* (d. Robert Favreau).

Pratley's appreciation of *Bonheur d'occasion* (*TS* 1987, 259) conforms to my impression: "The author's theme of the erosion of human faith and values in the face of poverty and industralization comes through with poignancy and purpose." Pratley points out that the 123-minute film version lacks consistency in the telling, because it is edited down from the five-hour television version. Like Carle's *Maria Chapdelaine*, the power and continuity of the tale and whatever depth of characterization there is in *Bonheur* . . . lie in the longer version, made for television.

While one may see gains and losses in this filming of one of Canada's greatest literary masterpieces, one can scarcely see any vast improvement over the novel. In the long run, the film *Bonheur d'occasion* (*The Tin Flute*) stands in relationship to the novel about like Sam Wood's filming of Hemingway's *For Whom the Bell Tolls*: it was a more-than-competent film, and it made the novel some-what more famous, but it certainly did not surpass it! Exactly the reverse is true of *Maria Chapdelaine*, as far as I am concerned. Others do not necessarily agree; indeed, many critics received the film with cold and even harsh words.

MARIA CHAPDELAINE (1983; d. Gilles Carle)

It seems unfair (for example) to characterize this film as nothing but a showcase for Carole Laure. Lever rather nastily asks: "... le spectateur pouvait-il voir autre chose que Carole Laure dans ce film où l'adaptation du roman célèbre ne se fit pas pour créer une oeuvre cinématographique, mais avant tout pour faire jouer une comédienne en mal de star-system? [... could the viewer see anything but Carole Laure in this film, in which the adaptation of the famous novel was not done to create any cinematographic work, but, above all, to give a part to an actress needing a star-system?]" (*Hist.* 1988, 469). This is strong, even though the casting of Laure in this role is questionable; she is a bit too luminous, a bit too frail to be believable in the hard menial tasks she is shown performing. (And what a contrast to the Carole Laure who strokes a penis as a tear rolls down her cheek in *Sweet Movie*! Or to the wife of Depardieu in *Get Out Your Handkerchiefs*.)

As a film that recaptures the traditional *québécois* past, *Maria Chapdelaine* is quite enjoyable, in spite of the largely negative criticisms it has received. It serves, also, as an excellent introduction to the Québec pioneer days for unknowledgeable students. The traditional material culture of the province is beautifully captured. I have spoken of this previously, but I will here remind my readers of the scene in which a load of oranges arrives in Peribonka on a sleigh. The orange — not a part of the material culture in the strictest sense — takes on the power of a sign in Québec film and literature depicting earlier times. It stands palpably for Christmas, for gift, for something exotic. It represents a rare and special treat from the warm climes, breaking with color and flavor into the harsh inhospitable winter. It was for the Québec child (as for many American children) of the early part of the century a prize to be savored and relished. We find this same sign not only in *Maria Chapdelaine*, but also, as we have just seen, in *Bonheur d'occasion*. And I remember attending a lecture by Suzanne Jacob (at a CIEF convention in Lafayette, Louisiana) during which she described the pleasure she would have as a child when she received her Christmas orange. She told how she would peel the orange most carefully and deliberately. This was analagous to the correct way to read a book or enjoy a poem, perhaps—like peeling away an artichoke leaf by leaf. Yet another very moving example of the use of the exotic Christmas orange (unknown to the Welsh home girl who, like many others, is brought as an orphan to work on a Canadian farm, and who, after finding her friend dead by suicide, places her orange in the snow on his grave) occurs in Allan Kroeker's *Heaven and Earth* (1986; 90 min.). It was written by Margaret Atwood and Peter Pearson and filmed by the BBC and the Ontario Film Development Corp.

But the material culture of early Québec is not all we may glean from *Maria Chapdelaine*: the religious practices of the family are of considerable interest, including the reciting of the rosary *en famille*. This not only evokes a true-to-life practice, but also a cinematic tradition. (The recitation of the family rosary has a similar iconic value in a much earlier film, *Le Gros Bill* [1949], a Québec film made by the French-born director, René Delacroix.) And, as we have seen, the French curé plays a very important role in the social portrait of the Carle film, as he certainly did in early pioneering community. He provides Maria with advice on the need to marry and have children, to forget about François Paradis and the city life offered by Lorenzo Surprenant, when he comes to the home to hear the confessions of the family and their hired help. He worries about a congregation on a stormy Christmas eve. He rejoices to learn he will be staying and will have his own parish. He also provides a bit of humor when he must have his tooth pulled, and the local telegraph operator and church organist distracts him with her music.

I have seen this film in several formats: first as a film entity, in French, in a theater in Ste Foye; next in the four-hour miniseries, dubbed—and extremely well—on CBC; then again as a two hour presentation, dubbed, on CBC; then as a film in French with English subtitles. The four-hour miniseries is greatly superior to the two-hour edited version, which cuts out a great deal of character study. Nevertheless, in my opinion, the film—both in the four-hour and the two-hour versions—is in many respects an improvement over the book, which I read a few years ago and found rather

Maria Chapdelaine. Photograph by Pierre Dury. (Courtesy Coll. Cinémathèque Québécoise.)

dry and stilted. The film profited from a more dramatic arrangement of events: it had a good deal of humor, and it was very beautiful to look at. Some criticized the mixture of accents. They should note how the angel in Scorsese's *Last Temptation of Christ* was the only persona to have a marked British accent. (Was this miscasting, or was there a snobbish meaning of some kind?) I am not enough of a linguist to have captured this putative mixture of accents the only time I saw *Maria Chapdelaine* in French. But one comical thing occurs in the dubbed version: the people from France (the Comartins, who are "foreigners" or "strangers" to the Québécois) have "French" accents, while none of the other characters do.

For me, *Maria Chapdelaine* is interesting as a study of the courtship of Maria by three very different men, including Lorenzo Surprenant. He represents the Franco-Americans who have gone to the United States and become corrupt, money-hungry atheists. Like Eutrope Gagnon, he is just a tad too unlikable, both of them suffering enormously from comparison with the handsome and charming Mancuso-Paradis, who willingly picks blueberries for the feast of Ste Anne, and bites the bullet in a terrible blizzard so that he may light himself a fire and survive to get back from the logging camp to Maria. However, Eutrope is more sympathetic in the longer TV miniseries version, where he whips his trotter to ruination, so that he must shoot it in the end, all in his efforts to get Maria's dying mother a doctor, who even so knows little but the crude medicine of the day. (Leeches would be his answer, were her illness not so deep.) Eutrope reminds us of Chief Joseph's proverb: "when a man seeks the prize of his heart he does not think to count horses."

Maria Chapdelaine is also moving by the tragedy of the true love's death and by Maria's efforts to run the household after her mother's death, and, finally, valuable as an evocation of a time gone by—a time of hard work, both in the clearing of the land and in the dangerous life of the loggers; a time when winter offered great hardships; a time when people sought to settle in a land of forbidding primal wilderness, haunted by the demons of loneliness, of cold, of anger, of bitterness, even the demons of love that prowled everywhere, as the narrator says. He tells us in the opening phase of the film that the people brought to the wilderness their prayers and their songs, while they might have done better to have learned the ways of the good savages. We proceed to find out why he holds this view.

But as this film is based on a French, not *québécois*, novel, I shall not dwell on it here. (Similarly, other Québec filmmakers have adapted literary works from France to the cinema: e.g., Claude Jutra, who in 1959 wrote a *scénario* for *Anna, la Bonne*, adapted from Cocteau; or Louis-Georges Carrier, who in 1972 filmed Georges Feydeau's *Léonie est en avance* under the title *Le P'tit vient vite* (shot on video and blown up to 35 mm; music by Jacques Peron); or Frédéric Back, who turned Jean Giono's *Man Who Planted Trees* into a prize-winning animated film. Nevertheless, any person who reads French will find Esther Pelletier's highly scientific analysis of Hémon's novel as compared to Carle's film quite useful.[9] She finds, for example, that the first meeting of Maria and François Paradis (whom, upon occasion, she calls François Paris) is, in the novel, "much more discreet than in the film. It is treated in a much more incidental, almost accidental way."[10] She also appears to believe that the viewer is given too much nonhierarchical information at the beginning of the film. She points out that Hémon's novel (which describes internalized emotions) would not be the kind that would generate action, which may explain why, for her, the film tends to put more emphasis on speech than on action. This, when combined with the absence of the loved object, was the specific problem that the adaptation of Hémon's novel posed. "Lack of action, anguish, absence, ennui are all abstractions that are difficult to present in iconic form . . .

for they are states, not actions. Carle and Fournier had recourse to various techniques such as the voice-off and the letter-writing to try to give life to their character (Maria), who was closed up in a guarded milieu, and was far away from the object of her desire . . . But it was not very convincing."[11] In sum, however, Pelletier believes that Carle and Fournier fell into the most obvious of traps: they remained too faithful to a text that by its nature resisted adaptation. How differently, then, did the readers of Anne Hébert react to the filming of her novels: they did not find them faithful enough!

ANNE HÉBERT; JUTRA; BEAUDIN; SIMONEAU

Indeed, the followers of Anne Hébert have been particularly dissatisfied with the filming of her works. Most have not seen the beautiful *Canne à peche*, a short, lyrical film about a young girl and her relationship to her father, a métis. It is based on a short story by Anne Hébert, whose novels have often been described as using cinematographic techniques.

It is of some importance to note that Anne Hébert herself spent several years writing radio scripts, in fact (and she has recently published two plays); and when Jutra came to film *Kamouraska*, it was she who worked on the *scénario*. It would have taken the author herself, in collaboration with Jutra, to imagine sequences in which the complex chronologies of the novel could be brought into visual form. Indeed, those unfamiliar with the novel confess to having some difficulty understanding the first few frames of the film. These are based on the opening pages of the novel, and involve flashbacks suggesting Elisabeth's tortured memory – a factor not entirely clear to the viewer, unless s/he has read the book.

Geneviève Bujold, however, brings Elisabeth vividly to the scene (in my opinion), and the dark, claustrophobic atmosphere of the book is adequately maintained by Jutra, whose vision may well have paralleled that of Hébert. And, one might add, this darkness is replicated in Jutra's 1981 filming of Margaret Atwood's *Surfacing*, where the theme of the quest for the father and for the self through deep-sea diving, and the intimations of the possiblity of drowning (which will be Jutra's own solution to his fatal illness) are not well captured, despite the excellent photography of Richard Leiterman.[12] Nonetheless, the acerbic tone and the surrealistic atmosphere of Atwood's *Surfacing* can have appealed to Jutra in deciding to make this film; for acerbic and surrealistic are adjectives that also apply to Jutra's earlier work, *Pour le meilleur et pour le pire* (1975), a comedy about marriage built around one couple, one day, one life, one period—a comedy which was not well received either critically or by theater-going audiences. *Surfacing*, an anglophone venture of Jutra's, made during his Toronto days (where he also made *Ada*; *Dreamspeaker*; and *By Design*), is interesting, then, mostly for its historical value and for yet another example of the malaise and disconnectedness that characterize Jutra's films from earliest times, with *A tout prendre*.

Indeed, this dark vision of Jutra, which coincides with that of Hébert, has been paralleled by Jean Beaudin in *Mario* (1984), based on Claude Jasmin's *La Sablière* (1983). And the sinister witchery we find in *Kamouraska* is not lacking, either, in Beaudin's filming of Yves Beauchemin's novel *Le Matou* (1984). In both of the Beaudin films there are marginal children (cf. Francis Mankiewicz's *Les Bons Débarras*, 1980). In the first, *Mario*, we have a seemingly autistic boy who, with his friends, builds a Moorish fort of *objets trouvés*, and, in the long run, through the love he bears him, allows his brother to urge him into a deathtrap. It departs considerably from the Jasmin novel.

MARIO (1984; d. Jean Beaudin; d'après *La Sablière*)

This tender film, which concerns the sanctity of the person, is centered on Mario, a mentally handicapped boy of ten, who is afflicted by mutism and pica. The nature of the affliction is not entirely clear. (In the book he speaks, sometimes stuttering. At one point we learn that the mother has been told by a "specialist" that his brain will slowly grow dim; little by little he will become like a vegetable.[13] While his father (both in the book and in the film) has little patience or sympathy with this poor child, his brother, Simon (called "Clovis" in the book), has such complete understanding of him that he invents games that they play together. They build a *châteaufort* and have war games of the medieval type, with Arabs against gentiles—the French of Poitiers and Tours in particular. When in the film Simon meets Hélène (in the book she is called Ramona), she wants to know why they have chosen to impersonate Arabs. "C'est ailleurs; ça vient d'ailleurs, comme Mario, d'une certain façon," replies Simon. ["Its from another place; it comes from elsewhere, like Mario, in a way."]

But as Hélène and the fourteen year old Simon grow together in a first love, Mario's relationship to his brother is threatened, and his jealousy is enflamed. First he charges the couple; then when Hélène leaves the vacation site that the Iles de la Madeleine (in the Gulf of the St. Lawrence) represent, the games resume. But Mario's violence causes him to push one of his playmates off the high scaffolding they have constructed. The child is seriously injured, as a result of which a social worker arrives and urges that he be put in an institution. As the father has consented to this, Simon tries instead to drown Mario. But he is unable to carry through his plan and fishes him back out of the water. Mario then is put into an orphanage, and Simon finally goes to get him. He takes him back to a shack by the sea, by the *sablière*, or sandbar, where he is reunited with his favorite games and with the coyote head and carcass he always has in tow. They eat potato chips and drink coke in the lean-to. In the morning, Mario arises and runs (in slow motion) into the blasting site of a columbium (or niobium) mine, followed by Simon. In a final scene he gives a war-hoot, calls out his battle cry quite clearly, and the two brothers, mounted on Arabian steeds and dressed as Arabs, as *corsaires*, fade into the horizon.

This sad tale lacks some of the qualities of the book: the intimacy of the first person narrative and therefore the point of view of the older brother, Simon-Clovis, are lost, for example. The fascinating episode in which the boys find a corpse on the beach is also eliminated. I feel, too, that while the natural settings of the film are unmistakeably Canadian, too much of the material culture alluded to in the book has been extrapolated. The question of conflict between anglophone and francophone peoples of Canada (1986, 189; 191) has been omitted, and the charm of "Simon's" efforts to get encyclopedias with Corn Flakes boxtops, so that he can add to their knowledge of (medieval) history, seems to have been suppressed for some reason. This not to mention the proofs of purchase he has collected from Crown Brand corn syrup, with which he has obtained toy metal trucks (1986, 194). The sugar maples and the products made from them tell us "where we are"; for they are in the environs when a *plombier* who has halfway befriended them allows the boys to take shelter in a *cabane à sucre* (1986, 202).

More importantly, the film seems blacker than the book, and more violent. Though Mario cannot talk in the film, as Elie Wiesel says, "violence is a language," and Mario and the film about his short life both possess this language. Moreover, in the book, Clovis only attempts to drive his brother into the explosion, but fails. Mario, rescued by a monk named brother Gabriel (messenger of God?; symbol of death?), agrees to enter a Trappist Cistercian monastery, where he will learn to make bread and cheese, to raise pheasants and geese, to prune apple trees, to recognize good mushrooms from poisonous ones (1986, 210). Clovis, invited to join the monastery too, refuses. Seeing his brother going through the gate of the monastery, with his hand in that of the monk, he wonders if Mario has found a third father (for Mario has previously told Clovis that he, Clovis, is his real father). Then Clovis hitches a ride into town with a cheesemaker, and here the story ends. It had to be so, for the story is told in breathless, short sentences *in the first person singular*, so that, like Camus's *The Stranger*, it could not end with the narrator's actual death. A more recent analogy with a somewhat different twist is Tahar Ben Jelloun's *Enfant de sable*. Though the main character, an androgynous woman masquerading as a man, seems to have died, this is only an invention of the narrator and an illusion therefore of the listener/reader. In the sequel we learn that s/he is not dead. By this I mean Mario may be dead at the end of the book, and maybe not. The symbolism of Gabriel and the gate are fluid enough to allow for his being dead, or for a sequel. Not so the film, it seems to me.

BEAUDIN AND *LE MATOU*

Evocations of Québec and the mentality of its people are not reserved to makers of direct cinema, such as Pierre Perrault with his cultural explorations, or of poetic documentaries, such as Jean Lafond with his *Voyage au bout de la route* (1987). In the 60s and 70s fictional film began to seek out what was quintessentially *québécois*, perhaps beyond the myth of *Séraphin*, and beyond the myths of logging, hunting, fishing, and fur-trading. As we have seen, or will see in other chapters, Jutra — after Gélinas — was among the first to show us what might be termed the inner tickings of the society. And the dark vision of Jutra, who represents the best in *québécois* filmmaking, has, as we have just seen, been paralleled by Jean Beaudin in *Mario* (1983–84), based on Claude Jasmin's *La Sablière*. Moreover, the sinister witchery we find in *Kamouraska* — both film and novel — is not lacking, either, in Beaudin's filming of Yves Beauchemin's novel *Le Matou* (1984). Indeed, as Clanfield says, the films of Beaudin are in the best Jutra tradition. It will be recalled that Beaudin also directed *J. A. Martin photographe* (1976), and *Cher Théo*, as well as *Cordélia* (1979). As we saw, in *Cordélia* the atmosphere and even the story are not unlike those of *Kamouraska*, also built on a real-life story. In most of his films, then, but especially in *J. A. Martin photographe* and *Cordélia*, Beaudin is recovering a certain mythic Québec; and certainly the infrastructure of *Le Matou* pertains to the Québec society versus almost all the rest of the world. The novel, of course, dictated this; but the very selection of this material by Beaudin is significant.

LE MATOU (1985; d. Jean Beaudin)[14]

In *Le Matou* we have a street-urchin, Monsieur Emile, a hard drinker, who goes to his death for the love of his cat. Can he be the incarnation of the Québécois? Does the story represent a fight to the finish for the *pays* and for autonomy? Perhaps. Significantly, *Le Matou* contains a Mephistophelean character named Ratablavatsky — referred to as the alley cat.[15] He, together with his anglophone partner Len Slipskin, seeks unsuccessfully to frustrate a young restaurateur Florent Boissonneault (played by Serge Dupire) and his wife Elise (played by Monique Spaziani). The villains get their just due, however, thanks to terrorist methods used by M. Emile (Guillaume Lemay-Thivierge), who has been taken in and loved by the couple.

Weinmann sees in *Le Matou* an imaginary bastion of Québec's long, almost racist "closing off" of the world. For him, the issue in both the novel and the film is how to keep Québec "pure" — how to keep out the immigrants, the Jews, the (inimical) Other (associated with vermin), indeed anyone who is not Québécois *pure laine* (Weinmann 1990, 154−55). In both the film and the novel Florent insists upon the purity of his blood. In the film he tells the clerk at Ratablavasky's hotel: "Je suis québécois pure laine" (as also in the novel, *AC* 1986, 39). At one juncture Gladu calls the French chef Picquot a "French asshole" (*AC* 1986, 150), or, in French, a "maudit Français." This insistence on *québécois* purity is manifested through the Boissonneaults' intention to offer in their Beanery a cuisine that is nationalistic and traditional, by serving beans, *tourtières*, shepherd's pie, meatball stew (*ragoût de boulettes*), cucumber salad, veal hearts, and omelets and *grand'mères* (potato pancakes) — (*AC* 1986, 20, 23, 27, 37, 52, 57, 67, and elsewhere). La Binerie Mont-Royal in Montréal appears to be the model for Beauchemin's Beanery, according to Nancy Lyon's article on Québec's cuisine.[16]

But the Boissonneaults are driven out of the business through the trickery of the anglo Slipskin (an "anglo asshole," *AC* 1986, 121), who is backed by the "alley cat" Ratablavasky — whom Florent also calls a "fucking foreign shithole"(*AC* 1986, 298), among other things. But they go into the antique business in Sainte Romanie and struggle to open another restaurant, called the Chez Florent, in which the bill of fare is Canadian, though this time enhanced by French dishes (*AC* 1986, 398; 515–6 in French), all prepared by yet another foreigner, the Frenchman Picquot, who in his turn abhors the Americans and their terrible food (e.g., *AC* 1986, 36, 284 and 399). When Slipskin, who, though an anglo, ironically has gained complete control of the original all-French-Canadian Beanery, tries to undersell Florent, and resorts to other methods to ruin him, Florent, assisted by the resourceful Monsieur Emile, completely destroys Slipskin. This is as it should be; after all, from the very beginning Slipskin was, as Florent says, his "*associé minoritaire,*" *minoritaire* having both financial and social levels of meaning. Emile and his *copains* plant cockroaches in the Beanery; and later Florent and his friend Ange-Albert plant rats in the cellar. Next Ratablavasky is finally put out of commission when Emile takes him in a "blood-bath" of canned tomatoes that he explodes. The Beanery must close, while the Chez Florent — which the couple had opened across the street — flourishes. This picaresque, at times droll, story ends on a bittersweet note. Florent and Elise have a fine baby girl; but M. Emile dies trying to rescue his cat Déjeuner from a roof.

Ratablavasky, whose name playfully contains the word rat (as opposed to cat; he's an alley cat; and he plays a game of cat and mouse throughout the novel), seems also to be Mephistopheles, with his goatee, his magical appearances and disappearances, and his foreknowledge of all manner of plans and events. And this returns us to an early Beaudin film: *Le Diable est parmi nous* or, *Possession of Virginia* (from 1971–2; with Louise Marleau and Daniel Pilon). A melodrama of romance, magic, and murder, built around mysterious deaths, this film supposedly dealt with the satanic in the wake of the great success of *The Exorcist* (Lever *Hist.* 1988, 249; 286). It may be more attributable to a constant taste for witchery in the *québécois*-Jutra-Hébert tradition, however. One might add that Ratablavasky may perhaps be an *article de la mort*, as well.

But just as important to the novel and to the film is the portrayal of the waif, who seeks to replace his own with a better set of parents. I see strong analogies between him and the waif in *Dick Tracy*. Except, in *Le Matou* the child is a more complex metaphor of the *sans abri*. He can be viewed as representing the embodiment of the "homeless" province of Québec, and as the emblem of its nationalistic longings for proper "parents," or proper government — one of its own choosing, that is. Note too, that small and alcoholic though

Le Matou. Photograph by Robert Marquis. (Courtesy Coll. Cinémathèque Québécoise.)

he is, he gives the anglophones and the immigrants who steal the Quebeckers' livelihood their comeuppance.

There are other issues besides provincialism versus federalism or continentalism at stake in both film and book — satire of the inertia of French Canadians and of the clergy (especially in the book), attack on the bureaucracy in the province, a statement regarding unemployment, snide references to the perpetual demolition going on in Montréal and Québec City (cf. Pool's *Anne Trister*) — all accompanied by large doses of snow and cold in the descriptions and, in the film, in the outdoor scenes. On the soundtrack one hears the cruel wind. (See *AC* 1986, 127–37; 171; 253.) These do not lessen what André Giguère refers to as "une atmosphère mystérieuse et fantastique," which pervades not only the novel but even more particularly the film.[17]

It is true that for the sake of economy, Beaudin has suppressed some of the *farfelu* and picaresque nature of the novel, achieved through the use of Emile and Florent, who when combined give us the *pícaro* of many employments, marginal, orphaned, and wandering. The bookworm, and gourmet, Father Jeunehomme, and his mother, Florent's aunt — who lives in Florida, and whom the Boissonneaults visit and even work for in the course of the novel — have not been portrayed, though in fact most of the characters have.[18] One readily grasps that this would have made this already longish film too long and cumbersome. (Thus, a book containing information on Ratablavasky with which Florent threatens him is found by Elise in a *librairie*, and not provided by Father Jeunehomme.)

But if homelessness is a theme in this book, as in this film, the very definition of home as a moral and not a geographical or even a physical space seems to be another deeper theme. Moreover, the story has some mythological infrastructure: one is reminded of E. T. A. Hoffman's *Nutcracker*, in which the horrible and machiavellian king of the rats plays such a role, and which gives us a battle between wooden soldiers and a battalion of rats. Why not, by extension, an "alley cat" and a "rat"?

While Weinmann's view of this film insisted on the Québécois-vs.-the-Other, Yves Picard views *Le Matou* from a political perspective, representing a shift from matriarchal to patriarchal concerns, or as a symbol of the recent Entreprenurial State. He writes: "In this film the vision of the State would surprise one, if it were not interlocked with a new mosaic of the *québécois* social *imaginaire*. The principal character of this film is not Ratablavasky, nor Elise, but Florent. Elise embodies the quiet State, the State that bears and contributes to the private enterprise of Florent. Florent has all eyes and smiles of sympathy turned on him and his dream. Florent obeys the new and recent functional logic: he has no identity or independence to acquire as did Rose-Aimée in *J. A. Martin photographe*, but an economic independence and emancipation to conquer. Indeed, all the new weapons that Florent enlists form a mental configuration that is opposed to the (concept of) State-Nation-Providence-Mother: it's a question, rather, of the (concept of) Entrepreneur-Individualism-Excellence-Father. At the end of the film he is literally a father."[19]

However much the *québécois* film may have changed in content and evolved in style along with the dynamics of the socio-political-economic picture in Canada and in Québec, that body of film continues to carry on the early charge of defining the culture and its values; it also continues to preserve the linguistic heritage of the French-Canadian people. One may find many examples of these traits in any number of *québécois* films; but *Le Matou* is a rich mine to explore from this perspective, as is the novel. This tradition of filming Québec for Quebeckers, and in the language typical of the region, is at once the attraction and the limitation of most *québécois* cinema. For those of us who love Québec, its literature, its film, its people, *Le Matou* is a delight. But one can see why its rather culture-bound character would cause it to have only limited appeal to the average American moviegoer. From a linguistic point of view, certainly, almost any American with standard training in French would be lost in viewing *Le Matou* without benefit of sutitles, it seems to me. It, like certain other *québécois* films, would even need subtitles in order to be screened in France. Even so, it would not take an expert to collect whatever universal message might be contained in the book and film. There *is* one, for sure (cat vs. rat, a recurrent metaphor throughout the book; the dichotomy of David vs. Goliath, dwarf versus giant, small versus large, good vs. evil, "or a mixture of the two, leading to perfection," as Ratablavasky puts it [*AC* 1986, 369].) The novel has now been translated into six foreign languages and sold nearly a million copies for its local color alone.

That is to say, and Pratley notwithstanding,[20] from Yves Beauchemin's novel *Le Matou*, which was an example of *québécois*-francophone *écriture* unfurled in the speech of the Québécois common people, Jean Beaudin has provided an outstanding image of the *québécois*-francophone society—an image that both defines and creates that society.

Recóvery of Québec's past and portrayal of its present are of great interest to Beaudin, then. In both *J. A. Martin photographe* and *Cordélia*, Beaudin used the "cellular structure of 'memory units' separated by fades to black, discreet camerawork, and underplayed acting that relied on glances and facial expression," (Clanfield 1987, 76) or closeups. This evocation of the past, as another dimension of portraying Québec in its history and in its culture, incorporates what would be supposed to be the speech of the French Canadian in the nineteenth century, and although for those to whom French is a foreign tongue the language of these two films is more difficult to understand than that of *Kamouraska*, it is certainly more believable. Of course, we might explain the differences by the disparate social and educational backgrounds of the women involved. In any case, these two Beaudin films are in a class with Jutra's not only through their tone, but also, through their effort to give a sense of Québec history through fiction (just as *Le Matou* and *Mon oncle Antoine* mirror the "present"). Stepping back a few years from *Cordélia* and *J. A. Martin, photographe*, let us look at Jutra's filming of Anne Hébert's[21] *Kamouraska*, generally viewed as a less successful enterprise than was his *Mon oncle Antoine*.

KAMOURASKA (1973; d. Claude Jutra)

The film opens in Québec City, with Elisabeth, the mother of eleven children, a bourgeois woman respected by everyone, keeping vigil over her husband Jérôme Rolland, who is about to die. From this perspective she relives her youth. Elisabeth's memories are, from the beginning, mixed with the present. It is raining and "Mme Rolland" is looking out the window and "seeing" her American boyfriend driving his horse and sled across the snow. She then returns to her dying husband and reads to him. In one of the earliest sequences she remembers her former arrest, imprisonment, and departure from prison in her former mother-in-law's buggy. A bit later she recalls her first husband, Tassy.

Finally, we have a true flashback to her youth. (The color shifts to an orangish sepia.) She is now Elisabeth d'Aulnières, born in Sorel, a river port between Montréal and Trois Rivières, where she is being reared by her mother and three maiden aunts.

A new flashback takes Elisabeth and us back to her youth with her aunts again.

Through Elisabeth's rememberings we come to know Antoine Tassy—a hunter for whom Elisabeth is the prey. In the novel he is so savage he may well be a "vampire"; at least his teeth seem bared. In the film he is boorish and cruel, a woman-chaser and a drunk. After several flashbacks we go "forward" in the past to their wedding and then to the newlyweds' departure for Kamouraska. Elisabeth recites the villages as they pass through them; it is not winter. This produces a magnificent litany-like effect, especially in the book. (And the horror of her wedding night is conveyed in both book and film.) A flash forward—but not to the film's "present"—shows her American lover "George" passing them; it is winter. Then she is at table with her husband and mother-in-law, where she is introduced to *anguilles* [eels], common fare in Gaspésie and one she is expected to learn to like.

Shortly thereafter we see a pregnant Elisabeth with her mother-in-law; the old lady is giving her lots of advice. Next, she is in bed with Antoine Tassy, her husband. He awakes and tells her of his dream of confession; he breaks a mirror; his violence of their wedding night is reconfirmed. There is a party at Kamouraska. It is a baptismal party for the recently born son; Antoine is not there. He soon shows up, however, and he is drunk, abusive, ugly.

Back in Sorel a drunken Antoine breaks through Elisabeth's barricade. He manhandles her. "Are you sick? You should see a doctor," he says. Dr. Nelson is called. A family scene ensues, in which Elisabeth, nursing the baby, is seated with Antoine and her aunts, who are discussing this Dr. Nelson, the "étranger" from a loyalist family. (The attitude is one that typifies a traditional insularism on the part of the Québécois, who had [and perhaps still have] little tolerance for the foreigner, the outsider.) Says Antoine: "He would be my friend if I had one." The statement is at once revealing and ironic. Antoine is speaking of his eventual murderer; but Antoine is also showing how little liked he is and how much he is aware of that fact.

A few scenes later we shift to a snow scene. Elisabeth comes alone to the doctor's house in her horse and buggy. She is wearing a great hat of beaver that frames her beautiful face. He shows her the house. Now we have a flashback within a flashback. Tassy and Nelson are seen as young academicians, playing chess. "I'll take his queen," says Nelson prophetically. We shift back to Elisabeth and George Nelson. They agree that he will take her to an upcoming party in his "traineau" [fine sled]. In the next scene, she is preparing for the party, while Antoine tries to prevent her. He slaps her. Then we have an overhead shot of black horses and sled on the white snow. The camera focuses on George's horse and sled. Elisabeth gets in; they ride along; she puts her head on his shoulder.

She tells him that her husband has hit her. Angry, he races his horse and they overturn. The two confess their love to each other. Antoine is already there at the party, flirting, when they arrive. As he dances, George looks on; he then confronts Tassy and they fight.

After love trysts recalled, we flash forward to the court scene (not to the present!). The "Mother of the accused woman" lies for her daughter: "They were never alone in her bedroom." Aurélie testifies: "She was often alone in closed bedrooms with the doctor."

After another love tryst in a barn, we are in the house in Sorel. Antoine has returned after a prolonged disappearance. "I'm going to make up with my wife," he annnounces. We shift to Elisabeth. Antoine: "We're going to make up." She: "Yes." As he penetrates her, she thinks of George. She starts screaming. The mother and aunts arrive and tell him to get out. He: "Elisabeth, ma femme, you'll not get away from me that easily. I'm leaving, but I'll be back; I promise." Shortly thereafter, Elisabeth sends Aurélie with a letter, to tell her husband she is pregnant by him, "même si ce n'est pas tout à fait vrai [even if it isn't completely true]." A few scenes later she tells Aurélie she is going to the doctor's house, though it's the middle of the night. ". . . I can come home any time . . . I have the key." Not long after her arrival at the doctor's house, she tells him she is going to blame Antoine for the baby. After making love, Elisabeth returns home in the broad morning light. Her relatives warn her of her honor. "A letter from Antoine has arrived. I burned it," says one.

Aurélie Caron, the servant (and witch), and Elisabeth are together. They drink wine. Elisabeth tells Aurélie she needs her; that she has to go to Kamouraska to poison her husband. When Aurélie objects, saying that that is a very big crime, Elisabeth promises that she will keep her all her life beside her. Nelson arrives and declares that he is going to Kamouraska, but Elisabeth tells him Aurélie will go. She's to seduce Antoine Tassy, then poison him. "If you succeed you'll never have to work again . . . . You'll pour the poison when he has an erection . . . ."

Shift of scene: Aurélie — in court — testifies. She tells the story, during which time we have several flashbacks. She is seen in a sled with Antoine; he is drinking; he has a severe pain. She leaves him for dead. Then we see her with George, who is angry with her because she has failed; Antoine is alive. He prepares to leave for Kamouraska, swearing, "I'll not fail. *Ce salaud* [That pig] . . . . I've told people I've gone to the U.S. where my father is ill." He puts on a gray wool coat, goes out the door, gets in his sled, and departs.

The arduous trip of the doctor through the snow is vividly conveyed to us. He frequently asks directions. (This trip through the snow is not unlike the mad ride of Antoine and Benoît in *Mon oncle Antoine*, another Jutra film.)

Elisabeth awakens with a start: "Antoine. Where is Antoine?" Where is she? Who is she? Antoine's wife? Mme Rolland?

Nelson finally meets Antoine. "I've brought news of your wife. Come in my sled." He shoots Antoine. Then he drags him to the floes and shoots him again.

Nelson, back in Sorel, tells Elisabeth it is over; Antoine is dead and now she is free; they are both free .... (Yet another irony, coupled with the fact that he, a doctor, has taken a life.)

Back to the present. Elisabeth's daughter Anne-Marie wakes her. She is very disturbed and lies back down, to dream again. And so we return to her fragmented reconstruction of the past. She arrives at Dr. Nelson's. His man tells her the police came this morning. "He said he must leave the province forever. He said before he left, 'It is that damned woman that has ruined me.'"

We return to the film's "present." Now she remembers the "machinations d'une bonne famille." Mme Tassy, Antoine's mother, "helps" her. "Raise your veil; we must be seen everywhere together .... You're innocent. Vous êtes condamnée à l'innocence [You are condemned to innocence]." And as Elisabeth thinks, Anne-Marie fixes her hair. "Dead. I am dead." She remembers how she

Kamouraska. Photograph by Bruno Massenet. (Courtesy Coll. Cinémathèque Québécoise.)

had received a letter from George: "You'll come ..." But the letter was intercepted by the judge. (She had been arrested as an accomplice, condemned to prison, but released 'sous caution.')

Elisabeth now goes up to see her dying husband Jérôme, whom she had married for convenience. He had given her "respectability," but she had always awaited the return of Nelson, her one true love. Elisabeth sits beside Jérôme. "Je suis là; rassure-toi [I'm here; don't worry]." Weeping is heard.

One may see the truth of the statement that Hébert walks a tightrope between melodrama and tragedy. By a curious irony, *Kamouraska*, in my opinion Hébert's best novel, has yielded a rather unsatisfactory film, steeped in melodrama. (Conversely, Jutra's masterpiece is *Mon oncle Antoine*. The latter is a film that does not depend upon a book for its impetus, and, moreover, does not have to combat the *parti-pris* of a novelist's devotees.) Still more ironically, Hébert's *Fous de Bassan*, far from her best work, yielded a splendid (and tragic) movie, in my estimation.

The orange-sepia hues set the tone and time of *Kamouraska*. The snowy scenes — all real — and the use of the fine horses and sleds, along with the great fur coats, set the time (1839) and place of the film (in a true prereferendum northern site and culture). But this film, unlike the film version of *Les Fous* ..., does not tell the story iconically, even though from time to time there are some visual details that could be called iconic (e.g., the plain cross in the protestant doctor's house as opposed to the crucifixes in the houses at Kamouraska and Sorel, which constitute a nonverbal manner of conveying the difference in religion between the inhabitants of the region and their loyalist "transient"). In due time I shall speak extensively of the powerful visual language in *Les Fous* ....

In the novel *Kamouraska* we undergo as readers a kind of deep-sea diving, down to the bottom, up to the surface, then down not quite so deep, then back but perhaps not to the surface, and then to the surface, and so forth, through various levels of experience framed by their own time. This technique, so effective in the novel, is not achieved in the film. Instead, the strategies for portraying the functions of memory lead to viewer frustration. Indeed, the film's grammar is mightily confused on several counts. As a matter of fact, some critics contended that linearity would have been preferable to flashbacks in this film: but how could they have expected scriptwriter Anne Hébert to do other than she did? This is her consistent approach to presenting reality and its conflict with memory and with illusions coming out of dream, drug, and sorcery.

The critics also contended that the historical evocation of the film was poor, and that the devastation of Elisabeth's relationship to Nelson was not well depicted: here the psychological dimension was, for them, *invraisemblable* (not believable).

If we were to indulge in a little nit-picking, we would probably like to ask about the linguistic world of this film. It seems unrealistic that most of the people involved should speak such Frenchy French. Granted they are educated intelligentsia of nineteenth-century Québec; but can it be that as we move from film to film, we find Cordélia Viau-Poirier (in *Cordélia*) and Rose-Aimée Martin (Monique Mercure in *J. A. Martin photographe*) speaking New World French, while Elisabeth, played by a French-Canadian actress, should show few or no traces of difference from a continental Frenchwoman, and not the slightest relationship to her "compatriots," Cordélia and Rose-Aimée Martin?

Kamouraska is an early novel (and film) about the battered wife, just as *La Petite Aurore*, even earlier, is a story about the battered child. The givens do not seem exaggerated: the question is, to what extent can a woman go (or have gone) to escape brutality? Of course, adultery would not have to be included in the escape. Nor murder, either. But we must bear in mind that it is a question of a nineteenth century Québec woman, well brought up, protected, isolated, whose options are not exactly myriad in this closed and tight-knit society. (Besides, the story is based on a real-life event.) But is it of its time alone? Perhaps. Still, it is interesting to see that in the United States women are sometimes now being acquitted of violent crimes against a brutal, tyrannical husband, and only recently it was announced that in some states the cases of women who are presently serving prison sentences for such crimes are to be reconsidered. And five or six years ago a Nova Scotia woman who had suffered unspeakable physical, sexual, and mental torture at the hands of her husband was nevertheless forced to serve a prison sentence when she finally shot him to death. Was Elisabeth's suffering commensurate with the crime in which she served as accomplice? Were the punishment and the loss of her lover merited? These are some of the questions we ask upon finishing the novel — and, it follows, at the end of the film. But regardless of all the moral questions we might ask, both as readers and as viewers we certainly undergo a coenaesthetic experience as we relive Elisabeth's ordeal, flash by flash, and suffer such mental anguish along with her. A riveting novel that studied psychological repression and guilt along with the pain of rejection was, if not completely captured, even so certainly *far from ruined* by the film.

In sum, *Kamouraska*, the film, perhaps because it is bound, or predetermined, so to speak, by the logocentrism of Hébert's novel—which mimes the process of inner mono/dialogue—does not transmit narrative with the same immediacy and power as Jutra's superlative signature and quasi-*auteur* films, such as *A tout prendre (Take It All;* or *The Way It Goes),* or *Mon oncle Antoine.* In these latter the director's focus and design remain quintessentially filmic. *Québécitude,* too, is more directly apprehended in such a film as *Mon oncle Antoine* than is the case in *Kamouraska,* which, as a novel, brought out in high relief the claustrophobic nature of the Québec society as it stood historically all the way through World War II. The proof may lie in the fact that *Mon oncle Antoine* was rejected by the Cannes film society in 1971, and had to be discovered by Canadians first, before the rest of the world came to see it as a four-star two-thumbs-up kind of film (Pratley *TS* 1987, 109). Since by the time of *Kamouraska*'s appearance *Mon oncle Antoine* had cemented Jutra's reputation, and since *Kamouraska* was already known to audiences through the novel, people were more drawn to *Kamouraska* from the outstart.

Beattie, as is always her approach, gives a large bibliography on the film *Kamouraska*,[22] and on Jutra in general through 1975; one may also consult Véronneau's thesis, which compares the film to the novel. Let us look at some of the specifically *critical* appraisals of *Kamouraska,* the film; they have varied considerably.

In *Films about and by Women* one reads: "A classic love story written from a woman's point of view. Its heroine, Elisabeth, is a tragic victim of a narrow-minded Victorian age when love was incidental and marriage was to last a lifetime. When the story begins, she is a worn-out, middle-aged wife waiting for her husband to die. In a flashback dream, Jutra reveals the past—a young girl's marriage to a rapacious, slow-witted hard-drinking Antoine Tassy, a man she hates; her love affair with a kind but possessive American doctor; the murder of the oafish husband, prison, and finally another loveless marriage. The result—a sweeping, passionate film set in nineteenth century Quebec and the story of a sensuous woman, bedeviled by an unobtainable love in a soul extinguishing family."[23]

And in *Variety,* 23 May 1973 it was said that *"Claude Jutra, after some semi-bio pix in the New Wave model, went back to more timeless themes of the past and scored with 'My Uncle Antoine,' a tale of a boy coming of age in the '40's in a backwoods town. Now he goes back to the nineteenth century to paint a romantic tale of a woman whose need for life is stifled by the mixed European and puritanical look of the time."*

"If familiar, and sometimes even conventional, it has a lift in the playing of Geneviève Bujold; and the rustic, harsh but sometimes bawdy look of the era despite its closed-in social narowness. The woman being used as an object by both men in her life could reflect on modern ideas ....

"French actor Philippe Leotard has the grossness as a product of his time and upbringing while Yank Richard Jordan is properly obsessed in his mad affair with a married woman in a little town where he is already suspect as a foreigner.

"Pic has fine production dress for good home consumption and its bow to this genre of ... romantic pic, with some deeper social and moral aspects could give it playoff legs abroad if needing harder sell and care in urban areas. Pic was invited by the Association of French Film and TV Critics as a noncompeter at the Cannes Fest."[24]

While admirably evoking Québec City, "Sorel," and the Gaspé penninsula (in particular the county of Kamouraska), this is nonetheless a film of mixed blessings. It has the value of telling a story we all know well from the novel; it has the value of giving us a pictorial concept of the work. We may not have imagined Tassy as quite so handsome, or Elisabeth as quite so beautiful; and certainly we regarded the novel as very complex from a spatio-temporal point of view. Could this be captured in a film? Michel Houle's reference suggests not. One reads as follows concerning the probelms involved in the making of this film and its reception:

*"*Kamouraska *had a running head-start by the fact of the great, indeed international success Jutra had enjoyed through* Mon oncle Antoine. *Moreover, the novel had been both a critical and a commercial success. Michel Brault's reputation was firmly established. Geneviève Bujold had consented to take a detour into Quebec on the road to her international stardom. The fact that it was to be a coproduction with a French producer meant there would be a larger budget that Québécois directors usually had at their disposal (at that only $750,000)."*

Houle does not seek to compare the novel with the film. His discussion is limited to the film. He goes on to say:

*"*Kamouraska *is a story of passion passed through the grill of memories. But the film is scattered in time and not sufficiently rooted in a historic space; it lacks psychological vraisemblance.*

"At the level of time, the construction in flashback cuts up a dramatic frame which would have been better depicted through linearity. As for space, the Quebec of the nineteenth century is more filtered than physically present in the decors. As for psychological

vraisemblance, ... one has difficulty in picking up the current of that passion ... which gnaws [Bujold-Elisabeth]. ... [T]he *inexpressive passivity of Richard Jordan's acting does not help her ....*

"When it first came out Kamouraska *experienced a critical reception comprised of the reservations that a comparison with the novel implied .... They underlined ad infinitum the quality of Bujold's acting and the pictures of Brault.*

"*The film was not the commercial success expected; by the time of this writing* [1978] *it had not yet been distributed in France.*" (Houle *Dict.* 1978, 146–47; my translation and paraphrase.)

Of course, the film, like the novel, revolves around adultery, murder and guilt. And, like the novel, it attempts to give us past events in layers, going intermittently back into the remote past, surfacing, but perhaps not to the present, going back again to the past, then returning to the present. Is this not, after all, the way the memory functions? We do not each and every time we think of the past go back to a given point and progress forward in time exactly as things happened chronologically. Still, for the viewer who has not read the novel, the film is (said to be) very confusing.

But, despite the implications of the above quotation, *Kamouraska* has a certain riveting, unforgettable effect; and for me Bujold's performance here outshone any other I have ever seen by her, even that of *Isabel*, or of *Dead Ringers* — though these, too, were near perfect. The same cannot be said of any number of other films in which she has starred; and, although some critics give rather high grades to *Coma* (1978; with Michael Douglas and Richard Widmark; three stars), I found that film rather absurd.

According to Lever (*Hist.* 1988, 289), *Kamouraska* was released in 1984 as a "*four* hour television spectacle," and to my certain knowledge it has been shown on Montréal television at least once since — since I was in the city when it was being aired. Clanfield claims it appeared in the "full *three* hour version through Pay-TV in 1983"; Pratley claims the "original" 173-minute version was shown on Pay-TV in 1984 (*TS* 1987, 208). Lever finds this three-hour version more consistent from the point of view of action and characters, but contends that it "loses the warmth of Michel Brault's 'image' (photography)" (*Hist.* 1988, 289).

Finally, two interviews from *Cinéma/Québéc* (March/April 1973), one between Euvrard and Bujold, the other between Tadros and Jutra, shed more light on the filming of *Kamouraska* than most other writings. Bujold attests to the genius of Jutra, and speaks of his use of many "plans-séquences," which allowed the actors to develop their characters. She also explains how playing Elisabeth was important to her: "... important to me as a human being, as a Québécoise, as a woman and as an actress — in that order — important to play a character conceived by a woman."[25]

Jutra, on the other hand, explains some of the problems he confronted in making this "first *québécois* period piece" (i.e., first, along with *Quelques Arpents de neige*). There was, for one thing, a problem in converting the story, told in the first person singular: "It was almost impossible. Then we decided to go slightly away from the subjectivism (of the novel). So we proceeded in that way."[26] He goes on to explain how they began with little flashbacks that became more and more important, and, towards the end of the film, introduced a great many more of them. It is of some interest to point out, however, that Jutra is not entirely correct in saying the novel is written in the first person singular. It is at times in the first person singular, for at times Elisabeth looks at herself as subject; but at other times, when she is considering herself as an object, the narration shifts to third person singular.

Jutra's commentary on the difficulties of finding appropriate exteriors is even more revealing. He laments the wholesale destruction of fine old *québécois* buildings in the name of progress.[27] (This theme is prevalent in the litterature of Québec; e.g., in Beauchemin's *Le Matou*.) So much is this the case that Jutra could find no suitable village in which to shoot the town of Sorel, so important to the novel. "It was Sorel that was our nightmare. We looked for a long time for a place that might represent Sorel; we didn't find one. We went to St-Michel; it was an approximation; but finally all those plans were dropped."[28] Because no town existed that was not cut up by wires or by a federal highway cutting through it, the film, he explains, could not adequately translate the evocation of the community of Sorel, of its sociological climate.

Jutra expresses his satisfaction with the three principal actors, however. Indeed, he agreed to film *Kamouraska* only on the condition that Bujold play Elisabeth. He found Jordan worked enormously hard to portray Nelson, who, in the novel was, in his view, almost at abstraction. "He is ideal but impossible love. She projected into him all her aspirations, and for that reason once the act has been committed, the supreme coitus completed — that is to say Tassy's assassination — then everything is finished, he disappears, he faints, he very simply ceases to exist. That's how it is in the novel, moreover: he is annihilated in the heart and memory of Elisabeth at the same time he is annihilated as a person."[29]

Editing, on the other hand, was one of the great problems

Jutra faced. On the first editing the film was three hours and forty minutes long; after the second cutting it was still two hours and thirty minutes long; then Renée Lichtig was proposed as editor, and he found her to be "terrific."

Though on the whole Jutra found Anne Hébert to be a compatible collaborator, he does confess that her demands that certain details regarding the trial, length of prison terms, and other kinds of information should be included took too much time when relayed in cinematic language, and, besides, were not only unnecessary, but also "added nothing to the dramatic structure of the film."[30] Where, then, would Anne Hébert stand in the filming of her *Les Fous de Bassan*, since there she was not even a coscriptwriter? And what would her reading public have to say of this transposition of a novel that some found outstanding, others poor stuff?

LES FOUS DE BASSAN (1986; d. Yves Simoneau)[31]

"THE LISTENING EYE"

It was Yves Simoneau's 1986 filming of *Les Fous de Bassan* (in English called *Shadow in the Wind*) that most raised the dander of Anne Hébert's readers, and at a meeting of CIEF in Montréal on 15 April 1988 Hébert herself added fuel to the fire, by indicating her displeasure with the results of the film. She contended that, whereas she had intended to make the little girls in her story the objects of the villagers' desire, the filmmakers had turned the situation into a sort of free-for-all in which "just about everyone viewed Stevens Brown as an object of desire." It seems, too, that Hébert's first preference as director was Mireille Dansereau, not Simoneau, but after Francis Mankiewicz dropped the project and the various scripts that had been proposed, Simoneau took it up. He prepared a script with Marcel Beaulieu, which it seems that Hébert agreed to, curiously enough. (All the politics surrounding the making of this film are narrated by Kathryn Slott,[32] but have no real bearing on a discussion of the final film product.) The least we can say of all this is that the plan to externalize and actualize large doses of internalized discourse — where action is buried in the word — was not without its problems, not to mention its hazards, whoever might undertake the project.

It is of some importance that we take a close look at this beautiful film, which Lever so correctly calls "the typical case of the film mistreated by the critics" (*Hist.* 1988, 429; my translation). He goes on to say: "Some praised it and others scorned it; the young director and the author of the novel were much interviewed. But no serious analysis has been done of it yet, and Simoneau will probably transport the same facile tricks and subconscious tics into his next films" (*Hist.* 1988, 429; my translation). I propose to make here such a "serious analysis" of this stunning film, created by a director who had shown an earlier taste for the study of crime and voyeurism through *film noir* (e.g., *L'Enquête*; *Pourquoi l'étrange monsieur Zolock s'intéressait-il tant à la bande dessinée?*), and who continues to display such fascinations in his latest thrillers — e.g., *Pouvoir intime*, of the same year as *Les Fous* ..., and *Dans le ventre du dragon*.

The film, like the book, portrays the descendants of loyalists who fled America for Canada at the time of the French Revolution. The characters are marginal by their geographical location on the tip of the Gaspé peninsula; by their language, English; by their protestant religion — which nonetheless in this story functions as the Catholic church does to characters in other *québécois* artworks, forming the basis of their morality and politics; and by their mentality, which verges on the kind of madness sometimes found among the isolated and the inbred.

On the evening previous to Hébert's appearance at the CIEF forum, there had been a showing of the film (14 April 1988), preceded by Prof. Mary Jean Green's commentary ("Filmer Anne Hébert: *Les Fous de Bassan* et le regard masculin"), in which it was claimed that Stevens Brown "rapes and kills both Nora and Olivia." But in reality he does not appear to be able to rape Nora in the novel; he writes to his friend: "pas eu le temps de jouir d'elle."[33] And under any circumstances the rape of Nora is not shown in the film. Nora humiliates him, by calling him a drunkard and a pig, and also, knowing Nora is attracted to him, while Olivia tends to spurn him, he rapes Olivia, at least "with satisfaction." What we might well insist upon is that the film opens with Nora crying "N'y va pas, Olivia; n'y va pas [Don't go there, Olivia; don't go there!]," and then shows Stevens raping and murdering Olivia, after which we have a brief flash forward showing Stevens old, and then a giant flashback. The warning that Nora gives to Olivia and that opens the film is in fact drawn from the novel (*Fous*, 244). However, I am not convinced that the film ever makes clear that in the novel we had a double murder, with Nora being the first to go.

Moreover, Green overlooked the fact that *le regard* — female and male, young and old, bird and human — is, in fact, a rampant sign, operative at every juncture of the novel, and in every scene of the film.[34]

Green also criticized the final scene, in which we see Stevens Brown and his half-witted brother Perceval seated together on the beach where the rape-murder has occurred. For her the scene represents Simoneau's "suppression of the feminine characters and the insistence on the feelings of the masculine characters." Still, it is only Perceval who seeks to join his brother and to console him. He is an idiot who does not wholly understand what has occurred. As the novel-Stevens says: "c'est fou ... ce que cet enfant m'est attaché. Ne me trahira jamais" [It's crazy how attached that child is to me. He will never betray me]" (*Fous*, 243). The final scene of the film seems to me also to be inspired by the text; there Perceval says: "Dormir. Rêver à mon frère Stevens qui est bon pour moi. Lui dire en rêve que je l'aime [To go to sleep. To dream of my brother Stevens who is good to me]" (*Fous*, 142). The film-Stevens is less attached to Perceval than Perceval to Stevens, perhaps, but he loves no one except Perceval. This affection between the two brothers is, then, grounded in the text. And moreover, the novel ends in this bonding, almost exactly the same way as in the film. Leaving aside the "P.S.," in which Stevens tells of his acquittal, he writes to his friend, as a conclusion to his letter (and thus to the novel): "je n'ai jamais aimé personne, même pas toi, old Mic, peut-être Perceval, cet autre moi-même. Je l'entends qui dit que je n'ai pu faire une chose pareille. [I have never loved any one, not even you, old Mic, maybe Perceval, that other me. I can hear him saying that I couldn't have done such a thing.]" (*Fous*, 249; my translations). In the case of the film as in the case of the book, it is up to us to grasp the ironies inherent in this mutual fraternal love.

Critics (especially Green) have also been put off by the omission of Pam and Pat — twin sisters of Stevens and Perceval — and claimed that these women painted the pictures "which appear without explanation in the film." However, the paintings in the film are being moved about, as would be the case with the ones painted in the novel by *Stevens* or by the *Pastor*, whose personae are fused at the beginning of the film. The pictures painted by the twins are on the wall and bordered in black and white with the fatal word and date "*été 1936*." In other words, Simoneau has retained the images suggested by the paintings of four of the novel's characters, and condensed the four painters into one. But in any event, the presence of these secondary characters was not indispensable in the book — even though we learn about the pastor and his will to sadistic domination partly through their eyes. In fact, it seemed a happy adaptation on the part of Simoneau to trim down the amount of

characters and to make the paintings a part of the rubble Stevens
Brown finds in the abandoned church as he returns to the ruined
village years after the traumatic events. Even more possibly, the
evocations brought about by the paintings may suggest to a film
audience that they are by Stevens Brown himself, who in the book
also paints. (See *Fous*, 235.)

In the beginning of the novel, it is the pastor who, at an advanced
age, contemplates the paintings — his own and those of the twins — as
he shuffles about in his decaying house. Likewise, at the end of the
novel, Stevens has turned sixty-six and is mentally "revisiting"
Griffin Creek. The film's opening fusion of the persons and the
recollections of these two similar characters, both of them painters
in the novel, and one of them a writer, is not offensive to me, but
rather facilitates the filmgoer's comprehension of the rapidly passing
images: four painters would be a bit much for the moviegoer to
absorb. And for readers of the book, the old Stevens seems to be
rummaging about in the pastor's *galerie d'ancêtres*. Such a fusion
is within the feel of the novel. The two voices of Stevens — old
(confessional) and young (brutish) — are also in the book.

The paintings of Pam and Pat do not constitute important feminine
"rapports," as Green asserted. Rather, both the film and the novel
propose that art is a truth beyond any torturer and beyond the
creator and is also a powerful, almost historical, but fallible, tool
of memory ... be it a painting, a journal, a letter. (Hébert's idea
of the transcendence of logos is present in her intensely dialogic
poetry, where she unfolds "le mystère de la parole" as she calls
one of her volumes.) Stevens is not without art in the novel: he is
sensitive to natural beauty, and takes great pains to describe the
wildflowers and other landscapes to his friend; and, as we noted
above, he did indeed learn to paint while in the Veterans' Hospital.
Beauty to him may not always be purely sexual. Though Olivia's
sex-tool is for him a "défaut caché [a hidden flaw]" that belies her
angelic goodness, he speaks of her as "la Beauté même [Beauty
personnified]" (*Fous*, 82). And he is more than a little disturbed
to discover she has a physical flaw that makes her like all other
women, whom he basically hates (*Fous*, 83; 88: "je déteste le
monde feutré des femmes ... [I loathe the world of women, soft
as felt ...]"). He hates everyone except Perceval, in fact.

The attribution of the paintings to Stevens is not so questionable
as his return as an old man; it is a violation of the text: "revoir,
revoir," he says in the film ["to see the place again; to see it again"].
But *in the novel* he tells his friend he has never returned to Griffin

Creek (*Fous*, 232), which seems as it should be. If the novel-Stevens knows of the present desolation of the site it is through descriptions he has received secondhand.

Professor Green was also concerned with the fact that in the film, when the pastor tells Stevens he is similar to the prodigal son, Stevens replies "I may resemble Christ, also." Still, in the novel (*Fous*, 88–9 and 230) the pastor designates him as the prodigal child, and Stevens Brown in his retort compares himself to Christ. In one part of his letter to Old Mic he uses the words of Christ blasphemously to describe himself. ("A little while you see me, and then a little while and you see me no more" [*Fous*, 88].) He imagines he is walking on water (*Fous*, 103). In any of these cases the meaning is not that Stevens Brown is a Christ figure, but that the megalomania of this noonday devil permits him the comparison. Moreover, his response shows the defiance of Church authority common to characters in the *québécois* film. As Nora says in the novel, he is a "maudit Christ" (*Fous*, 91) — the devil — and elsewhere she claims that while the pastor must "celebrate" his wife's own funeral service, "mon cousin [Stevens] n'a pas montré son nez ni à l'église, ni au cimetiére. Il craint les cérémonies religieuses et familiales comme un diable l'eau bénite [My cousin hasn't shown his nose in church, or at the cemetery. He fears religious and family ceremonies as the devil fears holy water]" (*Fous*, 130). In this assertion she compares him to the devil — without realizing he indeed is the devil. It is of some significance, too, that while the novel-Stevens scornfully calls himself "Christ," and speaks of "casting his pearls" (i.e., before the swine) even as he contemplates suicide (*Fous*, 236), he also calls *himself* the devil (*Fous*, 106).[35]

One of the chief arguments used against the film by some feminist critics is that the "importance of women in the novel" is deflated in the film. But, no, their importance is *not* deflated automatically by the use of one point of view, or the elimination of some of the figures: and Stevens Brown's hatred of women is made clear in the film. What is even more certain is that the tenderness that the film-Stevens displays toward his brother is not absent from the novel. Significantly, Marilyn Randall most convincingly rebuts all claims to a feminist reading of this novel,[36] while Suzanne Lamy not only saw it as an outstanding example of the "novel of irresponsibility," but also as a "facile book, a novel whose success was foreseeable, with a false modernity, a style full of tics and clichés, and which, moreover, conveys a macho ideology."[37] If so, and it may well be so, then Simoneau's reading, in stressing male bonding, is correct.

But Simoneau's *regard*, though inevitably masculine, does not make him a sympathizer with rape and murder.[38] The sickness of all the characters is adequately demonstrated by Hébert and preserved by Simoneau. For to some extent these descendants of loyalists *are* all marked, if not imbalanced: they are marginal figures, in maximum isolation; they are largely on poor terms with one another. Even Olivia and Nora dislike each other. Thus, to insist too greatly on the strictly "feminist" view of these characters and these events is to betray Hébert's text — in spite of what she herself may say is in the text.

Everyone knows that murder and rape result from the highly energized mechanisms of hostility, hate, and rage; and these, together with a thirst for power, are the basis of Stevens's deeds both in the novel and in the film. His will to dominate is carefully spelled out in many passages of the novel (e.g., *Fous*, 62—63 [village]; 92 [parents]). Lust, of course, cannot be dismissed as one of his major motivating forces.

Moreover, Mireille Dansereau's contention that had she directed the film she "would have preserved the interplay of voices"[39] brought about in the novel by the five people who tell the story (one from beyond this life) is very troubling. At what juncture did she make this remark? How can we know she would have done this? Would she have been able to adhere unswervingly to Hébert's proposed script? In the actual filming, these prescriptions may have proved not feasible. Would the film have had any visual impact at all if it had been held to "voices"? Dansereau's own *Vie rêvée* depends upon image, not dialogue! More perplexing still is Slott's final rhetorical question, after reviewing the film's rocky history: "Could the film have been constructed around a different perspective?"[40] The answer is obviously yes — but then we would not be talking about the same film.

If Stevens's is not the only voice (though it is likely he alone "speaks"), there are more than "five voices" in the novel; there are the voices in "Perceval's 'book' and that of some others"; there are the choric voices of the villagers (*Fous*, 157), and there is even a narrator's voice that floats in and out of the story at random. And do the voices of the men really represent death, while those of the women represent life, as Green claims? Perceval's voice does not represent death: he moves from gibberish to clarity in the novel, as he does in the film (*Fous*, 173). This is the "clarity" of the fool, who counsels the wise man in the Bible, in many pieces of Renaissance literature, etc.

Then, too, to claim that in the novel "woman's voice is privileged" (Green) is to stray from the basic facts: In the novel Stevens Brown, and Perceval, and the Pastor have much more to say than any woman, both by written and by oral word. That is the whole idea! Only an abused reader, then, can "privilege" the woman's voice. More to the point, Randall, in her magisterial article on *Les Fous* ..., sees the possibility of reading the novel so as to reduce these voices entirely into the one "book" of Stevens Brown, and claims that this is the one (book) the film presents. ("Le seul scripteur mis en scène dans le texte, finalement, c'est Stevens lui-même."[41]) But, in any case, it is not the loss of the supposed multiple voices that is to be regretted; there was nothing particularly new or unique in that, anyway.

Green's criticism of Simoneau's inclination to attribute certain psychological woundings to Stevens that make of him a "victim," and thus to explain his behavior, seems to suggest that there is no basis for this in the novel. Still, Olivia remembers the cruelty of Stevens's father (*Fous*, 206); Nora remembers it, too, and at length; and Stevens speaks of it as well (*Fous*, 239–40). Indeed, Green's idea that Stevens, as well as the pastor and Stevens's father, all get sympathetic treatment from Simoneau is not in accord with my reaction: I see all the characters as victims of a very dark inner world, and do not think that this deviates from the novel's structure, which, as some read it, seeks to show the events from various points of view, or tell them with different voices. The old Hebertian Jansenistic fatalism seems quite present and functional in this novel, and that as tone and determinator is carried into the film. This is quite evident in the screen version of the story as Nora and Olivia discuss Irene's suicide. Nora says: "Some people are made for *malheur* [unhappiness]" and Olivia responds, "Yes, but maybe she is now free"; then Nora in a tone of protest says significantly but quite unconvincingly: "Je suis faite pour le bonheur. Je suis faite pour le bonheur [I am made for happiness. I am made for happiness]." (Compare in the novel, her claim that she is made to live and thinks she will never die: "Je suis faite pour vivre ..." [*Fous*, 131].

THE USES OF COLOR

In *Les Fous de Bassan*, eros tyrannos and thanatos are involved in the same fatal struggle as in *Kamouraska*, where Mme Rolland, if she does not die, lives a life-in-death.[42] And this struggle is clearly preserved in the film version of *Les Fous* ...; for the

animus and the libido of Stevens and the pastor are in the same
deadly, if lyrical, focus here as in the novel. From the technical
point of view, the soft-takes, the use of filtered light, the blues and
blacks of the moonlight scenes effect this preservation.

Blue, in fact, seems to be a dominant "color" in the novel. But
the persistent lack of color—the pervasive chiaroscuro—is even
more dominant. Who painted the paintings? The question is in the
long run irrelevant. It is not one that bothers the viewer, really;
and as for the novel, Hébert is the master painter controlling all
the brushes. If one examines her pallette closely, one finds that in
the novel noncolor is more prevalent still than any color, the major
references being to black and white, with lots of gray and several
shades of brown. There are at least two hundred and five instances
of words suggesting noncolor, plus phrases such as *déteint, non
plus vert*, etc. And if blue describes the eyes of these Anglo-
Saxons, it is also used as a modifier of black. One should note also
that blue can have a strong negative force in the novel: Olivia's
brothers' eyes are blue to the point of being white (or blank), or
dirty gray (*Fous*, 100); and it is no accident that Patrick, one of
Olivia's jail-keeper brothers, has a blue beard! The color green, on
the other hand, being associated with life, appears infrequently in
the novel. It too can have a negative concept: the green teeth of
McKenna, for example. In the novel the green of life is often lost;
not only in the "compact blue" of the mountain in the distance,
but also when the algae are yellow, the pine trees are black.

Red would be the color of the truck in which Stevens dreams
of spiriting away his twin sisters and his brother. Similarly, Nora's
dream corrects the usual description of the sand as gray: in her
fantasy the sand is yellow. In this violent novel, red has a predominantly negative force, being associated with the spilling of
blood, with cheeks turned red or rosy with embarrassment, sexual
excitement, anger, or some other strong emotion. Red seldom has
a positive value, except in the case of Felicity's robe (which also
has hues of dark brown). Interestingly enough, three times red and
green are brought together.

The attention to these details of color and the fact that the
characters remember the vivid ones suggest at once their rarity
and also indicate the kinds of things one recalls, even though they
may have no intrinsic significance. Along this line, the significance
of the red hair of the pastor and Nora is not clear: does it mean
that they are nordic types? hot and temperamental? different from
the other people? Or is this, too, just one of those things one
notices? In any case, the significance or importance of the red hair

may have been lost on Simoneau, since Nora's hair in the film is not red.

Orange is, of course, noticeable as a key color in the murder sequences, for there is a harvest moon in the sky (and this is ironic, for there is no harvest!). The full moon, which seems like a ripe fruit (*Fous*, 134), does not last, however. At the time of the murders, it turns to white: milky white, in fact, and becomes metallic.

Because the grandmother is suppressed in the film, as is also Hotchkins, and as is also the reference to the calendar, strong colors — red, turquoise, yellow — when used positively, do not tend to be used in the film. Additionally, the colors of Anne Hébert's pallette are often modified or muted so as to attenuate their intensity, and prolong the feeling of colorlessness and drabness that dominates the novel.

Above all, the words black and white, frequently accompanied by the word gray, are often seen together, with the white dominating. This gives the novel a sense of the austerity that characterizes at least the external side of these people, and translates the dullness and sterility of their existence. It also underlines the theme of death so prevalent throughout the book. The word white appears in the first line of the novel and on the last page (white sea; white moon), the word black on the last page but one. The clothes of the clergyman in particular — the black suit and the white collar — are emphasized, of course (*Fous*, 15; 38; 44; 53).[43] (And it is interesting

Les Fous de Bassan. Photograph by Claudel Huot. (Courtesy Coll. Cinémathèque Québécoise.)

to note that similar clothing is described in the case of Elisabeth's aunts in *Kamouraska*, as well as the nuns in *Les Enfants du sabbat*.)

Of course, the gannets consolidate the black and white symbolism (austerity, weakness, death), being mostly pure white, with their blue-black eyes and their bar of yellow by the beak providing the contrast.

Now, this color code is incontrovertibly observed in the film. The dominant tones are dark blues and blacks with streaks and spots of white. Throughout the film one sees burnt or brownish oranges, siennas, dark blues, blue shadows against lighter blues, perhaps, the light blues of sea and sky — though at times the sea is even yellow and dark orange. Because the grandmother, Felicity, is suppressed in the film, we see little green. There is only an occasional splash of green grass; a very dark green bottle holds the liquor that Stevens and Olivia's brother drink. Dark browns of the clothes and brownish orange of the skin carry out the prescriptions of the novel. And the clothing descriptions are also quite carefully observed. We have Stevens in his dark brown jacket, his dark brown felt hat, his dark trousers .... Irene in a black-and-white dress and hat at church, but in the famous beige dress at the festival. We have the minister in black and white; the men on Sunday in their black and white. Olivia's father and brothers wear the white shirts she irons for them. We have Nora in the "faded blue dress." As in the novel, the houses are gray, without paint, as is also the church. Olivia wears the crocheted white hat, though Nora should have one also. The faces turn stark white in the lightning. And the silvery light of the full moon is exploited, together with the pure whites of the birds. If there is one noticeable deviation, Maureen is too blond, and the green shades at her windows are not apparent in the film. There is, however, a green drape at her bedroom "door." In fact, green is hardly to be seen in the film, except in a scene or two where grass is shown; and there is only one instance of red, I believe: this is the red of the fire in the stove that warms Stevens-old as he rummages among the paintings and reminisces. Here there are also touches of yellow as the light hits the stained glass windows; an irony to say the least.

Leaving aside color, what can be said of the role of desire in the novel and in the film? It seems to me unjustified to argue (as do Hébert, Green, and Slott)[44] that Stevens Brown is "transformed" in the film from an agent of destruction to an object of desire: the reverse seems more the case. But also, in fact, in the book the two little girls clearly feel desire, too, and this desire is primarily directed at Stevens Brown. (See *Fous*, 74 [Nora]; 216; 221–23

[Olivia].) We were never really talking exclusively about the rape and death of innocence, anyway; but of the looking and listening eye, of a power trip, of a society in which the males seek to dominate, oppress, imprison, and enslave the females. We were talking too, I believe, of the inappropriate socialization of these young girls, the one being over-protected, the other off in her dream-world, fantasizing over her Prince Charming, who would come in his shiny American car and spirit her away. (She cannot recognize the noonday devil — though at one point she proposes that Stevens may be the devil — in the film and also in the novel [*Fous*, 91; 130].) That the girls live in the realm of the fairy tale is clear: Olivia incarnates the story of Cinderella; Nora fantasizes the fortunes of Sleeping Beauty. From another point of view, although the cousins experience their own desire, their identifications with these legends cause their desire to be overlooked or else subsumed under that of the male (here, Stevens) for whom they project their passive and pitiful existential states, their innocence and seductiveness. Like Medusa to Perseus, so are they to Stevens: objects of his desire, perhaps, but also threats to the phallus, and thus to be conquered and then exterminated.[45]

The film's loss of the reference to grandmother Felicity is serious, as the critics contest.[46] Yet I do not think that the "counterpoint" between the male voices (called death by Green) and the female voices (called life) is lost. To say, as Green does, that the voice of Olivia de la haute-mer represents life is in itself a *contre-sens*, since at that juncture Olivia is dead. Moreover, there are female characters in the novel who are scarcely appealing or nurturing. Stevens's mother, Beatrice, for example, seems to hate him (*Fous*, 239) as much as his father does; they want to get rid of their children (give them to the minister, put them in institutions). Beatrice to Stevens is almost a witch, with icy hands, a polar womb, her breast a frozen fountain (*Fous*, 86–7). To Perceval she is also "glacée ... d'habitude" (*Fous*, 159). To him, too, she is almost a witch; and for that matter, so is her husband, as several characters recall (*Fous*, 84; 87; 114). But in the film, Beatrice is fused with Felicity, and therefore kinder, saying "tu es beau" to Stevens, and telling her husband not to beat Perceval, who has, symbolically, overturned a pail of milk (as he does in the novel). Thus, even though the grandmother is lost, Stevens's mother gains in the film, becoming fused with Felicity, and therefore kinder. In the film she is associated more or less with life, while in the novel she seems to me to be associated with cruelty and death. (It is true, however, that the film-Stevens remembers how cold his mother's hands were.) Irene in the novel seems to be associated more with death than life. She has never seemed alive, says Stevens; she is without color, without odor, without taste, as if stillborn, and corroborating this, Nora says: "she sleeps like a dead woman," i.e., all the time (*Fous*, 139). She is of course sterile, and because her husband is unhappy over this she commits suicide, thus choosing death over life, though some would argue she is driven to this. Pat and Pam are not associated with life; they are eccentric, dried-up old maids, given up by their parents to the will of the pastor. It seems that all the characters in the book (and not just the males) are associated with death, and that all are under the same Jansenistic fatality: *des éphémères*, as we read in the book (*Fous*, 98) — insects that last but a day.

One might add that certain male characters — Bob Allen and "Old Mic," or old Chum (to whom Stevens communicates his inmost thoughts) — have little to do with death, and also that in the film Bob Allen's part in the story has been substantially suppressed, while Old Mic seems to have been completely suppressed, even though they too might have been lamented because they provided "important *masculine* rapports." (My emphasis.) Yet inexplicably we have no regrets expressed by the various critics at *their* omission, or reduction. In any event, had Simoneau included Pat, Pam, Felicity, Bob Allen, "Old Mic," etc., such a proliferation of characters would have been extremely difficult for the viewer to follow.

In the end, the whole argument revolving around the novel-versus-film, male-voice-versus-female-voice issue, seems useless, since in reality it lies elsewhere. For the novel is in many respects a reconstruction, or deconstruction, of the myth of Demeter and Persephone, and of their association with Artemis, all violated by Hades and trivialized by Adonis.[47] And this mythic infrastructure may be what is most missing in the film. While in Christian terms Stevens is the Devil, identifiable by his dark brown felt hat, which almost always covers his face, and which gets lost (*Fous*, 213), by his laugh (*Fous*, 77), and by the fact that Nora sees him to be a pig,[48] Stevens-Satan-Hades-Adonis is also Charon, with his reconstructed "*barque*" in which he wants people to "leave" with him. Most significantly, he uses this "barque" to carry the dead girls out to sea. Thus, in the film, the scene where Stevens finds his "bark" in smitherines is less effective than it might have been, had the boat's profoundest symbolism somehow been conveyed.

The question, then, is whether the film has captured these mythic subtexts, for it is certain that it has surpassed the novel iconically or imagistically. The "cinematographic" nature of Hébert's novels is often pointed out; but Auerbach in his *Mimesis*[49] would argue that try though he or she might, the novelist cannot replicate the structure of film: one cannot achieve film's concentration of space and time. Film can capture spatio-temporal reference through a few pictures, pictures that in seconds can evoke a whole era, a whole country, a widely dispersed group of people. These effects can never be within the reach of the spoken or written word.

In the light of these mythic elements, let us return to the question of the male bonding between the two brothers, Stevens and Perceval, a bonding which, as we said, is perhaps underscored in the film. As demonstrated ealier, this closeness of the brothers was already present in the book. But the "positive" abduction of the brother (the reverse of the abduction of the girls) and the "fishing trip" that Stevens takes Perceval on in his bark are of mythic substance. Such a male and nostalgic activity is revisited by Lauzon in his *Night Zoo*. But, there as here, the bonding fails; there it is undermined by corrupted urban pursuits; here it is undermined by the father and ultimately by the abduction, rape, and murder that negate, indeed shatter any potential pastoral and piscatorial modes. For, although, as we saw, the embrace of brother by brother is the final "image" we have in both the book and the film, we feel that, as in *Night Zoo*, "il n'y a plus d'Amérique": great hunting and fishing expeditions by adventurous males are a thing of the past. Here the adventure is undertaken by a soon-to-be criminal rapist-murderer and his idiot brother. (Still, Perceval brings back a fish in the film, as in the novel, where Nora says that Perceval, Olivia, and she come out of the sea, "bearing fish" [*Fous*, 115].)

But that is not all. As regards the matter of bonding, both the novel and the film corroborate the view of the "real world" portrayed by Hélène Cixous in her *Sorties*.[50] Crime becomes the bonding agent for males, the noble, Promethean deed; sin is the attribute of females. And, with respect to this latter, in the novel the pastor, in an impressive *tour de force*, shifts the blame and accuses Nora of "sin." "Mon oncle Nicolas ... dit que je suis mauvaise ... que c'est par moi que le péché est entré à Griffin Creek [My uncle Nicolas ... says that I am bad ... that it is through me that sin came to Griffin Creek]" (*Fous*, 129). Thus, if the novel is "feminist" it is feminist by these inverse patterns of the world as it is and not as it should be, just as they are described by Cixous. We can add to this the notion that for Nicolas Jones, the son, and for Stevens, the grandson, Felicity is the phallic mother who has virtually incapacitated them. Stevens remembers that she has said

that "tous les hommes sont des cochons ... [all men are pigs]"
(*Fous*, 75); and both the pastor, who spies on his mother (*Fous*,
35; 38) and Stevens say that she has "always preferred girls [or: the
girls?]" (*Fous*, 37; 75). To claim, as some have, that in the novel
"woman's voice is privileged" is, then, to stray from the basic facts:
First of all, in the novel Stevens Brown and Perceval and the
Pastor have much more to say than any woman, both by written
and by oral word. In the novel what we have is a clash of views
among the chief speakers plus many other voices of undetermined
[sexual] identity who are choric representatives of the whole village.
All offer conflicting testimony à la *Rashomon*. Or, following
Randall, else these "voices" are filtered through Stevens — even,
perhaps, hallucinations of his. Hence, they become *his* representation of their testimony, and thus, in the long run, univocal. (Only
the reader, then, can "privilege" the woman's voice.) The layered
technique is common to Hébert.

Similarly, saying that Stevens Brown is an object of desire in the
film and not in the book is not valid; for this desirability too was
present in the book. For us he may not be an object of desire in
either setting; in the book he definitely is (or else perceives himself
to be) the object of the girl's desire. (*Fous*: Desire of Olivia, 80;
97; of Nora, 80−81; 90−91; 127; expressed by her, 124.) The
problem does not lie there, as some critics contend. Rather, it is
principally the telescoping if not the complete loss of the above-
mentioned mythic substructure of the novel that we miss in the
film. This loss comes from the reduction to the single point of
view and the suppression of the common grandmother as a focal
personality. By this I mean the failure to present scenes where she
might have been seen bathing with her granddaughters Nora and
Olivia; or an emphasis through some dialogue on her preference
for the female. (The grandmother does not have a voice of her
own in the novel.) But all the paraphernalia of myth, present in
the novel, are virtually scuttled: the concept of the women as sea-
creatures, Olivia's webfoot *as a sign of her otherworldliness* as well
as of her imperfection (cf. Oedipus). The voice of Olivia that
returns from the sea is the voice of the other world, the chthonic
side; she has left the bonded world, gone out to the high sea and
acquired what was missing — order and meaning — (as Joseph
Campbell expresses it[51]), and, ironically, returned as voice (not
eye). The feminist critics pretend that the sea is an instrument of
life; that the sea equals life. But here the sea and its storms seem
death-dealing, too, and wash death, its voices, its cadavers, to the
shore. All this seems lost in the film, though the fact that the

people's voices are drowned by sounds — the sounds of sea, wind, gannets, and other birds — is noticeable in the film. The suppression of the references to the grandmother, Felicity — references made in the novel by the pastor, Stevens, Perceval, and the maidens — is then the loss of the notion of the women as sea allies, allies of life-death cycles, as found in myth. Interestingly enough, Felicity is referred to once in the novel as "une *reine offensée* [an offended queen]" (*Fous*, 34); and elsewhere as "*une méduse géante* [a giant Medusa]" (*Fous*, 35) — probably with no reference to the meditations of Cixous on that subject. The film has not captured any of this mythic subtext, even though, as I stated above, it has surpassed the novel iconically and/or imagistically.

I have spoken of the characters in this film (also in the novel) as *marginaux* of the Québec society, and marginal they are in many respects. As a community, they represent the descendants of fugitive American loyalists (cf. George in *Kamouraska*); therefore, they are anglophone protestants (even though the story is told in French). One of the chief criticisms of the film was the fact that the director did not resolve the problem of the levels of language (Lever *Hist.* 1988, 329[52]). It is claimed that the two little cousins (not "sisters," as Lever says) speak with an accent that is so different from the rest of the family that all sense of reality disappears. Says Lever, the result is that the "viewer 'hangs up.'" But the linguistic situation is all pretend anyway: the fact is that all the characters in the film would in reality be speaking English to each other. It is, moreover, ironic that this film, so successful from a visual perspective, should have to "go down" over such a small point. And the girls in *Les Fous* ... are attending school, after all; Olivia even intends to become a school-teacher. And not only is this stated in the book, but it is clearly articulated in the film. In the scene where Maureen, Nora, and Olivia are making streamers for the festival, Olivia confides to Maureen the likelihood she will go to the "continent" next year to study, and may eventually become a "schoolmistress." But, to repeat, however much one wishes to criticize the various levels of French and the varying accents of the characters and actors, the issue is made irrelevant by the fact that in theory all of them are speaking English, anyway. The use of the French language is incorrect for the geographical-ethnic depiction, but necessary for the audience for whom the film has been made. (In film, so much about language is "pretend" and "simulation" that the whole issue could receive an entire book-length study. Here we only touch upon the subject at the most salient spots.)

Moreover, these people are not Latins; they are blue-eyed and blond, or red-headed, though Maureen is different, because she is not related to them; she has eyes of pale stone in a face of darker stone; she has dark hair. Nevertheless, all of them are immigrants — outsiders — and the degree to which they are related to one another suggests that they are inbred to the point, perhaps, that some are subnormal in mores, others in intellect. (But this portrayal of a microsociety in the film and in the novel is not unrelated to the macrosociety, as we shall see at a later point.)

The film-Stevens, like the novel-Stevens, an heir of this as-cendancy, had quarreled with his father and run away before his father's malediction could be hurled at him. Now, back from an America where he did not succeed, he looks down upon the community of Griffin Creek from a high hill: already his will to dominate and his voyeurism are clear. His hat shades his eyes, throwing a screen between him and the world; his man's boots could crush anything beneath them. (The hat, and the boots, symbols of his masculinity, are carefully portrayed in the film.) Voyeurism is, in fact, a trait of most of these protestant "elects" (*Fous*, 31). Arguably, the girls eye Stevens; but unequivocally, Stevens spies on the girls, as does the pastor. Here the statements of E. Ann Kaplan seem especially pertinent: "The difference between ... male voyeurism and the female form is striking. For the woman does not own the desire, even when she watches; her watching is to place responsibility for sexuality at yet one more remove, *to distance herself from sex*. The man, on the other hand, *owns the desire and the woman*, and gets pleasure from exchanging the woman, as in Lévi-Strauss's kinship system."[53] Stevens is in charge of all; he is focal and central both in the film and in the novel. The novel is not an example of *écriture féminine*, and to say that it is would be an instance of simplistic biological reductionism. And since Stevens is the focal preoccupation and object of desire of most of the principals (Maureen, Nora, Olivia, Perceval), Stevens's parents are, etiologically speaking, the troublemakers. It is not just Stevens who suggests this, but all major voices — whether filtered through him or not — agree. In the novel, these parents abuse Stevens and Perceval and reject the twins. In the film the abuse of the two brothers is evident; the twins, of course, have been omitted for purposes of clarity.

Perceval also spies on the girls while they are bathing (without their grandmother in the film — *Fous*, 129), as he does through the panes of the boathouse, on the minister and Nora, or the "homme noir-Nora," as he says in the film. He also spies through the panes

of Olivia's house (*Fous*, 174). He even thrusts his hands through
the glass and cuts them. But in the case of Perceval, the spying, so
well captured in the film, has to do with his marginality within this
marginal group: one is reminded of Guy, the retarded uncle of
Manon spying on Mme Viau-Vauchon in *Les Bons Débarras*.

Stevens's devilish nature is revealed, not only through his hat
(which the film-Perceval should not have been wearing), but, in
the film, through the treatment he gives to his cousin Maureen's
pregnant doe rabbit. The insertion of this cruel scene has been
viewed as gratuitous by some, who do not find its parallel in the
novel. Still, in the book he does say he kills and skins rabbits for
Maureen: "je tue et j'écorche ses lapins [I kill and skin her rabbits]"
(*Fous*, 69) — for her "civets," supposedly — as he "explains" to her
when she catches him killing the pregnant rabbit in the film. When
tired if not resentful of Maureen, the Stevens of the novel says:
"let her kill her own rabbits" (*Fous*, 157). (It is assumed he says
this; it could be other people, even Stevens's parents, saying this.)
More to the point, the abuse of animals, whether in the novel or
not, bespeaks his perverse nature, and forecasts his murderous
deeds. His sadism is clear in the book, and he thinks of fornicating
with Nora, who is both desirous and afraid of him: "She stops and
looks at me with eyes like a hare surprised by a hunter" (*Fous*, 90).
And Stevens has gutted fish for a living while "on the road" (*Fous*,
58). He speaks of "undressing" them (and women) to Bob Allen
and others in the film.

The rabbit scene in the film belongs in the cosmos of Hébert,
whether it figures in the novel or not. The "odor" of blood and
torn flesh seems to be in keeping with Hebertian tone, which varies
little from work to work. It tells us the hunt is on, the hunt for
defenseless foxes, guided by the pastor, no less! Other victims
include the *chevreuil*, or hind; the *orignal*, or moose; the salmon
(*Fous*, 40). Violence to animal life says that the pursuit and death
of the animal and the chase of Stevens and the pastor through the
taiga for the tender virgin are one and the same. This is the same
hunt that Hébert details in *Kamouraska* and again in *Les Fous de
Bassan*, and that Simoneau portrays. Additionally, the rabbit functions both in Hébert's story and in Simoneau's film as a threatened
fertility symbol, which the maidens are also. And they are symbols
also of sacrifice: in one part of the novel, Perceval may even eat
Nora, as if she were a (sacrificial) lamb (117). Similarly, when
Perceval hears Olivia's voice, he says it is cut off from her body
"as one cuts off the head of a fish" (*Fous*, 174). [In the film the

beheaded fish image occurs when Irene cuts the head off the fish she has been given for their supper "by Nora's father."]

In addition to Stevens, the pastor, the girls, and the twins in the novel all seem afflicted by some deficiency. But no doubt it is Perceval, whose name has a mystic charge (cf., the Perceval who sought the grail), who most bespeaks the tragic nature of this community and its inhabitants. Perceval is an *attardé*, played in the film by the brilliant young actor Lothaire Bluteau [now famous for his role as Jesus in *Jésus de Montréal*, and as Father LaForgue in *Black Robe*], in one of the most gripping performances in Québec film. In many respects, Perceval is an idiot savant (somewhat Dostoevskian at that), and he reminds us of another cinematic figure from Québec, the tragic autistic boy, Mario, in Beaudin's *Mario*. Perceval, too, has the bird's eye view, *the gannet's view*, from the hill. He too has an eye upon the girls, upon his brother Stevens, upon the village. It becomes clear that the "listening eye" I mentioned above is an important subtext of the novel, and it is this, I believe, that Simoneau has captured almost miraculously. For in the film, all the characters seem linked to the eye of this stunning bird. All look upon one another, indeed spy upon one another; and this *regard*, which is the major imagistic motif of the novel, present on every other page, is also the most fundamental characteristic of the film. If Stevens Brown is both a land and sea creature, so is the gannet. If the girls look upon Stevens with the interest of young adolescent females about to become women, their eyes are those of the seagoing gannet. If they are victims, so is the gannet, hunted almost to extinction by the inhabitants of the Gaspé and surrounding islands as a food supplement and as bait for codfish, but also for sport (as were so many of the waterbirds of the area).[54] A bird with dark blue, piercing eyes that seem to stare uncannily (like the pale blue eyes of Stevens), the gannet, or booby, moves over the ocean on air currents and nests in the cliffs, and thus it can be associated with both land and sea. And so can the girls, for Olivia is marine, since in the sea she, the web-footed duck/gannet, finds the mother-voice, the memory of warnings; Nora, on the other hand, claims to have been born in the sea and of the sea (*Fous*, 118). Yet both are clearly earthly creatures.

The close relationship of the birds to the characters[55] is carefully shown in the film by intercuts of these striking creatures. The technique operates almost like intertitles as used in silent films, explaining and clarifying the relationships of multiple human desires to the natural time and space in which they are lived. Similarly,

Hébert's insistent mention of Maureen's clock, as it ticks off time, and then stops at the moment of the girls' dark passion, is carefully portrayed by Simoneau. The film-Maureen sets the clock, winds it, stops it. But one might feel that in both cases the device is hackneyed, and in any event not in league with the visual and metaphorical use of the gannets. It is not an exaggeration to say that the gannets are among the principal players (or characters) of the film (though perhaps not of the novel). They are its "stars." They are also linked deeply on an anagogic level with Olivia. Not only does her web foot have a link to the concept of imperfection (Oedipus), but to the gannet (or Morus [Greek for foolish or silly] bassanus), which has a webbed foot, making it thus the "perfect" swimming foot, with its four toes webbed like the pelican's. Olivia, too, is linked to the sea, so that though dead, her voice comes back from the sea. (An irony that silenced woman gains voice when dead!)

Other birds are present too, both in novel and film — blackbirds, seagulls, maybe kittywakes, and wild geese (even a swan in Nora's dream). They represent, among other things, the tearing and hatred of these people one for another: the deafening clamor and the tearing of the claws and the beaks is quite present in many places (*Fous*, 166, 206, 207, 230). It is made clear as a sign early in the film as Stevens rummages through the paintings and the birds fly up. The tearing at flesh out of cruelty or out of defense is allied here (as in the name Griffin Creek): the novel-Stevens does not forget Olivia's nails (*ongles*) tearing at his flesh as he murders her (*Fous*, 248). In the scenes where the birds seem especially thick we are reminded momentarily of the *volées* in Hitchcock's *Birds*.

But until we have discussed the festival (the village dance) we have not quite completed our analysis of the mythic content of both film and novel. Reverend Nicolas Jones molests, perhaps rapes, Nora — first mother, Eve (*Fous*, 116; 118) — while the village festival, occurring in late summer, is in full course, mad violins playing, and people dancing with one another. The festival in the film, a harvest festival (in late August, or early September) is the centerpiece, the turning point: Stevens's appearance turns the dance to slow motion; the long flashback becomes, as well, a flashforward, the whole accompanied by the slow-motion reaction of the onlookers. The old and the young Stevens are fused, as he calls all the villagers "hypocrites" and urges Olivia to leave with him; if not, she too is a "hypocrite." As he departs in anger, the wind breathes the names of the maidens: "Olivia," it sighs, then

"Nora" it cries. (And the viewer has a sense of mystery and fore-boding at this moment.) The wind is Stevens's undoing. He cannot stand its disruption, its salt breath. And he lives out his father's proverb pertaining to sterility: "Sow the wind, reap the storm." Yet he also identifies with the wind: "On the shore, "j'étais fou et libre comme le vent ..." (*Fous*, 102). Perhaps the wind is only his excuse for his rage (*Fous*, 249); perhaps, though, he is the instrument of hereditary forces and the product of the isolation and hostility of the site. I do not mean thereby to enlist sympathy for him; but I am not sure the film-Stevens (or even the novel-Stevens) does not have a touch of the tragic in him, like the fallen angel, Lucifer.

At this festival, also, the minister's hypocrisy—he runs a close second to Gide's pastor in the *Symphonie pastorale*—is compounded by his peculiar connection with fertility myths. What is more, he is driven in part by his wife's sterility, or so he would have all believe. Stevens, the pied-piper, the magician-enchanter, perhaps a pederast—or pedophile—(*Fous*, 74) is complemented by the pastor, a subspecies of Stevens: *diable* and *diablotin*; Hades-Satan and his earthly priest. Ironically, the pastor's favorite Old Testament prophet is Malachi: and if you were to read the four chapters of this book, you would find that they have to do with purity and with marital fidelity, as well as with the last judgement, when the Eternal God will punish enchanters, adulterers, falsifiers, oppressors of widow and orphan, of foreigner or stranger. Is he not all of these?

Still, the minister does more than embody hypocrisy; we perceive, especially in the film, the irony of the religion he preaches, and that some of the villagers attempt to live. The church itself is at times nothing but a painted set, as is clear from at least one scene in the film. This stimulates in us the subconscious awareness that the building portrayed in the background (seemingly a set) is the static and iconic representation of a former political and religious center of community, now largely crumbling, or dysfunctional. And in one splendid scene in the film the minister stands outside the great church doors, which he then closes. His decision seems to be taken in that wordless gesture. As for the parishioners, "Praise to the Lord," they sing; as he tells them to seek first the kingdom of God (Matthew), and warns them of the Devil; and, most painful of all, Olivia hums the sweetest of protestant hymns, "Fairest Lord Jesus," as she irons. But where is this Lord when Stevens-Death-the-Nethergod comes to claim her? What the film may lose in myth it often gains in auditory and visual irony.

Simoneau's highlighting of the gannet underlines the links of the women to the sea, and stresses the notion of gaze, all important in the book. (As the pastor says of Stevens: "His piercing eyes gaze at sea and shore like the black eye of the gannet aimed at the surface and depth of the water, spying through the waves on everything that trembles with life, that promises a feast" *Fous*, 42; tr., *Shadow*, 29). The gannet, then, becomes an iconic vehicle for sea and even for that which is associated with land and sea alike, for the wings of desire, for the gaze, for the host or victim (cf. the rabbit), for innocence, for that which is high-perched and aloof, for that which is webfooted, and so forth. The intercuts of the gannet in scenes involving Olivia and Stevens, in scenes involving Perceval, and so forth, all translate this symbolic use of the bird. And from this perspective, the film version of the suicide of Irene (the minister's wife), in which she throws herself off a high cliff — after realizing her husband's seduction of his niece, little Nora — is like the dive of the water bird downward, though it is true, of course, that in the novel she dies by rope, a constant component of Hébert's imagery.[56] Nor are the howl of the wind or cry of these birds to be forgotten: they may be referenced in the novel; in the film they are auditory and visual realities. Finally, we should note that just as the earth lies barren and the houses of these mad people[57] stand deserted at the end, so also the nests of these "fous" are empty. No more will they brood or reproduce on these cliffs (*Fous*, 232); for no more can life find issue here: the barren womb of Irene predicted it.

However much the film may deviate from the novel (and I hope to have shown that most of these seeming deviations have some basis in the novel), *Les Fous de Bassan* is one of the most beautiful films, visually speaking, ever to have come out of Québec. The use of the Morus bassanus as a symbol of the "wings of desire" gave the film an iconography only hinted at in the title and in certain passages of the novel describing the cry of the birds and their plumage. Similarly, the use of the cliff as an instrument of Irene's suicide gave to the film a visual impact more startling and more dramatic than could have been effected through hanging. (It is true, as I said above, that Hébert's cord imagery, which haunts her every work, was thereby lost.) But let it be said once and for all, where the northern gannet played an almost imperceptible role in this tragedy as depicted in the novel, its presence in the film provides the perfect montage for the action that unfolds in this remote Gaspé village inhabited by the descendants of anglophone loyalists: a village whose name is not so imaginary as some would pretend. Called Griffin Creek, *l'enfer* (*Fous*, 243), both in the novel and in the film the name reminds us of the kind of clawing (Fr. "griffes") we observe in the relationships of these strange people (e.g., Olivia, who would like to give a *coup de griffe* to her cousin Nora [*Fous*, 219]; to claw her [*Fous*, "*la griffer*," 222], or the twin sisters who have scratched [*ont griffonné*] "*Eté 1936*" on the walls [*Fous*, 48]). It also suggests a place settled by anglophones and even a real location — probably not in view of Percé, as in the film — a place called Anse au Griffon.[58] But, again, the use of Percé not only afforded majestic perspectives, but also provided establishing shots (just as the Eiffel Tower would for Paris). Most viewers, seeing Percé, would know immediately that the action is taking place in Gaspésie. (And the [social] desolation of the site is characterized in the still from the film used in Abel.[59] But the long traveling shot later on in the movie that intends to show the bucolic nature of the fishermen's lives near Percé, as they smoke their pipes, sort their fish, mend their nets, stack the dry cod, etc., is one of the least fortunate moments in the film; it smacks of nostalgic and touristic documentary. And if its purpose is to contrast this peaceful interlude with the tempest coming out of the sea, the wind, and Stevens — all being one — I am not convinced that this is successfully conveyed.

While the strong rhythms and the preponderance of fricatives (f and v) and plosives (p and b) present in Hébert's vocabulary (*Fous*, especially 96–107; 124) and in the very names of the *fous* (Stevens Brown; Patrick; Perceval; Olivia; Felicity) are for the most part lost, the atmosphere of the novel is, I think, preserved. The introduction of several voice-overs for the purpose of capturing the book's breath, or "breadth," would have been as confusing as to have introduced every minor character etched by Hébert. And we must ask what Dansereau would have given us for the "chapter" in which Olivia's voice comes back from the high sea. Would we have had waves pounding on the shore and a woman's voice, over, reciting the pun-ridden text of the novel? This prospect sounds as visually exciting as a talking head on the television. Not a mistake Simoneau would make. For what this film lacks in mythos, or in depth, or breadth — if it does (and François Bilodeau claims it does[60]) — it makes up for in visual impact and in the contrast of the natural beauty of the scene with the sometimes sordid behavior of the characters and with the pain experienced by the contorted psyches of the characters, who are Hebertian to a fault. It is little wonder that the film took an award for its photography; other aspects of the film should have fared better than they did.

Yet another dimension of the film that no novel could attain is Simoneau's splendid auditory effects. Some of these were described in the book — the wind, the sound of birds. But description of sight and sound do not replace the "actual" experience afforded by film, and this film in particular gives us a wide range of both sights and sounds. We have, then, the sound of the birds' wings flapping as they fly up on the air currents. We have the shrill violin music that persists throughout, sometimes simultaneously heard with the cry — the cawing — of the birds. We have the clear ticking and chiming of Maureen's clock, telling us something will happen in time, the church organ and the singing of familiar protestant hymns, the clucking of hens, the sound of the wind, the beating and splashing of waves against the beach, punctuating the end of the film, and accompanied by the plaintive violin music. These sounds and sights of the ocean at the end of the film, that continue as the credits are given, speak to the desolation of the deed: male bonding is far from our minds, it seems to me. Only the empty feeling of hopelessness, and sorrow too deep for tears, seem fitting responses. The universal thrust of the story gains its sublimest statement in these final moments when all the sights and sounds come together to say that the ocean — site of original chaos — is greater than these people. For none of them is there any longer any future. Shadows in the wind they are. One could almost hear Olivia speak from the high sea if one strained one's ear at this instant. But thank heavens Simoneau chose not to introduce a voice-over into this moment of immense blackness and finality. In a book, yes; in a film, no.

The fact remains that the two works are in many ways mutually exclusive, and Hébert's linguistic and structural prowess, with its debts to eminent classical literary figures such as Bossuet and to her own previous works, is to a great extent lost in the film. She, on the other hand, is not a filmmaker, and all her verbal descriptions cannot equal the memorable photography of the movie. (One picture is worth a thousand words, they say.) Along this line, criticisms of the "hastily-done scripting and editing" of the film (Lever *Hist.* 1988, 329) do not seem to me justified; the editing of the film is, in fact, one of its glories, in my opinion. Finally, the words of Esther Pelletier on the adaptation of a novel to film seem fitting here: "The novelistic system and the filmic system are erected in part on the basis of a network of relationships between the characters and the situations which evolve in the time and in the space of the diegesis (recital of facts; narration) that is represented. These elements are so intimately tied together that, just as the theory of systems tells us, as soon as one of them varies, it brings about a modification of the other elements and even of the entire system."[61] Given this kind of domino effect, it was inevitable, then, that Simoneau's film could not be "told" in precisely the same "language" as the novel.

And have you not noticed how "faithful" film versions of great books very often tend to be dull?

Monique Champagne has discussed the filming of *Kamouraska* and of *Les Fous de Bassan*, in both of which she had a role; she says that in both films the difficulty was to portray personal conflicts and the things responsible for them. Québec nature (the struggle against that nature) she says, is inherent in the novels of Anne Hébert. "In both films the world of Anne Hébert had unleashed the elements against us."[62] It is curious she should say this; for it is an absolute fact that we are seeing in both films the harshness of the climate, in the one the harshness of the cold winters, in the other the harshness of the rugged sea coast at a northeastern tip of the continent. (That *nordais*, of which Stevens speaks; the wind and the sea and the gulls and the gannets all about!) But it seems to me that, even more importantly, *Les Fous de Bassan* – though it has as its protagonists those marginal anglophone loyalists of whom I spoke at the beginning of this analysis – reveals the Québéco-Hébertian psyche and the particular nature of Québec society as much as did *Kamouraska*, this time in a contemporary setting.

And that is my most important point. While on the surface the novel *Les Fous de Bassan* paints a marginal society, nevertheless on the sociological level it is not just these puritans who are depicted. Essentially, it is the *québécois* society that is at stake. We saw many of the same structures in *Kamouraska*, for that matter. On the superficial level, there is reference to the material culture we associate with Québec at large: fishing, knitting, berrypicking, *tourtières*, fiddleheads (*Fous*, 180), *soupe à pois*, and the general store (most of which we have encountered many times in other films). On a more profound level the institutional incapacity of the police and the Church are portrayed in the novel. The film captured only the second of these, having bypassed the investigation into the crime. There is, in addition, implicit socio-cultural criticism of the condition of women – controlled and at labor in the novel (*Fous*, 75, 215, 220, and elsewhere). And although the men are also shown at work, the criticism regarding them concerns their domineering ways, their drinking and philandering. Some if not all of this was clearly caught in the film. The drudgery of the women's lives and the behavior of the men are also depicted in *Kamouraska*, film and novel, where the mainstream *québécois* culture is portrayed.

On the deepest level, I believe that the fatality under which these people lived in the novel version was caught by Simoneau. Most of them were living in time: they had plans for September 1; but living time stopped at 7:30, 31 August 1936. Since that time all are dead; or all are living dead (*Fous*, 162). Olivia's disembodied voice is timeless, and yet caught in time. All characters of the village now have become "like green and blue birds in a cage covered up abruptly by a black cloth" (171). Simoneau alludes to the clock; but he does not belabor the point. And he caught the lunacy of the people, under the spell of the moon. Simoneau may have played down the supernatural elements of the novel, and submerged the mythopoesis and the symbolic potential inherent in the figure of the grandmother, but he replaced them with very real psychological tensions. He retained the dominant symbols drawn from nature. He even expanded upon them, and brought out their true power. He indisputably preserved the color, the tone, the feel, the social ills of this society as portrayed in the novel, and he did so coherently, but in the grammar of film, which is not the one of fiction.

Besides, for all that, the novel *Les Fous de Bassan* cannot be said to equal the complexities of *Kamouraska*, which complexities were also lost in the film — partially through a confusion brought about by the very effort to retain them. (On the other hand, *Le Premier Jardin* is a novel that represents Hébert at her worst. May it never be brought to film!) It may be of some interest to point out here that Hébert has recently published two more plays, *La Cage* and *L'Ile de la Demoiselle* (Paris: Seuil, 1990) which join a much earlier set of dramas (*Le Temps sauvage*, etc.). These latest plays are founded on the legend, or history, of Québec and deal with "a theater of revealed interiority." This would hardly be filmable, if indeed it is even tellable. Should some unfortunate *cinéaste* undertake to bring these plays to the screen, heaven help him or her, lest we see more disagreements between author and filmmaker than ever before.

Finally, the applications of cinema to fiction are a long-standing technique of Anne Hébert, at which she succeeds less well than France Daigle (*Film d'amour et de dépendance: Chef d'oeuvre obscur*). The applications of fiction to cinema are, on the other hand, not the *métier* of Anne Hébert, and are best left to those who fully understand the exigencies of this medium.

And is it not true that, in the long run, if we depart from the precept that the literary product is inviolable, we will never have much of a film? The one works with words, the other with images (as Simoneau himself says). And each must be taken, it seems to me, on its own terms. Above all, it is a travesty to say that when a film is condemned for being false to the essence of the novel — which *Les Fous* ... is seemingly not — one can at least praise it for increasing the novel's readership.[63] Such a claim suggests a hierarchy of values wherein cinema is the lesser medium, if not indeed the loser. I do not think Simoneau intended, in making *Les Fous* ..., to stimulate the literary public to return to the "text."

LE SOURD DANS LA VILLE (OR, *DEAF TO THE CITY*) (1987; d. Mireille Dansereau)

Now, if, as we saw above, Mireille Dansereau did not have an opportunity to try her luck at the "voices" in *Les Fous de Bassan*, she did, on the other hand, direct the highly successful filming of Marie-Claire Blais's *Le Sourd dans la ville*, an evocation of a universe where the clash between life and death, between innocence and evil is as much under scrutiny as in the novel and film *Les Fous* .... And, while in Chapter 3 I dealt with her *Vie rêvée*, *Deaf to the City* is an excellent example of fiction turned into film.

Florence, a sophisticated woman, married to Doctor Gray and living with him in a luxurious apartment, decides to leave him. She does not know where she will go nor exactly why she is leaving, although certainly to escape her memories of the past. She winds up at the "Hôtel des Voyageurs," and, worn thin, she moves in to take a rest, not knowing if it is for a short while or forever. There she meets and makes love with Charlie, as well as meeting the adolescent Mike, afflicted with a brain tumor, but uncannily able to see into the mental and physical sufferings of others. She also comes to know Gloria, Mike's mother, a stripper dying of cancer and the widow of a gangster, as well as the proprietor of the hotel. In the end, Florence and Mike become bosom friends, for she is looking for an escape, a final refuge, even unto death, while he, intent upon overcoming his pain and illness, is determined to live.

The film admirably captures the atmosphere of the novel, with its theme of eros and thanatos, of life and death in violent conflict. It also captures the portrayal of the society (one of Blais's constants) through such offbeat characters as a dancer (topless) and a bandit, a woman professor, a high society lady, and so forth. A ship of fools. All of them are more than mere automatons, however; we see to the bottom of their souls. All in all, it seems fitting that this outstanding woman director should have brought to the screen one of Blais's most famous novels, one that runs a close second to her masterpiece, now a classic of *québécois* literature, *Une Saison dans la vie d'Emmanuel*, which, incidentally, was made into a film by Claude Weisz under the title *Emmanuel*.[64] Of *Le Sourd dans la ville*, Gérard Grugeau wrote: "... un beau film aux multiples résonances poétiques, qui se nourrit du sentiment tragique de l'existence humaine. L'amour et la mort, l'art et la vie y forment un théâtre d'ombres et de lumières où se débat une humanité en proie au vertige [... a beautiful film with multiple poetic resonances, which draws upon the tragic sense of human existence. Love and death, art and life become, in this film, a theater of shadows and lights in which the human beings, preyed upon by their vertigo, are locked in combat]."[65]

Obviously, some of the stylistic characteristics of the book could not very well be replicated in a visual form. The most notable of these is the fact that the book is written as an inner monologue, made up of one long paragraph. But the images of death found in the book (cat pursued by boys, Hiroshima, Nazi death camps, gangsters gunning each other down, Mike wasting away, Florence shooting herself, an old dog destroyed by its old master) can be rendered, as also the life forces (Mike's mother Gloria, art transcending death by confronting it, Judith Lange—l'ange—an angelic presence, the young history professor who sees, suffers, and bears witness). As with the novel, so with the film: human identity unites victim and torturer through mythic truth (rather than through Christianity).

LES PLOUFFE (TV MINISERIES AND FILM) (1981; d. Gilles Carle)

In bringing Roger Lemelin's *Les Plouffe* to the screen, Denis Héroux[66] as producer introduced a formula for the treatment of "great works of literature," which was followed by the making of several other works, including *Maria Chapdelaine*, *Bonheur d'occasion*, and *Le Matou*. It would also be used for the filming of *Le Crime d'Ovide Plouffe*. This formula involved the creation of a full-length film for the movie theaters and a six-hour series for television, with financial collaboration—amounting to somewhat more than six million dollars—of IQC (Institut Québécois du Cinéma), SDICC (Société du Développement de l'Industrie cinématographique canadienne or Téléfilm Canada), Radio-Canada, Famous Players, and private investors. Gille Carle's *Crime d'Ovide Plouffe* followed this pattern. (The two last episodes, out of a total of six, constitute the movie house version; these were directed by Denys Arcand.) Roger Lemelin received $250,000 for his *scénario* version (Lever *Hist.* 1988, 294–5). And Héroux spent $300,000 to advertise *Les Plouffe* in Paris, without attracting many spectators who were not already "les amis du Québec" (Lever *Hist.* 1988, 375).

Most importantly, however, Lever contends (*Hist.* 1988, 327) that, with the exception of *Les Plouffe* — which is imbued with the style of Gilles Carle — none of these film adaptations added a thing to the original works, unless it might be their diffusion to a wider public. But Carle's film was a critical success. Some of this may be attributed to the nature of the original book version, which provided scenes of life in pre–World War II Québec. All those older values and traditions were present and come through in the film: the power of the Church and the provincial government over the lives of the people, their dislike of the English, etc. Like some of the films we examined in Chapter 2, and even earlier in this chapter, the whole saga of *Les Plouffe*, both in novel and in the various film versions, represents a search for the past, in this case often the urban past (of Québec City). This it has in common with *Bonheur d'occasion* (for Montréal). And if these films were not based on classics of Québec literature, we could as well have spoken of them in the context of a nostalgic "search for roots." *Les Plouffe*, a reconstruction of the society of the times, deemed more effective than Carle's similar attempt in *Maria Chapdelaine*, seems to have profited from the hand of the original author in the creation of a script; nonetheless the episodic nature of the originals comes through in both *Les Plouffe* and *Le Crime d'Ovide Plouffe*.

Historically, the self-taught Roger Lemelin wrote one of the first *québécois* works having close observation of the society as its foundation. This was *Au pied de la pente douce* (1944). It was a virulent satire that created something of a scandal. In 1948 he wrote its sequel, *Les Plouffe*. This work then went on to be enacted on the radio, where it was a favorite among French Canadians, who were very able to identify with the portrayal of life in the impoverished faubourgs of the working class (*les mulots*) and even the petit-bourgeois (*les soyeux*) of Québec City during the great depression. The author's depiction of the mores of these people through these episodic novels (for which Lemelin won a prize from the Académie Française in 1946) then came to be known by an even wider audience when he, Gilles Carle, and Denys Arcand brought this novel and its sequel, *Le Crime d'Ovide Plouffe*, first to the small screen and then to the big.[67]

There are, as I have said, several versions of *Les Plouffe*. There

is a four-hour version, which was the first to be shown, followed
shortly thereafter by a shorter version. There is also a two-hour
subtitled version. Then there is a six-hour version in French, also
dubbed in English (Pratley *TS* 1987, 132). I saw this work in a
Québec City theater in the shorter, French language — unsubtitled —
version in 1983. The dialogue, resting on the speech of the working
class Québécois, was at times rather difficult to understand. Thus,
the average American would be very much in need of subtitles, or
else a dubbed version, for full appreciation of either *Les Plouffe* or
Le Crime . . . .

LES PLOUFFE (OR *THE POLUFFE FAMILY*) (1981; d. Gilles Carle)

An evocation, as was the novel, of the working-class milieu
of Québec City in the 1930s and 1940s, *Les Plouffe* will give
the viewer a notion of society in the province before the Quiet
Revolution, although one should always bear in mind the specific
locus of the action, for the culture of Québec City is quite a different
thing from that of Montréal. (It is more insular; traditionally more
francophone; perhaps more conservative; and, physically speaking,
split between the upper [old] city — at the top of a steep mountain
slope — and the lower city, where the industry and the factories,
the railways, and the old post office are spread out along the
river.) If one drives around in certain sections of the lower city,

Les Plouffe. Photograph by Attila Dory. (Courtesy Coll. Cinémathèque Québécoise.)

near the river flats, one can almost imagine one is at the site of the novel/film. I recall the lower city in the 40s (a time when I first visited Québec and then even lived there), with its modest to poor living conditions. Not only did one see such conditions in the areas leading to Ste Anne de Beaupré, but also all along the river road below the Chateau Frontenac and the dock of the Lévis ferry, where now one finds elegant shops and charming restaurants. And these scenes, along with the respectable poverty of the family, the unwavering Catholicism of the strong woman Maman (Josephine) Plouffe, who nonetheless would have liked not to have to perform her marital duties so frequently, had not the priest threatened to withhold absolution, are very well transported from book to screen. (In *Le Crime* . . ., her husband Théophile being dead, she takes up smoking and would like to see some racy movies.) Present too are the ubiquitous Americans, who attempt to speak French with their terrible accents.

LE CRIME D'OVIDE PLOUFFE (OR, *THE CRIME OF OVIDE PLOUFFE*) (1984; d. Denys Arcand)

In this melodramatic episode in the life of the Plouffe family, Ovide is convicted of murder and sentenced to be hanged when his sensual wife Rita is killed in an airplane crash after the plane is blown up by his employer, Pacifique Berthet. Berthet, having installed himself with a pair of field glasses on a cliff overlooking Montmorency Falls, has spied on Rita as she makes love to Bob at a picnic. (It is a memorable scene to say the least!) "It hurts me to see you make love to someone else; I love you, too," Berthet tells her afterward, as he then tries to have Rita himself. When she spurns him, and calls him a cripple, he gets his revenge. He asks Ovide to get dynamite. The mysterious Frenchman Berthet—a watchmaker who had met Ovide in the hospital and then gone into business with him—makes a time bomb, hoping to collect his part of an insurance policy taken on Rita. He and other witnesses implicate poor Ovide, who tells his brother Napoléon that his "only crime was to have married Rita." "Everything depended on the credibility of Berthet, and the jury believed him."

But in the end Ovide is cleared, and Berthet, an ex-convict and a criminal who has been fencing jewelry and precious stones, and an unsavory, sexually frustrated type, whom the police have finally pinned through Interpol, is confronted. Berthet commits suicide with the remaining dynamite. Released, Ovide travels to France, where he gives lectures on the Montagnais.[68] There he is rejoined with Marie (the daughter of a singer hanged for her Nazi sympathies). He has always loved Marie, but has not touched her, because he was married — even though he has not loved Rita, and even though he has known she has cheated on him. (Earlier in the film he even spends an idyllic time with Marie up North, where he is selling gems, etc. to other jewelers. There they swing, fish for salmon, picnic on the shore; and in his dream he sees himself in Paris, spending a night in a chateau, making love. In that same dream, however, Rita shoots him. When he awakens he tells Marie: "I love you, but the fact that I'm married is holding me back.")

Pratley says of *Les Plouffe* that "in the last two hours, directed by Arcand and comprising the 'crime,' the story seems disconcerting in time, place, and plot, [but this] is explained by the fact that once again cinema audiences are suffering for the sake of television. This version is a two-hour segment of a six-hour miniseries, the cinema part being directed by Denys Arcand, the TV part by Gilles Carle, who directed the first *Les Plouffe*. These are enormously expensive and complicated undertakings with huge casts and period locations, involving private companies, the CBC, and the NFB, and which, in spite of shortcomings, are a tribute to the filmmaking capacities of Quebec province" (*TS* 1987, 151). Indeed, credits to the six-part series include International Cinema Corporation, Soc. Radio Canada; CBC, NFB, Filmax/Antenne 2, a part of Telefilm Canada [the government agency set up to develop the feature film industry]; the Institut Québécois du Cinéma, Famous Players; and Alcan.

In *Telerama* (January 1985) *Le Crime d'Ovide Plouffe* was summarized as follows: "The chronicle continues, this time concentrating on Ovide, the 'intellectual of the family.' Denys Arcand prefers strong images to long atmospheric sequences. There is a touch of Chabrol ... in this cruel story, told without any tenderness and even with a touch of lightness."[69]

And according to Pratley (*TS* 1987, 263), the story, set in Québec City in the 1950s, lacks the kind of social and historical documentation found in the novel. But this can be true only of the two-hour movie, directed by Arcand, since the first four hours of the TV miniseries, directed by Carle, are so rich in social, historical, and political references as to be almost overwhelming. Québec's blue flag with its white fleur-de-lys and white bars is just being made official during one of the episodes of the series, and one sees it everywhere: painted on barns, in the background at rallies, and so forth. Verbal reference is also made to it. Then, too, as in *Maria*

Chapdelaine, an old victrola, here playing 78 rpm's while Ovide discusses the new 33 rpm's with Marie, the Frenchwoman, serves to establish the time frame, as well as to show the longings of this self-educated man for "all things beautiful" — Poulenc, Sacha Guitry. Goethe's aesthetics.

Moreover, Carle brings in the backgroiund politics prevalent during the Duplessiste (and the Union nationale) régime. In fact, he shows Duplessis himself, seen here as a friend to Gideon Plouffe, who offers bribes of maple syrup to Duplessis's secretary, on whose desk one sees the flag of Québec. But Duplessis is also portrayed as a man who feels that the universities and the Church (esp. the Dominicans) are poltting against him. In the series, Carle uses actual newsreel footage when he deals with the Asbestos strikers; he depicts Monsignor Folbèche[70] offering high mass and a fund-raising rally in support of the strikers and shows him receiving Pelletier, Trudeau, and Jean Marchand, the latter of whom delivers an antiduplessiste speech from the pulpit, following the mass: this is broadcast to the *parvis*, in fact, where people stand listening, and Duplessis's antiriot police stand poised for action. Marchand declares himself a Catholic, nationalist, and francophone; but he also claims that the Asbestos mines are fighting injustices, and he calls for solidarity with the striking "brothers," regardless of the their religion. For this "hospitality" Monsignor Folbèche is banned to a small parish in the North Country, and will have to suffer, as Maman Plouffe puts it, from mosquitoes and black flies (cf. *Maria Chapdelaine*).

In the course of the series, snide cracks are taken at the "liberals" who, according to the arch-conservative Napoléon Plouffe, are as "dry as dust" — i.e., as he wishes his martinis to be. (The Plouffes are ardent supporters of Duplessis, but "times are changing.")

A host of other cultural allusions are included in the four hours Carle has provided: the saying of the rosary; the purchasing of a pew "for thirty years"; the gathering of the whole family for Sunday dinner (though now they are not so happy, as they speak of politics and the fact that Duplessis might lose); the love of movies, or *désir de cinéma* we have spoken of elsewhere, and also the Church's (Monsignor's) capitulation to the movies as having an educational potential.

While the French are brought to task through the characterization of the atheistic Berthet, the Americans are again ridiculed — as in *Les Plouffe* — this time in their contacts with Guillaume Plouffe, who has taken cover in the bush after having gone through terrible war experiences. Then, too, one should note the caricatural characterization of Ephrem Bélanger, suitor to the widow Manman (Joséphine) Plouffe and *commandant* of the Zouaves, "the glory of the French Canadian Catholics," whose uniform he wears so often that the Plouffes wonder if he wears it to bed.

Nor should one overlook the problem of alcoholism (one of the tools of colonialism), represented through the character of Tit-met. Nor the intentions of Berthet and Ovide to strike it rich (in true "American" style), by exploiting the Indians on the North Shore. They cynically set up headquarters (Bijouterie Ovide Plouffe) directly across from the Church.

And some of this is not without humor, as the scene in which Cécile is invited, along with the other "bowling girls," to see such silent pornos ("art films") as the *Mattress Rhumba*. Equally funny is the recessional from a funeral in which the poorly made six-handled coffin provided by Gideon begins to disintegrate. As the bottom begins to give way, first a bare foot of the corpse is seen, then a hand, and, as the pallbearers decide to make a run for it, the whole bottom of the coffin gives way and the corpse falls out on the church steps, its belly bloated, and in its undershorts, which have blue fleur-de-lys on a white background.

Perhaps most interesting is the constant portrayal of Maman Plouffe as the kind of strong ballast to the family we encounter in many other films and novels from Québec, including *Maria Chapdelaine* and *Bonheur d'occasion*, or *The Tin Flute*. Though in *Le Crime d'Ovide Plouffe* she has evolved enough to smoke and to want to see movies, she is the same woman she was in the earlier *Les Plouffe*: strong, enduring, unswerving in her conservative Catholicism. One of her sons remarks that times are changing, and that if Papa (Théophile Plouffe) were still alive she would not smoke, to which she retorts: "If Papa were alive I wouldn't <u>have</u> to smoke." And when, in the section directed by Arcand, Ovide Plouffe goes to his mother, she tells him how his father had had a mistress, and how she had in essence ignored this, in order to retain her position in the marriage and the family. She counsels him to forgive his wife Rita and adds that if they (Rita and Ovide) were both to go to confession it might help.

Such sacramental niceties as that are not at issue in *Laura Laur*, however. Indeed, here it is another world entirely.

LAURA LAUR (1989; d. Brigitte Sauriol)

Brigitte Sauriol's *scénario* and direction of Suzanne Jacob's *Laura Laur* produced a film that is at once confusing, because (like

Kamouraska) it relies too greatly upon the multiple flashbacks of
the book, and yet spellbinding in its dark and fatal atmosphere.
This is a story of cold sexuality and suicide that both in book form
and in film evoke the Hebertian cosmos.

The movie opens with a set that bespeaks the cold of winter. At
a racetrack our "heroine" picks up an old man (Gilles) and goes to
a bar with him; there they watch the nude dancers, whom Laura
likes, though her escort does not. As they leave, she gives him a
heavy kiss. He gets in the car with her; she drives wildly, comes
near an accident; he then takes over the wheel. They make a date
at a given auberge for six o'clock "next Saturday." She tells him
her name.

With some difficulty we realize that part of this story is being
told from the point of view of Laura's brother. We also come to
understand that Laura will not tell this "lover" anything about
herself and, through a flashback, that she is having considerable
trouble with her overly severe father.

Other scenes show the "lover" (Gilles) with his wife Agnès, who
is very unhappy; he tells her he needs her and always will. He
knows that Laura doesn't love him; he's fifty, after all, and she is
very young. In a scene between Laura and him, he calls her a
"salope." An overhead shot of them shows them lying on the bed;
he says over and over "tu n'existes pas," and starts to smother her.

He then proposes they go to the sea.

In a subsequent flashback, Laura's brother remembers when
Papa went to the hospital and Laura slept with Mama.

Next, Laura tells her "lover" that she can't go to the sea. He
asks her to promise she'll write or phone. She responds that she
cannot make promises she cannot keep.

In an abrupt shift of scene, Gilles is sparring at karate. He
relates his love afair to his sparring parther. He goes to get photos
of Laura, nude photos in fact, from Pascal the photographer, who
tells Gilles something of this mysterious woman. We learn that she
is suicidal. A flashback to a billiard scene shows her pulling a gun;
she wants to shoot herself, she wants to drown; Pascal saves her.
Says Pascal to Gilles, in a return to the present, "Vous ne la
connaissez pas [You don't really know her]."

Gilles meets his wife. He says to her, "I'm leaving," and she
replies, "Go! Laura will be somewhere (waiting for you)."

In a subsequent scene, Laura's brother is telling of his past to his
psychiatrist. Their father, we learn, was a surgeon. In a flashback,
narrated by the brother, we find that Laura had a miscarriage, or
an abortion. "The fetus was on the table. Was it the doctor's

baby?" "Au collège," says the brother, "tout le monde était au courant [At 'college' everybody was informed]" He continues, "As for me . . . I do not reproach her. I was ashamed."

The next scene shows Gilles among the prostitutes looking for Laura. Later we see him with Laura's picture on his pillow.

There is also a scene between Serge, Laura's brother, and his wife. She tells him that her friend Agnès's husband has come back to her and that it is a good thing not to spoil his life for a twenty-year old girl. (The suggestion is that they do not know the identity of Gilles's mistress.) In the next scene, Serge and his wife and Gilles and Agnès are dining. A discussion of Laura occurs. Outside there is a dreadful storm. In the next scene, which occurs in Gilles's imagination, he and Laura meet in the garden; the storm is ending. Next, Gilles goes into the room where Laura is in bed nude and on her stomach. He turns her over. She is dead. She has left a note saying, "Mon chéri. I will marry you some day." "That is all she has left."

Laura Laur was not a great novel; this is not a great film. Its contours are extremely blurred, its proposed study of a pathological case pretentious and not profound. Instead, we have mainstream "psychologization," resting upon such trite, soap-operatic themes as an unhappy love affair; sexual aberration; the problem of frigidity; marginality; suicidal preoccupations — indeed, the whole spectrum of psychosis and deviancy. But the music is excellent.

Laura Laur is a *québécois* film that deals in abnormal psychology, more than in political or social problems of the province. But even in that respect it does not come up to *Les Portes tournantes*, which for me represents a cornerstone film of paramount importance in its portrayal of individual, provincial and national psychology.

LES PORTES TOURNANTES (OR *REVOLVING DOORS*). (1988; d. Francis Mankiewicz)

Two stories of three or four generations are told in intertwining fashion: first, Céleste's through flashbacks stimulated by journals, tapes, and mementos, which are being read, listened to, and touched, intermittently, by her son Madrigal Blaudelle; then Madrigal's and that of his wife, Lauda, from whom he is separated, and of his son Antoine. Many of the characters are musicians, Antoine in particular; he is becoming a pianist under the tutelage of a European-born "professor."

In a voice-over we learn about Céleste. In flashbacks we learn of her family from Val d'Amour; of her mother, who cares for the traditionally large *québécois* family while Céleste practices on the piano—; and of Litwin's negotations. He comes looking for a musician to accompany the silent films. The father tells Céleste that Litwin wants her to play alone; she plays a composition of her own. Though "the work lacks imagination" he hires her. In another flashback Céleste is packing. Then mother and daughter say a tender and sad farewell. She drives off in Litwin's car with him at the wheel.

Again a voice-over and a flashback, this time to Céleste's arrival at the Royal Theater in Campbellton. A sign advertising a film with Mary Pickford is on display.[71] Litwin shows her to her attic room. Another voice-over, then another flashback. "I spent weeks learning my job. Cinema completely changed my life . . . . Evenings, I made dresses for myself, like those of the great stars. I knew everything about all of them . . . . . I read all the revues; I invented. It was as if every night I went to Hollywood."

Scenes from the life of Madrigal and Antoine intercut the flashbacks. New flashback. Céleste is dressed like a vamp. She crosses the street and walks toward the theater. A man [Pierre Blaudelle] drives up; he knows her. He asks to go in with her, "to get a better seat." She lets him go in with her, "even if he is rich!"

We next have a scene between Céleste and Litwin. Céleste: "You'll have to choose. Pay me more on Sunday, or I won't play today, and the theater is filling up." The people are pressing for the show—which is Greta Garbo in *Flesh and the Devil*. She sits Litwin out; he must agree. They go to the front of the theater. He introduces her and she takes the light, like a performer. Then she begins to play the piano and the old film comes on.

Next, Pierre Blaudelle invites her to a picnic in the country on Sunday. She speaks of her "career." "Every showing is a feast," she says. "Val d'Amour and Hollywood are the same thing in my head." Then, "Tu es comme le cinéma [i.e., silent]. You never say anything." Then, "There'll be a projection of a new film next week. If you want, I invite you."

Next comes the preview. Says Litwin to Céleste, "You don't need to play. Just watch." It is a sound film! Al Jolson sings "Mammy." [D. W. Griffith's 1923 *Mammy's Boy*—incomplete; *The Jazz Singer*, 1927.] Céleste comes unglued. Litwin gloats; Céleste is visibly shaken. There are tears in her eyes. Litwin laughs.

Now Antoine speaks to Madrigal of his plans to spend time with his French mother, Lauda.

Next a new flashback: a park, then a long traveling shot over an elegant interior with fine furniture. Céleste has married into the austere and wealthy Blaudelle family. Mother Blaudelle has ambitions for Céleste to be a concert pianist, and wants to arrange a program. Some Mozart; some Bach; "Some *beautiful* music."

Subsequently Céleste's depression increases. Pierre arrives in his car, asks the maid where she is. The maid indicates the river, and says that Céleste has been "like this" for quite some time (suicidal).

Next a benefit concert. Dowager Blaudelle announces Céleste Blaudelle, who will play some Chopin pieces. Céleste begins to play the Chopin—not too badly—but suddenly she stops in the middle of the piece. They all clap. She continues playing, but switches to "You don't kill the piano player." The people clap enthusiastically at her playing, but Mme Blaudelle is mortified.

Shortly thereafter, a pregnant Céleste is seen writing (her journal?) on the terrace. Pierre comes to say goodbye. "If it's a boy we'll name him Madrigal." She predicts he'll be a painter. The dialogue informs us that war is eminent, and that Pierre is a *volontaire*. The older Blaudelle—the patriarch—lays out the plans: He proposes that Céleste accompany Pierre while he and his wife care for the child; they want to get hold of the baby.

Next, Lauda is with Antoine; she asks him to come and live with her. But Antoine says of his father: "He can't stay alone. Someone has to care for him. He won't eat; he won't sleep. He lets himself die." In this scene we discover how Madrigal and Lauda met in Paris when he came there to study painting. Little by little he fell into his silences. "He laughed no more; he talked no more. He hid behind his paintings, as if they were a wall. When I got behind that wall I discovered a fragile, timid man, desperately looking for his mother. I realized that there were two of you who didn't talk: he who had stopped and you who hadn't started."

A fade-in and a flashback to a married Céleste holding her baby, Madrigal, as Pierre and M. and Mme Blaudelle stand with her at the train station. Simone Blaudelle takes the baby and the old stuffed animal; the baby cries plaintively. Céleste and Pierre get on the train, and are off to military camp. A voice-over of Céleste with the baby crying in the background narrates the tale: "Pierre went to the front and died six months later. 'J'ai fui: le camp, la guerre, le clan Blaudelle' [I fled: the camp, the war, and the Blaudelle clan]."

Now Antoine is on a train, an older man beside him. He shows the man (a stranger) Céleste's photograph. "It's my grandmother. I'm going to see her." An English-speaking conductor appears.

Les Portes tournantes. (Courtesy Coll. Cinémathèque Québécoise.)

Antoine explains to him that he is going to New York. When the conductor asks whether it is for business or pleasure, the stranger, as if to conspire with Antoine, answers, "Pleasure."

Meanwhile, Madrigal finds that Antoine is missing. He makes a phone call to Lauda, who tells him Antoine is not with her, and says she'll come right over.

In the depot, Antoine and the stranger separate; Antoine goes through the revolving doors as a woman who looks like Céleste goes in and he goes out. He thinks he recognizes her; he looks at an old flyer. A man sees him with the flyer; he seems to know Céleste, and without speaking he gestures to Antoine to follow him.

Meanwhile, Lauda arrives at Madrigal's. She tells Madrigal how Antoine thinks about Céleste all the time. Perhaps he has gone to New York?

The scene shifts to New York. John Devil, Céleste's black lover and "boss," is playing jazz on the violin, while Céleste accompanies him on the piano. She has greatly aged. John Devil presents her to the crowd (as Litwin had long ago). Antoine appears in the background with the man from the street who had shown him the way. He walks over to Céleste. Not a word is uttered in this last scene. Céleste touches the boy tenderly on the cheek, as if she were blind and seeking to come to know him.

The film ends here. The meaning of *Les Portes tournantes* appears
to be that what goes round must come round. We assume, optimis-
tically, that there has been a reunification of all the scattered
elements of the family by the film's ending. The embrace of the
desolate, even degraded, and extremely lonely grandmother and of
her grandson Antoine, a lonely young boy, seems to suggest the
probable return of Céleste to Québec. And the separated couple
(Madrigal and Lauda) seems to be on the verge of reuniting,
through the mutual fear that the two experience over the disappearance of their son.

Weinmann's chapter on this film is particularly unsatisfactory
and confusing. He wants to tell us that Jacques Savoie's book is
greatly superior to the script he wrote for the film. But it is hard to
separate Weinmann's references to the film from those having to
do with the book. If one has not seen the film, one thinks that it
ends with John Devil—the Devil—disappearing out of the life of
the star-struck Céleste through revolving doors. This is, however,
the book: no such scene occurs in the film. Indeed, Weinmann
points out that while the revolving doors are symbolic in the book
of unwelcome immigrants coming into Québec, and of the died-in-
the-wool Québécois leaving it, the symbol is little utilized per se in
the film, where only the set of revolving doors in the New York
depot is to be seen. Besides, in a book that discusses film, it is
peculiar to have the final sentences of this chapter referring to the
book and not the film. For those who do not read French, it is
perhaps useful to summarize here Weinmann's thinking on this
film.

The title of *Les Portes tournantes* defines Québec as a narrow
pass and also as a place of indecision. The functioning of the doors
is seen to be a problem for the immigrant, who can get stuck in
them. The Québécois also use these revolving doors, of course; in
their case the object is to come out, but they too can get stuck
(Weinmann 1990, 123–6). The *portes tournantes* also symbolize
for Weinmann the problem of the individual artist's crisis: e.g., the
crisis of the musician who accompanies the silent film *vis-à-vis* the
advent of the talkies (1927). And the individual crisis reflects the
crisis of the collective and political *imaginaire* of the Québécois.
Céleste's family crisis reflects the crisis of confidence and conscience
of the postreferendum Québécois society. Weinmann goes on to
say that "The work shows the trauma of the adventure of the
talkies in the life of Céleste, who had been an *in-fans*, unspeakingly
playing the piano to the silent screen." The whole question of
speech and silence is here explored at length. Then, of the disap-

pearance of Papa John Devil (Uncle Sam), Céleste's black American lover and employer at the end of the work, Weinmann says: "Le Québec n'a plus besoin de ces fantômes pour prouver son existence .... Il est, existe. Jeune, très jeune, sera-t-il un jour adulte? Oui, le jour où il aura chassé les fantômes du 'roman familial', une fois pour toutes. [Québec no longer needs such phantoms to prove its existence .... It exists. Young, very young, will it one day be adult? Yes, the day when it has driven out the phantoms of the 'roman familial' (i.e., the family novel, a concept taken from Freud) once and for all]." (Weinmann 1990, 137; my paraphrases and translations.)

But *lector caveat*! Weinmann's assessment refers to the book, and not the film. The upshot of Weinmann's discussion is that Savoie has betrayed his novel, in which the revolving doors mean the *entrance* into the culture, which for the immigrant is very difficult. Moreover, for Weinmann the central message of the book was the transmission of the culture from one generation to another: Three generations practice three kinds of art. (And art and culture are both narrow doors, through which only the few can enter.) But the doors also represent the site of exit for the Québécois themselves; this exit is also difficult. Weinmann supposes that the film does not depict these principles so well. He may be right; for I am not at all sure that the film dwells on the symbolism of the revolving doors to any degree. But the transmission of the culture from generation to generation; the expatriate status of Céleste; her preference for the world of dreams, silent film, and its stars over the real world of the talkies and her unhappy marriage; the potential assimilation of Céleste to Québec (and the Blaudelles to the rest of North America); the conflict between speech and silence, written and oral communication vs. music, etc. — all are certainly present in the film for the viewer who would find them.

One may say that many aspects of traditional *québécois* culture — though not the same ones found in *Les Portes tournantes* — are reflected in *The Sweater*. It is one of the few pieces of animation we will look at in this book.

THE SWEATER (OR, *LE CHANDAIL*) (1980; d. Sheldon Cohen)

Indeed, it would be no exaggeration to say that the most famous animated film of Québec is Sheldon Cohen's *The Sweater*, or *Le Chandail* (1980), a short work based on a Roch Carrier story. Part of the success of this film is explained by the fact that Carrier himself reads the story both in French and in English, in the two

Le Chandail. (Courtesy Office National du Film.)

versions; and the English narration is made especially charming by
Carrier's delightful accent.

While this animated film is one of the best known and most
winsome to come from the ONF, and stands on its own as a work
of art, the culture content, or cultural load, can be considered
heavy. The English-French conflict is shown and told humorously
(as in Carrier's "novel" *La Guerre, Yes Sir!*); here it is reflected in
his mother's dislike of the Eaton catalogue order form (there is too
much intimidating English); it is also seen in her fear of "offending"
Mr. Eaton by returning the Toronto Maple Leafs sweater that
arrives as a response to her letter (written in her fine schoolteacher's
hand). The subsumed status of the French Canadian in Canadian
society of the time is therefore not absent.

During the 40s, when he was a small boy growing up in the little
village of Ste-Justine (one thousand two hundred souls), two
events took primacy, Carrier says: hockey on Saturday night and
mass on Sunday. This rings true, for all of the inhabitants of the
town are involved in both pursuits, but the young boys in particular
are caught up in near worship of the "Culture Hero," Maurice
Richard, the hockey star. And all the adults are involved in the
"education" and moral upbringing of the young Carrier. Through
the film, therefore, we appreciate the disciplinary nature of his
Catholic education — the curate is at once the referee, the moral

and values guide, and the voice of authority. (Parental authority is pictured, as well.) He also doles out punishment. But I will not spoil the film by telling my reader how the humiliating situation in which Carrier finds himself — when he is forced to play hockey in his Maple Leafs sweater, instead of one showing the red white and blue of the Canadiens — is "resolved."

From a technical point of view, Sheldon Cohen has achieved a masterpiece: the curate, for example, looks enormous, as he stands over the boy and scolds him for his temper tantrum. (The curate is seen from the boy's point of view, looking up.) The round faces of the figures add to their general aura of "friendliness," though the curate's glasses make him look pretty stern. Their soft circular contours seem, moreover, to have something in common with the drawings of Caroline Leaf, who is among Québec's greatest animation artists.[72]

Before closing the door on this chapter, I would like to point out that the plays of one of Québec's most celebrated playwrights — Michel Tremblay (*Les Belles-Soeurs*; *A toi, pour toujours, ta Marie-Lou*, etc.) — have provided some of the characters in *Il était une fois dans l'est* (1973; d. André Bassard; screenplay by Tremblay and Bassard). The film shows the sordid and sometimes tragic night world of Montréal East. (See credits; see Pratley *TS* 1987, 215.) In 1976 Brassard coscripted his *Le Soleil se lève en retard* with Tremblay. And in 1989 Brassard published a book about Tremblay (*Les Trois Montréal de Michel Tremblay*), subsequently made into a rather average film.

And I would add, too, that in the wake of *Dances with Wolves*, *Black Robe*, and *Last of the Mohicans*, 1992 saw the appearance of a film version of one of Yves Thériault's most famous novels: *Agaguk, l'ombre du loup* or, in English, *Shadow of the Wolf* (1992; Jacques Dorfmann). Thériault, who figures among Québec's most prolific authors, has devoted most of his novels to the evocation of the Canadian North. This story, set in 1935, concerns the conflict between Agaguk and his despotic shaman father Kroomak, chief of an Inuit band (the Inuk). Agaguk flees the camp, taking with him the loquacious Igiyook, who nurses him back to life after he is seriously wounded by a white wolf — as has been predicted. Indispensable to the plot is Agaguk's clash with a man named Brown, who has exploited the "Eskimos" with unbridled sale of alcohol. When Agaguk kills Brown over ownership of a polarbear skin, the RCMP begin an inquest, headed by Henderson. Kroomak, however, kills Henderson, and orders him cut into five pieces, to be buried in five different places. Now Henderson's disappearance becomes the problem of a man named Scott, who, upon arriving in Kroomak's village confiscates all hunting gear until he gets a confession. Unexpectedly, Kroomak assumes blame not only for Henderson's death, but also for Brown's. He is arrested and taken away on a plane, from which he falls, turning into an eagle on his descent.

Janick Beaulieu finds *Agaguk* to be carefully researched (kitchen and hunting utensils; costumes; igloo building; chants; whale hunt) and beautifully photographed (dawn; sunsets; snow; the aurora borealis). In particular, he finds that the film is less psychologically oriented than the novel and more oriented toward the magico-religious (shamanic) practices of these people; he does not view this as a betrayal of the novel, however, but rather as "an anthropological explanation which sits well with the mentality of today's viewers."[73] However, he notes some miscasting and other flaws that we will pass over here.

Beaulieu's appreciation is fundamentally correct: the film seems almost a piece of documentarian ethnocinematography. It is, on the other hand, full of violence and action, and the final scene where the father falls from the plane and is transformed into an eagle is not only quite mythic but seems absent from the novel. I might add that *TV Guide*'s dismal appreciation of this film,[74] in which it is stated that we have in *Agaguk* an "Eskimo tribal soap opera," seems quite unjustified; and surely anyone who sees in it a comparison with *Dances with Wolves* speaks from what little he or she knows about the Inuit, about wolves, about Thériault, and all the rest.

Conclusion to Chapter 4

The foregoing essay has had as an essential discourse the distinctions between *res pictura* and *écriture*. It is a question not only of common sense but of ethical criticism that one bear in mind that film works by images, and literature — inescapably — by words. But what makes the productions of the seventh art even more complex is that they are (even when made through an *auteur*) team-produced; and, moreover, they draw on virtually all the other arts. Dialogue, for example, is generally important to cinema, and, in spite of what I have just asserted, can in some films become an even more dominant factor than image (as, for example, in *My Dinner with André*). Music contributes to the ensemble, too. Sometimes certain frames of a film will remind us by their composition and color of a Vermeer or a Matisse. Structure, sculpture, time, tone, space — all these figure into the film as well. (Shall we say that cinema cannot, however, be three-dimensional? It has tried!) Film by nature treats time differently from literature: it has a certain fixed duration not dependant on the viewer, while the novel has a fixed number of pages, whose reading length must vary according to the reader. And film can also move backward and forward visibly in a way that novel cannot. Simultaneity may be achieved in film, through split screen or superimposition of one image upon another. Though an author may strive for these effects through innovative stylistic devices, the question remains whether this can ever really be achieved: words cannot be superimposed upon one another and still be simultaneously assimilated. Similarly, the spatial dimensions of film are different from those of the novel. In cinema, objects and people move through (hypothetical) space, and theoretically cannot be "re-viewed." (Video however makes this possible.) This fact of motion is key, as the very word cinema implies. True motion cannot exist in the novel, as anyone knows. Yet the principle bears emphasizing here. Since everything is different, including the conditions of reception, it is perhaps fair to judge a film based on the novel only in terms of the story line.

Then, too, the transposition of told myth (story) into a dynamic, visual enactment is an aesthetic exercise that is very ancient: the plays of Sophocles, of Racine, or of Shakespeare do essentially the same thing that the *cinéaste* does when she or he brings a play or novel to the screen. It is easy to say one prefers Shakespeare to Belleforest; but seldom has film been said to surpass its source. Still, the process is of the same essence, and in most ages, people relate to the "story" more intimately when it is enacted. That the details'must be modified for the exigencies of the genre or medium ought not be lamented, if the tone, thrust, and message are not violated. For me, *Les Fous de Bassan* is an instance of enactment in which these criteria are met; it is also, for me, a film that surpasses the novel in many respects. *De gustibus* ...

Volker Schlondorf (in an interview excerpted before a TNT showing of *The Tin Drum*) makes the following observations regarding the issue at hand: First, he would prefer that the viewer receive the story "fresh," and he adds that "it is better not to compare the movie to the novel." Second, he believes that the movie "has to stand its own ground; it has to be a thing in itself." Third, he "supposes that the audience would be so much more receptive if they had never read the novel, or hopefully forgot about it." Schlondorf has been sharply criticized for his rendition of *The Handmaid's Tale*, a novel by Margaret Atwood. Perhaps I am wrong, but it seems to me that that movie, though not a good one, was as good as the novel, which was not so good as many thought.

On this note, I close this segment of my study, for I am digressing into questions of German film and anglophone Canadian literature, which are both somewhat removed from the central focus of my considerations, Québec and its portrait in cinema.

When all is said and done, the novel turned to film almost always represents the director's own metamorphosized "reading" of the written work; it images a kind of *superécriture*, it becomes a *super-orature-optature* presented to the viewer/listener — who is only a reader for possible subtitles or intertitles — on film, and not on paper. (Some critics and theoreticians have adopted the term *cinécriture*; others, holding that film is *écriture*, or text, seem to continue the "camera-stylo" formulation of Alexandre Astruc.) An entirely separate art, film is entirely different from, it is not, and it does not pretend to be *literature*; for in literature, one may go back and reread, while in film — not counting home video, of course — everything comes to the viewer in rapid succession.[75] Things cannot be too complex, too obscure, or one becomes either bored or lost. The reader of the novel who expects to see that novel packaged by the film in his or her own imagination ought to stay home and read the novel and leave the movie to us who are lovers of the sight of faces and motion, in other words film buffs. But the teacher of Québec literature may find a welcome complement to his or her presentations through these and other dramatized enactments of the stories the students have read. One may even invite one's students to discuss the values, the limitations, the "violations," the possible superiority of the film over the story. Contemporary students have grown up in an age of film and television; literature is made more alluring to most of them through an examination of the "film."[76]

5

Québec Film as a Mirror of Society:
The Couple; The Family;
Encounters with Death; Children

> Documentation . . . merely indicates a process. It is all history.
> It does not show all that is going on, or that has been going
> on. Nor does it indicate what will be going on. Processes will
> continue; the results, effects, names, and places will always be
> different.
> — Steven Dwoskin on Canadian film in *Film Is* . . . (104)

It is certainly no new thing to posit that film can be an effective
mirror of a society, and the *québécois* cinema is no exception to
that principle. Through film we may observe the broadest manifestations of a culture, and its minutest icons. These latter can
include the natural setting in which and through which the civilization
in question makes its livelihood and lives out its life (e.g., hot
desert with siroccos and blistering sands; seaside environments
with fishing industries, beaches and raging waters; long, hard, cold
wintry climates with deep snow and penetrating north winds; all
the flora and fauna connected with these settings, etc.). They can
also be material items that reflect the language and the values of a
given people. In the films we have examined up to this point many
of these issues have already arisen. And certainly most of those
films were in their way "mirrors of the Québec society." But they
were selected for some other salient characteristic, such as their
historic value, or their debt to the literature of the province.

In this chapter, we will study films that focus on the intimate life
of the Québécois, whose traditional view of the family as the
nucleus of the society is in a state of collapse. Modern life in North
America has impacted upon the older, more Catholic concept
of marriage as a sacrament and as a vehicle of procreation. In

229

most of the films we will be scrutinizing we find orphaned children, illegitimate children without fathers, single parents, substitute parents; we find couples without children, couples bent on pleasure, unhappy marriages, rifts between parents and children, and so forth. (It is obvious that, to some extent, family disruption and strife may not be any more prevalent in *québécois* society/family/ films than in other Western societies/films.) And one of the explanations for the presence of these patterns in film is that they make for a dramatic situation. Thus, we may find the semiorphaned or orphaned state not only in *Aurore*, or in *Benoît* of *Mon oncle Antoine*, but also in the early American silent, *Orphans of the Storm* (1922; d. D. W. Griffith), and in the early French silent *Ménilmontant* (1925; d. Dimitri Kirsanov). In like vein, *Eclair au chocolat* (1979; d. Jean-Claude Lord) depicts a single mother telling her illegitimate son about the absent father.

Of course, we cannot overlook the more pleasant view of life presented by some of the "comedies," those that feature children in contexts where the adults are not primary players, including such films as *La Guerre des tuques*, *Bach et Bottine*, and *Tadpole and the Whale*. Though these latter are manufactured with a clear intention to market them not only in Québec, but in English Canada and in the U.S. and elsewhere (they are often seen on the Disney Channel, which has also shown *Anne of Green Gables*, *Anne of Avonlea*, *Lost in the Barrens*, etc.), they are not, strictly speaking, "kid flicks," and are more than worthy of some consideration in this book.

An early example of troubled marriage and the star-crossed couple as sources for the plot of a *québécois* film is *Un Homme et son péché* (1949), which was based on Claude-Henri Grignon's very successful radio play.[1] The film, *Un Homme ...*, like its sequel *Séraphin* (1950), was directed by an immigrant Frenchman named Paul Gury, sometimes called Loic Le Gouriadec. A lengthy synopsis and details of reception of this film are given by Véronneau (*Cin ...* 1979, 35–46). The compelling message emanating from the criticisms quoted on these pages is that the film was, at least for Québécois commentators, "typically Canadian," and a "true Québec production." Others, however, found that there was a "penury of closeups which [would] help the audience to participate in the screen action," that the editing gave abrupt transitions, and that it was "banal" (*Cin ...* 1979, 42). So much for the critical reaction; the public reception was "délirant" (*Cin ...* 1979, 44). What strikes one, apart from the struggle that Alexis has for his Donalda—who is married to the vengeful and vicious miser and usurer Séraphin—, is the fatalism of the financial adversity undergone by Alexis (which makes us think of Ringuet or Anné Hébert), as well as the alcoholic responses he and others (Pit-Caribou) make to their misfortunes. (The theme of alcoholism is, in fact, a thread running through the *québécois* film almost from its beginnings; it is tied to the plot of *La Forteresse*, is witnessed through Adhémar in *J. A. Martin photographe*; and it forms a leitmotif in the films of Forcier.) Then, too, *Un Homme et son péché* shows the values of traditional rural life and its realities. Michel Brûlé (quoted by Lever *Hist.* 1988, 481) mentions, after Léon Franque, the *épluchettes à blé d'inde* (which Donalda must use to clean with, since her husband refuses to buy sponges and the like), the square dance, the curate bringing Viaticum, etc. But Brûlé significantly insists on the concomitant portrayal of the bankruptcy and wretchedness of these values (Lever *Hist.* 1988, 481; 482), and the triumph of capital as well as the appearance of reification in this film. In other words, the values tied to the country are no longer viable; they no longer correspond to the new economic reality. While the film appears to be celebrating rural values, it may very well be representing them while emptying them of their content. (It goes almost without saying that many seeing this film would not have been aware of this device, which one might call "subversion.") Brûlé is also quoted by Lever as saying that a similar statement may be made about *La Petite Aurore*, in which rural life is shown as rotten and sordid, while it is city folk (the State with its juridical apparatus) who come to succor and to avenge.

One of the first important films to depict *urban* life in the big northern city (Montréal) was *La Vie heureuse de Léopold Z.* (*The Merry World of Léopold Z.*). It is a highly regarded early piece, and is an excellent starting point for our discussion of *québécois* family life as depicted in film from Québec. In addition, in Houle's *Dictionnaire* we read that this film belongs to that small group of films (incl. Groulx's *Le Chat dans le sac*, Jutra's *A tout prendre*, Perrault's *Pour la suite du monde*) which "in the early 60s were the point of departure of a production of feature-length films in Québec and served as international calling cards for the nascent Québec cinema. Thanks to Gilles Carle's perseverance, this film, which in the beginning was to have been a short-length documentary on snow removal in the pure 'onefian' (ONF) tradition, became a fictional full-length feature film in 35 mm. The choice of this format, with what it contained in possibilities for commercial

La Vie heureuse de Léopold Z. (Courtesy Office National du Film.)

exploitation at the time, was capital" (Houle *Dict.* 1978, 301; my translation).

LA VIE HEUREUSE DE LÉOPOLD Z. (1965; d., Gilles Carle)

Léopold Z. Tremblay, "a plump, amiable, happily married man, drives a snowplow for the city of Montréal. It is Christmas Eve and the snow is falling heavily. Between cleaning streets, he takes out a loan with the help of a finance company, buys his wife a fur coat, and takes care of his relative, a [*chanteuse*, or] nightclub singer. Throughout his long and tiring day he is watched by his foreman, who suspects he is up to other things. This is a lively, spirited, deftly handled comedy with serious undertones, an auspicious beginning for Gilles Carle, who, if nothing else, had made winter and its snow seem entirely natural and frequently funny" (Pratley *TS* 1987, 183).

The film is, among other things, a comedy of manners and a fictional film, but one with a (direct) documentary background.[2] Léopold is an example of a film character who has no desire to revolt. He is a type of French Canadian, like Jean-Baptiste in

Patricia and Baptiste, molded by certain power games and certain historical forces: the Duplessis regime and Holy Mother Church. These two tenderly ironic portraits are both funeral eulogies and exorcisms. Both Houle and Clanfield point out that this film grew out of the earlier *Chat dans le sac*.

"Can Leopold Z. be the image of a whole Québec people, in that he is able to laugh at his misadventures, but unable to react against his situation as an exploited person? One would like to believe this along with Gilles Carle, who, when speaking about his character, mentions a 'sub-proletariat' that he wanted to make 'realistic' and 'tragic'" (quoted from *Cinema 72*, no. 170; Houle *Dict.* 1978, 301). But, far from being tragic, "the humor in which the whole film is bathed — and which gives it its unity and its entertainment value — is practically a publicity wink; moreover, the humor is neither corrosive nor denunciating. The whole film is pleasing to the eye and to the ear; and there is no trace of that grinding kind of satire that can be a distraction. Let us not forget that in the same period, Gilles Groulx, in *The Cat in the Sack*, which also was supposed to be about winter, gave an image of Québec that was much less reassuring and above all more necessary (or appropriate) in those years, ... which were not so tranquil as all that" (Houle *Dict.* 1978, 31–2; my translation).

Houle continues: "Jean Pierre Lefebvre probably had a taste for euphemism when he wrote that *La Vie* ... was a 'simple and realistic film which nonetheless did not lend itself to any extensive explicative developments'" (quoted from *Objectif* #35; Houle *Dict.* 1978, 302; my translation).

Lever writes that, from a technical point of view, "in *La Vie* ... the use of direct camera is put to the service of fiction. And while fiction is regarded by the director as the only means of really showing the ordinary person's imagination, ironically, *Léopold* is shot in the direct manner, giving the film its realism and truth" (*Hist.* 1988, 162).

It remains to be said that Carle is one of the most indefatigable portrayers of Québec society. We have seen how his *Maria Chapdelaine* attempts to recover visually the *habitant* (peasant) past of the province. And Noguez says of Carle's *Viol d'une femme douce* that it is "very *québécois*." Noguez points out that *Viol* ..., which concerns three traditional brothers and the supposed injury to their sister's honor, depicts the hiatus between two types of society: the traditional, closed, Catholic, sexually taboo society, versus the new one.[3]

Let us now examine an early Jutra film, concerned with the couple in a somewhat different way from *Léopold* ..., and see how it compares, technically and from the point of view of content.

A TOUT PRENDRE, AN EARLY EFFORT OF CLAUDE JUTRA (1961–63)

This film is considered as the apogee of the direct style, which we have seen to be the hallmark of a distinctly *québécois* movement growing out of the "documentary" style — for which Canadian film-makers are so noted. Jutra's film was also a critical success for the most part, earning the Grand Prix du Festival du Cinéma Canadien in 1963. However, according to Houle (*Dict.* 1978, 3–4), it received considerable negative reaction as well, especially from Jean Pierre Lefebvre in *Objectif*.

This feature-length film can be considered an *auteur* film, perhaps the first from Québec, as Jutra obviously had a heavy say in all aspects of it. But it also allies the techniques of the direct cinema (synchronic sound, natural lighting [!], hand-carried camera, cinéma vérité approach) with an aesthetic and ethical point of departure that differs radically from such contemporaneous films as *La Petite Aurore*. The intention in *A tout prendre* is largely to tell one's own personal story and also, no doubt, simply to make a film and to make statements on making films, since it is said early on in the film that "au nom de l'art, on va faire de la photographie [in the name of art, we are going to do some photographing]."

As far as the story line is concerned, it is a matter of Jutra's reliving in an improvised fashion and before the camera a love affair he had experienced several years before. He plays the role of Claude (as Johanne plays Johanne and Victor Désy plays Victor); and he tells the story, off-camera, in the first person singular. Amateurish in its technology — clearly the result of an ill-funded project and, perhaps, too much experimentation — the film is poorly lit and only occasionally suggests the greatness of its photographers, Michel Brault, Jean-Claude Labrecque, and Bernard Gosselin. Almost at this same time Brault was doing the splendid films of Perrault that I discussed earlier.

This said, one must nevertheless recognize in this film an important landmark of *québécois* cinema. As we read in Houle, "... le jeu ... des trois principaux interprètes recréant attitudes et dialogues à la lumière déformante de leurs mémoires, pondérant ce qu'ils ont été au baume de ce qu'ils auraient souhaité être, donne au film une touche particulière qui, aujourd'hui encore,

atteint le spectateur ... [The acting of the three principal interpreters — recreating attitudes and dialogues in the deforming light
of their memories, while pondering what they were through the
balm of what they would have liked to be — gives to the film a
particular quality which, even today, touches the viewer]" (Houle
Dict. 1978, 3). The allusion to "le Québec libre" on a background
sign that comes toward the end of the film — at the point where
Jutra is experiencing "le déclin de l'amour" and a rather liberating
breakup with Johanne — accompanied by the statement that "we
have to think of other things now," project the work into the
political arena, while intimations of suicide in the case of both
Johanne and Claude suggest the sorrowful end to which Jutra
himself was to come in the 1980s. Jutra will again treat the mix-ups
that the couple can get into in *Pour le meilleur et le pire* (1975).
And even before that he had done a more total study of the society
of Québec in his landmark film, *Mon oncle Antoine*. In both of these
films, as in an early animation of Norman McLaren, *A Chairy
Tale*, he appears as an actor. But in *A tout prendre*, said by Moffat
to be an autoportrait, his appearance was inevitable. Moffat, in
fact, gives one of the best analyses of this early work. Seeing it as a
fusion of two codes (direction and autobiographical fiction), he
finds it to be a filmic representation, like a mirror, turned frst toward
oneself (subject/object) and then toward others (objective reality).
It is for Moffat an exercise in cinematic self-portraiture, which
involves Jutra's confession of his homosexuality; his *désarroi* — that
of his age, but also one caused by his sense of difference and
otherness; his schizophrenia (in response to which he plays off all
the conflicting aspects of his personality with diverse masks);
and his realization of his preference for male bonding. Ambivalence
is present too. Moffat cites Denys Arcand's discomfort with this
film and with the fact of Jutra's homosexuality, expressed in his
article "Civilisation et Sexualité," published in *Parti-pris* (9/1;
1964).[4] Is it due to a change of perspective that one of Arcand's
most memorable characters is the (AIDS ?) afflicted homosexual
in *Le Déclin* ...; and that, besides, his name is Claude? Or that
Arcand's latest film, *Love and Human Remains* (1994), from the
play by Brad Fraser, deals primarily with homosexuality?
   Perhaps the right scholar will one day be able to show the extent
to which *Mon oncle Antoine* — Jutra's masterpiece, and indeed very
possibly Québec's cinematic masterpiece — is also an autoportrait
of an even younger Jutra; for the sexual formation of the young
Benoît spells future trouble. Of course, in such an analysis the

autobiographical elements of the scriptwirter Clément Perron would have to be separated from those of Jutra as director, for the two had very different backgrounds.

MON ONCLE ANTOINE (1971; d. Claude Jutra)[5]

It is little wonder that when those one hundred Canadian and American critics were polled a few years ago in an effort to establish which Canadian films ranked highest in their esteem, *Mon oncle Antoine* was ranked as the number-one film (as already quoted from *Variety*, 8 August 1984). At the time of its appearance, *Mon oncle Antoine* won many awards, including the Canadian Film Awards selection (Toronto, 1971) for best feature-length film, best direction (Jutra), best photography (Brault), best recording (Roger Lamoureux), best music (Jean Cousineau), best supporting actress (Olivette Thibault), best actor (Jean Duceppe), best screenplay (Clément Perron). It also won the diploma of honor at the International Festival of Film in Moscow, 1971 (Abel 1990, 314). It is more than a critics' choice, however. It is, as Weinmann attests, a masterpiece. Indeed, it is one of the great films of the world; and every teacher and student of French or francophone culture, not to mention every film scholar, every film buff, and every film critic, should not only view it, but also seriously consider its aesthetic and cultural load. It requires of us considerable reflection: students, and even persons otherwise usually appreciative of the cinematographic arts, often have difficulty in grasping the true import and stature of this jewel. They find it "strange," or "different," and I have even heard one French professor dismiss it as "mal fait"! Like *Les Bons Débarras* and like *Les Ordres*, *Mon oncle Antoine* is introspective and analytical; its pace seems "unnecessarily" slow to the American viewer. It is imperative that such unfortunate impressions be erased. Clearly, until we have viewed this motion picture (and reckoned with its aesthetic value) our acquaintanceship with the best specimens of the seventh art is incomplete.

Still suffering from a confusion with *Mon oncle* and with *Mon oncle d'Amérique* (though the title of the latter is only a reflection of an expression) — a confusion that causes many persons to believe they have "already seen it" — this 1971 film provides as exciting and as fruitful an inquest into the states of the young mind confronted with adult behavior as does Truffaut's *Argent de poche*.[6]

While Claude Jutra, who now several years ago disappeared and then was found in the river some time later — having probably committed suicide by drowning himself — directed this film, Michel Brault did the camerawork in his characteristic cinéma vérité technique.

Certainly this film was the first of Jutra's to truly capture the imagination and the admiration of moviegoers. Born on 11 March 1930, he studied medicine before turning to drama. He had been making films since 1957, when he collaborated with the celebrated Norman McLaren on *A Chairy Tale*. In 1963 Jutra made *A tout prendre* (*The Way It Goes*). This film, as we saw, is an intensely personal film, but its strong emotions and its internal dedication to the art of making films pave the way for the masterpiece to come.

The eight Canadian Film Awards that *Mon oncle Antoine* received shortly after it was made included, as I said above, one for best actor, Jean Duceppe, as Antoine. (Duceppe also starred in *Le Vieillard et l'enfant* from G. Roy. He died after his long and distinguished career only in the fall of 1990.) Claude Jutra himself plays the role of the store clerk, Fernand, and the celebrated Monique Mercure has a cameo appearance as a seductive client. The film was aired on many P.B.S. stations in the early 1970s and on CBC (in Windsor, at least) in 1989. There is an atrocious dubbed version that manages to virtually destroy the beauty of this haunting film; it is to be avoided at all costs, for the mouths and the words are at war with one another, and one is so distracted by this that the more important visual components of the film tend to be lost.

Mon oncle Antoine, which looks back, but not nostalgically, to the Québec of the 1940s, is a profound film on a rite of passage, by which the young adolescent Benoît moves from the notion that the adult world is joyous and appealing to a realization of its weaknesses, failures, vices, and hypocrisies. Because of Benoît's age and his trial "by fire," *Mon oncle Antoine* might have considerable appeal for (American) high school students — provided it is properly presented. But it is so complex that all viewers can find interest in it regardless of their age or station. The film has interlocking devices that portray many facets of Québec society, including the tensions between the anglo "boss" and the underpaid, overworked employees of an asbestos mine that physically and economically dominates the small community "dans la région de l'amiante." Jos Poulin's story, wrapped around the Antoine story, best reveals these tensions, which account for his departure for the lumber camp, only to return to his dead son, whose cadaver Antoine (funeral director and owner of the general store) has gone to St. Pierre to "remove." And one of the most poignant scenes, early in the film, shows Mme Poulin, the traditional Québécoise, on the inside looking out at the departing, soon to be absent, husband, as he gives orders to his children. Leaving aside the film's special allusions to cultural tensions and family relations, one can also learn from it the values, behavior, and morality espoused by Québec's small-towns, "about the same today as they were in the 1940s"! (Pratley *TS* 1987, 198). The story is set in Black Lake.

On a deeper level, the portrayal of Benoît's evolution from adolescence to manhood as presented in this gripping and highly visual film is one that lifts a potentially hackneyed subject into the sublime. The loneliness of this orphaned boy, living as a foster child with his uncle, is revealed through the vast expanses of snowy, moonlit fields, through his silent observation of those around him, through his coming to terms with the very real horrors of alcoholism, adultery, and death. While the film ends in a stark freeze-frame à la Truffaut, it has moments of humor and charm — especially at the beginning. These only serve to enhance the film's appeal and to make the tragic note upon which it ends all the more stark.

The two stories that come together here are skillfully fused, as are the abrupt juxtapositions of scenes revolving around birth and death. Beneath a picture of Jesus of the Sacred Heart, Benoît chases his coworker Carmen[7] (who is wearing a bridal veil) around among the coffins in the upstairs storehouse of his uncle's general store, where practically everything the village could need is sold, including well-known products such as Ritz Crackers, Salada tea, Simplicity patterns, and Coca-Cola. (The general store is like a microcosm of *québécois* society of the time; one sees this in *Maria Chapdelaine*; and, in literature, in Ringuet's *Thirty Acres*, for example.) Most of the action takes place on Christmas Eve, when Benoît and his uncle go to the Poulin farm in a mounting blizzard. Their hazardous trip — by horse-drawn sleigh at that! — is taken for the purpose of removing the corpse of the Poulins' eldest son, who has fallen ill, while his father has left the farm to seek winter work in a lumber camp — not an uncommon practice among Québec farmers of earlier days, and one we see François Paradis and several of Maria's brothers doing in *Maria Chapdelaine*.

Prior to this long episode involving the "epic journey" of Benoît and his storekeeper-undertaker uncle, a crèche has been set up in the general store, with a "broken" Baby Jesus at its center. (Weinmann sees this window display as theater for the villagers, a kind of parody of a medieval *mystère*, one supposes; but he also sees it as a criticism of the commercialization of Christmas —

assumedly held holy by Jutra — at the same time as he paradoxically and indefensibly sees the whole film as a rebuttal of Catholic authority [1990, 72; 79].)

In the final scene of the film, the image of the crèche is reprised, this time with the Poulin family playing the principals, in what might be called a negative nativity scene: the dead son in his coffin placed in the middle of the circle, with his father, his mother, and his brothers and sisters gathered around him. The lonely Benoît gazes through frosty window panes upon the scene. He is now more orphaned and more isolated than ever. The glass, in fact, sets him apart from the scene, and is an obstacle and a distorter — just as the display window of the general store separates the villagers from the crèche (and, one might add, just as the voyeurism of Guy in *Les Bons Débarras* and of Marcel in *Un Zoo la nuit* involves a "wall of glass"). But one is chilled by the presentation of this dead man and his mourning family (the subversion of the Holy Family — a pietà in fact; where the cradle is replaced by a coffin) as a conclusion to the film. Weinmann sees in this ending the message that the society, parental authority, state authority, and religious authority are dead; but he also sees, in the loss of the body and its recovery, the concept that "the dead (Antoine) cannot bury the dead, and also that death seeks out and demands the living." (But the reverse can be equally true: Antoine, Fernand, and Benoît go to get or find the dead body; elsewhere Jutra sees suicide as a solution to life's woes.) In Weinmann's view we have at the end of the film not the Holy Family, but the Québec family around a "crèche létale" (1990, 88). This is to find more sociopolitical statement in the film than I am willing to grant is present. Truly, the major motifs of life and death, and of becoming an adult, following an initiation that resembles the mystic's "dark night of the soul," are intertwined in a highly skillful fashion in this great film. This thrusts it beyond the narrow confines of the political and the parochial.

It seems, in fact, that the possible directions for analysis of this film are infinite. Brault's effective camera angles, the special nature of Québec French as a language, the ways of dress depicted, the village types, all contribute something to the ambiance of the film. Its visual impact; the preeminence of image over dialogue; indeed the silence and the *regard* of Benoît — contrasted with the angry "ivrogne!" ("you drunk!") that he finally hurls at his Bols-drinking uncle — all make a lasting impression on any sensitive viewer.

Not to be underestimated, either, is the beauty of the photography, giving us the majestic snow scenes under moonlight and the characteristic street scenes of the village that tend to remind us of a Clarence Gagnon painting, or of one by Jean-Paul Lemieux.

The role of the Catholic Church in the life of the people in the 1940s is integral to the comprehension of this film. Benoît is a server, and in the beginning of the movie, as in other instances, he apes the conduct of the priest. A swig from the bottle of communion wine — *unconsecrated* — is innocent enough; a prankish deed. A small snack on an *unconsecrated* host completes the snitch. Benoît has seen the priest take a nip or two; so why not he? The child imitates the man; it is characteristic of the longing the adolescent has to grow up. Some have, moreover, seen these gestures as a sign of his hunger. But it is more, and has little to do with a debunking of Catholic ritual and rite. For in contrast to this comical little deed, a later swig from his uncle's bottle during the desperate trip back to the village with the Poulin corpse (ultimately lost in a somewhat macabre turn of the plot) is less amusing, because now we are keenly aware that we are no longer dealing with a boyish prank, or, for that matter, with a "boy." Similarly, his flirtations with Carmen are innocent enough; they are the manifestations of his awakening sexuality. This is reflected, too, in the scene in which Alexandrine, the notary's wife and the village vamp, tries on a corset while Benoît and his friend Maurice look on. (One sees her bare breasts; this can be a manifestation of the "déshabiller la Québécoise" movement discussed in Chapter 3; still, some felt that the role was rather beneath the dignity and usefulness of so great an actress [Monique Mercure].) But Benoît's discovery of his aunt's infidelity, of her fornication with Fernand, chief clerk of his uncle's store, is a revelation to him of the ugly manner in which sexual activity can be "used" in adult life.

Loss of innocence and the growing awareness of the grimness of adult life and of death are the true subjects of *Mon oncle Antoine*. In a transition from innocence to the assumption of adult responsibilities, the choirboy becomes a "man": he learns about the adult world: drink, dalliance, death, and desolation. Surely the behavior of the adults whom this boy observes, silently for the most part, clashes with the catechism he must have been taught. Catechetics were never lightly approached in Québec of bygone years: the stories of Anne Hébert bear witness to that. And her *Kamouraska*, which Jutra also made into a film, especially shows the burden of French-Canadian Catholicism upon the psyche of the trapped Elisabeth. The impact of Catholicism on young lives is more sweetly and more amusingly shown by Roch Carrier. The animated version of his *Chandail* will nonetheless reveal the same sternness of that brand of education, and it is set at roughly the same period; but in viewing *The Sweater*, we are charmed; we will smile. There, but also here, in *Mon oncle Antoine*, we see the tremendous difference between the French-Canadian (Jansenistic) Catholic mentality and that of their protestant neighbors to the West and to the South. Weinmann has seen in the film a portrayal of a dead Church and of an irreverent young man (a young Québec) in rebellion against its authority, as evidenced (he thinks) by drinking the wine and eating the wafer, and serving mass in an empty church, or running across the top of the pews, rather than using the aisles. I have some problems with that; for it is to say that Jutra supposed that this vacuum existed in the 1940s, which it pretty clearly did not. (To repeat, the wine and wafer are consumed prior to the mass; the church is empty because it is daily mass; inattentiveness at mass and walking across the pews seem signs of carefree boyhood and normal to that state, etc.) Instead, and given the tempo of the film, which moves from humor (black, to be sure) to the end's grim finality — where thanatos has the upperhand — I think the boy, relatively carefree in the beginning, must grow up overnight as he finds the hypocritical adults in his world in deadly terror of death (which the Church holds to be a birth) and in *flagrante delecto* when it comes to intemperance and adultery (mortal sins), not to mention infidelity to the cult itself. For example, the aunt has adjured Benoît and his uncle to get back in time for Christmas midnight mass and meanwhile started her private *réveillon* with Fernand well ahead of any celebration of the Birth of Christ and in contradiction of its meanings. These adults — around whom various earthly trinities can be constructed — do not practice what they seem to preach. Weinmann's analysis of the film is very good up to a point; but it fails to see the evolution in Benoît's personality and behavior that I think is very clearly built into the work. (Weinmann throughout his book demonstrates little knowledge of Catholicism, moreover. He does not even know the difference between the Incarnation and the Immaculate Conception.)

It is also apparent that after the experiences of these some forty-eight hours, Benoît will never be the same again; any illusions he had entertained have been replaced by not-too-glowing realities. The stark realism of the setting, of the photography, and of the story permeates this film of initiation and the attainment of "manhood"; and the story itself can be on one level the story of one boy, and on another may stand for the coming of age or the raising of consciousness of Québec and its sense of authority and of history. (The loss and recovery of the dead body is symbolic, also. A disappearing corpse had been seen in Hitchcock and read about in Roch Carrier's *La Guerre, Yes Sir!*; but here it suggests the unsuccessful effort to shed one's past more than it makes a bid for black humor.) This political reading was obvious before the appearance of Weinmann's book, but Weinmann builds a real case for such an interpretation. What he misses however is the symbolic handing over of the reins that occurs during the *chevauchée fantastique*, as he calls it (1990, 81). In this, one of the most unusual sequences ever filmed, with magnificent scenes of eery, moonlit, frozen landscapes and camera shots that intensify the largeness and the power of the horse, youth takes over from the past generation. The mythic Québec that the uncle incarnates is exposed to be something of a fraud: in the snow, in his warm fur coat, seated in his sleigh behind his powerful horse Red Fly, as he goes forward to meet the face of death, he is unable to manage his horse, for he is afraid, he is a coward, he is a drunk. We know, too, that he is a failure — at business (things don't "add up") and at his marriage. It is time for a change. Benoît up until now has been viewing the ebb and flow of village life, and in particular of his "family" (which includes his aunt and uncle [for he is an orphan], as well as Fernand and Carmen), from behind his broom, or undercover in the attic of the general store, or in the church vestry. But now he sees this family and, in particular, those who are most meant to be his models very clearly, in all their nakedness and cowardice. The erstwhile comedy has come to an end. Tragedy now sets in. The keg of nails that has encumbered the passage of persons in the store can serve now to seal up his uncle's coffin. An ironic distortion comes in one advertising blurb for this film, which states: "What is surprising is the gentleness with which [Benoît] is taught [life's] lessons by Antoine." Can the person who wrote this possibly have seen the film?

Choosing the coming of age as a motif for a film could have been quite risky; it has been done again and again. But as Jay Cocks writes in *Time Magazine*, "Worn by repetition, the story of how a boy becomes a man can still be a revelation. So it is in *My Uncle Antoine*, an earthy substantial Canadian movie about a few days in the life of a lad called Benoît .... Director Claude Jutra approaches the excellent Clement Perron screenplay with such intuition and insight that he manages to make Benoît's initiation at once universal and unique .... *My Uncle Antoine* is indelible, the best chronicle of a coming of age since Truffaut's *The 400 Blows*." And, supporting this idea, Andrew Sarris writes in *The Village*

Mon oncle Antoine. (Courtesy Office National du Film.)

Voice, "... Not the least of the distinctions of *My Uncle Antoine* is that it chooses not to describe Canadian experiences in universal terms, but rather to describe universal experiences in Canadian terms. Ultimately, Jutra does not tell us everything we want to know, but what he does tell us he tells with such intelligence that we yearn to know more. I was moved."[8]

Universal and unique. But also — though incidentally — a political allegory. For there is in *Mon oncle Antoine* a probable symbolism in Benoît's coming of age that, while a universal human experience, may also stand here for the raising of consciousness that was occurring among the Québécois concerning their culture and their history at the time Jutra was making this, his masterpiece — a work substantially greater than his later *Kamouraska*. And the manner in which this transition and this *prise de conscience* are portrayed, through a *chevauchée fantastique* and through strange dreams is vitrually unique to this film.

THE DREAM SEQUENCE IN *MON ONCLE ANTOINE*

After the crucial return from St. Pierre in which Benoît cries to his uncle: "wake up, damn drunk (*réveillez-vous; ivrogne*); we've lost the body," but fails to rouse him, and after the scene in which he finds his aunt arising from her sexual encounter with the store clerk, Benoît climbs up on the counter and half falls asleep; at this juncture Jutra has inserted a dream sequence that involves a distorted rerun of Benoît's recent experiences with sex and death. Always seen from Benoît's point of view, no longer does death provide the amusing, slightly satirical early sight of Fernand the store clerk and Uncle Antoine, as undertakers, packing up their affairs; removing the rosary, the vest, and collar from the corpse; screwing on the lid of the coffin; and humming as they work. Now he realizes what he did not realize when we first met him. Surreal though the dream sequence is, through it we know that he has come to the apprehension that sex is lethal and that death is no laughing matter. He has learned death as a thing to fear; he knows now that his drunken uncle is a coward, afraid of death, and that his aunt, a lonely frustrated woman, has perhaps been pushed to her act of adultery, though nevertheless he does not seem to forgive her. When finally Fernand awakens him and takes him out to search for the body, he is perhaps more an adult than any one else in this little world. We do not forget his face as he peers through the Poulins' window — outdoors in the snow and the cold, outdoors looking in upon that scene of sorrow and poverty, upon that pietà — exiled, isolated, lonely: it is the face of a *puer senex*, a child old before its time. (The face of a young Jutra? The face of Québec itself?) Old, pinched with hunger, and wise. Beyond the technical effects of the freeze-frame lies the visual framing of a mental and physical state we can only call thanatosis. Benoît the child/adolescent has died to his adulthood, to the truth of death. Like Edvard Munch in his "Puberty," Jutra understood, and showed us here, that adolescence is the true starting point of loneliness, vulnerability and anxiousness. A very dark movie, in which the inner drama of the psyche and its processes are not described so much as portrayed.

Jutra has already done what R. Bruce Elder thinks is to come, when he writes: "We need a cinema that can deal with the here and now. Any cinema that wishes to deal with the experience of the moment must not offer description; rather, it must reveal how events come to be in experience, that is, the dynamic by which events are brought into presentness in experience."[9]

Pratley has summarized this film as follows: "At times Jutra ... seems to lose faith in his material and resort to technical devices. These do not detract, however, from this warm, personal and sympathetic study of a boy's growing awareness of life's realities, and of the people around him, honestly told, observant, refreshingly free from the clichés of Quebec cinema, and quite easily the best feature film the NFB has yet made."[10]

Many years later, and not long before his death, Claude Jutra returned to the theme of the abandoned child that subtends *Mon oncle Antoine* in *La Dame en couleurs*, which concerns abandoned or orphaned children who are sent to "un asile d'aliénés" [an asylum for the exiled; alienated; castoffs]. He himself said that *La Dame* . . . was "a film noir strewn with moments of happiness, in which misery in all forms — physical, intellectual, and human — is present as it is in life."[11]

Mon oncle Antoine is, then, a film that shows the *québécois* "family," even the society in crisis. Another director of a later film — *Les Bons Débarras* — will do no less and will do it no less effectively.

LEX BONS DÉBARRAS (OR, *GOOD RIDDANCE*) (1980; d. Francis Mankiewicz)

Like most *québécois* films, *Les Bons Débarras* is an introspective film, in the French vein, and for the most part lacks the kind of external violence and swift action that characterizes so many contemporary American movies. It is a study of desire and jealousy; at the same time it can be regarded as a political allegory and a psychological horror story. It is as thoroughly *québécois* in its social setting as it is harrowing in its emotional impact.

Desire and *Wuthering Heights* in *Les Bons Débarras*

Les Bons Débarras, though one of the truly great films of French Canada,[12] was, in general, poorly received by American critics. At the time of its screening on the CBC Windsor television station, *The (Toledo) Blade*, no doubt leaning on standard American ratings such as those of Leonard Maltin and his team, gave this masterpiece a mere two stars, even though in 1984 the team of American and Canadian critics rated the film as the third best ever made by any Canadian artist. (See the previously cited analysis in *Variety*, 8 August 1984.) Indeed, Leonard Maltin's *Movies and Video Guide*, for the past several editions, states the following about *Les Bons Débarras*, to which it awards two-and-a-half stars: "Fatherless [i.e, illegitimate] 13-yr. old girl (Laurier) idolizes and romanticizes her mother (Tifo), with tragic results. Cogent but overlong and repetitious drama about growing up, aided by a strong performance by Tifo."[13] If the movie were just about growing up, the put-down would be somewhat justified. But since it is about the intensity of young love, as well as masochism, accompanied by taboo desire and the impossibility of its being happily fulfilled, the repetitions — which set the pace and tone for tragedy — are not that unnecessarily numerous. The "overlong" impression is often attributable to a cultural conditioning. Such an impression is frequently experienced by Americans when viewing French-Canadian films, which are characteristically introspective and at times brooding. I have encountered similar reactions to *Mon oncle Antoine*, to *Le Déclin* ..., and in particular to *Les Ordres*, even though the slowness of pace is an integral part of that film's meaning. It may therefore be best, at least in a classroom situation, to at least prepare the viewers for a dialogue-oriented, slow-paced kind of film. Americans are so geared to visual violence and to speed in their films that it is difficult for them to relish the luxurious pace of many foreign films: the restlessness of the American spectators is perceptible and their impatience is analogous to their behavior in the face of a three-hour, five-course gourmet meal, as opposed to a preference for grabbing a quick takeout from McDonald's.

The film *Good Riddance* is, in fact, based on a script, or *scénario*, by one of Canada's most famous if also most eccentric writers, Réjean Ducharme (author of the complex and highly regarded novel *L'Avalée des avalés*, which has more than a few things in common with the film *Les Bons Débarras*). It concerns the tensions among the unwed mother Michelle, her twelve-year-old daughter Manon, and the mother's retarded brother 'ti-Guy. Manon is extremely possessive and jealous of her mother's attentions to any others, and to such an extent that one can safely assert that the major theme of the film is that of first love, in all its intensity and destructiveness.

Subordinately, the film, while containing the familiar but usually rich theme of the rite of passage, has a subliminal reference to the emergence of young Québec, and its ambivalence toward as well as its revolt against the greater motherland, anglophone Canada (and perhaps, too, against the concept of the queen, from whom the French Canadian has always been fundamentally alienated). One is tempted to suggest analogies not only to *Wuthering Heights*, but also to Aquin's *Prochain Episode*, where the question of failed Revolution, failed love, and a power struggle are also at stake. (And, incidentally, such titles are offered here as *analogies*, not intertexts, since in discussing film one cannot, properly speaking, present intertexts.)

But *Les Bons Débarras* also has further currents that are noteworthy, and that have nevertheless been largely overlooked in critical writings on this world-class film. For even though it is true that this film is in many ways as useful as *Mon oncle Antoine* for gaining insight into the language and culture of rural Québec, sadly enough *Les Bons Débarras* has apparently been viewed by some critics as merely provincial and limited in its focus. And indeed it embraces a lovely but locus-specific iconic portrayal of the remote Québec forests vividly colored by the fall leaves and almost breathing the cool crispness of that fall. (It has been called "the dark side of *Anne of Green Gables*," and there is room for that interpretation, among others.)

But those same critics, and others like them, succumbed to what must have seemed on the surface to be a story about the queer folkways of the Québécois woodsmen, whose squalid poverty provides a strong contrast with the beauty of those woods, so handsomely photographed by Brault, on Eastman-Color. (Lake Barette and St.-Jérôme provide the locus.) Still, close consideration of the film shows that Derrida's contention that meaning is elusive because it comes through the unstable vehicle of language, and depends on absences, upon the unstated as well as the stated, has applications here. Thus, while Manon loves to lie in bed and read passages from *Wuthering Heights* aloud as her sleepy mother only half listens, the analogy between the desire of Manon and the desire of Heathcliff is never openly stated, never completely articulated. Indeed, the strong similarity between Manon and Heathcliff assists the director in ascribing to Manon the status of frustrated lover; for Manon exhibits the same dark and stormy nature; she is temperamental, like Heathcliff; she is changeable, like him. She understands his hatred; it is one she has, univocally, toward her uncle, who poses a threat for her because he will be hardest to "get rid of." He poses an even greater threat than Maurice, the policeman; than Gaetan; than the gentleman on the road who proposes that her mother begin the operation of a motel. Moreover, Manon is in revolt, as was Heathcliff. A romantic of sorts, this little female twelve-year-old Heathcliff (just turning thirteen), like any child, sometimes exhibits adult postures: she smokes joints with her friend — a would-be suitor of her mother — and takes draughts of beer from her uncle's beer cans. And she has a disconcerting gift for sarcasm and cynicism, in one so young.

Precocious and fierce, manipulative and yet tender, "grave and gamine, secretive and keen, cruel and excusable, modern, solitary, friendless,"[14] she manages to get her mother to drive off (or "get rid of") her policeman-lover, by whom the mother has become pregnant, by making a preposterous claim that the lover has attempted to seduce her. Manon's love for her mother is jealous, destructive, and all-consuming, but also total, deep, and adoring, like that of Heathcliff for Cathy. Manon is willing to lie, cheat, and steal, and does not hesitate to be catalyst even of her uncle's death. Indeed, she will do anything to rid herself of anyone — her mother's lovers, or would-be lovers, and her uncle — so intense is her desire to be alone with her mother, and free of rivals. The all-consuming passion begins in semi-innocence, though always with erotic and even sexual overtones; it ends in a pathology. These points are made quite clearly in the ending of the film, where Manon, after answering the telephone, resumes her reading, while omitting to convey to her drowsy mother the message that her uncle has undergone a fatal accident. (Heathcliff, too, would "get rid" of everyone in order to have his Cathy; he does not succeed. Moreover, murder is not that far from the minds of persons in *Wuthering Heights*, as scripted by Ben Hecht and Charles MacArthur. "If Cathy died I might begin to live," Isabelle says; "Kill him, kill him, [i.e., Heathcliff]," says Cathy's brother to Isabelle; "Kill him [i.e., Heathcliff]," says Cathy to her husband Edgar.)

We should note, moreover, that a *dédoublement* of this ultimately impossible love (like Heathcliff's) is present in the alcoholic 'ti-Guy's pitiful aspirations for the unattainable life style of Madame Viau-Vauchon. In this fascination that the dim-witted and drunken Guy conceives, the tragic thrust of the film takes on a social meaning as well. All this is strongly portrayed by repetitions of his visual imaginings, in which he stretches toward her from his death agony, as if she were a goddess, or at least some angel. The record she is playing seems stuck on this bar; the picture repeats itself as if time and narrative progress have reached some everlasting and insurmountable obstacle or even, perhaps, apogee. Time, space, and desire are frozen or arrested here, as it were, at this moment when Manon's greatest longings for her uncle's destruction also are largely realized, ironically and to some extent unintentionally, through Guy's *liebestodt* and then his death. Appropriately, we should remember that Heathcliff, too, was not of Cathy's class. (And class conflict is the basis, too, of *Gianni Schicchi*, which provides the musical background for this scene.) From all of this, we can see that the assertion, sometimes made, that Guy has no role to play in the film, except to be the foil of the two women and their conflict, is completely erroneous. It is through him that we see the social sphere and its stiff structures mirrored; it is through him and his aspirations, so sadly unachievable given his mental lacks and his social standing, that the tragedy is funneled. He is, in a very real sense, the tragic pawn of the events portrayed in the film. He is, as well, the doubling, or mirroring, of Manon. He may also represent to us the way in which society at large tends to deal with the mentally handicapped. After all, says his sister, "Ce n'est pas sa faute [it isn't _his_ fault]": the handicap is the result of a bout with meningitis, and one supposes this catastrophe occurred long ago for such a dependency as he has upon his sister to have become so established. Guy's rage and frustration are, in any case, quite palpable, and they, too, complement the anger and the aspirations of Manon, while he is also the butt of her most injurious insults and her most aggressive hostilities.

Guy's voyeurism is an important part of the studies in pathology that the film presents. We have noted the importance of the _regard_ as a component in Pool's _Femme de l'hôtel_; we also observed the same phenomenon in _Les Fous de Bassan_; but it is no less operative here. Any one of these works may or may not have debts to Michel Foucault's theories on the glance, which he developed in _The Birth of the Clinic_, and elsewhere.

If, as I asserted above, Guy's link to _Wuthering Heights_ sheds light upon the film, Manon's is even more illuminating. Her oral recitation of the passages from _Wuthering Heights_ is tightly tied to the film and the passages have multiple functions. They remove the terrible events from the provincial, and lift them into the realm of a classic narrative well known to the literate world. Orality and literacy seem to be implicated, of course, and even at odds, for that matter. In fact, the gap between Manon's world and this literary classic would be so great as to make the readings incongruous, were it not that Manon builds bridges between the two, via her reveries and flights of fancy. But more importantly, the readings from _Wuthering Heights_ mirror (or else inspire) Manon's desires, shames, rebellion, and her violent mood swings. They also represent either a subversion of, or at least an allusion to, romanticism, with its emotional charge and passionate view of life, that of a prepubescent girl in the instance, experiencing the powerful push of desire and responding in kind. All that is savage and untamed in Heathcliff accrues to our small antiheroine. But unlike Heathcliff, she is a child and should perhaps not be judged by adult standards; her ethical code has not been formulated. She is operating strictly from the intention to have what she wants,

Les Bons Débarras. (Courtesy Coll. Cinémathèque Québécoise.)

and like a child or a rebuffed lover (Heathcliff) destroys what she cannot have, what hurts her, or what is in her way.

It seems that like all children Manon is at first innocent. Then, as Ducharme himself says, "tout se gâte, tout de suite après" [Everything gets spoiled right away afterwards]."[15] Can we say that the spoiling of everything comes from a conflict of desires or of wills, from a collision of agendas, as is the case in classical tragedy? While we must recognize that Michelle loves Manon, she is also baffled and frustrated by this problem child, who, more and more, casts a critical and implacable eye on life. (An ancient and yet altogether modern lot of motherhood to be baffled by one's child or children!) But more to the point, Michelle has other fish to fry. She loves and seeks to nurture her problem brother; she is a businesswoman, she has her work to do; she is expecting a child, whom, as she makes clear to her boyfriend, she does not intend to abort. (It is of some significance that for such an abortion she would "go to New York.") She must seek out her own pleasures in drink and dance. And these are areas of her life that do not include Manon. She has a professional, affective, and sexual life of her own, and she is outspoken in her opinions. She is not, of course, a superwoman. Rather, she has weaknesses that add to the depth of the characterization and prevent her from being a mere stereotype of the traditional movie mother.

Along this line, one must not forget the extent to which Manon gets slapped around and ordered to take on adult responsibilities ("bring back the $35.00"; "make your own sandwiches," says the mother). And clearly, Michelle gives to her difficult daughter many mixed signals: a slap on the face is followed by "je t'aime à mort"; a severe shaking is followed by a kiss on the mouth. It is certain that the mother often misses the cry for help issuing from the deepest recesses of this androgynous prepubescent "child" who, ironically, is often inclined to take on the role of the nurturer and caregiver (bathing the mother, caressing her, soothing her, telling her not to stay out too late, reading her to sleep — in short, giving her the treatment she herself longs for). It would seem, in fact, that through a process of sadomasochism Manon "hurts" her mother, in order to bring on the slaps and scoldings that at times seem to her appropriate treatment, considering her self-loathing. To be a "bad girl" is to get some attention from the mother, who, with her heavy load of concerns — work, brother, lovers, cigarettes, drink, pregnancy — does not set Manon very high up on her list of priorities. Interestingly, the editing techniques of the film bear out these "mixed signals." There are no dissolves, and the sharpness of the shifts in scene and situation gives a fractured effect that is at the emotional base of the film as well.

Now, a process of masochism linked to the mother-daughter relationship also helps us to access and assess Manon's true dilemma. Operative in the film, along with this masochism, is a case of cathexis (i.e., a concentration of psychic energy on some one thing or person). Manon is not a nascent lesbian; but she nonetheless exhibits the fixation on her mother (or any older woman) that many an androgynous teenage girl might. At least at present she is not a lesbian, but the frustration she is experiencing may lock her into that orientation. Rather, she reflects what psychologists see as a masochistic desire for complete symbiosis with the mother.[16] Hers is a pain that in one sense is becoming pleasure, and in another sense inflicting pain has become a source of pleasure (as her mother points out). Manon reflects the wish and the counterwish for fusion with and separation from the mother, which all of us experience to some degree in our youth. She shows the flight to and from the mother that is characteristic of her age and perhaps never wholly outgrown. A film about passage, this film. About loneliness. A film about the difficulty and the psychic disruption of "breaking away." For, after all, the mother and child were once one body; now they may stand for two parts of the self. On the artistic and affective level this notion of oneness and this dread of separation find their resonances in *Wuthering Heights*: Cathy says: "He's more myself than I am ... I am Heathcliff." Heathcliff regards Cathy as "his soul." Moreover, a curious correlation exists in a passage from France Vézina's *Androgyne* in which Isabelle painfully declares to Marie-Jeanne, her mother:

Je t'aimais, oui. Je sais. Tu m'aimais terriblement. Oui Mon corps-enfant agglutiné à ton corps-mère. Des instants souterrains. A l'abri. Des murmures. Mais le corps-enfant par la force des choses s'est mis à se décoller du corps-mère. Par la force des choses oui. Le corps-enfant aspirait au corps-femme. Et le corps-mère devint sourd. [*I loved you yes [when I was a little girl]. I know. You loved me terribly. My child-body, stuck to your mother-body. Subterranean moments. Private and sheltered. Murmurs. But the child-body, through the force of things, began to become unglued from the mother-body. By the force of things, yes. The child-body aspired to the woman-body. And the mother-body became deaf.*].[17]

We can almost postulate an "adult" Manon saying this to her mother in five or six years.

On one level, this film can be used to show life in modern rural Québec, and the ways of speech and behavior in that region. Not only is this film a sociological study in poverty and the strong contrasts between the haves and the havè-nots, but it depicts as well the pathos implicit in the opposition of the natural beauty of the landscape to the sordidness of the lives of Manon and the rest of her family.

But on a more profound level, a psychological level, this film concerns the power of first love, the possessiveness and destructiveness of desire and taboo longings. On the one hand the film offers an examination of Guy's voyeurism and a portrayal of his liebestodt. On the other, it looks deeply into Manon's psyche. Is she good? Is she bad? Should she be taken in hand; spanked? This fatherless child has had too much neglect, already. Moreover, Manon is actually showing the syndrome of the abused and neglected child.

Is there fetishism in the film? Certain transitional objects here seem to soothe the separation from the mother (the stolen dog collar; the dog itself; the stolen lipstick; the reading of the book). One should not substitute a perceived fetishism for the obvious symptoms implicit in Manon's kleptomania, but in either case a kind of substitution for the mother's attention and love is provided. Manon finds temporary solace in these objects, and forestalls a more drastic appeasement of her desires. It may be of interest to note, moreover, that the collar Manon steals represents not only the potential beautification of her dog, already Princess, but also a control device. In this child, who seeks to control her world and those about her, the sign is not trivial. Moreover, the selection of the lipstick from the store counter is a sign of the never-never condition in which she finds herself: a child taking on adult behaviors. But, whether fetishism is present or not, as Manon moves from theft to lie to ever more asocial acts, we strongly sense that there is a still more drastic step that must inevitably come. It is clear early in the film that Manon cannot accommodate this separation, or even the threat of separation. She must get rid of her competition at all costs, even by murder.

The use of the passages from *Wuthering Heights* is, as we saw, not accidental. Ducharme did not select the work or the passages at random. And similarly, the music that Mme Viau-Vauchon is playing on her phonograph at the moment when Guy decides to spy upon her — he, too, is pushed by an unrealizable desire for everything she represents in style, elegance, and feminine beauty, in something outside of and beyond his world — alludes to and even subverts the romantic, projecting something not only infantile and destructive, but also something painful, a necessary *étape*. Eros tyrannos grips *both* Manon and Guy, as also the mother, who seems to dissipate the poverty and hardness of her life through sexual contacts. The passages from Puccini's *Gianni Schicchi*, which underscore the pain and the longing of these desires, are tied to the romantic or postromantic undertow of fantasies manifested by the film's personages, and are closely related to the passages from the novel *Wuthering Heights*, which Manon is living out. Of course, the music's most poignant use is to juxtapose Mme Viau-Vauchon's life-style to the almost sordid existence of the poor retarded Guy, who nonetheless has his dreams, too, and, who, moreover, is deeply loved by his sister. What happens to him matters to her.

Gianni Schicchi. Has Bernard Buisson's selection of this music had anything to do with the film itself? One of my students who "knew opera" argued vehemently that it did not. Yet we should note at least in passing that great filmmakers and their colleagues do not generally work haphazardly; and so it is no coincidence, I think, that Gianni Schicchi is a peasant, but one who, unlike 'ti-Guy, has succeeded. And, above all, one must observe that the opera (like *Wuthering Heights*) has to do with social constraints. Rinuccio, of the wealthy Donati family, aspires to marry Schicchi's daughter; the relatives complain that Rinuccio should wish to marry outside his class, for Schicchi is (like Guy) "from the backwoods." Schicchi, in an involuted trick upon the Donati family, makes this marriage quite possible, however; and so in the opera there is a happy resolution of a conflict situation at crisis, the same conflict as that of Heathcliff and of Ti-Guy.

One can, moreover, easily see political meanings in all of this: the little province that aspires to the big country; the big country that wants to embrace the province; etc. The connections of *Gianni Schicchi* to *Les Bons Débarras* are tenuous, to be sure, but cannot be dismissed out of hand. The same score is used, along with others of Puccini's operas in *Room with a View*, but in that movie the scores add to the Florentine embroidery against which stiff Britishers lead their lives and to which one or two of them succumb. *Gianni Schicchi* was especially appropriate to that film because its action takes place in Florence; and perhaps, too, it was used to contrast Schicchi's origins and conflicts with those of the wealthy characters in the film.[18] But as to the use of this opera in *Les Bons Débarras*, even if we left aside the story of Schicchi we would have to note how the music itself marks the transfiguration of Guy, who is translated (from his condition of rage, hostility, anxiety, and frustration) into the promised land. The operatic number in and of itself (like *Wuthering Heights*, or any book that might be borrowed from Mme Viau-Vauchon's library) signifies the whole world of this elegant lady, who represents the realm of "culture," distanced, but also now desired, now resented by Guy and Manon. This distance is, in fact, represented in Guy's death scene by glass and water obstacles, by the pool occupying the space between Mme Viau-Vauchon's home and him, a distance he envisions overcoming as he moves toward her in slow motion — his vision of art, of paradise — though she always remains just out of his reach, just ahead of him. (Incidentally, the glass through which Guy "peers" at Mme Viau-Vauchon, evokes other pieces of literature and other films in which the poor, the have-nots, peer through panes of glass, often steamy or foggy, at the rich, the haves. One thinks of Baudelaire's "Les yeux des pauvres" or "Les pauvres devant un café neuf"[19] and of Jean Renoir's great silent classic, *Little Match Girl* (1928). Above, I also signalled the presence of glass as an obstacle or wall in *Mon oncle Antoine*, *Un Zoo la nuit*, etc. But note, too, the emphasis on "smallness," whether physical or mental, in both Renoir and Mankiewicz.)

The music thus serves to complement the architectonics of the scene: the auditory component complements the visual, or iconographic, impact; the learned, high-culture referents com-

Les Bons Débarras. (Courtesy Coll. Cinémathèque Québécoise.)

plement the base, the oral, the poverty-ridden, indeed the whole lived reality of these people. The specific aria is Puccini's *O mio bambino*; and for Weinmann, it underscores the adult child that Guy is, as an inversion both of Manon (a child-adult) and the *in-fans* Aurore in *La Petite Aurore* (1990, 99; 102; 104). Both of these girls can represent Québec, he contends; Aurore not having yet arrived at a state of complete rebellion against parental and Church authority, Manon in a state of total *refus global* (1990, 93–94).

Clearly, *Les Bons Débarras* is a masterpiece; but Mankiewicz's earlier film, *Le Temps d'une chasse* (1972) was not far behind it in capturing the lifestyle of the Québécois. In it, three men leave Montréal to go into the forest on the (mythic) moose hunt (i.e., on a bachelor week-end); but their style is cramped by the fact that Richard has brought along his young son. They spend the time in a motel eyeing the waitresses, sleeping off their debauchery and stalking moose. But when conflicts arise the atmosphere grows ominous and in the end they wind up stalking each other.

In *Variety* we read that the episodes in *Le Temps d'une chasse* "capture and reflect the Quebecois mentality." The same article gives high praise to the "technical excellence" of the image (as we would expect, with Michel Brault at the camera), and also to the acting, especially to Luce Guilbeault, as a waitress unable to perform the acts she's been paid to perform for the hunters, and to Guy

L'Ecuyer as a small, fat, drunken hunter who cannot keep up with the others, and so must content himself with stories about last year's bag.[20]

Le Temps d'une chasse had its merits as a global portrait of the Québécois male (and was, as we saw in Chapter 3, used by Anne Claire Poirier in her *Il y a longtemps* . . . . But some found this film "*maladroit*," while Mankiewicz's *Les Beaux Souvenirs* (1982) — based like *Les Bons Débarras* on a *scénario* by Réjean Ducharme — was judged something of a failure, despite high critical acclaim from some. For example, Pratley, both in *Variety* and in *Torn Sprockets*, gave the film high praise, finding the narrative compelling and stating that it "is one of those rare films that never takes a false step nor contains an unnecessary scene. Achingly real, beautifully written, honest and perceptive, it never compromises or exploits the weakness and despair of its characters. The cast is superb, the technique imaginative and unobtrusive (*TS* 1987, 205). To my way of thinking, Mankiewicz, whether before *Les Bons Débarras* or after, never made quite so nearly perfect a film as is *Les Bons Débarras*.[21] His recent *And Then You Die.* is a rather standard fare crime story — just a cut above the average. I conjecture that the relative success of *Les Bons Débarras* is due to the greatness of the particular script. (It was the most popular and widely seen feature from French Canada since *Mon oncle Antoine*. By now *Le Déclin* . . . and *Jésus de Montréal* have no doubt surpassed it.) It is, then, of some value to point out the compatibility of Mankiewicz's personality with that of Ducharme, even though he could not come up to the same high quality with the second Ducharme script as with the first. As Jean Blouin and Jean-Pierre Myette write: ". . . on comprend que Ducharme ait fini par écrire des scénarios: il vient d'ailleurs d'en terminer un troisième [*Les Bons Débarras*]. Qui pouvait mieux le mettre en images que Francis Mankiewicz? 'C'est un peu le double de Réjean, confie une connaissance: timide, humble, perfectionniste. Lui seul pouvait traduire cette intensité émotive, cette révolte nourrie de tendresse.' [(After the publication of *Enfantômes*, a novel from 1956 containing many references to film) it is understandable that Ducharme would wind up writing scripts. He has just finished a third one, moreover (that is, *Les Bons Débarras*). Who was better suited to put this into pictures than Francis Mankiewicz? 'He's somewhat the double of Réjean, confides an acquaintance: timid, humble, perfectionist. Only he could translate this emotional intensity, this revolt, nourished by tenderness']."[22]

Les Bons Débarras is, then, about as simple and about as provincial as *Manon des Sources* or *Jean de Florette*, which, while set in Provence and reflecting Provençal customs, raise the specter of human tragedy in all that that may suggest of "universality." The peculiarly American underrating of *Les Bons Débarras* may reflect a problem in hermeneutics, as well as a bias reflected in its eternal love of France (Mark Twain providing one exception, at least). And, even more serious, it may suggest a lack of attention to the subscriptions and the inscriptions that are at once unstated and yet are implicitly part of this rich and sensitive work, this masterpiece in the realm of psychological drama, a film that, like *Jean de Florette* or *Manon des Sources*, partakes of the very essence of Greek tragedy, with all its focus on taboo and passion, revenge and jealousy, desire and power, reason versus emotion, and, too, on the politics of youth versus adulthood, small versus big, wealth versus poverty, have versus have not, and so forth. Two rich and complete female characters, contemporary and plausible, are mounted here and shown in an almost mortal struggle with one another and with their destinies, a struggle that does not exclude the pessimistic charge of fatality.[23] For there is a kind of inexorable doom that hangs over this harrowing film like a black cloud at noon.

And the ending of the story leaves us in mystery, besides: for even though Manon seems to have succeeded in eliminating all of her present competition, one has even so to ask what she will do to or about the baby. Should there be a sequel?[24]

LE DÉCLIN DE L'EMPIRE AMÉRICAIN (1986; d. Denys Arcand)

On a different plane, cannot *Le Déclin* ... serve to show us the Québécois and his family, the Québécoise and her world in total inversion, if not collapse, something clearly on the horizon in *Les Bons Débarras*? And is not Arcand's film not only just as "universal," while also depicting a state of Western civilization that is widely presented in other films from other countries, in something of the same way, and yet quite uniquely and differently?

THE DECLINE OF THE AMERICAN EMPIRE IN WORLD CINEMA[25]

The sale of *The Decline of the American Empire* as a sex comedy raised a problem related to truth in advertising. Not only was this not Denys Arcand's greatest film — at least, not according to Louis-Guy Lemieux, who gives that honor to *Réjeanne Padovani*[26] — but it was far from being the "sex comedy" under which rubric it succeeded, at least commercially, at the level of popular film. And this without really being a popular film! Rather, *Le Déclin* ... fits into the more sober vision of Denys Arcand's earlier films. For it is, above all, a morality play in the purest sense of the word. Nor is it radically removed in its world view from a later work, *Jésus de Montréal*. The two films can be considered as reverse sides of a coin.

Viewed from this perspective, *Le Déclin* ... is related to several other classic and recent films that show how idealistic or highly valued "systems" are either in the process of crumbling or have crumbled already. The film has rightly been compared to *The Big Chill* (1983; Lawrence Kasdan), although *The Decline* ... is the greater film. In turn *Chill* has been justifiably compared to John Sayles's *Return of the Secaucus 7* (1980), although the connection of this film to the group under study here will not concern us. In other words, while *Le Matou* stood, as we saw, for everything *québécois*, and for the vulnerability of the *québécois* way, and although it approached "universality" only marginally, *Le Déclin* ..., although it specifically pertains to *québécois* society, is readily seen as a critique of continental American and even European (all Western) values.

The Decline ... has therefore also rightfully been compared to Jean Renoir's French classic *La Règle du jeu* (1939), in which the French aristocracy of the 1930s is shown to be on the verge of collapse. It has been likened to *La Ronde* (1950; d. Max Ophuls), as well, and I will show what *Le Déclin* ... has in common with that film too. I shall also incorporate into this "intertextual" study a British film by Alan Bridges, *The Shooting Party* (1984).

Why make these comparisons? First, to show that *The Decline* ... has been largely misunderstood when taken as a smacking, or dirty, movie, because it is more accurately characterized as a strong criticism of the society of our continent. The title, reflected early in the dialogue of the film, does say "American" (North American, Central American, South American), and not "*québécois*" or "Canadian." But the word "American" may also designate the U.S.A., and the influence of what the Canadians consider its vulgar culture, now declining, since that is apparently hypothetically possible.

The second reason for making these analogies is to underscore the fact that *The Decline* .. is no longer in the "nationalistic" tradition of the more parochial films of Québec that we have been looking at in the course of this study, films such as *Les*

Plouffe, *Maria Chapdelaine*, even *Mon oncle Antoine* (though I must reiterate here that *Mon oncle* ... has a strong "universal" charge as well). *The Decline* .\. does not entirely escape the sense of documentary characteristic of the Canadian film, both anglophone and francophone. So it does seem to some extent a sociological probe of at least one stratum of contemporary *québécoise* civilization, if not two.

But *Le Déclin* ... is, even so, a world-class film that accomplishes in its way much the same thing that the French, British, and American films I mentioned above do. It shows an aristocracy— whether titled, landed, or of the professional or intellectual sort— an elite that is decaying, decadent, falling short, falling out, dying, or taking its last futile and feeble gulps of air, gasping all the while. Laughter is not, when all is said and done, a proper response to any one of these films. But the films under scrutiny are not only interrelated by these somewhat similar moral perspectives. They also have in common a certain technical approach. They are not filmic movies; they are not visually appealing (as was, for example, that most beautiful of *québécois* films, *Les Fous de Bassan*, with its outstanding montages). They have little in the way of suspense and they have virtually no action (*The Shooting Party* perhaps being somewhat of an exception). Their dramatic appeal is in the strong emotional thrust of the dialogue; this is often charged. These films have in common, then, the fact that they are all talky. Arcand knew that to make a film that relied so heavily upon conversation was a risk, but, as it turned out, the marketing of *Le Déclin* ... brought people to see it in droves. Québec cinema houses were packed; the film gained more attention in the U.S.A. than any other film from Québec ever has. It is one of the very few films from Québec available in the video store in Bowling Green, another of them being *Blind Trust*, its reverse. This fascination with this particular film should never have happened for the reasons that it happened, but it did. For it is not because of the attention that the film commanded or the crowds it attracted that the film can be called world-class. Such a claim is possible because in its profound portrayal of despair it is as deftly handled as is the same theme in *The Big Chill*, to take our first comparison. Despair is, indeed, the leitmotif of *The Big Chill*. From the beginning the minister at the funeral of Alex, who has committed suicide, asks, "Where did Alex's hope go?" Likewise, the journalist Michael questions, "Where did hope go? Lost hope?"

Gathered together in a house where they prepare meals and sleep together, the couples in *The Big Chill* shift relationships among each other as often as do those in *The Decline* .... *The Big Chill* presents a complete picture of the emptiness of the lives of a group of promising alumni of the University of Michigan, who in the sixties thought to teach in the ghettos, to be of service, to be committed, who even participated in the "march on Washington," but who now are yuppies, cokeheads, pillpoppers, grass-smokers. They are promiscuous, sophisticated, materialistic. They are also *embourgeoisés*. In the group — a microcosm of sorts — we have (in addition to the suicide victim, who has, of course, left the scene and whose funeral is the impetus for the reunion) a woman doctor, Sarah, who is willing to lend her husband Harold as stud to Meg, a liberated if not feminist bachelor lady who wants to have a baby. We have Nick, the impotent Vietnam veteran, bitter and addicted, but who manages finally to link up with the suicide's giddy girlfriend Chloe. We also have the divorcé Sam Weber, a successful TV actor who hooks up with Karen after her husband Richard departs. Then there is Michael, the journalist, the manipulator, who does not score with anyone, but who in many respects is central to the film. The scene is one of elegance and luxury; and nearby the house in which most of the dialogue unfolds (the home of Harold and Sarah) there is a lake. Even the setting, then, is that of *The Decline* ..., whose locus is Rémy's chalet in the Lake Memphrémagog region. In both films the natural beauty clashes with the sordidness of the human outlook.

The two films also have in common the fact that the characters exercise furiously. They jog, lift weights, play ball, swim, etc.; and they both portray a sort of "last supper" scene, in which the group partakes of fine wines and good food. The obvious hedonism and the preoccupation with the body among these self-centered types is thus highlighted, as is also the talkiness of the film. People tend to converse around a table more than in other settings; hence the overuse of dialogue in both films is given more credibility. (Cf. *My Dinner with André*.)

Conversation around the table is only one of the things that *The Shooting Party* has in common with *The Big Chill* and *The Decline* .... What allows us to see *The Shooting Party* as a forerunner of *The Decline* ... (fixed, like *La Règle du jeu*, in the period just before World War I) is the very dialogue that articulates the disappearance of an era in which values and morality had some sway. Says one character, "If the landowner goes, everything goes"; whereupon one of the chief characters (Lionel Stephens, who is, significantly, considered to be very probably the best hunter of the party) replies, "I think an age, perhaps even a civilization is coming to an end." To this, Randolph Nettleby, the host (played by James Mason), says, "I believe it to be true. If you take away the proper function of the aristocracy, what can it do but play games too seriously. It happened at the end of feudalism, and it's happening now." If we were to substitute the word "intellectual" for "aristocracy" we might argue with force that these observations apply to the situation in *The Decline* ...: the proper functions of the intelligentsia are to lead, to direct, to mold. However, in modern society it is the monied, the money-seekers, and the corrupt politicians who lead. The intellectual must play games. And these games hardly differ from those of the characters in *The Big Chill*, in *The Shooting Party*, and *La Règle du jeu*. The games in *The Shooting Party* and in *La Règle du jeu* are those of the lives of empty, idle, vain, rich people. They include collecting toys such as musical birds and dolls, playing bridge, billiards, dancing, putting on competitive costume parties and masquerades, eating sumptuous dinners and breakfasts,[27] hunting — in reality participating in a mass slaughter, in which everything is shot — and, above all, swapping partners for sexual thrills, or, perhaps more pitifully, just to break the monotony of their empty lives. It is the portrayal of sexuality that is the principal thread tying together all the films we are looking at here: fidelity is disappearing with the pedigree, and the adage pronounced in *The Shooting Party*, that "it is better for a gentleman to mow his own fields than to ride over other people's fields," is rapidly losing ground in favor of diversity. As for the literal chase of fox and rabbit in *The Shooting Party* and at the weekend get-together at La Colinière in *La Règle du jeu*, that chase is readily supplanted by the metaphorical hunt, i.e., the erotic pursuits of all the characters in all these films to which are added, in *Le Déclin* ..., the frenzied, even tragic, cruisings of the homosexual art professor, Claude. In *La Règle du jeu* André asserts that there are "des règles" — rules to be followed — in this hunt that is their life; but in any of the societies portrayed, these are hard to discern, either because they have disappeared or because they never really existed beyond the stage of lip service.

In view of the foregoing, what must we conclude regarding the astonishing box office success of *Le Déclin* ...? In what subtle manner has this film departed from the more provincial fare of the Québec cinema? Or has it? On one level it is quite justifiable to assert that *Le Déclin* ... is not drastically different from many other Québec films, in that it partakes of the documentary, for which all Canadian film is known, and in which it excels (*Pour la suite du monde; Les Ordres; L'Acadie, l'Acadie*; etc.). Many of the scenes mimic documentary; some portray actual interviews; others simulate interviews, if not confessions. Moreover, the film is clearly making a sociological statement far more than any psychological ones. The visual impact is regional in nature and realistic in technique (scenes of Montréal, as in Léa Pool; scenes in the massage parlor and the gym, lakescapes, etc.).

But on yet another level, *Le Déclin* ... references other French classic films and other great American and British films (or books) regarding the decay of a society. Its very title evokes the decline and fall of the Roman Empire, which, in fact, fell for reasons similar to those shown in Arcand's work. It must be recalled that this ancient decline is the springboard for the portrayal of the modern decline. At the beginning of the film, Dominique, being interviewed by Diane, asserts that immediate gratification is her idea of happiness, that marriage is unrelated to the personal happiness of two individuals who are married to one another, and that indeed the concept of conjugal love begins to proliferate in the third century under Diocletian, just at the time when the structure of the Empire is crumbling! (Perhaps not coincidentally, *La Règle* ... was about the failure of a so-called "open" marriage, among other things.) For the historians in Arcand's film, then, history is repeating itself. Besides, over and above the allusions to the ancient fall implicit in the title of the film, the use of the word "American" intends to show a pancontinental if not worldwide collapse.

Therefore, the nationalistic flavor of most Québec cinema, leaving aside art films and experimental films, has taken the back seat to a wider view, in which postrevolutionary Québec mores, once so Catholic in their orientation, are not discernibly different from those of contemporary anglophone Canada or from those of modern America, both of which are predominantly Protestant. Intercinematic (intertextual) comparisons make possible the placing of this film among a whole series of films displaying a recurrent theme in cinema art. The presence of this theme in *Le Déclin* ... allows the film to enter the international scene in a very important manner. Not only was this film at its appearance the "most intelligent" of Arcand's films,[28] but it was also his most "international" film. Going a step further, it is permissible to say that it is also the most "international" of Québec films.

So if the public went to see a rollicking "sex comedy," that comedy was surely, and to their surprise, a "black" one, as its ending confirms. And technically speaking, they encountered not only a "black" comedy, but (probably to their disappointment) one that, like all the others we have been discussing here, is nonfilmic and talky,[29] characterized by dead scenes, and one that, as I have said, portrays an upper class in decay, devoted to the *body* as its main politic, as its unique desire and its sole obsession, a society dedicated above all to eating, talking, exercising, fornicating.[30] A microsociety that thinks itself very sophisticated, very cosmopolitan, and not xenophobic like the macrosociety.

There is not, therefore, an enormous difference between Max Ophuls's great film *La Ronde* (1950) and *Le Déclin* .... Both depict the sadness of a near Racinian *amour en chaines*; both end on a bitter note; neither provokes great belly laughs. This is equally true of *The Big Chill*, and even more so of *La Règle du jeu*, which latter, in addition to showing the decline of a society through its loose mores and its "aristocracy" on the loose, incorprates a death, foreshadowed by the mass killing of rabbits, and the killing of a cat. (It should be remembered that *La Règle* ... was even banned as depressing, morbid, and immoral. Effectively, the film can be regarded as a *danse macabre*.) Likewise, early death is almost certainly promised to the homosexual Claude, afflicted by some terrible illness (not AIDS) as also to the sadomasochist woman, Diane, in *Le Déclin* .... Suicide, the starting point of *The Big Chill*, may well be the ultimate solution of the dumpy, despondent, "betrayed" Louise (an "Yvette" of sorts; *Le Déclin*'s Karen). And when these deaths occur, will one or another of those left alive in their living death, their death-in-life, have license to say, with utmost cynicism: "He/she was only a pervert," or "only a little housewife," just as, in *The Shooting Party*, where competition and rivalry are the causes of the death, we hear said of Tom: "He was only a peasant" (i.e., "only a rabbit"; "only a fox")?

Le Déclin ..., then, is not a portrayal of Latin libido, as some have said: it portrays suicidal bent, despair, lost hope, physicality, promiscuity, greed, consumerism, materialism, selfishness, and superficiality, all reflected in the "witty dialogue" of these characters, who are almost stereotypes identifiable in or from several classics of the seventh art. Then, too, *Le Déclin* ... recalls the ritual or mythic supper before the sacrifice, or Trimalchio's feast perhaps, as do the other films we are examining here. The gourmet dinner is, in other words, the hedonistic festival before the fall.

A profound and troubling film, a modern morality play of sorts, *Le Déclin* ... has been underrated and misunderstood by the moviegoing public, unjustifiably criticized by certain feminists, one of whom ludicrously complained to me that she found no

Le Déclin de l'empire américain. Photograph by Bertrand Carrière. (Courtesy Coll. Cinémathèque Québécoise.)

lesbian in the scenario (though in point of fact the condition is at least discussed). Some of these feminists did not like to see the role reversals of the women in the gym and the men in the kitchen. Many argued that women characters and their dialogue were more of a male projection than a realistic representation of female lives or discourse. The film has also been decried by those who ridiculously eschewed the portrayal of Claude the homosexual as the only "sensitive" male character. These points are nit-picking, for at bottom it is not the least bit difficult for one to find enough types to serve as adequate examples of the theme, which is how fraud and deception lead to social decay. Véronique Dassas effectively debunks the critcisms of Louky Bersianik (in *Le Devoir*) and of Louise Carrière (in *Femmes et cinéma québécois*) regarding women in Québec film, and especially in *Le Déclin ...*, when she points out that *all* segments of society are targeted in Arcand's work, and that his pessimistic view is to be found in all his films including *Réjeanne Padovani*, *Gina*, *La Maudite Galette*, and so forth. She reminds us, too, that the feminist perspective is that of the ideologue, and therefore simplistic and weakened by its point of departure, which seeks to have reality enter a theoretical cadre (stranglehold) from which by definition that reality can only escape.[31]

One reads in the *Film Review Annual* that Arcand's intention is not really to highlight the differences between males and females but to show two Québecs, one the present, hedonistic and unaware of its history; the other, the unreconciled and repressed past, unrepresented but implicit.[32] Whether this is the case or not, to appreciate the thrust of *Le Déclin* ... one has only to take a long, hard look at this group of would-be aristocratic professionals with their pedigrees (their *pieds de grue*), their A.B.D.s and their Ph.D.s, and at Mario, the one unpresuming representative of a "lower class," who is at sea (or is he?) among this group of pretentious people. They pepper their "international" French with English phrases, speak of Woody Allen films,[33] drink special imported ales and *grand cru* wines, eat gourmet fare, and so forth. (Similar airs and affectations are to be found in the *personnages* of the other films we have been examining here.) All idle, empty, vain — "full up" with vanity, like La Bruyère's *caractères*[34] — the people in *Le Déclin* ... announce disaster for the whole affluent and amoral society that inhabits the American continent today. As we have seen, almost identical human specimens were shown with less brilliance in *The Big Chill*; and similar types from the 1890s populate the Vienna of *La Ronde*, while the same degeneracy in the elite of pre–World War I British society is the subject of *The Shooting Party*. And, in much the same vein, the upper class French society of the 1930s, with its strong strain of anti-semitism and its valueless snobbery, is memorably drawn in *La Règle du jeu*. Forever on the fox hunt, the chase, the cruise — epitomized by, but not exclusively limited to the images in the park that are adumbrated on the screen as Claude describes his painful pursuits — virtually every one of these characters in virtually every one of these films has forgotten the wisdom encapsulated in the adage of *The Shooting Party*. All — with what Arcand calls their "oceans of free time," are concerned with (their) "happiness," all are busily mowing "other people's fields."[35] They are the elite, who seek instant gratification; and they identify this (sexual) gratification with happiness. In *Le Déclin* ... they discuss all this in standardized French, by the way, and this is another example of their flight from the image of the Québécois of the old school; from regionalism. And *discuss* is the word, for they talk and talk. The dialogue, therefore, is more important than the visual impact of this film. But Arcand himself realized he was going against all the laws of cinema to illustrate his contention that the eye has seen everything, but the ear is still virgin. (So much for the issue of *regard* we have noted elsewhere in this book!)

Yet, before concluding this analysis, I should not fail to point out that not everyone sees in Mario a simple contrast to the other characters, as suggested just above. He is to some not natural but a parody of the macho type: he drinks beer, not wine; he likes only what is from Québec. On the other hand he himself is not and cannot be *homo quebecensis* in the flesh, as are the professors: he is the Other, the immigrant, the stranger. He is not Québécois *pure laine*. Rather, he is of some foreign extract, Italian, Latin American, Hispano-Italian, as his name, Mario Alvarez, reveals. Note, however, that the role is played by Marcel Arcand, the brother of the author-director, and a well-known Québécois actor ('*Bye See You Monday*, etc.), while one of the Québécois professors — turned international, of course — is played by the renowned actor of Italian descent, Pierre Curzi. But this is not the first time Curzi has embodied the Québécois — he did as much in *Maria Chapdelaine*, and in *Le Crime d'Ovide Plouffe*.

Such is the polysemy not only of the film but of Canadian society in general at this point in its history. And the merging (or non-merging) of all these cultures, along with that of the native peoples, is the biggest issue facing that nation at this time. It is one about whose resolution Arcand seems rather pessimistic. The question of a pluralistic civilization will return as a theme in Arcand's *Jésus de Montréal*. An *auteur* film, made on the modest budget of $1.3 million, *Le Déclin* ..., then, poses the central problem the individual has in facing the Other, either as a threat to one's integrity, or as a mirror through which one comes to self-knowledge.

And yet the real subject of *Le Déclin* ... is not the Other so much as deception: it illustrates, as several critics have pointed out and as the dialogue of the film itself reveals, how lies lead to social decay. It is, therefore, unmistakably *québécois* in its sensibility, "buoyant but introspective, uninhibited but graceful." It is a masterpiece by international standards.

While I would contend that these professors seem to have a more exciting life than most professors at Bowling Green State University probably have, that is really not the point. *Le Déclin* ... has been dubbed a sex film about intellectuals and an intellectual film about sex. (In that, it may be compared to *Néa* by Nelly Kaplan, for example.) And ironically, the American "empire" *enjoyed* Arcand's visions of its own decline. The film supposedly will be made in Hollywood, since, according to Arcand's assertions on television, dialogue in the film is important, and most Americans will not read subtitles.

Le Déclin ... did much better at the French box office, than did *Jésus de Montréal*. Did the titillating ads in *Le Monde* (and elsewhere) account for some of this? The illustration that accompanied the ad showed a couple, the man dressed in suit and tie, the woman a mere drawing, with breasts and nipples showing through her sweater. In both cases, the faces are blurred to suggest the "universality" of the characters. The film is rated for "14 ans indicatif" and above the picture we have quotations indicating that this film has been a success in Montréal, Toronto, and New York. Vincent Canby is quoted from the *N.Y. Times*, saying "spontaneously funny ... a comedy which expresses in a successful and amusing way the intelligence of its characters," while Bruce Kirkland of the *Toronto Sun* is quoted as writing, "*Le Déclin* ... is turn by turn amusing, cruel, tender, profound, funny, crude, surprising, demanding ... *Le Déclin* ... is a film which troubles the soul ... a masterpiece of finesse and wit." And Louis-Guy Lemieux, from *Le Soleil*, is asserting that *Le Déclin* ... is "A masterpiece ... a sparkling *comédie de moeurs*." The film is also credited with receiving the Best Canadian Film from the 1986 Toronto Festival of Festivals; the prize for the most popular film from the same festival; and the International Critics' prize from the Cannes Film Festival of the same year. Playing at the Place Charest and the Cinéma Lido, who would want to miss a movie with such a glowing come-on? Many of those attending may not have received the deeper message, however.

Let us sum up the situation of Arcand and his two renowned films as follows: *Le Déclin* ... was widely screened and reviewed on this continent and in Europe; it also fired a quite a lot of scholarly writing. After this success, Arcand's *Jésus de Montréal* inevitably was widely shown and commented upon. But if you want to know more about Arcand or his films, the last place to go is the *International Dictionary of Films and Filmmakers*.[36] Neither Arcand nor *Le Déclin* ... nor *Jésus* ... appear in this mammoth work. *La Règle du jeu* and *La Ronde* do. Does this mean that the authors see Arcand's films as too parochial, too rooted in Québec culture, thereby undermining the international popularity of the first (*Le Déclin* ...) and the generally favorable critical reception of the second (*Jésus* ...), as well as any claims to "universality" made by many reviewers and writers on Arcand? They are both, of course, mirrors of the society from which they emanate; but that is not all they offer, by a country mile.

In addition to the works we have already dealt with in this chapter, there are a number of other films from which we may learn much about the Québec society, and Jean Beaudin's *Cher Théo*, like his better known film *J. A. Martin photographe*, is a prime candidate for that role. In both of these works there is a brooding quality, along with a great sense of the past society; and in both of them the couple is threatened. But in both of them, too, the resolution seems to be happier than we find in the works of Arcand, while in *Mario* and in *Le Matou* the conflict resolutions Beaudin offers seem to be dictated by the works from which they are taken.

CHER THÉO (1975; d. Jean Beaudin)

In a documentary style, this fictional film reconstructs the *québécois* past and indeed the material culture of that past, while seeming to offer a postmodern suggestion that that past had values forgotten by the present generation of Québécois. In a larger sense, the film is concerned with a curious bonding that occurs between two women who happen to share a room in a hospital over a period of six weeks or more. They have very different values and very different life styles: Julie is young, artistic, sophisticated, while Josette is old, plain, countrified, simple. And yet they bridge these differences and come to a kind of love, before the death of Josette. The relationship has profoundly changed Julie by the end, and one of the most important ways in which she is changed is in her concept of the couple.

The antiseptic and usually impersonal atmosphere of the hospital is the setting for a warm communication between these two very opposite women. A series of tableaux that sometimes flow into one another, and sometimes have clear separation from one another — i.e., are without dissolves — tell the story of the evolution of this moving instance of "mother replacement.' At the beginning of the film, we see a young woman with head bandaged. Obviously, she has had a serious accident. Once she has revived, the conversations with the older woman in the next bed begin. Josette, the old country woman (who has a strong Québec accent) talks to Julie as she does her knitting, the eternal knitting of the Québécoise (using that fine wool still today so *demandée*, so in demand, by serious knitters). She writes to her husband, beginning with the formula from which the title comes: "Cher Théo." And she receives letters from him with such everyday information as "Aujourd'hui, j'ai ramassé des bleuets pour la confiture [Today I gathered blueberries for the jam]."

Josette confides in Julie, "We've always been together. ... Theo is eighty-one; we will soon have our fiftieth wedding anniversary." She tells her that Theo always names all the animals; at present he wants a name for his calf. She gathers the letters, as would a young lover, and ties them in a bundle with a reddish ribbon.

Julie, on the other hand, is an artist, and once she is on the mend, she at times sketches. She listens to cassettes. Her life is clearly fragmented and lonely. Her mother is on the way to Majorca, and cannot be held back because of this accident. Her husband visits her, but he must make several business calls during this short stop. Ironically, Julie has everything—but nothing. Josette has little, but has everything. She sleeps the sleep of the content; her husband does not come (cannot come) to see her, but he sends her letters and things. Indeed, a fine package of blueberries shows up, and Josette shares them with Julie. Later, Julie asks if Theo has named the calf yet. She suggests "Bleuet" (Blueberry), and the name is adopted.

Julie's life is like the sterile hospital in which she finds herself until she bathes in the warmth of Josette's smiling simplicity, her generosity, and her natural straightforwardness. The two begin to play games; Julie helps Josette make a cassette recording for Theo.

Julie's real mother, returned from Majorca, brings her a "beautiful present from Spain." But Julie finds she wants to stay with Josette, who represents the better, the ideal mother. Then Josette is removed in the night; when brought back, she is quite out of it. Julie grows more and more concerned, as it becomes clear that Josette's condition is worsening. Slowly Josette comes to: she puts on her spectacles and begins to read her letters. But again she is taken out of the room during the night. In the morning, the bed is returned, empty and unmade: the stark, striped mattress tells its own story. But the nurse brings Julie a letter from Josette. She has left Julie her pen; that is all she had with her; it is sixty years old, and has always written words of love.

Julie takes the pen and begins to write, "Cher Théo ... It will soon be daylight and ...." The camera moves away from her; her image recedes into the distance.

This is an extraordinarily beautiful short film. There is a soft sadness to it, and the night scenes are especially memorable: they have a strange luminosity, so that one remembers long afterward the blue and rose tones, the shining skin, the curtain moving in the breeze. Some might find the film a bit too obvious, a bit too sentimental. I found it direct, tasteful, and touching. James E. Page suggests that this film complements Margaret Lawrence's *Stone Angel*, which is only one more reason to view it.[37] One may categorically say that both *Cher Théo* and *J. A. Martin . . .* clearly outshine Beaudin's *Emilie*, which has been serialized on CBC television quite recently (shown in English in the early months of 1993). While having a certain compelling rusticity in its effort to evoke earlier times, *Emilie* never achieves the power of *J. A. Martin . . .* or, for that matter, of Carle's *Maria Chapdelaine*. But, like *Cher Théo* and *J. A. Martin . . .*, *Emilie* most clearly deals with problems of the couple, threatened by the arrival of many children, the alcoholism of the husband, and so forth.

But for those viewers who prefer to learn about Québec society through the very unsentimental vehicle of comedy and satire, the works of André Forcier do well. And of these, *Kalamazoo* may be the best choice. Not only will one laugh, but certain barbs directed at Americans will echo the general dislike of the United States often expressed in films from Québec (and from anglophone Canada as well). The immigrant, the Other (in this case the Italo-Jewish), who often figures in the *québécois* film, will play an essential role in this story.

KALAMAZOO (1988; d. Marc-André Forcier)

Forcier (Abel, 1990, 177) says that although Felix Cotnoir is fifty-three years old, he is still a virgin. This does not, however, prevent him from having a strong desire for love. He hopes he will soon "lose his virginity," in fact. But the reason he is still a *puceau* is that his capacity for love is too great to permit him to love a real woman. Having nearly killed Pascal Globenski with his Checker cab, he is deeply concerned about Globenski; but he also immediately falls in love with his victim's mistress, Helena Me(n)tana — I have seen it written both ways — whose picture he has glimpsed on the cover of her novel, entitled *Kalamazoo*. In the picture she is disguised as a mermaid. He takes this book (which Globenski has had published at his own expense for its author, Helena) from Globenski's Italo-Jewish delicatessen, whose chef, Wilfrid gives us one or two laughs. Cotnoir likes plants; he cultivates the rutabaga (rodevechhi).

In this film, sometimes reminiscent of the films of Jacques Tati (but never quite so funny), there is a curious fusion of dream and reality. At one juncture we find Felix (who calls himself Feliciano Montenegro, as an exotic rendition of his French name) and Helena traveling to St. Pierre and Miquelon, where they lunch on crackers and Kraft Velveeta cheese. The brand of the cheese transmits a sense of the cultural debasement of New World French countries when they (necessarily) come in contact with American culinary monstrosities.

In the dubbed version, this film comes off as poor stuff. But because it remains by and large ethnic in character, it gives a sense of French-Canadian life in its present complexity. Along with reference to *québécois* culture, there is some Acadian· content. The film relies heavily upon dialogue, is slow-moving, slow-paced, with poor timing, poor rhythm, little action, and so it is at times tedious. Yet for some reason one does not completely forget it. (By the way, is that Marilyn Lightstone's voice we hear in the dubbed version, behind Marie Tifo's acting?) Tifo's brillant acting is hardly showcased here, where, as a mermaid and goddess of love, she is supposedly making the dreams of the two men come true. (*I've Heard the Mermaids Singing* this is not!) From mermaid-disguise to real mermaid, in a rather grotesque "metamorphosis," Helena provides for Felix the possibility of imagining his rejuvenation through love, and this is the real lure of his amorous quest. Thus, he may perhaps slip the category of the unloved. Nevertheless, the fantasy gratifies the male's longings,·and is larded with misogynous implications.

Forcier's films are often compared to those of Jean Vigo, not only because he mixes the real with fantasy and the imaginary, but also precisely because he is interested, like Vigo, in "People whom life does not love."[38] His other films include *Return of the Immaculate Conception* (1971); *Bar Salon* (1973); a short called *Night Cap* (1974) concerning vengeance and murder among the working class of Montréal; *Hot Water, Cold Water* (1976); *Au clair de la lune* (1982); and his recent *Une Histoire inventée*, or *An Imaginary Tale* (1990), which had its United States premier showing in November, 1990 in Chicago, where a retrospective of his work was also being mounted, under the title "The Rabelaisian Cinema of André Forcier." One of the most remarkable things about *Une Histoire inventée* is the performance of an adult Charlotte Laurier, whose face and voice are not substantially changed from the days of her stunning performance as Manon in *Les Bons Débarras*. But beyond this, the film seemed to be a clear hit with the audience. Forcier's sense of humor has definitely evolved; it has been refined, now, and has turned from the burlesque to something more sophisticated. Significantly, Richard Martineau finds *Une Histoire inventée* to be "a profound work, which speaks to us of the difficulty of loving and of being loved." (The film was aired on CBC in spring 1993.)

The Return of the Immaculate Conception (1971; 80 min.), Forcier's earliest feature, captures the essence of one level of Québec culture. It pictures the dinginess and the frigid snowscapes of the winter season, and stresses the countrified nature of the members of society he is looking at, both through the main characters and through the music. The plot revolves around a group of young men whose adventures are at once raunchy, bizarre, and funny. Yet Forcier's dark humor already peeks through this film, suggesting the dead end these youthful figures may be headed for. An even earlier short film, entitled *Chroniques labradoriennes* (1967; 12 minutes), deals with revolution in Québec, shown through satire, and involving an invasion by neighboring Labradorians.[40]

BAR SALON (1974; d. André Forcier)

A film about a personal crisis, but also a generalized portrait of a society in decay, *Bar Salon* presents a "lushly textured black-and-white portrait of a dying culture."[41] Charles, the proprietor of the Montréal tavern where his daughter tends bar, is trying to save his business from bankruptcy. So he moonlights at a nightclub in the suburbs. He becomes quite dissipated. Then, in a grand gesture, he opens his tavern for his daughter's wedding reception. Some might claim that the comedy, much of which emanates from the gathering of *bons-buveurs à la Rabelais*, is both culture-bound and accessible. For others this movie might be called a "film noir," as is stated on the video jacket. For me, it is neither a comedy nor a film noir: the film, with its intensely alcoholic characters and its sordid sets, is a study in despair; and though the film is dark, it is not film noir as I understand it. Still more disturbing, it is not difficult to see how the tavern (and then the inn) can be the central *maison de palabres* for these unfortunates, and thus we have a microcosmic view of the Montréalais, and even of humankind.

Hardly anything is funny in this movie. It concerns bankruptcy, suicidal drunkenness, betrayal of friendships, and offers the viewer lots of drinking scenes, lots of car rides (and D.U.I.), lots of sex and/or nudity, lots of snow, quite a number of cats, and quite a lot of pottying. The humor, when it occurs, is quite black, not to say grotesque (e.g., a scene in which a cat weighing 4 lb., 8 oz. is sold for $4.80 to a Chinese cook for "spare ribs," which the cook claims to be "like chicken, like chicken").

On the broader level, there are several cutting allusions to the alleged domination of the English language in Québec. Major

Cotnoir, for example, runs the New Majestic Inn, and answers the phone in English. Charles must make a radio announcement of a forthcoming Saturday night performance by Western singers from Gaspésie both in English and French. (And, by the way, those Western singers from La Gaspésie really do show up to provide us with some pretty twangy music: it is a question of Libère Holmes and Josephat Berthelot, representing themselves.)[42]

Less noticeable, perhaps, is background radio dialogue during a morning breakfast scene between Robert and his daughter. In English, we hear a series of announcements, including one for Money Game; we also hear advertisements for Tang, for ChapStick, and for an American movie set in Chicago. ("Earl Williams is not hanging, as condemned to do, but is hanging around in Cook County," the voice says. The reference is to Jack Lemmon and Walter Matthau as reporters in Billy Wilder's *The Front Page* [1974], a Hecht-MacArthur play made into a film four times.) All this is followed by news of a rail strike and something about President Nixon that is not clear. The messages subliminally point to the domination of English language and culture, and particularly of American "culture." This is not the last time Forcier will stab at that. Nevertheless, he was willing to go to Chicago to meet and speak to the American Council of Quebec Studies and the Alliance Française, to be present at the American premier showing of his *Histoire inventée* (filmed in 1989), where he used the tactics of visible boredom and "boyish" rudeness to amuse (insult) the American audience. Looking very rumpled and unclean (read: bad boy-artist) as he fielded "questions," he was the cat, the moviegoers the mice. Nevertheless, Forcier says in Abel: "J'attends avec impatience le jour où l'on va me considérer moins comme un voyou qui fait du cinéma et plus comme un cinéaste qui n'a du voyou que l'apparence. [I await impatiently the day when I will be considered less as a bum who makes movies and more like a moviemaker who only seems to be a bum]" (1990, 177).

L'Eau Chaude l'eau frette (1976) is again a comedy set in Montréal, this time in a rooming house, whose occupants celebrate the birthday of a loan shark named Polo. Carmen pays off her debts to Polo with sex; she also runs the laundromat and has a daughter Francine, a teenager with a pacemaker that becomes the instrument of a con game invented by her boyfriend Ti-Guy, etc. The plot is complicated, and the humor blacker here than in Forcier's previous films. This is also true of *Au Clair de la Lune*, which stands both by its date and its conception somewhere between *Kalamazoo* and *Bar Salon*, having something in common with each of them.

Pratley finds that the characters in *Bar Salon* are observed "with a stark realism and a love for the 'lower depths' of cinema expressionism" (*TS* 1987, 217). *L'Eau chaude l'eau frette* (*A Pacemaker and a Side-Car*) is, for him "overdone and overstated" (*TS* 1987, 231). He does not even mention Forcier's *Au clair de la lune*.

AU CLAIR DE LA LUNE (1982; d. André Forcier)

Au clair de la lune is set largely in a Montréal bowling alley named Moonshine Bowling (or, in French Au Clair de la Lune — but the pun on moonshine is lost in the French name). Here Frank, a homeless albino who lives in a green Chevy and is addicted to elixir of terpin hydrate and codeine, which he blithely mixes with 1955 champagne, meets Bert, an ex-champion bowler, now "l'homme sandwich." Bert wears a sandwich board (a *pancarte*, ironically called at one point a *scapulaire*) to earn his living, for arthritis has cramped his bowling style. In the course of their friendship, Bert "saves" Frank's life and Frank "helps" Bert regain his championship, by getting behind the pins and knocking them over, so that Bert gets strike after strike. Again the black humor of Forcier is apparent. He intertwines sad situations and the stories of Frank, Bert (born illegitimate, and whose father is by now dead), and Léopoldine, an orphan by now. But in a flashback, Léopoldine is seen to have left her father after having worked diligently in his tire shop (which was in fact supplied with tires she had stolen). She left him because he could not break up with Margot, who makes candy at a sweet shop. By means of a voice-over in which Frank tells the sordid pranks and antics of Montréal's have-nots, Forcier, in this film as in *Bar Salon*, deals with the serious problems of homelessness and alcoholism on the level of a personal and personalized story. Yet on another level there is criticism of a continent so rich where there are such poor. Thus, on a sardonic plane Frank is shown to live in a car, where he does his cooking, eating, toileting, and sleeping. This is referred to sarcastically as "the magic comfort of America ...." Indeed, the social criticism is quite evident, and in the long run there is little to laugh at. This time Forcier includes a bit of blasphemy regarding the Church. For, says Frank, "the Albino prefers the goodness of blasphemy to unleashed sanctity, or holiness." And in a parodic religious ceremony Albert becomes Alberta, his twin sister. As in *Bar Salon*, there is lots of snow, and there are lots of cars; there is also quite a bit of urinating (again) and lots of drinking and drunkenness, as well as spitting; but there is a little less vomiting. Some of the dialogue is rather vulgar. (Sample: "Every night Maurice fixed himself up so he was as handsome as Elvis, to go to the "course" with his blonde; and every evening boredom saw love in the joining of two wads of spit on the pizza leftovers.")

One can argue that Bert, having put Frank in his debt by "saving his life," or "resuscitating him," reduces him to a sort of slavery. Apart from that, Frank, the creator of a cinema/story concerning his mythic utopia Albinia, is Forcier's alter ego. He floats; he flies; he has difficulty controlling himself; he insists on the illegitimate and orphaned state of his companions (cf., Aurore, Tit-Coq, Benoît); he tangles with leather-jacketed hoods, then organizes them. He speaks in oxymoronic metaphors and in verse: "Léopoldine — orpheline de la lune [et] aussi visible que l'ombre du destin arrivait à point. [Leopoldine, a girl-orphan from the moon (and) as visible as the shadow of destiny arrived in the nick o'.]" The rhyming observations at the end of the movie cannot escape us: "Il n'y a pas d'iv_resse_/ pour réchauffer l'espace trop fret de notre dét_resse_ ... [There is no drunkenn_ess_/ to warm the too cold space of our dist_ress_]"; and, Frank continues, "I think of _Léopoldine_ and all the _héroïnes_ who do not drink _codéine_ ...; of my other father (_père_) and the tenderness of _Albert_." A touch of optimism, however drab and grim, characterizes the very end of the film, when Frank says: "Albert, les vers ne mangeront avant l'été [Albert, the worms will not eat before summer]."

Richard Brouillette has some astute observations to make about this film: "_Au Clair de la Lune_ marks an important turn in Forcier's work ... and ... a return to the poetic and surrealistic mold of his first full-length feature, _The Return of the Immaculate Conception_. Forcier undertakes something miraculous and rare: he creates a mythology with a _québécois_ essence (whereas this has always been flushed out of the cinema from Québec) and he therefore succeeds in constructing the _québécois_ archetype with his paradoxical dreams and his reality, riddled with adversity. A mythology which will be found again in _Kalamazoo_ (1988)."[43] This is an accurate evaluation, if a bit of an exaggeration, as this mythology _can_ be found in many films prior to 1982.

Early in 1991, a segment of Victoria Tennant's Sunday Arts Entertainment (CBC) was devoted to Forcier, with added commentary on Pierre Falardeau's _Le Party_, set in prison. (This film gives a paradigm for class society [four levels], while dealing with sex, death, and freedom.) _Une Histoire inventée_ was also covered, as a study of unrequited male lust and love; it was compared to the neorealist films of De Sica. Forcier himself appeared in his unconventional dress, and the bourgeois faubourg where he lives seemed in sharp contrast to this renegade, somewhat asocial person, who states in the interview that he wants only to make films, and seems embarrassed by his fame.

Carnival and Lent — eros and thanatos — seem to be at odds in almost all of Forcier's work (another Rabelaisian trait, if you will). I am sometimes reminded in viewing Forcier of such a film as *King of Hearts* (1966; Philippe de Broca), one of Geneviève Bujold's early sorties, in which she played the frivolous Columbine-Coquelicot. His films also share something with *Cannery Row* (1982; David S. Ward). As a source of further information for my reader, I would also point out that Forcier's *Eau chaude eau frette* is the object of a complex analysis by Major (1982, 84–90). But as a final note, one might contend, if tentatively, that the Forcier film verges on being exploitative.

We have seen that *Cher Théo* provides us with contrasts between the old traditional Québécois couple and the threatened marriage of another, and Forcier's films show us societal drift. In this vein, the breakdown of the family and the plight of the single woman on the make are skillfully portrayed in a rather unknown but, in my opinion, excellent movie entitled *Au revoir ... à lundi*. Although one might call this film international, having both French and Québécois stars, the film seems to me sufficiently *québécois* to be included in my discussion here. In fact, one of its points of interest is that it was made following Carole Laure's performance in the cult film *Sweet Movie* (1974–5; video jacket erroneously gives 1984; video release 1989), and assists in redeeming her reputation. *Sweet Movie*, by the Yugoslavian director Dusan Makavejev, had Carole Laure rolling in melted chocolate and, in fact, drowning her lover in same, and the film brought an aura of scandal around Laure's name. As Marcel Jean tells us, Laure, after this, sought to star in films that "conformed more to the image of herself that she wished to project" (Coulombe 1991, 317–18). Thus, subsequent films in which she appeared, such as *Born for Hell* (1975–6; Denis Héroux), the memorable feminist film *Jument Vapeur* (1977; Joyce Buñuel), *Maria Chapdelaine* (1983; d. Gilles Carle), and a film showing the more contemporary Maria of *La Mort d'un bûcheron* (1988; d. Gilles Carle), along with *Au revoir ... à lundi*, helped to refigure this image. One might add that this effort was at once assisted by the discovery in France of Carle's movies, and undermined by Laure's role in *The Surrogate* (1984; d. Don Carmody). Although we might have discussed *Au revoir ...* in the chapter on Literature into Film, since it is based on a novel by Roger Fournier, it seems more appropriate to treat it in the present discussion of the couple and the breakdown of marriage and the family.

AU REVOIR ... À LUNDI ([*GOODBYE [OR BYE]* *SEE YOU MONDAY*)
(1979–1980; d. Maurice Dugowson)

It is the Christmas season, and that fact heightens the bitterness of the situations in which the two main protagonists find themselves. Lucy, a Montréalaise single woman, has been carrying on a love affair with Julian, a married man, who, when he learns she is pregnant and expects to keep the baby, disappears in a hurry. Nicole, on the other hand, is a French immigrée, who rooms with Lucy and who is having a very unhappy affair with a married man, Robert. It is readily apparent that this is a film about contemporary couples, about a lack of commitment (all the males in this film are quite disgusting), and about the collapse of marital values in modern (*québécois*) society. We may bracket the word *québécois*, because in the long run Nicole (a Frenchwoman), who goes to Robert's house where he is playing Santa Claus and in the process not only exposes their affair to his wife, but also loses him, finally links up with Frank, a wimp, a mama's boy, an uncommunicative American doctor who also refuses to make a long-term agreement with her, although he is ever so happy to transport her to Tampa, Florida (to the tune of Caribbean music), where he expects her to keep house for him and entertain his important guests. (In the dubbed version Nicole has a French accent, while Carole Laure has none; this is to show Miou-Miou as the "foreigner," victim nonetheless of the same sexism as her roommate. Frank's mother also speaks to her of her neatness, not what one would expect from a Frenchwoman.)

Meanwhile, Lucy, having lost Julian, meets up with Arnold, after having had sex (for which she tries to pay) with George the bartender, who has serviced both her and Nicole at low moments in their sex lives. Arnold, also a married man, seems to be involved in some shady business. Although Arnold courts Lucy, although he wines her, dines her, sleeps with her (naked with his gold cross conspicuously showing on a chain around his neck, as he unabashedly commits adultery), he, too, has deeper loyalties to his wife than to Lucy, and she must finally tell him to "go home."

The story ends with the reunion of Nicole, who has left Frank, and Lucy, who has lost her job because of her absenteeism, even though Jack, her boss—who has a soft spot for her, but who also upstages her in the radio-talk show—has tried to intervene.

One feels that the film, though directed by a man, has a feminist line to it that emerges as an endorsement of sisterhood. At the end, the two women are seen walking in the park with Lucy's baby, now a child of three or four, in a classic *québécois* scene — snow is everywhere. As the title suggests, in contemporary life, where the men want to have their cake and eat it too, there is little to look forward to except weekend kicks, after which comes the workaday world. Early scenes also show the conflicting values of the feminist, Lucy, and her sister, Juliette, who thinks Lucy is a whore. She herself is a self-satisfied if unhappy "Yvette," caught in a tedious marriage with Hector, a mild and sympathetic man who is among the many Lucy seduces or attempts to seduce in the course of these few years. (She even makes up to the policeman who questions her nighttime roamings.)

A major flaw of the film is that, in an effort to portray Lucy's promiscuity, there is a confusion of characters. But the sad, dark atmosphere of the film is unforgettable, and seems to translate "universal" contemporary problems. Pratley (*TS* 1987, 244) says: "This film is much superior to those that were being made then in North America about unconventional affairs and the changing patterns of love and marriage. Although the pace is somewhat slow, the treatment unimaginative, the situations and the talented cast give it a direct appeal and emotional depth." Certainly it has more depth than the recent American film, *Single Women, Married Men* (1989), in which a psychotherapist who lost her husband to a younger woman examines her life after forming a support group for women involved with married men. But then, *Au revoir ...* is more than a story about unconventional affairs and the changing patterns of love and marriage. It is about the gulf between the sexes brought about by the profoundly sexist attitudes of the men portrayed.

Yet another kind of gulf, between parent and child, is the subject of many Québec films. At times that gulf is bridged. In the next chapter, for example, we shall see two examples of father and son (male) bonding as portrayed in the crime drama. But in comic terms, *Gaspard et fil$* portrays the tensions of this relationship, tensions that are resolved in the course of the film's events.

GASPARD ET FIL$ (1988; d. François Labonté)

The father, Gaspard, represents everything repugnant to the son, Claude, whose meticulous French and discriminating tastes are in sharp contrast to the sloppiness of his father. Gaspard, threatened with being thrown out of the house by his son (who has inherited everything from his mother), has ostensibly won a six-million-dollar lotto ticket, which, however, he cannot find. They accuse one another of hiding the needed ticket; but Gaspard remembers he had the ticket in the pocket of a shirt he had given to Evelyne, his sister-in-law, who is collecting used clothing for her "clinique." Now the problem is to find the clinic. First, there is a search in Montréal; then in New York, where they learn from Evelyne's son, Maxime, that she is in Venezuela, and that her name is Evelyne Gutierez. But when they arrive in Venezuela, she is not at the hotel. Nevertheless, they stay in this five-star hotel while they continue to search for her. (Location scenes here are eye-catching.) Finally, father and son are informed as to the whereabouts of la clínica Amilcar, and when they locate her, and through her the ticket, the father pretends to eat it, commenting afterward that "It lacked salt." "But why did you do this?" asks the son, to which comes the answer, "I was hungry." (He is always hungry.) But the truth is soon out, and the father says to the son, "You didn't think I was that big a fool did you?" So after all this tension and irritation, their relationship is on new terms, as they drive off in Claude's car to collect the money and "live happily ever after."

Gaspard ... starts out with a plot similar to René Clair's classic *Le Million* (1931), but hardly holds up to the French film for depth of social commentary, charm, or quality. While *Gaspard* ... is, then, a thin film, it nonetheless has some amusing interludes and presents family conflict in a palatable format.

MANUEL, LE FILS EMPRUNTÉ OR *A SON BY CHOICE* (1990; d. François Labonté)

Manuel ... is another, more recent, film by Labonté dealing with the relationship of father to son and vice versa.

In his quest for an acceptable father figure (his own father, a Portuguese immigrant being brutal, rigid, and impatient) Manuel bonds to the Spanish Civil War refugee Juan Alvarez, a cobbler, who teaches him unworkable notions of anarchy, revolution, liberty, and justice, while Alvarez's wife gives the boy practical advice and some tenderness. The old man teaches him to read, and tells him stories of the civil war, and of a shepherd boy who saved his life. There are intercuts in black and white to depict the horrors of the war. But the lessons lead to the boy's revolt in the school setting and to his ultimate disillusionment when the Spaniard advises him to conform. Nevertheless, Manuel seems in the end content to remain in the Alvarez household; he has perhaps matured enough not to expect perfection.

The film depicts rather powerfully the adjustment problems of immigrants and the conflicts arising in the multiethnic Québec of today.

HOMOSEXUALITY IN QUÉBEC CINEMA

While we are in the process of discussing threats to the couple and breakdown in family life, we might look momentarily at an alternate life style as portrayed in the Québec cinema, that of homosexuality. We have seen some treatment of this while discussing women's films, and particularly those of Léa Pool. But one should not overlook an important film of the 80s dealing with male homosexuality. That is *L'Homme renversé*.

L'HOMME RENVERSÉ (1986; d. Yves Dion)

Like so many *québécois* films, this one combines the direct cinema, which contributed to the early formation of Dion, with fiction. In it, Dion allows for a great deal of improvisation. Though this is the first of Dion's fiction films, it is doubtless his most famous. But in all his films he calls for a better life with more justice, more dignity, more humanity, and more "normality" for all handicapped or marginal persons. He has dealt with cerebral palsy, deafness, cancer, and, here he lays bare the masculine condition.

Dion also participated in the making of the series, "La bioéthique: une question de choix," with *Perversion* (1988), which had to do with medical help in euthanasia, and in the series "Enfants de la rue," with *Danny* (1987), the story of a boy from a good family who, in spite of the interventions of a social worker (played by Gabriel Arcand), slips into delinquency (Yves Lever in Coulombe 1991, 152–53).

Lever says that *L'Homme renversé* was "the first *québécois* film to reveal, without making any excuses, the Québécois [man] in all his vulnerability, with all his fears and weaknesses" (*Hist.* 1988, 351). And Ignacio Ramonet says of this film: "Yves Dion, in *L'Homme renversé*, grapples with all the problematics concerning the individual: one's sense of self; affectivity; machoism; homosexuality. With a sort of Pirandello-like prowess, in which the director takes risks, he proposes a real autopsy of the *québécoise* soul, and offers, in a magisterial manner, the spectacle of its great disorder."[44]

This was not, however, the first time that the theme of male homosexuality had been treated in the Québec film. As we saw, Claude Jutra dealt with this "problem," which was his own, in *A tout prendre* (1963), while in 1965 Jean-Claude Lord made his *Délivrez-nous du mal* (1965), basing his *scénario* on Claude Jasmin. This latter film presents 1950s style stereotypes of homosexuals. It also is fashioned on the film noir of the 50s. In it André, a wealthy man, falls desperately in love with Georges, a bisexual business man. (The film stars Yvon Deschamps.) Humiliation and suicide are ingredients of this "sordid" film, as Lever calls it (*Hist.* 1988, 177). It was not shown commercially until 1969.

Two other recent films treating the subject are Jean Beaudin's powerful *Being at Home with Claude* (1991) and Mario Dufour's *Mortel Désir* (1992), the former concerning the murder of Claude by his lover, and the latter focusing on the testimony of HIV positive persons and AIDS victims, as well as giving the highly emotional reactions of their partners and their relatives.

EROS AND THANATOS IN FILMS FROM QUÉBEC

Threats to the couple and representations of death are, as we have been seeing, not uncommon in the *québécois* film. A rather early example might include the 1964 Gilles Groulx feature *Le Chat dans le sac*, where the racially mixed couple is on the verge of separation (Pratley *TS* 1987, 177−78). (The woman is an Anglo-Canadian Jew and the man a Québécois who is in search of his identity.) We might also have considered the highly poetic *Chambre blanche* (1970) d. by Jean Pierre Lefebvre. It is a film showing full acceptance of the Other. Peter Harcourt labels it "an extraordinarily intimate and original masterpiece."[45] We might even have studied Lefebvre's *Dernières Fiançailles* (1973). Or his *Ultimatum* (1973), where love and death collide. The possibilities seem endless. And of course we have already encountered the theme of death in a very real way in *Mon oncle Antoine*, to mention the most important example, and also in *Cher Théo*. We could look back, too, to an earlier NFB film, Fernand Dansereau's 1964 *Festin des morts*, a stark docudrama that shows the martyrdom of Jesuit missionaries by Huron Indians during the seventeenth and eighteenth centuries (Lever *Hist.* 1988, 163−64; Pratley *TS* 1987, 181, same still). In *Festin* ... (starring Jean-Guy Sabourin), the theme of death is linked to the question of religion. But in modern times it has also been shown in a metaphorical, even allegorical fashion in some less well-known films, as, for instance, *Sous les draps les étoiles*. In *Jacques et Novembre* we have a thoroughgoing study of death and dying. But one rather recent and certainly bizarre film that deals with dream, death, and coupling is *Trois Pommes à coté du sommeil*.

TROIS POMMES À CÔTÉ DU SOMMEIL (1988; d. Jacques Leduc)

In this film there are many flashbacks — the male protagonist is dreaming, and in his dream he sees three apples. One supposes the "apples" refer to the three girl friends he has (he has at least three): Madeleine; Oisille; Nicole.

Dialogues that refer to love and its end are in the ascendancy here ("J'ai cessé d'aimer"/"Est-ce qu'on s'aime encore?" the characters say to one another.) And like some of the characters in *Le Déclin* ..., they do lots of exercising, especially walking, jogging, and swimming, "pour garder la forme"; "pour dominer l'eau." The hero also talks to a "wise old man" who discusses water, stars, and other things. They also discuss "silence intérieur." The hypothesis is expressed that all <u>problems</u> begin with "p" (pauvreté, pollution), while all <u>solutions</u> start with "c" (copulation, compassion).

Madeleine is pregnant, but doesn't want to have a baby, especially with the protagonist. She wants to break up with him, in fact.

For our purposes, the observations on Québec are of special interest: the region is seen as a "pays de passage," and Montréal statistics are given to support this idea.

In a restaurant, the "hero" is speaking Polish (throughout it has gone through his mind). And a fête — the birthday party — is woven in and out of his dream. The old man is in the country; he comes to the city to the birthday party

The film ends as it begins — *j'ai cessé d'aimer* — and with a song. All the characters are singing. And Geneviève tells him: "This evening I'll take a good bath with you."

The most we can say of this is that this is a slender, postmodern film in which the state of dream is the main technological and thematic problem. Within this we have meditations on birth and death, separation and togetherness, love and its cessation, etc.

Still, note that Marcel Jean writes: "Leduc is a perceptive observer of Québec; his socio-political preoccupations are accompanied by thoughtful consideration of the interaction between cinema and experience, between fiction films and commentaries."[46]

SOUS LES DRAPS LES ÉTOILES (1989; d. Jean-Pierre Gariépy)

Sous les draps les étoiles opens with a party just ending. Next, a couple who has just met is copulating. She discusses leaving. He is just returning; he has "come back to sleep in the arms of Montréal." They are next seen in a bar. He doesn't want anyone to touch her. He is jealous, after just one night.

We next have the "inspector" (the concierge) and his pigeons on the roof (of the apartment building) with the male lead.

The woman then tells her mother she is going away.

The man gives the woman a check for "service rendu." She tells of a long-ago trip (to Spain?) in a crowded train, where she met a man with whom she had six months of paradise; then she returned. And, she adds, "... since I've been back, I tell myself a story to put myself to sleep. Je suis condamnée à mort [I am condemned to death]." Now there is to be a new voyage from which she cannot return. "Now I have one condition: that you go with me." We understand she is to die, and that she wants him to go with her.

Le Rongeur, the personification of death, appears: "Pour vous servir; je reviendrai; mes hommages, madame. [At your service. I shall come back. My respects, Madame.]" And he does return two or three times. The couple then goes to an old hangar, or barn, full of antiques, including a little old plane (it was her grandfather's). He breaks off a part (it's rusty). The antiquity of the escape vehicle is an impediment: "You want to leave and you can't." More existential dialogue ensues.

The scene shifts to a restaurant. The "hero" goes out (to the restroom?). Le Rongeur arrives. She says: "Go away or I'll tear out your eyes." He says: "I'm sick as a dog." The "hero" comes back in. More existential discussion, this time about *le disparaître* (disappearing; disappearance).

At a cookout she tells the concierge the trip is "on" again. The concierge, however, is concerned about his pigeon. He'd like to make the trip with Betty the pigeon, for "elle s'ennuie ici [she is bored here]." The concierge speaks of M. Le Rongeur. He takes him for a gendarme.

In bed she says, "You're boiling." He says, "I'm cold." In an archeologist's haunt the male has a full vision of death, including skeletons. The archeologist tells him to go before it's too late.

Then the couple is walking along. He falls, gasps, says: "Tu t'en vas. [You're going away.]" She: "Pour longtemps [For a long time]." He: "Moi, aussi [So am I.]."

As they are going downstairs, they meet the inspector with an empty rocker. (A woman had often been rocking with him on the rooftops; now, it seems, she is dead.) M. Le Rongeur is nearby.

This very postmodern film leaves an impression, despite its incoherence; one does not forget the feeling of gloom and doom hanging over it. But the allegory and the symbolism of the "gnawing" of death, its omnipresence, and of life (and death) as a "trip" are quite hackneyed. The strange dialogue is fragmented. Still it is clear that this film has to do with departure and return; with death and resurrection.

Another film, a much more important film, that deals with death and dying is *Jacques et Novembre*.

JACQUES ET NOVEMBRE (1984; co-d. Jean Beaudry and François Bouvier)

Jacques has discovered he is afflicted with an incurable and indeed terminal illness. Far from capitulating to this, he decides that he will keep a journal, which will also be a testament and an album. He will do this with his videocamcorder, focused on himself, predominantly. Friend Denis will also help him, with his 16 mm. camera.

In an interview with Léo Bonneville, Beaudry states that François Bouvier was really the director of this original and rare film. It was a low-budget film, costing $13,000 for the filming and in total only $225,000. Perhaps this is obvious, speaking technically, but at the same time, and as can be seen from the brief synopsis above, this is also part and parcel of the story: two young men documenting death with rather unsophisticated photographic equipment. Beaudry says in the same interview that the film deals with the portrayal of death, with the intention to say that "life is precious."[47] Since the man who discovers that death is imminent is a photographer, he decides to record this "event" on his videocamera. His video filming, then, differs in the final movie-product from the rest of the photography, shot by "Denis" in 16 mm color. The video film is grainy, in order to give the effect of a homemade product; it is in black and white. The purpose, as well as the effect, is to give Jacques's testimonial.

Janine Marchessault says that "the film reformulates the tension between documentary and fiction, a tension which constitutes one of the riches of *québécois* cinema. The irony and the nostalgia of the film reside in its conscious negation of that cinema, and its originality is in the proposition of a new paradigm which simultaneously is inspired by that cinema and yet does not bear the label of that cinema."[48] And Pascale Beaudet says of *Jacques et Novembre* that "the film oscillates between sadness, melancholy, and laughter; the tragic is avoided, as is also the grandiloquent."[49]

Beaudry has also made a film with Bouvier entitled *Les Matins infidèles* (1988), which was begun in 1985. It departs from a series of photos taken on the same street corner every morning in 1979 (à la Monet!). A break of a year and a half came in the making of this work, while François Bouvier photographed *Marie s'en va-t-en ville*. *Les Matins infidèles* is about Jean-Pierre, a photographer, and Marc, a writer. Jean-Pierre undergoes sudden death. But it is not the plot that matters in either of these Beaudry-Bouvier films; rather, it is the theme of death, of death-in-life and the ephemeral nature of life that counts. Fused to this is the problem of time, or *durée*.

But Beaudry has directed some films that are more lighthearted; among these we might mention the sequence in La Fête-Rock Demers's production of *Contes pour tous*. His most recent work in this realm is *Tirelire, Combine$ & Cie* (1992; 89 min.), in which Benoît Latour aims to become a millionaire before the age of fourteen!

Films for and about Children

Certainly one of Québec cinema's major roles as regards the United States has been its contributions to the American paid television channels' store of after-school specials. Making films for and about children is nothing new to the province; and one should no doubt single out from earlier times *Le Martien de Noël*, or *The Christmas Martian* (1971). Pratley reviewed this film in *Variety* (1971) and took it up again in his book, calling it (in both places) "a delightful film for young children, about a friendly Martian who lands in Quebec's northern woods at Christmastime; he is discovered, lost and cold, by two children who take care of him, and after a snowmobile chase by the villagers, send him on his way again in his twinkling red space craft" (*TS* 1987, 199). Pratley is not alone in seeing this as a clear forerunner to Steven Spielberg's *E. T.*

Also from the 1970s is François Labonté's comedy, *Le Château de cartes* (1979). In it, a detective sorceress investigating the disappearance of a scholar goes to a nephew who has built a chateau of cards in the forest. This is an amusing production, made for children; the characters are eccentric and the decor is picturesque.

Labonté, whose *Gaspard* ... and *Manuel* ... we discussed earlier in this chapter, is an interesting figure. Born in 1949 in Robertsonville, he is at once a director, an editor, and a producer. As producer, we will encounter him in the next chapter, where we discuss *Les Années de rêve*. He has directed a number of children's films, including *Henri* (analyzed below). Having been the assistant director to André Melançon for *Les 'Oreilles' menent l'enquête* (1974) and *Les Tacots* (1974), he ultimately turned to making children's films himself. Michel Coulombe says that whether Labonté tells the story of a doll or the adventures of very colorful characters in search of a disappeared professor, he seems influenced by the fanciful, characteristic of the programs of the great period of service to the young rendered by Radio-Canada television. Karoshevskaya, who was the unforgettable Fanfreluche of the small screen, figures in *Le Château* as the detective sorceress Varicelle. Far from the realism dear to Melançon, Labonté proposes a children's cinema that has no children. (Coulombe 1991, 290–91; my translation and paraphrase).

In more recent times, other "children's" films of considerable worth have appeared; among these are *The Peanut Butter Solution* (*Opération Beurre de pinottes*), *The Dog Who Stopped the War* (*La Guerre des tuques*), *Bach and Broccoli* (*Bach et Bottine*) — all of which have more than average merit — and, on a lesser level qualitatively, *Tadpole and the Whale* (*La Grenouille et la Baleine*). Two of the most illustrious directors of "films for children" are André Melançon, a francophone, and Michael Rubbo, an anglophone. Rubbo is seen in the beautiful video regarding Margaret Atwood's summer retreat (*Once in August* [1985]), where he and Merrily Weisbord converse with Miss Atwood about her literary creations.

Though French-Canadian film is like the literature, known as tending to concentrate on the dark side of life, we have seen that the films of André Forcier, like the writings of Roch Carrier, are inclined to laugh — sometimes lovingly, sometimes satirically — at the society, and, for that matter, at life. The treatment of children in the *québécois* film, and films for children, is similarly varied. Some films are dark and threatening (*Aurore*; *Mario;* *Le Matou*; or even the anglophone film, *The Mystery of the Million Dollar Hockey Puck*); some are light of heart; others come in between, being threatening, but in the final analysis happily resolved (*Henri*; *Bach et Bottine*). How the children live their experiences provides at once a window on the society and, upon occasion, a lesson or two for both children and adults of all nations (e.g., *Bach et Bottine*; *La Guerre des tuques*).

HENRI (1986; d. François Labonté)

Henri, set in St. Maurice, has a number of long sequences containing no dialogue. It deals with a case of a father's grief placed over everything else, a case of a severe and inattentive parent, so often seen in the Québec film (*La Petite Aurore*; *Laura Laur*; *Les Fous de Bassan*; etc.).

The opening scenes show the drowning of the mother and the near-drowning of Lili; she is fished out and carried away as the young boy Henri watches, dumbfounded.

The scene then shifts to a house and then to the interior, where a young boy arises in the early morning, departs cross-country through the cemetery, up a fire escape to a rooftop, into a building that turns out to be a hospital. He has brought his sister a hard-boiled egg, on the sly.

Then we see the school bus; our boy Henri tries to get on, but misses. He begins to run, and the young people on the bus bet on who will make it first to the school. He is picked up by Mlle Jeanne Painchaud, an older woman, a teacher, and he does make it to the school ahead of the bus.

In another scene, the father presents Lili with a gift; but she does not like papa or his gift. Henri arrives with some children and they present her with a birthday cake. Henri gives Lili a pendant. The father asks him where he found it, and he replies, "In mother's drawer." Lili throws a fit, and casts the pendant across the room, saying to her father: "Mama should have been saved, not me." Henri comforts her.

The scene shifts to Roch Chabot's gas station. Henri sits in Roch's jeep-like car. They then take a joy ride; Roch drives his car in circles, and Henri knows some pleasure in what is clearly an otherwise dark life. They talk about the upcoming race, the "course du village." Roch will participate in this race, in the running and sprint events, for Jeanne Painchaud, whom he likes.

As Henri returns home late that evening he sees that M. Martineau, the principal of the school, is visiting his father. The father confronts the young boy with cheating, but Henri simply runs out of the house; he goes to Jeanne Painchaud's home. (It is amusing to note that this schoolteacher has a pumpkin on her porch; she is obviously not too distracted to observe these little niceties.) It is night; she puts him up.

The next morning he goes to the hospital by his usual route, but cannot get in the window. He uses the regular entrance and discovers that Lili is worse; she is tied down, and he frees her. The father arrives. "Why is she hog-tied?" asks Henri. The father replies that it is for her own good. Now it is the father, M. Boivin's, turn to throw a fit. The doctor or director of the hospital tells him to get it together, to stop his mourning and be concerned for those who remain. The father does not receive this advice kindly. But Henri says to him: "You wanted her to die instead of mother, right?"

In a moment of "high drama," Henri runs and runs and runs, without getting on the bus; the bus leaves him behind; Painchaud wants to stop him; he finally falls. The father remarks, "Henri is the grand champion." And soon after, Henri is on a dock; he stares into the water. (Suicide? Memories?)

It is now the Ninth of October, the date of the annual cross-country race. Jeanne Painchaud presents Henri with a gift of running clothes; but the father tries to prevent Henri from running the race. "I'm your father," he protests. "Mon père? Toé, mon père," replies the lad bitterly.

In a subsequent scene of considerable importance, Henri speaks to Lili in the hospital, telling her that she must eat to be strong when he comes to get her; for they are going clear to China. The father arrives; they do not know he is there and he overhears Lili say, "Papa va être seul [Dad is going to be alone]," to which Henri replies, "C'est ça qu'il veut; c'est ce qu'il a toujours voulu [That's what he wants; that's what he's always wanted]."

The cross-country race is about to begin. Roch, Martineau, and others are all present, making ready the race. Henri joins in. And then the race! Henri, from in the rear, overtakes one after the other of the participants. At one juncture Henri sees his father with Lili; they both urge him to "go"! It's between Henri and Martineau, who is looking more and more like Mephisto. Henri sprints and beats Martineau. His father, Lili, and he all three embrace; they are reunited at the end — the time of mourning is over.

While this film, more realistic than Labonté's earlier work, has the gravity of many other films from Québec, it ends on a note of reform and optimism preferred, no doubt, in a film to be viewed largely by children. *Henri*—in which Jacques Godin and Eric Brisebois starred as the father-son couple (a combination we will encounter again in Ch. 6 when we discuss *Pouvoir intime*, made in the same year)—was followed by Labonté's *Gaspard et fil$* (1988). Starring Godin with Gaston Lepage, it, too, pertains to a problematic father-son relationship in which reconciliation is again the resolution.

Another film that ends on a note of reform, but one that is greatly superior to *Henri*, both for its technical accomplishments and for its warmth and charm, is *Bach et Bottine*.

BACH ET BOTTINE (*BACH AND BROCCOLI*) (1987; d. André Melançon)

The film begins with a dream sequence on snowy expanses, and this establishes the accident and trauma that will leave Fanny's parents dead, and her alone and unwanted. As a result of the accident, and because her grandmother is growing too old to care for her, this twelve-year-old, androgynous orphan girl moves in with her shy bachelor uncle Jonathan. She is accompanied by her pet skunk, named Bottine (in English, Broccoli). In an amusing early sequence, Bernice, who is sweet on Jonathan, gives him a bust of Beethoven, as he goes on sabbatical, but he has one already, as well as many pictures of him. Another charming scene involves the uncle and his charge celebrating their Christmas with a treat of lobster.

Sean, the next-door neighbor boy, who assists Fanny in her menagerie caretaking, gives a significant prod to the uncle's conscience.

This is certainly less a kid-flick, even, than is *The Dog Who Stopped the War* (q.v., below). The stiff uncle, an organist, is all for himself and for his amateur Bach contest, until, in the course of trying to place the irrepressible and imaginative Fanny in a foster home, he learns the most important lesson of his life: that of love. Moreover, he is a city man, and Sean is a city boy, and they must learn something of the country, which Fanny knows best. Sean, on the other hand, will teach her the city, which lesson affords us some wonderful scenes of Québec City. In fact, we see scenes here that would be specifically associated with Québec: outdoor steps leading to the second floor; cross-country ski-trip; Italian music being played on the bus, etc.

Bach et Bottine. Photograph by Jean Demers. (Courtesy Coll. Cinémathèque Québécoise.)

The film is rich in cultural material, as well as in theme. In general, it shares with *The Dog* ... an impression of brightness.

I have seen only the dubbed version of *Bach et Bottine*, alas, and was not well-impressed with the dubbing. If viewed in the original format, one's evaluation of this film might be even more positive. But what remains obvious is Melançon's love of telling a story, which he himself emphasizes. He attests to his early admiration of *La Strada*, which was "at the origin" of his love of cinema, and to his interest in telling the story of complex characters, accompanied by music, to make an "event." Indeed, so much is this his aim that he has grown tired, he says, of the sterile debate that accompanies every film opening, a debate that tries to point out some poetic or political "message" in the film. This is especially irritating because every film has its own personality. It is the *story* of *Bach et Bottine* that interested him from the outstart, when Rock Demers first proposed Bernadette Renaud's *scénario* to him; and all the choices of sequences were determined by "events that would advance the *récit* (tale). "The story must be lively so as to lead the viewer to receiving emotions ... and not necessarily to reflection," he says. And he is not interested in gaining a large public, but, above all, in speaking to children. But he also wishes to reach the adults, when possible. "I find it very interesting," he goes on, "that a child can say to an adult: 'Listen to me! I have things to say,' and to all adults, 'Darn it! if you will listen to children, maybe that will change something.'" Basically, in *Bach et Bottine* he is not interested in proposing miraculous solutions; he is not interested, either, in organizing 'child power'. He wants solidarity between children and adults, without any form of authority. Perhaps, he concedes, that is utopian, but it is not impossible.[50]

Melançon, unlike many creators of children's films, avoids the fantastic, the unreal, even though his first children's film, *Les 'Oreilles' mènent l'enquête*, features a child who can hear through walls. The only scene in *Bach et Bottine* that can be called surrealistic, he says, is the dream sequence at the beginning. At Guy Dufaux's suggestion, they used a short, 14-mm focal to accentuate the pictural character of the sequence. Part of his "realism," too, is to show his children in the Montréal milieu, in the common people's milieu (Hochelaga-Maisonneuve, Longueil, Outremont, Rosemont, le Plateau Mont-Royal). He avoids fable (or *"fabulisation"*) because for him *it is the story that is important*; it has a purpose, which is to make the viewers participate in an emotion, which can become a passion. He wanted to surprise people in *Bach* ..., but also to move them, and to draw them close to the two characters.[51] He confesses to the use of still photography in stimulating those emotions: in *Bach et Bottine*, photos have the function of connecting a moment that was lived six or seven years ago to the present life of Jean-Claude Parenteau. (In *Le Lys cassé* — in which he used the same child actors [Raymond Legault and Mahée Paiement] as in *Bach et Bottine* — photography is the door Marielle uses to return to her childhood.)[52]

An earlier film by Melançon, as impressive as *Bach et Bottine*, and one that has been widely shown in art films and Canadian (or Québec) film festivals, as well as on the Disney and other American premium channels, is *The Dog Who Stopped the War*, more imaginatively titled, in the original, *La Guerre des tuques (The War of the Stocking-Caps)*.

LA GUERRE DES TUQUES (THE DOG WHO STOPPED THE WAR) (1984; d. André Melançon)

Pratley, who calls this film, "charming and provocative" (*TS* 1987, 265), relegates it nonetheless to the realm of the kid-flick. But it is perhaps not just for children; one notes that it is generally included in Québec film festivals, and this is perhaps because on the deepest level the absurdity and tragedy of war become the

lesson these children learn outside the school walls — a lesson in
how pretending becomes a reality beyond control. It is one we may
all profit from. However, one may justifiably say that the ending of
The Dog ... undercuts the seriousness of the tragedy (and thus the
potential "message") that comes from their choosing up sides for
their war. As the fort is demolished, one of the children — Walter,
the Vietnamese "engineer" — remarks that there will be other forts,
thus suggesting that the lesson, however grim, will not stick, and
the song ("Love is on our side") that provides the closure makes of
an otherwise well-done film fit material for an after-school special.
It can be characterized, therefore, as entertainment with secondary
values: an antiwar message and a consideration of preteen sex
involvements. Various positions are taken, too, which reflect those
of adults in the face of a scuffle. The children represent various
human types, and the "battle of the sexes" is not the least of the
subjects touched upon. The boys are against the girls, the observers
or pacifists against the "warriors." Among the characters, Nicki
the Loon is particularly interesting. He won't join in the war; but
he pretends.

Multiethnic and multinational as well as cross-cultural allusions
are present: Catholic backgrounds; American radios; Walter,
the Vietnamese boy, and his little brother. There is, besides,
something in the tone of the film that is reminiscent of Truffaut
(*Argent de poche*).

The screen is well-lit and provides a different tone from that of,
say, *Mon oncle Antoine*, though both are concerned with a loss
of innocence. Among the beauties of the photography one might
cite the snow scenes — exploited to advantage here and contrasting
with the bright colors of the "*tuques*" or stocking-caps — and also
the fine textures of the old barn, which provides the children
with their meeting-place. Cross-country skiing presents another
opportunity for some good footage. The film was made with the
participation of the people of St. Urbain, Laval, and Baie St.
Paul; the Dominique Savio School of Saint Urbain was also involved.

An actor to begin with (*Partis pour la gloire* [1975], d. Clément
Perron; dealing with conscription), André Melançon has had a
distinguished career as a creator of "children's films" — usually with
a serious or pedagogical intent (Lever *Hist.* 1988, 251) — that
began in the 70s with some short films produced under the auspices
of the ONF. These included his *Les Tacots; Les 'Oreilles' mènent
l'enquête; Le Violon de Gaston*, later collected by Demers under
the generic title *Contes pour jeunes. Les Tacots* tells the story of
"une course de tacots, [où] les filles mènent le bal à la grande

honte des garçons [a rattletrap race in which the girls run the show to the shame of the boys]." In *Les 'Oreilles' mènent l'enquête* "six jeunes entreprennent une enquete à la suite du vol d'un magot [six young people undertake an investigation following the theft of some money]." In *Le Violon de Gaston*, "Un excellent joueur de hockey, également virtuose de violon, apprend qu'une partie importante coïncide avec un récital. Que fera Gaston? [An excellent hockey player, also a virtuoso violin player, learns that an important game coincides with a recital. What to do?]." In 1978 Melançon won the critics' prize for his film *Comme les six doigts de la main*. During the 80s he also made *Le Lys cassé*. It starred Jacqueline Barrette, Jessica Barker, and Markita Boies, and explored "violent conflicts and extreme émotions," as Lever characterizes it (*Hist.* 1988, 330). (Because it is a film about incest.) Speaking of this film, Melançon states that he himself would not have written a film on incest; but when he read Jacqueline Barrette's *scénario*, he was overcome by what happened to Marielle, and sensitive to the fact that the film could speak to men; for men avoid the subject, since they think the man is presented in this subject as a filthy beast, whereas he is often sick.[53]

Melançon has not been absent from the animation scene, either, as seen by his work in the creation of a charming piece entitled *Mascarade*.

But Melançon's reputation was in a sense solidified by *La Guerre des tuques*, the biggest financial success of the 1984–5 season, and the first film produced by Rock Demers in the series called *Contes pour tous*. This series also included the collected films done for the ONF. As we have seen, after making *La Guerre des tuques* he directed *Bach et Bottine* (1986).

Charles Caouette contends that all of André Melançon's productions show his interest in the human being and the quality of social relationships. In Caouette's view, Melançon does not seek to show any theories on childhood, but rather his work places the spectator in direct contact with childhood. *Les Vrais Perdants*, *Bach et Bottine*, and *Le Lys cassé* are all good examples of this.[54] Sylvie Halpern examines the relationship between adults and children in the films of Melançon.[55] And Pierre Véronneau's article on Melançon reinforces Melançon's confessed emphasis on the story and on the emotions; for Véronneau states that in his films "l'efficacité narrative occupe une place de choix: Melançon aime divertir .... [the narrative efficacy occupies the preferred place: Melançon likes to entertain ....]". His style is "fruité, naturel, and qui ne cause aucune aigreur ... on sent un cinéaste généreux, sensuel, aimant la vie, les sensations et les plaisirs, et pourtant critique. Il ne fait pas que divertir. Il témoigne dans ses films d'un humanisme constant qui se traduit dans les buts qu'il poursuit. [His style is like fresh fruit, natural, and leaves no sour taste ... one senses that he is a generous, sensual filmmaker, who loves life, sensations, and pleasures, and yet is critical. He does not just entertain. He demonstrates in his films a constant humanism, which is translated into the purposes he has in mind]."[56] In this same article, Véronneau is interested for the most part in Melançon's film for adults, *Des Armes et les hommes* (1971), in which the filmmaker has as his point of departure the hypothesis that firearms are the talisman of modern society. (Melançon himself speaks of this film in the interview cited above;[57] he sees it as his 'first true film'; one in which he applied the principle of Russian puppets; and he adds that his first preoccupation was to know whether the fact of having a weapon in one's hands changes something in an individual.) Véronneau recognizes in *Des Armes* ... one of the stylistic constants of the Melançonian film: a sense of humor. For after all, the notion of showing three humans as guinea pigs being shot while a university professor explains the effect of bullets on the human body is at bottom "invraisemblable," and inevitably brings a smile to our lips. But Melançon's humor has a function beyond the immediate one of making us laugh; for it suspends our understanding and assimilation. With his humor, says Véronneau, Melançon combines the tender and the nervous in the profound manner of a Chaplin or a Capra: Melo(drama) and smile. Melody and parody. Bach and broccoli. The two twins (Laurel and Hardy). A balance of ingredients. Melançon "appeals to certain surface structures in order to indicate other levels of meaning ... and this construction engenders an ethic of ambiguity .... In his series called 'Observation,' Melançon peels the skin off young people, in the light of their behaviors ...."[58] Melançon is also known for his collaboration on *La Grenouille et la baleine* and for his preparation of the French version of *Operation Peanut Butter*, a rather well-known work by the anglophone filmmaker, Michael Rubbo. (See Clanfield, 1987, 84.)

Filmed on the beautiful Mignan Islands, as well as in Rimouski and Florida, *La Grenouille et la baleine* is number six in Rock Demers's *Contes pour tous* (*Stories for Children of All Ages*) series, and while Melançon had a hand in the script, this time the director is Jean-Claude Lord.

LA GRENOUILLE ET LA BALEINE, or *TADPOLE AND THE WHALE* (1988; d. Jean-Claude Lord)

Tadpole is the nickname given to Daphne by her grandpa, Thomas. She is a little girl who has a special relationship with a dolphin. Daphne, who (according to Ann the biologist) has unusual sound perception abilities, being able to hear sounds others cannot, up to forty kilohertz, has befriended Elvar the dolphin; and from B Minor, a female humpback whale, she is learning to accompany, imitate, and call the whales with the use of her recorder. These friends of hers live in the cove near Old Manor, a resort inn that her Grandpa Hector operates and that she visits on her vacations. When Grandpa Hector threatens to sell the inn, Grenouille (Tadpole) will have to separate from her friends, of course. This, along with the rescue of a humpback whale tangled in a fisherman's net (whose distress sounds she hears courtesy of "Cries from the Deep," directed by Jacques Gagné, NFB), not to mention her own near-drowning and her rescue by Elvar, make for many dramatic moments. But all ends well, with Hector's estranged brother, Toby, saving the lodge, and Daphne rejoined to Elvar, who takes great leaps out of the ocean and over her as she swims with him. This film concludes with a song: "We are one," composed by Guy Trépanier, Normand Dubé, and Nathalie Carsen; it is Nathalie who does the singing.

The photography—especially the underwater photography and the scenes of the magnificent erosions at Mignan—makes this film well worth while, even though the acting and the plot are, over all, somewhat less striking than the works of Melançon discussed earlier. Still, director Lord himself is no newcomer to the *québécois* scene: he adapted Claude Jasmin's *Délivrez-nous du mal* (1965) and wrote, directed, and edited *Les Colombes* (1970), thus establishing himself as an *auteur*. After this he engaged in the making of commercial Hollywood-style films, ones "that exploit contemporary issues more for dramatic potential than as a basis for reflection" (Clanfield 1987, 73). Among his films we would have to mention *Bingo* (1974), *Parlez-nous d'amour* (1976), and *Panique* (1977)—three sociopolitical thriller films that Lever (287; 357) says made Lord into a local Costa-Gavras, and that were followed by English-language films such as *Visiting Hours* (1981); *Covergirl* (1982); *The Vindicator* (1984); and *Toby McTeague* (1985). He returned to the French language to make a CBC-TV serial in 1986—*Lance et compte* (*He Shoots, He Scores*). He has also made *Eclair au chocolat* (1979), "a sensitive, entirely natural child study, about a young son of a single mother who loves his absent father through the stories she tells of him" (Pratley *TS* 1987, 239). How many of these films have you seen? I thought so. Lord is not listed in Sadoul's *Dictionnaire des cinéastes*. Claude Jutra is. So are Denys Arcand ... Perrault ... Brault. We will nevertheless return to *Bingo*, which Pratley calls "the most important film of 1974" (*TS* 1987, 215).

An earlier film, also part of the Demers series *Contes pour tous*, but one first made in English and then provided in French is *The Peanut Butter Solution*.

OPERATION BEURRE DE PINOTTES (*THE PEANUT BUTTER SOLUTION*) (1985; d. Michael Rubbo)

Peanut Butter ... is a fantasy concerning a young boy Michael, who loses his hair through fright and is visited by some "witches," or "ghosts," who tell him he can get it back by smearing his head with (Skippy) peanut butter, but only in a certain recipe, which he forgets. Here we have a combination of things. Canadian content, embracing family conflicts and the multicultural nature of the characters (including a Vietnamese boy and a young African Canadian), figures heavily as in many children's films. (Lever *Hist.* 1988, 344: "Les 'minorités visibles' entrent sur les écrans commerciaux surtout avec les enfants." See the still [same page] illustrating this principle.)

But, more strikingly, the film entertains a parody of the stern discipline of Canadian teachers—of the pinched old maid type, Miss Prume, and of the math professor, the image of the scientist who, in the face of the miraculous or the supernatural, persists in giving statistics, etc., not to mention Signor, the "immigrant, foreign" professor who wants to stifle imagination. The plot revolves around a dream Michael has when he becomes unconscious: he turns the art professor, Sergio, into a boogeyman, the brother of Dr. Heinstein Epstein who had a scare (harem scarem).

Though my students compare the scene in Epstein's tyrannical sweatshop to a similar passage in *Chitty Chitty Bang Bang*, this allegory of the wicked witch, who is into torture, suggests to me the eternal metaphor of the giant versus the dwarf, with the dwarf winning. In a satisfactory comedy, Rubbo presents deep problems regarding child labor, and certainly deals with the matter of rebellion, and also the transfer of fright (i.e., the realization that it is mainly in your imagination). Besides, issues of art and imagination are important here: not only does the art professor tend to stifle the artistic process and the expression of the imagination, but he, like most teachers, is represented as diametrically opposed to the imagination. According to him, I should paint what I have seen (mimesis); but in truth, by enlisting my imagination — and not heeding the professor — I should attempt to paint something I have never seen.

In a more recent film, *Vincent et moi*, Rubbo returns to the question of nourishing artistic creativity and freedom in children, as he indicates in his interview with Léo Bonneville.[59]

VINCENT ET MOI (*VINCENT AND ME*) (1990; d. Michael Rubbo)

The work and dreams of Jo, a young artist from Motley who goes to Montréal to study art, have been inspired by Vincent Van Gogh. But the unscrupulous art dealer, Dr. Winkler, buys and then sells her drawing of some geese to Mr. Hirodake, a wealthy Japanese, as Van Gogh originals. This leads to international intrigue, with Jo and her friend Felix traveling to Amsterdam, where they meet Joris, and uncover an art theft. But, more importantly, in a dreamlike episode Jo meets the great painter in person. He is very kind to her, and gives her a painting of his bedroom. But when she returns to "reality," she prefers to trade the painting for her own drawing. Before returning to her home, she visits Mme Calment in Provence. There Mme Calment, a 114-year-old woman who really knew Van Gogh, visits with Jo. When Jo tells her how kind Van Gogh has been to her, Mme Jeanne Calment, who found the artist "rough, rude, and ugly," responds, "Il était grossier avec moi [He was not nice to me; he was crude]." In the end, Mme Calment cannot understand how a thirteen-year-old girl can have actually visited Van Gogh, long since dead.

This film, in which the reproductions of the paintings of Van Gogh and Rousseau are marvelously clear and sharp, follows the Rubbo pattern in its international flavor, and in its message, which is that a child — or anyone — should follow his or her own imagination, rather than to slavishly imitate others. Scenes in the art school in Montréal especially remind one of similar "poor teaching methods" of the sort we encounter in *The Peanut Butter Solution*.

In *Le Jeune Magicien* the leading role involves another kind of artist — a magician.

LE JEUNE MAGICIEN, OR *THE YOUNG MAGICIAN* (1986; d. Waldemar Dziki)

Briefly, *Le Jeune Magicien* concerns a young boy, Pierre, who studies magic and parapsychology, and through his interest discovers that he has powerful telekinetic powers. Yet he has little control over the power and effects of his gift. Nonetheless, he becomes the object of intense study by the medical profession, and is confined in a clinic, from which, however, he manages to escape, thanks to a new friend who is going to help him control his powers. All ends well when Pierre (Peter) is asked to move a bomb that has been placed in the local factory, and thus saves the city from impending catastrophe. Not entirely in the Demers style, this film has the traditional didacticism: children should be listened to when they give signs of having certain gifts. But *The Young Magician* lacks the complexities of plot and character of *Simon les nuages*.

SIMON LES NUAGES (1990; d. Roger Cantin)

Simon les nuages is the story of a young boy who thinks he can get to a dreamland inhabited by animals and birds that have become extinct either through natural causes or by some deed of civilization. In an exotic forest, he has adventures with six or seven boys and girls, until, suddenly, Simon sees a fantastic thing. In his final dream, he notices as he sojourns in Sainte-Lucie de Bagot that the clocks cannot keep time and Mr. Walker's garden never freezes in the winter. He realizes he has found the road to his dreamland, which is located behind the Third Wood. With his cousin and some friends he sets out on an expedition. But they must be careful, for no adults must see them; their glance would be fatal, especially Mr. Walker's. Mr. Walker frightens the children with his wooden ruler, an instrument that measures the length of the hands of any intruders who dare set foot in his garden. But when the children get to the Third Wood, the forest becomes a sea, and only Simon has time to swim in it, for the fabulous country dissolves by magic. When Simon wakes up, he is stretched out in the watertrough used by farmer Solis's animals. He is the adult who caused the imaginary country to disappear by his glance. But for the children this is just a break in their adventures, since they again get to the enchanted country, where they meet a Megacuriosauris, which terrifies them with his great roar, which he utters because of a terrible toothache.

(The dinosaur — ostensibly thirty-seven feet tall and weighing thirteen tons — was constructed by an animation filmmaker, Bill Maylone; in reality it weighed a pound and a half and was thirty-seven inches tall. It took him six months to make this animal. In all, it may compare favorably with Steven Spielberg's tyrannosaurus rex in *Jurassic Park*.)

Sylvie Beaupré characterizes *Simon* as follows: "... the pedagogical aspect ... is not as heavy as certain critics have given us to understand. Certainly, one feels that the future of the planet ... preoccupies the filmmaker, but this preoccupation is beginning to be a part of our lives .... And the acting of the children is better than that of other *québécois* films that have been made for children in the last several years."[60] One should add, however, that as with other children's films from Québec, an effort has been made to reflect the multiethnic nature of the contemporary society: in this film black children play with white children, as is reflected in the still that accompanies Beaupré's article.

In accordance with the widespread contemporary tendency to have an international team for the making of a movie, nowadays we find many films made through the joint efforts of the Québécois and the French. Such a film is *Treasure Train* (1981; d. Fernando Arrabal). Mickey Rooney received top billing for his part as the "emperor of Peru," a crippled old man named Tubal, who, as one of the last steam locomotive engineers, was able to relate to the fantasies of the children, though the adults found him to be half-crazy to the extent that the major, speaking for the Town Council, wants to put him in a rest home. The plot concerns the children's discovery of an old locomotive, "bigger than a whale," belonging to Tubal. He helps them to get the locomotive in order, so that they may travel to Cambodia, where Hoang can marry his mother. In all, the film has some good moments, but the editing has created a sense of incoherence and discontinuity that sadly mark this work. (Edith Butler was in charge of music, which was one of its weakest and most irritating features.)

Tommy Tricker and the Stamp Traveller (1988; first shown in Paris 24 October, 1990), is another work by Michael Rubbo (1987), and one that is a cut above *Treasure Train*. It, too, was first filmed in English, according to Abel (1990, 166); but in any case it belongs to Demers's series *Contes pour tous* (*Planet Earth*), as does also *The Great Land of Small* (1987).

TOMMY TRICKER AND THE STAMP TRAVELLER, OR *LES AVENTURIERS DU TIMBRE PERDU* (1988; d. Michael Rubbo)

This is an unusual tale, bent upon making children aware of foreign lands and foreign cultures and their music. Ralph's father owns a very rare stamp of the Bluenose schooner that has a man on the mast. The fatherless "waif" Tommy — related in some ways to M. Emile of *Le Matou* — tricks Ralph into trading the stamp for some other worthless stamps, and then sells the Bluenose for three hundred dollars. (We learn he is supporting his mother and siblings as best he can.) But when Ralph's sister, Nancy, goes to the stamp dealer to try to get the Bluenose back, instead he gives her an album as a consolation. It contains a secret letter telling that two very valuable stamps are "hidden on the other side of the world." To get there, Ralph stands on a stamp and shrinks. (Here, animation effects are outstanding.) He arrives first in China, but this has been an error; he then travels to Australia, where Tommy Tricker has also arrived by stamp. He has been seized by "Mad Mike," for "stealing" the rare stamps. Ralph must rescue Tommy and he does. In the long run, the two return to Canada with the rare stamps, and reparations are made to the father.

The film is quite memorable, perhaps because of the unusual fantasies in it. Obviously didacticism, present in other Demers films, is not absent from this work either: one should not steal; one should know more about one's fellow human beings on the other side of the world; even when one has been tricked, one should take pity on the trickster and help him or her if necessary; etc. This kind of Sunday School does not ruin the movie, even so.

Rubbo (in his interview with Léo Bonneville) confesses that he found *Les Aventuriers* ... more successful than *Opération beurre de pinottes*, because the *scénario* was richer. He goes on to tell that it was a coproduction with China, and contained several trips, including the rather important sequence in Australia. He tells how as a child he loved to collect stamps, and how they evoked exotic locales for him. And he adds that thanks to his film many young people began to collect stamps: in Québec alone, 30,000 people subscribed to a philatelists's club created by the Canadian Postal Society, after the film came out.[61]

In the same year as *Tommy Tricker*, Demers also produced *The Great Land of Small*, number 5 in the series *Tales for All*. It seemed to be dubbed in the version I viewed on the Disney Channel. For all intents and purposes. *The Great Land of Small* must be deemed inferior to *La Guerre des tuques*, or *Bach et Bottine*. The editing in *The Great Land* ... makes for a rather incoherent narrative. Still, it is well acted, and notable in the cast is André Melançon as the Keeper in The Land of Small.

THE GREAT LAND OF SMALL (1986–87; d. Vojta Jasny)

Fritz, one of the little people from the Land of Small, sleeps in the (Black Mountain) forest near grandfather's country house, not far from Waterloo. He loses his pouch of gold dust to Mimick, who is a "half-wit," halfway between Fritz's world and ours. Mimick in turn loses the pouch to hunters, including Flannigan. City dwellers David and Jenny are visiting grandfather, and they can see the "invisible" creatures their grandfather speaks of, because "they believe." Therefore, they come to know Fritz, who spends one of his wishes to bring their dog, Willy, to them. They are also able to accompany Fritz to his land, which is located in inner space, on the other side of the rainbow. There, the queen is [like] their mother (who in their real life is an acrobat). Fritz's twin brother is her husband/consort, and there are creatures in this realm called slime-os; they are created by being dunked in slime, and are quite gruesome. In The Great Land of Small, the children also meet a full-grown man who is called Keeper. Once in this Great Land of Small, the children cannot go home unless Fritz spends his last wish for this, and he does; but he cannot use the wish to get back his pouch of gold. Now the children must help him get back the dust, with the aid of Sarach, and of a likeable little "monster" named Munch, who is a shortened Flannigan (both played by Ken Roberts). In the long run, Fritz reappropriates the gold, and he returns to The Land of Small with Keeper, who uses *his* wishes to get Willy back to the children's city home and to get himself and Fritz back to the Land of Small.

Like most Demers films. *The Great Land of Small* ends with a song: "Life is like a dream, in the Great Land of Small," a song composed by Guy Trépanier and Normand Dubé.

The film seems to be quite thin, and in most respects lacking in the didactic content and artistry seen in *La Guerre des tuques*, or *Bach et Bottine*, unless the fact that Flannigan learns that he loves his daughter more than gold counts as the ethical message here. Other than that, there is perhaps an emphasis on the need to use our imaginations. But this is one grown-up child who found the going tedious.

CONCLUDING REMARKS ON CHILDREN'S FILMS

It is obvious from the above discussion that the French-Canadian children's films and films about children are numerous and in demand. Abuse (such as found in *La Petite Aurore*) has largely disappeared, and in its stead we have the dwarf versus giant topos. Can this have anything to do with the conflicts between Québec and the rest of Canada? Perhaps. But in any case it is of some interest that Lever should make the ironic statement that the less children the Québécois produce, the more they like to see them in the movies or on the television! (*Hist.* 1988, 348). And Clanfield remarks that, "With their magical transformations of both the natural and the urban world ... Quebec's films for children are close to the local traditions ... observed in the sixties films of Jutra and company" (1987, 85).

Such illustrious work bodes well for the future of French-Canadian films for children, and it is not without significance that the newest films about the famous French elephant, entitled *Le Triomphe de Babar*—indeed the first to move from album to cinema—is not only partially produced by Nelvana, the largest company of independent productions in Canada, but is also directed by Alan Bunce, a young Canadian who has worked closely with Laurent de Brunhoff, the son of Babar's creators, Jean and Cécile de Brunhoff. The first book about Babar was published in 1931.[62]

In short, Canadians do well with presenting children in film, and films for children. The episode on "Sesame Street" that aired on CBC on 21 June 1991, in which "Barbara Plum and the Notebook," modelled after "Barbara Frum and the Journal," traveled to Montréal for an in-depth report on the word *dormir*, must be a model that television will provide to children's movies, not only for its complete charm, but for its pan-Canadian spirit, which is needed for an overcoming of "The Two Solitudes." (*The Two Solitudes* is a splendid film in its own right.)

Marc Sévigny's dossier on "Le Cinéma pour enfants au Québec"[63] includes treatment of André Melançon (*Tou'l monde parle français*), Richard Lavoie (*Guitare; Cabane*), and François Labonté (*Babiole*). There is in this dossier strong criticism of the Disney tradition, which is characterized as marshmallowy,[64] while there is scarcely more tolerance in this discussion for Englishwoman Mary Field's action films or thrillers, which influenced anglophone *québécois* films such as *The Mystery of the Million Dollar Hockey Puck* by Peter Svatek and Jean Lafleur.[65] (Entertaining, but hardly a masterpiece, in my estimation, so improbable was the plot and so weak the acting.) Preferred by Sévigny are Sonika Bo's "poetic works," which "appeal to children's sensitivity and intelligence," and to which, according to the dossier, Québécois filmmakers have been most attracted, in their effort "to get as far away as possible from Disney stereotypes and American television." Bernard Gosselin in his *Le Martien de Noël*, which insists on *québécitude* in its poetic context, and Richard Lavoie in his *Guitare* and in his *Cabane* fall into the current; Labonté also, but with more stress on the fantastic and the fairylike, as in his *Babiole*.[66] Speaking from that American perspective from which I must view the corpus of Québec's cinema, I can only reply that while the Québécois do make admirable films for children, many of their makers must be rather glad for the Disney Channel as an inestimably important outlet for their films.

Conclusion to Chapter 5

In this chapter we have looked at films in which aspects of the *québécois* society that gravitate around individual, personal, and family concerns are treated. But in the next chapter, while bearing in mind that the two currents (personal and political or institutional) overlap, we will look at the society as portrayed in the broader context of politics and institutions. That issue is an engrossing one; for some of the finest films ever made in Québec fall into this general heading — a heading that includes such genres as "political film," "the thriller," the "crime drama" — while the films themselves may also treat such questions as immigration, emigration, and religion.

6

Québec Film as a Mirror of Society: Institutions

— Il nous faut agir sur le terrain du Cinéma en matière d'enseignement, mais il faut pénétrer le film tout entier d'un esprit nouveau.
C'est au Canada ... que reviendra l'honneur de prendre la tête
de cet important mouvement .... N'avons-nous pas avec nous
Dieu lui-même et la sympathie agissante de l'Eglise? Question
d'Energie et de persévérance, question de foi aussi, dans notre
idéal partagé déjà par une foule d'âmes d'élite. — Pierre Vachet
(*Le Devoir*, 5 sept. 1946).

— Dedans l'Eglise, point de salut.

Most if not all good films have a political base or stance: this is
not said as a revelation. The adage is as true for Québec film as
for any other. Documentaries, many of which were examined
in Chapter 2, are no exception to this general rule. As Jacques
Leduc has said, "Le documentaire, c'est un lieu de combat [The
documentary is a combat zone]" (quoted in Lever, 492). One
should add that the films that take up issues of gender, many of
which were treated in Chapter 3, have political implications, and
call for a complete restructuring of the polis along the lines of
greater equality. (Indeed, many of them have as their very point
of departure political and economic grievances.) Of course, the
family, too, is a social unit that functions within a political framework, and within political strictures, so that most of the films we
dealt with in the preceding chapter are not excluded from the
phenomena we will observe in films specifically treated in this
chapter. But here it is a question of how the *québécois* cinema
reflects institutions outside the family. One of the most salient
characteristics of the cinematographic treatment of these institutions, as of the family, is that they are frequently (but not always)

305

portrayed in recent films as being in a state of decline and even of collapse. In such films, the most "sacred" legacies of law and of other ordering agents of the society (such as religion, or more specifically the Church) are often handled subversively, and almost always critically. But we have seen that these legacies were already under attack, though somewhat more tentatively, as early as *Tit-Coq* and *La Petite Aurore*, and even sooner. These social and political agencies in their heyday established the rules of censorship of 1931 (see Lever's appendix) that continued to exercise influence into the 1960s; but by now the rules have been as seriously weakened as the forces that issued them.

Because several of the films to be discussed in this chapter deal with historico-political events that reflect Québec's longstanding and ongoing effort to gain independence from the anglophone Canadian "establishment," and because some of my readers may not be conversant with that particular chapter of Canadian history, a tableau presenting principal dates and events is found in Appendix A.[1] But one recent short documentary that affords an overview of that history, as it intertwines with the special grievances and needs of the province of Québec, is Dorothy Todd Hénaut's *Québec ... un peu ... beaucoup ... passionnément*. Not a feminist film, I treat it here for its survey of key events leading up to the "October Crisis."

POLITICAL FILM: THE OCTOBER 1970 CRISIS

The political and social struggles between the francophones and the anglophones of Canada, and more specifically within the province of Québec itself, are endemic. The conflict, which has hardly changed over the centuries, can be traced back to earliest colonists. These differences, which underwent scrutiny during the time of Québec's Quiet Revolution, finally erupted in the late 1960s. The more violent phase of the revolution continued through the early 70s. The stand taken by the Québecois has played an important role in the creation of works of art at the service of revolution. One inevitably thinks of Hubert Aquin, a revolutionary himself, who produced one of the literary masterpieces of the era with his *Prochain Episode* (1965). But this period is still the setting of certain notable works today; it still continues to haunt the imagination of Canadians. For example, Denis Lacasse published his first novel in 1990: It is entitled *Prélude d'Octobre*.[2]

And just as these events fed into the literature and the literature fed the revolution, so too the seventh art was used to express the thirst for revolution, and the horrors of Trudeau's enlistment of the War Powers Act, which demonstrated how easily a democracy might become a dictatorship. It also dealt with frustrations of such failures as the 1980 referendum, and, upon occasion, went back into history to state obliquely its views of contemporary events. Weinmann shows how a group of French-Canadian films[3] state more or less indirectly the sociopolitical attitudes and grievances of the Québécois vis-à-vis the English Canadians; but in so doing, he sometimes presents rather farfetched theories, and ones that may or may not apply to the films in question. In this chapter, therefore, I prefer to deal with those important *québécois* films that deal very clearly and unequivocally with the conflicts outlined above.

QUÉBEC ... UN PEU ... BEAUCOUP ... PASSIONNÉMENT (1989; Dorothy Todd Hénaut)

As I suggested, a good place to start a discussion of politics and the establishment is with Dorothy Todd Hénaut's segment from the English film, *A Song for Québec*, entitled *Québec ... un peu ... beaucoup ... passionnément*, which narrates the chief events of French-Canadian history and the struggle for independence from the perspective of Pauline Julien, a famous Québécoise *chanteuse à la* Edith Piaf, and her husband Gérald Godin, an equally famous Québécois poet and politician.[4] (The same device was used to convey the struggle of Québec in Robert MacNeil's *Canada: True North*.) Old footage showing Julien and Godin involved in their political activities is used. There is also footage from several important *québécois* documentaries, docudramas, and fictional political films, including segments from Robin Spry's *Action*, from Kramer's *The Inheritance*, from Donald Brittain's *Champions*, from Hugues Mignault's *Le Choix d'un peuple*, and even from Denys Arcand's *Le Confort et l'indifférence*, as well as from Perrault's *Un Pays sans bon sens!*. While the film dips back into the matter of the arrival of French Canadians to this continent, and to Wolfe's conquest in 1759, which left the Québécois "isolated in the middle of an 'English' continent ..., where at that time American power was already felt ...," the backdrop is a series of watercolors by George Geertsen.

We learn how the English minority dominated the culture, while the clergy protected the faith and the language. Godin, however, was one of the first to put the lay language into a literary setting. The couple grew up in the Duplessiste régime of the 1940s, when all was religion and flag. When in this period the workers attempted to establish their right to strike, Duplessis supported the bosses:

this was the "beginning of indignation." Duplessis's death in 1959 marked the "epoch of the great blackness." But in 1960 came Jean Lesage, with his "now or never" motto. The Church was put aside as a power; René Lévesque began to rise, and "pride in and of self was reborn." When in 1964 Elizabeth II came to Canada, Julien was invited to sing for her, and refused; the Queen symbolized English power. Julien and Godin, like many, endorsed the new slogan, "Québec libre." Remembered are the "Samedi de la Matraque," or the Saturday of the Truncheons (which refers to riots the day after the Queen's visit to Québec, in which the police are said to have struck citizens with their billy clubs); the Front de Libération du Québec's (or FLQ's) 1963 planting of the terrorist bombs on Wolfe's monument and other "English" symbols; as well as the 1965 visit of De Gaulle during which he pronounced the words: "Vive Montréal; Vive le Québec; Vive le Québec libre," which Godin says were an "unbelievable consecration." The English were, of course, offended by De Gaulle's cry, but, as Pauline Julien says, "the struggle was thus internationalized." This event, by the way, is also the subject of one of Canada's most important documentaries — Jean-Claude Labrecque's *La Visite du général de Gaulle au Québec* — "The best film for understanding how a piece of editing can become 'parole politique,' or political discourse," says Lever (*Hist.* 1988, 169).

Next, Hénaut's film takes up the 1968 separatist movement as it forms the Parti Québécois. Godin here suggests that Lévesque at the time embodied hope and change, while Julien claims that he revealed to the Québécois who they were and that is why they followed him.

Particularly stressed are events of 1970 forward, including the kidnapping on 5 October, 1970, of the British attaché of commerce, James Cross, and the subsequent kidnapping of Pierre Laporte, Québec government minister, after which the FLQ released its manifesto, widely supported by Québécois youth, and on through the 15 October invocation of the war powers act by prime minister of Canada, Pierre Trudeau. Julien tells how houses were sacked, offices as well. Godin himself was imprisoned. And once the dead body of Pierre Laporte was found, it was the "end of the FLQ." When the October crisis was over, they would, "never be the same again."

In 1976 Godin became an active elected politician running with Lévesque, on the Parti Québécois ticket. A top agenda item for Godin was, as it had always been, the establishment of the pre-eminence of the French language in Québec. The protection of the language was secured through law 101, which held that immigrants must go to a French school, and commercial signs must be in French. But the elation felt in Lévesque's 1976 defeat of Bourassa was dampened when Lévesque, inviting the people to a referendum on negotiation of their independence, was undermined by the pro-Canada federalists. They had incited the people to vote no, so that on 20 May, 1980, the day of the actual vote, 40.8% of the Québécois said yes, but 59.2 said no: in other words, only 4 out of 10 were for "negotiation." (What the film does not point out is that many people thought they were actually voting on out-and-out separation.) Hénaut here introduces the often-reproduced scene of a hoarse and apparently tearful Lévesque saying to the assembled crowd, "If I understand you correctly, you are saying, 'à la pro-chaine.' Very well then, 'à la prochaine' ['until next time']." But that was not to be: he died in 1987.

The film ends on a somber note. A quick glance at the last decade (the 1980s) suggests that while Québec has gained economic power and set aside its militantism, and while, thanks to law 101, French has become a language of work, and signs have been posted in French, nonetheless the 1988 challenge of law 101 brought about a ruling by the Supreme Court that the segment of law 101 that requires signs to be in French is "unconstitutional." The language, and therefore the culture, of Québec are once again threatened. (Subsequent to the filming of this documentary, of course, came Meech Lake and its defeat, events that confirmed the worries expressed at the end of the film. Jacques Godbout detailed the effects of this defeat in his *Mouton noir* (or *Black Sheep* [i.e., Québec], a 232-minute film made in 1992.)

DUPLESSIS ET APRÈS (1972; Denys Arcand et al.)

Another documentary that might well serve as a background to films devoted to the October crisis is *Duplessis et après*, often attributed to Denys Arcand. But a look at the credits shows that the persons responsible for the creation of this film are multiple, and are simply listed in alphabetical order.

The creators of *Duplessis et après* have used stills and old footage to show us the platforms of the chief politicians of the 1960s. These include Jean-Robert Ouellet (libéral); Robert Burns (Parti Québécois); Antoine Drolet (Crédit Social); Bernard Landry (Parti Québécois); Robert Quenneville (libéral); and Guy Pelletier (Parti Québécois).

What makes this film especially striking are the intercuts in which Robin Spry, with his strong English accent, reads sections from the 1838 Durham report contending that the French Canadians are fundamentally stupid, "mal éduqués," illiterate, and possessed of an irremediable inferiority, all of which in the long run proves their inability to participate in the democratic processes of greater Canada.[5]

The Durham report serves as a backdrop to passages in which the choir sings segments from the mass (Kyrie eleison, etc.) while the politicians affirm the need to preserve the language and the interests of the Québécois. These scenes, clearly ironic on the part of the filmmakers, are offset by passages in which Gisèle Trépanier reels off sections of the Union Nationale[6] "cathéchisme" of 1936 in the cathetical style (i.e., a man asks her questions; which she or a group of schoolchildren answers, as if by rote). Asked "Is agriculture in *la marrasse*?" she answers "Agriculture is always treated as a poor relative." Interrogated on taxes, she responds: "Québec is heavily taxed and deeply in debt." What is more, she explains, the big companies control the forest industries — the gas and oil, the paper, the aluminum, the telephone. Trusts are protected by the *québécois* governement. The political consequences are exploitation of the people and the suffocation of democracy. Moreover, freedom of opinion does not exist in Québec; there is a dictatorship, and abuse of power, even a control of the newspapers. As for justice, the treatment of accused persons is determined according to whether they have friends in high places or not. The worst is that the Church and the State are in the same boat, or in cahoots.

We are next shown newsreels and the like in which bishops and cardinals are "parading" with high-ranking political figures. Then the liberal party is shown promising work to the unemployed: posters read "Au travail; votons libéral [Back to work; let's vote liberal]," and the politicians are explaining that this work will *not* be for Westmount, Outremont, and the Grande Allée (i.e., for the rich [anglophones]).

Despite the many talking heads and the clips from endless political testimonials and speeches, this documentary allows one to see the course of events over a span of more than one hundred years and how it influenced the politics of the 1960s, just ahead of the devastating actions of 1970. It is of note that Landry is seen here predicting as difficult a time for the Québécois in Canada as the blacks had experienced in the U.S.A.

Certain anglophone films may also serve as a prelude to the examination of *Les Ordres* and *Les Années de rêve*. Among these is Robin Spry's *Action: The October Crisis of 1970.*

ACTION: THE OCTOBER CRISIS OF 1970 (1973; 87 min.; d. Robin Spry)

Although this documentary is in English and was made by an anglophone director, it is appropriate to include an analysis of it here, since it is usually mentioned in a discussion of films concerning the October 1970 crisis.

James E. Page characterizes *Action* ... as "An extraordinary film that depicts the desperate days of October, 1970, when it seemed as though Québec's Quiet Revolution might end in insurrection and repression."[7] The events depicted in this film are historically contextualized by rare archival footage and stock photos from earlier crises, such as significant occurrences during the pro-Church, pro-federalist (pro-establishment) Duplessis régime (the Asbestos strike; the Murdochville strike; the Radio-Canada Producers' strike, taking place in 1959, the date of Duplessis's death, which marks the rise of nationalism and separatism). Certainly here, as throughout the film, the commentary is inclined to be pro-separatist. It points out that historically the best jobs in Québec had always gone to the anglophones, and that even through the Duplessis régime, the Québéc province had remained "rural, subjugated, and poor." Although the right to strike had been an issue in the rest of Canada in the 20s it was not until the 40s and 50s, following the industrialization that came with World War II, that the right to strike became a strong issue in Québec.

The film seeks to give the background necessary for understanding the events of October 1970. It shows how the FLQ executed many bombings against English businesses and monuments throughout the 1960s, and how the Queen was treated during her 1964 visit to Canada, and includes footage of the Saturday of the Truncheons (Samedi de la Matraque). (Pierre Bourgault had denounced the Queen's presence to an angry crowd, which squared off against the police.). We are also told about Charles Gagnon and Pierre Vallières, two FLQ polemicists who demonstrated outside the United Nations in New York and were arrested by the Americans, only to be illegally deported and to serve three years in jail before being released on bail. Pierre Bourgault, running on the RIN (Rassemblement pour l'indépendance nationale) separatist ticket, is shown losing the 1966 election by 90% to the old conservative

Duplessis party (the Union Nationale), with Daniel Johnson the winner. We see De Gaulle in his famous 1967 utterance, in which he "confused his trip through Québec with the Liberation of France," as the narrator puts it. Also we have the struggles of Lévesque versus Trudeau, the attack on Trudeau on the eve of the 1968 St. Jean Baptiste parade (although he was elected the next day). We also learn how Lévesque and Bourgault joined forces, how the RIN disappeared into the new Parti Québécois, and are informed about the introduction of Bill 63, which required immigrants to learn French, as well as about the McGill/français movement.

After detailing the kidnappings of James Cross and Pierre Laporte, the film concentrates on the War Powers Act, invoked by the federal Prime Minister Pierre Elliott Trudeau, who is shown, his face "masklike," as he berates the "bleeding hearts" and the "weak-kneed" who decried his militaristic solution to the growing dissension—approaching insurrection and anarchy, or so he calculated—in the upstart province Québec. It was a time of terrorism, and behind the foment lay, among other forces, the powerful FLQ. (The situation had worsened, of course, and the anger of the FLQ had been fueled by the 'liberals' defeat of the Parti Québécois, with Robert Bourassa going in as the liberal leader. The deepest conflict between the ideologies of Lévesque and Trudeau comes a bit later. It is studied in *The Champions*.)

"Just watch me," Trudeau says in that interview: not only will he send in the soldiers, but he will resort also to an invocation of the War Measures Act, on 15 October in the middle of the night. We are given the complete reading of the manifesto of the FLQ on television. This manifesto was a call to revolution and a historical recall of the patriots of 1837–38, who were excommunicated by the Church. It was also a document in which certain demands were made in exchange for the return of Cross. This, of course, led to a declaration of martial law, which in turn is shown to have been invoked without appeal to the Federal Parliament, and which is said to have allowed police to search and arrest and/or seize without warrant, and to hold one prisoner for ninety days without charge or without trial. Most curiously, being a member of the FLQ was at the same time retroactively illegal, and punishable by five years in prison. The army is shown rolling in, and the soldiers are seen breaking into houses and seizing material, in scenes that at times are grimmer than those in *Les Ordres*. It is ironic to think that the Canadian prime minister went to these lengths when one considers that, according to David Lewis, M.P. and member of the New Democratic Party, clear plans for armed insurrection were never proved. Americans in particular should also note that John Diefenbaker, member of parliament, supported Trudeau, and criticized the former régime as being too permissive of revolutionary rhetoric. In the clip, he claims that the government should have acted long ago against these 'Americans coming in and preaching their doctrine of revolution.' And he adds that their protection of revolutionaries under the right to 'freedom of speech' has led to this situation.

But these measures, explained by Trudeau on national television on 15 October as necessary in the face of the "cancer of armed revolution," do not prevent the murder of Pierre Laporte by the FLQ. He is found dead, following receipt of a note from the FLQ telling where he is to be found, calling Bourassa "the federal government's valet" and Laporte the "minister of unemployment and the minister of assimilation." Laporte's execution shocks Québec. Trudeau calls for unification and labels the FLQ a band of murderers; he also expresses the "shame" Canadians feel for these acts. Following the event, Lévesque speaks for the Parti Québécois, saying Laporte's execution is intolerable; but he criticizes the federal and provincial governments for the hard line they have taken. He then expresses his hope for reconsideration by the government and for the surrender of the extremists. But he adds that Quebeckers will not regard themselves as impotent.

In the final scenes, we see the funeral of Laporte at the Church of Notre Dame with all the dignitaries, including Bourassa, attending. We learn of the apprehension of the kidnappers, the finding of Cross, and, at the end of 1970, the discovery of the Roses and Simard (leaders of the FLQ) in a tunnel in Saint-Luc. Says the commentary, they will battle the legal system, "calling it foreign and imposed." (Cf. *Cordélia* and *Kamouraska*, as well as *La Corriveau*.)

"A strong and gripping feature-length documentary," says Pratley (*TS*, 1987, 217). At the 1990 meeting of the American Council of Québec Studies, Pierre Véronneau discussed this film, calling it a "compilation film" (in French, *montage*), and questioning its objectivity, because of its Re-action (pun on the title) to the events, characterized as a time of "loss of liberty," and "loss of innocence." In reality, the events are characterized as bringing about a "sad and costly loss of innocence."

REACTION: A PORTRAIT OF A SOCIETY IN CRISIS (1973; d. Robin Spry)

In *Reaction* ... actual "groups" of anglophone Québécois, not identified by name but, rather, by their social or age class, discuss in heated terms their "reactions" to the "actions" taken by the FLQ and by Trudeau during the October 1970 crisis.

This film first gives a rapid summary of events, with Trudeau on television explaining why he has called upon the War Measures Act. A group of people from Westmount watch, and a hot argument ensues. If it could be done in Québec, it could after all be done in Ontario, or British Columbia. Children, too, discourse on violence and racism in what I found to be the most extraordinary segment of this piece. Professors discuss the pros and cons of the evocation and avow a sense of their political weakness as a minority. There is debate here over cultural identity and also the expression of fear that the United States will take over; fear, too, that *québécois* nationalism will allow them no place. (Some of the speakers are of English descent; others are immigrants.) The question is raised as to whether Canada is even a "nation." In "a poor neighborhood" of Montréal democracy is discussed. The point is made that the people did not, after all, vote on the use of the War Powers Act, which must raise concern for Trudeau's possible setting up of a police state. One woman, however, says she is glad for Trudeau's act; in her view the FLQ has gone too far, and she feels safer with the troops in place. But one man points out that the police are not there to protect them — the poor — they are there to protect the rich people's fancy houses. There is discussion, also, of the pros and cons of releasing the detainees, as requested by the FLQ. Finally, we have reactions of executives to Trudeau's measure. To them the government's behavior is "courageous and very right." Their thoughts on the mentality of the revolutionary are forthcoming. As virtually the parting word, one of them states that anglophones must put their weight behind the effort to preserve Québec.

For the person studying this pivotal political (and social) crisis through Canadian cinema, this short film — which is the *pendant* of Spry's *Action* ... — provides valuable information and important insights into what the anglophone *québécois* community was apparently thinking during this upheaval. It is, however, through the prize-winning and riveting fictional film *Les Ordres* that the most memorable and the most devastating picture of the events of those grim days emerges.

Less closely related to the October crisis per se, but also of great value for its portrayal of the political dimension of Québec culture is *The Champions* (1978—86; Part 1: 26 min., 31 min.; Part 2: 30 min., 31 min.; Part 3: 90 min.), an anglophone documentary, written, directed, and narrated by Donald Britten. It is a vast work, but, like the films discussed above, a very good one for backgrounding *Les Ordres*.

THE CHAMPIONS (1978—86; d. Donald Brittain)

Aired on television as a three-part miniseries, the cinematic triumph *The Champions* is not entirely unrelated to the several films about the October 1970 crisis that I have just treated. Using archival footage, still photos, and many interviews from participants of this troubled interlude in Canadian history, Brittain evokes the early life and the political career of two figures who sparred throughout a good segment of the twentieth century: Pierre Trudeau, the sophisticated liberal federalist who rose to be prime minister of Canada, and René Lévesque, the liberal separatist, who, after many vicissitudes, became the premier of Québec. Though both were of strong political integrity, events shown in the film forged them into ideological enemies.

The film shows how from their childhood forward these two men — both Québécois, both therefore having a bicultural heritage, both educated by the Jesuits — differed in their breeding and upbringing. Lévesque, who attended Brébreuf College, developed a certain style associated with the "gars brébeuf." Early in his career he even wrote a bad play regarding dictatorship. During the war he refused conscription with a strong *non serviam* that led him to the United States, for which he worked during World War II. Trudeau, on the other hand, was an elitist, also educated by the Jesuits. Ultimately he studied law (as Lévesque did also). Trudeau early developed a hatred of nationalism during his stay in Europe. While he showed a political sympathy with the strikers in Asbestos, Q., he demonstrated already in this affair his social distance from them. Brittain shows the main events of the Duplessis election and régime, and the roles the two men played during this era. Since Lévesque was a journalist during this period, and later (in 1967) had a role to play on Canadian television — through his appearance on "The Public Eye" — Brittain's film amounts among other things to a minihistory of the role of the Canadian media in its political life.

After the death of Duplessis (1958), the liberal Jean Lesage and the Equipe de Tonnerre were swept to power (1960), and the Quiet Revolution had begun. Among the ministers were Lévesque and Pierre Laporte. Lévesque, as a professor of law at the University of Montréal, mingled with Québec's artists, including Leonard Cohen, to whom Adrienne Clarkson devoted a program in 1991. By 1962 Lévesque had put in place his plan for nationalism, under the slogan "Masters in our own house," from which I derive the subtitle of this book.

At this juncture in the long documentary, a serendipitous segment offers scenes from the political parable, "Yesterday, the Children Were Dancing," by the established playwright Gratien Gélinas, whose *Tit-Coq* was discussed in Chapter 1, and who, as an actor, appeared in *Les Tisserands du pouvoir* (see below). The segment is meant to show the continuing politicization of the Québec scene and its culture.

Chief scenes leading up to the bitter confrontation are then examined: Expo; De Gaulle's famous "Vive Montréal; vive le Québec; vive le Québec libre," which is reprised, and said to have split the country in two. In the 1970s the Parti Québécois is formed, and Lévesque leads it to a majority position in the National Assembly, while, meanwhile, Trudeau remains Prime Minister through two elections. The role of Pauline Julien (who was to the Parti Québécois what Juliette Greco was to the Existential movement in France) is adumbrated. (Julien, with her husband Godin, formed the backdrop for Robert MacNeil's segment on Québec in the documentary series *Canada, True North*, in which all the major events of the referendum and the liberation movement are again rehearsed.) Then comes footage and commentary detailing the War Measures Act, by which Trudeau gave to the militia the power to search and arrest without warrant, to detain without charge and to detain without bail. All this we saw in *Action ...* or will in *Les Ordres*, but it is a cornerstone in this documentary, as it shows sharply the lines of battle that had come to be drawn between these two champions. We learn that of the 419 people arrested, 281 were never charged; but, as importantly, the Parti Québécois now lay in ruins. Lévesque condemned the violence and also the Trudeau overkill. He then had to rebuild the party.

The merit of Brittain's film lies in the differentiated portraits of the two men: Trudeau is viewed as intelligent, removed, and solitary. In isolation, he surrounded himself with a handful of senior civil servants who had access to him. (They were called the mandarins.) Possessed of Cartesian logic and an ability at Socratic dialogue, he was more in his element with the great men and issues of his time; he dreamed of Canada as an important player in the international arena. Lévesque himself characterized Trudeau as "a citizen not of Québec nor of Canada, but of the world." Meanwhile, Lévesque and his followers spoke of ethnic purity and dangers of cultural contamination. For Trudeau, this was cultural suffocation, a crime against humanity. The Lévesquians rammed through Bill 101, which was tantamount to calling for special status for Québec. But in this battle between two men, both showed that they had brilliant minds and passionate souls; there was, says Brittain, "a fine rage in each." They were, he finds, prisoners of each other.

The final segment of this fascinating documentary shows how in 1976 the second battle for Québec was launched, when Lévesque was elected its new premier, and he and his staff prepared for the referendum, which called for a separate nation in loose association with Canada. This truly frightened English Canada, and especially the English Canadians born in and living in Québec. (But the Québécois viewed the English as bent on cultural genocide, so that the Revolution was a matter of "survival.") Claude Morin drafted the question, which was so worded as to be ambiguous and to lose, perhaps because of this alone. (A "yes" for the referendum was a "mandate to negotiate the sovereignty of Québec" and to seek an economic association with Canada; and in a second referendum to approve any change. Voters were asked to vote yes or no to the question: "Do you agree?") But at this election, on 20 May 1980, 87 percent of the Quebeckers came to vote; it was the biggest turnout in Canadian political history. (The viewer may find it amusing to see Knowlton Nash as a very young man during this passage of the film.) And only 40 percent voted with Lévesque, for Trudeau had waged a powerful campaign against it, aided by Jean Chrétien, Trudeau's hit man, and a Québécois, now prime minister of Canada. Also, during the campaign for the referendum, Lise Paillette, a TV host and then Lévesque's cabinet minister, had spoken of the women in Ryan's camp, and of his wife, "Yvette sa petite soeur" — the stereotype (out of early primers) of the Canadian female child (and woman). In the primer she was a good little girl who looked forward to becoming a housewife, and who liked to cook and sew. This was a gigantic error on Paillette's part, for it made many people angry. Fifteen thousand women poured into the Montréal forum; Lise Paillette had galvanized the Yvettes, i.e., had harmed the possibility of the "yes" vote. But while it had a negative effect on the vote for the referendum, the incident was historic in the feminist movement of Québec.

In the postreferendum period, Trudeau occupied himself with the patriation of the Canadian Constitution, for Canada was still by definition a colony. Lévesque marshalled all the premiers behind him to stand tall for provincial powers; but Trudeau declared war on the provinces, and asked the British to deliver a Constitution to Canada. Lévesque, by joining the "gang of eight," an alliance of provincial premiers, surrendered Québec's right to veto. Trudeau, then, was obsessed by the question of the Constitution, while Canadians were worried about the price of gas. The "Civil War" was over, and Québec was still in the confederation.

This documentary was, as is obvious from the length of footage, intended for showing in three long segments on Canadian television. But by now one must view it as an important political and historical film that can be screened with great profit by all people involved in Canadian affairs or culture, and in particular by anglophone students and scholars. Although one must admit that the editorializing on the part of Brittain may skew the viewer's assimilation of this documentary, we know by now that this is really always the effect of a so-called "objective documentary." And, in any case, it is as engaging a portrayal of political events as anyone might find.

The film is, of course, limited to the dates mentioned above, so the viewer has no information on subsequent events. Supplementary information would have to be supplied to the potential viewer, showing that next would come the battle for the ratification in 1990 of the Meech Lake Accord, which delineated Québec, under the leadership of Robert Bourassa, as a special culture. This also failed, but apparently only for a time. And it would be important, also, to delineate how, as a result of these upheavals—not unjustified, of course—150,000 anglophones have left Québec in the past five years or so, while 300,000 are expected to do so within the next few years.

Marcel Jean (in Coulombe 1991, 71–2) calls Brittain the most famous anglophone documentary filmmaker of Canada. Though born in Ottawa, his treatment of Québec history and civilization is substantial. In addition to *The Champions*, he has made a film on Leonard Cohen (*Ladies and Gentleman: Mr. Leonard Cohen*, codirected with Don Owen, 1965) and on Norman Bethune (1964, codirected with John Kemeny), praised by Pratley for its "sheer power of detail and narrative control" (*TS* 1987, 93).[8]

In 1976 Brittain made a documentary called *Henry Ford's*

America, and in 1980 he made a film entitled *The Dionne Quintuplets*, thus adding to the list of films on this landmark event in the history of French Canada and of world medicine, more filmed by others than by French Canadians. In this present book, two important films of Brittain's are utilized from time to time: *Dreamland* and *Has Anybody Here Seen Canada?* And in Chapter 7, one will find a brief treatment of his *Volcano: an Inquiry into the Life and Death of Malcolm Lowry* (1976) viewed, like *The Champions*, as a "Québécois" film (Coulombe 1991, 72; 560).

With all these fine documentaries "under our belt," we are now well equpped to view *Les Ordres*, which, even so, can be understood as an entity, and in that case stand as a powerful cautionary tale about totalitarianism.

LES ORDRES (1974; d. Michel Brault)

Based on the testimony of 50 out of 450 victims of the War Measures law, arrested and imprisoned without charge, this is a gripping film showing the terror and inhuman treatment of half a dozen people coming from all walks of life. The film works like a documentary, with people supposedly giving interviews in which they narrate — by means of "flashbacks" — their brutal arrest and false imprisonment, carried out by the police, who say they are enforcing "orders" backed by a "loi spéciale." (Trudeau's famous 1958 statement that "all men are responsible when any man is accused unjustly" sounds like truculence when we see the effects of his invoking of the War Measures Act portrayed here.) Included are the experiences of Clermont Boudreau, who works in a weaving mill and handles grievances of union members, and of his wife Marie. The latter is arrested and put in jail when she cannot say where her husband is. (He has been suspended from his work in the mill, and is driving a taxi.) Their ordeal is interwoven with the story of Claudette Dusseault, a social worker, who has "always been a fighter," and with that of Richard Lavoie, a thirty-four-year-old unemployed man with a tenth grade education, who cares for his babies while his wife works nights as a waitress. For completely unexplained reasons, except to terrorize him, he is particularly badly treated; he is questioned for three hours in the middle of the night, and then led to believe he will be shot to death in three days. When he is taken down to a large room and shot at with blank bullets he faints and comes to in his cell; he is then put in solitary confinement. Also among the victims is Jean-Marie Beauchemin, a physician who has established a community health clinic for low-income families, and had once been a socialist candidate, but "was beaten." These persons undergo all manner of physical and mental humiliation; they sense a loss of identity through the uniforms they are obliged to put on. And the fact of being held indefinitely without any charges brings on psychoses that leave life long scars. Especially moving is the need Boudreau feels to see his dead father. After much hesitation on the part of the prison authorities, he is finally taken, handcuffed in a car with four guards, to the funeral home in St. Joseph d'Alma where his father lies in state. Here he kneels for a moment, then signs the register, and is returned to prison. Back in his cell he sings a plaintive song of St. Joseph d'Alma and of liberty, to keep from breaking down, a song his father taught him.

By use of long shots of prison corridors, of frame after frame showing bars, bars, and more bars, and of strange angles of the exercise courtyard — the architectural expression of imposed order — along with a very slow-moving pace, the film effectively captures the sensation of being in jail, where "you have no rights, but only privileges, maybe, if you behave." (The film was shot in an empty prison in Sorel.)

No discussion of this masterpiece would be of any point, were we not to speak first and above all of the architectural effects of the film. In the opening shots, all is in "order," if I might make such a pun. The view of the building where the Boudreaus live is characteristic of most québécois residential areas. But the particular angle suggests perfect symmetry. Three stories of the building are in view, with their orderly balconies, and on either side the outside staircases that lead to upstairs apartments. Squarely in front of the building stands Boudreau's taxi. This peaceful orderliness is no longer apparent when Boudreau returns to his home upon being released from prison.

Secondly, added to the slow pace and the long shots, the film emphasizes the tediousness of the situation by being photographed in sepia tones, with very little color. When color is used it is muted. (The film is not exactly in black and white and color, as Pratley states.)

And thirdly, there are many subtle ironies in this film, but particularly notable is the opening quotation of the highly rhetorical statement by Trudeau made in 1958, in which he declares (in John Donne-like style) that all men are responsible when any man is accused unjustly. Can he have remembered having said this when, almost like a dictator, he invoked the War Measures Act, and hurled out that defiant "Just watch me"?

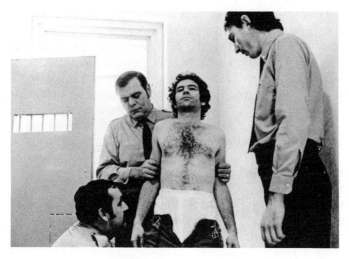

Les Ordres. Photograph by Daniel Kieffer. (Courtesy Coll. Cinémathèque Québécoise.)

Les Ordres usually passes for one of the great fiction films of Québec, one sharing the nature of a docudrama, tying with *The Grey Fox* for fifth place in the previously cited Critics' Survey (*Variety*, 8 August 1984), and receiving the Cannes prize for *mise en scène*, together with some seventy-five other awards. Clanfield, at the 1990 meeting of the American Council for Québec Studies in Chicago, presented a handout and spoke to the "unsaid, the unacknowledged, and the unknown," in this film, which is certainly "in the canon." It is, according to him, a "problem film" from the ideological, formal, and epistemological points of view, and one that takes a humanistic approach to the issues involved. The cycle, episodic and investigative, affords closure, but still the film says that the people will never be the same. The film also states that knowledge has been gained, but "we are not told what this knowledge is, the why and the who of it"; that is, the why and the who of it are not given—experience comes without knowing. Clanfield claimed that the film cycles, carefully and symmetrically framed, have disembedded the historic content; in other words, the film does not really speak of the historical event. And, in fact, it was his case that in the making, the NFB controlled the limits of the sayable, or that the film presents a "case of self-censorship."

Véronneau, speaking on that same panel, said much the same thing: while the film is gorged with emotion, it does not mention the real causes for the invocation of the War Powers Act, nor for

322 THE CINEMA OF QUÉBEC

the arrests. I must confess that I was troubled by Véronneau's assessments, because it is my opinion that the explanation *is* given in a postscript at the end of the film (not to mention a foreword); and above all, because I believe that it was Brault's intention to show the horror of sudden *unexplained* arrest and imprisonment with the added grotesqueness of police torture and brutality occurring in the midst of a supposed democracy as something that, frighteningly enough, could happen anywhere, even in Canada, where we assume democracy prevails and human rights are respected; and if in Canada, then even, for example, in France, or in the United States. And that was its great power. Its great beauty. Its great impact. While I do not agree with Pratley that the film "conveys [the humiliation of these people] *honestly and fairly*" (Pratley *TS* 1987, 217), at the same time he is right to say that it does convey the "humiliation of *innocent people, caught up in the backlash of a violent period of terrorist activity*." (My emphases.) But it is more than that; it is not confined to its period. This was surely the director's design, and explains why he left many questions about the how, who, and why unanswered for us. These problems of justice and injustice are treated not only by Brault in this film, but by Beaudin in *Cordélia* and Arcand in *Jésus de Montréal*. In the anglophone Canadian film repertoire, one of the best films on this subject is *Justice Denied*, concerning an Indian falsely accused of murder.

Les Ordres has been the subject of much critical commentary, including an article by Pierre Vallières that completely pans the film, and leaves Vallières looking very ignorant. He writes: "It really does not matter that Michel Brault's intentions were of the best in the world (which I do not doubt for an instant), the fact remains that his film is for me politically and morally unacceptable ... The fiction is no more *québécois* than it is Lebanese or Senegalese. It is nearer to enigmas in the style of Kafka than to the October 1970 crisis ... He drowned the social and political context of the War Measures Act in a melodrama leaning on a half-dozen individual dramas, unexplained and anecdotal. He could not choose between fiction and history ... Instead of [giving] the salubrious shock everyone urgently needs in these times, a film like *Les Ordres* contributes to the acceptance of apoliticism as an unavoidable fact. Moreover, it contributes to erasing from the memory of the Québécois and others the machiavellianism of a political power for whom lying, blackmail, and the army are inseparable instruments in necessarily keeping citizens in ignorance and submission."[9] But, of course, Vallières's political and social agenda would be at great variance with that of Brault. A journalist in Montréal, but no film critic, he was a member of the FLQ from 1965; accused of terrorist activities he fled to New York, where he was arrested in 1966 and deported back to Canada. He spent four years in jail (1967–71), during which time he wrote his famous *Nègres blancs d'Amérique*, a book that is full of rage and strong ideas. Yet, ironically, in 1971 Vallières renounced violence, and endorsed the Parti Québécois; and by 1980 he had joined a religious order that is under the Franciscan star.

One of the best analyses of *Les Ordres* still remains that of Michel Brûlé, which was published not long after the appearance of the film. In his article, entitled "Un constat d'impuissance à l'égard des groupes d'opposition," we are shown that in *Les Ordres* the prime minister and the minister of justice are two "characters" hidden behind the police, who give the orders so that the "system" be protected and upheld. The "system" represents unity and coherence; the people who are apprehended express no collective vision, and do not understand what is happening to them, nor the common denominator that has bound them together. *Brault's* point of view is that there was no crisis in the Québec population nor with the police; it was a crisis of those who had hold of the power. And those who had the power to give the orders lived out a crisis caused by the kidnapping of two political personalities. It was political power that felt menaced and that understood that it was necessary to defend, as well, the economic interests upon which it rested; that is, (a) the boss of the factory, (b) the gentleman who comes to seize the furniture, and (c) the interests threatened by the regrouping that FRAP constituted and by the socialist ideas already in action in the cadre of a people's clinic.

Brûlé finds there is a shifting of point of view in the film, from one personality to the other, including Brault's own perspective, and that the film is not political, in that there is nothing political at the explicit level. Still, there is another level at which political analysis occurs. This analysis reveals that *québécoise* society is divided into three groups: those who give orders and protect the "system" in its economic and politial components; those who oppose this system by political actions and by economic and social revindications; and those who are removed from both of these groups.

Brûlé's conclusion is that *Les Ordres* formulates a sort of report on the damaging facts of impotence with respect to the opposition groups, and is very pessimistic as to the capacity for reaction on the part of the whole of society as it faces manifest abuses of power. The crisis has past, but this just means that power is no longer in crisis. Still, one must wonder if it is very reassuring that that power is not afraid any more.[10]

With *Les Ordres*, Brault proved himself as great a director as photographer. Since then he has distinguished himself as director of four more films: *Les Noces de papier* (1989), *Diogène* (1990), *Sabbath Shalom* (1992), and *Mon amie* Max (1994). *Les Noces de papier* is an emotionally honest and fiercely intelligent Canadian drama that revolves around the same situation found in *Green Card*; it stars Geneviève Bujold as Claire, a disillusioned thirty-nine-year-old single woman, and university professor, who agrees to marry a Chilean political refugee simply in order to forestall his deportation. If she agrees to do this it is partly because she is bored with her long-term affair with a married man, and also because her lawyer sister persuades her to do it, presumably to save him for herself. However, the relationship takes an unexpected turn when Canadian immigration officials develop an active interest in the case. Forced to live together, and to find out details about each other, they quite unexpectedly come to realize the depth of their affection for one another. Most viewers of this film, myself included, find *Paper Wedding* to be quite superior in its conception and execution to *Green Card*.[11]

Jean-Claude Labrecque's *Les Années de rêve*, or *Years of Dreams and Revolt* (1984) is another film that, like *Les Ordres*, depends on some of the events we have been relating for its political content.

Labrecque began his study of social history through the portrayal of a single family in his 1975 *Les Vautours*, to which *Les Années de rêve* is, so to speak, a sequel. The three aunts, for example, were played by the same actresses, and Gilbert Sicotte and Anne-Marie Provencher also played in that film, as did Roger Le Bel. Pratley (*TS* 1987, 221) characterizes *Les Vautours*, in which a young man becomes the pawn of an artful political game played out during the corrupt Duplessiste régime, as "a shadowy and thoughtful film about human relationships and individual selfishness."

It is 1964. At the outset of the story, Louis, who marries Claudette — already two months pregnant — in a long, drawn-out, elaborate nuptial mass, wants to be nothing more than a photographer and a musician. But as time goes by he becomes involved in union and then in revolutionary political plots that bring him the loss of his job, a threat to his marriage, and finally ruin. Early on, we see him displaying great anger at a street blockade in honor of the Queen's visit, and not long after he is off to Montréal to see the De Gaulle visit. Through actual footage (some shown as if over television) we once more hear De Gaulle, from his high vantage point, speaking of "*Libération*," and crying out, "Vive Montréal; Vive le Québec; Vive le Québec libre."

Louis has questionable associates with whom he wastes a great deal of time, notably John-John, an expatriated American hippy. There are others, too, with whom he smokes pot and plays music. John-John's role allows for allusions to the Democratic Party Convention in Chicago, which is seen in another film regarding the flower people, the communes, etc. (Spry's *Prologue*). With yet another group, Louis is shown using his taxicab to transport explosives, and seems to have had some part in the Cross kidnapping. As he becomes more and more deeply involved, his wife, who has aborted their second child and gone to work for a Breton crêperie, threatens to leave him; he convinces her not to go. "Va-t'en pas," he pleads, and she capitulates. We are rapidly approaching the somber days of the October 1970 crisis. At a given moment toward the end of the film, Louis calls Claudette at work and tells her that he is in trouble and that she should go to their home and retrieve a package of explosives near the sink, and meet him below, where he will be waiting in his cab. She does so, and sets the wrapped package on the counter. The phone rings, and while she is answering it their five-year-old son (played by Guillaume Lemay-Thivierge, whom we encountered in *Le Matou*) opens the package, which explodes in the child's face and hands, and sets the building afire. She carries him to the cab and the three rush to the hospital (to the tune of some overly-dramatic music). There the doctor informs them there are facial injuries and the loss of several fingers. When Claudette returns to the child's room, Louis attempts to follow her in, but she shuts the door in his face.

One of the more interesting devices used to show that the marriage is over and the story at an end is the final set of montages in which a hand turns the pages in the picture album, as photo after photo of the couple's wedding passes by, until we reach the outside of the album called "notre mariage." Thus the wedding and its undoing seem to frame the film.

One might observe at this point that the Church wedding — coming shortly after the first scenes of the film, in which the couple are having intercourse (and Claudette is assumedly being impregnated) — seems to be a mere convention. Thus it showcases the disaffection of that generation of Quebeckers with the moral teachings of the Church. The negative attitude toward the Church is, of course, associated with the general political and social unrest of the times depicted. (If the people felt financially exploited, even colonized by government, and by anglophone establishment, they saw themselves, like many third-world peoples, as spiritually colonized by the Church, which sometimes even worked in tandem with government for additional financial exploitation. Still, according to some reports, many Quebeckers are now beginning to re-affiliate with the Church.)

Perhaps, too, Claudette's refusal to be "eaten" is indicative of the then-breaking feminism: she not only threatens divorce, but also goes for an abortion with the help of the aunts and of her workmate. (The scene between Claudette and her workmate reminds one a bit of similar scenes between Florentine and her friend and workmate in *The Tin Flute*.) In any case, the early scene in which the newlyweds each shout "Je suis libre" takes on an ironic flavor, in view of the end. It is only because Louis has a false sense of freedom, while Claudette matures beyond this "bébé," that the tragedy comes about. Francine Laurendeau writes that *Les Années de rêve* is "le constat doux-amer des espoirs trahis d'une génération [the bittersweet proof of a whole generation's betrayed loves]" (Coulombe 1991, 293).

If one were to reappropriate Brunette-Willis's Derridean study of film, one might say that this movie is choreographed around the concept of hymen (meaning the female membrane and marriage *à la Mallarmé*), with the Church having merely a perfunctory role in the connection between desire (dream) and fulfillment. Already violated by prenuptial gratification and "illegitimate" germination, Louis's "entrance" into the political arena effects final explosion, rupture, destruction, with accompanying loss of purity and virginity and the scattering of seed. The hymen (marriage-family and also the female membrane) signifies the "site of potential and perhaps structural and institutional violence performed on real women and the real world."[12] And, as well, the sexual-political acts symbolize the co-optation of the female body. Derrida himself says, "It is the hymen that desire dreams of piercing, of bursting, in an act of violence that is . . . love and murder.[13] In *Les Années* . . ., political violence "murders" love; the violence occurs across the hymen, threatening the fruit of the union, imperiling the family, and undermining the role of priest and ritual in the probable absolution of a sixth-commandment sin, as well as nullifying the ritual consecration of this precarious "sacramental" union. The concept of the Church as the Mystical Body, as the bride of Christ, is also co-opted, along with the "real woman in the real world."

Les Années de rêve, perhaps the best-known fully-fictionalized film dealing with the October 1970 crisis, is seen by Pratley to be more open than *Les Vautours*, since it moves to the streets; but nevertheless he finds that, "even though the whole is not lacking in passion and feeling, ... strangely it remains slight and superficial in spite of the creator's affinity with the period and the events set against it" (*TS* 1987, 263). I am less disappointed with the depth of the film than with the musical background settings (leaving aside the "songs of the period"), which seemed inappropriate, melodramatic, distracting, and, at times, just plain irritating and interminable (*Panis angelicus* at the wedding ceremony being only one of several notable examples). Interestingly enough, although musicians themselves are named, one cannot find any one individual to whom one might attribute this problem. But endless, too, seemed the postnuptial sex scene, and even unnecessary, unless one wished to show an early joy of the relationship and how it went sour; or unless one wanted to be sure to include sex as an arm of viewer interest (?). This is far from the greatest of Québec films, but it is nonetheless good enough that it merits serious attention. In the long run, *Le frère André* may be a better Labrecque film, if to say so is not to compare apples and oranges.

Two other feature-length fictional films that deal with these events of October 1970 are Jean-Claude Lord's *Bingo*, a film about terrorists, and Jean Cousineau's *Légende*. Cousineau's films are not easily seen — as attested by Lever — but Lord's *Bingo* is quite well-known.

BINGO (1974; d. Jean-Claude Lord)

In this film, two students, François and Geneviève, at the outstart happy and carefree (she frolics while he flicks her), become accidentally involved in terrorism, following the closing (selling) of the factory, Goldwater and Sons, in which François's father, Eugène, an employee of twenty years, loses his job. What begins as a strike ends up in terrorist activities, with the principals kidnapping businessmen, whom they strip of their clothes, and becoming deeply enmeshed in elections, utlimately won by Bernard Léger, who represents "le pouvoir du peuple." The two young people, who have been exploited, wind up dead; the truly guilty go free.

One might say that this documentary-like film has several levels, or agendas; Aunt Eva reflects the hope of the poor, the desire to win at Bingo, the wish to strike it rich without half trying. (A lighthearted wraparound song about Bingo belies the darkness of this film's message.) But Eva also recognizes she is a burden to her nephew. Still, as she says, she cannot resolve to go into the old people's home. Additionally, she represents the old-time (*simple*) Québécoise; she prepares food and strong coffee as an antidote to her brother's sufferings and alcoholism. The portrayal of Geneviève is enigmatic: she is a modern woman, but seems more an object to François than anything else. Still, she dies with him, and mostly because of his activities.

However, the major themes remain the treachery of the establishment, terrorism, exploitation, and right wing movements.

Bingo is mentioned by Lever several times; he insists on Jean-Claude Lord as Québec's Costa Gavras (*Hist.* 1988, 287; 288; 357), and finds that he studies the "conscience" of those in power. Pratley finds *Bingo* to be the most important film of 1974. He writes that it is "a disturbing dramatic fiction with documentary overtones set around the Front de Libération du Québec October crisis in Montreal in which two young students are unwittingly involved and then destroyed by politics and big business. Under its deceptively lighthearted title (which refers to an aunt's mania for the game), this picture brings out the ugliest aspects of French-Canadian nationalism ... Jean-Claude Lord has not since made a film of such power and purpose as this" (*TS* 1987, 215–16).

Marcel Jean asserts that *Bingo* was the first full-length fiction film inspired (but freely) by the October 1970 events, and although the film was a huge success with the public, the left wing intellectuals took it apart, reproaching it for its demobilizing effect, and for showing that terrorism serves the right. These reproaches came because, "constructed like a thriller, *Bingo* tells the story of a *cégépien* (a student) who joins a group of strikers manipulated by [Pierre], an activist who is in the hands of the rightists. The strikers kidnap some businessmen and also expose an affair implicating the morals of a minister, and a crisis ensues: repression begins, the police assassinate François, and the right comes out on top" (Coulombe 1991, 351).

Reinforced by *Bingo*'s success, Lord next brought out *Parlez-nous d'amour* in 1976. It was based on a *scénario* by Michel Tremblay. In 1977, Lord made another thriller, *Panique*, which dealt with industrial pollution. In *Eclair au chocolat* (1978), he again explored social problems (single parents; abortion). He is also the director of English-language films, and in Chapter 7 the reader will find a discussion of his film *Toby McTeague*, filmed in the region of Chicoutimi, and concerned with a boy obsessed by dog sled races.

Less well-known than Lord's films are those of Pierre Falardeau, said by some to be in need of recuperation, although to Lever (*Hist.* 1988, 273; 358), Falardeau's *Elvis Gratton* (1981) — codirected with Julien Poulin — contains gross satire and simplistic messages.

Yves Picard writes that *Gratton* is a "Portrait chargé du Québécois affligé de tous les travers de l'aliéné ... [et une] farce qui montre sans ménagement les conséquences — le confort et la bêtise — pour pointer du doigt les causes politiques [Loaded portrait of the Québécois afflicted by all the ordeals of the alienated person (and a) farce that shows without reserve the consequences — the comfort and the stupidity — of pointing one's finger at political causes]" (Coulombe 1991, 181). It has two sequels: *Les Vacances d'Elvis Gratton* (1983) and *Pas encore Elvis Gratton!* (1985). Falardeau's *Magra* (1975) is an antifascist film that deals with oppression and the negation of oppression; in it the police have the power. Other films of his include *A Force de Courage* (1976) and *Pea Soup* (1978). *Speak White* (1980; 6 min. — after the poem of Michèle Lalonde) denounces American imperialism and colonialism, while he has also made *Country Fried Chicken*, *Coca-Cola*, and *Le Party*, this last taking place in a prison milieu. (Early in 1991 a segment of Victoria Tennant's Sunday Arts Entertainment [CBC] was devoted to *Le Party*.) Falardeau himself speaks of this film, which stars Charlotte Laurier, saying "J'ai essayé de faire un film sur la liberté le plus librement possible. [I tried to make a film about freedom as freely as possible]."[14] It is extremely gross.

Lever, in his article "Une histoire à suivre, Octobre 70 dans le cinéma québécois," laid out in a very organized fashion the films dealing with the October crisis to that date (1974). He first looked at films using the October events themselves as their global or partial theme. Among these he included Fernand Dansereau's *Faut aller parmi l'monde pour le savoir*; as well as the films *Tranquillement, pas vite* (1972; ONF, Guy L. Côté); Jean-Claude Labrecque's *Les Smattes* (1972); Jean-Claude Lord's *Bingo* (1974); Brault's *Les Ordres*. In that category he also included *Action: the October Crisis of 1970* (ONF, Robin Spry); and Jean Cousineau's *L'Ile Jaune*. He then discussed a series of films that — without speaking of the events specifically — refer to it in some manner or other. These might include almost "all of Québec cinema," he says. But he finds that films made just after the crisis may exploit one aspect of it or another. Here he mentions Pierre Maheu's *Bonhomme* and Jean

Pierre Lefebvre's *Ultimatum*. He then treats some of the repercussions of these events on *québécois* cinema, and especially the
tightening of political censorship at the ONF. The affair of *24
heures ou plus* was the "summit," but the release of *L'Acadie,
l'Acadie* was delayed, and both *Québec: Duplessis et après* and
Richesse des autres underwent small cuts or changes. It was Lever's
impression, moreover, that Québécois filmmakers had become much
more careful, that the cameras did not go "parmi l'monde pour
savoir," and that the films (of the years between 1970 and 1974 at
least) dealt much less with the dream of a new society.[15]

The October 1970 crisis will not soon be forgotten in Canada.
Twenty years after the event the newspapers and other media
analyzed its meanings, and principal among these was the CBC
Sunday Report (7 October 1990), in which it was said that during
that period, "civil liberties evaporated," terrorism took hold, a
police state held sway, and "a certain innocence" was lost. All
was related: from the 24 June 1968 St. Jean Baptiste Parade in
Montréal, during which Trudeau, a symbol of Ottawa, becomes
a target but is spared, to the kidnapping of Cross; to Trudeau's
deploying of the army; to his invocation on 15–16 October of the
War Measures Act (which suspended Canada's Bill of Rights, and
gave to the police the right to search and arrest without a warrant);
to a detailing of the "deal" in early December whereby Cross was
to be freed for the release of six kidnappers (all of whom fled to
Cuba and gradually came back, one by one, to serve their sentences).
Especially revealing in this broadcast was the ensuing panel discussion with the journalists Peter Desbarats, David Halton, and
Lysiane Gagnon participating. Here it was advanced that most
people believed in the tough stands taken by the Trudeau government, and that the FLQ almost killed the *indépendantiste* movement,
for people became afraid. Halton argued that it helped by separating
the criminal fringe from the *indépendantiste* movement, while
Gagnon maintained that it was the death of Laporte and not the
War Measures Act that put an end to terrorism, for people were
horrified by these violent and bloody deeds. Desbarats capped the
discussion by observing how easily "we" can lose our rights; and
again he characterized the October 1970 crisis as a time for the
"loss of innocence" in Québec.

As a final note to our discussion of these political documentaries
and feature films, let us point out that Denys Arcand, so well
known for his *Déclin de l'empire américain* and *Jésus de Montréal*,
has made a documentary regarding the failure by Québec nationalists
to win a referendum on separation. This should come as no surprise,

since early on Arcand had done a free-lance "documentary" for
the National Film Board entitled *On est au coton*, which, according
to Ron Burnett, is an example of the "crisis of Québec's documentary films."[16] The more that polemical subjectivity entered the
Arcandian documentary, the more the National Film Board became
inclined toward "censorship." Even earlier than this, Arcand had
made some historical documentaries about Québec that had gotten
him into trouble with the Board. He had portrayed the Québécois
as conquered people, which was not agreeable to the Board. Arcand
describes these early conflicts of the 60s as follow:

> "The NFB thought that these films should be peppy and good for the
> morale of the people. Mild, smiling propaganda, of how happy we all
> are in Canada. I had some small conflicts in the making of the films,
> particularly with the commentary. Those with commentary were always
> refused and I had to rewrite them all the time. After three films, the
> NFB decided to drop the series."[17]

In *On est au coton*, made as a free-lance project after leaving the
Board as a regular employee, Arcand took a strong political stand
and in so doing shifted away from *cinéma vérité*. He makes no
attempt to hide his nationalism in this film; he simply foregrounds
conflict and contradiction with a call to action.[18] The NFB came
under pressure to censor this film, for in it Arcand included a half-
hour segment on how the president of Dominion Textiles lives in
contrast to his workers. That firm as well as the Canadian Textile
Institute, a lobby of all the textile companies, managed to provoke
a crisis at the Board that resulted in the banning of the film. Only
in 1976 was this ban lifted. Some see in this film signs of Arcand's
"subversiveness," but I would want to stress that in my opinion to
criticize is not necessarily to be subversive. *Le Confort* ... is the
subject of two useful articles in the special issue of *CopieZéro*
devoted to Arcand. One is by Michel Larouche, the other by
Gérald Godin.[19]

The idea of critiquing Québec society through film was, after all,
not exclusively Arcand's. One has only to point to J.P. Lefebvre's
Jusqu'au coeur of 1969 (Pratley *TS* 1987, 192) to show that the use
of film to raise questions regarding the society was already an
established tradition shared by most of the intellectual moviemakers
of Arcand's early career.

Even more importantly, Arcand's *Le Confort et l'indifférence* of
1981 deals with the political issues of the referendum while mixing
in fictional elements. As in *Jésus de Montréal*, the action of *Le
Confort* ... pivots around an actor who, here, plays Machiavelli.
The fictional moments that contextualize and explain preceding

footage are built around this "plot." Burnett finds that the documentary nature of this work is compromised by an attitude that is "profoundly cynical and relentless" in its "critique of the ordinary desires of ordinary people."[20] "As image after image passes by of silly politicians making frivolous promises and arguments about the future of Québec, and as Machiavelli intervenes to point out the grand stupidity of it all, the film becomes more of a condemnation of the working class as a whole than it does of their politics .... Its critique hardly glances at the root causes of fear, the unsettling worry which many Québécois had about the problems of trying to create a new country .... Arcand ... has taken the very traditional view of the worker as a representative of false consciousness; and as Machiavelli provides the 'grammar ... for the cynicism,' the petits-bourgeois are blamed, too, as are all the leaders. The most devastating criticism is laid at the feet of Prime Minister Trudeau, who is not only a traitor because he is French and a federalist, but because, for Arcand he is the fullest incarnation of the paternalism of anglophone culture."[21]

Unlike *On est au coton* (which was censored for its aggressive examination of the economic relations between Québec and Canada and because it was done in a voice that threatened the institution of which it was a part), *Le Confort et l'indifférence* managed to pass through the NFB. This was perhaps because of its journalistic look and tone, resulting from its new clip format, a conventional NFB collage-montage of events that are not analyzed in any great detail.[22] Arcand's film does not fit into the "direct" that I have discussed elsewhere; but according to Burnett it "mixes cinéma-vérité with an intense didacticism that would only be threatening if it could transcend its cynicism."[23] Why is it that we think of *Le Déclin* ..., and even of *Jésus de Montréal*, when Burnett writes, "Though it might be brutal to say this, the film is the equivalent of a Sunday morning show on television that looks with a pitiful eye upon the handicapped, trying to overwhelm the audience with guilt, filling them with easy categories of what is true and false, moralizing, endlessly ..."[24]? The transformation into a morality play of the complex problems facing Québec, a transformation that occurred already in Arcand's "documentary" *Le Confort* ..., seems to me to have been repeated in *Le Déclin* ... and *Jésus de Montréal*. Therefore, it is in my opinion more accurate to refer to Arcand as a moralist than as a subversive; and the two feature films, excellent though they are, distort the complicated realities of the province's political and social structures by virtue of their subjectivity and their exaggeration. This of course is the peril as well as the right—when intentional—of any portraiture artist (or any *auteur*).

The Work-Scene; Crime and the Law

To judge from *La Forteresse*, the early *québécois* crime thriller had little intention of criticizing the law enforcement agencies or the judicial system of Québec. After all, *Cordélia*, though based on a historical criminal trial, is a relatively recent film. Rather, *La Forteresse* was meant to present a mystery in the setting of Old Québec (City) and Montmorency Falls, and its photographic representation of the environment was one of its great virtues. Nevertheless, this film, this 1947 *roman policier* or *film policier* ("où tout finit bien"), directed by Fédor Ozep and produced by Langlais, or, better, L'Anglais (of the Q.P., or Québec Productions, Corporation), did present a dramatic element in the mystery revolving around three murders, "l'un véritable, l'autre suggéré, et le troisième deviné [one real one, another suggested, and the third guessed at]" and involving an American (woman reporter). It also featured lawyers and policemen investigating the crimes. And some of these ingredients will still be present in recent crime films, now set more often than not in Montréal.

A full report on this film is to be found in Véronneau's *Cin* ... (1979, 7–30),[25] including a long synopsis and many critical assessments given at the time of its appearance. While the acting of the Canadians was generally applauded (Nicole Germain, Paul Dupuis, Jacques Auger), as was the photography, the English-language version (*Whispering City*, with Mary Roberts, Helmut Dantine, Paul Lukas) was less well received. In addition, the French-language version was recognized to have been made on too low a budget, and, especially interesting was the fact that the French language film was severely criticized for its atypical speech, its lack of Canadian accents, its academic discourse. (We saw a similar criticism made of *Les Fous de Bassan*, by the way.) *La Forteresse* is, as Lever says (*Hist.* 1988, 98), an early *québécois* attempt at "film noir à la manière américaine." But later thrillers will be much more sociologically oriented, and will intend strong criticism of the police and the judicial system of the country; they may well show the criminal in a sympathetic light, and they will often take on the aura of political films as well.

L'Anglais produced and Jean Devaire directed another crime melodrama in 1950, entitled *Son Copain* (in English, *The Unknown from Montreal*). Set in Montréal, Québec, and Paris, this film involves a chase. A RCMP has a friend who knows a murder suspect whom the RCMP wishes to arrest. The film was made in two versions, French and English, with the same stars (Renée Dory; Patricia Roc; Paul Dupuis; Albert Miller; Guy Maufette; Armand Leguet; Jacques Langevin). (See Pratley *TS* 1987, 166.)

Another film that deals with crime was *La Corde au cou* (1966; 93 min.). Directed by Pierre Patry, it was based on a novel of Claude Jasmin, who wrote the *scénario* for the film. (I might have analyzed this film in Ch. 4; it fits in either domain — literature or crime thriller.) *La Corde* ... tells the story of Léo (played by Guy Godin), who, one night at a party, murders his girl friend. He runs away from the scene, and from then on is a fugitive from justice. (Details and cast found in Pratley *TS* 1987, 183.) The negative reception the critics gave to this film contributed to Patry's decision to cease directing, though he had been the founder of Coopératio and had worked for a long time in the ONF. He did continue to produce, and also made a few educational films following this failure.

Denys Arcand, too, ever on the watch regarding ills in his society, has not failed to give us stories of crime and murder in the family. This comes out not only in his filming of *Le Crime d'Ovide Plouffe*, whose crime has its origins in an incident that occurs during a picnic at Montmorency Falls, but also in his *Maudite Galette* (1972). This is a *film noir* concerning a poor plumber, his wife and children, and a hired hand and lodger named Ernest (Marcel Sabourin), and involving the robbery and murder of a rich old uncle. Pratley blames its pace for preventing this film from becoming a "superior crime thriller" (*TS* 1987, 202).

A far less successful film about murder made in the same year (1972) is Jean Beaudin's *Le Diable est parmi nous*. (See Pratley *TS* 1987, 204). In the genre of *film noir* one of the most recent *québécois* contributions is Gabriel Pelletier's *L'Automne sauvage* (1992; 105 minutes), in which Régis Santerre, an Indian, is accused of the murder of two whites. It fails by being too crammed with "intrigue." But an absolute classic of crime drama, again by Arcand, is *Réjeanne Padovani*.

RÉJEANNE PADOVANI (1973; Denys Arcand)

Réjeanne Padovani is a melodrama dealing with corruption in the *québécois* construction business. "Vincent Padovani is an entrepeneur in construction and has just finished the first trunk of a turnpike crossing the downtown area. To celebrate the event, he invites a certain number of political personalities to dine at his home. He has spared nothing to please his guests, from whom he is getting important contracts. Padovani is a 'godfather.' During the dinner, which will be followed by an opera spectacle and fireworks, his two aids inform him of the unexpected return of his exwife Réjeanne, who has left him several years ago to marry the son of the leader of a rival clan, Leny Tennenbaum. Padovani had consented to the divorce, on the condition that Réjeanne leave the city. But she has come back because she wants to live with her two children, who are being cared for by Vincent. Moreover, she has decided to leave Leny, who has a serious illness. But Padovani's aides convince him that Réjeanne must not come back. Vincent had loved this woman a great deal, and the aides look upon the return of this rival with an evil eye. At his wit's end, Padovani says he no longer wishes to see her. Réjeanne is then liquidated without the guests knowing, the noise of the shot being fused with that of the fireworks. Her body is then poured into the concrete of the turnpike, which is to be inaugurated the next morning."[26]

The film has, as Pratley says, "strong political overtones and caustic comments about businessmen and their deals with governments" (*TS* 1987, 208). (What film of Arcand's does not?) Having as its forebear Arthur Lamothe's *Le Mépris n'aura qu'un temps* (1970), *Réjeanne Padovani* is a highly-regarded film. It was shown at the Cannes Festival, along with Carle's *Mort d'un bûcheron* and Jutra's *Kamouraska* in 1973. Ginette Major analyzes the social import of this film, especially its themes of family breakdown and power politics. She finds, too, that the film is, by its setting and structure, something like the Kammerspiel, and that the characters make one think of Tennessee Williams's. She also compares Réjeanne, in her white clothes and thick make-up, to the "ange exterminé." She does not appear to see the debt of the film to the crime drama, or the thriller, however.[27]

In his preface to the *scénario* of this film, Arcand has said some things that are pertinent to the present discussion. His remarks show us exactly how the crime thriller and the film of socio-political commentary can be combined in the hands of a master: "*Réjeanne Padovani* is a sort of reflection on the present state of civilization, on the detour of a gangster story—for I am personally convinced that the West is in decadence, on the way to disintegration. It is a film on venality and on terrorism, on daily violence, and on tragedy which comes on abruptly and disappears without leaving a trace .... I did not want to give out such and such a piece of information in a precise or particular way. I wanted the film to be one which a person comes out of with the impression that we are governed by madmen, by wicked madmen who are manipulated by profiteers of all kinds" (R.P., préface, 11).[28] Hardly anything different is said in Jésus de Montréal, almost twenty years later.

In Variety, Réjeanne Padovani was described as "a cold, but never calculating or overstated look at governmental and business collusion that does not try to make it general but emerges as a coldly disturbing detailing of one particular event . . . . The characters are blocked out with a cold, visual precision that gives them the air of decadent Romans as well as shrewd exploitive locals. It is not clinical, but more a tale of the misuse of power . . . . Well-acted, directed with tact . . . ."[29]

Other films, sometimes loosely tied to the October 1970 crisis, but more concerned with (social) politics and with crime than with a specific historical event, have become well known in the canon of québécois cinema, and are certainly worth our attention here. Among such "thrillers" one would include Red, Lucien Brouillard, Pouvoir intime, and Un Zoo la nuit.

In Red (1970; d. Gilles Carle), the protagonist, a homeless, restless, rootless young man, part Indian, part Québécois, has one violent encounter after another with women and with the establishment. His death is deeply symbolic, but the film is not found by critics to be a true reflection of French-Canadian society. "A strange collaboration between Gilles Carle and the Italian writer Flaiano has resulted in a film that sounds French, looks Italian, and follows the violent traditions of American cinema" (Pratley TS 1988, 194).

The 70s also saw the appearance of two rather offbeat films by Jacques Godbout, both tied to the genre we are looking at. One was La Gammick (a thriller), the other was IXE−13, a parody of the spy film. The latter is a tale that falls halfway between musical comedy and a comic strip. In an interview with Richard Gay, Godbout also admits his debt to documentary, especially in Kid Sentiment; but he says his real departure in filmmaking was IXE−13, which was an enterprise identical to La Gammick, for both were "pop films"; both had the cadre of the musical comedy, to which he tried to add something else (as a cultural given) than simply comedy.[30] He recognizes, too, that the public had trouble putting the form and the context of IXE−13 together. Godbout then asserts that he will not accept the idea that the only gangster

IXE-13. (Courtesy Office National du Film.)

myths offered to Quebeckers are on the one hand those found in *Serpico* and the *French Connection*, or, on the other hand, in French films starring Lino Ventura and Jean Gabin. "I have the impression that we have a right to our own projections of our imaginations."[31] The making of *IXE−13* provided a "demy[s]thification" of the agent IXE−13 for those who had known him: Godbout had to show how ridiculous he was. But at the same time he "mythified" the story, by the sets and the musical side of the film. He sought to give to the Québécois the proof that they have an imagination (or a life of the imagination) that can offer meaning to their lives and to their experiences as these unfold in the province of Québec.

Departing from parody and musical comedy, and returning to serious film, let us now look at yet another *québécois* film about crime and justice, and one that raises the question of executing a possibly innocent man — *L'Affaire Coffin*.

L'AFFAIRE COFFIN (1980; d. Jean-Claude Labrecque)

In this only partially successful film, a crime thriller with political overtones situated in the Gaspé (Murdochville), we have the blame pinned on Coffin, an anglophone protestant (played by August Schellenberg, part Swiss, part amerindian, with an unusual accent, who also appears in *Qui a tiré sur nos histoires d'amour*? [1986] and in Robin Spry's *One Man* [1977]).

Based on a true story, the film opens with a view of Percé as an establishing shot. It is June 1953; three American bear hunters have been murdered, and Capitaine Forget wants the three murders placed on Coffin's head, although he has reason to suspect Coffin is not guilty. Forget must get these murders "solved" quickly; there are pressures on him, and this crime does not bode well for the tourist trade. Circumstantial and surrounding evidence is mounted against Coffin: he is a Protestant; he is the father of an illegitimate child by Maureen Patterson; and, above all, he stole field glasses and a *canife* (instrument having spoon, knife, etc.) belonging to the murdered men. (This does not, after all, make a murderer of him.) The issue of a carbine is woven in and out of the story. Coffin tells Bourdon, one of the policemen, about a rifle; Bourdon tells Forget, who pretends not to hear him. After the inquest, Coffin again tells about the rifle, and a search is begun. But despite the efforts of the defense lawyer, Courtemanche (played by Gabriel Arcand in an entirely different kind of style from his usual), Coffin is found guilty. Coffin denies his guilt; breaks out of prison; is convinced he must return if he's to prove he's innocent. So he returns, but to no avail. He is given last communion in the Anglican rite and hanged in the Bordeaux prison in Montréal in 1956.

Lever (*Hist.* 1988, 291–92) informs us that although the film did not succeed too well, this "cadaver" brought back a huge journalistic discussion of judicial error (with Jacques Hébert as the principal herald). Because the murders occurred during the Duplessiste régime — as is pointed out in the film — there is probably a political intention to indict the judicial system of that era, as well.

Curiously enough, Jean Beaudin's *Cordélia* came out the same year as *L'Affaire Coffin*, and no viewer can help but see in the two films a very similar theme. Here the accused is, like Camus's Stranger (or Outsider), an outsider, and, like Meursault, his guilt is "proved" by irrelevant issues. (Drinking a cup of coffee at one's mother's wake is as much proof of guilt as having an illegitimate son; and, worse, we know that Meursault killed the Arab, while in the case of Coffin, there is "reasonable doubt.")

Lucien Brouillard is less rife with political and moral overtones, and yet was a more successful film. (I personally found *L'Affaire Coffin* quite riveting, however. *De gustibus* ...)

LUCIEN BROUILLARD. (1983; d. Bruno Carrière)

Lucien Brouillard is the hero of the Montréal blue-collar workers. He combats injustice and political and legal trickery with anger, and his physical and verbal attacks upon them lead him into prison. According to Henri-Paul Chevrier, Lucien is capable of alerting public opinion to social injustices, but he is somewhat irresponsible, in that he is more preoccupied with others than with his family (Coulombe 1991, 84–5). His wife, Alice, and their baby seem to get set aside for Brouillard's "more important" concerns.

The plot is centered on Lucien's relationship with his friend Jacques Martineau, whose final turn about is unexpected. Through the vehicle of this friendship, the machismo quality of the film is extended. Certain side scenes focus upon the almost derelict nature of some of the characters, who for reasons no doubt not intended evoke such teams as Laurel and Hardy, or Abbot and Costello. The late Jean Duceppe, who played the uncle in *Mon oncle Antoine* and the old man in the film of the Gabrielle Roy tale (*Le Vieillard* . . .), is, as always, especially effective.

Chevrier makes the following assessment of *Lucien Brouillard*: "Even if the social drama is lost behind the psychological drama, hence bringing to the screen a "hollywood-type spectacle," *Lucien Brouillard* remains a very generous work" (Coulombe 1991, 85; my translation). The first of Carrière's feature-length films — following works on social issues such as *Le Scrapeur* (1976); *Les Récupérateurs* (1977); *Vous 'santé' vous bien?* (1978), in which he looks at recycling of waste, work safety, and its repercussions on blue-collar families — *Lucien Brouillard* is a "film of transition, but gets rid of the militantism of the 70s to deal more firmly with woman, the strong figure of the 80s" (Coulombe 1991, 84–85; my translation). *Au bout du vent* is another, more recent of Carrière's films.

A psychological thriller and an incisive social drama, *Lucien Brouillard* is, as Pratley says, "only thinly disguised when it comes to describing the Quebec social scene" (*TS*, 1987, 258). But he finds that the film is "marred by a contrived assassination attempt and by the fact that the character of Lucien becomes so unlikable that audiences are likely to lose patience with him." Pratley also declares that Lucien's plot to assassinate the premier of Canada (which he likens to *The Manchurian Candidate*) is "a political subplot that is farfetched and unconvincing, true though some of its implications about political double crossing may be" (*TS* 1987,

151−5). ("Inachevé," or unfinished, is Lever's assessment, *Hist.*
1988, 301.) I personally found this film to be very run-of-the-mill
as far as its plot and execution were concerned. In any event, it
could scarcely equal the compelling and memorable Simoneau
film, *Pouvoir intime*, either a thriller, or else a parody of a thriller,
and a film involving the same two principal actors.

POUVOIR INTIME, OR *BLIND TRUST* (1986; d. Yves Simoneau)

"This year's sleeper" says Eliott Stein in *The Village Voice*, "A
nonstop explosion," says *Variety*; "Well-crafted . . . gripping," says
Newsday; "An intelligent thriller," says *The N. Y. Times*.
These are some of the descriptions we may read of this film,
quoted on the video jacket of the dubbed version. It is all of these,
and yet none of these; for most accurately, it is a critique of
contemporary Québec society set in a context of crime, decay, and
debris. Misplaced trust and criminal power are the focal points,
just as the French and English titles describe. The people trust
their money to Trust; Trust trusts its empolyee, Thomas, who will
help in the heist of its armored car. The robbers trust in Thomas,
but he becomes ill and is replaced by Martin. Neither society nor
Trust should trust in the homosexual Martin (in French, Martial),
but as it turns out he was most to have been trusted, for he defends
unto his death the armored car in which, as it turns out, he is
captive. (In some ways, he reminds one of Jerry, the caricaturized
reactionary security guard for Pinkerton, who is disgusted by the
radical turn of events in *Yes or No, Jean-Guy Moreau* [see Ch. 7].)
Having trusted his lover, Janvier, when the latter shows up to try
to talk him out of the car, Martin gives over to the trick momentarily.
But when one of the crooks — Jerry — gives him a blow on the
head, he returns to the truck, where he dies, even before Jerry
drives the truck out of the garage, being deluded that the police
are after him. Michel Coulombe (in Coulombe 1991, 237) finds
that Robert Gravel, who plays Martin (Martial), is at his best as
this pathetic type, in which he plays, very convincingly, "a security
guard cornered in the armored truck for which he is responsible,
and [who] knows himself trapped by the love he secretly bears for
a young man. Here we find the very essence of Gravel's acting, at
his best when playing characters who appear to be solid, but whom
one always senses to be on the verge of cracking."
But the most ironic of all things about this film is that those who
are most in the public trust, Morrow (Meursault) and his superior

H. B., a cokehead, are in reality criminals who "mastermind" this heist gone awry. H. B. is, in fact, Head of Internal Security, and was formerly empolyed by the Ministry of Justice. His superiors "trust him," as he says, although he is involved in many shady deals, and now is not so much after the money in the armored truck, as he is after a particular bag carrying papers concerning him. But when things go wrong, and he goes out to take matters in his own hands, he fails to get the papers, and in the process is arrested. Morrow, or Meursault, played by Jean-Louis Millette, who has been driving him to the scene, and who is a very disingenuous, creepy customer — indeed, an "outsider," or "stranger" like Camus's antihero — is killed in a crash with the escaping armored car, driven by Jerry. (We associate Millette's dissipated-looking face with Simoneau's Stevens Brown as an old man in *Les Fous de Bassan*; he will also be the megalomaniac director of the pharmaceutical consortium in Simoneau's *Dans le ventre du dragon* [q.v. infra], as well as a talk show reporter in *Jésus de Montréal*.) Morrow, who dreams of a golden retreat in customs, and almost realizes this dream, first engages Théo the crook to be in charge of the robbery, just as he is being released from jail after serving a three-year term. He recommends that Théo get his son Robin to help him. And indeed that is what Théo does. We see both the trust of the criminal who believes the ringleaders have worked out all the details, so that the crime is foolproof, and also the trust of the son that his father is going to protect him from some vicious-looking people who are pursuing him first in a poolroom and then down an alley for reasons he does not know. (One assumes the plotters may have sent these unsavory types in order to "persuade" the son that he needs his father.) Robin believes his father, hides first in a warehouse scattered with litter of all kinds, and then agrees to hold the gun on the armored truck drivers in the projected robbery; with the loot, he and his father will "get away". However, he is obliged to kill several of the guards when things go wrong, and, later, in the theater workshop where the armored truck has been hidden with Martin still inside, he takes one of Martin's bullets and dies. Subsequently his father, Théo, commits suicide.

Among the critical statements being made in *Pouvoir intime* about the fragmented and decaying society, it seems the film contains a running commentary on the degeneration of the theater. Jerry, a set designer for what seems to be a summer stock theater, must supplement his income with acts of armed robbery. Is this what becomes of the contemporary artist? Fragments and debris of this profession clutter various scenes of the film, for the major part of the action takes place in the workshops behind the stage. Strewn about and backgrounding many scenes are props (mannequins, masks, candelabra, a statue of an elephant, etc.) and painted sets. (Toward the end of the film, Janvier and Roxanne, fleeing the police, appear on the stage momentarily, and look out on the empty seats.) These allusions to theater refer to Simoneau's past experiences in that field. While they make statements about the deterioration of theater, they also show the involvement of the theatrical artist with profit, as will be the case with some of the protagonists in *Jésus de Montréal*. Painted sets or posters are used by Jerry and Roxanne to cover up the word TRUST on the panels of the armored truck. And the name of the theater for which Jerry (Théo's former cell mate) works is, significantly, the Théâtre Immobile; it is going nowhere, getting nowhere, in a society now more interested in other recreations (such as television and cinema?).

At the end of this film, only two people from among the principals are alive: Roxanne, who was Jerry's friend, and Janvier, Martin's lover. This bears some commentary. Roxanne is an androgynous type. She used to have long hair; it is now cropped close, like a man's, and she wears tall boots, slacks, and a leather jacket. She used to run (away); this time, she tells Jerry, she is not running. Not a lesbian, as some contend (there is no evidence of this), she must be androgynous as an exigency of the plot. It is because she dares to go into the men's restroom (when the line proves too long at the women's) that she discovers the relationship between Martin and Janvier as well as Janvier's name. While in the restroom she sees Martin give Janvier a knife and tell him "See, I've had your name, Janvier, engraved on it." She also sees Martin embrace Janvier and make a date with him. Later, when the criminals cannot get Martin out of the armored car, Roxanne devises a plan for flushing him out: she will go to Janvier and tell him that Martin is locked in the car and is calling for him. Janvier, suspicious, pulls the famous knife and fights with Roxanne, getting away her gun. (The homosexual wins out over the androgynous woman in this film that depicts, above all, the world of male violence, epitomized early by the poolroom scene, a place of reunion for thugs and idle drifters.) He then agrees to follow her. One stray woman amongst all these violent men. She alone intervenes to tell Théo to stop his merciless pounding on the armored car, saying that one wouldn't even treat an animal like that.

Janvier, on the other hand, provides a contrast to Martin. He denies that he is Martin's "lover" and, ironically, winds up with part of the money Martin has died trying to save for the rightful owners.

The closing scenes take place in a church, abandoned since a fire, that now becomes a hideout for Roxanne and Janvier. (The abandoned church may well be symbolic: the French film *Le Repos du guerrier* [1962] ends with the two lovers, who hand been at war, coming to peace in a ruined church. For me, this did not bode well.) Here among these shambles, Roxanne and Janvier meet and divide the few bags of money that have spilled out when Martin momentarily emerged from the armored vehicle. (In them were the papers H. B. was trying to recover, and that finally exposed him.) The empty church as a hideout for a homosexual and a woman "gone bad"? A sign of the crumbling society, of one of its hitherto most important institutions, no doubt. The church door opens wide onto the outdoor scene (as in *Les Fous de Bassan*). Outside there is fresh air and sunshine. Carrying along her share of the take, our antiheroine drives off in a red convertible (offered by Janvier) into the unknown. We trusted the old Québécoise *habitante*; but can we trust her, inasmuch as she seems to be a type of Québec's "new woman," willing to assume the clothes and the role of a man, unwilling to assume a relationship (with Jerry)? She appears to represent the "Modernization (perhaps the Americanization) of Yvette."

Tifo, who has made five films with Simoneau, is to me least convincing in this role, which Henry Garrity finds to subvert the "traditional Hollywood-style female icon ...."[32] Perhaps, but in that this is a "thriller," why does the portrayal of Roxanne not conform to the Hollywood portrayal of the gang moll? Or why does it not have affinities with the somewhat masculine or androgynous women we see in Hollywood *film noir*? Lauren Bacall seems angular and tailored enough in *The Big Sleep* (and her voice was always overly husky), and no one, to my knowledge, ever claimed Joan Crawford (in *Mildred Pierce*, or elsewhere) to be a paragon of femininity. There may be more parodic satire than subversion in the character Roxanne; she may be a caricature of the modern, feminist type, rather than the subversion of a "film icon." See, this is what she can offer: no love, no sex, no homecooking; only companionship in crime, and at that she works for herself! The near-comic ending of this film supports the concept; in a bit Simoneau will produce another thriller, *Dans le ventre du dragon*, openly labeled a comedy, but nonetheless carrying a charge of stinging misogyny.

Carrying out the themes of the scattering of the society and its commodities — reflected in the accumulation of debris in the theater, in the empty warehouse, and seen also in the empty Coca-Cola can and the photos of Martin and his lover, Janvier, floating in the water (with which the criminals hope to drown Martin) inside the armored truck, as well as in the crash scene between the armored truck driven by Jerry and the car driven by Morrow — are the shattering sound effects, such as the balls crashing together in the pool hall and then going in all directions (noted by Garrity), or the screech and the thundering noise of the train as it pulls into the Montréal central station. But note also the name of the company for whom the armored car is transporting money. "TRUST, Security Since 1869" it says on the side of the truck; and, not without significance, in some scenes the first T of TRUST is blocked off. This date, 1869, is two years after the formation of the Canadian Confederation, which the new "province" of Québec entered into at the time. Now, the film seems to say, Québec, indeed the whole confederation, is fragmented; corrupt officials and criminals double-cross one another. The wealth of the nation, left to the care of deviants, is up for grabs; and filthy lucre is what is most craved by most. Moreover, there is no accounting for "types": while one homosexual is deserving of trust, another is less so. The androgynous woman is the only source of softness here (although, to tell the truth, she is the only woman present at all, except for a couple of tourists waiting their turn in front of the women's restroom). But, then, as this androgynous, modern woman has allied herself with the criminals, can she be trusted, even though she is a survivor?

As the scattering occurs, so each of these persons is alone and isolated in his or her own little compartment, be this a prison cell, or the "four walls" of the armored truck, or the glass walls or windows of the office buildings, etc. (Similar devices used to convey isolation and to provide a "huis clos" effect are found in Lauzon's *Night Zoo*.) Music and especially sound heighten the emotion of this film, and, as I have said, contribute to the sense of fragmentation and scattering everywhere present. Above all, there is cleavage at the film's end, for the only remnants of the "society" — such as they are — the untrustworthy (unfaithful) homosexual and the androgynous woman are going their separate ways. The trust that she had placed in the mob to forge her new identity is ironically betrayed and yet realized. Earlier, just after the heist, she had said to Jerry, "If we get out of this, I'll go to the States with you," and he had replied, "Count on me, we'll get out OK." In the end, she must count on herself. The small society of the gang is shattered;

most, who counted on group action to realize their dreams of weatlh, are dead; only one remains and he, too, is alone.

Garrity sees this film as representing a "study in subversive discourse, which undermines the very bases of society and state in modern Québec."[33] If the film does show variations on the standard police film, in which the police should be honest and should win, it is nonetheless a police film, in which Simoneau may also be portraying the society as he sees it. It is not *he* who undermines these bases, but the society, as it devours itself and its institutions (art, law, order, church, marriage [the traditional couple]). For, according to Yves Picard (Coulombe 1991, 497), Simoneau is not interested in "disassociating himself" from the genre of the thriller, or *film noir*, through his exploration of it. (He studied it during his stay in New York in 1980.) Rather, he wants to succeed in this genre according to "the American approach," which seeks originality within the limits fixed by the genre (i.e., which seeks to be internationally and commercially successful). Simoneau has been viewed as too American by Paul Warren and others. Warren decries Simoneau's *Dans le ventre du dragon*, and calls Simoneau a "Spielberg québécois." Warren also expresses his dislike of *Les Tisserands du pouvoir*, and states that what the Québécois do best is films like *Jacques et Novembre*, or the films of Pierre Perrault, or, lacking that, films like *Alias Will James*, where "our fascination for America is explained."[34] (But that negative view of Americanization and of its Hollywood star system appears to me to be one of Warren's hobby horses, continued in his recent book.) In fact, *Pouvoir intime*, like *Night Zoo*, uses an apparently American film genre to analyze fundamentally *québécois* sociopolitical conditions. Moreover, Picard says that *Pouvoir intime*, which was written in New York, stresses psychology within the framework of the thriller. The care brought to the photography and to the editing shows through; and the work Simoneau has done in directing stage actors is apparent (Coulombe 1991, 497).

In a rather loose way, *Pouvoir intime* has qualities in common with a classic of *québécois* cinema — *O.K. ... Laliberté* (1973; d. Marcel Carrière and photographed by Thomas Vamos; 112 min.; ONF). In *O.K. ...*, forty-year-old Paul Laliberté, having quarreled with his wife, leaves his job and moves into a rooming house, run by an obsequious and oily landlady. There he meets both Ti-Louis, a bandit, and Yvonne Cousineau, who loves quiz shows and bingo. Paul and Yvonne become lovers; Paul takes a job as a pest exterminator, but cannot satisfy Yvonne's expensive tastes. He loses his job, and, needing money, the three of them stage a pitiful holdup at Paul's former boss's business. The police are there, but to get Ti-Louis, not Paul. "*O.K.* . . . *Laliberté* does not tell a story. It shows us a series of moments, correctly felt, correctly described, correctly translated by inspired actors (Jacques Godin, Luce Guilbeault, Jean Lapointe). Carrière hits the bulls-eye on all scores. Passages like the party in the car, Yvonne's song, and many other sequences are irresistibly funny and moving. It is the smiling tableau, done with a sometimes off-color humor, of a milieu rarely shown in the Québec cinema: people in their forties who are neither bourgeois nor blue-collar workers. Carrière's long experience in direct cinema is certainly not foreign to the climate of spontaneity that characterizes this film. Unlike Labrecque in *Les Smattes*, Carrière was able to shepherd his past as a filmmaker of direct cinema when he approached fiction" (Houle 1978, 213).[35]

While the plot of *Pouvoir intime* taxes one's credulity, its social criticism gives it, even so, an aura of docurealism that should not surprise, when we remember that in 1980 Simoneau produced *Plusieurs tombent en amour*, a documentary on prostitution in Montréal. One must agree in any event that *Pouvoir* . . . , which was both a critical and a popular success, leaves us pondering its deeper implications, as will the equally fascinating *Un Zoo la nuit*, a thriller that in 1987 took dozens of Canadian prizes and a Belgian one as well (for which see Abel).

UN ZOO LA NUIT (*NIGHT ZOO*) (1986–87; d. Jean-Claude Lauzon)

A story about Montréal's underworld, *Un Zoo la nuit* narrates the struggle of Marcel Brisebois, a leather-jacketed tough, but also a musician ("artist"), to escape the stranglehold of crime and desolation and to make peace with his dying father. Having come out of prison, where he had been raped by envoyés of Charlie and George — a corrupt, anglo homosexual policeman — he meets with their repeated and violent attempts to get the money he holds from previous drug activities, and for which he has taken the rap. But far more important to the film is the growing warmth of his relationship to his father, who has been taken in by Italian immigrants.

From a cultural perspective, it is notable that we are in part depicting an Italian milieu through the people with whom the father resides; and this is indeed an irony, as the father is a reactionary "pure laine" Québécois, while they are the immigrants. The Italian population is not an insignificant element in the Montréal society.

It is alluded to in many films — *Bach et Bottine*, for example — and has been portrayed most completely in *Caffè Italia* (Chapter 7). The Italianness of the characters in *Zoo* ... is a pure fiction, however, even though the parts of Tony and Angelica are played by Italians. (There are also several small parts played by Italians.)

Equally notable here is the negative portrayal of the establishment. As in *Pouvoir intime*, we have in *Zoo* ... the corruption of authority, of government (here embodied in the anglophone! police), as well as the marginality of the homosexual, shown as a policeman in both films, though in this one George, the cop, is the incarnation of evil, while in *Pouvoir intime*, the gay policeman shows a macho heroism uncommon to the others. (In *Pouvoir intime* we also have the father-son relationship shown in a criminal context; there the father leads the son to crime and death.)

Perhaps *Zoo* ... is so referential as to remain culture-bound. But to me, it is a very powerful film. As I observed in the introduction to this book, American critics sometimes have difficulty with *québécois* films, and this is one — like *Les Bons Débarras* — that Leonard Maltin's guide cuts down. In the 1991, and still in the 1994 edition we read: "French-Canadian melodrama, wildly over-rated on its home turf, unconvincingly mixes a moving story of love between excon Le Bel and his father with a brutal tale of sex and drugs unfolding in Montreal. Title refers to a ludicrous climax at the local zoo. Graphic sex scenes almost reduce this one to exploitation-film level."[36] The film receives two stars. But wait! Can we pay attention at all to such incompetence? Not only is this an insensitive assessment of the film, but the reviewer does not know Roger Le Bel from Gilles Maheu. Nor is the climax in the zoo exactly "ludicrous." Rather, it, like *The Decline* ..., shows the degeneration of the Québec society and the reversal, so to speak, of the mythology of the co-operative hunt by father and son. (The film deals with many forms of attempted retreat and recovery.)

Then, on the very jacket to the film we read: "This videocassette contains graphic sex and violence. Viewer discretion advised." But the sexual scenes are not in the realm of "exploitation." They are not there to titilate, but are carefully motivated. Raped in jail, Marcel in turn virtually rapes his girl friend on his return. These are the attitudes towards and the uses of sex and women in the hard world of crime.

Weinmann rather arcanely finds the shooting of the elephant in the zoo symbolic of the killing of memory (the memory of Québec; an ironic sign of its motto, *je m'en souviens*). But I believe that, far

more importantly, it tells us that the hunt is a degraded myth:
that once the hunt that provided food is now, ironically, merely
gratuitous, a meaningless and empty sport. The killing of the
elephant is also criminal: the son, to "save" the father's image of
himself leads the father (land) into a life (before death) of crime.
The father's picture, which Marcel takes with his polaroid, is, of
course, standard: one must bring back the photo of the big-game
hunter posing with his victim.

Unlike Maltin's reviewer, other American critics of the film have
been more generous: "Extraordinary. Damned good filmmaking
... slick, furious, and erotic," said the *N.Y. Post.*; "A brooding,
disturbingly graphic, *new wave* thriller ...," wrote Kathleen Carroll
in the *N.Y. Daily News.*[37] And Clanfield, the distinguished Canadian
critic, writes: "Lauzon has declared his debt to the eccentric underground world of André Forcier's films, and yet his first feature ...
is equally reminiscent of Beneix (*Diva*) or the new British Channel
4 New Wave films for its combination of sordid violence and
moments of sentiment in a story about an ex-convict's efforts to
keep the drug-deal proceeds he had hidden before being caught"
(1987, 82–83).

Outstanding in this film are the sound effects that accompany
the establishing shots of the river and the lake—we hear in some
cases the cry of gulls, yet the absence of sound is equally effective.
So the great tranquility and calmness, the total silence of the river
and the lake—which background many scenes—contrast very
markedly with the interior and inner violence of the sex and
murder scenes. Sound is, in fact, the dominant notable technological
characteristic of this film, while the silence and peace of the water
not only provide contrast but also give references to the myths of
Québec as a "Truly Northern" country. Moreover, these romantic
icons of nature recall a sweeter past, and function to evoke such
romantic portrayals of nature as we encounter in poems such as
"Morning on the Lièvre" by the nineteenth-century anglophone
poet Archibald Lampman, so handsomely brought into a film
"version" by David Barslow (NFB, 1961). The photos of the river
and the wildlife, of the boat and the two men in *Morning* ... are
for all the world those of *Night Zoo*. Additionally, in *Night Zoo*,
the idle piles of logs along the side of the river sign Québec's great
forests and vast logging enterprises, first imperiled by over-cutting,
but, as an industry, now threatened—even more ironically—by
North America's compelling need to recycle.

There is, also, an extraordinary use of animal symbols in this
film: the father's loneliness is dissipated by his love of Florida, his

Un Zoo la nuit. Photograph by Lyne Charlebois. (Courtesy Coll. Cinémathèque Québécoise.)

pet bird. Of course, throughout the film we hear the chirping of Florida and the noise of jungle animals, the rattles, the cries; and at times their shadowy forms play on the screen. Warm tropical settings and the escape that Australia could offer are obliquely enlisted. The analogy between the corrupt urban milieu and a jungle — or else a zoo — is, of course, the central symbol of the movie.

But it goes without saying, bonding and "love" occur in the jungle, as well as in the human city, even though the bonding that occurs in this film is too little too late, and of a sort not expected. I might add that the bonding of the father and the son is sharply contrasted with other types of bonding, in particular with the ties that exist between the American criminal who, once out of prison himself, assists Marcel in the murders of George and Charlie, and, as he leaves for Nebraska on Marcel's motorcycle (his reward), offers him a "line," and embraces him, while telling him that he should look him up if ever he gets to Nebraska. This curious foreign aid from America, which comes in the form of a drug-addict and a criminal, seems to tell us what kind of help Québec can expect from its neighbors to the South, i.e., about the same kind of friendly help that comes from the anglo policeman and the Japanese who have taken over Canadian markets — using cast-off soup cans to make Toyotas and electronic devices. Nevertheless, the competition from the Italians seems to be viewed more benignly. They are into demolition and reconstruction; they are also into love and charity, at least temporarily. Whatever the case, the romanticism of the lake scenes provides another contrast with the realism of these scenes of prison, murder, violent sex, and sex thrills by video and voyeurism obtained by dropping coins in a slot, thereby permitting the "curtain" to go up on the pornographic scene.

Realistic also are the sounds of background conversation in the cafeteria scene, and upon occasion an ambulance in the background. This adds to the eeriness and the loneliness of the film; the impersonality of the city is everywhere. We do not know the exact topic of these conversations; we do not know whom the ambulance goes to seek, anymore than we fully understand why this film portrays the "criminal" as sympathetic. We are struck, really, by the idea that tenderness might surface as a guiding emotion between a criminal and his old father. We see the mother blamed, the woman spurned in favor of a bonding, a veritable love affair, with the father. Psychologically speaking, the feminist would say, "here the father and the son get married and undergo their liebestodt": not a scenario the feminist cares for. But whatever else we might say, as a theme, the desperate effort of a son to communicate with his father is rare in Québec literature and film; notable examples are Robert Lalonde's *Le Fou du père* in literature and *Un Zoo la nuit* in film. Thus, the film inverts the stereotypical family situation so common to francophone Canadian literature, in which the father is absent or removed. Here the mother is absent. I would like therefore to propose that this reactionary father, who dislikes the invasive Japanese and who replaces the drug money he has found hidden in a duct in his room with a statue of Jesus (of the Sacred Heart), stands for a mythical father (land). The mother ([m]otherland) is "locked out" and lost to her child, her son. She is, indeed, one of those "femmes infidèles" of whom Jacques Brel sings at the end of the movie. And she, too, is (a country) lost in the urban scene of violence, crime, and drugs. All this is supported by a scene in which the father gives the son his wedding band ("gen de mariage"), and not the girlfriend's, as he at first claims, and by a very significant scene in which the remains of the mother are literally scattered, through the acquistion and destruction of a packet the mother has left for the son, containing various items including a bottle of perfume — a sweet remembrance of the mother's odors. In his *Léolo* [1992; 107 minutes], Lauzon presents a sympathetic if bizarre portrayal of the mother figure, played by Ginette Reno. The film, partaking of a fusion of poetic dream sequences and grossly realistic scenes, has had a very mixed reception, as is witnessed in the two disparate reactions of Janick Beaulieu and Johanne Larue.[38]

It remains for the son (in *Un Zoo* ...) to see, then, if he can reconstruct the image of a father who is integrally attached to the myth of hunting and fishing — in which the competitiveness between the (Québécois) father and the (Italian) immigrant is sharply etched. In the first lake scene, the father is initiating the son into the art of fishing; what weather is the best (rainy), and so forth. The "city boy" wants to see a moose, and persuades his father to make the sound of the moose. And the father tells the son, too, of the ways of the moose, its true habitat and its mating habits. Meanwhile, they fish in a boat on a magnificent lake that shows Québec as "la belle Province," a land of the "True North," a land of great natural beauty. (Add to this that the father wears a"classic" red-and-white mackinaw, but not the son; and later, during their return on Marcel's motorcycle, the father is wrapped in a red-and-black Hudson bay blanket that is used as a "traditional" source of warmth at several junctures in the film.) But "le temps d'une chasse" is over — the son does not land his fish, despite the father's directions. It was nothing but a dream, then, nothing but a myth. Later, as the father lies dying, the son invades the hospital in the dark of night, and shows his father a film (within a film), again portraying the lake and the noble moose. He then takes his father (in the antique Buick now replacing his bartered motorcycle) to the Grandby zoo. There he uses a wheel chair he has no doubt stolen from the hospital to push him about the zoo. Not finding a moose, he allows his father to kill an elephant instead, the biggest though the most innocent of all catches; bigger than anything his Italian rival Tony has ever caught, in spite of all the trophy heads hanging on the wall of his *caffè*. Besides, Tony, or 'Spaghetti,' as Marcel's father calls him, may eat too much lasagna to be able to continue his success as a deerhunter. Though the myths of hunting and fishing fail, Marcel achieves a manhood that has as its meaning the fact that the son has become the father of the man, the father being magnificently played by Roger Le Bel, who has a much more significant role here than in *Les Bons Débarras*. Marcel quiets his father's fears that anyone should "drive us from our house." (The father has been evicted by the Italians by now: they need the space; they take it from the *pure laine* Québécois.) The son also helps the father in the illusion that he has killed the "biggest game" ever. A powerful bonding has resulted.

This is in fact the only bonding that seems possible in the film (other than the affection between two lesbians who background

Marcel's first out-of-jail encounter with George, the anglo homosexual policeman, who seems to represent the ultimate in vicious
sexual perversion as a form of power greater than that of the
policeman and the authority he could represent within that role).
The sole love scene (actually a heterosexual sex scene) of *Un Zoo*
... strikes one, also, as cold, lonely, and brutal; perhaps of the
animal in the jungle, and without bonding. Some critics regard this
scene as a virtual rape. The fact that Marcel's girlfriend is a hooker
does not eliminate the central issue, which seems to be her attraction
to him and his intention not to become involved with her, even
though the sadistic torture inflicted upon her by Michel's "colleagues" brings him up short. Jacques Rendu has twice complained
that in this film "Les femmes sont loin d'avoir le beau rôle [Women
are far from having a beautiful role]" and indeed, in the first of his
two accountings, he says that the film "has us discover ... the
jungle of the shadier quarters of Montréal and the persons you
would not want to meet who populate these quarters at night. The
homosexual scenes in the film are unfortunately treated with a
strong flavor of sadomasochism. Not to mention the love scene
between Marcel and his former girlfriend, which conveys love in
name only ... There is a whole world between the Marcel who
seeks to tie up a relationship with his father and the Marcel of the
underworld of Montréal, as if there were two persons: one Dr.
Jekyll, the other Mister Hyde. We are interested in the first one;
we can do without the second."[39] This seems to me to suggest only
a rudimentary grasp of Marcel's personality; but the assessment of
the "love scene" is on the mark.

So we might well ask the question: In this struggle of money
versus love, which will really win out? Well, really, neither, because
instead of Julie, whom he would take to Australia, but who is by
now tired of his vacillations, Marcel opts to choose his father as
an object of his pursuit and desire. He would take his father to
Australia, where the kangaroos live. Lacking this flight, he regales
the father with expensive gifts: an antique Buick, an antique gun.
(These objects again hark back to the romantic past.) And in the
final frames of the film, what can only be called love scenes are
projected. Tenderly, Marcel washes his father's naked body, and
the cloth across his genitals and the angles of the photography give
us the feel of a deposition scene). After the father's death, Marcel
lies naked, his cheek against the naked father's, tears streaming
down his face. The effort to regain the myth of the father and the
myth of hunting-fishing has been a lost cause (a farce, in fact, a
fiction for the happiness of the father); these are aspects of the

Québécois's former life that are not regainable. Nor is the beauty of the landscape outside the city to be recovered: "Il n'y a plus d'Amérique," as Jacques Brel sings at the end, and the magnificent but unpeopled lake scenes close the visual component of the film.

Garrity sees this film — and, as we have noted, *Pouvoir Intime* as well — as subversive of the police-film genre. (They are classified as thrillers by the merchants.) In his conclusions, Garrity also calls *Un Zoo* ... a thriller, as well as a psychological drama akin to "other Québec political films." Not only does Garrity deal with Lauzon's "subversion" of the icons of authority and of the family as well as subversion of language in the society per se (though I would rather say that it is not a subversion but a rendering of what Lauzon sees as present-day *québécois* realities), but he also places *Un Zoo* ... within the context of the genre. He says, for example, that Lauzon seems to subvert the Hollywood image of the police tandem, the two-man team of the traditional buddy picture.[40] I would rather think that the statements about film made in *Un Zoo* ... are very much more complex. Though no doubt it does "subvert" the police film genre, there are details within the film that show us further contrasts over the ones we have already seen (calmness versus violence; country versus city; various types of bonding; etc.). The romantic, or at least idyllic, film that Marcel shows his father in the hospital is in marked contrast to the peep shows and sex videos suggested in the scene where he goes to rescue Julie from the sadistic torture of his enemies. Is it that he would leave his father with a better image of the world than he himself can have? Is it that Lauzon is showing us the degradation of the use of film in modern society (echoed in the bizarre use of the trophy photo in the zoo scene)? Similar "misuses" of other technologies seem evident in the film; remote control by "tokens" (!) allows not only the viewing of pornographic scenes but also rewinding and listening to one's answering machine (*répondeur*) from the impersonality of a telephone booth. Moreover, the use of the answering machine is of significance as replacement for face-to-face communication.

Garrity also finds in the film evidence of subversive language, criminal argot that allows for the encroachment of English into "pure *québécois* French." Again, this is not so much a subversion on the part of Lauzon as concrete and realistic evidence of this linguistic intrusion; for the use of English words in French dialogue is not restricted to George and Charlie. Garrity points out the use in French of the words "lunch" ("*mes heures de lunch*") and "smoked meat" by George and even by Charlie. But *smoked meat* is entered by Bergeron in his *Dictionnaire de la langue québécoise*, as is also *lunch*, not to mention the verb form *luncher*.[41] And Marcel and his father talk about the father's "*boîte à lunch*" (also given by Bergeron as a replacement for "*musette*"). (The father has hidden the disputed loot, found in the duct of his room at the Italians' home, in this lunch box.) Incidentally, not only does this kind of breakdown in language signal the end of Québec's isolation from the English-speaking world, but it also bespeaks the nostalgic past of the father, in this case a proletarian who once upon a time carried the standard black lunchbox to his work. The father is now too sick and too old to work. His courage and strength are tied up now in the use of his lunch box to carry the criminally gained money to and fro, first to the prison and then to Marcel's apartment.

In the long run, the film seems to be as Proustian as it is New Wave: as we have seen, multiple devices, many of them sensory, are used to stimulate the characters to "remember" the past; but here none can succeed. The past of Québec as innocent, isolated, its "True Northern" beauty crowned by cool lakes and forests of pine and spruce, is not recoverable.

And what of film traditions? Are they recoverable, according to this film? When it comes to analogues, my students have found rapports with *Tangerine Dream* and *The Leaf*. But more to the point, one might ask what connection there could be between this film and Perrault's 1982 *Bête lumineuse*. It is the time of a moose hunt; the characters on the hunt are urbanized, city types ... *they* are the savages. They find again the violence of their primal senses through this hunt: they get in touch with their senses; with their contradictory emotions of cruelty and tenderness. *La Bête lumineuse* has transfiguration. Does *Un Zoo* ... have that? I think in some ways yes, because of the rebonding. In some ways no, because the bonding, like everything else, seems in the end to lead nowhere but to loneliness and destruction.) If in this comparison I draw Lauzon into Perrault's world of documentary and of documentary technique, the analogy is not unjustified, because of the similarity of statement, and because of the social realism in the mirror-image Lauzon obtains through story and camera. Thus, I believe that *Un Zoo* ... has demonstrable debts to the documentary genre, whose contribution to Canadian films is so strong, even in the realm of fiction.

Jean Charbonneau, a physician, in his short article on *Un Zoo* ..., excerpted from a lecture he delivered in March 1988 concerning the suicide of young adults in Québec,[42] has some interesting points to make about this film, though many others are self-evident. Charbonneau used *Un Zoo . . .*, in fact, to illustrate the phenomenon of suicide, by insisting on the role that the image of the father plays in the *québécois* culture. Especially arresting is his notion that various images of the Québec father are present in the film, including the persecuting homosexual police, who represent the diabolical form of father; the real flesh and blood father of Marcel, who is old and ill; the idealized father Marcel sees in him at the beginning, not as a limited and fallible human being suffering from his wife's absence. Marcel adopts a process of idealization, transforming the father into an elephant hunter. The central problem of the film, then, is whether the real Marcel (without the aid of cocaine) will ever meet up with the real Albert. Charbonneau also finds that the violence is not present to give the film an American ring, but, rather, to translate Marcel's struggle with this father, who is at once protector and also a jealous and authoritarian man, both diabolical and godlike. In any event, when the wife appears, pardon takes place, and a triangularization of the situation occurs. "The death of the father brings the son to make up an ideal of life, a social morality, a personal mythology which gives a sense to his father's life and his own."[43] Charbonneau then goes on to speak of the father in traditional Québec culture(as portrayed in film and literature), often presented as unstable, frail, and vacillating, on whom one could not count and with whom one could not identify. Albert fits the list, which includes Maria's father in *Maria Chapdelaine*, the deceiving Théophile of La Famille Plouffe, and even Séraphin Poudrier of *Un Homme et son péché*, who shows no sign of "genitalization," and behaves like a wicked mother to poor Donalda. In the literature, there are some solid men (Didace, Menaud [*maître draveur*]), but they find no son to succeed them. *Un Zoo . . .* is a product of the culture, and yet in conflict with it. A culture that has problems with the father's image.

It is usually somewhat irritating to have a film end with a "song" that is meant to prolong the tone and teach the lesson. The use of this technique, or cap, in *The Dog Who Stopped the War*, and, in fact, in many *québécois* children's films, is notably annoying. Yet, the use of Jacques Brel's "Voir un ami pleurer," with the lake scene in the background, provides an unforgettable closure to this outstanding film, whose sweetness and sad power depend upon our willingness to believe in Marcel's complex sensibility, and also upon our suspension of femininist demands that eschew the portrayal of exclusive, esoteric male bonding and violent sexual scenes—rape and peep shows—in this or any film or fiction. (Witness the feminists's feelings concerning *Les Fous de Bassan*.)

Weinmann provides a stunning analysis of this film and its themes of the search for the father; the absent mother; the raped prostitute; the sadism and misogyny; the portrayal of the English versus the French Canadian. He also discusses the dialectic of speech and silence running throughout. Though Weinmann is always and everywhere stimulating, for those who read French, he is especially useful in the chapter on *Un Zoo* ... (Weinmann 1990, 107–120).

This is, then, a "postmodern" film: nostalgia for the good old days, in light of the corruption and decadence of the present; the initiation "rites" inherent in the fishing trip (cf Jean Renoir), contrasted with the life the protagonist leads and the circumstances in which he finds himself; ethnic fragmentation of the society; the inversion of the traditional moose hunt, turned into the wounding of a captive elephant. But, as Weinmann points out, the elephant remembers; is the elephant Québec? (Weinmann 1990, 120),

Finally, the lake scenes—in broad daylight, unlike the dark night of the "zoo"—give a sense of mysticism and transfiguration, even though they are also poignantly nostalgic and noticeably emptied of life. They contrast, too, with the motifs of entrapment and solitude seen in the prison bars, the dark interiors, the walled peep shows (and the walls the Italians are breaking down), and with the psychological dead-ends suggested by the long empty streets down which our protagonist rides his motorcycle. A rich and splendid film.

(TWO ANGLOPHONE CRIME FILMS BY FRANCIS MANKIEWICZ)

Before ending this discussion of crime (melo)drama, I would like to mention two anglophone films by Francis Mankiewicz, *And Then You Die.* (1987) and *Love and Hate* (1989). The former is allied to two films we have just looked at, *Pouvoir intime* and *Un Zoo la nuit*; the latter is a suspenseful and absorbing tale about crime in high places.

AND THEN YOU DIE. (1987; d. Francis Mankiewicz)

There is no question in the viewer's mind that the locus of this crime drama is Montréal; establishing shots and scraps of dialogue betray the francophone infrastructure of this society, which in the course of the film falls prey to severe criticism at the hands of the director and his colleagues. As an opening, the skyline of the city is shown across the river while criminals drop a bloodied corpse into the river; shortly thereafter we see Habitat, and later Old Montréal with its horse-drawn *calèches*. Eddie Griffin, the "Irish" drugrunner who is trying to maintain a grip on his world, orders his lunch in French; Wally and he both read a tabloid newspaper in French, and we hear Prego say "*zut alors, hein?*" when called away from a party to the telephone. Signs also cue the scene: a roadside restaurant called "Marcel Cloutier"; a video shop for "adultes seulement," advertised on the street sign as having "videos explicites"; and the headquarters of Eddie's gang, room 18 of Le Motel. When a bomb goes off in an apartment house killing several people, the TV reports that the police claim they have seen "nothing like it since the days of the FLQ [Front de la libération du Québec]."

Like *Un Zoo* ..., *And Then You Die.* deals in violence both with the underworld drug scene and with the underworld crime syndicates that seek to control it. Will it belong to the Anglo-Irish/Scotch, the Italians, or the Québécois *pure laine*? Also, as in *Un Zoo* ..., we have film-within-film. By showing videos and using TV coverages, as well as newspapers, the filmmaker conveys information to the characters and to the spectator. The realistic feel of documentary is also thus procured. The events of the main film are seemingly projected out onto a wide public.

The good cop, James McGrath, seeks to quell the rackets, but the crooked cop (this time a French Canadian) is prepared to sell out for profit. As in *Pouvoir intime*, things fall apart; the crime world fails because of the criminals' misplaced trust. Says Eddie to Wally, who has betrayed him, "Mikey trusted you, Wally; so did I." As in *Pouvoir* ... (where it is also a question of "trust"), we are surprised to see the survival of the weakest, here Wally the grave robber, and not surprised to see that for most people crime does not pay.

Meanwhile, the penetration of an American cultural stratum is suggested by Eddie's drinking Coca-Cola from a bottle and from McGrath's drinking coffee from a paper cup bearing the MacDonald logo, and going to phone for someone to claim Eddie's body from a booth nearby Scot's Kentucky Fried Chicken shop. America's criminal contributions are spelled out by Eddie's sending Jimmy to Miami to "score," and later hearing by phone that Jimmy can get "twenty kees" there in Miami. It also seems to be suggested by news coming from New York television, news that relays the death of the godfather, Frank Vitello. Now it is a question of whether

Eddie shall deal with the unsavory Salvatore Prego, who eats *coniglio cacciatore* (rabbit stew) washed down by gulps of red wine while he explains that Frank had to be done away with: it was a decision of the *famiglia*, because Frank stole wedding presents. Prego insists that from now on Eddie will deal with him exclusively, and drop his prices by 20 percent. But Eddie believes that Buccelli, who has connections with the Old Country, and [Harold] Scaglia, or Scalia, who has connections with New York, are number one and two, while Prego is a distant third and fading fast. When Eddie balks at Prego's commands, Prego attempts a drive-by murder of Eddie and his son Danny. His wife Liz is outraged and cries to him, "Fix it, Eddie, just fix it."

In fact, throughout the film Eddie's activities disturb Liz, who fears for his life as well as for her own and their son's. Thus, the story presses for our realization of the threat this disintegrating society poses to the family. And when Eddie gets Prego killed (his blood spatters all over a white statue), he is then free to deal with Scaglia.

The Italian màfia is in control of the drugs; the Dutchman Vanderkeist, hoping to get a share of the take, lends his warehouse to Eddie and his gang as a place to unload a shipment of Sun Glo pineapples from Mexico, under which thirty to forty millons of dollars worth of coke (thirty kilos) are hidden. McGrath has found that Wally is double-crossing Eddie, and so he uses him to get information on this huge shipment, and convinces his colleagues to bring in the RCMP from Ottawa (the "feds") because the Montréal RCMP (the "provincials") may be on the take. But Peter begins to buckle later on after the raid, and after Harold tells Eddie that his "biggest problem is Peter, he is not to be trusted, Peter must be killed by a huge explosion brought about by the remote control of a bomb through a VCR delivered to Peter's mistress Soulange." Eddie and the others use the French-Canadian Garou and his man for hired killings. (But Nick Garou wants to be Eddie's partner.) Nick's man will ultimately kill Eddie and save Wally, just as Eddie is about to kill him for betraying him to McGrath—a betrayal Eddie has learned about through the work of his best man, Cliff.

"There are cracks in the foundation; they're startin' to show, kid," says McGrath to Eddie when Wally angers at McGrath's needling. (Is the word "kid" reflective of *film noir* lingo, e.g., from Bogart's "Here's looking at you, kid."?) Things fall apart, as William Butler Yeats said in his poem "The Second Coming." In the beautiful fall. And it is as beautiful and as much in contrast to the sordid story as in Mankiewicz's *Les Bons Débarras*. The blazing autumn, caught there by Michel Brault, is here captured by Richard Leiterman. The end of the season, the end of a time, the fall of the anglos — the fall of the Others? — the re-instatement of the franco-phones, now debilitated, if not handicapped? I do not want to push my ethnic interpretations too far, especially since here the good cop is an anglo (although he is very aware of ethnicities himself, referring to "the wop" and "the Irish"); but the use of the crime drama to make these statements has been seen elsewhere, after all.

Marty Simson's music is one of the powers of this film. The distorted "Doxology" ("Praise God from whom all blessings flow ...") playing in the background at the funeral parlor where the crooked Michael's body lies in state is a touch of effective black humor. Ditto for the use of "It's a Long Way to Tipperary" at Aunt Peg's birthday party. And one might add that this terribly long cast of characters is cause for considerable confusion on the part of the viewer. But what is most interesting about this is that the characters are ethnically diverse, and yet the actors themselves do not necessarily fit the ethnicity they are projecting. I do not believe any Italian or Italian Canadian plays an Italian, for example.

LOVE AND HATE (1989; d. Francis Mankiewicz)

This is a TV drama, but is very acceptable cinema even so, as can sometimes be the case. I always recall the power and charm of *Love Among the Ruins*, with Laurence Olivier and Katharine Hepburn, as American TV film at its best. But the Québécois pride themselves on their ability to make TV dramas, and even serial or soap-opera films, a case in point being *Le Temps d'une paix*, a "téléroman" that the French Canadians, unlike other Canadians, have apparently preferred watching to *Dallas* or *Dynasty* (Lever *Hist.* 1988, 222–23). *Love and Hate*, however, has the added special fascination of being a true story, though the film-makers admit they have embroidered upon it here and there for heightened impact.

Telling a story that involves the marital disputes and child custody battles of the high ranking government minister Colin Thatcher, this film painfully portrays Thatcher's ugly temper, his vicious and vindictive ways, his episodes of rage and wife-beating, his efforts to poison his children against their mother by praising their family heritage and stimulating their love of the Saskatchewan land they will inherit, and finally, his attempts to have her murdered, which finally succeeded in 1983.

The film is based on Maggie Siggins's best-selling book, which studied the true story of (Wilbert) Colin Thatcher. Born in Toronto in 1938, he was the son of (Wilbert) Ross Thatcher, who was Liberal premier of Saskatchewan (1964–71). Colin became a Liberal MLA in Saskatchewan in 1975. In 1977 he switched to the Conservative party and then became minister of energy and mines. He appears to have thought himself above the law, and because of his overbearing personality and erratic behavior, he made enemies and was forced to resign in 1983. He was arrested and convicted in 1984 for the brutal murder of his ex-wife.[44]

The film version projects Thatcher's very unsavory character, inclined to rages and assuming at times the "innocence" of a clever poseur. Though in reality Thatcher protested his innocence, the film leaves us with no divided opinions about his guilt. His accomplice, Jerry Anderson, may have done the actual murder, but he turned crown witness in exchange for immunity. Thatcher was further compromised by his ex-girlfriend, whom he had promised to marry but did not, and, more tellingly, had beaten. She, along with his former colleague, Dick Culver, who testified against him at the eleventh hour, helped to get him convicted. Both in the film and in reality he was found guilty and sentenced to life imprisonment, without possibility of parole before twenty-five years (a sentence he is now serving).

Despite the riveting nature of this piece of work, the film, being made for mass audiences, has a straightforward narrative style, and the photography is quite uninventive. There is quite a bit of panning, as in the court scene, where the faces of the people in attendance are shown as if to give us the sensation that we ourselves are present and watching their reactions. But the device is ineffective, and strikes one only as quite hackneyed.

Love and Hate has aired on CBC more than once, while *And Then You Die*. has been screened on premium channels (HBO) in the United States. To say the least, Mankiewicz's interest in violence, torture and suffering had new outlets through his turn to filming in English.

Horror

In the Québec film, crime thrillers and horror films are the forte of Jean-Claude Lord and Robin Spry, among others. (For Spry's *One Man* see Chapter 7.) Lord, as we know, is chiefly a director of francophone films such as *Les Colombes* and *Bingo*; and he has also made such films as *Panique* (1977), a story that feeds our worst fears about industrial pollution. Nevertheless, he has offered some rather gruesome films in English as well. In 1977 he directed *Visiting Hours*, a big budget film with an English-language cast intended for the international market. The plot of this thriller revolved around a psychopathic killer. And in 1984, Lord made *The Vindicator*, filmed in Montréal and starring Terri Austin, Richard Cox, Pam Grier, Maury Chaykin and David McIlwraith. It is a sci-fi film in which Carl, a scientist, gets mixed up in a plot to find immortality. He is transformed into a cyborg when the computer is connected to his brain, but Gail, the laboratory assistant, fails to put the remote control unit that governs him into his belly (cf. Cronenberg's *Videodrome*). Carl becomes self-operating and all-powerful, and nothing will kill him, not even the efforts of Hunter, the female troubleshooter. He is compelled to kill if touched, but in the end, after reprogramming himself in the lab, decides to kill White, his creator, as well as himself. One of the highlights of this film is the metallic monster created by Stan Winston. This film, which I found tedious, though it was only eighty-eight minutes long, was, of course, made before the other, better known cyborg film *Robocop*. It is not unlike David Cronenberg's films, particularly in the theme of scientific overreach, here resulting in the accidental fusion of a living human brain attached to and preserved in an indestructible, mobile body. Indeed, the sets seem like a meld between *The Brood* and *Scanners*. (*The Vindicator*, originally called *Frankenstein* and said to be a remaking of that story, can be rented in most video shops and has aired on Fox TV.)

But if horror films are somehow related to themes of crime as an antisocial phenomenon, and if David Cronenberg[45] — a Canadian whose first two full-length features were made for Cinéprix in Montréal (*Shivers* [1975] and *Rabid* [1976]), and whose *Scanners* [1980] was also made in Montréal — is one of the world's masters of this genre, one does not even so find any outstanding examples of this genre in other Québec film. One might argue, of course, that the darkness of some films, and the portrayal of fear, as well, are related to the horror film as we understand it; but strictly speaking an element of fantasy/surrealism ought to be present. One example we shall study here that seems to fall into the generally accepted definitions of the genre is *Dans le ventre du dragon*.

DANS LE VENTRE DU DRAGON (1989; d. Yves Simoneau)

Caught in the meshes of alcoholism, tobacco addiction, too much work, or other forms of entrapment, Bozo dreams of the perfect woman; Steve dreams of travelling to another planet; Madame Côté, prisoner in a special kind of clinic, dreams of "dying in a real house, in a real bed, next to someone who loves her a lot"; and Lou dreams of getting away from the *train-train* of life, "faire le tour du monde, voyager." It is the dissatisfaction of Lou that unfurls a series of horrors, for he sells himself over to be a guinea pig in the mad experiments of Dr. Lucas, who, herself, dreams of activating the dormant part of the brain, so that a new human race will emerge: one that knows all.

The "director" of the medical factory, where "medicine of tomorrow is developed" and where Dr. Lucas is employed, sends Mireille to spy on Lucas, as he suspects things have gone astray. And yes, Mireille discovers the terrible condition of the patients. They are shackled, and they are given injections and drugs that age them. Within a short time, Lou has become very old (he responds under sedation that he is more than one-hundred years old). He is wrinkled and nearly bald, and the little hair he has left is gray and wispy. Drunk with her success, Lucas exclaims that now she must extend her research to children, for she is on the verge of penetrating "une autre réalité," the imagination in all its purity. Her leaning toward Lou is not without erotic and castrating overtones, or undertones: does Lu-cas now have Lou's *cas*? She kisses him as he is under sedation, and injects him with a needle (a phallic symbol?).

But Lou has sent a letter to his old pal Steve via Jean-Marie, Lou's former roommate at the research clinic, and Steve, accompanied by a timorous Bozo, goes to Lou's rescue in a paddleboat. (The interaction between these two *marginaux* reminds one a bit of Laurel and Hardy.)

With the exception of Tifo, Mercure, and LaHaye, the acting in this film is exaggerated to the point of caricature, and one is not really ever afraid. The attendants at this clinic, both female and male, are stiff and obedient; one of them is played by Steve Banner, who had the lead role in Simoneau's *Fous de Bassan*. No doubt, also, there is a misogynous flavor to *Dragon* (cf. *Les Fous de Bassan*?), when one considers that Dr. Lucas is a vicious professional-type woman, who, Eve-like, tempts Lou with promises of fortune and long life, not to mention great knowledge. With his axe, this prototype of Adam, or even of Christ-the-Savior, threatens Lucas, saying "Je vais couper la tête du dragon avant qu'il avale tout le monde [I am going to cut off the head of the dragon before it swallows up the whole world (or everyone)]." Note, too, that the doctor's laboratory is complete with snakes, which terrify the Bozo-Steve team. Lou almost destroys the temple, then runs off; Mireille seizes Lucas and calls in the "Director," who gives the "out-of-control" Lucas a good scolding, calling her a "sale égoïste," who has "ruined everything." In the end, the Bozo-Steve team arrives to deliver Lou and Mme Côté. Once out of the stinking atmosphere of the drug factory and experimental clinic, Lou throws a magic dart at the bizarre edifice, which in some ways resembles a prison; and all the escapees, looking on the transformation, declare they have found their dream: "C'est ma maison [It's my house]," says Aube Côté; "c'est ma planète [it's my planet]," says Steve; "c'est ma femme [it's my wife]," says Bozo. Thus, horror is dispelled and in this happy ending the film takes on the aura of an allegory. Is this another representation of simple Québec *marginaux* and their triumph over technology, power, and authority? I leave it in the realm of a question. Whatever the case, as a thriller (though viewed by some as a comedy) this film does not come near *Pouvoir intime*; needless to say it cannot compare with *Night Zoo* either.

Labor and Management

In the course of this study we have encountered many dissatisfied workers, reflected in the films of Jutra, Arcand, and others (in *Mon oncle Antoine*; *Les Plouffe*; *On est au coton*; *Bonheur d'occasion; Lucien Brouillard* etc.). In the past, six hundred thousand French Canadians migrated to industrial cities of New England to work in the textile mills. So much was this true that quarters grew up in these cities that came to be called "Le Petit Canada." Notable among such cities is Lowell, Massachusetts. Documenting this phenomenon is a short film entitled *Le P'tit Canada* (1979; 28 min.; Nanouk Films, Ltée.), in which the historian Richard Santerre explains how and why these events occurred, and how the people maintained their customs. It could serve as a brief introduction to the gargantuan production that *Les Tisserands du pouvoir*, a fiction on the same theme, represents.

LES TISSERANDS DU POUVOIR (1988; d. Claude Fournier)

A television series that follows the lives and fortunes of three families, this work is more than worthy of entry here, where we are speaking of "cinema." And it should be noted that the *Mills of Power*, *Bonheur d'occasion*, and *Maria Chapdelaine* are works that were widely shown on television, but also were packaged for rental or purchase on videotape; some were also offered in streamlined versions, *Maria Chapdelaine* and *Bonheur* ... both suffering enormously from the surgery.

Although *Mills of Power* could be discussed in terms of literature into film, since it is based on Claude Fournier's novel, the social commentary and the depiction of the conditions of the [Québécois, or Franco-American] working class in conflict with [French and American] management at the turn of the century and in the early part of the twentieth century are so strong that it seems fitting to look at this monumental work as one of the best such cinematographic studies of the subject.

The story concerns the Lamberts—a poor farm family that emigrates from Québec to Woonsocket, Rhode Island in 1907 in search of work—and their encounters with the Roussels, a wealthy family of French mill owners, who in turn conflict with an upper class Montréal family, the Fontaines.

Part 1.

*Baptiste Lambert (Gratien Gélinas), now a very old man well into his eighties, is angry at the powers-that-be for taking away the French television programs and threatening him with eviction from his house on Maple street and with being committed to a home. He holes himself up in the abandoned building of the Lorraine textile mills, and holds the officials of Woonsocket at bay with a rifle and a bomb, while he tells Richard Laverdière, a television journalist, the story of his life, while also reiterating his demands that the television programs in the French language be restored. He goes back over his long life to his family's departure from Québec and their new beginning in the United States. Through the convention of flashbacks he tells the story of his family's arrival in Woonsocket, of the conflicts between the Irish workers and the "Francos [Franco-Americans]"; and of the hardships he and his family suffered in the mill, run by the extremely powerful and wealthy Roussels of Roubaix, France.

A shift to France shows Auguste Roussel preparing to send his son *Jacques (only eleven years old) to Montréal, where he will receive his education and learn the mores of the French Canadians, so that one day he may operate the plant in Woonsocket. (His brother, Pierre, has already been sent to Indochina).

Yet another shift to an upper class Montréal family introduces us to *Emile, to his sister Simone, and to Henriette, their mother. The father having just died, Emile, who is bent on studying medicine, is taken by a priest-cousin to a seminary. (The mother is a musician, as is Simone; she will give piano lessons in order to survive.)

Lambert is hungry. He tells Richard to get him some good food; some *ragoût de pattes* (pig's feet stew) from the restaurant in Le Petit Canada (the French-American quarter in Woonsocket). In another flashback, we are in 1914, and Abraham Gauthier has just become mayor of Woonsocket—the first Franco to be elected to that office. It is the time of the St.Jean Baptiste parade, a French-Canadian holiday (24 June), which the Franco-Americans persist in celebrating. The children fight, the Francos versus the Irish. Says Mme Lambert, "We have been in the U. S. for seven years, and we are still foreigners."

In another shift, it is eight years later in Montréal: Jacques Roussel and his friend, John Elliott, are graduating; at dinner with his father, Jacques suggests he does not necessarily have his heart set on being an industrialist and running his father's American mill in Woonsocket. Meanwhile, Emile Fontaine graduates from medical school. He announces to his mother that he will practice in Woonsocket, where he is needed. Suddenly, the church is on fire. It is surely the Ku Klux Klan behind this deed. (We know of their strong anti-Catholic biases.)

Auguste Roussel, still on visit to America, has gone to Woonsocket with his son, Jacques. A St.Jean Baptiste parade is in process, with the Québec flag waving—the white cross on the blue field, with the four fleurs-de-lis. (Is this right? The flag was adopted on 21 January 1948 and sanctioned by legislation on 9 March 1950—but the scene in the film takes place before World War I.) The two Frenchmen then go to the head office of the mill, where the president explains to Roussel that the workers have taken off half a day. Roussel is not happy about this, and cannot accept the notion that the employees should regard this as their "national holiday," when they are in America. (He proposes that since they work for a French company they should observe Bastille Day.) A flash forward to the present shows Baptiste telling Richard Laverdière that they never had to observe the 14th of July French Holiday, but, he adds, "we were being pushed to become Americans."

A new flashback. Jacques and his father have returned to France; Jacques's mother gives him a Bayard automobile; they go off together to join the rest of the family at the seashore. Here, at table, the family discusses the fact that war is in the air. Pierre is back from Saigon and wants to leave Indochina permanently. Mlle Caroline Motte arrives with her brother to visit the family; she and Jacques fall in love.

It is now mobilization; occupation soon follows. The Roussel sons have gone to war. The German soldiers ask Auguste Roussel to start up his textile mill; he says all his workers are at war, and is told to use women and children, then. When he says, "Ask them yourselves," he is "arrested." (He will spend three years in prison.)

Two years after this arrest, Auguste's son, Jacques, is wounded in France; and his badly injured leg and indeed his life are saved by Dr. Emile Fontaine.

Jacques returns to his home. His father is there, as are the other sons, all in uniform. The father explains that the mills, destroyed by the enemy, will be rebuilt. When, shortly after this discussion, Jacques goes down to the beach to sun himself, Caroline, now a film actress, suddenly appears. They indulge in an affair, but cannot reach an agreement about her going to America. They part company, and Jacques arrives in Woonsocket (it is now 1920) to take charge of the mill. Here he encounters even stronger prejudice in the upper echelons of the plant against the French Canadians, who are said to be unintelligent: they cannot read or write.

The scene shifts to the interior of the mill, where Baptiste's hand gets caught in the machinery. Dr. Emile Fontaine cares for him and then goes to the mill, where he speaks angrily (and in Jacques's presence) of the butchery and the exploitation going on in the mill. It is especially the women and children who suffer, "while you don't care for their health or even for the life of those who work for you." His sarcasm reaches its zenith, when he says, "History has its peculiarities: Americans died for you French in the war, for the safeguard of humanity; and now you French come to the United States to turn industry to your profit, without caring in the least about humanity. 'Ce n'est pas tout à fait le même geste.'"

On a sojourn to Montréal, where Jacques wants to encourage French Canadians to go to the U.S. to work ("it is better than starving, after all"), he attends a soirée of the St. Jean Baptiste Society. He takes up briefly with his old friend, John Elliott (John Wildman), who, through the lesbian Fidélia, introduces him to the beautiful chanteuse, Simone Fontaine (Dr. Fontaine's sister!). It is the *coup de foudre* [love at first sight]. He sends her dozens of roses.

Emile Fontaine comes to Montréal to visit his mother and sister. When he learns that Simone's new love is Jacques Roussel he is furious.

In the next scene, Simone is being scrutinized by the clergy, who is, at the order of the Vatican, preparing a "dossier" on her, for, as it is explained, the Roussel family is one of the greatest Catholic families of France, and this family and the Vatican have a "privileged relationship." She is asked if she still has her "integrity." Angry with these *grands scrutins à l'Inquisition*, she climbs on his desk, spreads her legs to the *chanoîne*, and tells him to see for himself.

Back in France, Jacques's parents are concerned about this daughter-in-law-to-be — her bohemian environment, her friend who is "practically a man," etc. But as the scene shifts back to America, we see that, although Simone is not happy about her *"enquête"* with the *chanoîne*, Jacques is going to persist; he kisses her passionately. The next morning, Fidélia finds Simone in Jacques's bed at breakfast time, and is told that they are going to be married as soon as possible. (The poor lesbian loses out — temporarily.)

Part 1 closes with the most powerful scene of the 116 minutes. As the priest is joining Simone and Jacques "in holy matrimony," a group of people arrive in the church and interrupt the ceremony. They have been brought there by Dr. Emile Fontaine. All are young people, maimed in the mill: one is blind; another scarred; and the one-armed Baptiste is included. At the wedding reception, as Emile speaks critically to Jacques, Simone says to him: "Emile stop! you don't know Jacques." "Oh yes I do!," replies Emile. "You don't recognize me? I recognized you very well!"

Part 2. "La Révolte"

Part 2 opens in present-day Woonsocket, with citizens debating the merits of Lambert's actions. (He has barricaded himself in the small gatehouse of the abandoned mill.) There is a circus of spectators, and finally Soeur Bernadette and Lambert's friend Cléophas Larouche arrive. They propose to talk him out of his stubborn stand, but instead he takes them hostage. Through a photograph he has with him, we get a flashback to 1921. Jacques Roussel is now in charge of the plant, and Baptiste's father Valmore Lambert is organizing the workers for a walkout strike. After the walkout, the workers go to Roussel's house. The police arrive, but Roussel pretends there is no trouble. He gets hit by Lambert; his wife tells him that no matter what he does he cannot make friends with the workers. Ultimately, Baptiste and his father are put into prison, and Baptiste's sister, Madeleine, goes to Jacques on her own. She tells him she'll do whatever he wants if he gets them free.

Valmore, out of prison, is preaching solidarity and unity, and saying that only four or five men are needed to get a revolt going, when Jacques Roussel arrives. He tells Valmore and his wife that he will pay for Madeleine to study with the Sisters.

The film begins to pick up the heavy involvement of the Church in (labor-management) politics: we learn that the Vatican is calling for the establishment of Catholic high schools in New England and that the "Francos" are refusing to assimilate — though the Irish do. Emile angrily reads to a gathering Bishop Kenney's "orders" that English must be the only language used in Catholic schools. A bit later, we witness the "initiation" of a group of men, including Valmore, into a secret society for the preservation of Franco-American culture. Emile conducts the initiation into this "Order of the Crusaders," and then introduces the "Grand Commander of the Order," his Eminence Cardinal L.-P. Bourguoin of Québec! The mission of the society is said to be to work in secret for the advancement of Franco-Americans, and the motto-password is "moins de discours, plus d'action [less talk and more action]."

Meanwhile, Fidélia is hanging around with Simone (as is also John Elliott). Fidélia and Simone become lovers, and soon after, Jacques learns that Simone has sold her jewels to help her brother. Feeling that she is "singing to the walls" or to deaf ears, she leaves Jacques and goes to New York City to continue her career. There she lives with John Allen and prepares to sing for the Metropolitan Opera.

On the other hand, Simone's brother, Emile, has vowed to take a stand against the Irish-American Bishop Kenney. He founds a newspaper, *La Sentinelle*, and hires Valmore Lambert to work for him. The curate is sent away from the parish (Ste Anne) for his "collaboration" with Emile. Emile decides to fight Kenney in the courts; he loses. The parishoners, now in revolt, refuse to put money in the collection baskets, and when the new priest refuses the Lambert family the eucharist, Valmore forces him to serve them. In the scuffle, the priest falls and hosts fly all over the floor. The non-Catholic moviegoers who shouted "sacrilege" at poor Benoît when he ate an unconsecrated host (*Mon oncle Antoine*), should know that Valmore's actions from beginning to end are sacrilege; and nothing would have shocked a devout Catholic of the period so much as to see all these consecrated hosts (body of Christ) strewn about on the floor.

Soon it is open warfare between some of the Francos and the Church; Valmore, thinking to serve Emile, plants dynamite intended to kill Bishop Kenney; instead he gets Canon Allen. He had taken the dynamite from the plant; his wife tells him he must leave the town, for they know it was he who stole the dynamite. She gives him money and he departs, never to return home again.

Emile goes to Rome to present a petition bearing fifteen thousand signatures of people who protest Bishop Kenney and his methods. He is told that these are but fifteen thousand rebels (out of a diocese of one hundred twenty-five thousand). His paper is forbidden and he is excommunicated along with all his collaborators for the assassination of Canon Allen. Only Kenny can get the excommunication lifted. Immediately following Emile's departure, the cardinal who had interviewed him sends a telegram to Auguste Roussel saying, "Dear Friend, You will be happy to learn that ...." Obviously, Rome is in cahoots with the powerful wool merchant and his family. But towards the end of the film we find Emile asking pardon of the Church and the bishop, so that he can return to the sacraments. He kisses Bishop Kenney's hand and slipper; the bishop releases him from the excommunication, and shortly thereafter he is seen taking holy orders.

In the meantime, Madeleine shows up at Jacques's. She has left the convent and wants to stay with him. He suggests she go to a convent in Montréal to finish her studies. "I don't want to go to Montréal. No one is so important to me as you." They become lovers. A few scenes later, she, together with Jacques, her mother, and Baptiste, go to Valmore's hiding place. There Baptiste finds his father hanging in an old abandoned barn. Madeleine and Jacques are drawn closer and closer together. Ultimately Jacques leaves the factory, they marry, and she bears him a child.

On this note, we return to the present. A swat team arrives and surrounds the area. A woman from "Home Entertainment" proposes that they get Jacques Roussel in Palm Beach to speak to Lambert on the television. With some persuasion, and the promise that his demand for reinstatement of the television programs in French will be looked into, Baptiste allows his "hostages," Cléophas Larouche and Sister Bernadette, to leave. He himself ultimately comes out, having learned from Roussel that this television representative is his great-niece (Roussel's granddaughter) — even if she does not speak French!

In a final scene Baptiste is visiting Roussel in Florida. As they walk along the beach, Jacques tells him he will not have his programs in French. "I should have set off the dynamite, and blown myself up" says Baptiste. As Roussel goes on about how Baptiste should accept things as they are, and try to adjust to changes, or go to Montréal where he can hear and speak French, Baptiste cries out, "You don't understand now any better than you did in the past; you'll never understand!" But, says Roussel, your family has been here now for three generations, etc. And to this, as a last word, Baptiste declares that "a hundred years from now we'll still be fighting, and have something to fight for."

In an article by Pierre Hébert, we learn that Claude Fournier's story was based in fact, and that Emile Fontaine was modeled after Elphège J. Daignault, who, in reaction to the Church's treatment of the Francos, as French-American immigrants were called, founded La Sentinelle. (Daigneault told his story in his book entitled *Le Vrai Mouvement sentinelliste en Nouvelle Angleterre 1923–1929 et l'affaire du Rhode Island* [Montréal: Editions du Zodiaque, 1936].) Hébert finds that Fournier's cadre (Lambert demanding his TV programs in French) was very timely. "Does Claude Fournier have a crystal ball? For the appearance of the *Tisserands du pouvoir* coincides perfectly with an agitated period in which it is a question, in the context, of present-day linguistic problems, of relations between minorities and majorities, whether they be anglophones or imigrants to Québec, Québécois in North America, or francophones outside Québec. One is always somebody's minority, and Claude Fournier's novel proposes a realistic reflection on that fact: in this matter, one does not have rights too often except when numbers justify it.[46]

Eloïse Brière's Québec Heritage Series seems in some sense an answer to New England's Jean-Baptiste Lamberts. The work of CODOFIL in Lafayette, Louisiana, and of some of the professors of Southwestern Louisiana University serves a similar need in the descendants of French Canadians living in that region of the United States. It was there that *Bélisaire the Cajun* was filmed; it has its own kind of ethnic charm and clash. And at times it gives off the feel of a documentary on *guérisseurs*, or healers, who practiced (and still do) not only in Louisiana, but in certain regions of French Canada, as the works of Antonine Maillet readily show.

One might point out, too, in passing, that Michel Brault, with A. Gladu, has done an extensive series of films on French "Americans." ("Le son des Français d'Amérique": 13 episodes from 1974–6 and 14 episodes from 1977–80.)

Education

If there is a Québécois Mr. Chips, or Miss Bishop, or Miss Brooks, or, for that matter, even a Nabokovian-type professor like the sick Dr. Humbert Humbert (James Mason) of *Lolita*, the fact has not come to my attention. In Québec, the priest has traditionally been the educator, and if he is celebrated — or criticized — in film, it is not solely as a teacher, but in his dual role that we see him. (A good example of this is *The Hockey Sweater*. Another is a film telling the fact-based story of the priest Father Murray — founder of Notre Dame College in Regina. He is pictured as the hockey coach and teacher in Ken Mitchell's *The Hounds of Notre Dame* [1981]. Of course, neither the story nor the film is from Québec.) Nuns, too, did the teaching. But the role of teacher does not seem to arise too often in Québec film. Even in my examination of the horror film in Québec, a Mlle Hélène (of Claude Chabrol's *Le Boucher*) did not surface.

Although we do get many scenes of provincial school rooms in such films as *Henri*, *The Peanut Butter Solution*, and so forth, education does not seem to be a cinematic theme for the Québécois, either; nor does the school room or the university seem to be the prime locus of a film. This is curious, considering the fact that the school curricula have been the subject of much debate in the province for several years, the central question being enforced bilingualism, or, "Must the public education be offered only in French to all citizens?" Of course, I except here such a film as *Le Déclin* ..., although certainly the state of the North American university, with its undervaluing of students and its overvaluing of "research" and "publication" is one of Arcand's subthemes. Weinmann makes quite a point of this, in fact, attacking conference-goers (1990, 155), and later resuming this approach when he observes how, in the film, the vast hall of the University is empty, except for a student who roller-skates along in jeans, to the sound of Handel's "Concerto Grosso, opus 5; no 6"; for "apparently, the professors profess, the students study; the administrators administer ... like functionaries, like mechanical dolls" (1990, 170). And, he asks (ibid.), "What can professors who have lost faith in what they profess profess? Who will educate the educators?" Weinmann then launches into a tirade concerned with the motto "publish or perish" and with much more about higher education, all of which he derives from this film, and only some of which is justified.

Of note, nevertheless, is Michel Brault's *Seul ou avec autres*, a new wave, *cinéma vérité* documentary (1963; 65 minutes), coproduced with the Association Générale des Etudiants de l'Université de Montréal, in which Brault—using a script by Denys Arcand and Stéphane Venne (also responsible for the music)—follows the lives of several students, who tell Brault's camera their thoughts and their problems. It is comparable to *Christopher's Movie Matinee* (1969). Brault, a proponent of the *cinéma direct* style, made *Entre la Mer et l'eau douce* (his first feature film) a bit later (1968). It concerns a climber, an opportunist (played by Claude Gauthier), who exploits a pretty waitress (played by Geneviève Bujold) and then abandons her. Somewhat reminiscent of Jean Lévesque in *Bonheur d'occasion*, wouldn't you say? Or even of *An American Tragedy*.

In the same period as *Seul* . . . came Jean-Claude Lord's production of *Trouble-Fête* (1964; d. Pierre Patry; scripted by Patry and Lord; 95 min.), a fictionalized film dealing with a college student in Montréal who rebels against all authority, as well as against his family and his friends. He, like so many (students) of the 60s, is seeking the meaning of his life, or, more broadly, of existence.

Other films that might be examined for student life would include *Comment Savoir* (1965) by Claude Jutra (Pratley *TS* 1987, 180); *Entre tu et vous* (1969) by J.P. Lefebvre, about student protests (*TS* 1987, 195); and, also by J.P. Lefebvre, *Avoir 16 ans* (1979), concerning student fears and anxieties (*TS* 1987, 127). This last film is analyzed at length by Peter Harcourt. According to him, *Avoir 16 ans* was at first going to be a documentary on school vandalism; "but when every school refused him access to their buildings, Lefebvre was pleased . . . to have the greater formal authority of fiction. Though based on an actual event, *Avoir 16 ans* is less about school vandalism than the institutional repressions that stifle our lives." Harcourt demonstrates, too, how the use of slow zooms translates the feeling of imprisonment the students feel, as a result of the regimented aridity of the educational system. He finds that in the long run the film has much to do with the impersonality of authority, and the lack of humanity with which authority always imposes itself. Moreover, Harcourt draws parallels between the humiliations of the protagonist Louis and the humiliations inflicted on the Québécois in the 60s and 70s. The film thus becomes emblematic of the political situation in Québec at the time of the film's creation. But, Harcourt adds, "At the same time, the systematized repressions, the categorization of human knowledge, and the impersonal futility of most of what is offered as secondary education throughout North America cannot help but make the film meaningful to all kinds of people. By creating a 'tone poem to the prison we call adolescence,' Jean Pierre Lefebvre has universalized these experiences. Like all great art, *Avoir 16 ans*, while speaking directly from the specificities of its own time and culture, speaks to the world."[47]

Claude Jutra's concern for youth and its education is the subject of discussion in Noguez, where it is stated that Québec's youth has always been one of his chief interests, from his *Mouvement perpétuel*, made in 1949 when he was only twenty, throughout most of his career, including his pedagogical concerns in *Les Enfants du silence*, which he made with Michel Brault in 1962. While *Comment savoir* (1965) dealt with modern educational techniques, it is Jutra's *Wow* (1970) — which focuses on the professor's role — that especially concerns Noguez. He finds that *Rouli-Roulant* (ONF, 1966) and *Wow* show a parti-pris for the adolescent even more than Gilles Groulx's 1961 *La Lutte*. (Noguez finds that Jutra may in fact be a closet educator.) As with the *scénario* that Jutra wrote for Pierre Patry's 1962 *Petit Discours de la méthode*, where Paris is seen from the point of view of a young Canadian, in *Wow* Montréal and the whole society are seen from the point of view of a handful of Québécois adolescents, in whom one can discern a poignant nostalgia or a refusal to grow old. In *Wow*, Noguez claims, everything jumps — house, family refrigerator, jalopy. It begins where Antonioni's *Zabriskie Point* ends. A cautionary film, it suggests that apologetics and submission of youth to established values are not synchronized with their own concepts of themselves as recorded in school newspapers. Only Flis, the most *cégépien* [i.e., typical of the students of the Collège d'Enseignement général et professionnel, a postsecondary institution begun in 1967], warns that violence is inescapable. Obviously, the film was made two years after the great educational upheavals and authority-bashing that occurred throughout the Western world. But Noquez finds that the point of view in *Wow* is extremely ambiguous, as is even the film genre in which it is cast: Is it documentary? investigative reporting? If so, how do dream sequences (*à la Christopher's Movie Matinee*) fit in? How can one have sequences that are neither interview nor dream, such as the memory of a trip, at the beginning? What of Jutra's clear interventions, which sometimes seem to moralize (as, marijuana makes one an iconoclast and apolitical)? And why did Jutra choose these nine young people? Because they were representative of a kind of youth? (which one?), or because they were not representative?

It is in any case clear, says Noguez, that Jutra is stating that

Léolo. Photograph by Roger Dufresne. (Courtesy Coll. Cinémathèque Québécoise.)

young people have more in common among themselves, regardless of their differing social or educational experiences, than they do with adults of their own milieu, and that youth of the Western bourgeoisie are finding it more and more difficult to assimilate to Western society, are more and more centrifugal. And if there is a perspective in *Wow*, it is Jutra's didactico-tactical and aesthetic perspective. His approach is to be distinguished from that of Jacques Godbout in *Kid sentiment* (ONF, 1968), in which Godbout allows four young people to improvise, to act, before us. Jutra, rather, puts his protagonists in situations of passivity. *Wow*, like *A tout prendre*, announced the masterpiece that was to come with *Mon oncle Antoine*, and it also showed some of the special interests of Jutra (adolescent psychology, dream analysis, formation of youth) that would surface again in *Mon oncle Antoine*.[48]

Finally, Jean-Claude Lauzon looks at the education of children (among other things) in his 1992 film *Léolo*. The importance of Lauzon's "attack on the Québec school system" in this film is recognized by Lauzon himself when he says: "If I had one sole message to send in *Léolo*, it was probably to tell teachers to really help and encourage their pupils." And he adds that a little shove from a professor would have been useful in his own case, as far as that's concerned.[49]

Of course, the education of minorities has been the focus of some attention in the documentary, and among these minorities, especially the placement of Native Canadians in special schools. On this subject the anglophone filmmakers both of Québec and of other provinces have been especially effective. But a twist to this may well come in the establishment by the Native Canadians of schools tailored to their needs. *The Cree Way* (1977; d. Tony Ianzelo, NFB; 25 min.; 18 sec.) is a film concerning the school and cultural center at Rupert's House in northern Québec, showing how the school's approach has been to allow the children to relate to their own cultural milieu, while involving the parents in the educational process. James E. Page finds what is being done here to be "a model for learning everywhere in Canada .... Clearly the approach taken here is much sounder culturally than taking Native children out of their communities for ten months of the year to study a foreign culture in a residential school."[50] Along with this film, the NFB has released *Our Land Is Our Life*, also about the Cree of the Mistassani area of northern Québec. Especially in part 3 do we see how the school system, under the control of the Department of Indian Affairs and Northern Development, is based on the needs, wishes, and values of the Whites, who are "out of touch with the cultural aspirations of the Native people."[51] The film explores "how a whole generation of Cree children raised in the residential schools have lost touch with their own roots."[52] (Martin Defalco directed an inferior movie on this subject — a fiction film entitled *Cold Journey*, made in 1975.) Many recent documentaries on CBC, including the week-long series on "The Journal" (Fall, 1990) insist on the disaster this approach to assimilation (in truth, a colonization of the most brutal sort) has been. The series included testimonies not only of the obvious alienation of the individual from his or her roots, but, in addition, of sexual and other physical as well as psychological abuse by authorities charged with raising and educating these children. The standoff of the Okas in the summer of 1990 appears to have forced Canadians into taking a longer and harder look at their Native peoples (something the Americans should also do).

Religion in Recent *Québécois* Film

If education gets rather scant attention in Québec's cinema, the same cannot be said of religion, which is amply dealt with.
    Treating questions of religion is, of course, nothing new in cinema,

but what is of interest to us in this study is how the Québécois regard the collapse of the Church's power mentioned in the early pages of this chapter. Postwar Québec saw a reversal of perspective and tone that allowed for the *mise en question* of government, and also of religion, which through the CIF (Confédération internationale du film) had up until then had a tenacious hold on films produced.[53] In the recent film *Le Déclin de l'empire américain*, the characters certainly show little belief in the moral or theological teachings of the Church, and, in fact, express their disaffection with the whole issue. But even prior to *Le Déclin* . . ., and without clearly articulating the aspect of liberation, there were several films that could "for their time, be called 'useful catalysts' of the imagination, and that contributed to the mental and spiritual evolution [of the Québécois] by their gesture of original cultural affirmation" (Lever *Hist*. 1988, 453). Some of those films questioned the Church's assumptions; others, of course, merely valorized the distinct culture of Québec, and included in their picture the role of the priest in that culture. It is Lever's contention that among such pioneering films we could count *Le Père Chopin* (1944; Charles Philippe/J.A. DeSève), *Un Homme et son péché* (1949; Paul Gury), *Aurore* (1952; Jean-Yves Bigras), *Le Curé de village* (1949; Paul Gury), and *Le Gros Bill* (1949; René Delacroix).[54] Certain contemporaneous assessments of these films would agree with Lever. For example, Renaude Lapointe wrote in *Le Soleil* of *Le Curé de village*: "Il n'est plus question d'imiter Hollywood; il est question d'être nous-mêmes. [It is no longer a question of imitation of Hollywood; it is a question of being ourselves.]."[55]

Le Curé de village (1949; d. Paul Gury), was based on a radio play written by Robert Choquette (1934), who then wrote the screenplay for Québec Productions (Paul L'Anglais). Noteworthy is the fact that its photography was directed for the first time by a Québécois, Roger Racine. While technically speaking the curé is not the main character in this film — rather, it is Juliette Martel — he is nonetheless pivotal. It is through him that the other characters must process their behaviors, so that he becomes the guiding moral conscience of the inhabitants of Saint-Vivien, when a stranger, the Franco-American Leblanc, arrives from Detroit and threatens to reveal secrets about the father of the orphan, Juliette. The curate must stop these revelations, and also put a stop to Mme Théberge's opposition to the marriage of her son, Lionel, to Juliette. As the official synopsis puts it, "M. le curé prend charge de la situation; il met la main au gouvernail . . . [et] à présent que Leblanc a parlé, M. le curé fera peser toute son influence sur l'esprit de Mme

Théberge" ["The curate takes charge of the situation; he puts his hand to the helm ... [and] now that Leblanc has spoken, the priest will make the full weight of his influence felt on Mme Théberge's mind.]"[56] He therefore pulls Mme Théberge aside and adjures her to look into her heart, and to recognize that the real reason for her opposition is that she herself loves Lionel and that she is jealous. The curate is the soul of "tact and wisdom" throughout all his ordeals; he must hear all kinds of sorrows, and listen to revelations regarding the material difficulties of his flock. As the synopsis states: "Il lui faut diriger la barque, faire en sorte que ses paroissiens évitent les écueils de la vie qui n'est pas toujours facile, allez. Est-il plus beau rôle? [He must guide the boat; see to it that his parishioners avoid the reefs of life, which is not always easy, you know. Is there a more beautiful role?]"

Houle notes that Le Curé de village — which was adapted from the radio play and broadcast by CKAC from 1934 forward — is a film that surprises the viewer by the mastery of cinematographic language that Gury demonstrates. The movements of the cameras (the long traveling shot accompanying the curé as he traverses the town), the angles of the shots, the narrative or symbolic effects that today seem facile, nevertheless cut through the general platitude of the scenes in this first industrial epic of the québécois cinema. But beyond these qualities, what constitutes the real sociological interest of this film is the erection, as principal subject, of the theme of the clergy's omnipresence and omniscience that underlay all cultural production of the period. The curé always appears in time to prevent or repair mistakes, push aside anything threatening his flock, and to redirect souls in distress into the straight and narrow path of Christian virtues (Houle 1978, 64–5. My paraphrase and translation).

We may conclude that Le Curé de village, though it presents "truly French-Canadian content," has little inclination to criticize the society, and less to portray the clergy in any but flattering tones. After all, under the influence of the arch–Catholic Dutchman Leo Janssens in the CIF (Confédération internationale du film), and following the Confédération's marriage to RFD (Renaissance Films Distribution), Québec films were submitted for approval by the Vatican; included in this list was Le Curé de village.[57] No critical perspective here, then! Instead, in Le Curé ... the priest is "the religious head, counselor, and final authority in the town" (Pratley TS 1987, 163); i.e., unquestioned. Instead, as Jean Béraud said in La Presse, the movie "exposes, explicates, demonstrates, and then again takes up the commère (biddy; busybody) of the village, so that we will be sure to understand that she is talkative; it shows us the village again and again so we can be sure we're out in the country; and it follows the curate's every step, shows us every button on his cassock so we can be very sure he is a curate."[58] Even the stills from *Le Curé* ... (*Cin*, ... 1979, 52–3) show the almost Flemish-Catholic nature of some shots, as, for example, that of the death of Juliette's grandfather, priest present and a huge crucifix over the bed; they show also the larger-than-life presence of the priest at the film's moment of crisis. (But can the caricatural sketch of the curé first appearing in *Le Front ouvrier* really be by Claude Jutra, as Véronneau claims? If so, why is it signed Jutras?)[59]

Roland Lelièvre complained, as did others, of the slowness of the film, saying that every heartbeat of the village was listened to through a bad stethoscope.[60] But, more significantly, this portrait of the priest is not only positive, it is also generic, as the very title shows: the village priest (not the priest of the village [St. Vivien].) Perhaps, then, one must wait for the 60s to experience (negative) criticism of the Québécois clergy, criticism such as is probably embodied in the procrastinations of the priest in *Aurore*, or in the scene in which *Tit-Coq* stands up to the priestly authority of the chaplain. This initiative is there, to be sure, and it continues through the 70s. Is one not justified, for instance, to see in such a film as *L'Amour humain* not only a "daring" subject — meant to be searing — but also one that largely suggests a disrespect of the [Québécois] clergy?

L'AMOUR HUMAIN OR *THE AWAKENING* (1971; d. Denis Héroux)

Pratley writes of this film: "This is Cinepix's heavyweight socio-serious entry into the sex stakes, and the result looks gloomy. The principals are a priest and a nun. He suffers from illicit dreams and she sighs sensually every time she sees a sex symbol. They leave their orders, meet again and marry, and eventually come to adjust themselves to their feelings of guilt over being able to enjoy sex freely. There is a poignant and searching subject here, but it is cheapened by treatment slanted to the sensational rather than to serious consideration. Given the right atmosphere, most audiences might find it funny."[61] In other words, this film is not in league with Maria-Luisa Bemberg's 1985 *Camila*, not even with *The Thornbirds*, nor *The Robe*. Lever gives a scathing assessment of the work, when he writes: "Denis Héroux y cherche un effet de scandale avec son affaire de coeur et de soutane, mais ne l'obtient pas, car son scénario — risible — demeure déconcertant de mièvrerie. [Denis Héroux tries to give a scandalous effect with his affair of heart and cassock (soutane), but does not succeed, for his script — laughable — remains disconcerting for its (marshmallowy) affectation]" (Lever *Hist*. 1988, 284; my translation).

No more satisfactory was a film satirizing religious hypocrisy, *L'Apparition*, directed by Roger Cardinal (1972). But, with *Le frère André*, the small jewel directed by Jean-Claude Labrecque (1987), it seems the subject of religion was finally treated with measure, distance, and taste. Indeed, for reasons that are not entirely clear, in the last couple of decades there has been a wave of films dealing with serious religious themes, but not always with a religious intent. Among the most notable are *Jesus of Nazareth* (1977 — a high caliber, star-studded television miniseries of sorts; and d. Zeffirelli); *The Last Temptation of Christ* (1988; d. Scorsese); *Thérèse* (1986; d. Cavalier); and two *québécois* films *Jésus de Montréal* and *Le frère André*, the latter being an excellent, tasteful film, not at all sentimental.

LE FRÈRE ANDRÉ (1987; d. Jean-Claude Labrecque)

For the uninitiated, a bit of background concerning the "culture hero," Frère André, may be in order. He was born in St.-Grégoire d'Iberville L. C. (Lower Canada) on 9 August 1845 and died in Montréal 6 January 1937. He joined the Congrégation de la Sainte Croix (CSC), and in 1904 his admirers — many of them blue-collar workers — helped build a chapel on the spot that is now the site of St. Joseph's Oratory, the huge basilica on the mountain that overlooks the lower city of Montréal. The Oratoire, built between 1924 and 1955, is a site of pilgrimage for North American Catholics, and especially for French Canadians. Even La Sagouine, Antonine Maillet's Acadian charwoman who lives far off in a small New Brunswick town, talks of the Oratoire and its magic oil. This "miraculous" oil, said to have come from the lamp of St. Joseph, to whom Frère André had a special devotion, was dispensed by the simple onk to the suffering and the sick. Finally, he came to be regarded as a holy man. He was declared venerable in 1978 and beatified on 23 May 1982. Though no doubt it was not the director's purpose in making the film, perhaps *Le frère André* will expedite the ultimate canonization of this saintly figure. But, in fact, the film intends, among other things, to show the red tape and the petty jealousies of André's coclergymen, who attempted to put him out of commission.

As we have so often seen in the *québécois* film, this one, too, partakes of the documentary to a very large extent, and intentionally so. It opens with archival footage of Lowell Thomas announcing the death of Frère André in Movietone News; we see the actual headlines of *Le Devoir* and of other newspapers bearing the dreadful tidings. As is declared, mourning is general throughout Canada and New England; and in an apotheosis one million persons pass before his remains.

In flashbacks, we learn about the life of Frère André. As he tells his story to a niece who has come to visit him—at nighttime, to the song of the whippoorwill—we hear of the miracles that have come from this oil he has been collecting. He would have applied it to the old priest who was dying, but the doctor was furious: he commanded that the "frottage à l'huile de St. Joseph" (massage with St. Joseph's oil) cease immediately. Obviously we have at stake here a conflict between science and faith. But in the tramways, in the crowds, he went about distributing that oil. Says André, "The last tramway gone, I looked at the mountain—Mont St. Grégoire—St. Joseph wanted it; it was gotten."

On the mountain, a small chapel was erected for André "to meet his people." And André says, "the chapel grew and grew."

André is the epitome of the grace-driven humble man. A journalist asks: "Why did Ste. Anne de Beaupré fail, while St. Joseph worked?" The answer of the simple, of the humble is given: "Perhaps she was *débordée* [overwhelmed]." André takes no credit, but gives it all to St. Joseph; "I was only his tool," he says.

The priests of his order become concerned: these deeds of his, this veneration of him, may amount to heresy or blasphemy. A council is held: "He has to be sent to Memramcook [New Brunswick]," says one; "he must relearn submission and modesty. His devotion to St. Joseph has become a *sous-religion*, or a subreligion. The people continue to idolize him—even to (con)fuse him with St. Joseph. They press to be near him; they flood to his chapel; then to the Basilica." (And do yet today, as the priest in *Jésus de Montréal* explains to Daniel.)

Francine Laurendeau writes: "Film de commande, *Le frère André* n'est pas, comme on aurait pu le craindre, l'édifiante hagiographie d'un personnage falot, mais plutôt un film sobre et émouvant .... [... *André* is not, as one might well have feared, the edifying hagiography of an odd and colorless character, but rather a sober and moving film ....]" (Coulombe 1991, 293). Be that as it may, such a film is not to everyone's liking. Still, the message of a need for humility and simplicity, the setting aside of the pomp and circumstance, as also of the overly-nice theological trappings of the Church as institution, are the message this film transmits, to the person lucky enough to have seen it. The same message is central to *Jésus de Montréal*; but, as we shall see, this latter is a layered film, with criticism not only of the clergy — the visible Church — but of many other institutions and professions: medicine, law, theater, advertising, media, and so forth. Frère André was of an earlier generation, when vices and virtues were perhaps more readily identified; and the film about him evokes that era. The setting — St. Joseph's Oratory, where people have purchased their Frére André curative oil and left behind their crutches — is still the same in *Jésus de Montréal*, but the society has by now, in 1989, become a wasteland.

JÉSUS DE MONTRÉAL (1989; d. Denys Arcand)

Denys Arcand's *Jésus de Montréal* is a statement about contemporary Québec, prolonging the portrait of contemporary corruption and decadence that was the subject of *Le Declin* ..., but adding a suggested antidote to this corruption. Like all good works of art, it is concerned with the local and the universal, the particular and the general.

This film reminds one more than anything else of Jean Rotrou's *Saint-Genest*, both being the story of an actor in a religious pageant who winds up taking on his role of sanctity: illusion becomes reality. (But the reader is reminded that Arcand used a similar framing device in *Le Confort et l'indifférence*.) Arcand's film, like Rotrou's play, deals not only with philistines — modern society — and their behavior in the face of art, with hairsplitting literalists (pharisees) opposed to the spirit of the law, with money-grabbers and lenders juxtaposed to the spiritual, and, essentially, with falsehood flying in the face of truth. The jacket of the published *scénario* correctly states that "once more Denys Arcand has succeeded in allying in a single story the deepest tragedy with the most hilarious comedy; parody and emotion; realism and the sacred." But this film does more; it also allies the parochial and the universal, or, as the jacket says, "it is a great tableau of our epoch; a ferocious and funny tableau, having a satire of the world of the theater, and of the commercial world in which the players are both actors and victims. But it is also a tender tableau, by its portrait of the hero and his companions, by the evocation of their joys and their miseries, by the fragile complicity which unites them." Yes, community, or collectivity, is certainly one of the themes; as are also injustice and homelessness. What is more, the film contains all the qualities we associate with Denys Arcand's style: "sobriety, precision, a sense of dramatic cohesion, vivacity, originality, humor mixed with compassion."

This is not a reenactment of the passion, crucifixion, and resurrection of Jesus Christ. This is not liturgical drama cut and dried. It is a reliving, a transposition of the story of Jesus — he who lived historically in the Holy Land — into a modern setting, this being not by chance the city of Montréal, formerly called Ville-Marie, the city of Mary, the city of Christianization and hospitality. These virtues, seemingly lost, have some hope of being reborn if the citizens can only recapture the charity taught by Christ and exemplified in the protagonist Daniel, who plays the role of Jesus in a liturgical drama performed at the St. Joseph's Oratory, the site where Brother Andrew originally dispensed his cures, including St. Joseph's magical oil, a place of pilgrimage and healing for North American Catholics.

Even more closely connected is Arcand's beautiful 1965 film on the early days of Ville-Marie, entitled simply *Ville-Marie* (NFB, 27 min. 38 sec.; color).[62] It underscores the holiness of the city's beginnings, a city, originally a private space, founded in 1642 in honor of the Virgin (to save souls), on the Ile de Montréal (Mont Royal), which had been purchased by the Société de Notre-Dame under the influence of the Sulpician priest J. J. Ollier and De la Dauversière. The film shows the trials of Chomedey de Maisonneuve and the extreme dedication and austerity of the Sisters of Mercy, including Marguerite Bourgeois and other nursing sisters, who came to create a purely spiritual link between France and the new world, between the governor of Nouvelle France and themselves, and who came, too, for the salvation of the Iroquois, who thought differently. This film evokes the early history of the city (as the historical-minded Arcand likes to do) through sacred music and icons, including a Veronica, a powerful crucifix, and a recurrent photograph of a very old statue of Our Lady; it also uses photography of present-day scenes, of paintings — especially those of Father Gandon (Boschlike at times) —, of drawings, of scenes in the wax museum, and of filmed reenactments by students and others.

Ville-Marie affords us the possibility of comparing and contrasting the early Arcandian film statement with *Jésus de Montréal*: the theme of charity is emphasized, in the quotations from Marguerite Bourgeois, who stresses that in the fortress charity toward one another is passionately invoked. Moreover, as the film draws to a close, we learn how greed of the fur traders undermined the town,

who saw it as a vital and indispensable strategic center. The "voice"
of Marguerite Bourgeois — whose name (Daisy; in Fr., Marguerite)
is associated with the interspliced photographs of fields of pure
white chaste daisies, which I have often seen blooming wild in
certain areas of Québec[63] — is heard to say that the early purity of
the town has disappeared; because France has had to send thousands
of soldiers to fight the Iroquois, people have grown as sinful and
corrupt "as in France." And finally the narrator states that "it
is ironical that in the end this town should be taken over by a
materialism it was founded to combat ... Yet the voices of its
origins still echo [through the city] ...." The tombs of the sisters
flash across the screen, cross after cross after cross. Whether we
can fully identify the main players in *Jésus de Montréal* with Biblical
figures or not, it takes a viewing of *Ville-Marie* to know that
Arcand is saying much the same thing in both films, and that
subversion is not the main thrust of *Jésus* ....

Nevertheless, the "actors" in the life of Jesus *can* be identified,
though Arcand has taken care not to make the equivalents too
rigid. Had he done this, the film would have lacked the dynamism
and fluidity that characterize it. Daniel, of course, represents Jesus;
his first name alludes, additionally, to the Old Testament Daniel:
Daniel in the lion's den, among the philistines; Daniel in the fiery
furnace. His last name, Coulombe, brings up our association with
the Dove of Peace, not only the Holy Spirit (which he is not), but
also of Jesus as the Prince of Peace. ("Lamb of God, who takes
away the sin of the world, grant us peace," one says at mass just
before communion.) Constance loosely represents Mary. She has
an illegitimate child; she is the "mistress," almost the handmaiden
of the feckless Père Leclerc, whom she allows to her bed through
"charity." More importantly, she is the *constant* and unswerving
friend of Daniel. She is also Mary Mother of Jesus by her last
name, giving the sonic effect of the word azure; not only was Mary
"heavenly, celestial," but blue is her color. She, with Mireille,
sings the *stabat mater* at the end of the film, as they collect money
in a cigar box for their newly founded theater-church. Mireille —
formerly a *putain* — is Mary Magdalene. (The name Mireille is a
form of Miriam or Mary.) As Daniel picks up his actors for a
performance of the liturgical drama, we see the vocation, or calling
of the disciples, in the prime, in the middle of life, all around
thirty — like Daniel and the women. Many, by the way — both men
and women — are called in *this* vocation away from their secular
and pornographic acting careers to the field of pure theater. First
it is Peter, called Martin Durocher (the rock! on which the non-

institutional, universal, and all-inclusive "church" was built); then René Sylvestre, as narrator "for scientific documentary," who doubts, like Thomas, and then is *reborn* (re-né); and so forth. René works in a *mixage* studio, so this provides a pretext for an insert, into the main film, of a film on the big-bang, complete with cosmic effects, a film that in the narrative conveys the idea that man was not necessary to the earth (*scénario*, 40−43). No truer thing was ever suggested, and David Suzuki would readily back this idea up. The ring of the text is that of Carl Sagan, and even of Pascal or Teilhard. Curiously, the bright star toward the beginning of the insert evokes the Star of Bethlehem in this context. But the makers of this film-within-the-film are not Creationists. Rather, their text and optic fireworks bear much in common with the cosmic ride afforded by the 1990 PBS video called *The Creation of the Universe*, by the award-winning journalist Timothy Ferris.

Jésus de Montréal opens with Pascal Berger playing a scene from Dostoevsky. This permits us to become aware early on that there are many levels of "play" in *Jésus de Montréal*; Pascal's play-within-a-play presents us with a profane representation of evil, through the figure of Smerdiakov, to whom Pascal is not completely equated, though Weinmann implies so. But the scene from Dostoevsky is also the forerunner to Daniel's play—a preplay, the first play-within-a-play, and one in which man is seen without God. But within the film, there is also the sacred or divine theater, the liturgical drama in which Daniel "plays the lead role," and beyond that the sacred and mysterious unraveling of Daniel's own passion, which is itself a play *to us*; this not to mention film-within-film; allusion to television, and so forth. We have at once a reenactment and a reliving. A play, too, that shows us how the actor can become the being he or she is portraying. So prismatic is this play/movie about plays/movies—this meditation upon theater—that the possibilities are endless. But that Daniel has started a theater is equated to Christ starting a church, for his theater is of the purest, the most essential nature. Like the theater of the Greeks, it is for ritual catharsis and didactic edification and has no commercial objective. (Alas, like the Church, it *will* have!)

Be it said that the false and corrupt media give messages, but messages with conflicting information, whereas the "*théâtre mystique*" (as it is called ironically but correctly by Jerzy) is the essence of theatrical purity. In the second play-within-a-play (the video of the bad pageant) we are amused and put off. In the third play-within-a-play, Daniel's version of the passion, we reach the profoundest level of theatrical mimesis, and grasp, through the illusion, the

power of theater to teach, influence, and reform while seeming
to be "reality." The real messages emerge without the taint of
commercial or manipulative intent. The diagram below shows
how many levels of "reality" — how many illusions of reality — we
experience through this film.

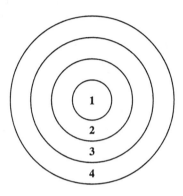

1 Daniel's mystery play in which actors (Bluteau)
  are playing actors (Daniel) playing roles (Jesus).

2 Spectators at D's play; Actors within Arcand's
  film.

3 "Reality" of actors and other Québécois' lives;
  actors playing real Montréalais of today.

4 External spectators (us) watching play and
  also several plays - within - plays.

The outer and inner realities (illusions) tend to overlap and to
become blurred. We are, complexly, spectators of the external
play regarding contemporary *Montréal*, spectators of the video of
the early, crude pageant play, spectators of the spectator Daniel in
this last instance; we are also spectators of all the commercials
being made; we are spectators of the spectators at Daniel's play
who themselves have complex identities both as actors and as
spectators; we are, of course, ourselves spectators of Daniel's play,
the mystery play at *Jerusalem* — a play soon to be censored — as we
also were of the film-within-a-film about the creation of the universe,
of the first play-within-a-play featuring the soon to be corrupted
Pascal, and of the video of the "bad pageant." Reality and illusion
are so blurred in Daniel's performance that in one instance a
Haitian woman spectator — an actress, in reality — takes the story
for real and intrudes upon the action. (Note she, like others,
represents the "foreign" element — the Other — in Québec today.

We shall return to this issue later on in our discussion of *Jésus de Montréal*; it will also be the subject of my Chapter 7.)

It is around this schema that the multiple warring stimuli that accost us daily are "organized." As Arcand says in the preface to his *scénario*: "I wanted to make a film full of rupture ... in the image of life around us, exploded, banal, contradictory. A little like the supermarkets in which one can find on a ten-meter shelf novels of Dostoevsky, toilet waters, the Bible, porno videocassettes, the work of Shakespeare, photos of the Earth taken from the Moon, astrological predictions, and posters of actors or of *Jesus* ...."[64] Yet the film is organized concentrically around these conflicting realities. And the characters, too, reflect these realities.

Weinmann has identified the character Pascal with Mammon; with Lucifer (1990, 190; 192; 207). But is he not, rather, the forerunner (*avant-coureur*), the one who came before, John the Baptiser, a shepherd (Pascal's last name is Berger!) dressed in beasts' skins ("l'Homme sauvage"), who said he was not to be confused with the true prophet, Jesus, who was to come after him, and whose sandal-laces he was not worthy of tying? (So Pascal tells Garibaldi and Miroir that not he but Daniel is the "real, or the good actor.") Certainly it would be unlikely that John the Baptist would be excluded from this story, for the Quebeckers have a special devotion to him, as we have noted at various junctures in this book. It will be remembered that the fête de St. Jean is Québec's national holiday.

Iconographically one sees the Baptist pointing to the (Pascal) lamb and saying, as does the priest at mass: "Ecce, Agnus Dei," or "Behold the lamb of God." John himself is often shown with lambs, since he tended them; and, moreover, he is not unlike the Pascal lamb, Jesus, through his martyrdom. And Arcand's Pascal is referred to as the "médiateur." Moreover, Denise Quintal, the publicity director, says of him, "I want his head" (to advertise "l'Homme sauvage"). She is equivalent to Hérodias/Salomé; and indeed, at the end, as Daniel, speaking of apocalypse and the final judgment, goes down into the metro station (hell, the underworld), the "head" of Pascal/Baptist is seen on a large ad, behind the figure of Daniel. The Baptist would have been in hell when the harrowing occurred. One may suggest this reading, for the real Satan of the play is Richard Cardinal (whose name gives us an ironic reversal); he is the one who tempts Daniel. (Viewed another way, there is a touch of Satan in all the characters, other than Daniel, who represents purity and integrity. The little children [Rosalie] readily come unto him.)

Among other Biblical figures and scenes, Joseph of Arimathea appears to be represented in the ambulance driver[65] who takes the injured Daniel to the crowded hospital emergency ward. It is true — in the *scénario*, at least — that, as Weinmann says, the ward's lack of a blanket to cover Daniel speaks to the miserable state of care provided in most emergency rooms of North American hospitals (1990, 235); but after all, in the New Testament, Jesus came into the world nude and without a home — Daniel is alone, without a biological family, and seemingly left exposed and abandoned. (He says at one point, like Christ on the cross, "My father abandoned me.") Jesus went out of the world nude and without a tomb of his own. Joseph of Arimathea provided the wherewithal for his burial. The donation of the blanket from the ambulance — a winding sheet, if you will — replicates this situation. (In addition, the ambulance driver "carries" the body, as did Joseph of Arimathea.) At several points in the film one sees such allusions: not only to the statement of Jesus that "I was naked, and you clothed me," which is suggested in the ambulance driver's gesture, but also to the statement that "I was hungry and you fed me," which is realized in Arcand's *scénario* by the donation of pizza (on credit) by the "immigrant" Italian restaurateur.[66] The Good Samaritan appears more than once in

Jésus de Montréal. Photograph by Pierre d'Aillon. (Courtesy Coll. Cinémathèque Québécoise.)

this film. Constance herself takes the homeless in; soup kitchens are depicted, etc. But in the final version of the film, the Italian pizza vendor is omitted; instead the group eats a pizza supper together at a table in an unspecified location, with Daniel bringing out the bottle of wine, while much later in the film they are seen having their "last supper" together in the form of a picnic of pizza and wine consumed on the lawn near the oratory.

Similarly, the washing of Daniel's body by Mireille compares to Mary Magdalene's anointing of Jesus' feet with oils and perfumes — a deed Jesus sanctioned. Arcand has blurred the figures of Mary, the Mother of Jesus, and Mary Magdalene; he is giving us the spirit, not the replication. Therefore, the pietà is replaced with a scene where Mireille, not Constance, takes the head of Daniel onto her knees.[67] Mireille takes on something of the character or attributes of Mary, Mother of Jesus, elsewhere, for her last name suggests Mary, Fountain of Grace; and she "yields" to the spirit — the Holy Spirit — when she pinches the buttocks of the man wearing Esprit #7 perfume. This would represent a reduction of the fiat, of course. The function of Mireille's veils is not clear. This may allude to any Biblical woman, of course; veils in the Catholic Church bespeak virginity, but they also suggest Salomé, more clearly embodied in the figure of Denise. Mireille, then, takes on an ambiguity, standing for both Mary, Mother of Jesus, and Mary Magdelene. Put another way, the virgin-whore split of traditional Western representation (described by Kaplan[68]) is reintegrated into a single image in her.

After the storm that accompanies Daniel's death (as one did when Jesus gave up the ghost) comes the eucharistic sacrifice of Daniel-Jesus. It seems quite complete: his flesh is given through his body parts (heart and eyes, if not more) and his blood too seems to have been collected for "distribution." As Dr. Rosen at the Jewish Hospital where Daniel is finally received, but too late, says, it is "type O; a godsend" (!). That is, this (eucharistic) blood, sent through the Holy Spirit, is rare and saving. In this way, Daniel's death profits humanity. The "gift" may seem encumbered, however, by the fact that Daniel does not donate his body parts of his own volition. The gift is solicited by the doctor; the two girls, friends of Daniel, consent. It is to be assumed, however, that they act as Daniel would have, had he been conscious. (We will return to this issue in a moment.) Thus, Daniel as donor provides the parts (Orphic at that), which are given out to all, much as if he were Savior of the world. He is like Christ, who commanded apostolic propagation, as he also cautioned that he must be consumed with salvitic purpose. (But does the global nature of the recipients also suggest a Québec devoured by Others?)

Within the framework of Daniel's passion, and of the passion within the passion, we are able to see the corruption of society and its reactions to Daniel-Jesus. In a scene that occurs at the top of a skyscraper and replicates Satan's temptation of Christ on the mountain, Cardinal wants to tempt Daniel and his troupe with money, fame, and power. For a moment they are seduced by his values, and, like Jean Lévesque in *The Tin Flute*, like Balzac's Rastignac even, or like Celeste in *Les Portes tournantes*, they stand above the city dreaming of domination. But in this case, the characters do not give in. It is obvious that, like literature, film can simultaneously portray the ills and poisons of the society, and still propose medicine, a cure — as is the nature of a pharmakon (Weinmann; Brunette & Wills). *Jésus de Montréal* offers such binary opposites for the viewer's consideration.

Hypocrisy of the Church-on-earth is present here, largely shown through Leclerc, whose name, like that of others, means and stands for what he represents (the clergy). Through Leclerc, the old adage, "Hors de l'Eglise, point de salut," or, "Outside the Church, no salvation," is subverted. Rather, Arcand seems to be saying: "Dedans l'église point de salut [Inside the Church there can be no salvation]." Leclerc likes to be comfortable, i.e., to have all the creature comforts at his fingertips. He wants to compromise. As for the two other "witnesses," they too stand as pharisees. The intentional allegory wrapped in Leclerc's name is replicated elsewhere, of course, by such names as Fameuse, Célebre, Constance, un juge: this is substantially one of the procedures of the early mystery play.

We ought of course to insist that Daniel's anger at the philistines and his chastening of the commercial exploitation of human talent and body, as well as his clear attack on the clergy, not only present his own milieu, but also replicate rabbinical corruption in the times of Jesus. (Daniel's preaching to them — in the exterior, his audience — from the interior of his play is based on Matthew 23). Daniel's destruction of the recording studio recalls, of course, Christ's cleansing of the temple, by his expulsion of the money-lenders; but this, like Daniel's statements regarding the clergy, is also aimed at contemporary conditions in society.

For the fact remains that the person who would go to this film unequipped would not realize the extent to which the Montréal society is being criticized. From his early career on, Arcand has been speaking for the underdog. As we have already seen, in his "colossal" *On est au coton* (1970) he had highlighted the phenomenon of the closing of textile mills, while showing the daily life of workers in that industry, and had portrayed the struggles of and the strikes conducted by these workers, in their effort to get out of their situation. This film brought censorship and bitter debates.[69] But it is perhaps useful to point out to those who consider Arcand subversive that he claims in an interview with Gerald Godin that *On est au coton* was didactic for all: that the workers, that indeed everyone learned about Madeleine Parent; that it was a history lesson, too, in former beatings by the police; but that it was also a critique of the left, which speaks of the working class without knowing the degree of its alienation. Arcand adds that sometimes the leftists irritate him more than "management."[70]

Corruption in the Québec construction business had been the subject of his 1973 film *Réjeanne Padovani*, in which he criticized pork-barreling and other abuses of political figures and businessmen. Again in *Gina* (1974–75), Arcand attacked the textile mills, using the format of a film-within-a-film. Here Arcand shows the rape of a visiting stripteaser who performs in the motel of a small town, where a group of filmmakers (whose leader is played by Gabriel Arcand) have come to make a documentary on the local textile industry. The perpetrators are punished by her pimp. This film, while it attacked working conditions in a textile mill, also showed hapless dancers sent to the four corners of the province. For Houle, *Gina* synesthetically leaves a bitter taste in the mind, and Arcand's humor is barely present, if at all (1978, 5). For his trouble, Arcand saw this film undergo censorship.

We have seen that *Le Déclin de l'empire américain* is a general and universal satire of *québécois*/Western morality (or lack thereof) in the late twentieth century. In *Jésus de Montréal*, the social commentary continues. It embraces the media, whose representatives — Garibaldi, Miroir, Malouin, etc. — are caricatures of real Québécois "stars." Also under attack are the hospital system (on overload); the legal system (also on overload); the clergy (hypocritical and bound to creature comforts); the decay of institutions; the difficulties of bilingualism (the English-speaking hospital to which Daniel's friends must take him); and that is not all. Indeed, so extensive are the local references, and so important is Montréal as *a* if not *the* "main character" of the movie, that some critics have been inclined to see in this the possible explanation as to why this film did not take in Paris, as *Le Déclin* ... had done. (I would be inclined to think, however, that the apparent subject matter had something to do with this.) The film is so localized, on one level, that one may assert with confidence that Daniel himself incarnates not only Jesus but also Québec. On another level, it deals with a historical event — the life of Jesus — while at the same time showing the application of the history to present-day life in Québec, or of any place in the "developed" world of the twentieth century. In this, it restates the relationship between history (the Roman empire) and the contemporary scene (America), already asserted in *Le Déclin* .... The film also adumbrates the epistemological problems of telling history. Scholars differ on the exact date of the crucifixion: our knowledge of Jesus is sketchy. Even in contemporary, eye-witness reporting there is flagrant contradiction.

However, it seems that the profound message of *Jésus de Montréal* could not escape any sensitive viewer. And that message is that we should not and we cannot — but we do — undermine charity and true artistry. And that we must come to know the true from the false. We cannot be like Pontius Pilate (in the film, *un juge*, played by Denys Arcand himself): we cannot stare truth in the face while asking what is true. Justice and its systems stand on trial here, as they did in the times of Christ. Can we really have our "rights" read to us? And, by the way, the insertion of the reading of the rights (Miranda) seems somewhat peculiar in a Canadian film; was this for the satisfaction of a larger, international, or at least American, audience? Or something Arcand endorses? I have seen a policeman on CBC television speaking of having read rights to a suspect; but according to Chris Braiden, 'Nothing in the law requires that the police issue a warning about the rights of a suspect to remain silent before he or she is interrogated. Nor does the law oblige the police to prepare a thorough and reliable record of an interrogation, although both these issues are addressed in a recent working paper by the *Law Reform Commission of Canada*. If, in a judge's view, a suspect's rights have been violated in the process of gathering evidence, the admission of such evidence must be disallowed."[71]

One may also assert that Arcand prolongs the socio-critical intent traditional in *québécois* film but known, too, to early French and American cinema. Has he perchance passed through the sieve of D. W. Griffith, who in 1916 made *Intolerance*, the first few sequences of which concern the savage repression of strike, the third part of which concerns the Passion of Christ? Certainly, too, Arcand continues to embrace that "documentary style" characteristic of early film, and found not only in American, or *québécois*, but also in French movies—for example in Jules Dassin's *Du Rififi* (1955).

There are doubtless further messages of fraternity and ecumenism in *Jésus de Montréal*. Weinmann, himself an immigrant, sees Arcand calling upon the Québécois to be more open unto the world, more willing to accept the immigrant and assimilate him or her to their traditional died-in-the-wool, blood brother kind of provincialism. The film also invites the Québécois to accept with greater tolerance the marginal or the fringe elements (that Daniel and his friends seem to represent) into this closed society. It will be recalled that, according to Weinmann, this closed society is one of the themes of *Les Portes tournantes*. In any event, one may suppose that the film conveys the idea that a man of good faith, of good will, taken by the example of Jesus, can very well "follow in his footsteps," rejecting Mammon, and leading a life of charity and selflessness. Some see this as a socio-political signal meant intrinsically for the Québécois. Weinmann, for example, states that the film seeks to purge Québec of its egoism, its narcissism, its ethnocentric sufficiencies, and to push it to charity, to the hospitality and openness to the Other that it once practiced in its colonial days, when Montréal was called Ville-Marie, or Mary's City (Weinmann, 1990, 255).

One should not, however, look for ascensions, or resurrections (although the heart of Daniel does "*ascend*" in a plane as it is being flown to Mr. Rigby). One should not look for the *merveilleux chrétien*, for Arcand is telling the story of a man and his brush with the mystery of Jesus through a contagion of faith, emanating from his role as an actor, and passed on to his intimates. Had the director shown us Daniel going up through the sky toward pink clouds, saying "Lo, I am with you always, even until the end of the world," with heavenly choruses singing in the background, we would have said "ho-hum; this is yawn and sleepy time." Such an "ending" would have caused the film to *descend* into the maudlin, the pious, the syrupy, even into the realms of incredulity—CBN style. The solution of a lesser artist.

There can really be no missing the core meaning that informs all facets of this film. Lying, hypocrisy, jealousy, and wastefulness are forms of narcissism bent on protecting or projecting the ego. They incline to power play, and spell forms of corruption and unlove (acerbically displayed in *Le Déclin* ...). It is love only, love of Other that can redeem this world and save it from itself, its pollution, its corruption. Daniel as an avatar of Jesus and as a Christian (*tout net, tout nu*) is called to give from the deepest self, from the center of self (as preached by St. Matthew and also by St. Paul). And this Daniel does, 'giving' his very heart, first as a legacy to Constance and Mireille, who then in turn are called upon (by a Jew, no less!) to share that heart, that love; to give that love up, or at least to give it over. We are talking of the literal and figurative heart of Daniel, the (sacred) heart of Jesus, flesh, blood, and spirit. Through sacrifice and renunciation, through the esoteric, centripetal Christ that resides in the inner self, and through love of that self — and yet, paradoxically, also through the eccentric, centrifugal Christ of love (i.e., of service and outreach) — Québec/the world may yet continue, but now on a new and better course. These are the "delicate and sublime acts of the Holy Spirit," left behind by Christ to function for the world after his crucifixion, death, resurrection, and ascension. The world, yes, for the Central Mountain of the vision (quest), the Holy Place, the Holy Land is, as Black Elk said, "everywhere." And Daniel knows this.

Arcand, in the long run, never said anything different, from his earliest work on. Only here he said it better and more fully than ever before. If some are "offended" by Arcand's transposition, transsubstantation (as they were by Scorsese's *Last Temptation of Christ*), being happy only with the passion plays of Oberammergau or Spearfish, or with the Las Vegas school of Biblical dramas such as *Solomon and Sheba* — starring Gina Lollobrigida! — or with Franco Zeffirelli's *Jesus of Nazareth* (great though it was), then they have forgotten, or never knew, St. John of the Cross's assertion that "there are many ways in which God awakens in the soul: so many that, if we had to begin to enumerate them, we should never end."[72] Such viewers are perhaps to be likened to the Judas of *Jesus Christ, Superstar*, who painfully but truthfully laments, "I don't know how to love Him." Daniel did, even through the dark night of the soul he underwent (as had Aurore so long ago). Of this there can be no doubt.

Garrity sees the film as continuing in a subversive tradition characteristic of *québécois* film in general.[73] Whether he is right or not is a matter of point of view. For me the film is not necessarily "subversive," except as one might so label its clear criticism of several aspects of Québec society. This would include its bureaucracy, the difficulty of getting treatment in a Montréal hospital,[74] the inefficiency of the system of justice, the worldliness of the clergy.[75] As I said, this criticism has always been evident in Arcand's films, from *On est au coton* to the present.

Arcand sets the Christian mythology in a modern perspective, forces it to blend with "what we know," since he obviously perceives, with Joseph Campbell, that mythology must keep up with knowledge if it is to put us in harmony with the universe.

For all its beauty, this film has not drawn the international audiences to the extent that *Le Déclin ...* managed to do. *Jésus de Montréal* has been less talked about in the United States, and it has not been a success in France, having drawn only one hundred thousand viewers by March, 1991. Olivier Lefebure du Bus sees the arguments raised by Scorsese's controversial *Last Temptation of Christ* as a contributing factor in this poor reception.[76] A somewhat farfetched explanation, it seems to me; one is not kept from one film from one country and director by the work of another director from another country, is one? But is the story line just a bit on the arcane side? Are the principals too deviant? The establishment figures too unilateral, too stereotypical? Are most Frenchmen too far removed from any interest in Jesus? And if *Jésus de Montréal* contains the strong criticism of *québécois* society that Weinmann claims it to have, does it remain, for some persons, too localized? Is there a simple answer to the question of reception, lying in the unattractiveness of the title, as Emile Talbot has suggested in a conversation with me? (For who is drawn to see a film called *"Jesus of Montreal"*?) In addition, and as with many other *québécois* films, such as *Mon oncle Antoine* and *Les Bons Débarras*, the deep structures of *Jésus de Montréal* are not readily apprehended; this is at once their greatness and their shortcoming for the one time or the uninformed viewer.

Regardless of reception, a word here about the performance of Lothaire Bluteau is certainly in order. This young man, whom we encountered playing bit parts in *Rien qu'un jeu* and in *Les Années de rêve*, starred in *Les Fous de Bassan* as the mentally retarded Perceval, his first great role. His performance here in *Jésus de Montréal* carries out the promise of that tour de force. Marcel Jean (in Coulombe 1991, 55) maintains that the fragility of Bluteau and the interiorization of his acting give to Perceval [in *Les Fous ...*] an impressive dimension that surpasses the person in Hébert's story. Whether Perceval is important, even indispensable, to the story of *Les Fous ...*, or not, may be debated; but the importance of Daniel/Christ to "the story" of *Jésus de Montréal* may not; and here in *Jésus de Montréal* we observe that same fragility and that same internalized acting that gives this film (as well as *Les Fous ...*) its special quality, a quality that conveys a very real sense of pain and suffering, not to mention an ethereal and compelling presence.

Bluteau, by the way, has more recently appeared as the saintly priest, Father Laforgue, in Bruce Beresford's *Robe noire* (1991; 100 minutes), based on the 1985 novel of Brian Moore, who also wrote the screenplay. Filmed in the unspoiled reaches of the Saguenay River, which substitutes for the St. Lawrence as it was 350 years ago, this film concerns the relationships between the Jesuits and the Huron nation and, according to Vincent Canby, it surpasses in profundity the "over-decorated, pumped-up boy's adventure yarn [of such a film as] *Dances with Wolves*."[77] *Black Robe*, which was the opening film of the 1991 Toronto [Film] Festival of Festivals, has also been discussed at some length by Terrence Rafferty. He finds Bluteau's performance the weakest aspect of a film he otherwise admires![78] Other (copycat?) reviews as well fault Bluteau's acting in this film as not being sufficiently interiorized. I agree in no way with such an indictment, having found his realization of the tormented Jesuit father completely convincing. It is, incidentally, also of some interest to note here that Yves Simoneau, whom we have discussed in connection with *Les Fous de Bassan, Dans le ventre du dragon, Pouvoir intime*, etc., spent considerable time attempting to prepare an adaptation of Brian Moore's *Black Robe* for the producer Denis Héroux, without coming to terms with the project.

Finally, the question of *Jésus de Montréal*'s tone arises. When this film was presented to a group of professors at a 1991 CIEF meeting in Tucson, there was a lot of laughter at times when this did not seem the proper response. (There is quite a bit of intentional humor present, of course, such as the video of the past enactment of Leclerc's passion-pageant, or René's misplaced insertion of Hamlet's monologue into the script of the passion—even though it curiously enough seems to fit, under scrutiny.) One can never account for the reactions of a given audience, each audience being made up of its own special chemistry. But while the video scenes of the crude ur-pageant ought to evoke laughter in any audience, the temptation scene with Cardinal in the skyscraper (on the mountain) should not, it seems to me; nor should the frames showing Daniel's arrest as he hangs upon the cross (though when a policeman realizes he is missing a form, there is irony in his exclamation: "Christ, I forgot!"). What provokes this laughter? An awkwardness on the part of the actors? Assumed cases of black humor such as we find in *Le Déclin* ...? These mixtures of tone—the high and the low—would, then, be a part of the film's postmodern aura, proposed by Weinmann and others. It *is* postmodern by this ambiguity of tone, and the multiplicity of its ranges [high/low; old/new; comic/tragic]; it is also so by its seemingly unstitched, unfinished quality, including its lack of a clear point of view. But do we not also have here an inability on the part of the audience to contextualize these events either historically or contemporaneously? An incapacity to see the multifaceted and nuanced flavor of the film? This univocal view of the film is reflected in the following quote from the *American Video Review*: "Told with humor, verve, and irony, this is a surprisingly sprightly comedy-drama, a wittily observant look at modern life with virtually none of the sober touches associated with the religious or moral tales of French director Robert Bresson. We always know where *Jesus of Montreal* is going, and it arrives with charm."[79] The moralizing Arcand seems to be overlooked in this simplistic assessment of what may well be a pivotal Québec film. But Paul Salmon gives a more balanced assessment when he says that the film "is an impassioned exploration of the spiritual exhaustion and artificiality of the modern age and of the urgent human need for spiritual fulfillment and sincere artistic expression. In a rich blend of social realism and religious allegory, Arcand has woven a modern-day parable susceptible to interpretation on many levels. Thematically and stylistically, the film succeeds in integrating a serious social critique, poignant human drama, sophisticated humor, and a wealth of rich allusions to the history of Western culture."[80]

Whatever the answer to these questions about audience reception, and in spite of its over-fast editing, *Jésus de Montréal* is a work of art, both through its rich text that works on many levels (politically, socially, locally, globally, poetically) and its beautiful photography. Certain of the scenes as they flashed before my eyes (especially some of the early ones) reminded me of many of the stained glass windows I have seen throughout my life — in France, in Québec, in the United States — as, I suppose, have Arcand and Guy Dufaux. Some theatergoers were especially touched by Yves Laferrière's music.

Marie Naudin, who views *Le Déclin* ... and *Jésus* ... as post-modern films (though in reality they also criticize the postmodern condition), captures the true tone of these two films, which, while they provoke laughter, nevertheless portray persons who are on the lookout for their individual happiness, and who pursue a hedonism that is fragile. She writes: "The precariousness [of an equilbrium "achieved" in the life of the hedonist] is signalled in *Le Déclin* ..., [a film] in which children are almost totally absent and considered as impediments, and in which the duration of love in all its fullness seems reduced to two years; in which the enjoyment of one's comfort is, at bottom, only a route taken by those who feel incapable of bringing off an important work, or — as in *Jésus* ... — for those who are afraid of losing what little they have acquired. In fact, this postmodernity when fully lived and felt by the Montréal intelligentsia joins forces with the malaise that inhabits Western society and constitutes a sort of dance on a volcano, a smile masking a troubled anxiety."[81]

Yes, that is the nature of Arcand the moralist's black "humor." Paradoxical because for many *Jésus* ... is a scathing social critique of Québec; for some little more than humorous; but for a few this film may well be (like *King Lear*) a story of the rebirth of Christianity against a pagan background. Paradoxical, and for some, at times, even cynical.[82] These are ranges of interpretation that in and of themselves bespeak the postmodern nature of the film. Equally so is Arcand's *De l'amour et des restes humaines*, a work whose *scénario* is adapted from the Brad Fraser play about a Canadian serial killer. Ironically Arcand selected to release this film as an entry in the Toronto (Film) Festival of Festivals (beginning 9 September 1993), rather than to run it at the virtually simultaneous Montréal Cinéfest, or 17th World Film Festival (beginning 26 August 1993).[83]

Conclusion to Chapter 6

In the course of this chapter, we have been able to see the extent to which the contemporary Québec cinema reflects at once the *québécoise* society in its institutions, and the condition of modern Western man. Crime in relationship to law and justice is a subject of choice. And, too, the issues of political turmoil as they pertain to the struggle that the francophone Québécois have mounted against the forces of anglophone exploitation and monopoly for now two hundred years are extensively explored. We have also been able to appreciate the power of Catholic dogma and clerical authority in the lives of the Québécois as reflected in their films, and to see both the waning of that power and the possible refiring of religion, or at least spirituality, in Québec civilization, this time perhaps with less faith in the Catholic Church as a source of absolute guidance in the formation of the national conscience.

The films we have examined, both in this chapter and in those preceding, have often shown the Québec society as somewhat closed, and the francophone Québécois as somewhat intransigent with respect to the admission of people of other nationalities who were not born speaking French, i.e., who are not "*pure laine*."

Upon occasion a film is made that either calls for an opening up of that society, or else seems to be intent upon reflecting what is the ultimate reality of that society: I mean its multicultural nature. It is especially in the children's films of Rubbo, Melançon, et al., that we have been able to apprehend this appreciation for multiculturalism and a message of antiracism. But the fact remains that in many works of animation, widely seen by the public, the filmmakers not only embrace these ideals, but are themselves of many nationalities. And the fact also remains that this multiplicity of nationalities is characteristic of many of the younger directors of recent documentaries and films of fiction: they, of course, are particularly bent upon reflecting their own ethnicities and the complexity of present-day Québec society in general. These characteristics will form the basis of discussion for my final chapter.

7

Other Voices — Voices of the Other

(Films by and about Québec's Anglophones and Other Minorities)

On the subject of the Other, the Outsider in Québec society — whose *pure laine* citizens have historically had a certain antipathy for the immigrant, and borne as their motto "Le Québec aux Québécois" — one will gain a good appreciation by reading Mordecai Richler's witty piece, "Inside/Outside."[1] Here one grasps the anti-Semitic flavor of Québec nationalism. We saw this at work in the first chapter of this book with the doctrines of the Church as promulgated through L'Action Catholique founded by l'Abbé Lionel Groulx, who held the Church to be against film and its putative evils emanating from foreign influences (American) and Jewish business interests. But Richler also traces the whole recent history of the antianglophone, *indépendantiste* movements, and the frustrations coming from the failure of the Meech Lake accord. We see the Outremont population of Québec in rebellion at finding the Hassidic population, once negligible, to have grown to such a degree that it asked for rezoning in order to construct a temple. It was denied. Some argue(d) they were not against Jews in general, but against the anglophone Jews, never mind the point that most Jews in Montréal are — almost *de rigueur* — anglophone, and many have now quit the city. Some francophone Sephardic Jews have, however, immigrated from North Africa in more recent times, thus replenishing the city's Jewish community. As we shall see, both communities are portrayed in Québec cinema.

In the course of this book, we have occasionally touched on some aspects of the minority life pictured in the Québec film. We have also dealt with a few English-language political dramas and documentaries—for example, *Action: The October Crisis of 1970* and *Reaction*. We have looked as well at a few children's movies of importance made by anglophone directors. And, space permitting, we might well have spoken not only of many French-Canadian but also of important anglophone Québécois animation experts, such as Eve Lambart, and of the many immigrants working at the ONF as animators, including the Belgian Frédéric Back, the American-born Caroline Leaf and Lynn Smith, and German-born Lotte Reiniger, the creator of the world's first full-length animated film in 1923—24, and of the beautiful animated silhouettes she uses in her *Aucassin et Nicolette* (1975; 15 min., 39 sec.) and in other works. We would also have included in such a treatment Viviane Elnécavé, an Egyptian-born artist who is famous for her work with the ONF, in particular *Luna, Luna, Luna* (1981), which took prizes in Zagreb and Lausanne. (See Coulombe [1991, 173] for further information and a still.)

In this chapter, however, we will focus in on Québec cinema in the light of alterity, while bearing in mind that any examination of provincial cinema and cinema about the province would have to include some of the most famous of anglophone *québécois* films, including documentaries both in French and in English about Québec and the world and about minority populations living in Québec, and it would also embrace certain works by anglophone feminists. As we approach this subject, it is well for the reader to keep in mind the concept of the traditional Québécois *pure laine* as somewhat closed to the world and unreceptive of the immigrant, for many of the films we are looking at here reflect this social dynamic. The NFB's documentarist John Howe's *Strangers at the Door* (25 min., 2 sec.) translates these problems into a strong, half-hour documentary. It tells how Jan Laluckey and his family, after making a hard journey to the New World, arrive in Québec full of hope for a new and better life. But the immigration officials refuse to permit Kasia, Jan's daughter, to land, since, during the routine medical exam, she is found to have an infectious eye disease. She is sent back home alone. The story is repeated ad infinitum in the immigrant-oriented film; a rather similar *scénario* is shown, for example, in musical (comedy) style in certain segments of *Caffè Italia*, which we will be examining in due course.

The forms that these anglophone films take is as varied as the Québec francophone film: we have experimental film; documentaries and films of fiction by women about women's concerns; general social, historical, and political documentaries by anglophone filmmakers; documentaries and long fiction films about the Jewish,

Italian, Latin-American, and Native Canadian communities; and so forth. We also have fictional anglophone films from Québec that are entertainment oriented, and do not necessarily seek to expose some social truth about the province or about Canada.[2]

EXPERIMENTAL FILMS

Coulombe in his list of film credits cites several experimental films from the anglophone community, including *The Cage* (1972; d. Vartkes Cholakian & Richard Ciupka), *The Divine Right* (1985; d. Richard Raxlen), and *End Game in Paris* (1982; d. Veronica Soul).

Vartkes Cholakian was born in Syria, and worked in the United States before going to Toronto, and then finally to Québec, where he lived from 1972 to 1980. At that time he made *Nora* and *Nora in the Park* (1973), as well as *The Cage* (1972; with Richard Ciupka) and *The Basement* (1974), the last two being films that explore alienation and psychosis *à la* Kafka. We might mention, too, his coproduced *Rappelle-toi* (with Mireille Dansereau, 1975), which portrays a character, played by Luce Guilbeault, who cannot bring her past into harmony with her present. He has also made *A Simple Complex* (1978). His work, says Michel Larouche (Coulombe 1991, 97), is experimental, very personal, and of considerable aesthetic quality; but unfortunately it remains unknown and misunderstood.

The Divine Right was based on *The Golden Bough* (J. Frazer). Michel Larouche states that *The Divine Right* — unlike Raxlen's earlier work — has a narrator, who "tells a story," and that this film was made from an earlier video that had the same title. In 1988 Raxlen made *Horses in Winter*, about his childhood; the narrative structure of the film is built around perceptions of childhood that are strung together. Larouche concludes: "The work of Raxlen gives off a profound poetry, very much tied to new perceptions made possible by experimentation. It is also very interesting for the study of *métissages* (crossings) that come from the encounter of cinema with video, and which are determinants for the understanding of new images" (Coulombe 1991, 462).

It is again Michel Larouche who comments on Veronica (or Veronika) Soul (Coulombe 1991, 501–2), telling us that she was born in Baltimore (U.S.) in 1944 and went to Québec in 1971, at the age of twenty-seven. Her prowess, clear in her first film — *How the Hell Are You?* — involves mixing techniques (collages, designs, or drawings on film, etc.), and a minimum of material: a few photographs, a few maps, and some excerpts of letters written by a homosexual. With Caroline Leaf she codirected a film entitled *Interview* (1979), a documentary portrait of two women filmmakers. In 1982 she made *End Game in Paris*, the adaptation of a portion of Ian Adams's novel by the same name, in which the idea of the double is explored. Imagination and memory play important roles in this film. The images are complemented by a complex sound track, which gives a rich texture to the film. (Her independent films are part of the film collection of the National Gallery of Canada and the Ontario Art Gallery.)

Pratley speaks of no one of the three films credited in Coulombe; Clanfield does not mention Cholakian or Raxlen, but he does mention the collaboration of Soul with Caroline Leaf on *Interview*, telling us that in this film each filmmaker embarked on an exploration of the other. Clanfield also speaks of Joyce Borenstein's *The Plant*, codirected with Thomas Vamos, in which a man takes a plant from the snow into his home, with startling results. This film is entered as a French-language animated film (1983; 13 min.) in Coulombe (1991, 586).

ANGLOPHONE FEMINIST CINEMA

Mention of Caroline Leaf and Joyce Borenstein evokes the whole spectrum of anglophone feminist cinema, which is such an important aspect of the Québec film industry. Outstanding among these women directors is American-born Bonnie Sherr Klein.

Klein, who obtained a degree from Stanford, filmed the United Farm Workers first strike under Cesar Chavez while she was still in the United States. In 1967 she joined the National Film Board's program, Challenge for Change, for which she directed several socially-oriented films in the 60s and 70s. She returned to the United States for a time and then, in 1975, returned to Montréal, where she worked in the NFB's English studio for women. Here she made *Patricia's Moving Picture*, about a woman who, after having been married and having raised seven children, undergoes a personal crisis, in her longing for freedom and independence. In 1979 she made *The Right Candidate for Rosedale*, dealing with the campaign of the liberal Anne Cools. Then in 1981 came *Not a Love Story — A Film about Pornography*, one of the most successful productions in the history of the NFB, partially because the view of pornography taken in the film raised a controversy. Klein builds the film (produced by Dorothy Todd-Hénaut, whom I spoke of in Chapter 3) around the former *effeuilleuse* (stripteaser), Linda Lee

Tracey, who gives the viewer a guided tour through pornographic spots, funneled through director Klein. As Klein explores with Tracey the world of peep shows, strip joints, and sex supermarkets, the two attempt to determine why pornography exists, what forms it can take, and how it affects intersexual relations. Both those who earn their living through the porn trade and those who criticize it are featured. In this often explicit and disturbing film, Klein appeals first to the emotions, notably when she bombards the spectator with aggressive images, then to the mind, by proposing a reflection on the impact of pornography. The film marked an important moment in feminist cinematography; it was very successful with the public, and forced the feminist movement to deepen its reflection on pornography. *Not a Love Story* ... took an award in Barcelona. (Diane Poitras writes on Todd-Hénaut in Coulombe 1991, 522–23; Mary Alemany-Galway on Klein, in Coulombe 1991, 286.)

Klein resumed the same formula in *Speaking Our Peace* (1985, with Terri Nash), a film for world peace. This is an hour-long documentary filmed in Canada, Britain, and the USSR. Featured in the film are Rosalie Bertell, Marion Dewar, Muriel Duckworth, Ursula M. Franklin, Darlene Keju, Margaret Laurence, Solanges Vincent, and Kathleen Wallace-Deering. These women interview Russian women, and exchange views on war and peace with them. Included are scenes of women in mass demonstrations in Canada and England, and footage of ordinary citizens confronted with health and environmental problems caused by arms buildups and testings. (The film took an award at Walnut Creek.) In 1986, Klein made three films on the same subject.

Pratley points out that the film *Not a Love Story* ... is peculiarly more about pornography in New York City than in Canada. He goes on to say that "because it was made by women film-makers ... and reflects the feminine point of view, it received well-deserved support. However, male critics who found the film lacking were severely castigated by women's groups and individuals for not being sympathetic to the way women feel and for exhibiting feelings of male superiority. The film was banned from commercial exhibition in Ontario" (*TS* 1987, 134).

As important as *Not a Love Story* ... is Gail Singer's *Abortion: Stories from North and South (1984; 55 min.)*. Singer works for the NFB, Studio D, for which she has also made the films *Loved, Honoured and Bruised* and *Portrait of the Artist—as an Old Lady* (1982). *Abortion* ... (1984), which might be compared with the work of Anne Claire Poirier on the same subject—especially for its picture of a generalized problem—is also presented by the NFB in

French. Filmed in Ireland, Thailand, Peru, Colombia, and Canada, the film reveals how abortion transcends race, religion, and social classes. Women from all walks of life and of many nationalities seize the opportunity to make their position known. The film not surprisingly calls for safe medical procedures to be set at women's disposal. *Loved, Honoured and Bruised*, about the battered woman, has, among other things, extraordinary self-justifying testimony by an abusive husband, while *Portrait* ... is nothing if not charming.

On the other hand, native-born Québécoise Helen Doyle's *Scars of Memory* or *Tatouages de la Mémoire* (1984; 23 minutes) is a lyrical spiritual piece. Although a video—a format I have for the most part omitted from this study—I include it here because of its subject matter, and because Doyle, as a cofounder of Video Femmes in Québec, is a foremost Canadian video artist, vitally concerned with social and political issues. *Scars* ... deals with the layers of memory, stripping them away to reveal the core of Sarah, the main character in the tape. The director describes the film as being an intimate voyage of discovery verging on the indecent ... an invitation to the fantasies of a world outlined in myth and colored in dreams. Doyle is discussed in *Cinéma au féminin*,[3] where it is stated that she was born in Québec in 1950, and where her work *Le Rêve de voler* (1986) is analyzed; it is a two-part film concerned with the trapeze artist's *métier*. Doyle is discussed as well by Jeanne Painchaud in Coulombe (1991, 159); there her contribution to cinema is brought out; in 1981 she codirected with Nicole Giguère *C'est pas le pays des merveilles* (1981), a documentary-fiction on cultural factors that cause women to go insane.

Also a native of Québec, Montréal-born Margaret Wescott collaborated, as we have seen, on *Some American Feminists* (1977). Her *Eve Lambart* (1975) is a charming video about the great anglophone animation artist who lives in Québec. Still, even more remarkable is her *Behind the Veil* (1984; NFB, Studio D). One can speak more cogently of the Catholic Church's brutalization of women throughout history, as well as their inestimable contribution to the execution of its mission, after viewing this piece of work. Though we already knew these "facts" in a general way, Wescott brings out vividly, through use of art work and of contemporary footage, many insights, including the role of the pre-Christian cult of Brigid and of female saints of the Irish (Celtic) Church in giving the one-vote margin that declared women to have souls when a vote on the issue was taken at the Macon Council of Bishops in the year 900. She looks at other outstanding women "monks" and saints (e.g., Hildegard von Bingen), and takes us into a present-day Benedictine cloistered convent (Ste Marie des Montagnes) in Québec. And among iconic representations used is a brief slice from *Les Filles du Roy* (q.v., Ch. 3). I could not emphasize enough the indispensability of this documentary to women's studies groups or to Church staffs anywhere.

Noteworthy among these women directors is Cynthia Scott (see Coulombe 1991, 489–90), whose recent film, *Strangers in Good Company*—also known as *The Company of Strangers*—(1990–1) has won critical acclaim. This is a deeply sensitive film, at once humorous and pathetic; it studies the reactions and conversation of seven previously unacquainted women of widely diverse ethnicities and social backgrounds, who are thrust into exchanges and challenges to survival when their bus breaks down during an expedition. All of these women are sixty or over (one is ninety and facing death); none of them is portrayed by a professional actor, and each portrays herself, while conveying the problems and joys of her life. The dialogue of this bittersweet work is to a large extent ad lib, and very natural; the photography exceptional. *Strangers* ... has been successfully distributed in the U.S., and aired on many PBS television stations on 21 December 1992.

Before setting aside the films of feminist orientation, we might mention here contrasting films such as *The Masculine Mystique* and *90 Days* (q.v. infra) and also the documentaries of Douglas Jackson, an anglophone Montréal-born filmmaker who is well known for his study entitled *Why Men Rape* (1979; 40 min.), in which ten men convicted of rape tell their stories, and lawyers, policemen, teenagers, and men and women in a singles bar are interviewed. In the process, these interviewees touch on multiple issues related to sexual behavior and attitudes. Patrick Wilson is the on-camera commentator. The film, which won the American Film Festival Award, was produced by Jackson and Roman Kroitor. Jackson has made many other documentaries on many other subjects, as a glance at Bernard Lutz's article devoted to him testifies (Coulombe 1991, 273). There we see that he has made such films as *Norman Jewison, Filmmaker* (1971); *The Huntsman* (1972); *The Sloane Affair* (1972); and *La Gastronomie* (1973). Pratley treats the Jewison film (*TS* 1987, 40) as well as Jackson's fiction crime thriller, *The Heat Wave Lasted Four Days* (1973) (*TS* 1987, 214), and lists his work for the NFB (285). *The Art of Eating* (1976) is apparently confused with *The Art of "Acting"* in Coulombe.

OTHER ANGLOPHONE DOCUMENTARIES OF NOTE

Leaving aside films with a feminist orientation, many anglophone documentaries from Québec are as remarkable as are the francophone. I chose to include a couple of the politically oriented ones in Chapter 6, where I studied films having to do with the October 1970 crisis. But this by no means exhausts the subject. The material used is far ranging, so that we are looking here not only at politics, but also at ecology, history, and so forth.

A documentary that deals with world ecology, and compares favorably with such excellent nature programs as those of David Suzuki (*The Nature of Things*), is Terri (Terry; Terre) Nash's *If You Love This Planet*, even though Pratley (*TS* 1987, 143) states that it is "no more than an illustrated lecture by Dr. Helen Caldicott on the need for nuclear disarmament." Her picture is shown in a still taken from the film in Pratley (*TS* 1987, 147). But it is significant that Coulombe (1991, 572) retains this film as a sufficiently important example of *québécois* cinema to be listed under his master list of credits. Born in British Columbia (1949), Nash has worked with Studio D of the NFB since 1975. Nash's work is discussed by Marco de Blois in Coulombe (1991, 393) where one reads that *If You Love This Planet* was labeled as propaganda by the Reagan administration and that any American viewing it might be accused of criminal activity. Nash made *Mother Earth* in 1991; in this film one again encounters her feminist and ecological convictions.

Another documentary, one of the greatest ever made in Canada, is *Volcano: An Inquiry into the Life and Death of Malcolm Lowry* (1976), directed by Donald Brittain and John Kramer. This film took the Canadian Film Award for best documentary of 1976, a great year for the anglophones we are considering here, as the prize for best animation was taken by Caroline Leaf, and Marilyn Lightstone also took a prize for her role in *Lies My Father Told Me*. In fact, *Volcano* ... took awards in New York, Oslo, Hollywood, Toronto, and Montréal. It is a very disturbing portrait of this troubled genius.

To quote from the NFB itself, "Author of one of the major novels of the century, *Under the Volcano*, Malcolm Lowry fought a winning battle with words, and a losing battle with liquor. On-location shooting in four countries, photographs, readings by Richard Burton from Lowry's novel, interviews with the people who loved and hated him, give the film a terrifying immediacy. More than a portrait, it is a reflection on the greater agony of man."[4] It should be remembered that Lowry himself was a script writer. He wrote the film script of Fitzgerald's novel, *Tender is the Night*, which is considered an extension of his own fiction, especially of *Under the Volcano*. Lowry's cinema work (*The Cinema of Malcolm Lowry*) has been edited by Miguel Mota and Paul Tiessen.

THE SOCIAL DOCUMENTARY

An outstanding documentary about the successes of one labor union, *Temiscaming Quebec* (1975; d. Martin Duckworth) concerns the closing of a Canadian International paper mill in 1972, and tells how the people saved their town. Local 233 was especially instrumental in this salvation, brought about through a restructuring of the mill, with coownership being introduced, divided among management, workers, town, and the government. We see the demonstrations, and learn how after fourteen months workers have their jobs back. It was, in fact, the nation's first big experiment with coownership, and after the conflict, despite the old equipment, production is rolling, especially because the men working the mill know it through and through. I found some of the technical features of this documentary to be memorable, and in particular the color photography.

Réal La Rochelle (Coulombe 1991, 165) tells us that Duckworth (b. in Montréal in 1933) is a sensitive filmmaker who is always *engagé*, and that he always gives deep-structured portraits. Here it is a question of forest workers and miners; but he also made a documentary about prisoners (*Cell 16* [1973]); and he collaborated with Sophie Bissonnette and J. Rock on *Une Histoire de femmes* (1980), the prize-winning documentary about women in struggle. He was also photographer for a very important Don Owen film, *The Ernie Game* (1967).

HISTORICAL FILMS BY A HUNGARIAN IMMIGRANT

Age of the Rivers (1986–7; approx. 60 minutes; d. Albert Kish), while less successful than Arcand's *Champlain*, is nonetheless a useful work that traces the history of the early days of Cartier, the arrival of the French at the Ile des Oiseaux (Funk Island, Newfoundland) and at the Lachine rapids, and the encounter in 1534 with the Iroquois Indians, who are shown in drawings. The arrival of Roberval is then discussed; we are told how his men suffered from disease and starvation, and how the Iroquois taught them a cedar-tea remedy for scurvy. The fishing expeditions of the Portuguese, Spanish, and French are included for the purpose of telling of methods using salt to preserve the catch, especially cod, all of which amounted to a new food source for Europe. We learn, too, of modifications in ship construction that involved squaring the back of the ship to carry large cargoes. (The ship became a kind of warehouse for the transporting of barrels of cod and whale oil.) Beaver fur, too, is shown to have become another important resource sought by the Europeans.

We learn in this film about the Port Royal habitation in Nova Scotia; about Champlain and his astrolabe, which measured latitude; and how in 1608 Québec City was the center of his fur trading empire. When, finally, the English discovered Hudson's Bay, a new fur-trading center was created that then competed with that of the French. The narrator goes on to tell that the landing of the pilgrims at Plymouth Rock in 1620 also brought new threats to the French: there is now a New England to rival with New France. The French therefore built a series of forts to protect themselves (including Fort Chambly, built in 1667).

By 1713, with the Treaty of Utrecht, the French lost Newfoundland and Acadia. They built the walled city at Louisbourg (NS), with a social order imported from France. Then, on 11 May 1745, a volunteer army of 4000 New England militiamen, engaged by the English, attacked and captured Louisbourg, which was finally occupied by the British until 1749, when was is returned to the French. The English then build a rival fort at Halifax. Here in 1759, 14,000 British troops assembled to attack Louisbourg, which, after seven weeks, was taken again in 1759. Québec fell, and the era of New France ended. In 1760, the film goes on to show, Louisbourg was blown up. But in 1959 reconstruction was begun by the Canadian Government.

Additionally we learn of *voyageurs* who traveled in canoes to Fort William and back by using a circular trading system; and we are told how the Northwest Company rivaled with the Hudson Bay Co. and then finally amalgamated. We are shown how the introduction of the York boat ended an era and how, finally, in later years, as an answer to the problem of rapids and in order to facilitate river transportation, the Rideau Canal was constructed; we are told that it is one of the oldest still in use.

This documentary, although certainly not among the finest ever produced by the National Film Board, is an excellent visual device for classroom presentation, and provides pleasant and accessible background material for courses in (French)-Canadian history, geography, and general literature and civilization. I recommend it.

Marcel Jean, in his article on Kish (Coulombe 1991, 285–86), does not mention this film, but it serves as an example of Kish's work. A Hungarian immigrant known for writing history with film, Kish has directed *Historic Sites* (1969), *Time Piece* (1971), *This Is a Photograph* (1971), and *Louisbourg* (1972), whose story also figures importantly in *Age of the Rivers*. In 1973 he made *Our Street Was Paved with Gold*, which Jean describes as offering "a ... personal vision of history," for "in it the director visits the Boulevard Saint-Laurent in Montréal, and confronts what he sees there with his memories, those of an immigrant, for whom this artery is the meeting-place of numerous ethnic communities." Kish has also made *Los Canadienses* (1975), a documentary on the one thousand two hundred Canadians who took part in the war in Spain as an arm of the International Brigades. He directed *Bread* (1983), a silent documentary, and *The Age of Invention*, which Jean describes as "a cinematographic poem on the coming of age of the machine on the eve of World War One." We may add to the list *Ports Canada* (1969) and *Hold the Ketchup* (1977). (See Clanfield 1987, 32.)

Pratley (*TS* 1987, 40) speaks of Kish's *The Image Makers* (1981) as a brief but informative history of the NFB's first forty years, calling it one of those films that is "indispensable in the study of Canadian film history."

The reader might be reminded at this point of another Hungarian-born Québécois *cinéaste* whom I have frequently mentioned: Thomas Vamos, a francophone, who has directed some fiction and some documentary film. We found him as the ONF cameraman for *Jusqu'au coeur* (Lefebvre); *Mon Enfance à Montréal* (J. Chabot); *IXE-13* (J. Godbout); *O.K. ... Laliberté* (M. Carrière); *Mario* (Beaudin). He has also directed *L'Exil* (1971); *La Fleur aux dents* (1975; starring Claude Jutra); *Les Héritiers de la violence* (1977); *L'Enfant fragile* (co-dir. with C. Hazanavicius, 1980). As chief operator he has collaborated on a number of other films I have studied in this book, including *Le Vieillard et l'enfant*; *The Peanut Butter Solution*, and *Les Portes tournantes*.

POLITICAL FILMS BY ANGLOPHONE FILMMAKERS OF QUÉBEC

In the course of this book I have looked at certain important anglophone works in the context of a subject. This was particularly true of the passages where I talked about children's films (Ch. 5), and also where I analyzed Québécois political film (Ch. 6). There I included *Prologue*; *Action: The October Crisis of 1970*, and *Reaction. Action* ..., by Robin Spry, is an NFB film very much in demand, and one often consulted and screened as a prelude to discussions of separatism. As we saw, it constitutes an ideal introduction to *Les Ordres*, the fictionalized film that nevertheless has all the feel of the documentary about it. There we looked at the stunning documentary of considerable scope and power entitled *The Champions*, by the filmmaker Donald Brittain, who also made the film *Dreamland*, about the early film industry of Canada (referred to in Chapter 1). (See Clanfield [1987, 28] on Brittain; he claims he is "the best of NFB's narrative historians.")

A few anglophone films less closely related to the October 1970 crisis nevertheless should be studied for their portrayals of certain political phenomena of the province. Among them I would include *Democracy on Trial: The Morgentaler Affair—1970—6* (1984; d. Paul Cowan).

This film concerns Dr. Henry Morgentaler's 1970—6 challenge to abortion laws through the Québec courts. Using old newsreel footage, interviews, and dramatic reenactments (in which Morgentaler and his lawyer play themselves), this docudrama unravels the complexities of the case that began as a challenge to Canada's abortion law and turned into a precedent-setting civil rights case. The film also offers insight into the physician's motivation for defying the law and reveals how Québec's judicial system responded to this emotionally charged challenge of the controversial abortion law.[5] (See Clanfield [1987, 32] for other films of Cowan's, not necessarily related to Québec.)

In a class with Brittan and Cowan is Michael Rubbo. In Chapter 5, I looked at his "children's films"—*The Peanut Butter Solution* and his *Vincent and Me*—as well as at his *Tommy Tricker and the Stamp Traveller*, a segment of which was filmed in this anglophone Québécois's native Australia. But Rubbo's output is extensive. He has done documentary-like but nonetheless subjective films that treat local or Canadian issues, such as his *Persistent and Finagling* (1971; 56 min. 3 sec.), concerning Montréalaises housewives who organized a media event to publicize the wanton industrial pollution of the city; or his *I Hate to Lose* (1977; 57mins.), dealing with the views of Westmount inhabitants during the provincial election of November 1976. These two films are thoroughly covered by Page, who finds them important for their political content, for their demonstration of the power of political organization, and for their portrait of Québec's anglophone minorities and their tensions with their francophone countrymen.[6]

Rubbo's *I Hate to Lose* covers the candidacy of George Springate (Liberal), Harold Fairhead (Union Nationale), and Nick Auf der Maur (Democratic Alliance) in the Westmount Riding Campaign of 1976, which Springate won. His victory speech is inserted here and through its editing is put in juxtaposed contrast to the Lévesque victory statement made simultaneously in the Paul Sauvé arena. This effect "points out more clearly than any other section of the film the relative positions of the French and the English in the province and the dramatic differences which exist between those communities," says Page.[7] Elsewhere he says, "It is worth knowing that even though the Parti Québécois did run a candidate in Westmount, he does not appear in the film. The reason, according to the filmmakers, is that he did not really campaign in the English sections of the riding, and was never in face-to-face confrontations with the major candidates."[8] (See also *Reaction*, discussed in my Ch. 6, for anglophone Québécois political positions.)

Especially amusing is Rubbo's *Yes or No, Jean-Guy Moreau* (1979), in which he reveals, on the eve of election, "The Two Solitudes" — a telling phrase that refers to anglophone Canada "versus" francophone Canada. The film is at once a piece devoted to the art of Jean-Guy Moreau the caricaturist, being squired about by Rubbo as Moreau prepares to give his first performance in English and in Toronto, and devoted also to the politically charged prereferendum atmosphere throughout Canada, among seven-generation anglophone Québécois, among immigrant Jews, Portuguese, and so on, and among the French Canadians themselves. While we see Moreau imitating various characters, which he describes as his "tools," including Trudeau as a pharoah-hunting separatist, Gilles Vigneault as a leading voice for independence, Chartrand a leftist labor leader as a prophet, Jerry a security guard disgusted by the radical turn of events and an avatar of his father, it is the tremendously funny caricature of Lévesque, being impersonated by Moreau, that is the highlight of this film. Moreau captures Lévesque's habits — his cigarette smoking, his fishing through papers, the hand gestures, the facial grimaces — as "he" sounds out the crowd with a trial referendum, and later as he speaks English to a crowd at a "news press conference." Rubbo, who describes himself as a transplanted Australian filmmaker with a bilingual kid who wants to know if there's a place for him in the new Québec, introduces Moreau to various people to give him new insights (e.g., various immigrants, including the Portuguese, and the filmmaker Guy Fournier, who passionately declares that he wants to be a French-speaking North American, and predicts the referendum will lose). Rubbo also helps Moreau rehearse in English for his "news press conference"; then we have the "press conference" in performance. "We are frogs," says "Lévesque"; "but we are frogs who want their own independent pond." Those francophone Canadians who do not live in Québec should come home, they cannot have their cake and eat it too; they cannot live inside and outside Québec at the same time. Finally, when one man asks if this is a gathering devoted to politics or to political satire, the answer comes that those two things often coincide. The impersonation ends with Moreau-Lévesque singing a very comical song "I'm just an ordinary guy." (Which he was not.)

Besides these political films about Canada, we should also note Rubbo's stunning if enigmatic portrait of the preoccupations and character of the anglophone Ontarian writer, Margaret Atwood, in his 1985 *Margaret Atwood: Once in August*. It is compelling.

Rubbo is also visibly concerned with world problems. He has gone to Indonesia to film his *Wet Earth and Warm People* (1971), Australia for his *Man Who Can't Stop* (1974), and Cuba for his *Waiting for Fidel* (1974), and for *I am an Old Tree* (1975). Rubbo's international perspective was demonstrated early in his career by his locale shooting of *Sad Song of Yellow Skin* and in the trip he made to France for the filming of *Solzhenitsyn's Children ... Are Making a Lot of Noise in Paris*. (A large still of this NFB film is to be seen in Pratley [*TS* 1987, 110].)

Sad Song of Yellow Skin (1970) is a documentary that illustrates the subjective nature of Rubbo's approach to "reality." This film was shot in Saigon, in the middle of the Vietnam war. While showing the broken and chaotic life in Vietnam, it also brings out the people's hopes and fears, not shown by the media. The film, which won the Robert Flaherty prize, became a model for average-length documentaries with political content, according to Piers Handling (Coulombe 1991, 482−84.)

I Am an Old Tree (1975; 56 min. 50 sec.) finds Rubbo examining various facets of communist Cuba. The doctor featured in the film — Dr. Grande, who studied and practiced in the U.S. but returned to a day care center in 1963 as an act of conscience — gives the source of the title, when he asserts that the old tree is a [rigid] capitalist, but that the young tree can be shaped. The state-run supermarket is revealed as having little choice, no fancy packaging; the people are shown making old cars run and reshaping old parts off other old cars, as a need resulting from the blockade. Still the people envision a good future for their children. Rubbo takes in a meeting of the CDR (Committee for the Defense of the Revolution), at which it is asserted that the people want to give Dong, the visiting Vietnamese dignitary, a great welcome. Fascism is discussed, as are also other acts of law of the CDR; but Rubbo finds the meeting "flat and doctrinaire." Another meeting devoted to International Women's Day is covered; this gives rise to the question of how one can make the individual feel needed in a socialist society. We attend a floorshow in Havana, and a tobacco farm. As well, a teacher testifies that the children study more now because they participate more. On the farm, all the adults are learning to read and do arithmetic, too.

This well-done documentary is nonetheless very dated at this point, with the fall of Soviet communism and of the Soviet economy and the resultant need of Cuba to find supporters elsewhere in the world.

Solzhenitsyn's Children .... Are Making a Lot of Noise in Paris (1978) is, as its title suggests, a political documentary about communists (or at least far-left philosophers) in Paris. It is called Rubbo's "most ambitious film," by Piers Handling. Dissatisfied with his previous style, Rubbo takes a new departure, allowing himself to participate in the actual events more than had been his wont. This style is even more pronounced in *Yes or No, Jean-Guy Moreau* (1979) and in *Daisy: The Story of a Facelift* (1982). (Translated and paraphrased from Coulombe [1991, 483].) *Solzhenistyn ...*, like other important documentaries first made in English (e.g., *Action: the October Crisis of 1970*, by Robin Spry, called by Lever "un intellectuel humaniste de gauche et bien informé [a humanist intellectual on the left and well informed]" [*Hist.* 1988, 234]), was rapidly translated into French and widely broadcast throughout the province as *Les Enfants de Soljenitsyne ... y a pas à dire, font du bruit à Paris.*

According to Clanfield, Rubbo reflects the documentary style of the NFB's Unit B: his films "emphasize and extend Unit B's epistemological uncertainties and self-reflexive tendencies. Rubbo's films highlight his presence as speculative participant and his own voice-over often reveals his doubts about the value of his interpretations. He recounts his contact as an outsider with societies in flux around the world: daily life in wartime Vietnam, a visit to Indonesia, or a trip around Cuba with two Canadian politicians. In Canada, he chose times of intense political activity — anti-pollution campaigns, the 1976 election, or its subsequent independence re-

ferendum (*Yes or No, Jean-Guy Moreau*, 1979) — and concentrated
on the elusive feelings, the ambiguous identities, and the sense
of isolation of those caught up in the process, images that confirm
and reflect his own ambiguous status as participant-observer" (1987,
29).

Other sociopolitical works originally done in English but quickly
translated into French and widely broadcast, would include Gilles
Blais's *Le Journal de Madame Wollock* (1979), about Sophie
Wollock, the owner of the anglophone Québec magazine, *The
Suburban*, whose son gives a purely racist analysis of contemporary
Québec; Terri Nash's *If You Love This Planet*; Cynthia Scott's
Flamenco at 5:15 (1983), about the Robledos's flamenco class at
the National Ballet School; and, of course, Donald Brittain's *The
Champions* (q.v. above; in French called *Le Combat des chefs*);
not to mention Bonnie Klein's *Not a Love Story — A Film About
Pornography* (q.v. above; called in French, *C'est surtout pas de
l'amour*); Gail Singer's 1984 film on abortion, *Abortion: Stories
from North and South* (in French, entitled *L'Avortement, histoire
secrète*); and Paul Cowan's *Democracy on Trial: the Mogentaler
Affair* (q.v. above).

JEWISH LIFE

Documentaries regarding the past and present life of Jewish
immigrants to Canada are not lacking. One such well known work
is *Falasha, Exile of the Black Jews* directed by Jamie Boyd, with
Simcha Jacobovici. Pratley assesses this film as "A well-intended
but labored and confused study of the Falashas in Ethiopia and
Israel" (*TS* 1987, 263).

While most Jewish citizens of Québec are anglophones, an influx
of francophone Jews has been occurring in recent times. Thus,
Jacques Bensimon (b. Morocco, 1943) has made *20 ans après*
(1977), a documentary on the North African francophone Jewish
community in Québec (Coulombe 1991, 42–3). Bensimon immigrated to Canada in 1958, studied cinema in New York, and
returned to work in the English section of the NFB in 1967. His
contribution is largely the expression of cultural plurality in Québec
and the promotion of tolerance and of the acceptance of differences. He has done several films on Morocco (*Carnets du Maroc:
Mémoire à rebours*).

L'Arbre qui dort rêve à ses racines (1992; 81 minutes), an ONF
documentary, is notable as a film of unusual beauty by a new

guard, neo-Canadian woman director, the Jewish Tunisian Michka Saäl, who made the film with a Lebanese Arabic woman living in Montréal, Nadine Ltaif. Their friendship is explored here as a vehicle for the expression of the possibility of transcending the "différends irréconciliables" of the Israelis and Moslems. It is therefore only tangentially concerned with Québec problems. *L'Arbre* ... is a documentary on tolerance seen from a feminist, pacifist, and humanisitic viewpoint.[9]

But *Dark Lullabies* (1985), directed by Irene Lilienheim Angelico and Abbey Jack Neidik, is arguably the most powerful English-language documentary from Québec to deal with Jewish life.

This is a film about survivors of the holocaust, and about survivor guilt. Irene Lilienheim Angelico probes her father Henry Lilienheim's manuscripts written in 1947 just after his encampment in Dachau. She also inserts those gruesome pictures of the concentration camps, archival footage from Washington, D.C. and from the NFB, and private and public photographs. She travels from her home in Montréal to Jerusalem for the world gathering of survivors and children of survivors of the holocaust. There she visits the holocaust museum. She then travels to Germany, the "source," where she speaks to other "survivors"—survivors of Nazi fathers and grandfathers who must come to grips with the deeds of their ancestors; scornful young members of neo-Nazi organizations who deny the proof of the holocaust contained in photos, calling them an example of "photomontage." They think of the holocaust as a Hollywood film, a fairy tale, and ridicule the portrayal in the actual film, stating that the uniforms of the actors were not accurate, etc.

The directors' goal was to examine the reverberations of the holocaust on second-generation Jews. For me this film came close to *Shoah* for the horror of the images, but I was also shocked by the arrogance of some contemporary Germans. From a technical perspective, however, the sound quality (at least of the copy I viewed) was very poor. But the music, especially the use of the lullabies—Brahms's and the Jewish "Leila; Leila"—, was painfully moving.

Bonjour! Shalom! (1992; 60 min.), directed by Garry Beitel, is another quite recent anglophone documentary, and one that goes a long way toward describing the fears and misgivings of the francophone residents of Outremont, as they watch the neighborhood becoming ghettoized and "taken over" by the very private and reactionary Hassidic Jews. The film does show attempts of the younger generations of the two communities to reach out to each other, but the possibility of assimiliation or even of any real understanding certainly seems bleak, in this vehicle at least.

Together with documentaries, there are several anglophone films of fiction concerned with Québec Jewish life. I am not speaking so much about those based on the works of Mordecai Richler, anglophone, Québécois, Jewish Canadian, although his works provided the impetus for such well-known films as *The Apprenticeship of Duddy Kravitz* (Ted Kotcheff, 1974) and *Joshua Then and Now* (Ted Kotcheff, 1985) — , these being about Canadian (or any) entrepreneurship. For although *Apprenticeship* ... and *Joshua* ... concern Jewish-*québecois* life, these films were not made by Québécois; Kotcheff is from Toronto. Indeed, when it comes to Richler, only Caroline Leaf's short animated film *The Street* seems to have been made by an inhabitant of French Canada. (This film concerns a young boy's initiation into death and its consequences, some of it taught by his sister, some by "Duddy Kravitz.")[10]

Still, a sizable article is devoted to Ted Kotcheff by Jose Arroyo (Coulombe 1991, 286–88). He shows Kotcheff as a director who has had a long collaboration with Richler, dating from *Life at the Top*(1965), when they scripted Jack Clayton's sequel to *Room at the Top*; going through his efforts in England to bring about the adaptation of two Richler novels, *Cocksure* and *St. Urbain's Horseman*; and culminating with his direction of the highly successful films *The Apprenticeship of Duddy Kravitz* (1974) and *Joshua Then and Now* (1985). Both portray efforts to get out of the ghetto. These two films are musts for the student of Canadian film. They were filmed in Montréal and the Eastern Cantons, and although the principal male roles are played by foreign actors (Richard Dreyfus in *Apprenticeship* ... and James Wood in *Joshua* ...), Québécoises actresses play the main female roles (Micheline Lanctôt in *Apprenticeship* ..., and Gabrielle Lazure in *Joshua* ...). The presence of francophone women in these films provides a dose of cultural reality to a plot already very believable for its portrayal of Montréal Jewish life. The two films need no introduction to American audiences, of course, nor does Ted Kotcheff, who in 1974 went to Hollywood, where he made *Fun with Dick and Jane* (1977), again with Richler collaborating on the script. There Kotcheff also made *Someone's Killing the Great Chefs of Europe* (1978), *First Blood* (1982), and *Uncommon Valor* (1983).

Within this anglophone, Jewish-Canadian framework we have one of the most beautiful — if to some overly sentimental — films in the *québécois* portfolio: Jan Kadar's *Lies My Father Told Me* (1975).

Perhaps the most memorable thing about this touching film is the portrayal of the relationship between the small boy, David, and his grandfather, who drives a horse-drawn wagon, and is an old-time ragpicker. The bonding is so intense that the boy tolerates only with great difficulty the passing of the old man.

The fine performance of Marilyn Lightstone gives strength and a stable quality to the story and to the film. The role is somewhat comparable to the one she assumed in *Bonheur d'occasion*, though there she was required to be more snivelling than we might have wished. It is always a pleasure to see Lightstone, wherever she appears; and upon occasion this may well be in an American television program.

The boy's initiation into sexual matters is one of the sources of warm humor in this charming film, which captures with intelligence and sensitivity the life of Montréal's Jewish quarter and the gentle old Jewish man's personality. A believable story. The conflict of an old ethnic way of life and urban values; problems with the neighbors concerning the horse's quarters in the Old Montréal neighborhood that wants to progress into the modern era — all these are issues that come into play. Scenes of Montréal in the winter, the narrow streets of the quarter, the park, and the autumn woods, flood to the memory when one thinks of this film. It is no surprise that it was a nominee for an Oscar, and took several prizes. Ted Allan (born in Montréal in 1918) wrote the *scénario* for this film from his play of the same title. He has also been the scriptwriter for *7 fois ... par jour* (Denis Héroux, 1970) and for *Bethune, the Making of a Hero* or *Bethune, naissance d'un héros* (Philip Borsos, 1988; 1990).

THE ITALIAN COMMUNITY

In addition to cinema concerning the Jewish population of Québec (Montréal, in particular, which, as we have said, has a large and colorful Jewish *quartier*), one should be aware of films dealing with other minority populations of Québec. Their efforts to adapt to this rather unapproachable society have often been as difficult as have those of Jewish peoples.

The Italian population in Québec is quite significant, especially in Montréal, but for that matter everywhere in the province; and it has had considerable difficulty integrating into the community. (In

1968, as Richler shows, the Catholic school board in Montréal's Saint-Léonard responded to the desire of parents to have their children learn English by attempting to deny education in English to the Italian population, as a result of which ugly riots broke out. A year later Bill 63 was introduced by the provincial government; this bill allowed parents to choose the language of their children's education. But this bill in turn enraged the nationalists. Thus a commission was formed to conduct an inquiry into "language rights; and the province began sinking into that linguistic quagmire that has yielded Bills 22, 101, and 178, and a disconcertingly tribal society."[11])

It is not surprising to find this large Italian community, much of which is located in Saint-Léonard, a suburb of Montréal—alluded to in many films: in *Bach et Bottine*, for example, or in *Un Zoo la nuit*. (And in his more recent film, *Léolo* [1992], the most expensive *auteur* film ever made in Canada, Jean-Claude Lauzon deals intimately with the Italian population of East Montréal. He admits to an admiration of the Italians and to the felt influence of such greats as Visconti and Fellini.[12]) But it probably does not occur to the ordinary moviegoer that one of the province's most famous and most distinguished "stars," Pierre Curzi, is of Italian descent. For that matter, some Italo-Québécois even make films on the scene. As early as 1963 we have *Le Chat ici et là* by Cioni Carpi. And there has also been considerable cooperation between this Canadian ethnicity and the Italians of Italy. (Véronneau has written of this in an article entitled "Mariage à l'italienne."[13]) Moreover, Pierre Patry, whose *Corde au cou* we mentioned in Chapter 6, participated in the making of *Luciano* (1962; G. V. Baldi), within the framework of the collaboration between the ONF and Italy. Another rather well-known work involving Canadian-Italian cooperation was *Una Giornata particolare* or, *A Special Day* (1977; Ettore Scola).[14] Also among the French-Canadian and Italian-Canadian collaborations with the Italians (as well as with the French, British, and Americans) is *Caro Papa* (*Cher Papa*, or *Dear Dad*, d. by Dino Risi, 1978; 110 min.). Starring Vittorio Gassman, Stephano Madia, Aurore Clément, and Andrée Lachapelle, it concerns an Italian businessman, not very attached to his family, who learns that his children belong to terrorist organizations. Through the problems of a bourgeois family, this film portrays conflicts in the Italian society that would not be unknown in Québec. According to Pratley (*TS*, 126), *Caro Papa* was said to be one of CFDC's great Canadian coproductions. But Pratley's tone puts the assertion in doubt.[15] Also notable among these collaborations is *Notes sur une minorité* (or, *Note su una minoranza*) by Gianfranco Mingozzi (Québec-ONF/Italy, 1965), though in his filmography Véronneau lists several other works of note, including *Antonioni, Documents et Témoignages* (Québec-ONF/Italy, 1965).[16] These films were shown on the December 1990-January 1991 program of the Cinémathèque, along with many other Italian, Franco-Italian, and Italo-American films.

One should not, of course, overlook the important contribution of Italian actors to the cinema of Québec; notable among these would be the Italian-born Nick Mancuso, who made his name in the riveting film *Ticket to Heaven* (1980; d. Ralph L. Thomas), but whom we have particularly spoken of in Chapter 4 for his role as François Paradis in the film *Maria Chapdelaine*. An anglophone actor, in *Maria ...* he was obliged to speak in the voice of Claude Gauthier.

Another anglophone Italian-born actor, and also producer, is Saverio (Sam) Grana, who starred in the strange Giles Walker trilogy, *The Masculine Mystique* (1984; codir., J. N. Smith); *90 Days* (1985), and *The Last Straw* (1987). In these films, which are to be examined later in this chapter, Grana plays Alex, a macho type whose sperm are of great value.

Probably the most important film dealing with the Italian minority in Québec is *Caffè Italia Montréal* (1985), directed by Paul Tana, who was born in Ancona, Italy in 1947 — though Bachand refers to him as Swiss (and also misspells his name).[17] *Caffè Italia* won the prize of the Association québécoise des critiques de cinéma (Montréal) in 1986, and also the L.E.Ouimet-Molson prize (see Abel 1990, 322). In this history of Montréal's Italian community, Pierre Curzi, who takes multiple roles, speaks of himself in a conversation with Toni Nardi as an Italian. It is an engaging film and one that shows this 'ethnic' side of the *québécois* film industry, while also detailing the experiences of the large Italian immigrant population living in the big cities of the province. By its title, *Caffè Italia*, we are reminded of an Italian restaurant in Montréal that was the locus of much of the action in *Un Zoo la nuit*.

Tana immigrated to Canada in 1958. He made his name with his docufiction on the Italians of Montréal, but he has since done other works in collaboration with Bruno Ramirez, the historian, such as *La Sarrasine* and *Le Rêve de Joe Aiello*, the story of an immigrant's desire to transmit his cultural heritage. In 1988 he directed *Marchand de jouets* (story by Naïm Kattan, *scénario* by Clément Perron; starring Marie Tifo and Gilbert Sicotte).

Using testimonials, old archival photos and films, theater sketches, and fictional scenes, Tana achieves a remarkable and memorable work with *Caffè Italia*, and one in which the sufferings of the Italian immigrant are vividly painted. The theater sketches are taken from "La Storia dell'Immigrante" by Toni Nardi and Vincenzo Ierfino (directed by Nardi), and the archival photos and films come from North America and Italy.

The film opens with habitués of the *caffè* watching a soccer team being televised. They tell their stories one by one: a woman brought to Petite Italie in 1954, and a man who immigrated in 1951. Old footage (and/or simulated old footage) shows the difficult crossing, and a voice tells how after forty days in a steamship, the immigrants saw the Statue of Liberty. (From N.Y. they traveled to Montréal). Simulation of old film shows a man writing a letter to Rosa, in the old country; he complains of the cold, tells of his *pension* (rooming house) with thirty other *paisani*, none of whom speak French. "We speak Italian," he tells her; "Don Cordasco sent us to work on the railroad; in 5 months I have saved 130 piastres — and am sending you 100. ... After a year, I'll be back with enough money to buy some land."

Old footage shows railroad workers, mostly Italians. We learn much more of Don Cordasco, and of how he gathered workers and sent them to the *chantiers*. This "King" Antonio Cordasco is depicted in a movie insert, in which workers demonstrate, praising him outside his house, and bringing a crown to him, while inside he is lying in bed ill, but surrounded by his henchmen. Speaking Italian, like the godfather he was, he discusses photos that his "sons" present, to be put in the paper. Bianco, however, has refused to pay off Cordasco, so Cordasco threatens to put his picture in upside down. Antonio is "crowned," while being informed that the "contremaîtres et ouvriers" (of the railroad) are offering the crown to the immortal memory of their king and benefactor, Antonio Cordasco: "viva il re; viva Cordasco."

Says Cordasco, "You around me are the lieutenants in our army of picks and shovels ... I thank you for the honor you do me today. Outside the soldiers of work acclaim me, but I cannot greet them, as I am ill with rheumatism. So tell them for me that in the spring we will need thousands of workers. Mr. Burns of the Canadian Pacific Railways, *our* (CPR) has just told me this." Burns stands; they all cry: "Long live Mr. Burns. Long live CPR."

A speech is delivered in Italian, and then translated for Mr. Burns: they must come to Cordazco, or they will get no work. He will keep them in his records (i.e., they must come to him and pay him for their work). They will be "glorified" like him, if they are faithful to him.

One by one they tell their story. One of them tells how Italians like to have their own *potager* (garden), so needed for large families. They tell how they used to work very hard, but now are lazy "like the Canadians." The 1930s fascist movement in Montréal, which supported General Italo Balbo and Il Duce, is then considered. Balbo is shown going to America in 1933, with his twenty-four airplanes. He went to Montréal, too; carrying letters. Through old newsreels we see and hear Il Duce exclaiming, and also see a woman writing to her son, that Balbo intends to show the world that Italy is better under fascism, under Il Duce. Eleven million Italians have emigrated, but one need no longer leave Italy. Indeed, Mussolini has stopped emigration. ("But," says the woman, "I think you did well to leave, for there is not enough to eat here.")

Then Gentile Dieni shows an old photo of the fascists of Montréal greeting Italo Balbo as he gets off the plane. There were fifty thousand people, including seventeen thousand Italians, there. Everyone stopped working to go and see Balbo landing at Longueuil. All went to see the great progress of the fatherland. They were happy to see the best planes of the time.

In old newsreels from 1940 Mussolini declares war. The armies of Il Duce are on the march. We are shown headlines in French from contemporary papers: the device is a convention, of course. Inevitably, raids by Canadians on "dangerous" *immigrés* begin. "People would come to your door, tell you to dress, to get your smokes, and come with them." People who had done nothing were arrested — some Italians and Germans spent months in camp in Petawawa; they knew fear, tears, and worries about their family.

We return to the movie about the Italian immigrants. A character named Moresco says to an anglo policeman who looks like Bogart, "I've done nothing," to which the policeman replies, "Moresco shut up." A naturalized shoe manufacturer is being interviewed by an official (Curzi): "Are you a fascist?" "No." The official shows him a photo and a letter, "You are a member, or not." "We did nothing wrong; I called meetings, took care of the money." "What did you do with the money?" "Sent it to Il Duce." "Do you realize that Il Duce is an enemy of Canada?" "We organized parades, festivals; we hurt no one; I pay my taxes." "Are you proud?" "No, just us who respected Italy; even the mayor of Montréal; everywhere in Canada, especially in Québec." The official: "That's finished." Shoemaker: "I didn't declare the war." Official: "What's done is done. You're a menace."

Now Moresco meets the shoemaker, to whom he says, "You've got us in a fine mess, you fascists. It's your fault we're arrested." Shoemaker: "Italians like you make me sick." Moresco: "I'm more Italian than you; I fought in WWI, I've been decorated. You just make parades." Shoemaker: "We honored Italy; not you." Moresco: "Go play your fascist games in Italy."

Shortly hereafter we have a stage play, a musical comedy, in progress in Halifax. It is Toni Nardi's and Vincenzo Ierfino's *Storia dell'Immigrante*. In it Curzi portrays an officer. The characters sing of work and sweat, of dreams of being rich; but all had to work. And besides, the women worked double, the men were freer.

A discussion between Tony Nardi and Curzi shows both men to be of two cultures. Nardi finds he is not integrated; he finds the atmosphere too "*serré*; too rigid." He clearly articulates an identity problem. But other Italians — especially younger ones — claim that Italy is not their reality. Though they may have gone to anglophone schools, English culture is not their reality either. (They live the Québec reality.) Aldo Nova, a musician born in Montréal, finds he is a curious *mélange*: he was raised as an Italian, speaks French as his native language, but sings in English. Curzi testifies that he was born in Montréal; and through his conversation with his father, Alfredo Curzi (who arrived in 1923), we learn that he is to play Cordazo in the film, from which segments were shown earlier. For him, playing this role is "fantastic": it allows him to discover another universe. He tells his father he must speak Italian, and asks his father to coach him. (In the background is a poster of *Lucien Brouillard*.)

Caffè Italia is a touching film, and indispensable for a grasp of the situation of the Italian immigrant, or the person of Italian descent, as it was for him or her in the past or is even in Québec today.

Tana has recently directed another film regarding the life of Italian immigrants in Québec. Entitled *La Sarrasine* (1991; 109 minutes), it revolves around the murder of a French Canadian by Antonio Giaconne, a tailor who is condemned to capital punishment for the crime. (It is the Montréal of 1904.) The film adopts the viewpoint of Ninetta Moschella, and deals with the need for the immigrant to be respected while not betraying his own origins and customs. Interestingly enough, sixty percent of the dialogue of La Sarrasine is in Italian and Sicilian. For the reader of French, there is an excellent interview of Tana, conducted by Carlo Mandolini in *Séquences*.[18] *La Sarrasine* is reviewed in the same issue by Janick

Beaulieu, who finds the acting of Nardi and Enrica Maria Modugno to approach "great art," and the theme to be one in need of airing.[19]

THE LATIN AMERICAN COMMUNITY

FRANCOPHONE HAITIANS

In *Haïti-Québec* (1986; 59 min. 20 sec.; produced by the ONF, supervised by Roger Frappier), director Tahani Rached has drawn a portrait of the life of black Haitians who have fled the horrors of their country, and are living in Québec. There are about forty thousand such exiles; they come to francophone Canada (as the Jamaicans, such as those shown in *Milk and Honey*, come to anglophone Canada) in the hope of finding work and a new land. But the welcome they receive as depicted in Rached's film pinpoints the racism that plagues Canada, and reorients our occasional characterization of Québec as a closed society, often hostile to the immigrant.

Rached has made another film with the ONF about Haitians, a twenty-eight-minute documentary that deals with the Haitian "democratic" election of 29 November 1987. It is called *Haïti, nou là! nou là!* Other films of his include *Beyrouth! A défaut d'être mort*, and *Rends-moi mon pays*.

And here I would also recall to the reader the film *How to Make Love to a Negro without Getting Tired*, a fictional film based on the novel by the Haitian author, Dany Laferrière. I had occasion to discuss this in terms of censorship and marketing of Québec films in my first chapter.

SPANISH AMERICANS

Marilú Mallet, a well-known Québécois director from Chile, has been discussed in Chapter 3. The reader is referred to that passage for information on her films. But she is certainly not alone as a Spanish-American presence on the Québec film scene. For example, there is German Gutierrez, a director and *chef opérateur* who was born in Bogotá, Colombia, in 1955 and came to Canada in 1975, settling in Montréal. His first film, *Café* (1983), was a documentary and a social study on the production and distribution of coffee. With the ONF he has made *La Familia latina* (1985), which is

Le Grand Jack. (Courtesy Office National du Film.)

concerned with the Other in Québec society. His research into the question of the integration of Latin-Americans into the province of Québec brought him a prize at Yorkton (Coulombe 1991, 251–2).

FRANCO-AMERICANS AS SEEN BY THE QUÉBÉCOIS

As we have seen, Curzi stands at a confluence of cultures, as did the Franco-American, Jack Kerouac. Of French Canadian and, even more remotely, of Breton origins (origins common to many French Canadians, so beautifully evoked in Perrault's 1967 *Le Règne du jour*), Kerouac has been literally appropriated by the French Canadians. (Witness *Un Homme grand: Jack Kerouac at the Crossroads of Many Cultures*, by Pierre Anctil et al., published in revised form from interventions at the International Jack Kerouac Gathering [Québec City, 1987].) Kerouac is celebrated in Herménégilde Chiasson's overdramatic film, *Le Grand Jack* (1987). In the realm of filmmaking, as also in poetry, Chiasson, an Acadian, has made a considerable name for himself. (It appears he takes his pseudonym—first name only—from a great early Québécois filmmaker, Herménégilde Lavoie [1908–73], about whom Richard Lavoie made a 53-minute black-and-white documentary in 1976.)

Chiasson's film on Kerouac was supported and produced by the ONF, and has garnered considerable attention. A work that truly captures the darkness of Kerouac's vision, while somewhat over-romanticising his personality and his life, it is one of the few *québécois* films advertised by Facets, where it is available in English.

Doubtless, the American interest in Chiasson's film is due to the stature of Kerouac as an American writer. But there is also interest among Quebeckers and Americans in the Franco-American heritage per se. Other films have dealt with this question, and especially *The Mills of Power*.

NATIVE CANADIAN COMMUNITIES

The anglophone filmmakers of Canada have produced several films of quality in which Native Canadian, including Inuit, peoples are concerned, e.g., *Justice Denied*, or *Where the Spirit Lives*. This sort of film is virtually nonexistent in the *québécois* community. Still, we might note in the area of animation the collaboration of Co Hoedeman with several Inuit artists on the superb story of *Owl and Raven*, and his rendering of the Inuit legend about the lemming and the owl, as well as Caroline Leaf's charming *Owl Who Married a Goose*.[20] These films have their francophone versions, and one may well study any of them in one or the other language. The problems of the métis, notably as depicted in *Riel* (but also in *Red*), have already entered into my consideration.

Of course, francophone cinematographers have also produced documentaries on the Inuit and other Native-Canadian communities, including Gilles Blais's *Yesterday-Today: The Netsilik Eskimo*, or *Esquimaux* (1971; 57 min. 51 sec., produced by Marc Beaudet). In this film Zachary Itimignac and his family are shown as having lived a nomadic life in the Pelly Bay region of the Arctic, up until the mid-1960s, when the Canadian government decided to provide "modern" facilities to these Inuit hunters. The film shows a day in the life of this family, and reports on the impact these changes have brought upon them. The narration of this film clarifies that the family has done the acting without any prompting or intervention from the crew. Archival footage is inserted to show how things had been in the past, before "the coming of the white man." (Obviously an illusion, since it is not possible to have film from that era.)

We might mention here Claude Gagnon's *Visage pâle* (or *Pale Face*). Gagnon also made a film in Japanese about the place of women in Japanese society. It is called *Keiko*, the name of the main character (1978). Gagnon is married to a Japanese, Yuri Yoshimura, who is his coproducer.

In addition, Clanfield discusses the work of activist Arthur Lamothe and his connections with the Marxist CIP-Champ Libre group. Lamothe made an important documentary film series in which he portrayed the Montagnais Indians. It is entitled *Chronique des Indiens du Nord-Est du Québec*. The series consists of the eight-part *Carcajou et le péril blanc* (1974), and the four-part *La terre de l'homme* (1980). Says Clanfield, "Yielding to the grievances and testimony of the Indians themselves in these films, he revealed to the Québécois—at the height of their aspirations to a just redress of their own historic grievances—the fate of the Indians whose land, language, culture, and heritage had been, and were being, irrevocably destroyed by white Europeans of French as well as of English extraction. Made with anthropologist Rémi Savard, these films gave voice to Indian experience and make Perrault's films seem coy or distant by comparison. But if Lamothe's films disclose Indians' grievances in a more confrontational setting, and imply a tougher social analysis than Perrault's, his curious, almost surrealist juxtapositions within the frame, his symphonic editing style, and a tragic sense of destiny reveal common roots with a Québécois tradition" (Clanfield 1987, 51−2). Of Lamothe's *Mémoire battante* (1983), which deals with the Montagnais Reservation in Québec, Pratley gives an unflattering assessment, calling it "another of this film-maker's long and talkative anthropological studies" (*TS* 1987, 263).

Then, too, Maurice Bulbulian, of whom I spoke in Chapter 2, used the "direct" camera as a tool of "*science et conscience*" to portray the condition of Canadian Inuit and "Amerindians"—and indeed he is said to have given the most pertinent documentation of natives seeking a vindication of their rights since Lamothe produced his series on the Montagnais (Coulombe 1991, 74−5; Lever *Hist.* 1988, 237−9). He has made *Ameshkuatan* (1978), *Debout sur leur terre* (1982) and, recently, *L'Indien et la mer* (1992) and *Nitinaht* (1992).

And Tony Ianuzielo—in Pratley, spelled Ianzelo [*TS* 1987, 122; 285]—has made a number of films for the NFB concerned with the Crees and with other issues of the Far North. Notable is his *Cree Hunters of Mistassini*, which is known in French as *Chasseurs cris de Mitassini* (with Boyce Richardson, 1974).

Yet another series called *Légendes indiennes du Canada* was made by a Frenchman (from France), Daniel Bertolino, while the Turkish *cinéaste* Asen Balikli has made films on the Netsilik Inuit.

In a time when the report of the Manitoba Commission charged with an inquiry into justice for Native Peoples has declared their treatment by the justice system of Canada "an international scandal" (a finding issued on 29 August 1991), and also following the demonstrations of the Oka Indians in Québec in the summer of 1990 that have caused them to become known for more than cheese, one can look for more visibility in the treatment of the questions (and for more than a ghostly presence of native peoples) in *québécois* films of the future, be they by filmmakers of English, of French, or of Amerindian descent (or of any other national background for that matter). Indeed, one such film made since the events of Oka is Gabriel Pelletier's *L'Automne sauvage*. It involves the voyage myth. In other words, the director has sought, as he himself explains it, to recreate the voyage found in Joseph Conrad's *Heart of Darkness*, a novel that also fed *Apocalypse Now*. But Pelletier's film was not well-received critically.[21]

NATIVE CANADIAN DIRECTORS

One must note as well a few already extant, if isolated, examples of outstanding films by Native Peoples themselves, and particularly the documentaries of Alanis Obomsawin, an ethnocinematographist. Obomsawin, surnamed Ko-li-la-wato (She-Who-Makes-Us-Happy), is an excellent example of an anglophone (Québécoise) Native director and producer concerned in her films with the life of Native Canadians. Born on the Odanak Reservation in 1932, member of the Abénaquise band, she acquaints us with the culture, history, and aspirations of her people. Working predominantly for the National Film Bureau, she has made several documentaries of note, her first one being *Christmas at Moose Factory* (1971). In 1977 she made *Amisk*, a documentary about a festival organized by a Montréal group, which was in support of the Cree Indians and their opposition to the projected development of a hydroelectric plant on the James Bay. In the same year, she made *Mother of Many Children*, comprised of testimonies of "Indian" and Inuit women revolving around the concept of the primordial role of woman in the transmission of tradition. For this she won the Grand Prix at the International Festival of Arctic Film in Dieppe, France. (See Denise Pérusse in Coulombe [1991, 394–400], parts of which I have translated and paraphrased in the preceding paragraph.)

Alanis Obomsawin's *Mother of Many Children (Mère de tant*

d'enfants) (1977), an album of native womanhood, gives portraits of several women through testimonials and archival still photos as well as drawings; all provide interesting, sometimes moving visuals. Some of the testimony is given in French.

The women tell of the residential schools, which were closed in 1969. The birth of a baby to an adolescent Cree mother is shown; and the women speak of the healing arts and herbal medicines known to these people for centuries, much of the knowledge having been transmitted through women. The Inuit woman is shown, too; and a woman's initiation rites in the Ojibway band is depicted through dolls. The initiate is taught to do things quickly and neatly and to finish what she starts. She must learn herbs and how to preserve foods, and how to do her hair as a woman. It is her aunt who instructs her.

The scene shifts to a Chippewa woman studying at Harvard University, and to her classroom, where a black professor tells his class how minorities must fight oppression.

Another woman urges women to raise themselves up. "It takes women to get things going, and to get things done," she says.

The film informs us also of a law (Sect 12−1B of the Indian Act) that ruled that a native woman marrying a white man would lose her rights with the band. When the law was contested by one Indian woman, it was found discriminatory, but her case failed in the Supreme Court.

Again, we see Indian women gathering wild rice with two sticks, so that some will fall in the dugout and some in the water ... "you must seed as you go." An Ojibway male then dances on the rice to hull it; a woman must not.

The advances of women are shown when Potts runs as chief on her crutches. Her three oldest daughters are attending university, she says, for there is a "need for them to be independent, even if they are girls."

Examples of native art are presented, as is a woman broadcasting from a radio station that carries sixty miles, and informs the people of the surrounding area of important news.

Women are seen making prints from stones carved by men and women; the prints will go to a co-op in Montréal. At this co-op we see baskets being made that are so tightly woven one can carry water in them. We learn about throat singing. We meet the first Indian girl to work in Indian Affairs; now an older woman, she tells how she was hired as a bookkeeper and then finally promoted to Accountant Grade I.

While some have made this kind of progress, other "Indian" and some métis women tell of their problems with alcohol; we see the inside of the Portage Correctional Center (or Provincial Gaol) in Manitoba, which some find hard to leave, because then they are put on welfare, and given a small amount of money on which it is difficult to survive.

But most outstanding in this film is the 108-year-old Cree woman who married a nonstatus Indian and lost her own status as a Cree. She tells of snaring partridges and rabbits to survive, and recounts how the Great Spirit created woman and gave her many children. She says that when a woman speaks she should be respected and so should her children, because they are precious. Finally, Merle Baptist, also a Cree, dons traditional clothing, and we are regaled with a woman's dance.

"We are special, and should keep our traditions, our identity," is the concluding message; for all are agreed that following traditions can be a source of strength in their changing positions and conditions. The film ends with a woman singing an ancient song to a group of young people.

After making "Sounds from Our People," a series of six television films (1979), Obomsawin won the Order of Canada decoration (1983). She then directed *Incident at Restigouche*, a documentary relating the confrontation between the Micmacs of the Restigouche reservation and the Sûreté du Québec (Québec Security). This disagreement revolved around the fishing rights of Indians on that reservation. The film depicts with irony the fight of the government to assure its autonomy while repressing the fundamental right of the Indians on their own territory.

More specifically, *Incident at Restigouche* (1984), an NFB film, uses drawings, testimonials, and stills to depict the consequences of the request of the Québec government, made on 9 June 1981, that the Micmac salmon fishermen remove all nets from the estuary. As the band resisted, on 11 June the government sent ninety wardens and three hundred Québec police to raid the settlement and to confiscate and destroy the nets. Another raid was mounted on 20 June. But the native people set up blockades over the bridges, and drew support from all over North America. Some were arrested and fined, but by 1983 the convictions were overturned, for "facts and errors of law committed during the trials." This 1984 documentary uncannily foretells the incidents outside Montréal involving officials and their efforts to manage the Oka Indian blockades in the summer of 1990.

In 1986, Obomsawin made *Richard Cardinal: Cry from a Diary of a Metis Child*, about a metis child who committed suicide after being shuttled from home to home. And in 1987 Obomsawin filmed *Poundmaker's Lodge — A Healing Place* (1987; 29 min. 27 sec.; NFB). *Poundmaker's Lodge* . . . is concerned with alcohol and drug abuse by native peoples who finally wind up in Saint Albert (Alberta), where they can recuperate at Poundmaker's Lodge, named for Chief Poundmaker, a historic figure who taught that the Indian could overcome all obstacles. Using archival films and stills, as well as testimonials, this disturbing documentary shows young men (of an average age of twenty-five) who have been victims of great upheavals in their environments, of destruction and despair, of racism, rejection, betrayal, and loss, as they themselves tell it. They have been abandoned, or removed from their parents by white welfare workers, and if they attempt to return to their native villages, they are aliens. Murder and attempted suicide, and the suicide of parents and siblings, are common experiences for them. They have also lived a life of extreme violence. Alcoholics and drug addicts, they have come to understand all too well how alcohol was originally given to them by white men "in order to get their land, their women, and their furs away from them." It was introduced by the Europeans as a poison, says one of them. One encounters this classic colonization device in many contexts.

But at Poundmaker's Lodge these men have found hope and fellowship; they look at their past and, by freeing themselves from alcohol and drugs, they then begin to live their lives. The healing process at this lodge includes a return to native culture and ancient traditions. For example, they use the ancient custom of the sweat lodge for comfort and for purification. By passing through the sweat lodge they are cleansed of the storm of terrors; all is clear, and that is the "medicine." They learn love of brothers and sisters, and make appeal to the Great Spirit. When asked for the word for "sin," one Cree replied, "there is no word for 'sin;' our children are our future, and the shattering of the future is a 'sin'." This is by way of saying that the Crees must have a future. And the film ends with the affirmation that "We can make it and still retain our own culture, belief, and values."

The "applewine song" — telling of how wine stole away their life and advising that one eat the apples from the tree before they turn to wine — runs through the program, and it, along with a reading that expresses a longing that 'they go back to Cut Knife Hill' (to the old traditions) heightens the emotional impact of this remarkable work.

ANGLOPHONE FICITION FILMS AND ALTERITY

As the reader can readily appreciate, the issues we are looking at here are fit subject for a whole separate analysis, and can only be treated in passing here. Nevertheless, they do show to what an extent Québec, along with the rest of Canada, is becoming, or already *is*, truly multicultural. We can no longer speak of a *Québécois pure laine*, that is, one died in the wool, as the exclusive spokesman for the province; and the xenophobia the members of this province have historically felt toward the stranger and the immigrant may well be disappearing, as the francophone birth rate in the province decreases, and the need for population to do the work and provide the services grows. An effort to foster acceptance of the foreign, the Other, may well be one of the chief subjects of the relatively recent masterpiece, *Jésus de Montréal*. But the message is a subtext in many of the highly successful children's films where the marginal and the immigrant are incorporated into the story. Thus, the Vietnamese child of such a film as *The Dog Who Stopped the War* (*La Guerre des tuques*) is important to the visual and psychological impact he will have on the viewer.

In the eighth art, or animation, the American-born Montréalaise Caroline Leaf stands out for her *Owl Who Married a Goose* (1976), which relies upon Amerindian legend for its story and upon the Inuit language for its memorable sound track. In *The Street*, mentioned previously, we have her wonderful swirling visual effects, used to tell a very short story that deals with a Jewish boy's contact with death. Her work draws, then, on the culture of at least two large ethnic groups found in Québec, and throughout Canada for that matter. Leaf made an unusual documentary on the singing sisters, Kate and Anna McGarrigle (1981), into which she inserted some of her animation. However, she herself was not entirely satisfied with this film, and decided she was not a "bonne monteuse . . . ."[22] Indeed, this documentary falls well beneath her other work in quality; it gives the feel of having been made in the 60s, rather than in the 80s. Moreover, one should not forget that the McGarrigles were given their first exposure quite some time ago by Lena Spencer, the driving force behind Caffe Lena, a small coffee house and theater in upstate New York that also provided a showplace for the as-yet unknown artists Bob Dylan, Arlo Guthrie, David Bromberg, and David Amram. The story of this woman and her café is told in the documentary *Caffe Lena*, which aired first on American PBS stations in January, 1991. (It was hosted by Kate McGarrigle.) Kate and Anna McGarrigle also appear in the PBS program (now video), *Songs of the Civil War*.

These many minorities, the immigrants so marginal in their condition, so resented and yet so ambivalently wanted by many Québécois of French descent, are a part of the movie scene; and, as I said, some of the films made in Montréal may either portray such minorities, or may well even be the product of a divergent ethnic group. Nevertheless, all these works have what we would call "true Canadian content," because it is actually within the nature of Canada to have a pluralistic society—which, in fact, constitutes both its strength and its cross. Trudeau claimed that harmony between the two races (francophone and anglophone) was the crucible of the Canadian experience (*"la réalité canadienne"*). Some onlookers would have difficulty seeing the melting. Indeed, in Canada the melting-pot philosophy is eschewed by most ethnic groups.

Thus, when Céline Dion, the rising Québécoise *chanteuse* refused a prize for best anglophone Québécois recording a few years back, on the grounds that she was a francophone Québécoise, she offended many people by her oversimplification. Not only had she overlooked the fact that she was using English to further her own career—as did Mankiewicz, and as Jutra attempted to do with *Surfacing* (1981), and with *By Design* (1981) (a very bad movie about two American lesbians who decide to have a baby)—but she overlooked as well that one can be an anglophone Québécois with as much authenticity as a francophone one. It is important, then, to note that just as certain francophone Québécois filmmakers have made films in English, both in Québec and elsewhere, so also there is a group of anglophone filmmakers who are native Québécois; and by that fact (if for no other, such as being of an Italian or Jewish or Native-American background), they constitute a minority group. And even though they may belong to one of these "minority" groups, these filmmakers do not necessarily devote their attention to their own group, but, rather, to Québec society in general, or just to a story, as is the case, for example, with George Bloomfield, who was born in Montréal in 1930. As we saw, he directed *Riel*, which in turn dealt with a métis rebel!

We are not speaking here, of course, of such blockbusters as *Meatballs* and *Porky's*, which were great money-makers, and are well known to American audiences—who, however, probably do not even realize these movies are Canadian. Similarly, Harvey Hart has used the Québec scene in his *Fortune and Men's Eyes*, an "American" film, shot in Montréal, taken from John Herbert's play about men in prison. Jewison has done likewise with *Agnes of*

God. But I am speaking here of films made in Québec having true Canadian content, films that reflect Canadian life and values, and are not easily equated to American works. In this way, some anglophone Canadian directors may sometimes set their fictional story in Québec, but with the purpose of showing something about Québec. For example, Eric Till is British-born, but interested in using a Montréal story upon occasion. Often working on international projects with adequate budgets, he is responsible for *A Great Big Thing* (1968), a Montréal-made but American-financed film about a day in the life of a Montréal drifter, who is sometimes compared to Don Owen's Ernie (of *The Ernie Game*).[23]

The reader of French may profitably consult Thomas Waugh's lengthy article on anglo-québécois film.[24] In it, Waugh discusses the clout this body of film has, and the amount of visibility afforded to this "powerful" anglophone community, considering the small population its cinema represents. Waugh finds that since 1976 this cinema is eclectic, schizophrenic, anguished, and marginal — a good reflection of the situation of a community that lost its electoral power to francophone Québec and its economic power to Toronto. He also finds that the new blood, coming from an influx of anglophone immigrants, has shaken up the old monolithic anglophone culture and economy. Early cinematographic reflections of that culture and questions regarding it are found in George Kaczender's *Don't Let the Angels Fall* (1968). Other reflections are seen in Robin Spry's *Prologue* (1969) and in Ted Kotcheff's *Apprenticeship of Duddy Kravitz* (1974), which criticized Jewish immigrants' sons and their dreams of success. Don Owen's *Ernie Game* (1967) is for him another important work. But he finds that this cinema is, at this point, often mediocre (*Surrogate*, 1984), and is dominated by the ONF and by the presence of immigrants: Americans (such as Bonnie Klein and Caroline Leaf); English (Derek May, John Smith), Australians (Michael Rubbo), Hungarians (Robert Lantos, Albert Kish), or Canadians originally of other provinces (Martin Duckworth, Giles Walker, Donald Brittain). Waugh cites, also, cinema by women (*I'll Find a Way*; 1977; d. Beverly Shaffer); *If You Love This Planet* (1983; d. Teri [sic] Nash) and *A Twentieth Century Chocolate Cake* (1982; d. Lois Siegel) "... ni féministe, ni sérieusement diffusé ... [neither feminist nor seriously distributed]"; and he mentions trendy films such as Walker's *Masculine Mystique*, *90 Days*, etc.[25] Two important children's films, according to him, are Michael Rubbo's *Peanut Butter Solution* and Theodore Flicker's *Jacob Two-Two Meets the Hooded Fang* (1977). Certain political autoportraits that we have studied in these pages are cited by

Waugh. These include *I Hate to Lose*; *Yes or No, Jean-Guy Moreau*; *Riel*; *The Champions* (Brittain being the "best artist of the lot . . ."). *Bingo* also is mentioned, as well as *Lies My Father Told Me* (the "reverse" of *Joshua Then and Now*), and *Two Solitudes*. As *"couples-paraboles"* Waugh selects *One Man* of Robin Spry and the televised version of *Balconville* by Mark Blandford (1983), based on the play of the anglo-québécois Marxist author David Fennario. I agree with Waugh that this latter was a very fine performance indeed of a memorable play, in which situations in working-class neighborhoods of Montréal (Verdun, a suburb, and Pointe-Saint-Charles) underscore the conflicts (the solitudes) between the francophones and the anglophones. (Comparisons between different social classes were, incidentally, the subject of Jean-Claude Lord's French-language film *Les Colombes* [1972; 117 min.], starting Jean Besré, Lise Thouin and Jean Duceppe. In it Lord shows two families, one from the working class, living in East Montréal, the other from the bourgeoisie, living in West Montréal. The theme is in fact rampant.)

Waugh closes his article with a list of twenty important anglophone films produced between 1975 and 1986. They are: *Balconville*; *The Champions*; *Empire, Inc.*; *I Can Hear Zimbabwe Calling*; *Incident at Restigouche*; *Jacob Two-Two Meets the Hooded Fang*; *Joshua Then and Now*; *The Long Sleep and the Big Good-Bye*; *The Masculine Mystique*; *Mother Tongue*; *Not a Love Story: a Film about Pornography*; *One Man*; *Or d'ur*; *Rubber Gun*; *Solzhenitsyn's Children Are Making a Lot of Noise in Paris*; *Speaking Our Peace*; *The Street*; *Suzanne*; and *Temiscaming Québec*. We have discussed a number of these, and will shortly look at one or two of the fictional films he mentions.

But, first, let us consider one of the most famous of anglophone Québécois directors, Paul Almond, born in Montréal in 1931. Though Waugh makes little or nothing of his work (and his trilogy is too early to figure in Waugh's list), Almond is one of the most talented and one of the most profound of the anglophone Québécois filmmakers.

The Canadian/French-Canadian experience is surely brought into focus in *Isabel* (1968), a stunning anglophone Québec film made now many years ago by Almond, and starring Geneviève Bujold (then Almond's wife). She was right for the role, the action of which was set in Gaspésie (the Gaspé peninsula, along the south shore of the St. Lawrence, east of Québec City), Bujold's place of origin. The story involves the return of a young girl to her home in a remote region of the Gaspé, where she begins to notice strange things. Pratley (*TS* 1987, 189) writes: "Beautifully photographed, sensitively acted and directed, splendidly brooding and atmospheric .... Paul Almond tells a fascinating tale of suppressed sex, subjective fears, and psychotic fancies."[26]

Backed by American distributors Columbia and Paramount, Almond selected Paramount, because it allowed him more latitude; from paramount he received a $250,000 budget. He began shooting in April 1967 at Shigawake on the Gaspé coast. In general, the film was a critical success in French Canada as well as in America: *Time Magazine* at the time of its release called it a first-rate success. But in Toronto and the rest of anglophone Canada the film received many negative reviews. (We should remember, however, that anglophone Canadians, who deem themselves rationalists, prefer clear-cut documentary-style films rather than a blurred and metaphysical approach such as that of Almond's.) The Canadian Film Development Corporation retrospectively rewarded Almond in the amount of $12,300 for his work on *Isabel*; Bujold received the award for best actress and Gerard Parks for best actor at the International Film Festival in Vancouver (1969).

Isabel is part of a trilogy, the other two being *The Act of the Heart* (1958) and *Journey* (1972). *The Act of the Heart*, about the love of a protestant woman for a Catholic priest, is said to bring out the coldness of Montréal and Rivière du Loup; *Isabel*, the harshness of Gaspésie. In *Journey*, a young woman is found unconscious and brought to a community in which the people live cut off from the rest of the world. She finally returns to civilization. The film displays the majesty of the Saguenay River. It was filmed along the river's shores just north of Tadoussac. Michel Euvrard has written an article in which he discusses the cold reception this film received from the critics.[27]

Isabel is, as Almond himself said, a "study in fear." Almond's theory is that, in order to rid themselves of paralyzing fears, people must return to their origins and question their past existence. *Isabel* is an examination of such a return journey. In this film, he also portrayed the repressive force of religion in Québec society, and particularly its inhibiting effects on young women. Finally, the film also depicts spring emerging with difficulty from winter, a topos of the woman emerging from her troubled childhood.

Viewing this film, we confirm what we already knew, which is that fear is internal and can be of an imagined source, but is very real to the person under its spell. We also learn about the quasi-Jansenistic repressions of the Québec Church, and in particular of the wasted womanhood of Isabel's sister. Through the villagers

we learn that, as in many small towns and rural areas, gossip in
Gaspésie is a pastime. The villager's life is unsavory beneath the
rural routine, the eerie and sinister effects of the film managing to
punctuate this. The dialogue, too, is spare, and was in fact one of
the things that brought critical acclaim for this film. Indeed, the
nonverbal communication of the characters intensifies the moody,
chilling motif of fear.[28] As regards the climate of the Gaspé, we
can see that winter locks these people in, and that in this rugged,
storm-swept coastal setting, the climate and topography reflect
Isabel's own and the entire society's repressions. The photography
of Georges Dufaux is, as usual, excellent.

The ending of *Isabel* is somewhat ambiguous. Janet Edsforth
interprets it as follows: Isabel is making love to her father, brother,
and grandfather through Jason; and all these men had been objects
of mystery and fear. Now she accepts and absorbs them, first
internalizing, then externalizing them, then laying them to rest. In
other words, she exorcises her demons, and emerges a total woman,
capable of love and of being loved.[29] But Piers Handling has
contended that the ambiguity of the ending is a structural weakness.[30]

Edsforth writes of *Isabel*: ". . . some understood it, some didn't,
some loved it, some hated it, some did both. There were, it
seemed, as many opinions and interpretations as there were facets
of the film itself."[31] Some people who have viewed this film with
me find it dark, haunting, and extremely impacting. As do I.

Yet, the authenticity of these films of Almond's, cast in English,
is questioned by Geneviève Bujold herself in her interview with
Michel Euvrard when she says: "But Isabel . . . Martha, they are
not me; first of all the sole fact of not speaking in my language!
Didn't it shock you, in *The Act of the Heart*, to hear Monique
Leyrac and Geneviève Bujold speaking to each other in English?
No, it would have been better if those characters had been acted
by someone else."[32]

It may come as a surprise that at least one Québécois immigrant
who makes feature-length films in the province of Québec is
American-born! Frank Vitale's fictional work, also from the 70s, is
entered in both Coulombe and Pratley; it is *Montreal Main* (1973–
74). Pratley describes *Montreal Main* as "a well-intentioned but
depressing story about a relationship between a mature man and
an adolescent boy, set in an artists' colony in Montreal, in which
everyone is thoroughly unhappy about life" (*TS* 1987, 210).

According to Michel Euvrard, *Montreal Main* "is a low-budget
film that tells the story of a brief friendship between a bohemian

photographer and a young boy from a good family. Through them the film shows the two life-styles of Mont-Royal, Westmount and the Saint-Lawrence boulevard, the anglophone and the francophone, and the gay and the straight. The friendship lasts until the boy's father, who is troubled, asks Frank not to see his son anymore. However, Frank and his friends have shown themselves to be totally respectful of Johnnie's physical and moral integrity, and offer him a richer milieu, more favorable to his development, than school or his family. In a perspective that is more impressionistic than documentary, the daily life of the characters, the milieu, the *quartier* are painted ... through episodes whose rhythm and atmosphere are put into place in a seemingly spontaneous fashion, but, in fact, are carefully prepared. Through his directing, through the calm and sustained intensity of his interpretation of Frank, opposite a Johnnie who is gracious, concentrated, of a perfectly natural dignity, Vitale secures ... the continuity of the film. In the anglophone cinema of Montréal, *Montreal Main* is a shooting star, a film without ancestors and without posterity" (Coulombe 1991, 541–2; my translation).

Other films of Vitale include *Penny and Ann* (a documentary; 1974), about a rehabilitation center; *East End Hustle* (1976), about a prostitute who, having escaped the sidewalk beat, wants to help other women; and *The Rubber Gun* (1977). Vitale now works in New York. (On Vitale see also Pratley *TS* 1987, 209; 231.)

Robin Spry is another, even more prominent filmmaker who has offered Québec through an anglophone's vision. Leaving aside his important political work, we have, as his most famous fictional film, the thriller *One Man* (1977). When Montréal TV journalist Jason Brady discovers a shocking case of corporate negligence that permits emission of dangerous pollutants that cause the death of children, he must decide whether to risk his job, his marriage, his family, and possibly his life — for he is threatened by corporate and political interests. This is a gripping feature film about one man's confrontation with himself, his ideals, and the realities around him. Pratley says: "A compelling and concerned drama ... Much of what it is has to say later came true with the discovery of the contamination of Love Canal in Niagara Falls, N.Y." (*TS* 1987, 234). I personally found this film to be very absorbing and, indeed, suspenseful.

I would remind my reader of Spry's *Prologue* (1969), as well as his *Action: The October Crisis of 1970* (1973), and his *Reaction: a Portrait of a Society in Crisis* (1973), discussed in my Chapter 6.

Marcel Jean, who views Spry as a Québécois filmmaker, follows the career of this talented director, actor, *chef opérateur*, editor, producer, and script-writer, born in Toronto in 1939. Spry, says Jean, "is a first-class anglophone filmmaker, who in the beginning was able to perceive the cultural and political reality of Québec, though his films are some of them good, some not so good. But his recent films have lost this cultural vision" (Coulombe 1991, 504–5). Also of interest is the fact that Spry coproduced *A corps perdu* (1988), the full-length fiction film by Léa Pool (q.v., Ch 3).

Lever makes some pertinent remarks about Spry's anglophone vision in *Action* ... (see Ch. 6), saying that francophone Quebeckers might have wanted to make this story, but would have been accused of "apprehended nonobjectivity." Spry's film, he says, shows how far the understanding of a progressive intellectual can go (*Hist.* 1988, 219). The NFB did, in fact, give the mandate to make a film on the events of the October 1970 crisis to this anglophone, ironic though that may be. Therefore, though the film is honest and informed, it lacks a ture political interpretation embodied in the lived experience of a Quebecker (*Hist.* 1988, 234).

I recently saw Spry's *Obsessed* (1987 — Coulombe gives 1988; 2 hours), which a fellow-viewer considered to be "typically Canadian," meaning, as explained, "after justice." Starring Kerrie Keane and Daniel Pilon as Max, her estranged husband, the film concerns a violent struggle between an American hit-and-run driver and the Montréalaise mother of the victim, her twelve-year-old son who has died as a result of the accident. The mother seeks — despite frustrating international laws (and a stern judge played by the recently expired Colleen Dewhurst) — to bring the perpetrator to justice. It is worthy of the two stars it received in *TV Guide*.

Less striking than *One Man* is the film *Gabrielle*, by Lawrence L. Kent. Kent was born in Johannesburg, South Africa, in 1937, and moved to Montréal in the 1960s. He is known for his films made for the ONF: *Cold Pizza* and *Sakatchewan — 45° Below*. His works often deal with student life and with the problems of youth, as is the case with *High* (1967), about irresponsible youth — a film that was censored for its extensive pornographic content (Pratley *TS* 1987, 190; Lever *Hist.* 1988, 208).

Although we found few films about students among the francophone offerings, in *Gabrielle* (1979) it is a question of an American medical student at McGill, and of his efforts to stay on the hockey team, court Gabrielle — in spite of their religious and cultural differences — and, by remaining in Canada, avoid the army and the war in Vietnam. The action takes place in 1967 Montréal (and in Madison, Wisconsin).

Matt, after having been expelled from McGill for cheating and for a prank that brings injury to a professor, decides to stay in Canada with his beloved "Gabbie." But when he realizes that his father died for his country, and when his grandfather comes to appeal to him, his guilt catches up with him, and he goes back to the States to join the army. Boot training is ugly, but he will join Gabbie soon, and they will be married as soon as he gets to Montréal. However, at the eleventh hour he is shipped off to Vietnam, and subsequently is reported killed. Gabrielle, in the meantime, is pregnant. She must raise the child alone, but her parents, who at first opposed her relationship with an anglophone protestant American, help her. When the child is about two or three, she makes a trip to Madison to meet Matthew's parents. There she learns that Matthew is not dead after all, but in a VA Hospital, a cripple who evidently preferred to have her think him dead. Nonetheless, she rejoins him and presents the child to him — a strange surprise ending to this conventional plot that is less than satisfactory.

The filmmaker takes advantage of the period setting (the 1960s) to weave in every conceivable conflict of the day, including the exodus of American youth to Canada during the draft-dodging era of the Vietnam war, as well as tensions between the French-speaking and the English-speaking Canadians, reflected through signs, such as "Speak French," and "100 years of oppression," and also through the blasé and disrespectful attitudes of the English-speaking McGill students (mostly male). Gabrielle's brother Claude embodies the revolution, spouting lines about the people, the workers, and "négres blancs," and seeing in Matthew the anglo-phone enemy. Curious and unbelievable scenes in the classroom at McGill (not to mention a preposterous scene in the library) add little to the plot, much less the ambiance. Scenes depicting conflicts between Gabrielle and her family, including her brother Claude, over her involvement with this American, are contrasted with many scenes of love-making and pretty *ballades* in horse and buggy through the parks of Montréal and visits to the *jardin botanique*. Establishing shots of the Université de Montréal and of McGill are played off against scenes in the cemetery in Madison, with the grandfather (Eddie Albert) and his daughter-in-law (Cloris Leachman) reminiscing on the greatness of Matt's father. Family pride, cultural conventions, religious persuasions, and national heritage pull at both of the main characters. We have here a very

banal story told in a very straightforward, conventional, and predictable way. And to make matters worse, I had the dubious
pleasure of viewing this film in a version dubbed into French!

Among the minorities of Québec is a large, sometimes unfelt
group of francophones, Acadian in origin, who fled to the province
of Québec at the time of the *grand dérangement*, while others fled
to Haiti and then to Louisiana, to become the Cajuns. A very
respectable if small body of literature has arisen among the Acadians,
first in their own provinces (New Brunswick, Nova Scotia, and
Prince Edward Island), and then as expatriot artists, who find a
better intellectual milieu and greater support in Québec than at
home. Notable among these is Antonine Maillet, born in New
Brunswick but now living much of the time in Montréal. Her *Pélagie-
la-Charrette*, which took the Prix Goncourt in 1979, was scheduled
to be brought to the big screen in 1983. It is my understanding that
the agreements for the making of this film are at bay, the con-
tracting (filmmaking) company having gone bankrupt. On the other
hand, it is worth mentioning that another Mailletian masterpiece,
La Sagouine, which originated as *a pièce de théâtre*, was very
successfully serialized and shown on Canadian television; the
Québécois, though they sometimes look down on Acadians, had
no difficulty understanding the underdog position from which La
Sagouine (played by Viola Léger) was speaking. Videos of *La
Sagouine* are available.

Anglophone Acadian life is the subject of a rather good film
entitled *The Bay Boy* (1984; d. Daniel Petrie), starring Kiefer
Sutherland. Daniel Petrie grew up in Nova Scotia, where the film
was made. It concerns a teenager and his coming of age in a rural
Canadian community (Nova Scotia; Acadia) during the 1930s.

Pratley classes this film with *The Tin Flute*, *The Grey Fox*, and
several other illustrious Canadian films. He views it as a truly
Canadian film (genuine), and one worth knowing. (I agree.) He
describes it as a gentle and loving story of Petrie's own boyhood
days (*TS* 1987, 264). Petrie, after working in Hollywood for many
years, returned to Nova Scotia to film this story.

The film shows us much about the beauty and isolation of the
Nova Scotia fishing village. It also gives us a disturbing portrayal of
the clergy, but scandals among priests in Nova Scotia and in an
orphanage and a parish in Newfoundland, recently exposed, give
the episode between the young man and his "host" some believ-

ability. One should not think of this as exclusively Canadian, of course; only a very few years ago scandal arose when many a contributor to the cause of homeless boys learned that he or she had been supporting a priest's expenses for wining and dining these boys in order to get sexual favors. Other cases both in the U.S. and in Canada have since come to light. Additionally, to read Marie Claire Blais's *A Season in the Life of Emmanuel* is to come to know of this sexual aberration among priests of (Québec) boys' schools.

The protagonist's first sexual encounter with a girl is less believable, I'm afraid. And his witness to violent acts by a devilish "villain" adds a dimension of suspense to the intrigue.

Maltin's 1991 *Guide* gives this film two stars. He writes that it is a "well-meaning but hopelessly predictable portrayal of a teenager and his coming of age in rural Canadian community during [the] 1930s." And the *Guide* goes on to say: "You've seen this one many times before; Ullmann in particular is one-dimensional as Sutherland's hardworking mother." Is this assessment valid? I personally find it too harsh, and think it should be modified. Up by half a star, or maybe by one more whole star? In any event, Pratley's view is more useful than Maltin's: the film is truly "Canadian" in its atmosphere, its cultural load. A film about passage, like *Who Has Seen the Wind?* and *Mon oncle Antoine*, but not so great, *The Bay Boy* can nonetheless complement the other two; for the same theme is presented in three different Canadian cultural settings! The three shown together could give us quite a view of what it is (was) like to grow up in Canada, depending on the region.

On the other hand, in *Crazy Moon*, by the anglophone Québécois filmmaker, Allan Eastman, Keifer Sutherland (son of the Canadian superstar Donald Sutherland, and himself an up-and-coming actor, very much appreciated by young American moviegoers) turned in a performance considerably superior to that in *The Bay Boy*. Or was it that that film script brought about a context in which his talents were better showcased?

Yet another very good film about anglophone Canadian adolescence (this time not Acadian) and about rites of passage, that additionally involves a difficult father-son relationship, is *Toby McTeague* 1985; 1987; d. Jean Claude Lord).

Rural Québec is the setting for this family story, in which the teenager tries to win a dog-sled race in order to save the business

of his widowed, injured father. The boy is assisted by the wisdom
of Sam, an aging Indian, whom he has helped.

This is arguably Jean-Claude Lord's most important English-
language film, but he also made *Visiting Hours* (1981); *Covergirl*
(1984) — a failure; and *The Vindicator* (1985). I have seen *Toby
McTeague* both in English and in a dubbed French version (entitled
Toby), and it is quite entertaining. I am confident that young
people would enjoy this film.

GILES WALKER AND MINORITIES

The films of Giles Walker show yet another side of Québec life,
the life of minority ethnicities; and they involve rather strange
goings-on.

In *The Masculine Mystique* (1984; d. Walker with John N. Smith)
we first meet Alex of the Walker trilogy, which also includes *90
Days* and *The Last Straw* (1987). In Walker's *90 Days* (1985), two
characters from the director's *Masculine Mystique* (1984) return:
one (Blue) to wed a mail-order Korean bride, the other (Alex) to
be a donor to a sperm bank. Blue has found Hyang Sook in the
Cherry Blossoms magazine and has been writing to her. When she
arrives we have a clash of cultures, codes, and customs. She gives
him a large box; he gives her a baseball glove. She has a ninety-
day visa, in which time she must marry or go back; additionally,
we are privy here to ninety days in the life of two nonfrancophone
Montréalais, one of Italian descent, the other seemingly Polish
(Blue's real name is David [Lisenski]?). The social infrastructure is
totally lacking: these people seldom interact or even intersect with
the francophone majority population. The two police (played by
Michel Brunet and Pierre Goupil) who stop him speak English;
one without an accent.

Alex characterizes his wife Joanne, who has kicked him out
of the house, as a "rotten typical woman." He meets Laura. In
tailored suit and all business, she is a lawyer. She wants Alex to
donate sperm to a single woman who wants a child. Ten thousand
dollars are to be had for the right man; but he must be of Italian
descent. Alex gathers his sperm to background music from *Madame
Butterfly* and fantasizes. Laura comes to his room late at night to
tell him the results: he has lazy sperm.

By the time that Blue decides upon his Korean friend, she is
getting ready to leave for the airport. Alex will drive her. He
appears; she won't listen to Blue. Laura happens to be there to tell

Alex that there was a mix-up in the lab, and that he does not have lazy sperm, but, *au contraire*, one of the highest counts (2.2 million per milimeter). She is willing to raise the fee to twenty thousand dollars per pregnancy. In any case, when Laura sees the difficulty the two men are having with Hyang Sook, who is threatening to leave, she offers to intervene, and, of course, succeeds in getting her out of the car. Blue explains that he loves her. In the end, we have a protestant wedding with a "minister." Laura and Alex are the attendants.

The confessional scenes are awkward, it seems to me, with Blue telling his story to an unidentified confidant (us?). Pratley (*TS* 1987, 266) finds the film "in doubtful taste." I found it rather boring, also, but it brings out the loneliness of the Korean bride, as another minority figure in the largely francophone province of Québec.

Yet another sequel, called *The Last Straw*, was made in 1984; in it the most fertile man in the world (Sam Grana) is hired by an artificial insemination clinic.

A relatively recent Giles Walker film, *Princes in Exile* (1990; 103 minutes), aired on CBC Windsor in 1991. It is set in Camp Hawkins, a summer camp for young people who are afficted by life-threatening diseases. Ryan, a moody seventeen-year-old, remains aloof, in his own private world, and is given over to some extent by bitterness, until he meets Holly, also attending the camp. Thanks to her, Ryan discovers that love holds the key to many "miracles."

This film, which won the ecumenical prize at the 1990 Montréal World Film Festival, is regarded by some as a sensitive, uplifting story about the power of the human spirit to overcome adversities, and Gerald Pratley confided to me in person his admiration of the film. I found it touching, but far from great.

As noted above, John N. Smith, a Montréal-born director and producer, collaborated in the producing and directing of *The Masculine Mystique*. Smith is known for his studies of ethnic groups and marginal cultures. In 1977 he directed a film called *Happiness Is Loving Your Teacher*, which dealt with handicapped persons, and in 1981 he made *First Winter*, which concerned immigrants. He is also interested in the arts, and has made several films dealing with dance, theater, and music — for example, *Acting Class* (1980); *For the Love of Dance* (1981); *Gala* (1982); and *First Stop, China* (1985). His best known films are, however, *Train of Dreams* (1987) and, especially, *Sitting in Limbo* (1986). Like most Canadian directors, Smith clings to the documentary style, and this is especially apparent in *Sitting in Limbo*—a film that tells the story of the ups and downs in the everyday life of four black teenagers living in the Caribbean ghetto of Montréal. The tale, told with warmth and humor, features Pat, a feisty, outspoken eighteen-year-old who shares an apartment with two Jamaican teenagers living on welfare with their babies. The film combines documentary-style shooting techniques with nonprofessional actors and improvised dialogue, and comes up with a candid portrait of life as lived by this segment of the Montréal population.

Some contend—and among them Yves Rousseau—that *Train of Dreams* (1987; 89 min.; fiction) is Smith's best film. It, too, relies on documentary techniques, using a mobile camera that scrutinizes the bodies, a dry editing technique, and a realistic vision of the world, depicting a marginal hero who is a musician in the bargain. Like *Sitting in Limbo*, it stresses the difficulty young people have in believeing in themselves, as well as the importance of pedagogy. *Train of Dreams* was the first full-length English language film to earn the L.E. Ouimet-Molson prize. Smith's latest film is *Welcome to Canada* (Coulombe 1991, 499; my translations and paraphrases).

Other anglophone films worthy of note are: *Eliza's Horoscope* (1976; d. Gordon Sheppard; 121 min.); *Free Fall* (1964; d. Arthur Lipsett; 9 min.; Experimental); *Gala* (1982; d. John N. Smith; 91 min.; documentary); *Liberty Street Blues* (1988; d. André Gladu; 80 min.; documentary); *The Rising Tide* (1949; d. Jean Palardy; 31 min.; documentary, b&w); *Roughnecks* (1960; d. Guy L. Côté; 21 min.; documentary, b&w); *The Quest for Fire* (1981; d. Jean-Jacques Annaud, 100 min. [international project]; *Urgence-Emergency* (1988; d. Colin Low w/Tony Ianzelo; 35 min.; fiction, color).

Conclusion to Chapter 7

In the first chapter of this book, I mentioned the film *How to Make Love to a Negro without Getting Tired*, based on the novel by the Haitian Dany Laferrière (1989). It is of interest to note that Denis Bachand mentions this film, as well as those of Paul Tanna (sic), Léa Pool, Claude Gagnon, et al., as works that are not intent upon showing the old Québécois *"pure laine tricottée serrée"* of former days. Rather, Bachand contends, the cultural landscape (of the film, as of the society) has been modified "without having to deny its origins as a result."[33] I would agree totally with this assessment. But the question needs to be pushed a bit further. So complex has this multicultural spectrum become that the *québécois* film industry includes artists from all over the world, and not just Westerners: not only do they come from Ontario, England, France, Italy, Switzerland, Hungary, Haiti, and the United States, but from Africa, the Orient, and the Near East: Lebanon, Israel, and Syria. Francophone film directors make movies in French and in English; anglophone filmmakers do likewise. Sometimes a film is made in quite another language (Italian, for instance). Thus we would have to include in our rostrum not only the Syrian-born Vartkes Cholakian, of whom we have spoken in these pages (*Rappelle-toi*, with Mireille Dansereau [1975] or *A Simple Complex* [1978]), but also the younger Syrian, Bachar Chbib, who was but ten years old when he arrived in Québec in 1967. Having studied first at McGill, he turned to learning the art of filmmaking at Concordia University, and produced shorts such as a film on male prostitution, *Or d'Ur*—whose title puns on the French words *or dur* and *ordure*—(1983), and *Amour impossible* (1984), a documentary on marginal figures, transvestites, and neofascists. He has also made a number of long films, *Clair Obscur* (1988) being perhaps his most famous. Under the name Bashar Shbib he now films in the United States, where he has made *Julia Has Two Lovers* (1989), *Love and Greed* (1991), and *Lana in Love* (1991). (Michel Euvrard treats him in Coulombe 1991, 96–97.) More and more, French-Canadian moviemaking is becoming an international enterprise, as is true for other countries as well.

In any case, the multicultural nature of the Québec scene in many ways reflects that of greater Canada. If one wished to truly appreciate this and other facets of the Canadian mentality (distrust of and resentment over the penetration of American culture and values into Canada; a sense of uncertainty and, perhaps, inferiority; the frustrations and even schizophrenic absurdity of bilingualism) in a brief and humorous format, the best film one could view would be *Propaganda Message* (1974; 13 min. 18 sec.; NFB)—an animated film that stresses the heterogeneous nature of Canada and Canadians, and also the way federalism makes everything hold together. The many dissenting voices present in this conglomerate are made evident in the film; the tensions of bilingualism are also conveyed through the alternating (arbitrary) use of English and French.

But in reality the multiculturalism of the province, as of the whole nation, is not a laughing matter. It is at once a major asset and a source of great frustration, and even leads to serious problems of hostility (against assimilationism) and racism. This includes the frictions between Native Canadians and Quebeckers (which is old), between anglophone and francophone people (which is almost as old), and between the settled population and newly immigrated people who, because of the strict language laws and the unwelcoming atmosphere, often tend to land in the province and move on to other parts of Canada (all of which is relatively new). All these points of view are reflected on the Québec screen, and will no doubt continue to be. It is to be hoped that cinema will help to resolve such problems, as it documents the virtues and contributions of the various ethnicities. For it is no exaggeration to say that film can form as well as reflect attitudinal variations in a society.

Meanwhile, mainstream francophone cinema itself presents in masterful terms the civilization it seeks to mirror — not as a monolith, but as a polysemic, complex, contemporary, sophisticated, urbanized society with a language, a literature, and a history to be expressed to its people and to the world — regardless of what the Durham report had hoped to convey.

Concluding Remarks

Except for Québec, I have absolutely nothing to say.
　　　　　　　　　　　　　　—Claude Jutra (1970)

We have to stop talking about "losers."
　　　　　　　　　　　　　　—Jean Beaudin (1985)

It has come out in the pages of this book that the francophone
Canadian film follows the course of Canadian film in general by
its strong use of and (in the case of fictional movies) its debt to
the documentary in its distinctively national form, called "direct
cinema." Canadian, too, is the identity quest we observe in many
of the Québec films. But more particularly, the province of Québec
offers the world a corpus of film that echoes the longings of its
people for freedom from "colonization," for "sovereignty," for
"sovereignty association." That body of film therefore tends to
have an agenda that is often more sociopolitical in nature than is
the rest of Canadian film. The theme of pride as a died-in-the wool
Québécois is seen now to be countered by that of the multi-ethnic
voices that characterize the social scene in Québec; and those
many ethnicities are complements to the rise of the woman's voice
in both the francophone and anglophone productions of Québec
cinema. New women directors seek to show the history of entrapment that women have known through Church and society and
to mount a gender-marked cinema. As identity crises mount in
both the majority and the minority populations of the province, a
search to show what Old Québec was like and how history and
roots have determined the distinct nature of the *québécois* society
has come into play in the cinema. While horror and crime have
perhaps always been a part of Québec cinema, extreme visual
violence is to some extent new and still rare.

Noguez epitomizes the *québécois* cinema when he points out that
Québec is the almost exclusive subject of Québécois filmmakers,
from Perrault forward. In essence, Noguez contends that these

447

filmmakers are not concerned with Man with a capital M: they are not humanists (thank God, say Noguez); they are not aesthetes (more's the pity); nor are they formalists. Problems of the self (*le moi*), stormy and broken hearts, and little intimate Proustian or Gidian things hardly ever show up in the films from Québec, unless in some collective way. Films that are purely narrative do not prosper in Québec (and that's for the good, since there are too many of that kind anyway). And except for Lefebvre's work, formal research has little place, when compared to the French and Italian film. In short, in 1970 something was clarified in the *québécois* cinema. More and more filmmakers shied away from the candid-eye style, and came to prefer the cinema that relies on fable (or myth—i.e., that which is passed down by mouth) rather than on cinema that "reflects reality." And in that same era, cleavage occurred between filmmakers who were just in it for the money and the "real filmmakers"—the ones who are, as Flaherty had said as early as 1926, "lovers, amateurs, in the literal sense, passionate people, who undertake things without a financial end." A struggle between the rose and the reseda, between those who believe in "dough" and those who do not.[1]

That is a struggle that, in my opinion, goes on to this day. And among the latter films we might count the 1991 filming of the life of one of Québec's greatest poets (if not *the* greatest). For Robert Favreau in his *Nelligan* continues in the tradition of his predecessors with an exploration of Québec's mythology and culture, whether this film appeals to the international film-going community or not, whether the international filmgoing community even knows who Nelligan is or not. As Léo Bonneville writes, "You must hurry and see this film. It is not a trial, nor an opera. It is the vibration of a life turned to ashes by the interior fire of poetry. It is the sincere testimony of a genius from our own homeland, inscribed in our History. *Nelligan* is a film that does honor to the cinema of our province."[2]

The future of *québécois* cinema seems further assured by the fact that a goodly number of young filmmakers have surfaced in the past few years. Not only do these reflect the multicultural nature of the society today, but many of them are more preoccupied with the notion of continuity than with the notion of rupture, according to Richard Martineau.[3] The person who can read French will learn a great deal about five young filmmakers and their recent products in the January 1991 issue of *Séquences*. There, one will find interviews with three young women directors—Jeanne Crépeau, Catherine Martin, and Johanne Prégent—and two young men—Olivier

Asselin and Jean-Pierre Gariépy—as they converse with Gilles Carle and Martineau (representing *Séquences*). In general, they show their appreciativeness of existence of the National Film Board (ONF), but also express their problems with getting producers to invest in their works. They defend the making of shorts and documentaries, but lament the difficulty of getting them shown. (A special theater is needed as an outlet for this kind of cinema, says Carle.) What surfaces is that these young people are proposing a new vision of the child and of woman; and that they are attentive to problems of daily life never dealt with before. Says Carle, "You approach subjects that were not approached in the times of direct cinema."[4] Gariépy and Johanne Prégent among them are especially mindful of the dangers of a cinema that is too individualistic, too oneiric, one that would present a reductive vision of things. Says Prégent: "It is very fine to say that one no longer has a social cause or great ideas; but that must be put into a context. One should not forget that for a long time the *québécois* cinema spoke only of social causes and militantism .... Who knows? Maybe we are exorcizing that period right now. Maybe we must go to the very depths of our imaginations (*imaginaire*) to uncork something. For example, right now I happen to be interested in the relationship between men and women. But I won't be doing that all my life. One must watch out not to label people and films too much. That is what happens here: as soon as two or three of our filmmakers make an aesthetic film, it's called a current. People then say that 'everyone is making aesthetic films; we see only lofts in the movies nowaday.'"[5]

These young artists would be for the formation of a Cinema School [INIS, or Institut national de l'image et du son]—and they discuss the possible modalities of such a school. As for making commercial films, films adapting novels, Martin is not opposed, while Gariépy exclaims that it is not easy to adapt a novel. (Have I not shown this in my Chapter 4?) And, very interesting is Gariépy's complaint that in the universities, filmmaking professors suggest to their students that they will (soon) be creating (nothing but) *auteur* films, whereas this does not reflect reality, for the *auteur* film is only one of the many facets of cinema. Carle tends to agree, contending that people who are obsessed by the idea of the *auteur* film do not recognize the collaboration necessary for making a successful film. (And no more money is made when three people write a *scénario* than when one does). Crépeau sums up the interview by saying, "Cinema is not the work of a single person: it is the work of a team. One must underline that fact."[6]

Among the new films and directors let me cite in particular
Cargo by François Girard, who started his career as assistant of
production and *stagiaire* (person under instruction) at the camera
for Léa Pool's *La Femme de l'hôtel*. His first work was a six-minute
film called *Le Train*, which won seven or eight international prizes.
Cargo (photography, Daniel Jobin) is the product of a team, according to Girard, who also expresses his admiration for Orson Welles,
Hitchcock, Polanski, Antonioni, Wenders, Fassbinder, and Ruiz,
and is pleased with the success of André Forcier's *Une Histoire
inventée!*[7] Richard Martineau reviews *Cargo*, and declares it to be
about slavery and liberty, old age and youth, and claustrophobia
and vertigo. The story is of an older man who makes a voyage in
a sailing ship, accompanied by his daughter and his son-in-law.
Haunted by the death of his wife and obsessed by his work, he
tries in vain to establish a relationship with his daughter. The sky
grows dark, a storm breaks out, and the young people drown. It is
only then that the father decides to face his fears and to pass
through the mirror, at least long enough to exchange a few words
with his own father's ghost.[8] Girard's *Thirty-Two Short Films about
Glenn Gould* garnered four genies in 1994.

Two other films by young *cinéastes* of Québec are *La Femme de
Pablo Ruiz*, d. by Bernard Bergeron[9] and *La Liberté d'une statue*
(1990; 90 minutes), d. by Olivier Osselin. It is noteworthy that the
latter is quite clearly an *auteur* film: Osselin not only directed this
film, but he also did the photography, edited the film with Claude
Palardy, collaborated with others on the sets and costumes, and
played the role of Pyrrhon. Johanne Larue points out that both of
these films represent explorations into and exploitation of the
silent film. Thus, both endorse cinematographic continuity. And
La Liberté ... can be thought of as a "limpid treatise on the very
origins of cinema." (It concerns the reconstruction of an old silent,
using films found somewhere in Egypt.) As a testimony to the
strength and vigor of recent films by young filmmakers from Québec,
Larue concludes her article by saying: "*La Liberté d'une statue* is
the best *québécois* film I've had the good fortune to see in a long
time. Let us hope that the institutions that have made life hard for
the filmmaker will be more visionary in the future."[10]

Not only does one find young directors coming forth, but also
actors and actresses, among whom Geneviève Rioux and Denis
Bouchard stand out.[11] Rioux has starred in theatrical performances
of *Romeo and Juliette*, *Ruy Blas*, and *Les Misérables*, and in the
films *Le Crime d'Ovide Plouffe*, *Qui a tiré sur nos histoires d'amour?*,
Le Déclin de l'empire américain, *Cruising Bar*, *Blue la magnifique*,

and *Cargo*. She also played in *L'Héritage*, shown on Canadian TV. Denis Bouchard has been seen in *Cordélia*; *Le Château de cartes*; *L'Homme de papier*; *Une Histoire inventée*; *Ding et Dong, le film*; and *Le Crime de Lulu*. He appeared in *Les Matins infidèles* as Jean-Pierre, who cannot keep his engagements, until the day he commits suicide. Bouchard also had a part in the television film *Un Autre Homme*, as well as in *Les Tisserands du pouvoir*, and in *Les Fils de la liberté* (a television series). He collaborated on the script-scénario for *Rafales*, in which he also plays a role.

Then, too, in an interview with Léo Bonneville, Montréalaise Joan Pennefather, an important animation artist (*Why Me?*; *The Tender Tale of Cinderella Penguin*), as well as the president of the NFB (ONF) and commissioner of cinematography for the government, outlines her plans for the ONF of the future. These include the recovery and distribution of all that remains of the fifty years of filming by the ONF, including nitrate-supported films that have been transposed to nonflammable film; the encouragement of young filmmakers in the production of both long films of fiction and documentaries through support and better distribution; a greater amount of translation from French to English and English to French (though not always, as auudiences can differ grealty depending on the film); a special program (already established) for young directors — in the French section — to be directed by established directors of ONF (Colin Low and Wolf Koenig); more use of minority crew, as well as more attention to minorities in the films per se; and greater employment of young filmmakers, both anglophone and francophone. The ONF, in her opinion, "undeniably has a future."[12]

New talent is definitely on the horizon, then. But the older film directors also continue to produce. The *Annuaire du cinéma québécois* for 1989 listed twenty films in the English language; fifty-six full-length films, forty-two of which are fictional. Just a very few years ago, Gilles Carle released his new film, *Le Diable d'Amérique* (1990; 73 minutes); Abderrahmane Mazous created *La Fille du Maquignon* (1990; 82 minutes); Michel Langlois gave "... *Comme un voleur*" (1990; 83 minutes); Velcrow Ripper has written, produced, and directed *I'm Happy, You're Happy, We're All Happy, Happy, Happy* (1990; 80 minutes); and Léa Pool showed her new films, *Hotel Chronicles* (1990; 75 minutes) and *La Demoiselle sauvage* (1991; 100 minutes). To mention but a few more — whether good, bad or indifferent — we have: André Melançon's *Rafales* (1990; 87 minutes); Giles Walker's *Princes en exil* (*Princes in Exile* — 1990; 104 minutes); Yves Simoneau's anglophone film

Perfectly Normal (1990; 110 minutes); Richard Roy's *Moody Beach* (1990; 90 minutes); Tahani Rached's *Au Chic Resto Pop* (1990; 85 minutes); Michel Laflamme's *Vent de folie* (1990; 81 minutes); André Forcier's *Une Histoire inventée* (1990; 100 minutes); Robert Favreau's *L'Ange noir* (*Nelligan* — 1991; 100 minutes); Roger Cantin's *L'Assassin jouait du trombone* (1991; 100 minutes); Jean-Pierre Lefebvre's multiethnic film entitled *Le Fabuleux Voyage de l'ange* (1991; 102 minutes); Richard Boutet's *Le Spasme de vivre* (1991; 90 minutes); Vojtech Jasny's *Pourquoi Havel?* (1991; 100 minutes; coproduced with Czechoslovakia); Bernard Bergeron's *Pablo qui court* (1991; 80 minutes); Michel Brault's *Yamachiche* (1991); Sophie Bissonnette's *Des Lumières dans la grande noirceur* (1991; 90 minutes); Robert Ménard's *Amoureux fou*, starring Rémy Girard (1991; 100 minutes); Christian Duguay's *Scanners II: Le Nouveau règne* (1991; 104 minutes); Alain Chartrand's *Ding et Dong, le film* (1990; 96 minutes) and his *Un Homme de parole* (1991; 56 minutes); Marcel Simard's *Love-moi* (1991; 97 minutes); Jacques Godbout's *Pour l'amour du stress* (1991; 59 minutes); Vincent Ciambrone's *Montréal interdit* (1991; 84 minutes); Jean-Claude Lauzon's *Léolo* (1992; 107 min.); Jacques Dorfmann's *Agaguk*, or *Shadow of the Wolf* (1993; 111 min.); Paule Baillargeon's *Le Sexe des étoiles* (1993). The list is long and continues to grow.

Whether directors are young or old, whether the *québécois* cinema is made in the *auteur* style or as a team effort, whether the present-day products are individualistic or socially-oriented, we are confronted today with a cinema that must be reckoned with. World-class directors are producing world-class films that are often able to gain widespread attention. But distribution remains one of the problems of this cinema (as it does with all highly original films, such as America's *Camelon Street*, which has been critically deemed one of the ten best films ever made in America, and yet cannot find a distributor).

And the place of critical journals and critics in calling attention to good fiilms cannot be underestimated either. Certainly the journals are there. Among the most important, Véronneau cites *24 images*, *Ciné-Bulles*, *Cinéma Canada*, *Copie Zéro*, *Lumières*, and *Séquences*.[13] Of these, four have come into existence since 1979. But the American reader may find more and more reviews by American critics in such places as *Variety*, *The New York Times*, *The Christian Science Monitor*, and other more unexpected corners. Similarly, the province of Québec has produced several established film critics and scholars, Véronneau being one, Clanfield another,

Warren another. In the United States, an unprecedented but halting attention is beginning to be paid to this body of film both by movie buffs and by critics and scholars. Nevertheless, there is still much consciousness-raising to be done; it is hoped that this book will have contributed to that need. For the general public in America still tends to avoid Québec films, when and if they are ever offered.

What is the future of cinema in Québec? Can it only grow stronger under a separatist star, as some maintain? Will loss of those federal dollars have an impact, in the case of secession? Has the industry planted itself firmly enough to be able to continue under either political format? What is its future in the North American market? Uncertain, it seems to me. With free trade already implemented, the problems of distribution in the United States still remain, and will remain those of the past even after education has taken place. The linguistic problem persists: Americans still do not want to read the subtitles, and dubbing has its drawbacks too. As for the French market, we have seen that many *québécois* films have difficulty in France, as was the case for *Jésus de Montréal*, to take a glaring example. Bachand attributes these problems of reception to the fact that the French have not followed changes in the *québécois* society that occurred in the 70s and 80s, so that their image of that society is petrified in the folklore of the 60s. The French it seems, preferred films that looked into a past with nostalgia, or asserted resistance and a will to see the survival of a French culture in North America. (Whence in part the success of *Les Ordres*.[14]) Films dealing with the "Americanness" of the Québec culture must be less appealing. The self-portrait of a new reality that deals with women's place in that society and with the "*virage éthnique*," which embraces the life styles and problems of newly arrived immigrants who help to forge in Québec a new cultural *métissage*, must also be less appealing to the French, and probably are of no great appeal to most Americans either. But the films of the future will continue to reflect these characteristics of the new society; they will also turn to new problems created by new social and political realities.

Some of the factors needed to drive that cinema may well be a superstar system (although about this I wonder; the *je* and the *nous* become further divorced through the Hollywood approach); better technology (that is, better financial support); and, above all, better distribution, which has always been one of the biggest problems of Québec cinema. But certainly Jay Scott's prescription would spell anathema for Canadian film's future in America: He arrogantly claims that "Canadians have yet to recognize a law to which the British have profitably adhered for years: Yanks will queue up for highbrow insults."[15] Certainly Forcier offended and even alienated quite a number of Americans at an ACQS reception and then at the American premier of his *Histoire inventée* in Chicago with his "highbrow insults." We are not so insensitive nor so stupid as the formula, which borders on an ethnic joke in bad taste, implies.

Festivals are also a way that the films of Québec directors, especially those in French, can be brought to the attention of film critics, and from there, perhaps to the public. Such, as André Bazin suggests in *Le Cinéma de la cruauté*, was the route that led to the mounting of Italian neorealist films; it may well have been the route that brought the work of Buñuel and the Japanese film to the filmgoer's attention as well.[16] Bazin also traces viewer reaction to the foreign film. He speaks of the geographical and mental distance between cultures, and the hazardous conditions of distribution that make it likely that the viewer may have seen only one or two films of that country, and does not, cannot, place these films in the whole spectrum of the country's film production. But the viewer may not be aware, either, of the foreign nature of the film being viewed. For example, Americans may not be aware of the extent to which the Japanese have assimilated Western techniques while remaining fundamentally oriental in their world view. Thus Americans view Japanese films, especially those of Akira Kurosawa, with "pleasure." (Yet these particular films may not necessarily always be the most prized in Japan.[17]) This is in part the Japanese ability to overcome distribution problems. But, also, Americans have come to value things Japanese. The American intellectual will even read the subtitles of a Japanese film. And American intellectuals will certainly flock to see films by Mexicans (Buñuel in particular). Now, Arcand's films have profited from greater distribution than any other Québec films; but I still do not see the American movie buffs flocking to see *québécois* films. A correction is due, then, not only in Québec, but also in America . . . a greater international consciousness, a greater realization of the presence of something profoundly "foreign" in that which seems superficially altogether familiar, a greater identification with neighbors across the border, and a greater understanding of shared experiences with (French) Canadians and of the ways in which (French) Canadians differ from Americans.

Gilles Thérien's "L'Empire et les barbares" claims that Québec has a relationship with the United States that is fraught with problems, but one of continuity with France.[18] When we read in

Pratley's *Torn Sprockets* (1987, 179) that François Villon sings *La Ballade des Pendus* in Pierre Patry's *Caïn* (1965), we should conclude that this continuous nourishment of Québec by its spiritual mother France — as evidenced in the use of the poems of the great medieval French poet François Villon in *québécois* cinema — is little grasped not only by Americans but is just as lost on anglophone Canadians. One would suppose at first blush that a North-American film product would be readily grasped by most North Americans. But no. (Is Buñuel, really?) The continent shared is not enough. There is an exoticism here, in the Mexican and Québéc film, hinging upon a language and cultural barrier; there is a strangeness to be overcome. I submit that even though the ONF can have done a film series on the impact of America on the Québec identity (and called the series "L'Américanité"), that identity remains by language and heritage to some extent "un-American" or different from what we usually associate with the word "American." It is an amalgamated culture formed from first French, then British, and then other North-American traits (including those coming from the United States) — and this not to mention many other ingredients, emanating from minority influences, such as Native Peoples (Indian and Inuit), Italian, Jewish, etc. It is this particular hybridization, or *métissage*, that renders Québec's francophone culture — though distinctly non-European — nonetheless distinct and unique from other American subcultures. And it is this uniqueness that marks this province as special, as fascinating, and as different from all others. With a population no larger than the state of Ohio, it aspires to be a total country with a competitive G.N.P. and a stable economy, with an independent government (a "sovereign associate" to the rest of Canada, to use their oxymoron), an illustrious literature, and a competitive film industry. These last two it already certainly has. For though one may compare Jutra to Godard for his long, slow-paced sequences — that to some are tedious — or to Truffaut for his evocation of the universal problems of growing up, Jutra is still Jutra. And (within the scope of his best work, which is shaped by and reflects *québécois* realities, but which also looks inward toward himself and outward toward the world) he is conceivably as great as either of these two cinematographic geniuses.

Louise Carrière, in her dossier on Québec cinema mediates on the question as to whether we will witness the decline or even the death of Québec cinema. Finding that this body of film is the heir of two great impregnating cultures (American and French), she claims that *québécois* film hesitates today between derision and a mere copy of models, between the return to the past and the "spectacularisation" of the present, between the intimist cinema of European *auteurs* and the *cinéma rodé* (cinema that is ground out) by the great American machine. Québec's cinema comes from a film industry without "stars": that is at once its glory and its problem, depending on the person who interprets this condition. Above all, says Carrière, for a long time the *cinéma québécois* presented a people in anger, a confrontation of hero with Power. Québec dramaturgy is not inclined toward action; rather, it moves slowly to its tragic end. Sometimes, too, the different angles the directors choose as an approach to the subject prevent the viewer (who finds the director using methods and rhythms appropriate to the documentary) from identification with the film's action or situation. This can increase the viewer's discomfort (as, for example, with *Mourir à tue-tête*, or *L'Affaire Coffin*). But in the documentary, too, the Québécois *cinéaste* shakes up the rules and conventions. While the viewer is expecting an on-the-spot report, the director inserts a bit of fiction (as in *Caffè Italia*, for example). Or the director plays with quid-pro-quo, or allows a *mise-en-scene* as luxurious as that of a fiction film (as is the case with *La Bête lumineuse* or *Le Confort et l'indifférence*). Or the director presents herself or himself in the film (as with *Jacques et Novembre* or *Journal inachevé*).[19] These can be obstacles to the viewer's pleasure, it seems.

If, following the 1956 move of the NFB from Ottawa to Montréal and the establishment shortly thereafter of the French Production Unit, the cinema of Québec gave us some of its best work in the late 60s and early 70s (in part because, at that moment, the *"je"* of the filmmakers and the *"nous"* of the people coincided), toward 1975 the illusion that there was a great country to be built began to crumble, and things appeared to be manifestly more complex. This was the period of stark realism and political drama. Now, today (according to Carrière), the dream of lost childhood, the desire to travel, the search for identity, and the quest for new rituals are brought to the screen (*Lucien Brouillard*; *La Femme de l'hôtel*; *Anne Trister*; *Sonatine*; *Pouvoir intime*).[20] The failure of the Parti Québécois and the "no" vote to the referendum in 1980 had a certain effect upon the cinema, which perhaps had temporarily been given some spine by the prospect of national sovereignty. From these shambles we have *Le Déclin de l'empire américain*, in which Arcand takes inventory of a Québec without a social project and wholly centered on hedonism.

Yet, the end of the overvalorization of the national question also permits the filmmakers to find other *enjeux* (stakes) and other cinematographic procedures, other authors and other genres.[21] New filmmakers are appearing, and with them an outburst of various points of view and styles.[22] In all frankness, says Carrière, Americanization and decrease in population menace the Québec scene. But Québec is not a homogeneous nation, and the many interests, groups, and cultures are more differentiated than ever. Such a new configuration has scarcely lit the imagination of the scriptwriters, yet. But the young Québécois choosing movie and television careers are more numerous than ever. This in itself may be a sign of a will to live, in a community which, having been colonized, is eager to inscribe its own marks on the luminous screens, and to do so at all costs.[23]

It seems to me that Carrière sums up the accomplishments of the past Québécois filmmakers and the goals of the present ones in a succinct fashion. In the preface to Carriére's dossier, Dominque Noguez has characterized the product of Québec as "un cinèma plus direct que les autres."[24] We saw all these things that Carrière and Noguez claim, and more besides, as we explored the highways and the byways of Québec filmmaking, from its earliest days forward. Carrière's assessment, written six years after the defeat of the referendum, and now several years ago, could not foresee that the sovereignty question was not yet over, however; and it may again dominate the film.

Documentary; animated film; literature turned to film; fictional film; film for children; gender-marked, race- and root-marked film: in all, the directors and other collaborators of the *québécois* cinema have been and are "Masters in Their Own House" — and should as well be regarded abroad as masters of cinematographic art. Who would deny the filmmakers of Québec such an epithet?

Appendix A

Principal Political, Historical, and Social Events in the History of Nouvelle France and the Québec Province

HISTORICAL AND POLITICAL OUTLINE

1534 — Jacques Cartier lands on the shores of the St. Lawrence (in Gaspé[sie]). He takes possession of this land in the name of the King of France.

1608 — Samuel de Champlain and the settlement of La Nouvelle France. Under his command, on 3 July, a group of Frenchmen establish themselves in a spot called Québec (Kébec), Amerindian for "the spot where the river becomes narrower."

1629 — The colony is attacked by English vessels. (Between 1629 and 1760 they will undergo five sieges from the English fleet.)

1634 — Champlain requests Laviolette to establish a post at the confluence of the Saint-Maurice and the St. Lawrence, upstream from Québec.

1642 — Paul de Chomedey de Maisonneuve founds Ville-Marie, later to be called Montréal. It is a small colony having a fort, a hospital, a chapel, and living quarters for seventy people. Marguerite Bourgeois is among these early settlers, who must fight the Iroquois and who come close to defeat.

1755 — *Le Grand Dérangement* (*La Déportation*; *L'Expulsion*). The English expel the Acadian French people living in Nova Scotia, Prince Edward Island, and New Brunswick. They, as well as other Acadians who come overland, settle in Louisiana; these are the ancestors of the Cajuns. Those francophone Acadians who remain in or return to Canada will have a growing sense of their identity, until, in the late 60s, uprisings and demonstrations will begin to occur in these parts of Canada as well as in Québec.

1759 — On 13 September, during the so-called Battle of the Plains of Abraham, Québec City is besieged by the English. The British troops of Gen. James Wolfe (1727–1759) are pitted against the French troops of Louis, Marquis de Montcalm.

1760 — Montcalm falls into the hands of the British troops, and the British Conquest is completed. Sixty-five thousand "Canadiens" experience this conquest. At this time, there is little inclination for the francophones to revolt.

1763 — Treaty of Paris signed by the King of France ends French administration in North America. Many administrators return to France; the people remaining must submit to English government, for this treaty, following French and Indian Wars (involving American forces), gives the province and other French holdings to Great Britain. The Royal Proclamation of 1763 institutes the state-controlled organs proper to Québec.

1774 — The Québec Act. Reflects the British intention to recognize the French-Canadian identity. Under it, the French system of jurisprudence — already in place — and the Roman Catholic religion are to be protected and respected. As early as this act, we have Québécois people singled out as a "distinct society," a concept that will be at issue in the (failed) Meech Lake Accord (1990).

1775 — American forces besiege Québec City, under Generals Richard Montgomery and Benedict Arnold. Montgomery is killed; Arnold flees, abandoning hopes of conquering Canada.

1791 — By a Constitutional Act, Québec becomes Lower Canada. (Ontario will be called Upper Canada; its capital York, today Toronto.) While this act establishes a parliamentary regime in Canada, and recognizes that French Canadians have the right to a national "foyer," this "acte d'union" was in effect an effort to control the action of the francophones and the number of francophone deputies in the government.

1837 and 1838 — Early 19th cent. — a growing resentment of the English by the Québécois. *Patriote* rebellions, at the instigation of the French Canadian Party, led by Louis-Joseph Papineau (1787–1875), and seeking autonomy for Québec, are crushed by the British Gen. John Colborne (1778–1863), colonial administrator of Upper Canada (Ontario). Lord Durham in 1839 recommends a policy of assimilation.

1840 — The Act of Union joins Lower (Québec) and Upper (Ontario) Canada under a single government.

1839 to ca 1939 — French Canadians are rather resigned, and allow themselves to be led by the Roman Catholic clergy; nationalism amounts to mere preservation of traditions. (*Survivance*, or survival, is the name of the game.) French Canadians arc urged to have many children and to keep the faith. These attitudes are advocated as strategies for the preservation of their identity.

1867 — The British North America Act establishes a Canadian confederation, comprised of Ontario, Québec, Nova Scotia, and New Brunswick. The newly created "province" of Québec enters the Canadian confederation, but retains jurisdiction over education and civil law. This confederation makes the francophone society even more "distinct." Nonetheless, within the province, the anglophones, though a minority, dominate economically and will do so until well into the twentieth century.

1917 — Women vote for the first time in federal elections. In the provincial elections of Québec, they will not get the vote until 1940.

1900 to 1920—Urbanization and the industrial revolution are in full swing. These threaten the "traditional" values of the society.

1945 to 1960—Transition between tradition and modernity. Gradual erosion of old mores and of Church power; secularization; rise of media.

1960 to 1966—The Quiet Revolution. Balthazar describes this as "The modernization of Québec, including important changes in the way the province was governed and in the way French-Canadian society was organized" [p. 7]. This modernization has been incubating for quite some time, however. In 1959, with the death of the *Union nationale*'s conservative premier (Maurice Duplessis), long-needed reforms are introduced by Jean-Paul Sauvé, who, however, dies early in 1960; his reforms are not aggressively pursued by Antonio Barrette, his successor. Then, on 22 June 1960 the Liberals take over.

Jean Lesage and his Liberal team work for provincial autonomy, but always emphasize the positive nature of their policy: Reform of civil service, revamping of the educational system, establishment of a public hospital insurance program, and creation of a department of cultural affairs. State intervention is urged upon the Québécois as a positive and beneficial thing.

During this time of the "Quiet Revolution," the Québécois come to a new economic consciousness and power; they also become more internationally active, especially in establishing contacts with France.

1963—The federal government sets up a Royal Commission of Inquiry to look into the problems of bilingualism and biculturalism in Canada. Its report stresses the notion that Canada has two dominant cultures embodied in distinct societies. The report does not delight English Canada.

30 January 1964—A red truck is involved in the FLQ's (Front de la Libération du Québec's) $20,000 theft of arms from the Fusiliers Mont-Royal Armoury.

1965—Québec signs an agreement with France establishing cultural and educational cooperation. (And, consequently, disputes with Ottawa over Québec's role in international affairs arise.)

The role of the Catholic Church in the everyday lives of the citizens of Québec begins to lose ground.

During the Quiet Revolution, the issue of Québec's sovereignty—its insistence on special status—is hotly debated. The Québécois claim "double identity."

1968—Pierre Elliott Trudeau becomes the leader of the Liberal Party and the new Prime Minister of Canada. It is thought that he, a strong federalist, will rescue Canadian unity. He pushes for pan-Canadian bilingualism, but at the same time refuses to recognize any special status for Québec, his native province. His policies fan the fires of Québec nationalism; the separatist movement grows, and in that same year the Parti Québécois—a party committed to political sovereignty for Québec—is created. Separatism—which had already had its organizations (e.g., the Rassemblement pour l'indépendance nationale, or R.I.N.)—reaches the proportions of a very real movement.

1967 — René Lévesque leaves the Liberal Party and founds the Mouvement souveraineté-association (M.S.A.), which wants political sovereignty for Québec and economic association with the rest of Canada.

1968 — The M.S.A. becomes the Parti Québécois (P.Q.).

1970 — Twenty-three percent of the voters cast a ballot for the P.Q.

October 1970 — two kidnappings, one ending in murder, illustrate that for some the revolution is not so "quiet." Though the violent Québec Liberation Front (F.L.Q.) probably does not have a large membership, general panic if not pandemonium sets in.

The outcome of these terrorist acts is an enlistment of the War Powers Act, by which Trudeau suspends civil rights. Persons may be searched and arrested without warrant, and are.

During the 1970s a polarization of the province occurs, among federalists (Trudeau supporters) and separatists (Lévesque supporters). Also active is the Québec Liberal Party, of which Robert Bourassa becomes the leader in 1970. He hopes to reach a compromise; but he antagonizes the federal government and specifically Trudeau; this leads to further strengthening of the Parti Québécois.

1974 — The Assemblée nationale of Québec declares French the official language of Québec, under Law 22.

1976 (15 November) — The Parti Québécois wins a majority of seats in the Québec National Assembly.

1977 — Bill 101 (called "The Charter of the French Language") is passed; it states that French is the official language of Québec. It requires immigrant parents to send their children to a francophone school. Signs must be in French. Also, by law, every person has a right to receive services in French from all public organizations and from the various private enterprises doing business in Québec.

1980 (20 May) — A referendum is held; Quebeckers are asked whether the provincial government has a "mandate to negotiate" a new agreement between Québec and Canada with respect to political sovereignty and economic association. Many voters think — and indeed are made to think by certain parties — that they are actually voting on separatism, and the referendum fails resoundingly. Trudeau, believing himself victorious, then proceeds to impose his constitutional vision of Canada upon the Québec people, although their "no" to the referendum is not intended to invite that either.

1981 (November) — A new constitutional package is formulated at a federal-provincial conference, that consists of the patriation of the federal constitution, a formula for amending that constitution, and a Canadian Charter of Rights and Freedoms. It is accepted by all of the provinces except Québec. Its leaders (from the P.Q.) object to the amending formula in which Québec will not have a veto and to the Charter, which appears to infringe on Québec's own charter of rights.

Throughout this period tensions between the province and the rest of the nation are exacerbated; conflicts between Lévesque and Trudeau come to a boiling point.

1984 — Trudeau resigns.

1985 — Lévesque resigns. In September, Brian Mulroney, a Conservative, becomes Prime Minister of Canada; in December Robert Bourassa, a Liberal, becomes premier of Québec.

1987 — The Meech Lake Accord is formulated. Included is a proposed amendment to the Canadian constitution stating that the "existence of French-speaking Canadians, centered in Québec . . . and English-speaking Canadians, concentrated outside Québec . . . constitutes a fundamental characteristic of Canada; and . . . that Québec constitutes within Canada a distinct society." This accord, signed by all provincial premiers must be ratified, after three years, by the Parliament of Canada and by the legislatures of each province.

1990 — In spring and summer of 1990, the Meech Lake Accord fails to be ratified. Bourassa establishes a commission (headed by Allaire) from all sectors of Québec to consider the matter of "sovereignty association."

1990−1 — The Allaire commission brings out a controversial report in which Québec continues to make demands on the federal government. Separatist sentiment increases. A new party, the Bloc Québécois, made up of the federal members of parliament who defected from other parties in order to fight for a sovereign Québec, and, with the support of the Parti Québécois, will figure in new elections, along with a party from Western Canada, called the Reform Party. There are now at least five parties in Canada: The old Liberal and Conservative Parties; the recent but established New Democratic Party (socialist in nature), and the new Bloc Québécois and Reform Parties. This multiparty system epitomizes the balkanization of Canadian politics at present.

18−21 January 1992 — Constitutional conference in Halifax is boycotted by Québec. Discussed is the transfer of many powers to all the provinces, while retaining a central government. From this conference emerges the new term, asymetrical federalism. Though there is a growing consensus on this notion, there is also fear that asymetrical federalism may devolve into special status for Québec.

25−27 January 1992 — Conference on Senate reform in Calgary.

22 August 1992 — Provincial premiers and other leaders agree to a sweeping political reform package (the Charlottetown Accord), with proposals destined to respond to needs and demands of Québécois and native people. It is also designed to head off a secession referendum in French-speaking Québec. Bourassa agrees to the package: in exchange for agreeing to a powerful, directly-elected Senate in which each of the provinces would have six seats, Québec is guaranteed 25% of seats in the influential lower House of Commons.

26 October 1992 — The accord fails in federal elections intended to ratify the package. Bourassa may propose a new referendum, to be voted on by Québec's citizens.

THE CINEMA OF QUÉBEC

15 June 1993 — Kim Campbell assumes duties as Tory party leader and new Prime Minister of Canada, following resignation of Mulroney. Enforcement of law 101 appears to be softening; bilingual signs may now be allowable in Québec.

1994 — The separatist Jacques Parizeau is elected premier of Québec, and promises a referendum on secession in 1995.

DESCRIPTION OF THE TERRITORY

The province of Québec, of which Québec City is the capital, forms a huge triangle of approximately 1,357,810 km., only one-third of which is inhabited. It has 900,000 — 1,000,000 lakes and rivers, and many islands, including Anticosti (the largest), and those of industrial or historical importance, in particular the Ile de Montréal, the Ile Jésus, and the Ile d'Orléans. Hudson Strait and Ungava Bay border the north; the James and Hudson Bays are on the west; and the Gulf of St. Lawrence edges the southeast.

The province boasts three distinct topographical regions: the Laurentian Plateau, the Appalachian Uplands (which include the Eastern Townships, or the Cantons de l'Est, and three important rivers — the St. Francois, Nicolet, and Chaudière, which all flow northward to the St. Lawrence), and the St. Lawrence Lowlands. In the far north only grasses, mosses, and lichens cover the hills and valleys. These lands will be under dispute in the case of separation. Will they go to the rest of Canada, to the Native Canadians now living there, or to Québec?

Québec has approximately 6,500,000 inhabitants, of which 80% are francophone and 12.8% anglophone; 5.4% speak some other language. The provincial flower is the Madonna White Lily (*Lilium candidum*); the avian emblem is the large snowy owl (*Nyctea scandiaca*). The flag, bearing four fleurs-de-lis and a white cross on a blue field, was adopted on 21 January 1948 and sanctioned by legislation on 9 March 1950. Québec also has a coat of arms, adopted under a mandate from Queen Victoria in 1868 and modified by the provincial government in 1939. The escutcheon bears three gold fleurs-de-lis on a blue field, representing the first political system in New France; a gold leopard (symbol of the British Crown), standing for the second political system; and a three-leaved maple branch, symbolizing one of the province's main natural products.

The highest point in the province is Mont Jacques Cartier (1,268). Drivers must be sixteen if they have had training, otherwise they must be eighteen. The legal age for consumption of alcohol is eighteen; package liquor is sold only in government-controlled liquor stores; drinks only (not bottled alcoholic beverages) are sold on Sunday.

RELIGION AND ECONOMY

In Québec the Catholic faith has the strongest foothold of any religion or denomination (as in all of Canada; for 45% of all Canadians claim they are Catholic). Losing strength during the Quiet Revolution and the 80s, the Church is said to now be regaining a following, with 90% of Quebeckers declaring themselves at least nominal Catholics, and a surprising 58% of Montréalers—and an even more impressive 69% throughout the province of Québec—stating in a recent survey that they are practicing Catholics, who, leaving aside marriages, baptisms, and burials, have attended at least one religious service in the last twelve months. Moreover (as in the United States) enrollment in courses in theology and religion is gaining ground (*Journal Français d'Amérique,* April 1991, supplement on Québec: 11).

The Catholic Church of Canada has a clergy at present more interested in ecumenism than in fighting the traditional issues of abortion, choice, right to life, etc. These issues are fought on the level of the laity in Canada. (For an excellent portrayal of the Catholic Church of Canada, see: Michael W. Cuneo, *Catholics Against the Church: Anti-Abortion Protest in Toronto 1969–1985* [Toronto: University of Toronto Press, 1989], 280 pp.)

Major holidays of Québec are: New Year's Day; Good Friday; Easter Monday; Victoria Day—May 24, if on Monday, or else the closest prior Monday; Saint-Jean Baptiste Day—June 24; Canada Day—July 1; Labour Day—September, on first Monday; Thanksgiving—October, on second Monday; Remembrance Day—Nov. 11; and Christmas—Dec. 25. The Winter and Summer carnivals are also important.

The Québec economy is built on (1) energy; (2) minerals, mining; (3) lumber and paper; (4) fishing and related trades; (5) agriculture, especially along the St. Lawrence River (dairy; hay, rye, oats, barley, corn, potatoes, beets, apples, melons, strawberries, blueberries, tobacco, maple sugar); and (6) breeding farms (raising fur-bearing animals). In the event of separation, a large share of Québec's economy would be drawn from the export of energy to the eastern seaboard of the U.S.; but this assumption is threatened by recent ecological movements in New England that have caused and will cause voters to defeat the intention of their governments to import energy from HydroQuébec.

HISTORICAL SKETCH OF LA RUE ST.-DENIS (MONTRÉAL)

Let us consider now a little urban history, revolving around La Rue St.-Denis, a history that will serve as background to films situated in Montréal. This street, today thought of as the Quartier Latin of Montréal, was in origin a residential area of the Montréal French-speaking elite, who were for the most part professionals of nationalist inclination. One of the richest and most influential families of Montréal included the donors of the lands that the street was to occupy. These were the Vigers, to whom two other powerful families are connected: the Papineaus and the Cherriers. The street developed between 1818 and 1852; it then extended as far as Sherbooke St., and had wooden sidewalks, bordered by several stone and brick houses, suggesting that the inhabitants of this street were well-off. At the time, two of the most densely populated quarters of Montréal were clustered around St.-Denis: St.-Louis and St.-Jacques. In these quarters lived artisans, small-business merchants, and blue-collar workers. St.-Denis is in strong contrast to its environment. Throughout the nineteenth century, the residential and luxurious nature of the street prevailed; little by little, small deluxe commerces sprang up (fine grocery stores; florists' shops, art galleries, etc.). A religious and academic infrastructure began to develop: St. Jacques Church was erected in 1823, and Laval University of Montréal was established in 1878. Industrialization was in full swing all around this street (tannery, foundry, sawmill, soap factory, slaughterhouse, and brewery). 1873–1929 was, however, a period of unemployment and depression.

In the late nineteenth century, the street was extended from the downtown area toward the east. Extension of the street was accelerated as time went by. The appearance of the street changed. More commerces sprang up (bookstores, printers, publishers, and even a business not related to the activities of the area — Franco-American Chemicals). A new phenomenon arose: rooming-houses appeared.

As the street got busier and more congested, the traditional clientele progressively sought calmer quarters, many of the former occupants moving to Outremont. From then until now, the street has become a place of commerce and boarders and roomers. Thus, once the neighborhood of the French-Canadian elite, it has been transformed into a commercial and touristic artery, in which it is not always pleasant to live. The life of this street and the surrounding quarters has been completely swallowed up by uncontrolled expansion of the downtown toward the east, the inhabitants having had to make room for business, automobiles, roads, and turnpikes. It is sometimes referred to as the "lost Montréal." The process continues, as speculators and mega-projects claim more and more parts of the Old City.

Founded by Maisonneuve (1642), and at first called Ville-Marie, Montréal is, today, the second largest French-speaking city in the world. Of its 2,800,000 inhabitants, 1,800,000 plus habitually speak French. There are, in addition to French-speaking quarters, the anglophone neighborhoods, a Chinese quarter, a Greek quarter, an Italian quarter, a Jewish quarter, etc.

Books on Québec culture — both in English and in French — are cited in the bibliography. One of the most recent and most objective, though in French, is Françoise Tétu de Lapsade's *Le Québec: un pays, une culture* (*Québec: Boréal; Paris: Seuil, 1990*).

Appendix B

Film Credits

90 DAYS (1985; 100 minutes)

d. Giles Walker * production — Walker; David Wilson; & Andy Thomson w/ NFB * gaffer — Roger Martin * script — Walker; Wilson * photography — Andrew Kitzanuk * sound — Yves Gendron * location sound — Yves Gendron * additional sound — Serge Beauchemin * editing — David Wilson * original music (stylized Latin and oriental) — Richard Gresko. ** Cast (Characters/Actors) Blue — Stefan Wodoslawsky; Hyang-Sook — Christine Pak; Alex Rossi — Sam Grana; Laura — Fernanda Tavares; Joanne Rossi — Janine Basile; Blue's mother — Daisy De Bellefeuille; Shelley — Katy de Volpi; Minister — Anthony Kent.

ACADIE, L'ACADIE, L' (1971; 117 minutes)

d. Pierre Perrault & Michel Brault * produced — NFB Prod. & release (Guy L. Côté; Paul Larose) * camera (b&w) — Michel Brault * editor — Monique Fortier * sound — Serge Beauchemin * re-recording — Roger Lamoureux.
(Shown at week of Canadian Cinema, Cannes Festival, 1971)

A CORPS PERDU (*STRAIGHT TO THE HEART*) (1988; 92 min.)

d. Lea Pool * scénario by Léa Pool and Marcel Beaulieu, based on the novel *Kurenwal* by Yves Navarre * producers — Denise Robert and Robin Spry * photography — Pierre Mignot * sound — Luc Yersin * music — Osvaldo Montes * editor — Michel Arcand.
** Cast: Matthias Habich, Johanne-Marie Tremblay, Michel Voita, Jean-François Pichette.
Prizes for Young Readers at the Third Festival in Namur, Belgium (1988) and for Best Drama at the Fourth Atlantic Film and Video Festival in Halifax (1988).
[See Leboutte (1986, 56) and Abel (1990, 302).]

467

ACTION: THE OCTOBER CRISIS OF 1970 (1973; 87 min., 9 sec. — NFB)

d. Robin Spry * producer — Tom Daly, Normand Cloutier, Robin Spry * commentary — Robin Spry * sound editing. Bernie Bordeleau * rerecording — Jean-Pierre Joutel; Michel Descombes * camera (black and white) — various photographers; archival; stock * editing — Shelagh MacKenzie and Joan Henson.

ACT OF THE HEART, THE (1970; 103 min.; color)

d. Paul Almond * production — Almond & Peter Carter * script — Almond * photography — Jean Boffety * sound — David Howells * music — Harry Freedman * editing — James D. Mitchell. ** Cast (Characters/Actors): Martha Hayes played by Geneviève Bujold; Father Michael Ferrier — Donald Sutherland; Johane Foss — Monique Leyrac; Coach Ti-Joe — Gilles Vigneault; Adèle — Sharon Acker; Diedrich — Ratch Wallace; Choirmaster — Eric House; Party Guests — Jean Dalmain; Claude Jutra; François Tasse. The Northern Stars — Members of Les Hurricans de Ville-Emard. Church choir — Members of St. Philips Church.

AFFAIRE COFFIN, L' (1980; 100 min.)

d. Jean-Claude Labrecque * production company — Films Ciné Scène; Les Productions Videofilms * released by — Corporation des Films Mutuels * producer — Robert Menard * camera — Pierre Mignot * editor — André Corriveau * music — Anne Laubert. ** Cast (Characters/Actors): Wilbert Coffin — August Schellenberg; Capitaine Forget — Yvon Dufour; Maureen Patterson — Micheline Lanctôt; Ben Menard — Jean-Marie Lemieux; Maître Alain Courtemanche — Gabriel Arcand; Chauffeur de taxi — Raymond Cloutier.

AGAGUK, L'OMBRE DU LOUP (SHADOW OF THE WOLF) (1992; 111 minutes; Fr/Cand.)

d. Jacques Dorfmann * production — Claude Léger * screenplay — Evan Jones, Rudy W urlitzer, based on the novel of Yves Thériault * photography — Billy Williams * editing — Françoise Bonnot * music — Maruice Jarre * sound — Richard Schorr * sets — Wolf Kroeger * costumes — Olga Dimitrov. ** Cast (Characters/Actors): Agaguk — Lou Diamond Philips; Igiyook — Jennifer Tilly; Kroomak — Toshiro Mifune; Henderson — Donald Sutherland; Brown — Bernard-Pierre Donnadieu; Big Tooth — Raoul Trujillo.

ALIAS WILL JAMES (1988; 88 minutes)

d., scénario, recherches — Jacques Godbout * production — ONF * photography — Jean Pierre Lachapelle * editing — Monique Fortier * music — Robert M. Lepage * sound — Richard Besse. ** Voice of Will James — Jean-Guy Moreau * Modern Cowboys — Michael Bénard, Daniel David, his wife — Carole David, with participation of artist and singer Ian Tyson.

AMOUREUSES, LES (1992; 99 min.)

d. Johanne Prégent * producer — Louise Gendron * scénario — Prégent * photography — François Protat * editing — Dominique Fortin * music — Pierre Desrochers * sound — Richard Besse * décors — Louise Jobin. ** Cast (Characters/Actors): Léa — Louise Portal; David — Kenneth Welsh; Marianne — Léa-Marie Cantin; Nino — Tony Nardi; costumière — Sophie Lorrain; actor — .David LaHaye; actress — Macha Limonchik.

AMOUR HUMAIN, L' (THE AWAKENING) (1971; 90 minutes)

d. Denis Héroux * producer — Cinexpix * exec. prod. — Claude Héroux * screenplay — Roger Fournier * camera — René Verzier * editing — Jean Lafleur * music — François Cousineau. ** Cast (Characters/Actors): Constance — Louise Marleau; Julien — Jacques Riberolles, with Charlotte Boisjoly, Ovila Légaré, Jean-Pierre Compain, Germaine Giroux, Nana de Varennes, Denise Proulx, Simone Piuze, Yvan Canuel et al.
    (Shown at Cannes Festival, 1971.)

AND THEN YOU DIE. (1987; 1 hr. 40 min.)

d. Francis Mankiewicz * script — Wayne Grigsby and Alun Hibbert * photography — Richard Leiterman, C.S.C. * original music — Marty Simson * editing — Gordon McClellan and Alfonso Peccia * sound editing — Kevin Townshend * assoc. prod. — Harris Verge * exec. prod. — Bernard Zuckerman * producer — Brian McKenna. ** Cast (Characters/Actors): Eddie Griffin — Kenneth Welsh; Wally Dreagan (Eddie's sidekick) — Wayne Robson; Michael (Mikey) — Graeme Campbell; Sal(vatore) Prego — George Bloomfield; Frank Vitello — Donald Davis; Peter Vanderkeist — Tom Harvey; Nick Garou — Pierre Chagnon; Scarecrow — Guy Thauvette; Tremblay — Alpha Boucher; Liz (Eddie's wife) — Maggie Huculak; Cheryl (Liz's friend) — Barbara Kaye; Jimmy (one of Eddie's men) — Thomas McCamus; Dave (one of Eddie's men) — Jefferson Mappin; Danny (Eddie's son) — Joran Van Lange; Cliff (Eddie's most trustworthy) — Dennis O'Connor; Harold — David Bolt; Mom (Wally's mother) — Linda O'Dwyer; Aunt Peg (Mikey's mother) — Patricia Armstrong.

ANGE NOIR, L' (NELLIGAN) (1991; 100 minutes)

d. Robert Favreau * producers — Marie-Andrée Vinet, Gérald Ross, and Robert Sésé * *scénario* — Aude Natais, Jean-Joseph Tremblay, Robert Favreau, and Claude Poissant * photography — Guy Dufaux * editing — Hélène Girard * music — Marie Bernard * sound — Serge Beauchemin * sets — Louise Jobin and Pierre Perrault * costumes — François Lapointe. ** Cast (Characters/Actors): Emile young — Marc St-Pierre; Emile adult — Michel Commeau; Emilie Nelligan (mother) — Lorraine Pintal; David Nelligan (father) — Luc Morissette; Eugène Seers (priest)/Louis Dantin — Gabriel Arcand; Arthur de Bussières — David de La Haye; Idola St-Jean — Dominique Leduc; Robertine Barry — Andrée Lachapelle; Eva Nelligan — Isabelle Cyr; Gertrude Nelligan — Lysanne Gendron; Charles Gill — Jean-François Casabonne; Joseph Melançon — Patrick Goyette; Jean Charbonneau — Christian Bégin; Gonzalve Désaulnier — Luc Picard; Albert Ferland — Martin Drainville; la soeur supérieure — Denise Filiatrault; Dr. Brennan — Aubert Pallascio; Archbishop of Montréal — Jean-Louis Millette.

ANNÉES DE RÊVE, LES (YEARS OF DREAMS AND REVOLT) (1984; 96 minutes)

d. Jean-Claude Labrecque * released by Les Films René Malo, Inc. * video release by Vidéoglobe * producer — Claude Bonin, Films Vision 4 * production director — Daniel Louis * script and dialogues — Robert Gurik and Marie Laberge, based on a story by Labrecque * artistic director — Vianney Gauthier * camera — Alain Dostie * editor — François Labonté * sound — Serge Beauchemin * assistant director — René Pothier. ** Cast (Characters/Actors): Claudette Pelletier — Anne-Marie Provencher; Louis Pelletier — Gilbert Sicotte; Aunt Yvette — Monique Mercure; Aunt Adèle — Amulette Garneau; Aunt Marie — Carmen Tremblay; Armand (Député to National Assembly) — Roger Le Bel; John — André Mathieu; John-John — John Wildman; Mathieu at 2 1/2 years — Alexandre Guertin-Aird; Mathieu at 5 years — Guillaume Lemay-Thivierge. [First shown at the Cannes Film Festival (Directors' Fortnight).]

ANNE TRISTER (1986; 102 min.)

d. Léa Pool * production — Roger Frappier; Claude Bonin * *scénario* — Pool; Marcel Beaulieu * photography — Pierre Mignot * sound — Richard Besse * music — René Dupéré and Daniel Des-haime * editing — Michel Arcand. ** Cast: Albane Guilhe; Louise Marleau; Hugues Quester; Lucie Laurier; Nuvit Ozdogru; Guy Thauvette; Kim Karoshevskaya.

ARBRE QUI DORT RÊVE À SES RACINES, L' (1992; 81 minutes; documentary)

d. Michka Saäl and Nadine Ltaif * production — ONF * *scénario* — Michka Saäl * producer — Josée Beaudet * photography — Nathalie Moliavko-Visotsky * editing — Fernand Bélanger * music — Jean Derome * sound — Claude Hamel and Francine Poirier with Michka Saäl and Nadine Ltaif.

A TOUT PRENDRE (1963; b&w; 99 min.)

d. Claude Jutra * producer — Claude Jutra, Robert Hershon * *scénario* — Jutra * photography — Michel Brault, Jean-Claude Labrecque, Bernard Gosselin * sound — Michel Melaieff * music — Maurice Blackburn, Jean Cousineau, Serge Garant * editing — Jutra. ** Interpreters: Johanne Harelle, Claude Jutra, Victor Désy, Tania Fédor, Guy Hoffmann, Monique Mercure.

AU CLAIR DE LA LUNE (1982; 92 minutes)

d. André Forcier * producer — Bernard Lalonde; Louis Laverdière (with assistance of the ONF) * script — André Forcier, Jacques Marcotte, Michel Pratte, Guy L'Ecuyer, Michel Côté * photography — François Gill, André Gagnon * sound — Alain Corneau, Marcel Fraser * editing — François Gill * music — Joël Bienvenu/Catherine Gadouas. ** Cast (Characters/Actors): Frank — Michel Côté; Albert (Bert; Bolduc) — Guy L'Ecuyer; Léopoldine Dieumegarde — Lucie Miville; Maurice Dieumegarde — Robert Gravel; Margot — Varo; Alfred (Fred) — J.-Léo Gagnon; Alfred's dog — Ti Beu; philosopher — Michel Gagnon; Linda — Louise Gagnon.

AU REVOIR ... Á LUNDI ([GOODBYE [OR 'BYE]] SEE YOU MONDAY) (ca 120 minutes; 1979–1980. A Canada-France coproduction)

d. Maurice Dugowson * produced by — Somerville House (Canada) and Fildebroc-Capac (Canada) * story based on a novel by Roger Fournier (*Moi, mon corps, mon âme*, published by Albin Michel) * editor — Jean Bernard Bonis * dialogue consultant — Myra Clement * photography — François Protat * musical score — Lewis Furey and Jean-Daniel Mercier * song sung by Leurs Furey and Carole Laure * costumes — Michèle Hamel. ** Cast (Characters/Actors): Lucy — Carole Laure; Nicole — Miou-Miou; Frank — David Birney; Arnold — Claude Brasseur; Robert — Frank Moore; George — Gabriel Arcand; Hector — Raymond Cloutier; Lucy's mother — Renée Girard; Lucy's father — Murray Westgate; Jack, Lucy's Boss — Alain Montpetit; Juliette — Andrée Pelletier; Woman at airline — Denise Filiatrault; Frank's mother — Mignon Elkins; Julian — Pierre Dupuis; Policeman — Robert Gravel; Robert's Wife — Francine Vézina; Baxter Fry (Arnold's "client") — Pierre Dufresne; Drunkard — Lewis Furey.

LES AVENTURIERS DU TIMBRE PERDU

See Tommy Tricker ...

BACH ET BOTTINE (BACH AND BROCCOLI) (1987; 1 hr. 40 min.)

d. André Melançon * producer — Rock Demers * scénario — Bernadette Renaud, André Melançon * editing — André Corriveau * photography director — Guy Dufaux * sound — Serge Beauchemin * assistant director — Mireille Goulet * script — Johanne Prégent * artistic director — Violette Daneau * costumes — Huguette Gagné * makeup — Diane Simard. ** Cast (Characters/Actors): The Uncle — Raymond Legault; Fanny — Mahée Paiement; Sean — Harry Marciano; Bernice — Andrée Pelletier.

[Bach and Broccoli has been frequently shown on the American premium channels, and is readily available and very inexpensively through Walden Video, and elsewhere.]

BAR SALON (1974; 84 min.)

d. André Forcier * producer — Jean Dansereau * script — Jacques Marcotte and André Forcier * photography — François Gill, Claude Racine * sound — Hughes Migneaut, Dominique Chartrand * music — André Duchêne * editing — François Gill * special assistant — Jean-Claude Labrecque. ** Cast (Characters/Actors): Charles — Guy L'Ecuyer; Cécile — Lucille Belair; Robert — Jacques Marcotte; Michèle — Madeleine Chartrand; Larry — Gélinas Fortin; Lisette — Michèle Dion; Leslie — Françoise Berd; François — André Forcier; Amélie — Louise Gagnon; Major Cotnoir — Albert Payette.

BAY BOY, THE (1984; 107 min.)

d. Daniel Petrie.

Stars Kiefer Sutherland, Liv Ullman, Peter Donat, Mathieu Carriere, Isabelle Mejias, Alan Scarfe, Chris Wiggins, Leah Pinsent.

BINGO (1974; 116 min.)

d. Jean-Claude Lord * production, Les Films Mutuels, Pierre David, Jean-Claude Lord, and Louise Ranger, Société du Développement de l'Industrie Cinématographique Canadienne * script — Jean-Claude Lord, Roch Poisson, Lise Thouin, Michel Capistran, Jean Salvy * photography — Claude LaRue, François Protat * sound — Henri Blondeau * music — Michel Comte * editors — Jean-Claude Lord, Lise Thouin. ** Cast (Characters/Actors): François — Réjean Guénette; Geneviève — Anne-Marie Provencher; Fernand — Claude Michaud; Hélène — Alexandra Steward;

Pierre — Gilles Pelletier; Eva — Manda Parent; Madeleine — Janine Fluet; Eugène — Jean Duceppe. With Roger Le Bel.

BONHEUR D'OCCASION (THE TIN FLUTE) (1983; 120 – 123 minutes)

d. Claude Fournier * exec. producers — Marie-José Raymond, Robert Verrall, Dorothy Courtois-Lecour, W. Paterson Ferns * director of production — Sylvie de Grandpré * *scénario* — Fournier and Marie-José Raymond, from the novel of Gabrielle Roy * director of photography — Savas Kalogeras * Fournier's 1st assistant at the camera — Jean-Marie Buquet * sound engineer — Jacques Drouin * music — François Dompierre * Original song ("Bonheur d'occasion" or "Touch me," by Dompierre) sung by Diane Tell * Jazz music played by Eastman Jazz Ensemble of the Eastman School of Music (Rochester, N.Y.) * editing — André Corriveau * editing for English version — Yves Langlois * chief decorator — Charles L. Dunlop * assistant director — Mireille Goulet * script — Monique Champagne * artistic director — Denis Boucher * costumes — Nicole Pelletier * makeup — Marie-Angèle Protat * hair dresser — Gaétan Noiseux * *habilleuse* — Michèle Dion * sound editor — Bernard Bordeleau * *perchiste* — Jean-Guy Normandin * musical recording — Paul Pagé; Louis Hone * *mixage* — Hans Peter Strobl * *photographe de plateau* — Attila Dory. ** Cast (Characters/Actors): Florentine Lacasse — Mireille Deyglun; Rose-Anna Lacasse — Marilyn Lightstone; Jean Lévesque — Pierre Chagnon; Azarius Lacasse — Michel Forget; Emmanuel Létourneau — Martin Neufeld; Yvonne Lacasse — Charlotte Laurier; Danny Lacasse — Thomas Hellman; Marguerite (Florentine's "friend") — Linda Sorgini; Docteur Katz — Howard Ryshpan; Jenny — Liliane Clune.
[This film has been shown on television in its five-hour miniseries form (1984); it was filmed in French and in English. I have seen it in the dubbed five-hour and two-hour forms; I have also viewed it in the two-hour French language form.]
[*Bonheur d'occasion* took the International press prize for best Canadian film outside the competition at the World film festival (Montréal), 1983; it also received recognition at the International Festival of Film Moscow.]

BONS DÉBARRAS, LES (GOOD RIDDANCE) (1980; 109 to 114 minutes)

d. Francis Mankiewicz * producers — Marcia Couelle, Claude Godbout * *scénario* — Réjean Ducharme * script — Marie LaHaye * camerawork — Michel Brault * sound — Henri Blondeau * music — Bernard Buisson * editing — André Corriveau * asst. directors — Lise Abastado, Alain Chartrand * artistic direction — Michel Proulx * costumes — Diane Pâquet * makeup — Marie-Angèle Protat. ** Cast (Characters/Actors): Manon, the daughter — Charlotte Laurier; The mother — Marie Tifo; Guy — Germain Houde; Mme Viau-Vachon — Louise Marleau; Maurice (the policeman), boyfriend — Roger Le Bel.

[Winner of eight Canadian Genies (Canadian equivalent of Oscars); ranked as the third best Canadian film ever made in the *Variety* survey cited.]

CAFFÈ ITALIA MONTRÉAL (1985; 81 min.; color—documentary/fiction)

d. Paul Tana * producer—Marc Daigle * production director—Suzanne Girard * script—Paul Tana, Bruno Ramirez * research—Bruno Ramirez * photography—Michel Caron * sound—Serge Beauchemin with Dominique Chartrand and Thierry Morlàas-Lurbe * sound editing—Yves Chaput * music—Pierre Flynn, Andrea Piazza * artistic direction—Gaudeline Sauriol * costumes—Huguette Gagné, Marianne Carter * makeup—Diane Simard * editing—Louise Surprenant. ** Interpreters: Pierre Curzi, Toni Nardi * Voice-offs: Frédérique Collin, Pierre Curzi.
[Made with assistance of La Société générale du Cinéma du Québec; Téléfilm Canada; Bellevue Pathé Québec Inc. 1972; in collaboration with La Société Radio-Canada and the Association coopérative de productions audiovisuelles 1985 (ACPAV).]

CAGE, THE (1972; b&w; 18 min.)

d. Vartkes Cholakian; Richard Ciupka * production—Cholakian * script—Frances Gallagher * photography—Ciupka * sound—Jack Goodsouzian and Peter Benison * music—François Cousineau * editing—Cholakian.

CAP TOURMENTE (1992; 110 min.)

d. Michel Langlois * production—Bernadette Payeur * screenplay—Michel Langlois photography—Eric Cayla * editing—Jean-Claude Caulbois * sound—Richard Besse * sets—Frances Calder * music—Claude Beaugrand * costumes—Denis Sperdouklis and Louise Dubé. ** Cast (Characters/Actors): Alex O'Neal—Roy Dupuis; Alfa O'Neal—Elise Guilbault; Jeanne O'Neal—Andrée Lachapelle; Jean-Louis Mackenzie—Gilbert Sicotte; Barbara Kruger—Macha Limonchik; Monsieur Simon—Gabriel Gascon; Wilfrid Bourgault—Luc Picard; Jos—André Brassard; Madame Huot—Michele Deslauriers.

ÇA PEUT PAS ÊTRE L'HIVER, ON A MÊME PAS EU D'ÉTÉ (IT CAN'T BE WINTER; WE HAVEN'T HAD SUMMER YET) (1980; 87—90 min.)

d., prod., script—Louise Carré * production company—La Maison des Quatre, H. J. A. Lapointe Films * camera—Robert Vanherweghem * editor—André Théberge * music—Marc O'Farrell. ** Cast (Characters/Actors): Adèle Marquis—Charlotte Boisjoli; Germain Lafond—Jacques

Galipeau; Lise — Céline Lomez; Camille — Mireille Thibault; Jean-Pierre — Serge Belair; Martin — Daniel Matte.

(Prizes: International prize for Canadian full-length film at Festival of Films of the World in Montréal, 1980. Anglican Church prize [Germany; 1981]; Bronze award for first feature at the Houston festival, 1981.)

CHAMPIONS, THE (1978—1986; part. 1, 26 min. and 31 min.; part 2, 30 min. and 31 min.; and part 3, 90 min.)

directed, written, narrated — Donald Brittain * production — Donald Brittain, Janet Leissner, Peter Katadotis, Paul Wright * photography — Andreas Poulsson * sound — Claude Hazanavicius, Hans Oomes * music — Art Phillips, Eldon Rathburn * editing — Steven Kellar, Ted Remerowski, Richard Bujold.

CHAMPLAIN (1964; 28 min.)

d. Denys Arcand * production — ONF * *scénario* — Denys Arcand * illustrations — Frédéric Back * photography — Bernard Gosselin, Gilles Gascon * recording — Joseph Champagne * *mixage* — Ron Alexander, Roger Lamoureux * animation camera — Doug Poulter, James Milso, Murray Fallen, Jean Couinard * editing — Werner Nold; Bernard Gosselin * music — executed by the Brass Quintet of Montréal and Kenneth Gilbert. ** Female voiceover — Gisèle Trépanier * Male voice (Champlain) — Georges Dufaux.

CHANDAIL, LE

See *The Sweater*.

CHÂTEAU DE CARTES, LE (1979; 91 min.)

d. François Labonté. ** Cast: Kim Yaroshevskaya, Denis Bouchard, Marcel Sabourin, Paul Dion, and Gaston Lepage (as Bazooka).

CHER THÉO (1975; 49 minutes)

d. Jean Beaudin * *scénario*; dialogues — Jean Beaudin and Jacques Jacob * images — Pierre Mignot * son — Claude Hazanavicius * *montage* — Jean-Pierre Joutel * produced — ONF, Paul Larose. ** Cast (Characters/Actresses): Josette — Germaine Lemire; Julie — Julie Morand.

[Filmed in the Orthopedics Dept. of the Hospital of the Coeur-Sacré. Available in dubbed version.]

COMMENT FAIRE L'AMOUR AVEC UN NÈGRE SANS SE FATIGUER (HOW TO MAKE LOVE ...) (1989)

d. Jacques Wilbrod Benoît * production — Richard Sadler, Ann Burke, Henri Lange * script — Dany Laferrière, Richard Sadler * photography — John Berrie, Yves Binette, Takashi Seida * sound — Serge Beauchemin * art director — Gaudeline Sauriol * costumes — Ginette Robitaille * makeup — Michèle Dion. ** Cast: Isaach de Bankolé, Roberta Bizeau, Maka Kotto, Antoine Durand, and Myriam Cyr.

CONFORT ET L'INDIFFÉRENCE, LE (1981; 109 min.)

d. Denys Arcand * producers — Roger Frappier, Jean Dansereau, Jacques Gagné * photography — Alain Dostie * sound — Serge Beauchemin * editing — Pierre Bernier. ** Interpreters: Jean-Pierre Ronfard et al.

CORDÉLIA (1979 [1980, acc. to Pratley]; 115 min.; color)

d. Jean Beaudin * *scénario.* Jean Beaudin and Marcel Sabourin from *La Lampe dans la fenêtre* of Pauline Cadieux * assistant director — Jacques Wilbrod Benoît * production — National Film Board, Jean-Marc Garand with participation of Société Radio-Canada, Jacques Gagné, Roger Frappier * director of production — Laurence Paré * editor — Jean Beaudin * camera — Pierre Mignot * artistic direction — Vianney Gauthier, Denis Boucher * music — Maurice Blackburn * music editor — Roger Lamoureux * sound — Jacques Blain, Richard Besse * sound editor — Bernard Bordeleau * costumes — Louise Jobin * makeup — Brigitte McCaughry. ** Cast (Characters/Actors): Cordélia Viau — Louise Portal; Samuel Parslow — Gaston Lepage; Isidore Poirier — Pierre Gobeil; M. Jean-Dominique Leduc — Gilbert Sicotte; Joseph Fortier — Raymond Cloutier; Judge Taschereau — Jean-Louis Roux; Hangman Radcliff — James Blendick; Jailer Groulx — Rolland Bédard; Mme Viau (Cordélia's mother) — Marthe Blackburn.
    Cameo appearances of the following: Judge Bossé — Gratien Gélinas; Judge Ouimet — Jean Duceppe; Judge Wurtele — Jean Gascon; Judge Hall — Gilles Vigneault; Judge Blanchet — Doris Lussier.
    [Gaston Lepage (playing Samuel) took the prize for male actor at the International Festival of francophone film (Brest, 1980); Louise Jobin a Genie for best costume (Academy of Canadian Cinema, Toronto, 1980).]

CRAC (1981; 15 min.; b&w)

d. Frédéric Back * production — CBC and Société Radio-Canada; Hubert Tison * script — Frédéric Back * sound — André J. Riopel * music — Normand Roger * camera — Claude Lapierre; Jean Robillard * editing — Jacques Leroux.

CRIME D'OVIDE PLOUFFE, LE (THE CRIME OF OVIDE PLOUFFE) (1984; 105 min.)

d. Denys Arcand * prod. co. Ciné-Plouffe II, Inc.; CBC * producer—Justine Héroux (with Gabriel Boustani, Denis Héroux, John Kemeny, Jacques Bobet, and Ashley Murray) * *scénario*—Roger Lemelin and Denys Arcand, after the novel by Lemelin * camera—François Protat * editor—Monique Fortier * editors for the TV series: Pierre Bernier, Jacques Jean * music—Olivier Dassault * sound—Claude Hazanavicius, Michel Guiffan, Jean-Bernard Thomasson. ** Cast (Characters/Actors): Ovide Plouffe—Gabriel Arcand; Rita Toulouse-Plouffe—Anne Létourneau; Pacifique Berthet—Jean Carmet; Marie—Véronique Jannot; Maman Plouffe—Juliette Huot; Napoléon Plouffe—Pierre Curzi; Jeanne Plouffe—Louise Laparé; Cécile Plouffe—Denise Filiatrault; Guillaume Plouffe—Serge Dupire; Stan Labrie—Donald Pilon; grand avocat—Roger Le Bel; agent de voyage—Dominique Michel; jeune avocat de la défense—Marcel Leboeuf.
[Shown at Cannes Film Festival (Market).
(My discussion is based on the six-hour dubbed television version broadcast by CBC-Windsor; this included the film.)]

CURÉ DE VILLAGE, LE (1949; 85 min.)

directed, adapted, edited—Paul Gury (often called, as in this film's credits, Le Gouriadec) * QP (Québec Productions; L'Anglais) * director of production—Richard Jarvis * screenplay—Robert Choquette, based on his radio play * photography—Roger Racine * music—Morris C. Davis * music director—Jean Deslauriers. ** Cast (Characters/Actors): curé—Ovila Legaré; Juliette Martel—Lise Roy; Lionel Théberge—Denis Drouin; [Marten] Leblanc—Paul Guèvremont; the notary—Camille Ducharme; the Beadle—Eugène Daignault.
[Pratley says the director was Richard Jarvis, who was, in fact, "director of production." He also misspells Drouin as Droulin and then alphabetizes the error.]

DANS LE VENTRE DU DRAGON (1989; 1 hr. 40 min.)

d. Yves Simoneau * exec. producers—Monique H. Messier, Lorraine Richard * producer—Michel Gauthier * *scénario* and dialogues—Pierre Revelin, Marcel Beaulieu, Yves Simoneau * special effects director—Bernard Lajoie * head of makeup and aging effects—Pierre Saindon * director of photography—Alain Dostie * sound—Michel Charron, Paul Dion * editor—André Corriveau * editor of negative—Jim Campabadal * artistic director—Normand Sarrazin * costumes—Michèle Hamel * original music—Richard Grégoire ** Cast (Characters/Actors): Lou—David LaHaye; Mireille—Monique Mercure; Dr. Lucas—Marie Tifo; Steve—

Rémy Girard; Bozo—Michel Côté; Madame Côté (or Aube)—Andrée Lachapelle; Jean-Marie—Roy Dupuis; Le Boss—Pierre Curzi; Le Directeur—Jean-Louis Millette; Agent de sécurité No. 1—Steve Banner; Agent No. 2—Gaétan Nadeau; Agent No. 3—Michel Thériault.

DARK LULLABIES (1985; 81 min.)

d. Irene Lilienheim Angelico and Abbey Jack Neidik * producers—Irene Lilienheim Angelico, Abbey Jack Neidik, Edward Le Lorrain, Bonnie Sherr Klein with NFB * editors—Irene Lilienheim Angelico and Abbey Jack Neidik * executive producer—Kathleen Shannon * coproduction by NFB, Studio D and DLI * photography—Susan Trow * location sound—Jean-Guy Normandin * narration written by Irene Lilienheim Angelico and Gloria Demers * original music—Lauri Conger and Michael Beinhorn * music recording—Louis Hone * music editing—Diane Le Floch * sound editing—Abbey Jack Neidik and André Galbrand * rerecording—Jean-Pierre Joutel and Adrian Croll.

DÉCLIN DE L'EMPIRE AMÉRICAIN, LE (1986; 1 hr. 42 min.)

d. Denys Arcand * producers—René Malo and Roger Frappier * scénario—Denys Arcand * photography—Guy Dufaux * editing—Monique Fortier * music—François Dompierre, based on themes by Handel * associate producer—Pierre Gendron. ** Cast (Characters/Actors): Pierre—Pierre Curzi; Rémy—Rémy Girard; Claude—Yves Jacques; Alain—Daniel Brière; Dominique (femme)—Dominique Michel; Diane—Louise Portal; Louise—Dorothée Berryman; Danielle—Geneviève Rioux; Mario Alvarez—Gabriel Arcand.
(With the participation of Téléfilm Canada, La Société Générale du Cinéma du Québec, and with the collaboration of the Société Radio-Canada. Available with subtitles: MCA Home Video.)

DEMOCRACY ON TRIAL: THE MORGENTALER AFFAIR—1970–1976 (1984; 59 min.)

d. Paul Cowan * production—Adam Symansky, Jefferson Lewis, Paul Cowan, Robert Verrall, Andy Thomson * script—Jefferson Lewis * photography—Paul Cowan, Mike Mahoney * sound—Jacques Drouin * music—Alex Pauk, Zena Louie, Louis Hone * editing—Paul Cowan.

DEMOISELLE SAUVAGE, LA (1991; 100 min.; Swiss/Québécois)

d. Léa Pool (with Laurent Gagliardi and Michel Langlois) * producer—Denise Robert * scénario—Pool, Gagliardi, and Langlois, loosely inspired by the novella of S. Corinna Bille * photography—Georges Dufaux *

editing — Alain   Belhumeur * music — Jean   Corriveau * sound — Alain
Belhumeur * sets — Vianney   Gauthier * costumes — Christiane   Tessier.
** Cast (Characters/actors): Marianne — Patricia Tulasne; Elysée — Matthias
Habich; Maurice, Elysée's colleague — Roger Jendly; Police chief — Michel
Voita; Marie Chappaz, attorney — Lénie Scoffié; Elysée's wife — Séverine
Bujard.

DIVINE RIGHT, THE (1990; 12 min.)

d. Richard Raxlen * production — Main Film and Raxlen * story based
on *The Golden Bough* (James Frazer) * photography — Raxlen * sound —
Raxlen and Yoland Houle * music — Houle * editing — Raxlen. * Narrator — Jack Messinger.

DUPLESSIS ET APRÈS (1972; 114 min.)

d. often attributed to Denys Arcand, but credits show persons responsible
for creation of film are listed in alphabetical order: Denys Arcand, Serge
Beauchemin, Pierre Bernier, Jacques Drouin, Alain Dostie, Réo Grégoire,
Pierre Letarte, Pierre Mignot, André Théberge * produced by Paul Larose
(ONF) * music — Deschambault Church Chorus, directed by Elise Paré.
** Interpreters: for *catéchisme* — Gisèle Trépanier; for the Durham re-
port — Robin Spry.

EAU CHAUDE L'EAU FRETTE ..., L' (1976; 94 min.)

d. André Forcier * producer — Bernard Lalonde * script — Forcier and
Jacques Marcotte * photography — François Gill * sound — Hugues Mig-
nault * music — André Duchesne * editing — André Corriveau. ** Cast:
Carmen — Louise Gagnon; Francine — Sophie Clément; with Jean Lapointe,
Jean-Pierre Bergeron, Réjean Audet, Anne-Marie Ducharme, Albert
Payette, Guy L'Ecuyer.

ECLAIR AU CHOCOLAT (1979; 105 min.)

d. Jean-Claude Lord * production — Films Mutuels, Pierre David and
Robert Menard Production [for Productions Mutuelles Ltd. and Les
Productions Videofilms Ltd.] * *scénario* [based on a novel by Jean Santa-
croce] — Lord and Jean Salvy * photo — François Protat * editing — Lord *
music — Richard Grégoire [based on Diane Juster]. ** Cast (Characters/
Actors): Marie-Louise Prenant — Lise Thoin; Petit-Pierre Prenant — Jean
Belzil-Gascon; Lucien Prenant — Jean-Louis Roux; William Sinclair —
Colin Fox; Dominique — Danielle Penneton; Uncle — Aubert Pallascio;
Robert — Olivier Fillion; Fabienne — Valérie Deltour.

ELVIS GRATTON (1981; 30 min.)

d. Pierre Falardeau and Julien Poulin * *scénario* — Falardeau and Poulin * production — Bernadette Payeur * photography — Alain Dostie * sound — Serge Beauchemin * editing — Falardeau and Poulin. ** Cast: Julien Poulin, Denise Mercier, Little Beaver, Marie-Claude Dufour, Pierre Falardeau.

EMILIE (1992; TV serial)

d. Jean Beaudin * photography — Thomas Vamos * editing — Jean-Guy Montpettit * screenplay — Fernand Dansereau, based on a novel by Arlette Cousture. ** Cast: Marina Orsini — Emilie; Roy Dupuis — Ovila, with Pierre Curzi and Germain Houde.

END GAME IN PARIS (1982; 17 min.; color)

d. Veronica Soul * produced — Wolf Koenig and Robert Verrall * photography — Wolf Koenig and Ian Adams * sound — Jean-Guy Normandin * editing — Veronica Soul.

ET DU FILS (1972; 84 min.)

d. Raymond Garceau * producer — Pierre Gauvreau * screenplay — Garceau and Gauvreau [tr. from English and French translations of the Czechoslovakian of Vladimir Valenta] * camera — Michel Thomas-D'Hoste * sound — Joseph Champagne. ** Cast: Ovila Legaré, Jacques Godin, Réjean Lefrançois, Maruska Stankova.
[Filmed in 16 m and blown up to 35 m.]

ÉTIENNE BRÛLÉ, GIBIER DE POTENCE (E, B., THE IMMORTAL SCOUNDREL) (1951 Coulombe; Véronneau]; 1952 [Pratley]; 102 min., 15 sec.)

d. Melburn Turner * producer — Melburn Turner * production company — Carillon Pictures * associate producer — Richard Mingo-Sweeney * director of production — Jean Sweeney * *scenario* — Jeannette Downing, adapted from the book by J. H. Cranston, *E. B., Immortal Scoundrel* * script — Madeleine Lévesque * camera — Melburn Turner, Georges Delanoë, Claude Rondeau * sound — Stanley Clemson, Tom Derbyshire * costumes — Tanyss Malabar and Mme A. New Canoe * makeup — Pearl Gates. ** Cast (Characters/Actors): Étienne Brûlé — Paul Dupuis; Samuel de Champlain — Jacques Auger; Aĝonsa, Huron Princess — Ginette Letondal; Gayonena, Huron Princesse — Paulette DeGuise; Janendo, Huron Warrior — Gabriel Gascon; Serge Pelletier — Guy Hoffman; Père Jean de Brébeuf — Lionel Villeneuve; Sagida, Huron Doctor — Louis Thomas; Ojekwa (Prat.) or Ojikwa (Vér.), Iroquois Chief — Pierre Dulos; Odonéo, Huron Chief —

Aimé Maior (Prat.), or André Major; Nika, Huron Warrior—Thomas Taylor; Amiral Kirk(e)—Donald McGill; Aide-de-camp de l'amiral—Peter Jennings; Un chef indien—Tom Grand Louis, or, William Grand Louis; Mousquetaires—Pierre Rondeau and Réal Lemieux.
(Véronneau [*Cin. de l'ép. dupl.* 1979, 100]: Major played both Ojikwa and Odonéo.)

FEMME DE L'HÔTEL, LA (1984; 89 min.)

d. Léa Pool * production—Bernadette Payeur; Marc Daigle * *scénario*—Pool, Michel Langlois, Robert Gurik * photography—Georges Dufaux * sound—Serge Beauchemin * music—Yves Laferrière * editing—Michel Arcand. ** Cast: Louise Marleau, Paule Baillargeon, Marthe Turgeon, Serge Dupire, Gilles Renaud, Geneviève Paris, Kim Yaroshevskaya.

FILLES DU ROY, LES (1974; 57 min.)

d. Anne Claire Poirier * production—Poirier, produced by the ONF * script—Poirier, Marthe Blackburn, Jeanne Morazain * photography—Georges Dufaux, assisted by Suzanne Gabori * sound—Joseph Champagne * music—Maurice Blackburn * editing—Eric de Bayser.

FILM D'ARIANE, LE (ARIADNE'S MOVIE) (1985; ca. 60 min.)

d. Josée Beaudet * produced by Telefilm and the Société Générale du Cinéma du Québec for the Société Radio-Canada * script—Josée Beaudet * original idea—Christine Larocque * producer and sound manager—Denis Dupon * editing—Louise Michaud * original music—Jérôme Langlois and others. ** Ariane's voice—Monique Miller.

FILM FOR MAX, A (1970; 74 min.; documentary)

d. Derek May * production—Tom Daly * photography—Martin Duckworth * sound—Pierre Letarte, Henry Zemel * editing—Derek May.
[This intimate journal, full of "erasures" celebrates the director's young son, family, and communal life, and friendship.]

FOUS DE BASSAN, LES (1986; Alliance Vivafilm/MCA video rel. 1987; 107 min.)

d. Yves Simoneau * executive producers—Justine Héroux, Jean Nachbaur * adaptation—Marcel Beaulieu and Yves Simoneau * *scénario*—Sheldon Chad "d'après" Anne Hébert * photography—Alain Dostie * montage—Joelle Van Effenterre * music—Richard Grégoire. ** Cast (Characters/Actors): Stevens Brown—Steve Banner; Stevens old—Jean Louis Millette;

Olivia — Charlotte Valandrey; Nora — Laure Marsac; Irene Jones — Marie Tifo; Maureen — Angèle Coutu; T. J. — Paul Hébert; Nicolas Jones — Bernard-Pierre Donnadieu; Perceval — Lothaire Bluteau; Père Atkins — Roland Chenail; Patrick Atkins — Guy Thauvette; Sidney Atkins — Pierre Powers; Bob Allen — Henri Chassé, with Denise Gagnon and Joselyn Bérubé.

(Credits: Adriadne, Téléfilm Canada, Société Générale du Cinéma du Québec, Société Radio Canada, Société de Radio-Télévision du Québec, Super-Ecran.)

[Premier Choix: TVEC Inc.]. [Prizes: Genie for photography; also Prix Manuel Alves Castella, XVe Festival international du cinéma — Santyarem, Portugal, 1989 (Abel 1990, 324).]

FRÈRE ANDRÉ, LE (1987; 1 hr. 26 min.)

d. Jean-Claude Labrecque * producers — de la Montagne, Pierre Valcour, Téléfilm Canada, Société Générale du Cinéma Québécois; et al. * prod. délégué — Daniel Louis * sound — Michel Charron; Roger Guérin * photography — Michel Caron * artistic director — Ronald Fauteux * music, written and directed — Joël-Vincent Bienvenue * *scénario* and dialogues — Guy Dufresne * editing — André Corriveau. ** Cast (Characters/Actors): Frère André — Marc Legault; Marie-Esther — Sylvie Ferlatte; père Hupier — André Cailloux; père Louage — Michel Cailloux; curé provençal — René Caron; frère Léon — Raymond Cloutier; père Dion — Jean Coutu; frère Henri — Jean Lajeunesse; Monsieur Coutu — Guy Provost; père Econome — Jean Doyon; père Sorin — Roger Garceau; journaliste — Roger Larue; père Clément — Roland Lepage; docteur Charette — Gilles Renaud; mère de Guillaume — Linda Sorgini; docteur Parizeau — Guy Thauvette; père Gastineau — Michel Trouillet-Collet; frère Aldéric — Jacques Zouvi; Guillaume — Guillaume Lemay-Thivierge; Soeur Gertrude — Mireille Thibault.

[Prix de la Société générale du cinéma du Québec (prime à la qualité — Montréal, 1988, ex aequo with *Un Zoo la nuit*.).]

GABRIELLE (1979; video copyright, 1984; 90 min.)

d. Lawrence L. Kent * producers — John Dunning, André Link * assoc. prod. — Lawrence Nesis * script — Bill Lamond; John Dunning * music — Paul Baillargeon * editing — Debra Karen * photography — Richard Ciupka. ** Cast (Characters/Actors): Matt Kramer, McGill medical student — Vincent Van Patten; Gabrielle, his French Canadian lover — Claire Pimparé; Matthew's mother — Cloris Leachman; Matthew's grandfather — Eddie Albert; with Daniel Gadouas, Nicholas Campbell, Jack Wetherall, Jacques Godin, Marthe Mercure, Gerard Parkes.

GRAND REMUE-MÉNAGE, LE (1978; 1 hr. 10 min.)

d. Sylvie Groulx with Francine Allaire. [Coulombe erroneously writes Francine Dallaire] * coproduced—Les Productions de l'Envol and Le Centre d'Essai Conventum, with the Institut Québécois du Cinéma, Phyllis Lambert, and the ONF * camera—Bruno Carrière and Serge Giguère * sound—Noël Almey, Alain Corneau * editing—Jean Saulnier, Jean Gagné * music—Conventum * executive producer—Régis Painchaud. ** Participating in this film were Paride "Champ" Baldassare, Suzanne Roy, Richard Gogui Rochard (9 years old), Chantal Rochard, and "Les travailleurs de tricot partout."
* 3 and 7—"le numéro magique"—done by Marie Ouellet, Catherine Brunelle, and Ginette Bergeron.

GRANDE ALLURE, LA (1985; Pt. 1—60 min. 7 sec.; Pt. 2—73 min. 5 sec.)

d. Pierre Perrault * producers—ONF, Louisette Neil, Hélène Verrier, Jacques Vallée.
[Both parts of *La Grande allure* were coproduced by the ONF and the National Audio-Visual Institute (the INA), together with the Québec Ministry of Cultural Affairs, the French Ministry of Culture, the Saint-Jean-Baptiste Society of Montréal, and Société Radio-Canada.]

GREAT LAND OF SMALL, THE (1986–7, ca. 90 min.)

d. Vojta Jasny * producers—La Fête, Rock Demers * idea—David Sigmund * photography—Michel Brault * editing—Hélène Girard * music—Guy Trépanier, Normand Dubé * sound—Serge Beauchemin * line production—Lorraine Du Hamel. ** Cast (Characters/Actors): Jenny—Karen Elkin; David—Michael Blouin; Fritz—Michael Anderson; Mimick—Rodrigue Tremblay (Chocolat); Flannigan/Munch—Ken Roberts; Keeper—André Melançon; Grandpa—Gilles Pelletier; Grandma—Françoise Graton; Linda/Queen—Lorraine Desmarais; Sarah—Michèle Elaine Turnel; Willy the Dog—Bayou; Merlin the Horse—Unknown.

GRENOUILLE ET LA BALEINE, LA (TADPOLE AND THE WHALE) (1988; 90 min.)

d. Jean-Claude Lord * produced by Rock Demers (Les Productions La Fête with the participation of Telefilm Canada, La Société Générale du Cinéma du Québec and La Société Commandite Bach et Bottine) * screenplay—Jacques Bobet and André Melançon, based on an idea by Jacques Bobet * photography—Tom Burstyn (Abel adds Michel Brault) * editing—Hélène Girard * music—Guy Trépanier, Normand Dubé * line producer—Lorraine Du Hamel * sound—Serge Beauchemin. ** Cast (Characters/Actors): Daphne—Fanny Lauzier; Michael—Denis Forest; Julie—Mariana Orsini; Alexander—Felix-Antoine Leroux; Grandpa Thomas—Jean Lajeunesse; Anne, a biologist—Lise Thouin; Mother—Louise Richer; Father—Thomas Donahue; Grandpa Hector—Roland Laroche; Matthew—Pierre-Olivier Gagnon; Bernard—Jean-Pierre Leduc; Elvar—Nat; B-Minor—"Unknown."

[Prizes (listed in Abel 1990, 326) are numerous, including one from the Soviet Union for female interpretation (Lauzier), several French prizes, and the Golden Reel Award (Toronto, 1989).]

GUERRE DES TUQUES, LA (THE DOG WHO STOPPED THE WAR) (1984; 89 min.)

d. André Melançon * producers—Rock Demers, Nicole Robert (*Contes pour tous*) * director of photography—François Protat * music—Germain Gauthier * editing—André Corriveau * sound—Serge Beauchemin * assistant director—Alain Chartrand * script—Janine Sénécal * artistic director—Violette Daneau * costumes—Hughette Gagné * makeup—Diane Simard. ** Cast (Characters/Actors): Paul—Cédric Jourde; Marc—Julien Elie; Sophie—Marie Pierre (Maripierre) A. D'Amour; Nicki—Mathieu Savard; Walter—Duc Minh Vu; Cleo the dog—Luc(y).

HENRI (1986; ca. 2 hrs.)

d. François Labonté * producer—Claude Bonin * *scénario*—Jacques Jacob * music—Denis Larochelle * editing—André Corriveau * director of photography—Michel Caron * sound—Alain Corneau * ass. director—Alain Chartrand * script—Monique Champagne * artistic director—Jean-Baptiste Tard * costumes—Blanche-Danielle Boileau * makeup—Diane Simard. ** Cast (Characters/Actors): Henri—Eric Brisebois; Raoul Martineau—Yvan Ponton; Roch—Claude Gauthier; Joseph—Jacques Godin; Liliane—Lucie Laurier; Jeanne Painchaud—Marthe Turgeon.

HÉRITAGE, L' (1960; 58 minutes, 35 seconds; b&w)

d. Bernard Devlin * producers—ONF with Léonard Forest * adapted from Ringuet's novella by Bernard Devlin and Léonard Forest * editing—Bernard Bordeleau, Marc Beaudet * photography—François Séguillon * music—Robert Fleming. ** Cast: Albert Millaire, Marthe Mercure, Rolland D'Amour, J.-Léo Godin.

HERMÉNÉGILDE, VISION D'UN PIONNIER DU CINÉMA QUÉBÉCOIS — 1908 – 1973 (1976; 53 min.)

d. Richard   Lavoie * production — Richard   Lavoie * photography — Herménégilde Lavoie, Richard Lavoie, Pierre Pelletier * sound — Yves Saint-Jean * editing — Richard Lavoie. ** Narration: Paul Hébert.

HISTOIRE DE FEMMES, UNE (1980; 73 minutes)

d. Sophie Bissonnette. ** Voices of Paule Baillargeon, Markita Boies, Rita Lafontaine, Claudia Pharand and Gisèle Trépanier.
[Made with the support of contributions ranging from $5.00 to $1,000.00. This film won the "Prix de la critique québécoise" in 1981.]

HISTOIRE INVENTÉE, UNE (1990; 100 min.)

d. Marc-André Forcier * producers — Claudio Luca and Robin Spry * *scénario* — Forcier and Jacques Marcotte * photography — Georges Dufaux * editing — François Gill * music — Serge Fiori * sound — Marcel Pothier * décors — Réal Oulette * costumes — Gaudeline Sauriol. ** Cast (Characters/Actors): Gaston — Jean Lapointe; Florence — Louise Marleau; Soledad — Charlotte Laurier; Lentaignes — Marc Messier; Tibo — Jean-François Pichette; Alys — France Castel; Toni — Tony Nardi; Gros-Pierre — Marc Gélinas; Alfredo — Louis de Santis; Slim — Warren Williams; Roland — Donald Pilon; Nicole — Léo Murger; Arlette — Louise Gagnon; Théodule — Angelo Cadet; accordeur de piano — Denis Bouchard.

HOMME ET SON PÉCHÉ, UN (1948 – 9; 80 min.)

d. Paul Gury Le Gouriadec * producer — Paul L'Anglais * *scénario* — Claude-Henri Grignon; based on his radio play * photography — Drummond Drury * music — Hector Gratton. ** Cast (Characters/Actors): Seraphin — Hector Charland; Donalda — Nicole Germain; Alexis — Guy Provost; Jambe de Bois — Henri Poitras; Artemis — Suzanne Avon; Bill Wabo — George Alexander; le père Laloge — Ovila Légaré; le père Ovide — J. Eugène Daignault; le père Zime — Arthur Lefebvre; Pit Caribou — Armand Leguet; Caroline — Juliette Béliveau.

HOMME RENVERSÉ, L' (1986; 97 min.)

d. Yves Dion * production — ONF, Suzanne Dussault, Roger Frappier, Michel Gauthier * *scénario* — Yves Dion and Yves Gingras * photography — Pierre Letarte * editing — Yves Dion * music — Fernand Bernard. ** Cast: André Lacoste, Yves Desgagné, Johanne Seymour.

HOTEL CHRONICLES (1990; 75 min.; doc.)

d. Léa Pool * production — ONF, Eric Michel * text and narration — Pool * research and interviews — Pool, Laurent Gagliardi * photography — Georges Dufaux * editing — Alain Belhumeur * music — Robert M. Lepage * sound — Richard Besse.

IF YOU LOVE THIS PLANET (1982; 26 min.; doc.; color)

d. Terri Nash * production — Edward Le Lorrain and Kathleen Shannon * photography — André-Luc Dupont, Susan Trow, and Don Virgo * sound — Jacques Drouin. * music — Karl L. du Plessis * editing — Terri Nash.

IL ÉTAIT UNE FOIS DANS L'EST (1973–5; 101 min.)

d. André Bassard * producer — Pierre Lamy * *scénario* — Michel Tremblay and Bassard * camera work — Paul Van der Linden * editing — André Corriveau * sound — Jacques Blain * music — Jacques Perron. ** Cast (Characters/Actors): Hélène — Denise Filiatrault; Pierrette — Michelle Rossignol; Lise Paquette — Frédérique Collin; Carmen — Sophie Clément; with André Montmorency, Jean Archambault, Gilles Renaud, Manda Parent, Claude Glaude Gai, Amulette Garneau, Rita Lafontaine, Bétrice Picard.

IL Y A LONGTEMPS QUE JE T'AIME (1989; 88 min. 31 sec.)

d. Anne Claire Poirier * production — auspices of the ONF (Programme: Regards des femmes) * idea — Anne Claire Poirier * editor — Dominique Sicotte * sound — Lise Wedlock * sound editing — Myriam Poirier * "Original" music by Marie Bernard often represents variations on the old folksong: "Il y a longtemps que je t'aime, jamais je ne t'oublierai ...", from which the film takes its title.

INCIDENT AT RESTIGOUCHE (1984; 46 min.; color)

d. Alanis Obomsawin * production — Andy Thomson, Alanis Obomsawin, Robert Verrall (NFB) * photography — Roger Rochat, Savas Kalogera * sound — Yves Gendron, Bev Davidson * music — Luc Plamondon, Edith Butler, Willie Dunn * editing — Allan Collins, Wolf Koenig.

ISABEL (1968; 108 min.)

director, producer, writer — Paul Almond * camera — Georges Dufaux * editor — George Appleby * music — Harry Freedman. ** Cast (Characters/Actors): Isabel — Geneviève Bujold; Jason — Marc Strange; Uncle

Matthew—Gerard Parkes; Eb—Elton Hayves; Vila—Ede Kerr; Herb—
Albert Waxman.

IXE-13 (1972; 114 min.)

direction, *scénario*—Jacques Godbout * inspired by the novels of Pierre
Saurel * production—Pierre Gauvreau * music—François Dompierre *
photography—Thomas Vamos * sound—Claude Hazanavicius and Michel
Descombes * editing—Werner Nold * sets—Claude Lafortune. ** Ac-
tors: Louise Forestier, André Dubois, Serge Grenier, Marc Laurendeau,
Marcel Saint-Germain, Louisette Dussault, Carole Laure, Luce Guilbeault.
[Shown at the Cannes Festival.]

JACQUES ET NOVEMBRE (1984; 72 min.; b&w and color)

codirectors—Jean Beaudry, François Bouvier * production—François
Bouvier, Marcel Simard * screenplay—Beaudry; Bouvier * photography—
Serge Giguère, Claude de Maisonneuve, and Bouvier * sound—Marcel
Fraser, Diane Carrière, Dominique Chartrand, Christine Lemoyne, Michel
Charron, Gilbert Lachapelle, André Dussault, François Reid * music—
Michel Rivard * editing—Jean Beaudry. ** Cast (Characters/Actors):
Jacques—Jean Beaudry; with Carole Fréchette, Marie Cantin, Jean
Mathieu, Pierre Rousseau, Reine France.

J.A. MARTIN PHOTOGRAPHE (1976; 101 min., 13 sec.) (Date varies between
1976 and 1977, from Houle to Coulombe to Pratley to Clanfield. Made in
1976; premiered in early 1977)

d. Jean Beaudin * production—co./released by National Film Board * producer—Jean-Marc Garand * directors of production—Michel Dandavino
and Françoise Berd * *scénario* and dialogues—Jean Beaudin and Marcel
Sabourin * camera—Pierre Mignot, assisted by Jacques Tougas and René
Daigle * editing—Jean Beaudin and Hélène Girard * music—Maurice
Blackburn * musical recording—Roger Lamoureux * script—Monique
Champagne * assistant director—Michel Gauthier * decor, costumes,
props—Vianney Gauthier, assisted by André Loiseau * hairdressing and
makeup—Brigitte McCaughry * lighting—Kevin O'Connell * *mixage*—
Jean-Pierre Joutel. ** Cast (Characters/Actors): J. A. Martin—Marcel
Sabourin; Rose-Aimée—Monique Mercure; Mother Martin (Mémère)—
Marthe Thierry; Dolores Martin—Catherine Tremblay; friend—Jean
Lapointe; neighbor woman—Mariette Duval; Mathieu Martin—Denis
Hamel; David Martin—Stéphane L'Ecuyer; Hormidas Lambert—Jacques
Bilodeau; Madame Lambert—Colette Courtois; Tante Aline—Marthe
Nadeau; l'habitant—André St-Denis; hotel landlady—Denise Proulx; hotel
landlord—Robert DesRoches; Raoul—Guy L'Ecuyer; the old man—

Charlie Beauchamp; Madame Beaupré—Luce Guilbeault; Beaupré—
Denis Drouin; a lady customer—Madeleine Pageau; a man customer—
Eric Gaudry; Uncle Joseph—Yvan Canuel; Aunt Demerise—Germaine
Lemyre; Adhémar—Jean Lapointe; M. Wilson—Walter Massy; Julien
Tremblay—Denis Robinson; Scott Henry Raimer; a worker—Jean
Mathieu; M. Tremblay—Pierre Gobeil * Musicians and dancers. (See
Lever, "Pour une mémoire . . .": [16]).
(Prize: best film of 1977 [Canadian Film Award])

JÉSUS DE MONTRÉAL (1989; 120 min.)

d. Denys Arcand * *scénario*—Denys Arcand * camera—Guy Dufaux *
editing—Isabelle Dedieu * music—Yves Laferrière. ** Cast (Characters/
Actors): Pascal Berger (Smerdiakov)—Cédric Noël; France Garibaldi—
Pauline Martin; Roméo Miroir—Jean-Louis Millette; Régine Malouin,
TV star—Véronique Le Flaguais; Richard Cardinal, lawyer and artists'
agent—Yves Jacques; Denise Quintal—Monique Miller; Daniel Coulombe
—Lothaire Bluteau; Raymond Leclerc, religieux du Sanctuaire—Gilles
Pelletier; Constance Lazure—Johanne-Marie Tremblay; Martin Durocher
—Rémy Girard; René Sylvestre—Robert Lepage; Mireille Fontaine—
Catherine Wilkening; Aurore Léger, librarian—Paule Baillargeon; un
juge—Denys Arcand; Sophie de Villers, psychologist—Andrée Lachapelle;
Sam Rosen—Ron Lea; Mr. Rigby—Dean Hagopian; Italian Recipient—
Anna-Maria Giannotti; Italian doctor—Paul Tana.
(Prizes: [See Abel 1990, 327]: Cannes, Montréal, Toronto, Halifax,
San Remo [Italy], Chicago, Abitibi, Puerto Rico [1989].)

JEUNE MAGICIEN, LE (THE YOUNG MAGICIAN) (1986; 95 min.)

d., written—Waldemar Dziki * producer—Rock Demers' *Contes pour
tous* #4 (La Fête); coproduced by the Polish company Unité de Production
Tor [for Zespoly Filmowe] and Les Productions La Fête, with participation
of Téléfilm Canada, Société Radio-Canada, and CFCF Télévision, Inc.) *
delegated producers—Anne Burke, Michal Szczerbic, Jacek Szeligowski *
director of photography—Wit Dabal * artistic director—Violette Daneau *
special effects—Louis Craig, Mark Molin * music—Krzesimir Debski *
editing—André Corriveau * sound—Claude Langlois * French adaptation
of song—Guy Trépanier, Marc Desjardins * interpreter—Betty Eljarat.
** Actors: Rusty Jedwab, Edward Garson, Natasza Maraszek.

JOURNAL INACHEVÉ (1982; 48 min.)

d. Marilú Mallet * production—Dominique Pinel and Mallet * screenplay—
Mallet * photography—Guy Borremans * sound—Julian Olson * editing—
Mallet; Pascale Laverrière, Milicska Jalbert. ** Cast: Mallet, Michael

Rubbo, Nicolas Rubbo, Maria Luisa Segnoret, Isabel Allende, Salvator Fisciella.

KALAMAZOO (1988; 84–90 minutes)

d. Marc-André Forcier * producers — Jean Dansereau and Louise Gendron * script — Marc-André Forcier and Jacques Marcotte * music — Joël Vincent Bienvenue * editing — François Gill * photography director — Alain Dostie * sound — Richard Besse * artistic director — Michel Proulx * costumes — François Laplante * makeup — Bob Laden. ** Cast (Characters/Actors): Cotnoir — Rémy Girard; Helena — Marie Tifo; Globenski — Tony Nardi * with Gaston Lepage.

(Marie Tifo took the Guy L'Ecuyer prize for best actress for her part in this film [Montréal, 1989]; and the L. E. Ouimet-Molson prize was granted to the film by the Association québécoise des critiques de cinéma for the best full-length fiction film [Montréal, 1989].) (Abel 1990, 326.)

KAMOURASKA (1973; 119 minutes)

d. Claude Jutra * producer — France Film (Société Parc Film of Paris — Productions Carle-Lamy of Montréal), Pierre Lamy, Mag Bodard * screenplay — Anne Hébert and Claude Jutra, from Hébert's novel * photography (Eastmancolor) — Michel Brault * editor — Renée Lichtig [say Pratley and Coulombe; Renée Lighting, says Houle in *Dict.*], assisted by Françoise London, Madeleine Guérin, Susan Kay * art direction (sets and costumes) — François Barbeau * music — Maurice Leroux (or Le Roux) * sound — Serge Beauchemin; Jacques Blain. ** Cast (Characters/Actors): Elisabeth — Geneviève Bujold; Nelson — Richard Jordan; Antoine — Philippe Léotard; Jérome — Marcel Cuvelier; Aurélie — Suzie Baillargeon; Mme d'Aulnières — Huguette Oligny; Aunts — Janine Sutto, Olivette Thibault, Marie Fresnières; Mme Tassy — Camille Bernard.

[There was some French input into the making of this film. Also, at the end, under credits, one reads: "We thank the city and parish of Crèvecoeur."]

(Reviewed but not competing at Cannes: 13 May 1973.)

[*Kamouraska* can be rented at New Line Cinema — with subtitles; it has been shown on Montréal TV; video — rent from Vedette Visuals.]

LAURA LAUR (1989; 92 min.)

d. Brigitte Sauriol * written by Brigitte Sauriol, based on novel of Suzanne Jacob * production — Nicole Robert with ONF, Telefilm Canada, Société Générale, Super Ecran, Bellevue Pathé Québec; Société Radio-Canada * photography — Louis de Ernsted * editor — André Corriveau * art director — Jean-Baptiste Tard * sound — Marcel Fraser and Jean-Pierre

Joutel * costumes — Nicoletta   Massone * original   music — Jacques Corriveau. ** Cast (Characters/Actors): Laura — Paula de Vasconcelos; Gilles — Dominique Briand; Serge — André Lacoste; the psychoanalyst — Jean Pierre Ronfard * with a special appearance of Andrée Lachapelle as Agnès.

LÉOLO (1992; 107 min.)

d. and *scénario* Jean-Claude Lauzon * production — Lyse Lafontaine and Aimée Danis * photography — Guy Dufaux * editing — Michel Arcand * music — Richard Grégoire * sound — Yvon Benoît and Marcel Pothier * sets — François Séguin * costumes — François Barbeau. ** Cast (Characters/Actors): Léolo or Léo Lozeau — Maxime Collin; mother — Ginette Reno; father — Roland Blouin; grandfather — Julien Guiomar; "le dompteur de vers" — Pierre Bourgault; narrator — Gilbert Sicotte; Bianca — Giuditta del Vecchio; professor — Germain Houde; psychiatrist — Andrée Lachapelle; the young Léolo — Francis St-Onge; counselor — Denys Arcand; Fernand — Yves Montmarquette; Fernand's enemy — Lorne Brass.

LIES MY FATHER TOLD ME (1975; 102 min.)

d. Jan Kadar * production — Anthony Bedrich, Harry Gulkin, Bill Cohen * script — Ted Allan (after his own novella) * photography — Paul Van der Linden * sound — Henri Blondeau * music — Sol Kaplan * editing — Edward Beyer; Richard Marks. ** Cast (Characters/Actors): David — Jeffrey Lynas; Zaida — Yossi Yadin; Harry Herman — Len Birman; Annie Herman — Marilyn Lightstone; Mr. Baumgarten — Ted Allan; Mrs. Tannenbaum — Barbara Chilcott; Mrs. Bondy — Mignon Elkins; Uncle Benny — Henry Ramer; Edna — Carole Lazare; Cleo — Paskal.

LOVE AND HATE (1989; ca. 3 hours)

d. Francis Mankiewicz * asst. dir. — Pierre Houle * producer — Bernard Zukerman * written by Suzette Couture, after the book *A Canadian Tragedy* by Maggie Siggins * associate producer — Gail Carr * production manager — Lars Dahl * editor — Gordon McClellan * photography — Vic Sarin, C.S.C. * additional photography — Thomas Vamos * sound recording — Gerry King * costumes — Hilary Corbett * senior set director — Peter Ragmovsky * makeup — Mario Cacioppo * special effects — Gus White * original music — Eric N. Robertson * music recorded by Hayward Parrott. ** Cast (Characters/Actors): Colin Thatcher — Kenneth Welsh; Thatcher's wife, JoAnn — Kate Nelligan; Tony, JoAnn's second husband — Cedric Smith; Greg Thatcher (son) — Dungan Ollerenshaw; Regan Thatcher (son) — Noam Zylberman; Stephanie Thatcher (daughter) — Vicki Wauchope; Jerry Anderson — Eugene Lipinski; Dick Coliver (former colleague of Thatcher) — Thomas Peackocke; also stars Brent Carver.

LUCIEN BROUILLARD (1983; 88 min.)

d. Bruno Carrière * producer — René Gueissaz * production and co/release — ACPAV * *scénario* — Carrière and Jacques Jacob * camera — Pierre Mignot * editor — Michel Arcand. ** Cast (Characters/Actors): Lucien Brouillard — Pierre Curzi; Jacques Martineau — Roger Blay; Alice Tanguay — Marie Tifo; André Morin — Paul Savoie; Premier Provencher — Jean Duceppe.

MANUEL, LE FILS EMPRUNTÉ (A SON BY CHOICE) (1989; 80 min.)

d. François Labonté * producers — Francine Forest and Nardo Castillo * production — Cléo 24, Les Productions EGM and NFB * screenplay — Gerald Wexler * French shooting script — Monique Proulx and Nardo Castillo * photography — Karol Ike * art director — Normand Sarrazin * costumes — Denis Sperdouklis * location sound recordist — Dominique Chartrand * supervising sound editor — Viateur Paiement * editor — François Gill * music — Osvaldo Montes * production manager — Jean-Marie Comeau. ** Cast (Characters/Actors): Juan Alvarez — Francisco Rabal; Manuel — Nuno DaCosta; Rose Alvarez — Kim Yaroshevskaya; Manuel's father, Vasco Estrada — Luis Saraïva; Manuel's sister, Estella Estrada — Isabel Serra; Jimmy — Gaston Caron; Michèle Leblanc [or Leclerc] — Ginette Boivin; Mr. Fortier, the teacher — Robert Toupin; the principal — Michel Dumont; Pablo — José Barrio; Simon — Jean-François Leblanc; Angèle — Simon Guévillon-Loisel; Costa — Marc Lavoie; with Eric Brisebois, Pedro Marques, Marisa Martinho, Nardo Castillo, Marco Ramirez.

MARIA CHAPDELAINE (1983; 108 min.)

d. Gilles Carle * production — Astral Film Production; released in collaboration with CBC and La Société nationale de programmes (TF 1) in France * exec. prod. — Harold Greenberg * producers — Murray Shostak and Robert Baylis * *scénario* — Gilles Carle, Guy Fournier, based on Louis Hémon's novel * camera — Pierre Mignot * editor — Avdé Chiriaeff * music — Lewis Furey. ** Cast (Characters/Actors): Maria — Carole Laure; François — Nick Mancuso; Eutrope Gagnon — Pierre Curzi; Marie-Ange — Marie Tifo; Father Cordelier — Claude Rich; Laura Chapdelaine — Amulette Garneau; Samuel Chapdelaine — Yoland Guérard; Lorenzo Surprenant — Donald Lautrec.

MARIE S'EN VA-T-EN VILLE (MARIE IN THE CITY) (1987; 75 min.; 16 mm. ext. to 35 mm.)

d. Marquise Lepage * collaborating director — Jean Beaudry * production — Les Productions du lundi matin, Inc. * production director — Claude

Cartier * producer—François Bouvier * *scénario*—Marquise Lepage with François Bouvier, Pierre Foglia, Micheline Lanctôt, Jacques Leduc * photography—Daniel Jobin * sound—Marcel Fraser * sound editor—Marcel Pothier * sound recording—André Turcotte * postsychronization recording—Paul Gagnon * dialogue editor—Marie-Claude Gagné * artistic director—François Séguin * props—Simon LaHaye * costumes—Nicole Pelletier * makeup—Micheline Trépanier * photography editor—Yves Chaput * original music—Michel Rivard ["Méfiez-vous du grand amour"] * English subtitles—David Gold. ** Cast (Characters/Actors): Marie—Geneviève Lenoir; Sarah—Frédérique Collin; Paul—Denis Levasseur; Serge, the brother—Robert Boivin; the brunette prostitute—Geneviève Filion; radio voice—Dominic Frégault; television voice—Jean Beaudry; mother's voice—Francine Ruel; customer in car—Alain Gendreau; snack-bar waitress—Viviane Pacal; saleslady—Louise Richer; the first deaf man—Jacques Hamon; the second deaf man—Michel Lepage; first passerby—Jean-Pierre Gonthier; second passerby—Jean Beaudry; flower saleslady—Marquise Lepage; Marie's sister—Delphine Collin-Vézina; café waitress—Marie Charlebois; man with newspaper—Pierre Foglia; bistro waiter—François Lacoste; bus passenger—Gilles Marsolais; customer in the street—Jean Turcotte; . . . in the arcades—Richard Bertrand; . . . in the sushi bar—Shig Abe, Tri Du, Katsumito Inoue; . . . in the snack bar—Jean-Pierre Filion, Michel Oullette * Prostitutes—Nefertari Belizaire, Suzanne Bouchard, Chantal Desjardins, Geneviève Desrosiers, Sylvie Durant, Francine Guénette, Rachel Roy, Patricia Tulasne, Thérèse Blais.

MARIO (1984; 97 minutes)

d. Jean Beaudin * producers—Hélène Verrier, Jean Beaudin, Jacques Bobet, Denis Héroux, John Kemeny * An NFB production * *scénario*—Arlette Dion, Jean Beaudin, Jacques Paris (d'après *La Sablière* de Claude Jasmin) * images (photography)—Pierre Mignot, Thomas Vamos * sound—Richard Besse * music—François Dompierre * editing—Werner Nold * special effects—Gregg Curtis, Jacques Godbout, Gary Zeller * makeup—Mikie Hamilton. ** Cast (Characters/Actors): Mario—Xavier Norman Patermann; Dimon—Francis Reddy; Hélène—Nathalie Chalifour; le père—Jacques Godin; la mère—Murielle Dutil; social worker—Claire Pimparé; receptionist—Christiane Breton; thérapist—Marcel Sabourin; Denis—Jonathan Palmchaud; Benoît—Sylvain Cormier; Pierre—Marc André Vigneau; father's associate—Michel Gauthier; Sylvie—Geneviève Gauthier; Marie—Michèle Lapiere; M. Gauthier—Alcide Palmchaud; souvenir salesman—Yvon Boudras.

MASCULINE MYSTIQUE, THE (1984; 87 min.)

d. Giles Walker, John N. Smith * production—Smith, Walker, Robert Verrall, Andy Thomson * script—Smith, Walker, David Wilson * photography—Andrew Kitzanuk * sound—Jean-Guy Normandin * music—Richard Gresko * editing—David Wilson. ** Cast: Stefan Wodoslawsky, Char Davies, Sam Grana, Eleanor MacKinnon, Felice Grana, Stefanie Grana.

MATINS INFIDÈLES, LES (1989; 90 min.)

d., written and produced by François Bouvier * Productions du Lundi Matin, Téléfilm Canada; Société Générale, Radio-Canada, Commanditaires de la Société en Commandité Duluth * assoc. prod.—Claude Cartier, Marc Daigle * camera—Alain Dupras * editor—Jean Beaudry * music—Michel Rivard * sound—Claude Beaugrand, Esther Auger * set decoration—Karine Lepp. ** Cast: (Characters/Actors): Marc—Jean Beaudry; Jean-Pierre—Denis Bouchard; Laurent—Laurent Faubert-Bouvier; Julie—Violaine Forest; Pauline—Louise Richer; Young Woman on Corner—Nathalie Coupal.

MATOU, LE (1985; 141 min.)

d. Jean Beaudin * coproduced by Canado-Française, Cinévidéo, Inc.; La Société de Radio-Télévision du Québec; Société Radio-Canada and Initial Groupe Film A2; AAI-TV2, with the financial assistance of Téléfilm Canada and La Société Générale du Cinéma du Québec * exec. prod.—Denis Héroux; John Kemeny * prod.—Denis Héroux * director of production—Justine Héroux * script—Lise Lemay-Rousseau (d'après Yves Beauchemin) * director of photography—Claude Agostini * sound—Claude Hazanavicius * editor—Jean-Pierre Cereghetti * original music—François Dompierre. ** Cast (Characters/Actors): Florent Boisonneault—Serge Dupire; Elise—Monique Spaziani; Ratablavasky—Julien Guiomar; Picquot—Jean Carmet; Monsieur Emile—Guillaume Lemay-Thivierge; Slipskin—Miguel Fernandes; Mme Chouinard, Emile's mother—Johanne Fontaine; Rosario Gladu—Julien Poulin; Ange-Albert—Francis Reddy; Rosine—Isabel Lorca; Beaumont (antique dealer)—Paul Savoie; Mayor Meloche—Jean-Pierre Masson.
    (Several prizes [see Abel 1990, 322], the most notable being, perhaps, for music. François Dompierre took a Genie for the musical score. One of the songs, *Monsieur Emile*, "le beau petit caribou," is charming. Lever [*Hist.* 1988, 456 and elsewhere] insists on the high cost of this film—Beauchemin received $300,000 for the rights, etc.)

MAUDITE GALETTE, LA (1972; 108 min.)

d. Denys Arcand * producer—Pierre Lamy, Marguerite Duparc * *scénario*—Jacques Benoît * photography—Alain Dostie * sound—Claude Hazanavicius * music—Michel Hinton, Gabriel Arcand, Lionel Thériault * editing—Marguerite Duparc ** Cast: Luce Guilbeault, Marcel Sabourin, René Caron, J.- Léo Gagnon, Gabriel Arcand, Jean-Pierre Saulnier, Andrée Lalonde, Maurice Gauvin.

MON ONCLE ANTOINE (1971; 104 min.)

d. Claude Jutra * producer—Marc Beaudet * production—Gendon Films of Montréal for the NFB * screenplay—Clément Perron * adaptation— Claude Jutra/Clément Perron * camera—Michel Brault * editors—Claude Jutra/Claire Boyer * music—Jean Cousineau * sound editing—Jacques Jarry * sets and props—Denis Boucher, Lawrence O'Brien * makeup— Suzanne Garand, René Demers. ** Cast (Characters/Actors): Uncle Antoine—Jean Duceppe; Aunt Cécile—Olivette Thibault; Fernand— Claude Jutra; Benoît—Jacques Gagnon; Carmen—Lyne Champagne; Jos Poulin—Lionel Villeneuve; Madame Poulin—Hélène Loiselle; Alexandrine —Monique Mercure; Le grand patron—Georges Alexander; Le curé— René Salvatore Catta; with the people of Black Lake, Québec, Canada.

MONTREAL MAIN (1973; 88 min.; b&w)

d. Frank Vitale * producers—Frank Vitale and Allan Moyle, with Kirwan Cox * *scénario*—John Sutherland and the cast * photography—Erich Block * editing—Frank Vitale; * sound—Pedro Novak * music—Beverly Glenn-Copeland. ** Improvisations by a nonprofessional cast: Frank— Frank Vitale; Johnny—John Sutherland; and also Dave Sutherland, Anne Sutherland, Peter Brawley, Pam Marchant, Allan Moyle, and Jackie Holden.

MORT D'UN BÛCHERON, LA (1973; 115 min.)

d. Gilles Carle * production—Pierre Lamy * screenplay—Carle and Arthur Lamothe * camera—René Verzier * sound—Henri Blondeau * music— Willie Lamothe * editing—Gilles Carle. ** Cast (Characters/Actors): Maria—Carole Laure; François Paradis—Daniel Pilon; Charlotte Juillet— Pauline Julien; Armand St.-Amour—Willie Lamothe; Ti-Noir L'Espérance —Marcel Sabourin; Blanche Bellefeuille—Denise Filiatrault.

MOTHER OF MANY CHILDREN (MÈRE DE TANT D'ENFANTS) (1977; 57 min. 50 sec.)

d. Alanis Obomsawin * producers—Obomsawin, Don Hopkins, and Douglas MacDonald * produced by ONF in collaboration with Indian and Northern Affairs, the Secretary of State, and the Minister in charge of Multiculturalism.

MOURIR À TUE-TÊTE (SCREAM FROM SILENCE) (1979; 96 min.)

d. Anne Claire Poirier * production—Jacques Gagné, Anne Claire Poirier, with ONF * *scénario*—Anne Claire Porier and Marthe Blackburn * camera—Michel Brault * sound—Joseph Champagne * music—Maurice Blackburn * editing—André Corriveau * "clitoridectomy" scenes from Alain de Benoist. ** Cast: Julie Vincent as the nurse Suzanne; Germain Houde as the rapist. With Paul Savoie, Monique Miller, Micheline Lanctôt, Luce Guilbeault, Christiane Raymond, Louise Portal.

NOCES DE PAPIER, LES (1989—90; 90 min.)

d. Michel Brault * producers—Aimée Danis and Danièle Bussy * screenplay—Jefferson Lewis and Andrée Pelletier * editor—Jacques Gagné * photography—Sylvain Brault. ** Cast (Characters/Actors): Claire—Geneviève Bujold; Pablo, a Chilean political refugee—Manuel Arranguiz; Milosh, Bujold's married former lover—Teo Spychalski. Also starring: Dorothée Berryman, Gilbert Sicotte, Jean Mathieu, Monique Lepage.

NOT A LOVE STORY—A FILM ABOUT PORNOGRAPHY (1981; 69 min.)

d. Bonnie Sherr Klein * production—Dorothy Todd Hénaut, Kathleen Shannon, Micheline Le Guillou * script—Irene Angelico, Andrée Klein, Bonnie Sherr Klein, Rose-Aimée Todd * photography—Pierre Letarte * sound—Yves Gendron * music—Ginette Bellavance * editing—Anne Henderson.

ONE MAN (1977; 87 min.)

d. Robin Spry * production—Michael Scott, Roman Kroitor, James de B. Domville, Tom Daly, Vladimir Valenta, with NFB * script—Robin Spry, Peter Pearson, Peter Madden, Vladimir Valenta * photography—Douglas Kiefer * sound—Claude Hazanavicius * music—Ben Low * editing—John Kramer. ** Cast (Characters/Actors): Jason Brady—Len Cariou; Alicia Brady—Jayne Eastwood; Marion Galbraith—Carol Lazare; Colin Angus Campbell—Barry Morse; Ernie Carrick—August Schellenberg; Ben Legault—Jean Lapointe; Rodney Porter—Sean Sullivan; Dr.

Gendron — Terry Haig; Leo — Marc Legault; First Hood — Danny Freedman; Second Hood — Gilles Renaud; John, a TV Announcer — Bob Girolami; Jaworski — Jacques Godin.

ON EST AU COTON (1971; 159 min.)

d. Denys Arcand * producers — Guy L. Coté, Pierre Maheu, Marc Beaudet * photography — Alain Dostie * sound — Serge Beauchemin * editing — Pierre Bernier. *

OPERATION BEURRE DE PINOTTES (THE PEANUT BUTTER SOLUTION) (1985; 87 min.)

d. Michael Rubbo * original idea and screenplay — Michael Rubbo, Voltech Jasny, Andrée Pelletier, Louise Pelletier * production — Rock Demers, Nicole Robert (Productions La Fête; Conte pour tous #2), Les Productions Pascal Blais (d. Pascal Blais) * executive producer — Rock Demers * first assistant director — Jim Kaufman * script — Marie Théberge * photography — Thomas Vamos * film editor — Jean-Guy Montpetit * music — Lewis Furey * artistic director — Vianney Gauthier * costumes — Huguette Gagné * makeup — Marie-Angèle Breitner-Protat * set decorator — Martine Drapeau * sound — Claude Langlois * sound editing — Claude Langlois * sound man — Serge Beauchemin * hair special effects — Roger Cantin. ** Cast (Characters/Actors): Michael — Mathew Mackay; Connie — Selick Saysanasy; Suzie — Alison Podbrey; Billy — Michael Hogan; The Signor — Michael Maillot; Mary — Helen Hughes; Tom — Griffith Brewer; Dr. Epstein — Harry Hill; The Rabbit — Edgar Fruitier; Miss Prume — Pat Thompson; Mr. Gringras — Terrence Labrosse; Art Supply Owner — Doug Smith; More — Nick Manexas; Little William — Patrick Saint-Pierre; Jeremy — Jeremy Spry; Jessica — Cheryl Zaman-Zodir; Alice — Alice Grant; Vicki — Vicki Lee; Man Ling — Njoka Takamtng; The Mother — Anna White; Jim the dog — Patches.

ORDRES, LES (1974; 107 min. 29 sec.)

d. Michel Brault * producers — Bernard Lalonde, Productions Prisma * scénario — Michel Brault * photography — François Protat and Michel Brault * editing — Yves Dion * sound — Serge Beauchemin * music — Philippe Gagnon * art direction — Michel Proulx * subtitles — Marcia Couëlle. ** Cast (Characters/Actors): Clermont Boudreau (Clément[sic.] in Pratley; Clanfield correctly says Clermont) — Jean Lapointe; Marie Boudreau — Helen Loiselle; Richard Lavoie — Claude Gauthier; Claudette Dussault — Louise Forestier; Jean-Marie Beauchemin — Guy Provost.

PAS DE RÉPIT POUR MÉLANIE (1990)

d. Jean Beaudry * Productions La Fête * *scénario* — Stella Goulet * photography — Eric Cayla * music — Jean Corriveau. ** Cast (Characters/Actors): Mélanie — Marie-Stéfane Gaudry; La Petite Noire — Kesnamelly Neff; Madame Labbé — Madeleine Langlois.

PAYS SANS BON SENS!, UN (WAKE UP, MES BONS AMIS!, OR A RIDICULOUS KIND OF COUNTRY!) (1970; 117 min. 7 sec.)

d. Pierre Perrault * production — ONF, Tom Daly, Guy L. Côté, Paul Larose * photography — Bernard Gosselin, Michel Brault * editing — Yves Leduc * sound — Serge Beauchemin * assistant — Guy Dufaux, Pierre Mignot * *mixage* — Roger Lamoureux. ** Participants: Didier Dufour, docteur en sciences; Maurice Chaillot, docteur en lettres; Benjamin Simard, biologist; André Lepage, mechanic in Sept-Iles; Donald Carrick, lawyer in Toronto; Allan Dale, professor in Winnipeg; René Lévesque, head of the Parti Québécois; Pierre Bourgault, journalist; Marjorique Duguay, draveur et bûcheron (logger). * Caribou hunters: Charly O'Brien, Albert Gagnon, Paul Beauchemin, Didier LeHenaff. * People of Ile-Aux-Coudres: Marie Tremblay, Léopold Tremblay (trocanteur), Louis Harvey (farmer), Laurent Tremblay (captain of a voiture d'eau) * Indians: Jean Raphaël; Xavier Raphaël (99 years old); Victoire Basile-Raphaël (90 years old); Marie-Jeanne Raphaël; Madame Jourdain (from Sept-Iles). * Bretons: Meavenne (Parisian journalist), Michel Delahaye, M. Delamer-Delahaye, a Breton sailor, Jacques Cartier (through his *Brief Récit*).

PETITE AURORE L'ENFANT MARTYRE, LA (1951–2; 104 min.)

d. and editing Jean-Yves Bigras * production — l'Alliance Cinématographique Canadienne (i.e., De Séve) * production director — Roger Garand * *scénario* — Emile Asselin, based on a play by Léon Petitjean and Henri Rollin * photography — Roger Racine * original music, composed & played on the organ — Germaine Janelle. ** Cast (Characters/Actors): Aurore — Yvonne Laflamme; Marie-Louise — Lucie Mitchell; Théodore — Paul Desmarteaux; Catherine — Jeannette Bertrand; Abraham — Jean Lajeunesse, Le curé — Marc Forrez; Le docteur — Roland L'Amour; Maurice — Roch Poulin; Tante Malvina — Nana de Varenne. With J. Léo Gagnon.

PLOUFFE, LES (THE PLOUFFE FAMILY) (1981, 255 min.)

d. Gilles Carle * production company — International Cinema Corporation — Ciné-London, released by Ciné 360 * producer — Justine Héroux * exec. prod. — Denis Héroux, with John Kemeny * *scénario* — Roger Lemelin and Gilles Carle, — based on Lemelin's novel * camera — François Protat * editor — Yves Langlois * music — Stéphane Venne. ** Cast (Characters/ Actors): Théophile — Emile Genest; Josephine — Juliette Huot; Cécile — Denise Filiatrault; Ovide — Gabriel Arcand; Napoléon — Pierre Curzi; Guillaume — Serge Dupire; Denis Boucher — Rémi Laurent; Rita Toulouse — Anne Létourneau; Monsignor Folbèche — Gérard Poirier.

PORTES TOURNANTES, LES (REVOLVING DOORS) (1988, 100 min.)

d. Francis Mankiewicz * produced by ONF * Delegate producer — Monique Létourneau * production — René Malo, Francine Morin, Lyse Lafontaine, Jacques-Eric Strauss, Louise Gendron, Marc Daigle, Pierre Latour * *scénario* — Jacques Savoie (from his novel) * editing — André Corriveau * director of photography — Thomas Vamos * sound — Paul Dion; Bernard Aubry * music — François Dompierre * artistic director — Anne Pritchard * costumes — François Barbeau * makeup — Jocelyne Bellemarre. ** Cast (Characters/Actors): Céleste — Monique Spaziani; Madrigal — Gabriel Arcand; Lauda — Miou Miou; Antoine — François Méthé; Pierre Blaudelle — Jacques Penot; Simone Blaudelle (Mother) — Françoise Faucher; M. Blaudelle (Father) — Jean-Louis Roux; M. Litwin — Rémy Girard; with Rita Lafontaine, Hubert Loiselle, and Marcel Sabourin.
[Silent films used: *The General* — Buster Keaton; *Sally of the Sawdust* — D. W. Griffith; *The Jazz Singer* — Alan Crosland.]

POUR LA SUITE DU MONDE (THE MOONTRAP; or *SO THAT THE WORLD GOES ON)* (1962; 105 minutes; b&w)

d. Pierre Perrault; with Michel Brault * production and distribution — ONF, Société Radio-Canada; producer — Fernand Dansereau * *scénario* — Perrault * camera — Michel Brault, with Bernard Gosselin * editing — Werner Nold * sound — Marcel Carriére * music — Jean Cousineau (guitar), Jean Meunier (flute) * *sonorisation et mixage* — Pierre Lemelin, Ron Alexander, Roger Lamoureux. ** Cast: Alexis Tremblay, played by himself; Léopold Tremblay; Abel Harvey; Louis Harvey, and Joachim Harvey; The people of Ile-aux-Coudres.
Recording of the belugas' sounds done by William E. Schevill, of the Oceanographic Institute in Woods Hole, Mass., USA.
[In québécois French, with subtitles in standard French; but also available with subtitles in English. First shown at the Cannes Film Festival in 1963 as the official Canadian entry.]

POUSSIÈRE SUR LA VILLE (DUST FROM UNDERGROUND) (1968; 90 min.)

d., edited — Arthur Lamothe * production — Pierre Lamy * written [in 1953] — André Langevin * editor — Lamothe * photography (b&w) —

Guy-Laval Fortier * sound — Claude Pelletier * music — Gilles Vigneault.
** Cast: Alain Dubois (played by Guy Sanche); Madeleine (played by
Michéle Rossignol); with Henri Filion, Gilles Pelletier, Nicolas Doclin,
Roland Chenail.

POUVOIR INTIME (BLIND TRUST) (1986; 86 min.)

d. Yves Simoneau * production — Vision 4 International association with
the National Film Board, Téléfilm Canada, SGCQ and La Société Radio-
Canada * producer — Claude Bonin * assoc. prod. — Raymond Frappier *
exec. prod. — Francine Forest * script — Yves Simoneau and Pierre Curzi *
photography — Guy Dufaux * music — Richard Grégoire * editing — André
Corriveau * sound — Michel Charron * sound effects — Andy Malcolm *
special effects — Jacques Godbout * art director — Michel Proulx * set director — Normand Sarrazin. ** Cast (Characters/Actors): Roxanne —
Marie Tifo; Gildor (Jerry, in English) — Pierre Curzi; Théo — Jacques
Godin; Robin — Eric Brisebois; Janvier — Jacques Lussier; Martial (Martin
in English) — Robert Gravel; Meursault (Morrow in English) — Jean-Louis

PROLOGUE (anglophone; 1969; 87 min. 39 sec.; b&w)

d. Robin Spry * production — Tom Daly, Robin Spry * script — Michael
Malus * photography — Douglas Kiefer * sound — Russel Heise * music —
William Books, Michael Malus, The Ventures * editing — Christopher
Cordeaux. ** Intepreters: John Robb, Elaine Malus, Gary Rader, Peter
Cullen, Christopher Cordeaux, Henry Gamer.

QUÉBEC ... UN PEU ... BEAUCOUP ... PASSIONNÉMENT (1989; 54 min.)

d. Dorothy Todd Hénaut * production — Josée Beaudet with ONF * pho-
tography — Zoe Dirse * editing — Huguette Laperrière, Suzanne Shanks,
Werner Nold * commentary — Marthe Blackburn * sound — Marie-France
Delagrave, Esther Auger * Narration — Ariane Emond.

QUELQUES ARPENTS DE NEIGE (1973; 94 min.)

d. Denis Héroux * camerawork — Bernard Chentrier * music — François
Cousineau. ** Cast (Characters/Actors): Simon de Bellefeuille — Daniel
Pilon; Julie Lambert — Christine Olivier; Monsieur Lambert — Jean
Duceppe; Laura — Mylène Demongeot; Victor — Frédéric de Pasquale.

QUEST FOR FIRE, THE (1981; 100 min.)

French and Canadian film, d. by Jean -Jacques Annaud. Starring Everett
McGill, Rae Dawn Chong, Ron Perlman, Nameer El Kadi.

QUI A TIRÉ SUR NOS HISTOIRES D'AMOUR? (*A QUESTION OF LOVING*) (1986; 92 min.)

d. Louise Carré * production — La Maison des Quatre. ** Cast (Characters/Actors): Madeline — Monique Mercure; Renée — Guylaine Normandin. With August Schellenberg.

REACTION: A PORTRAIT OF A SOCIETY IN CRISIS (1973; 58 min.)

d. Robin Spry * producers — Tomy Daly, Normand Cloutier, Robin Spry with the NFB * editing — Shelagh MacKenzie * photography — Douglas Kiefer.

RED (1969–70; 101 min.)

d. Gilles Carle * producer — Pierre Lamy * *scénario* — Carle and Ennio Flaiano * photography — Bernard Chentrier * sound — Réjean Giguère, Raymond Leroux, and Don Wellington * music — Pierre F. Brault * editing — Yves Langlois. ** Actors: Daniel Pilon, Geneviève Deloir, Gratien Gélinas, Fernande Giroux, Paul Gauthier, Claude Michaud, Donald Pilon.

RÉGNE DU JOUR, LE (from 1965 to 1967; 118 min.)

d. Pierre Perrault * production — ONF, Jacques Bobet, Guy L. Côté * photography — Bernard Gosselin, Jean-Claude Labrecque * editing — Yves Leduc, Jean Lepage * music — Jean-Marie Cloutier * sound — Serge Beauchemin, Alain Dostie * sound editing — Yves Leduc, Guy Bergeron * *mixage* — Ron Alexander, Roger Lamoureux, ** Players: Alexis Tremblay (from Ile-aux-Coudres), Léopold Tremblay, Marcellin Tremblay, Simon Tremblay, Marie Tremblay (b. on Ile du Nord; married on the Ile-aux-Coudres), Marie-Paule Tremblay, Diane Tremblay, l'abbé Jean-Paul Tremblay, Louis Harvey, Louis Lemarchand, Carleton Ray, Raphael Clément, Louis Brosse, Robert Martin, Françoise Montagne, Christiane Greillon, Blanchon (the beluga whale).
    (Shot on location in 1965 on Ile-aux-Coudres, in N.Y., Paris, and France: St. Brieuc, La Rochelle, Angoulême, and Chartres. World première, Cannas, May 1967.)
    (Does not seem to have a subtitled version.)

RÉJEANNE PADOVANI (1973; 90 [94] min.)

d. Denys Arcand * production — Jean Pierre Lefebvre * *scénario* — Arcand, Jacques Benoît * camera — Alain Dostie * editors — Marguerite Duparc, Arcand. ** Cast (Characters/Actors): Vincent — Jean Lajeunesse; Réjeanne Padovani — Luce Guilbeault; Jean-Léon — Roger Le Bel; Dominique —

Pierre Thériault; Hélène — Frédérique Collin, with Gabriel Arcand. [Shown at directors' fortnight, May 24, 1973).]

RIEL (1978–9; 147 min.)

d. George Bloomfield * production — CBC and Green River Pictures Association * producer — John Trent * *scénario* — Roy Moore * camera — Vic Sarin * editor — Myrtle Virgo * music — Willaim McCauley. ** Cast (Characters/Actors): Louis Riel — Raymond Cloutier; Gabriel Dumont (Riel's general; narrator) — Roger Blay; Sir John A. MacDonald — Christopher Plummer; Bishop Bourget — Jean-Louis Roux; Ritchot — Marcel Sabourin; Taylor — Arthur Hill; Barker — William Shatner; Crozier — Leslie Nielsen; MacTavish — Barry Morse; Dr. Schultz — Lloyd Boachner; Smith — Don Harron; Wolsley — John Neville; Dr. Roy — Claude Jutra; Ouellette — Don Francks; Nolin — Normand Chouinard; Middleton — Chris Wiggins.

RIEN QU'UN JEU (*JUST A GAME*) (1983; 86 min.; Pratley says 100 min.)

d. Brigitte Sauriol * producer — Ciné-Groupe, Monique Messier, Yvon Michon, Jacques Pettigrew * delegate producer for Ciné II (1982) — Claude Bonin * *scénario* — Brigitte Sauriol, Monique Messier * camera — Paul Van der Linden * editing — Marcel Pothier * music — Yves Laferrière. ** Cast (Characters/Actors): Mychelle Vézina — Marie Tifo; André Vézina — Raymond Cloutier; Catherine Vézina — Jennifer Grenier; Julie Vézina — Julie Mongeau; Maude — Julie Desjardins; pianist — Jimmy Bond.

SAD SONG OF YELLOW SKIN (1970; 58 min.)

d. Michael Rubbo * production — Tom Daly * script — Rubbo * photography — Martin Duckworth, Pierre Letarte * sound — Pierre Letarte * editing — Torben Schioler, Michael Rubbo.

ST-DENIS DANS LE TEMPS (1969; 84 min. 3 sec.)

d. Marcel Carrière * producer — Robert Forget, ONF * script — Marcel Carrière, Gilles Thérien * *recherches historiques* — Edith de Villers * camera — Thomas Vamos, Bernard Gosselin * music — François Dompierre * sound — Claude Hazanavicius * sound editing — Jacques Jarry * editing — Werner Nold * *mixage* — Roger Lamoureux, Michel Descombes. ** Cast: Marie-Claire Nolin, Gilles-Philippe Delorme, M. Donovan Carter, M. Jackson Juirk.

SARRASINE, LA (1991; 109 min.)

d. Paul Tana * producer — Marc Daigle * *scénario* (based on a *fait divers*) — Bruno Ramirez and Paul Tana * photography — Michel Caron * editing — Louise Surprenant * music — Pierre Desroches * sound — Jacques Drouin and Claude Langlois. ** Cast (Characters/Actors): Ninetta Moschella — Enrica Maria Modugno; Giuseppe Moschella (or Antonio Giaconne) — Tony Nardi; Alphonse Lamoureux — Jean Lapointe; Félicité Lemieux — Johanne Marie Tremblay; Théo Lemieux (the victim) — Gilbert Sicotte; Pasquale Lopinto — Gaetano Cisco Cimarosa; Celi — Nelson Villagra; Salvatore Moschella — Biago Pelligra; Melo Ingressia — Franck Crudell; Joe Ingressia — Domenico Fiore.

SÉRAPHIN (1950; 101 min.)

d. Paul Gury (Loic Le Gouriadec) * producer — Paul L'Anglais * director of production — Jean Boisvert * *scénario* — Claude-Henri Grignon. * music — Arthur Morrow * photography — Drummond Drury * sound — Oscar Marcoux * editing — Jean Boisvert * costumes — Marie-Laure Cabana. ** Cast (Characters/Actors): Séraphin — Hector Charland; Donalda — Nicole Germain; Alexis — Guy Provost; Artémise — Suzanne Avon; Jambe-de-bois — Henri Poitras; Mlle Angélique — Antoinette Giroux; Wabo — Arthur Lefebvre; le docteur Cyprien — Marcel Sylvain; un révolté — Claude-Henri Grignon; Pit Caribous — Armand Leguet; le curé Labelle — Eddy Tremblay; Zacharie Lapaille — J.-Léo Gagnon; le notaire — Camille Ducharme; le père Ovide — Eugène Daignault.

SIMON LES NUAGES (1990; 80 min.)

d. Roger Cantin * producers — Claude Bonin, Ian Boyd * *scénario* — Roger Cantin * photography — Michel Caron * editing — Yves Chaput * music — Milan Kymlicka * sound — Dominique Chartrand * sets — Claudine Charbonneau * costumes — Huguette Gagné * special "in camera" effects — Roger Cantin * special effects — Louis Craig, Claire Brisson, René Patenaude. ** Cast (Characters/Actors): Simon — Hugolin Chevrette-Landesque; Pierre-Alexandre — Patrick St-Pierre; Picard — Benoît Robitaille; Laperle — Naad Joseph; Carole — Jessica Barker; Hélène — Isabelle Lapointe; Michelle — Anaïs Goulet-Robitaille; Paul — Charles-André Therrien; M. Walker — Edgar Fruitier; Mlle Margot — Kim Yaroshevskaya; M. Cadotte — Bernard Carez; Mme Cadotte — Louisette Dussault; le fermier Solis — Alain Genreau.

SOLSHENITSYN'S CHILDREN .... ARE MAKING A LOT OF NOISE IN PARIS
(1978; 87 min.)

d. Michael Rubbo * production—Marrin Canell, Arthur Hammond * photography—Andreas Poulsson, Michael Edols, Michel Thomas d'Hoste * sound—Joseph Champagne * editing—Michael Rubbo.

SOME AMERICAN FEMINISTS (1977; 56 min.)

d. Luce Guilbeault, Nicole Brossard, and Margaret Westcott * production—Kathleen Shannon * photography—Nesya Shapiro * sound—Ingrid M. Cusiel * editing—Margaret Westcott.

SONATINE (1983; 90 min.)

d. Micheline Lanctôt * production—Corporation Image M and M Ltée * producers—Pierre Gendron and René Malo (Films René Malo) * *scénario*—Micheline Lanctôt * music—François Lanctôt * editing—Louise Surprenant, Lucette Bernier * photography—Guy Dufaux with Yves Drapeau, Michel Bernier, and Michel Girard * sound—Paul Dion, Michel Charron, Claude Langlois, Viateur Paiement * assistant directors—René Chénier, Michèle Forest * script—Claudette Messier * costumes—Hélène Schneider * makeup—Jocelyne Bellemare. ** Cast: Pascale Bussière, Marcia Pilote, Kliment Denchev, Pierre Fauteux.
[Mostra international de cinéma in Venice (1984). Micheline Lanctôt took a Genie for best directing (1985). Silver plaque at the XIVth International film festival in Figueira da Foz, Portugal (1985).]

SONIA (1986; 53 min.)

d. Paule Baillargeon * production—ONF/Michel Gauthier, Roger Frappier, Suzanne Dussault * screenplay—Baillargeon, Laura Harrington * photography—André-Luc Dupont, Roger Martin * sound—Serge Beauchemin * music—Yves Laferrière * editing—Yves Dion. ** Cast: Kim Yaroshevskaya, Baillargeon, Lothaire Bluteau, Paul Buissonneau, Marc Messier, Raymond Cloutier.

SOURD DANS LA VILLE, LE (DEAF TO THE CITY) (1987; 97 min.)

d. Mireille Dansereau * production—La Maison des Quatre, Louise Carré * script—Dansereau, Michèle Mailhot, Jean-Joseph Tremblay (from Blais's novel) * photography—Michel Caron * sound—Dominique Chartrand * music—Ginette Bellavance * editing—Louise Côté. ** Cast (Characters/Actors): Florence—Béatrice Picard; Charlie—Pierre Thériault;

Mike — Guillaume Lemay-Thivierge; Gloria — Angèle Coutu. With Han Masson, Claude Renard, Sophie Léger.
[Prizes: Special mention: Organisation Catholique Internationale du Cinéma (OCIC) — Festival de Venise, 1987.]

SOUS LES DRAPS LES ÉTOILES (1989)

d. Jean-Pierre Gariépy * *scénario* — Jean-Pierre Gariépy * production — Vision 4 of ONF, Suzanne Hénaut, and Doris Girard * special effects — Jacques Godbout * cameraman — André Luc Dupont * images — Pierre Letarte * sound — Richard Besse * editing — Yves Chaput * music (original music) — Jean Vanasse. ** Cast (Characters/Actors): Thomas — Guy Thauvette; Sylvie — M.-J. Gauthier; Concierge — Marcel Sabourin; Le Rongeur — Joseph Cazalet. With Gilles Renaud and Hélène Loiselle.

STOP (1971; 85 min.)

d. Jean Beaudin * production — ONF/Pierre Gauvreau * screenplay — Clément Perron * dialogue — Minou Petrowski * editing — Sidney Pearson * camera — Georges Dufaux * music — Pierre F. Brault. ** Cast (Characters/Actors): Charles — Raymond Bouchard; Françoise — Danielle Naud; Diane — Marie Tifo.

STREET, THE (LA RUE) (1976; 10 min.)

d. Caroline Leaf * production — Guy Glover; Wolf Koenig * animation — Caroline Leaf * editing — Gloria Demers.
[Prizes: numerous, including second place among 50 best films of animation in the world (Animation Olympiades, Los Angeles, 1984).]

SWEATER, THE (THE HOCKEY SWEATER OR LE CHANDAIL) (1980; 10 min.)

d. Sheldon Cohen * production — Marrin Canell; David Verrall; Derek Lamb * script — Roch Carrier (after his novella) * music — Normand Roger * editing — David Verrall. ** Narrator: Roch Carrier.

TEMISCAMING QUEBEC (1975; 64 min.; color)

d. Martin Duckworth, with French Canadian Collaboration * production — Dorothy Todd Hénaut and Len Chatwin * photography — Martin Duckworth and Serge Giguère * sound — Benoît Fauteux and Hugues Mignault * music — Bob Robb (original music) * editing — Duckworth, Michael Rubbo, Gérard Sénécal and Ginny Stikeman * Narrator — Michel Garneau.

TEMPS DE L'AVANT, LE (1975; 88 min.)

d. Anne Claire Poirier * production — [ONF; En tant que femmes] — Poirier * *scénario* — Louise Carré, Marthe Blackburn, Poirier * photography — Michel Brault * sound — Joseph Champagne * music — Maurice Blackburn, Angèle Arsenault * editing — Jacques Gagné, Christian Marcotte. ** Interpreters: Luce Guilbeault, Paule Baillargeon, Pierre Gobeil, J.-Léo Gagnon, Marisol Sarrazin, Nicolas Dufresne.

TEMPS D'UNE CHASSE, LE (1972; 82 min.)

d. Francis Mankiewicz * produced by ONF and Pierre Gauvreau * *scénario* — Mankiewicz * camera — Michel Brault * editor — Werner Nold * music — Pierre F. Brault * sound — Claude Hazanavicius ** Cast (Characters/ Actors): Willy — Guy L'Ecuyer; Lionel — Pierre Dufresne; Richard — Marcel Sabourin; Michel — Olivier L'Ecuyer; Young waitress — Frédérique Collin; The redhead — Luce Guilbeault.
[Shown at Canadian Film Awards, Toronto, 3 October 1972, special jury prize to Mankiewicz for his direction, and best cinematography to Brault.]

TERRE PROMISE, LA AKA *LES BRÛLÉS* (*THE PROMISED LAND*) (1958; 112– 4 min.; b&w)

d. Bernard Devlin * production — ONF, under Léonard Forest and Guy Glover * *scénario* — Devlin, based on Biron * photography — Georges Dufaux * editor — David Mayerovitch * sound — Bernard Brodeleau. ** The actors, not named in the credits on the video through which I saw the film (in a not-too-badly dubbed version), are given by Morris as follows: Félix Leclerc, Jean Lajeunesse, J.-Léo Gagnon.
(According to Morris [*CFF*, s.d., 8], the film was produced in and around Montréal in 16 mm in 1958. It was released in four parts on TV and as a single film non-theatrically by NFB. The English version [97 minutes] was prepared and released in 1962.)

TERRIBLES VIVANTES, LES (*FIREWORDS*) (1986; 84 min., 35 sec.)

d. Dorothy Todd Hénaut * production — NFB, Studio D. (Women's program) * animation — Michèle Pauzé * painted characters — Francine Gagné.
(No subtitles; available with English voiceover under the title "*Firewords.*")

TISSERANDS DU POUVOIR, LES (1988; Part 1: 116 min.; Part 2 [La Révolte]: 116 min.)

d. Claude Fournier * producers — Marie-Josée Raymond, René Malo * script — Claude Fournier, based on his novel * music — Martin Fournier * editing — Yurij Luhovy, Claude Fournier * director of photography — John Berrie * sound — Normand Mercier and Jean Quenelle * asst. dir. — Mireille Goulet * artistic director — François Laplante, Guy Lalande, et al. * costumes — Michèle Hamel and Christiane Cost * makeup — Michèle Dion. ** Cast (Characters/Actors): (Jean-)Baptiste Lambert — Gratien Gélinas; Soeur Bernadette — Juliette Huot; Valmore Lambert — Michel Forget; Auguste Roussel — Jean Desailly; Jacques Roussel — Aurélien Recoing; (Mother) Evelyne Lambert — Andrée Pelletier; Madeleine Lambert — Charlotte Laurier; (Mother) Henriette Fontaine — Dominique Michel; (Dr.) Emile Fontaine — Pierre Chagnon; curé Pollard — Paul Hébert; Maire Rochon — Donald Pilon; Cléophas Larouche — Gérard Paradis; Simone (Fontaine) — Gabrielle Lazure; Richard Laverdière, journalist — Francis Reddy; Frank Généroux — Vlasta Vrana; John Elliott — John Wildman; Fidélia — Anne Létourneau; Caroline Motta — Corinne Dacia; Julien — Francis Lemaire; Chef Gilbert — Dennis O'Connor; Emma Leclair — Denise Filiatrault; Clem Tardiff — Paul Berval; Beauchamp — John Boylan; Baptiste at 20 — Denis Bouchard; Baptiste at 13 — Carl Boileau; Baptiste as a child — Felix La Ferté; Jacques Roussel at 12 — Amaury de Frémaux; Pierre Roussel — Yves Mathieu; Député Fontaine — Clément Richard; Maire Gauthier — Rémy Girard; Monsignor Kenney — Peter Fernandez; Special Guest Appearance of Madeleine Robinson as Betty Roussel, Jacques's sister-in-law.
[In French; also in French with subtitles. Shown on Canadian TV as a six-part miniseries.]

TIT-COQ (1952; 104 min.)

d. René Delacroix * co-director — Gratien Gélinas * producer — Gratien Gélinas * assoc. prod. — Paul L'Anglais * screenplay — Gratien Gélinas, from his play * photography — Akas Farkas * b&w camera — José Mena * sets — Michel Ambrogi * music — Morris C. Davis, Maurice Blackburn * editing — Anton Van de Water. ** Cast (Characters/Actors): Tit-Coq — Gratien Gélinas; Marie-Ange — Monique Miller; Father Desilets — Fred Barry; Padre — Paul Dupuis; Germaine — Denise Pelletier; Jean-Paul Desilets — Clément Latour; Aunt Clara — Juliette Beliveau; Mother Desilets — Amanda Alarie; Camp Commander — George Alexander; Léopold Vermette — Jean Duceppe; Rosie — Corinne Conley; Uncle Alcide — Henri Poitras.

TOBY MCTEAGUE (1985; 1987; ca 2 hrs.)

d. Jean Claude Lord * producer—Nicolas Clermont * executive producers —Peter Kroonenburg, David J. Patterson, in cooperation with Telefilm Canada, Société Générale du Cinéma du Québec, La Société Radio Canada, and CBC * story—Jeff Maguire, Djordje Milicevic * *scénario*— Jess Maguire, Djordje Milicevic, Jamie Brown * photography—René Verzier * original music—Claude Demers * costumes—Blanche Boileau * editing—Yves Langlois * production director—Wendy Green * special effects—Bill Orr * artistic director—Joceyln Joli, assisted by Raymond Dupuis * makeup—Gillian Chandler * costume decorator—Michèle Hamel * hair dresser—Bob Pritchett. ** Cast (Characters/Actors): Toby— Yannick Bisson; Toby's widowed father—Winston Rekert; Sam—Andrew Bednarsk; Sara—Stephanie Morgenstern; Jenny—Lilian Clune. With Timothy Webber.
(Aired on CBC Windsor on 10 February 1991.)

TOMMY TRICKER AND THE STAMP TRAVELLER (LES AVENTURIERS DU TIMBRE PERDU) (1988; 101 min.)

d., written—Michael Rubbo * production—La Fête, Rock Demers (Series—*Planet Earth*) * original music—Kate, Anna, and Jane McGarrigle * additional original music—St. Sauveur des Monts * line producer—Ann Burke * animation and special effects—Les Productions Pascal Blais * art director—Vianney Gauthier * photography—Andreas Poulsson * editor—André Corriveau. ** Cast (Characters/Actors): Ralph—Lucas Evans; Tommy—Anthony Rogers; Nancy—Jill Stanley; Albert—Andrew Whitehead; Chen Tow—Chen Yuan Tao; Mau Ling—Han Yun; Chery— Catherine Wright; Cass—Paul Popowish; Cree—Cree Rubbo.

TRAMP AT THE DOOR (1985; 90 min.)

d. Allan Kroeker * produced with the assistance of Téléfilm Canada and Winnipeg Video Inc, Burbank Prod., and Can. West Broadcasting Ltd. * producer—Stan Thomas * exec. prod.—Don Brinton * narrated by Melissa Dixon; based on story of Gabrielle Roy * editor—Lara Mazur * director of photography—Ron Orieux * sound—Leon Johnson * music composition, arranged by Randolph Peters—"Ephrem Brabant" themes by Pierre Guérin. ** Cast (Characters/Actors): Tramp ("cousin Gustave"; "Brabant")—Ed McNamara; Albert—August Schellenberg; Madeleine— Monique Mercure; Gabrielle—Joanna Schellenberg; Lemieux—Eric Peterson; Hébert—Jean-Louis Hébert.
[An award-winning work, which was shown at the Venice Film Festival.]

TREASURE TRAIN (1981; ca. 2 hrs.)

d. Fernando Arrabal * screenplay — Fernando Arrabal, Roger Lemelin * directors of photography — Ken and Romaine Le Gargeant * music — Edith Butler. ** Cast (Characters/Actors): the "emperor of Peru" — Mickey Rooney; Toby — Jonathan Starr; 'Liz — Anick; Uk Hoang — Ky Huot Ut; Fédérico the duck played himself; children's aunt — Monique Mercure; husband of the aunt — Jean-Louis Roux.
[Video released by Samuel Goldwyn; a fairly well-dubbed version.]

TROIS POMMES À CÔTÉ DU SOMMEIL (1988; 96 min.)

d. Jacques Leduc * producers — Suzanne Dussault, Pierre Latour * production — René Malo and ONF * *scénario* — Michel Langlois, Jacques Leduc * photography — Pierre   Letarte * sound — Claude   Beaugrand * music — René Lussier, Jean Derome (using Bach) * editing — Pierre Bernier. ** Starring: Paule Baillargeon, Normand Chouinard, Hubert Reeves, Josée Chaboillez, Paule Marier, Michel Nadeau, Frédérique Collin.

VAGABONDE FRAPPE À NOTRE PORTE, UN. See *Tramp at the Door.*

VIE HEUREUSE DE LÉOPOLD Z., LA (1965; 68 min.; b&w)

d., written — Gilles Carle * produced by NFB; Jacques Bobet * camera — Jean-Claude Labrecque * sound — Joseph Champagne * editing — Werner Nold * music — Paul de Margerie. ** Cast (Characters/Actors): Léopold — Guy L'Ecuyer; Théophile — Paul Hébert; Josita — Suzanne Valéry; Mme Tremblay — Monique Joly; The Son — Jacques Poulin.

VIE RÊVÉE, LA (DREAM (ED) LIFE) (1972; 85 [90] min.)

d. Mireille Dansereau * produced by — L'Association Coopérative de Productions Audio-Visuelles (A Faroun Film Release) * script — Mireille Dansereau and Patrick Auzépy * camera — François Gill * editor — Danielle Gagné * music — Emmanuel Charpentier. ** Cast (Characters/Actors): Virginie — Véronique Le Flaguais; Isabelle — Liliane Lemaître-Auger; Jean-Jacques — Jean-François Guité; Yves — Guy Foucault.
[This film, Dansereau's first, is 85–90 min. long; a three-reeler. I saw it twice, in dubbed version; in most scenes, the dubbing was unobtrusive, but the sound track was not clear.]

VIEUX PAYS OÙ RIMBAUD EST MORT, LE (1977; 113 min.)

d. Jean Pierre Lefebvre * production—Marguerite Duparc and Hubert Niogret for Cinak, Filmoblic, and the Institut National de l'Audiovisuel * *scénario*—Mireille Amiel [for the French characters] and Jean Pierre Lefebvre [for the Québécois] (See, Harcourt, 146) * photography—Guy Dufaux * editing—Marguerite Duparc * sound—Jacques Blain * music— Claude Fonfrède * *mixage*—Stephen Delby * sets and costumes—Nicole Rachline * song ("Le Vieux pays")—Mireille Amiel, Claude Fonfrède * musical arrangements—Claude Duhaut, the Dolphin Orchestra. ** Cast (Characters/Actors): Abel—Marcel Sabourin; Anne—Anouk Ferjac; Jeanne—Myriam Boyer; Yves—Mark Lesser; Anne's mother—Germaine Delbat; Anne's husband—François Perrot; Jeanne's father—Roger Blin; Viviane—Viviane Lesser; taxi driver/painter/picture dealer—Jean-François Stévenin; M. de Cassant—Jean Turlier; Mme de Cassant—Rita Maiden; florist—Joëlle Maline; troubadour—Claude Fonfrède; drunken soldier— Stephan Macha; policeman—Robert Darmel.

(*Le Vieux Pays* ... was made with France, and not released in the United States until 1984. It was shown in a limited way in 1982 on a double billing with Lefebvre's *Fleurs sauvages* [1982]—a film about tolerance—at the Thalia Repertory Cinema in NYC. The film tied with *Wavelength* for thirteenth place out of thirty in the critics' poll. [See *Variety*, 8 August 1984.] Cost of the film was $350,000—considerably high for a Canadian film. It was produced and edited by the director's wife, Marguerite Duparc, with whom he founded the Cinak company.)

VILLE MARIE (1965; 27 min. 38 sec.)

d. Denys Arcand * a National Film Board Production * script—Andrée Thibault * photography—Bernard Gosselin and Michel Brault, assisted by Jacques Leduc * editing—Monique Fortier * sound editing—Pierre Bernier * music—Renaissance Singers of Montréal, conducted by Donald Makey * electronic music—Pierre Henry, Pierre Schaeffer * advisers— Gustave Lanctôt, Maurice Careless * English adaptation—Stanley Jackson, Daisy de Bellefeuille * special effects—Gilles Tremblay * re-recording— Joseph Champagne, George Croll * executive producer—André Belleau.

VINCENT ET MOI (*VINCENT AND ME*) (1990; 1 hr.; 40 min.)

d. Michael Rubbo * script—Michael Rubbo * production—Rock Demers, Productions La Fête—*Contes pour Tous* (*Tales for All*) #11 * photography—Andreas Poulsson * paintings—Michael Rubbo * editing—André Corriveau * art director—Violette Daneau * original music—Pierick Houdy * musical administrator—Christian Lefort * sound—Yvon Benoît * sound designer—Claude Langlois * line producer—Daniel Louis * cos-

tumes—Huguette Gagné * makeup—Micheline Trépanier * hairdresser—
Réjean Forget * special effects—Les Productions de l'Intrigue. ** Cast
(Characters/Actors): Jo—Nina Petronzio; Vincent Van Gogh—Tcheky
Karyo; Felix—Christopher Forrest; Dr. Winkler—Alexandre Vernon
Dobtcheff; Tom—Matthew Mabe; Joris—Paul Klerk; Mrs. Wallis—
Andrée Pelletier; Mr. Hirodake—J. G. Ho; Tom Mainfield—Matthew
Mabe; grandmother—Anna-Maria Gianotti; Burt—Wally Martin; Mr.
Carruthers—Michel Maillot; Silva—Tamara Witcher; Frank Purvis—
Charles Pitts; Jo's mother—Dora Petronzio; Jo's father—Vittorio Rossi.
    (A Canada France Coproduction; crews for Amsterdam, France, and
Québec.)
    [A dubbed version of *Vincent et moi* has aired on the Disney Channel,
in the U.S.A.]

VOITURES D'EAU, LES (WATER CARS) (1968–1970; 110 min.; b&w)

d. Pierre Perrault * production—ONF/Jacques Bobet, Guy L. Côté *
story—Pierre   Perrault * camera—Bernard   Gosselin * sound— Serge
Beauchemin, Marcel Carrière * editor—Monique Fortier.
    (Shown in the Critics' Section at the Cannes Film Festival, 1970 [Pratley
TS 1987, 193]. Available with subtitles.)

VOLCANO: AN INQUIRY INTO THE LIFE AND DEATH OF MALCOLM LOWRY
(1976; 99 min.)

d. Donald Brittain, John Kramer * production—Donald Brittain, Robert
Duncan, James de B. Domville * script—Donald Brittain * photography—
Douglas Kiefer * sound—James McCarthy * music—Alain Clavier and
Art Phillips * editing—John Kramer.
    (Sponsored by the NFB; took the Canadian Film Award for best
documentary of 1976.)

VOYAGE AU BOUT DE LA ROUTE, LE (LA BALLADE DU PAYS QUI ATTEND)
(1987; 72 min. 10 sec.)

d. Jean-Daniel Lafond * *scénario*—Jean-Daniel Lafond * production—
ONF/Eric Michel * exec. producers—Eric Michel and Jacques Vallée *
images—Martin Leclerc * editing—Babalou Hamelin * sound—Claude
Beaugrand * sound editing—Alain Sauvé.

VOYAGE EN AMÉRIQUE AVEC UN CHEVAL EMPRUNTÉ (1987; color; 58
min.)

d. Jean Chabot * produced by ONF * delegate producer—Michel

Bandavine * *scénario* and commentary—Jean Chabot * sound—Claude Beaugrand * editing—Catherine Martin * music—René Lussier.

VRAIE NATURE DE BERNADETTE, LA (1972; 97 min.; 35 mm.)

d., script, dialogues, and editing—Gilles Carle * production—Productions Carle-Lamy * photography—René Verzier * sound—Henri Blondeau * music—Pierre F. Brault * sets—Jocelyn Joly. ** Cast (Characters/Actors): Bernadette—Micheline Lanctôt; Thomas—Donald Pilon; Rock—Reynald Bouchard; Antoine—Willie Lamothe.

WHISPERING CITY (1947. 91 min.; fiction; b&w)

d. Fédor Ozep * production—George Marton, Paul L'Anglais, Roger Wood * script—Rian James, Leonard Lee * photography—Guy Roe * sound—Edward Fenton * music—Morris C. Davis * editing—Leonard Anderson, Douglas Bagier, Richard J. Jarvis. ** Cast: Mary Anderson, Helmut Dantine, Paul Lukas, Joy Lafleur, John Pratt, Mimi d'Estée.

YES OR NO, JEAN-GUY MOREAU (1979; 58 min.)

d. Michael Rubbo * coproduction by NFB and WGBH-Boston * producers—Judith Vecchione, Tina Viljoen, and Barrie Howells * executive producer—Barrie Howells * script—Rubbo * assistant director—Judith Vecchione * photography—Pierrre Letarte * location sound—Yves Gendron * sound editing—Bernard Bordelau * picture editing—Tina Viljoen * rerecording—Jean-Pierre Joutel.

ZOO LA NUIT, UN (NIGHT ZOO) (1986–7; 116 min.)

d. Jean-Claude Lauzon * production—Roger Frappier, Pierre Gendron, Louise Gendron, NFB, in collaboration with Téléfilm Canada, SGC, Société Radio-Canada * script—Lauzon * photography director—Guy Dufaux * editor—Michel Arcand * music—Jean Corriveau * art director—Jean-Baptiste Tard * sound—Yvon Benoît * "With the kind participation of Dominique Michel and Denys Arcand" ** Cast (Characters/Actors): Marcel Brisebois—Gilles Maheu; Albert, the father—Roger Le Bel; Tony, the Italian restaurateur—Corrado Mastropasqua; Angelica, Tony's wife—Anna-Maria Giannotti; Julie, the girlfriend—Lynne Adams; George—Lorne Brass; Charlie—Germain Houde; The American—Jerry Snell.

Notes

Chapter 1. Introduction and Orientation

1. Gerald Pratley, *Torn Sprockets: The Uncertain Projection of the Canadian Film* (Newark: University of Delaware Press; Toronto: Associated University Presses, 1987), 148; and elsewhere. (Hereafter cited in my text as Pratley, *TS*.)

2. Leonard Maltin, *TV Movies and Video Guide* (New York: Signet, Penguin Books, yearly), 1989 Guide, 599; 1991 Guide, 654.

3. Lysiane Gagnon, "French Culture in Quebec," *Canada Today/Canada Aujourd'hui* 20:1 (1989). [Washington, D.C.: Canadian Embassy, 1989]: 6–8. See in same issue Richard Gay's article "Canada's Young and Diversified Film Industry," 19–20.

4. Georges Sadoul and Emile Breton, *Dictionnaire (microcosme) des cinéastes*, 4e ed, mise à jour en octobre 1989. (Paris: Collection de Poche, 1989 1990).

5. *Séquences* 147–48 (September 1990):3.

6. Léo Bonneville, "Interview with Jean Beaudry," *Séquences* 147–48 (September 1990):25.

7. Marie-Christine Abel, André Giguère, and Luc Perrault, *Le Cinéma québécois à l'heure internationale* (Montréal: Les éditions internationales Stanké, 1990), 112. (Hereafter cited in my text as Abel.)
See also Yves Lever, *Histoire du cinéma au Québec* (Montréal: Boréal, 1988), 305. (Hereafter cited in my text as Lever *Hist..*)

8. Joseph M. Boggs, *The Art of Watching Film*, 2nd ed. (Mountain View, Calif.: Mayfield Publishing Company, 1985), 354.

9. See John Pielmeier's introduction to his play, *Agnes of God* (New York: New American Library, 1985). Here he mentions in passing the *fait divers* that turned on the current for his play (vi); he also points out that it was Jewison's idea to set the action in Montréal, an idea he agreed with, since "Quebec is still a very Catholic province ... filled with convents and monasteries built in the nineteenth century to house hundreds of nuns and monks .... There is a feeling of stopped time in these places, a sense of medieval isolation in the middle of French-speaking America that I felt was ideal for telling sister Agnes's story" (x).

10. Sadoul and Breton, *Dictionnaire (microcosme) des films*.

11. Houle and Julien, *Dictionnaire du cinéma québécois* (Montréal: Fides, 1978). (Hereafter cited in my text as Houle.)

12. "Study Thy Neighbor." *Detroit Free Press* (31 May 1990): 1F–2F.

13. The survey was analyzed in *Variety*, 8 August 1984. Obviously, a new survey, since the production of several excellent new Canadian films, might produce different titles but not necessarily different results in distribution between anglophone (extra-*québécois*) and francophone films. The ranking was as follows:

513

[1] *Mon oncle Antoine* (1971); [2] *Goin' Down the Road* (1970); [3] *Good Riddance*, or *Les Bons Débarras* (1979); [4] *The Apprenticeship of Duddy Kravitz* (1974); [5–6] *The Grey Fox* (1982), tying with *Les Ordres* (1974); [7–8] *J. A. Martin photographe* (1976), tying with *Pour la suite du monde* (1963); [9–10] *Nobody Waved Goodbye* (1964), tying with *La Vraie Nature de Bernadette* (1972); [11–12] *Les Plouffe* (1981), tying with *Réjeanne Padovani* (1973); [13–14] *Le Vieux Pays où Rimbaud est mort* (1977), tying with *Wavelength* (1967); [15–19] *Between Friends* (1973), tying with *Le Chat dans le sac* (1964), with *Videodrome* (1982), with *Warrendale* (1966), and with *Wedding in White* (1972); [20–27] *Les Dernières Fiançailles* (1973); *Lonely Boy* (1961); *Neighbours* (1952); *Pas de deux* (1967); *Bar salon* (1972); *Kamouraska* (1973); *Outrageous* (1977); and *Ticket to Heaven* (1981).

14. David Sterritt, "Behind the Scenes at a Canadian Passion Play," *Christian Science Monitor* (24 May 1990): 10.

15. Robinson and Lloyd, Ed, *The Illustrated History of the Cinema* (New York: Macmillan, 1986), 399.

16. The film is based on Dany Laferrière's novel, which is "an ironic, Rabelaisian portrayal of pretense and hypocrisy in various Montréal communities," according to Johnathan Weiss, *French-Canadian Literature* (Washington, D.C.: ACSUS Papers, 1989), 55.

17. Julia Nunes, "Researching the ratings." *Comment faire l'amour ... The (Toronto) Globe and Mail* (Friday, 15 June 1990), A12[N].

18. Heinz Weinmann, *Cinéma de l'imaginaire québécois, de* La petite Aurore *à* Jésus de Montréal (Saint-Laurent, Québec: l'Hexagone, 1990). Hereafter referred to in my text as Weinmann.

19. Pierre Vallières, *Les Nègres blancs d'Amérique* 3rd ed. (Paris: Maspéro, 1968; 1969). Translated into English as *White Niggers of America*, 1971.

20. David Clanfield, *Canadian Film* (Toronto: Oxford University Press, 1987). Hereafter cited in my text as Clanfield.

21. Pierre Véronneau, *L'Histoire du cinéma au Québec*, 3 vol (Montréal: Cinémathèque québécoise, 1969–1988).

22. This means that the Lumière brothers lost no time in getting their work to the New World. A Lyonnais, Antoine Lumière presented the first cinematographic showing, an invention of his brothers Louis and Auguste, in the back room of a Parisian café in that same year, 1896. Ten short films were shown; they were viewed by an audience of thirty-three persons, who left 33 francs 60 sous in the *caisse* (*Journal Français d'Amérique* [22 Feb.–7 March, 1991]). One franc per person was not much in 1896.

23. See Lever, *Hist.*, 1988, 28. See also Yvan Lamonde and Raymond Monpettit, *Le Parc Sohmer de Montréal, 1889–1919* (Québec: Institut Québécois de Recherche sur la Culture, 1986).

24. Germain Lacasse, *Les Dossiers de la Cinémathèque*, 15 (1985), 48–49.

25. The first Canadian talkie (Gordon Sparling's *Rhapsody in Two Languages*, with an original Canadian musical score) was not made until 1934. It showed impressions of Montréal night-life. Curiously enough, it could not be shown in Montréal, for the Québec censors found it too daring, even though the film was shot around the corner from them. (Segments and commentary found in *Dreamland*.) See article on Sparling in Michel Coulombe and Marcel Jean, *Le Dictionnaire du cinéma québécois* (Montréal: Boréal, 1988; 2nd Ed. 1991), 502–1. *Dictionnaire* hereafter cited as "Coulombe" in my text.)

26. Lamonde and Hébert, Eds, *Le Cinéma au Québec: Essai de statistique*

historique (1896 à nos jours) (Québec: Institut Québécois de Recherche sur la Culture, 1981), 55.

27. The story of Evangeline was the subject of a 1929 film starring Delores Del Rio as the heroine and Roland Drew as her lover Gabriel. *Variety* (31 July 1929) stressed the beauty of the production, calling it "educational" but hypothesizing that "the fan mob is likely to stay away." The article goes on to say that it is artistically a credit, pictorially a smash, romantically a rave, indeed, "one of those pictures the literary minded will laud and the entertainment seekers pass by." However, for the critic, Delores Del Rio, a paprika Latin girl, doesn't seem to fit with the role of the saint-like maid of Grand Pré. Additionally, though it is "fatally lacking in drama" there are three or four admirable songs, including one by Al Jolson and Billy Rose. (See also *Variety*, 15 August 1919 and 22 August 1919 for earlier film.)

28. René Bouchard, "Un Précuseur du cinéma direct," *Cinéma/Québec*. Part I: 5, vol. 6; 1 (1977), 19–24, Part II: 52, vol. 6; 2 (1977), 27–33. Part I studies Mgr. Albert Tessier's photographic and cinematographic work; Part II is an interview between Bouchard and Tessier a few months before his death. Bouchard's "biography" of Tessier (33) is also an essential filmography.

29. Pierre Demers, "La Leçon du cinéma 'nature': L'abbé Proulx et le cinématographe," *Cinéma/Québec*, 4:6 (1974); 17–33.

30. Yvan Lamonde, "Indirectement le cinéma direct: réflexions autour d'un cinéma," *Cinéma/Québec*, vol. 4: 1 (December 1974), 23.

31. See Yves Lever (*Hist.* 1988, 63–8) for a discussion of the (Church's) role in the history of the Québec film industry.

32. One can find definitions of this term (*cinéma direct*) in almost all books dealing with Canadian film. Evolving from the 50s and 60s, the term originally was adopted officially by MIPE-TV of Lyon, but by March 1963 designated a new type of documentary that sought through its portable (or handheld) (16 mm.) camera to capture the speech and gestures of the person being studied while he or she is in action, in a natural context, and to show an event at the exact moment of its occurrence. It prized the quest for reality; nevertheless, the final product was inevitably a product of the aesthetic intentions and the ethical views of the filmmaker. The movement embraces other related techniques, such as candid eye, *cinéma vérité*, living camera, *cinéma vécu*, etc. The all-important move of the ONF (Office national du film; in English NFB, or National Film Board) headquarters from Ottawa to Montreal in 1956, which some mark as the beginning of Québec film as we know it, is seen as a key date in the appearance of *cinéma direct* in Canada. Following this move, certain of the young francophone filmmakers of the time (Brault, Groulx, Jutra) worked first on an anglophone series called "Candid Eye," and then went beyond this experience — Brault in particular — to emphasize use of the wide-angle lens, so as to pin down the event from the interior. Québec "direct cinema" accompanied and captured the movement of nationalist affirmation, and it was in the style and technique of the direct cinema that the great documentaries of Brault and Perrault were realized: "a type of documentary through which a breath of authentic poetry traveled." Whatever the approach, fundamental to the nature of this type of documentary is the responsibility assumed, as is also the respect by the filmmakers for the reality they are observing.

In the 70s, some of the films of this movement came to be more "subversive," for example, *On est au coton* of Denys Arcand (1970), after which some filmmakers turned to existential issues, while others turned to the private sector. In the course of my book, many of the filmmakers who follow this style will be discussed (Brault, Perrault, Arcand, Lamothe, Bissonnette, Gutierrez, Duckworth, Tana, etc.). Finally, one must not overlook the impact that this documentary style has had on fictional films of Québec, giving to them the sense of stark reality and the social portraiture so characteristic of their tone and thrust. (My discussion here is based primarily on the article by Gilles Marsolais [in Coulombe 1991, 103–10]. See also definition in Houle ["Cinéma direct; cinéma documentaire": 1978, xvii-xviii], as well as the article on Brault in Houle [1978, 27–28] and also on his film *Les Raquetteurs* [Houle 1978, 262–3], which is seen as inaugurating the *cinéma direct* at the ONF; here one reads that "this movement is defined by a will to participate in the events 'from the interior,' and by the care the filmmaker took to catch people in their daily lives." The best entire book on the subject may well be Gilles Marsolais's *L'Aventure du cinéma direct* [Paris: Cinéma Club Seghers, 1974]. Marsolais has also written a monograph on *Michel Brault* [*Cinéastes du Québec*, no 11, CQDC, or, Conseil Québécois pour la Diffusion du Cinéma, 1972].)

33. Gerald G. Graham, *Canadian Film Technology, 1896–1986* (Cranbury, N.J.: University of Delaware Press, 1987).

34. Christine Tremblay-Daviault, *Structures mentales et sociales du cinéma québécois (1942–1953): Un cinéma orphelin* (Montréal: Québec/Amérique, 1981).

35. A word on Gélinas himself (as seen in *Profiles* #3: 1989–1996): From 1950 to 1952 he was a member of the Board of Governors of NFB; in 1953 he made *Tit-Coq* into a film with himself as producer and as an actor, playing the title role. (This film was produced in a subtitled English version.) In 1956 he played the role of Juvénal Boldec in the TV series of *Les Plouffe*. In 1969 he was named president of the Canadian Film Development Corporation, and he retired in 1978. An admirer of Shakespeare and of Pagnol for their ability to oppose successively the comic, the pathetic, the dramatic, and even the tragic, he made *La Dame aux camélias*, a parody, of which only a partial print remains. But he is better known for *Tit-Coq*.

36. Lillian Gish's *Broken Blossoms* was taken from the short story by Thomas Burke, "Cutie Beautiful," published in *Limehouse Blues*.

Chapter 2. A Search for Roots

1. Peter Morris. *NFB: The War Years*, 29.

2. Tom Conley, *Film Hieroglyphs* (Minneapolis: University of Minnesota Press, 1991).

3. Piers Handling, *Canadian Feature Films: 1913–1969* (Ottawa: [Canadian Filmography Series No. 10] Canadian Film Institute, 1975), 21.

4. Dominique Noguez, *Essais sur le cinéma québécois* (Montréal: Editions du Jour, 1971), 200.

5. *Répertoire Vidéo* (Textes by Louise Dugas) (Montréal: Office national du film du Canada, 1988), 95.

6. Gerald Pratley, *Variety* (9 June 1971) (New York: Garland Publishing, Inc. 1983) vol. 13, n.p.

7. Guy Sylvestre, *Anthologie de la poésie québécoise* (Montréal: Librairie Beauchemin, Ltée., 1974), 377–81.

8. Brunette and Wills, *Screen/Play: Derrida and Film Theory* (Princeton, N.J.: Princeton University Press, 1989), 73 ff.

9. The story of the hardships of Champlain is also told in documentary-style

animation, drawn in color by Robert Doucet, in an effective short called *Dreams of a Land* (1987; 8 min.). Reminiscent of the style of Frédéric Back, creator of *Crac* and *The Man Who Planted Trees*, it is available on VHS from SUNY.

10. For the reader desiring more background, the rebellions of 1837 are described in the *Canadian Encyclopedia* (1831 ff.), and an impressive watercolor of the *patriote* insurgents, painted by Mrs. E. Ellice, is reproduced there.

11. [J.-P] Tad[ro]s, *Variety* (7 March 1973) (New York: Garland Pubishing Inc., 1983) vol. 13, n.p.

12. *Lone Cowboy*. The first two chapters of this 1930 novel were (re)published in Yves Alix's French translation under the title *L'Enfance d'un cowboy solitaire* (Montréal: Boréal, 1989). *L'Enfance* . . . contains a preface by Jacques Godbout.

13. Jean Larose, "Le Cheval du Réel." *Québec Studies* 9 (Fall 1989–Winter 1990): 38–47.

14. Hérménégildc Chiasson. This Acadian artist has published several books of poetry (*Mourir à Scoudouc; Prophéties; Rapport sur l'état de mes illusions*) and directed several other films (*Toutes les photos finissent par se ressembler* [ONF]; *Cap-Lumière* [Ciné-Est en Action]; *Acadie Parole* [ONF]).

15. Pierre Véronneau disputes its having been the first in *Les Dossiers de la Cinémathèque*, vol. 7 (*Cinéma de l'époque duplessiste*) (Montreal: Le Musée du Cinéma, 1979), 101, note 19. (Hereafter cited in text as *Cin* . . .).

16. One may profitably consult the following for additional information on *Etienne Brûlé* : Pratley (*TS* 1987, 167); Lever (*Hist* 1988, 99); Véronneau (*Cinéma de l'époque duplessiste*, 1979: 99–104). Véronneau, *L'Histoire du Cinéma au Québec, I et II : Les Dossiers de la Cinémathèque, vol. 3 (Le Succès est au film parlant français*) (Montréal: Cinémathèque québécoise, 1979), 128.

17. Peter Morris, *Canadian Feature Films: 1913–1963* Part 2. 1941–1963 (Ottawa: [Canadian Filmography Series, No. 7] Canadian Film Institute, n.d. [after 1969]), 8.

18. Lucien Fortin, "Les expériences de Gilles Carle," *CopieZéro* 37 (October 1988): 35–6.

19. Léo Bonneville, "Une visite chez *La Postière*," *Séquences* 156 (January 1992): 31–3.

20. Ginette Major, *Le Cinéma québécois à la recherche d'un public. Bilan d'une décennie: 1970–1980* (Montréal: Presses de l'Université de Montréal, 1982), 111–18.

21 Peter Harcourt, *Jean Pierre Lefebvre* (Ottawa: Canadian Film Institute, 1981), 147.

22. Peter Rist, *Magill's Survey of Cinema (Foreign Language Films)* (Englewood Cliffs, N.J.: Salem Press, 1985), V, 2263.

23. Ibid., 2262–63

24. Ibid., 2264–65.

25. Ibid., 2263.

26. Claude Jasmin, *Rimbaud, mon beau salaud* (Montréal: Editions du Jour, 1969). (Quoted from *Ensemble*, Ed. Raymond F. Comeau et al., 2nd ed. [New York: Holt, Rinehart and Winston, 1982], 137.)

27. Jean-Pierre Tadros, *Cinéma/Québec* 49; 5:9 (1976): *avant-propos* (foreword).

28. Ibid., 13–29.

29. *Canada on film and video.* (Catalogue of Canadian Film Distribution Center, SUNY Plattsburgh, N.Y., n.d.).

Chapter 3. Women's Cinema

1. *La Châtelaine* (April 1990): 32.

2. *Zoom sur elles* (Montréal: Office National du Film du Canada (Winter), 1990): 35.

3. Thérèse Lamartine, *Elles cinéastes ad lib 1895–1981* (Montréal: Ed. du Remue-ménage, 1985).

4. Louise Carrière, "En tant que femmes ...". *Femmes et cinéma québécois*, Ed. Louise Carrière (Montréal: Boréal Express, 1983): 145–49 and 225–45.

5. Patrick Leboutte, "Une simple question de déplacement: Rencontre avec Léa Pool." (Propos recueillis à Paris le 28 mars 1986 par Patrick Leboutte.) Ed. Patrick Leboutte. *Cinémas du Québec au fil du direct* (Crisnée [Liège]: Editions Yellow Now, 1986): 55.

6. Jacques Kermabon, "Cinéma d'intervention, dit-elle.A propos du documentaire." (Propos recueillis par Jacques Kermabon.) In *Cinémas du Québec ...*, 53.

7. Accused of killing two (or perhaps even seven) husbands by pouring melted lead into their ear while they were sleeping, La Corriveau was (like Elisabeth in *Kamouraska*, and like Cordélia in the film we will be discussing) judged by an English-speaking military court, just after the defeat of Québec on the plains of Abraham. In the (political) intention of asserting its power and of giving an example, the new government, according to British custom, hanged her and then suspended her cadaver enclosed in a cage from a tree on a crossroad in Pointe de Lévis. La Corriveau is written of in Philippe Aubert de Gaspé's *Les Anciens Canadiens* (1863) and is the subject of a book by Andrée Lebel (*La Corriveau* [Montmagny: Libre Expression, 1981]); and Gilles Carle made *La Corriveau* into a film he regards as a failure [1986]. (Professor Kathryn Slott is presently doing extensive research on La Corriveau, and presented a paper on this woman as she appears in Québec literature and film, especially in Anne Hébert's writings [incl. *La Cage*], at the CIEF convention in Morocco in July 1993.)

8. Jean-Pierre Tadros. "Grand remue-ménage pour une fondamentale remise en question," *Cinéma/Québec* No 58, vol. 6; 8 (September–October 1978): 15–17.

9. Jean-Pierre Tadros, as quoted from *Le Devoir* in *Cinéma au féminin* (Montréal: [Cinéma Libre] Bibliothèque nationale du Québec, 1990): 51.

10. *Cinéma au féminin*, 1990: 51.

11. *Zoom sur elles*, 50.

12. NFB International Film and Video Guide — U.S. Edition, 1987: 6. (In *Zoom sur elles* [Hiver, 1990: 60], the films used are listed in the order in which they appear in Poirier's work.)

13. Peter Rist, "Primal Fear," *Magill's Survey of Cinema* (*Foreign Language Films*) (Englewood Cliffs, N.J.: Salem Press, 1985) V; 2461–6.

14. Denise Pérusse, "*Mourir à tue-tête.*" *Le cinéma aujourd'hui — Films, théories, nouvelles approches*, Ed. Michel Larouche (Montréal: Les éditions Guérnica, 1988), 81–96. Categories of her discussion are: *Film comme matière fugace; Le découpage technique; Pour une première lecture du film; La structure temporelle; L'ordre et la durée; Le jeu de la focalisation: La séquence du viol; Quand discursifs en mêle; Les cinq premiers plans du film; Les documents d'archives; La séquence du tribunal; Les procédés de spatialisation.*

15. *Cinéma au féminin*, 81.

16. Quoted from *CinémaAction* in *Cinéma au féminin*, 81.

17. *Unfinished Diary* [1986; 55 min.] is available in English; it can be purchased from Cinéma Libre or rented from Women Make Movies, Inc. [NY]. Quotation from 1992–93 catalogue, 40.

18. These releases are reviewed by Stephen Godfrey (*The [Toronto]Globe and Mail*; 15 June 1990): A12[N]

19. Kaye Sullivan, *Films for by and about Women* (Metuchen, N.J.: Scarecrow Press, 1980; 1985), 86.

20. Agathe Martin-Thériault, "Jeunes femmes en proie aux images," *Cinéma/Québec* (November 1972): 31.

21. *Variety* (16 October 1972).

22. Permission to reprint this passage on Pool has been granted by Prof. Joseph Donohoe, Jr. of Michigan State Univ. It was originally published in *Essays on Québec Cinema*, edited by Joseph Donohoe, Jr. (East Lansing: [Can. Series #2] Michigan State University Press, 1991): 157–67.

23. *Les Fous de Bassan*, discussed in Chapter 6, does, incidentally, portray the "wings of desire" better than Anne Hébert's somewhat sordid and certainly conventional novel upon which it is based, perhaps because of interspliced clips of the stunning Morus bassanus, or northern gannet, shown in positions of courting and flight, or with beak upward as it seeks the currents and poises to take flight.

24. Léa Pool's filmography includes an earlier avant-garde film, *Strass Café* (1979), which has not been analyzed in this book.

As I note in my text, Pool is not a native Québécoise. She is from Switzerland, and so the final departure of the heroine in *Anne Trister* for a trip to Switzerland, where she will be reunited with her boyfriend, may, like other factors in the film, be somewhat autobiographical. Pool's lack of "*québécois*" content has been the focus of some criticism; yet we may call this a *québécois* film, since many, if not most, of the collaborators on Pool's films are Québécois. By now she herself is a citizen, in deed if not in fact, of that province. In another sense, we might call any of her works made in Québec "French" films, since they are made in the French language, and are "international feminist films" in the way that Nelly Kaplan's film, *Néa*, filmed in Switzerland in the French language by a French Jewess, and dealing with similar identity crises, could be called "international."

25. In view of the preoccupation with film that *La Femme* ... offers, it is important to note Léa Pool's claim, in her interview with Aaron Bor (*Québec Studies*, 9), that American film has not influenced her. Clearly, she could not avoid such influence, if only subconsciously; if she were not under the influence of American film directly, she would have to be so indirectly. But even more telling are the marks of the Garbo tradition on *La Femme* ...: the mysterious woman whom Andrea seeks to show in her film is even supposed to cherish her solitude in true Garbo fashion, as I have shown in my text. See also Roland Barthe's 'On the Face of Garbo' in *A Barthes Reader*. Ed. Susan Sontag (New York: Hill and Wang, 1982): 82–84. Interestingly, Pool's latest film, *Mouvements du* désir (1994), had Barthes' *Discours amoureux* as its point of departure.

26. The brilliant Baillargeon is also a successful director. *Le Sexe des étoiles* (1993), is the story of a girl named Camille, who seeks out her father (played by Denis Mercier). He has become a woman through a transsexual operation, and is now named Marie-Pierre. The story is based on the novel; screenplay by Monique Proulx. (See Bonneville, *Séquences* 163 [March 1993]: 10–12.)

27. Specifically by Mary Jean Green in a paper at ACQS (1986) in Québec City

(published in revised form in *Québec Studies*, 9). In this paper she also argued for the "inscription" theory, and the "privileging" of the feminine, discussed at a later point in my text.

28. Léa Pool herself maintained this in an interview she conducted with Suzanne Gaulin ("Pool's Splash"), published in *Cinema Canada* (October 1984): 8. Here she is quoted as having said: "The three women, in my view, make up a fourth, who is the woman." Then, among other things, *La Femme de l'hôtel* represents an effort to "define" woman, the essence of woman, and this effort to define woman is continued in *Anne Trister*, where, as will be seen, there are similar *dédoublements* of the three main female characters.

29. The themes of marginality and alienation as a Jew and as a woman are more strongly underlined in *Anne Trister* than in *La Femme* .... Even though Estelle says to Andrea (Richler): "Vous êtes juive?" the fact of the question tends more to function as a moment of "recognition" than to draw attention to a "marginality." The question establishes a common ground between the two women, so that their difference from the majority of other Québécoises is shared. Curiously enough, the external spectator, unlike Andrea, may not always be aware of this ethnicity, but only of an aura of exoticism. Consequently, this ignorance liberates his or her scopophilia from any religious or racial taboos or prejudices. Andrea Dworkin and others have studied the fate of the Jewish beauty in society and in art at great length and with some very revealing results; their studies include the particular victimization of the Jewess by the Germans during the holocaust.

30. This was Green's phrase in the above-cited paper.

31. *Maclean's* (15 September 1986): 44.

32. *Spirales* (Summer 1987): 8.

33. *Rencontre* with Patrick Leboutte, 56.

34. Professor Donohoe, during discussion at his Québec Film Symposium, suggested that the tripod, representing stability, indicates to the viewer that sessions with Sarah are being filmed. But one should add that the tripod also alludes obliquely to the art of film and photography, which recurs at the end of *Anne Trister*, and which therefore affords a significant link with the preoccupations of *La Femme de l'hôtel*.

35. This lack of resolution regarding the lesbian issue raised by *I've Heard the Mermaids Singing* appears to be a condition of the film that disconcerts Cameron Bailey. (See his review in *Cinema Canada* [November 1987]: 25.) Lacan would respond by signaling the multiple shapes and forms of feminine desire.

36. Not too surprisingly, expatriot sentiment and the strong sense of exile are not unusual themes in feminist films. Particularly in the Québécoise Marilú Mallet's *Journal inachevé* (1983), exile is the primary theme that links all the stories and substories to all of the characters, who are faced with the problem of choosing a place in which to settle down or "put down their roots." In this picture we also have the theme of the woman filmmaker, seen in *La Femme de l'hôtel*. Mallet's depiction of the theme has the arresting dimension of portraying husband and wife, both of whom are moviemakers, in conflict not only on the gender level, but also on the level of art: they are, so to speak, going in opposite directions. Mallet herself describes the film as "une recherche sur l'expression de la culture des femmes" in her "Notes sur *Journal inachevé*," in *Femmes et cinéma québécois*, 264.

37. Claire Johnston, *Movies and Methods*, ed. Bill Nichols (Berkeley: University of California Press, 1976), I: 210.

38. Varda and Pool have the theme of wandering in common. One might pose

the theory that Varda is marked by her Greekness, while Pool is also marked by her ethnicity.

39. As claimed by Green, *Québec Studies* 9: 56.

40. Jeanne Deslandes, "*La Demoiselle sauvage*," *Séquences* 155 (November 1991): 56–7. (My translation and paraphrases.)

41. Lynn Fieldman Miller, editor and interviewer of *The Hand that Holds the Camera* (New York, Garland Publishing, 1980), writes: "The women sometimes use work created by others or sometimes write their own scripts based on auto-biographical material or the lives of others. But always the choice is to work with personal and intimate thoughts, feelings, and experiences of women in dilemmas that are specific and transcend the specific. ... This selection of personal material often characterizes the best of the work of women filmmakers and video artists, whether they are independent filmmakers or filmmakers who produce feature-length films." Though Miller scarcely has Pool in mind, the passage applies to Pool's work, as it addresses her own observations on *les désordres de l'amour* most uncannily.

42. Maurice Elia, "*Hotel Chronicles*," *Séquences* 150 (January 1991): 97–99.

43. All four are quoted in *Cinéma au féminin*, 27–28.

44. Joseph I. Donohoe, "*Sonatine* in Context: A Neglected Film of Micheline Lanctôt," *Essays*, 157–167.

45. Ibid., 162, 163, and 164.

46. Ibid., 166.

47. *CopieZéro* (30 August, 1988): 36–37. (My paraphrase and translation.)

48. Janick Beaulieu, "*Les Amoureuses*," *Séquences* 164 (May 1993): 49. (My translation.)

Chapter 4. Literature into Film

1. Teachers of French—Canadian literature should be aware of the series on authors done by the National Film Board, or Office National du Film. While these films will not be discussed in this book, they are extremely useful classroom aids, but, in general, should be introduced only to the advanced student, as they are seldom if ever subtitled. Mostly found in the series called "*Profession écrivain*," the titles include: *Alfred DesRochers, poète*; *Anne Hébert: dompter les démons*; *Antonine Maillet: les gages de la survie*; *Deux épisodes dans la vie d'Hubert Aquin*; *Gabrielle Roy: une âme sans frontières*; *Gaston Miron: le haut-parleur*; *Gérard Bessette, l'observateur*; *Gratien Gélinas: le gagnant*; *Jacques Ferron: le polygraphe*; *Jacques Godbout: le présent singulier*; *Marcel Dubé: l'identité des siens*; *Marie-Claire Blais: le feu sous la cendre*; *Michel Tremblay: les cris de ma rue*; Michèle Lalonde (in the film *Speak White*); miscellaneous writers in *Nostalgie*, vol. 8 (*Théâtre et littérature au Québec*); in *La Nuit de la poésie*; *Réjean Ducharme l'illusionniste*; *Yves Thériault: vivre pour écrire*.

The film on Hubert Aquin (*Deux épisodes ...*) is an NFB film made in 1979 and directed by Jacques Godbout. It should be remembered that Aquin, in addition to being one of Québec's most important novelists, was also a film director and scriptwriter. He wrote the TV spy film *Faux Bond*, presented in 1967; excerpts of it can be seen in Godbout's documentary on Aquin.

Note also *En scène*, dealing with the plays of Michel Tremblay and Michel Garneau. There is also an ONF film on Roch Carrier, entitled *Une Terre ingrate*, in which he returns to his native village of Sainte-Justine. He speaks to the old people on the square, and gives us his impressions and his memories. This film, made in 1972, was directed by Cynthia Scott, an eminent Canadian filmmaker.

Les Ecrivains québécois is a series from the audiovisual repertoire of the Québec government. It includes a videocassette on *Alain Grandbois* (1971; d. Roger Frappier; 29 minutes, 43 sec.); on *Yves Thériault* (d. Claude Savard; 32 min. 6 sec.); on *Félix-Antoine Savard*, entitled *Le pays de Menaud* (1971; d. Claude Grenier; 28 min. 20 sec.).

Most are available from SUNY or Québec Cultural Services.

2. My paraphrase and translation of the plot of *Poussière sur la ville* come from Edwin Hamblet, *La Littérature canadienne francophone* (Paris: Hatier, 1987). Hamblet also gives an excerpt from the novel [109—10].

3. Louise Portal, cited in Abel, 1990, 245—6.

4. Pratley wrote essentially the same words in *Variety* (9 June 1971) (New York: Garland Publishing, 1983). Vol. 13, n.p.

5. For *Et du fils* see Tad[ro]s, *Variety* (1 November 1972) Here paraphrased. (New York: Garland Publishing Inc., 1983). Vol. 13, n.p.

6. Background on Canada in the Great Depression and World War II is provided by the National Film Board documentary, *Twilight of an Era (1934—1939)* (1960; 29 min.).

7. Gabrielle Roy, *Bonheur d'occasion* (Montréal: Stanké, 1977). (Written in 1945.) Philip Stratford's English translation is used: *The Tin Flute* (Toronto: McClelland and Stewart's New Canadian Library, 1980; 1982), 170 (Chapter 15). Hereafter cited in my text as *TF* 1982.

8. On NFB films that treat historic relationships of French Canada to English Canada and to England, see James E. Page's *Seeing Ourselves: Films for Canadian Studies* (Montréal: National Film Board of Canada, 1979—1980), 18—20.

9. Esther Pelletier, "Texte littéraire et adaptation cinématographique: la rencontre de deux systèmes," *Les Dossiers de la Cinémathèque* 12 (1983): 37—42.

10. Ibid., 40.

11. Ibid., 42.

12. Richard Leiterman is one of Canada's leading cameramen. One of his best-known pieces of work is *Who Has Seen the Wind?* (1976—77; d. Allan King), based on a story by W. O. Mitchell, with *scénario* by Patricia Watson. This film is also an example of provincial cooperation in the Canadian movie industry; the Saskatchewan government contributed $300,000 in support of it, since it was shot in Saskatchewan. Yet one cannot really speak of a Saskatchewan cinema, in the way one can of an Ontario cinema, or a Québec cinema.

13. Claude Jasmin, *La Sablière (Mario)* (Ottawa: Leméac/Poche-Québec, 1986; first pub. in 1979), 205. Hereafter cited in the text.

14. The discussion of *Le Matou* was delivered in abbreviated oral form at the Conseil International d'Etudes Francophones conference in Tucson (1991).

15. Yves Beauchemin, *Le Matou* (Montréal: Ed. Québec-Amérique, 1985. First copyrighted in 1981 by Editions Québec/Amérique, Montreal). Translated as *The Alley Cat*, by Sheila Fischman (New York: Henry Holt and Company [Owl Book Paperback], 1986), 236; 254. Hereafter cited in the text as *AC* or as French version.

16. Nancy Lyon, *The New York Times* (Sunday, 8 December 1991): xx6.

17. Abel, 14.

18. The reader of French is referred for further discussion of this novel and the film to Catherine Saouter, "*Le Matou*," in *Voix et Images* 36 (1987): 397—98.

Here she quotes the article in *Séquences* 122: 38, which underlined the fidelity of the adaptation, the servility to the novel being for Saouter only apparent, since the Florida sequence of the novel is only in the TV version, while Father Jeunehomme is in neither, etc. A whole issue of *Voix et Images* has been devoted to Beauchemin, while in yet another issue of the journal, Neil Bishop, studying the stereotype of the Frenchman in Québec literature, gives an excellent analysis of Picquot, although in my opinion he is less in "allegiance" with Quebeckers than the author suggests. (Neil P. Bishop, "Le personnage français dans quelques romans québécois contemporains," *Voix et Images* 37 [automne 1987]: 90−91.) Picquot for Bishop is a stereotype (but so are most of the characters, and intentionally so: they are comic parodies). In any case, Picquot is a chef, a womanizer, and he is also anticlerical, atheistic, cartesian, *fanfaron*, and antiAmerican. He likes his cognac and is for "*qualité*" in all things.

19. Yves Picard, "Les succès du cinéma québécois des 10 dernières années: des rendez-vous réussis avec l'imaginaire instituant d'ici," *Dialogue*, Eds., Pierre Véronneau, Michael Dorland and Seth Feldman (Montréal: Mediatexte Publications Inc. et La Cinémathèque Québécoise, 1987): 105.

20. Pratley states that *Le Matou* is an "involved and difficult tale," and that it is also a "rambling adaptation [that] . . . slip[s] into a state of lethargy" (*Intl. Film Guide*, 1987: 111).

21. Not only did Anne Hébert collaborate with Jutra on the *scénario* for *Kamouraska*, but before this she had worked for the ONF, which she entered in 1954. There she drew up the commentaries for *La Femme de ménage* (1954; L. Forest), and *Midinette* (1954; R. Blais). Jean-Marie Poupard finds the tone of these commentaries lyrical, stamped with a marked interest in social facts and characterized by a sharp concern for people of modest condition (Coulombe 1991, 227). Besides *Canne à pêche* (1959; d. F. Dansereau), she also wrote the *scénario* for *Saint-Denys Garneau* (1960; d. Louis Portugais). (S. D. G. was her cousin.) Of the script for *Kamouraska*, Poupard (in Coulombe) tells us that the critics found the filmstory more sentimental, less resolutely "feminist," and a bit edulcorated (that is, sweetened, as with saccharine). He himself claims that, although the script remains faithful to the spirit of the book, one cannot help but notice that it does not have the novel's violent lustfulness. But obviously, in view of my discussion of *Les Fous* . . . , one cannot agree with Poupard (in Coulombe) when he claims that Hébert seems satisfied with Simoneau's adaptation.

Poupard also points out the film in the series "Profession écrivain" made by Claude Godbout (1983) and entitled *Anne Hébert: dompter les démons*.

22. Eleanor Beattie, *The Handbook of Canadian Film*, 2nd edition (Toronto: [PMA/Take One Film Book Series] Peter Martin Ass. Ltd., 1977), 102.

23. Kaye Sullivan, *Films for by and about women* (Metuchen, N.J.: Scarecrow Press, 1980; 1985), 167.

24. G. Mosk[kowitz], *Variety* (23 May 1973) (New York: Garland Publishing, Inc., 1983: vol. 13, n.p.

25. Michel Euvrard, "Le rôle d'acteur, malheureusement," (Interview with Geneviève Bujold) *Cinéma/Québec* (March/April, 1973): 11−14. My translation.

26. Jean Tadros, "Un[e] Espèce de joie dans la création," (Interview with Claude Jutra) *Cinéma/Québec* (March/April 1973): 18. My translation.

27. Ibid., 16−17. My translation.

28. Ibid., 17. My translation.

29. Ibid., 16. My translation.

30. Ibid., 18. My translation.

31. My discussion of *Les Fous de Bassan* was presented in abbreviated oral form at the Chicago conference of the American Council for Québec Studies (17 November 1990).

32. Kathryn Slott, "From Agent of Destruction to Object of Desire: The Cinematic Transformation of Stevens Brown in *Les Fous de Bassan*" *Québec Studies* 9 (Fall 1989): 17–28.

33. Anne Hébert, *Les Fous de Bassan* (Paris: Ed. du Seuil, 1982), 245. Hereafter cited in the text. Tr., *Shadows in the Wind* (Toronto: Newpress Canadian Classics, 1983).

34. The regard in *Les Fous* ... The eyes are the scouts of desire and love; at the same time they are the tool of spying. Stevens's eyes are repeatedly characterized as "pale" and "piercing," Maureen's as velvet, the Grandmother's as green, the girls' as blue, like blue fruit—blueberries? The eyes in the novel show the efforts on Hébert's part to show ethnicity: these are anglo-saxon types we are talking about. The topos is all-pervasive in the novel, and is admirably caught by Simenon.

35. Remarkably enough, Yves Simoneau directed the made-for-TV film *Till Death Us Do Part* (1992; ca 90 min.), a real-life story in which a cunning and manipulative killer with a Jekyll-and-Hyde personality (played by Treat Williams) floats in and out of the hands of the prosecuting attorney, Vincent Bugliosi (played by Arliss Howard), in a most diabolical fashion. This work is quite effective, the photography and musical score complementing the skill of the actors and the finesse of the director.

36. Marilyn Randall, "Les énigmes des *Fous de Bassan*: féminisme, narration et clôture," *Voix et Images* #43 (Fall 1989): 66–82.

37. Suzanne Lamy, "Le Roman de l'irresponsabilité," *Spirale* #29 (November 1982–83): 3.

38. Slott, 24.

39. Ibid., 24.

40. Randall, 77.

41. According to Slott, p. 24, Hébert privileged Olivia's point of view in her own proposed screenplay, but, "When questioned at the CIEF about the film's reconstruction of the diverse narratives into a singularly masculine focus, Hébert replied: 'Le metteur en scène étant un homme a vu le film d'après sa vision d'homme.'" But Randall finds the novel itself to present only one point of view— a masculine one, Stevens's.

42. Cf. Janis L. Pallister, "Eros and Thanatos in Anne Hébert and Marguerite Duras: *Kamouraska* and *Hiroshima mon amour*," *Dalhousie French Studies* 10 (Spring–Summer 1986), 56–71.

43. As a branch of Simoneau's retention of novelistic details, we should note the extent to which he retained the items of clothing upon which Hébert insists. Thus, Stevens is often wearing his hat, and even uses it to gather berries in; we see him donning Maureen's dead husband's clothes in preparation for going to see his parents. The girls wear their crocheted berets; Perceval his "salopette" or coveralls, the parson his "soutane." The men in Olivia's family wear the white shirts she irons.

44. As Anne Hébert said at the CIEF meeting (15 April 1988): "Pour moi, c'est un livre sur le désir, et les objets du désir, c'étaient les deux jeunes filles. Mais dans le film, c'est vraiment Stevens qui devient l'objet du désir de presque tout le monde dans le village. C'est une transformation." Hébert forgets some

passages in her novel and exaggerates the situation in the film; Slott subsequently seems to lean in Hébert's direction.

45. Teresa de Lauretis, *Alice Doesn't (Feminism, Semiotics, Cinema)* (Bloomington: Indiana University Press, 1984), 133, 148, and elsewhere.

46. Slott, 26–27.

47. See Janis L. Pallister, "Satanism, Jansenism and Greek Myth in *Les Fous de Bassan*," *Carrefour de Cultures*, Ed. by Régis Antoine, Sorbonne (Tùbingen, Germany: Gunter Narr Verlag, 1993).

48. For satanic symbolism of hat and pig see François Ribadeau Dumas, *Dossiers secrets de la sorcellerie et de la magie noire* (Paris: Éditions Pierre Belfond, 1971), 32.

49. Erich Auerbach, *Mimesis* (Garden City, New York: [Doubleday Anchor Books] Doubleday & Company, Inc., 1957), 492.

50. Hélène Cixous (and Catherine Clement), *The Newly Born Woman (Sorties)* (Minneapolis: University of Minnesota Press, 1986), 110.

51. Joseph Campbell (with Bill Moyers), *The Power of Myth*, Program Five: *Love and the Goddess* (Mystic Fire Video [Parabola], 1988).

52. Mentioned also by Yves Picard in Coulombe, 437.

53. E. Ann Kaplan, *Women & Film: Both Sides of the Camera* (New York: Methuen, 1983), 27.

54. See the video *Home of the Birds*, directed by Blad Hansen (CBC, 1986) (Featured on *The Nature of Things*, David Suzuki.)

55. André Brochu finds that the characters of the novel are "oiseaux du sabbat" — birdlike and not psychologically studied at all. André Brochu, *Le singulier pluriel* (Montréal: l'Hexagone, 1992), 157–60.

56. In the novel, not only does she buy the cords expressly in order to hang herself (hanging by cord is present early in Hébert's poetry), but ironically she stands on the milk stool — an object linked to fertility. Milk is frequently referred to in the novel: the Reverend Jones drinks warm milk before retiring, and he also sucks on his pipe and thinks of breasts; Perceval tips over a pail of milk; etc. These metaphors can be retained in the film, but the viewer will perhaps not notice them, especially on first (or one) screening. See also Lever, as well as Janis L. Pallister, "The 'Esguillette nouée': Renaissance Forebears of Anne Hébert's *Enfants du Sabbat ...*," *Il tema della fortuna nella letteratura francese e italiana del rinascimento* (Florence: Leo S. Olschki Editore, 1990).

57. Who are "les fous"? The word "mad" is applied not just to the birds (*fous* = boobies). Some of the characters in *Les Fous de Bassan* — especially Perceval — might be regarded as lunatics; they are associated with lunar settings, or the moon itself, both in the novel and in the film. Indeed, both in the novel and in the film, there are more *fous* than the birds (*Fous* 166).

58. Abel, 199.

59. An ardent researcher would probably find in the journals of the area an event very similar to that of *Les Fous de Bassan*. Brochu opens his article by stating that the story is based on happenings in Griffin Creek, even though Anne Hébert suggests in an opening *avis au lecteur* (*Fous*, 9) that the story has no connection with any real fact happening between Québec and the Atlantic ocean. (Brochu, 156.)

60. Bilodeau François, "Le Cauchemar d'un fils déçu: *Les Fous de Bassan* d'Yves Simoneau," *Spirale* 68 (1987): 15.

61. Esther Pelletier, 38. My translation.

62. Abel, 149. My translation and paraphrase.

63. André Bazin, *What Is Cinema?*, Ed. & Tr., Hugh Gray, Vol. 1. (Berkeley: University of California Press, 1987), 65.

64. See *Cinéma/Québec* 2; (7 June 1972), 31.

65. Quoted from *24 Images* in *Cinéma au féminin*, 36. My translation.

66. It is worthwhile to note that Denis Héroux, the executive producer of *Les Plouffe* and of *Le Matou*, as of *Le Crime d'Ovide Plouffe*, and even of *Atlantic City*, is also a talented director. In 1974 he directed an extraordinary film of international reputation, entitled *Jaques Brel Is Alive and Well and Living in Paris*. Héroux was born in Montréal in 1940.

67. Some information in this paragraph taken from Hamblet, 96–98.

68. *The Montagnais* are members of an Indian tribe whose culture subsists in spite of all efforts to "tame" them. They have been portrayed by Arthur Lamothe in his *Train du Labrador* (1967) and in his color film *Mémoire battante* (1983; 55 minutes). Lamothe is the subject of a lengthy article in Coulombe. Recently we have been treated to his *Conquête de l'Amérique* (1991–92; 146 minutes), the second part of which is called "La Culture des Montagnais et la Mémoire du passé." It is discussed in *Séquences* 159/160 (September 1992): 54–55.

69. Quoted in *La Revue de la Cinémathéque*, program 5 [February, March, April, 1990]: 21. My translation.

70. Monsignor Folbèche. Pratley (*TS* 1987, 246) erroneously gives this character as "Pastro Foibeche"; that is, Pastor Folbèche.

71. The allusion is worth noting: Mary Pickford was a Canadian, born Gladys Smith, 8 April 1893, in Toronto. She made it big in American film. She is also a star who fell from the sky, after several failures. She retired from the screen as early as 1933, and is reputed to have ended in a descent into alcoholism (cf. Greta Garbo). Nevertheless, Pickford received a special Academy Award in 1975, not long before her death in 1979, for her contribution to American film.

72. Two of Carrier's stories have been published in book form, both in French and in English, by Tundra Editions (Editions: Livres Toundra): *The Sweater*, and also *The Boxing Champion*, illustrated by Sheldon Cohen. We can look for an equally charming animation on this story of the boxing champion. Roch, on a morning in April when the spring arrives and the ice begins to melt on the rink, begins a new sport: boxing. But he always gets a bloody nose.

73. Janick Beaulieu, "Agaguk," *Séquences* 163 (March 1993): 35.

74. *TV Guide*, 12 June 1993: 34.

75. Literature and film. Brunette and Willis (61–76) recognize that cinema's line of communication is "particularly indirect and complicated." Based on Derrida, they assert that film is a type of writing, "to the extent that it is language," even though cinema "can never be directly spoken," because "it is always written," and, being written, always leaves something material behind. This idea inscribes film within the domain of the textual. Yet for me there are impediments to these theories. If film were merely textual, the novel and the film could and perhaps would be identical. Film is more than language, more than text, and something different: only by a loose concept of written (pictures "written" on film) could one arrive at the conclusion that film is "written" and therefore "textual."

76. Other works of (Québec) literature that have been adapted for the screen include *Kurwenal* by Yves Navarre (which became Léa Pool's *A corps perdu*, treated in Ch. 3); *Le Chandail* (from Roch Carrier's *Les Enfants du bonhomme dans la lune*); *Les Bottes* (from a novella by Jean-Yves Soucy); *Divine Sarah* (by Jacques Bederwellen); *Évangéline Deusse* and *La Sagouine* (plays by Antonine

Maillet); *Le Dernier Havre* (by Yves Thériault); and *Tinamer* (inspired by the novel *l'Amélanchier* by Jacques Ferron).

Michel Tremblay's *Il était une fois dans l'est* (d. André Brassard) is treated in Carrière's *Femmes et cinéma* . . . (104–7). Carrière, who seems quite unsympathetic toward this film, claims that women in *Il était* . . . are "swallowed up, defeated, destroyed, as are men who are in the feminine 'pole,' and jilted lesbians."

Interestingly enough, sometimes a foreign literature is invoked for a story: such is the case with *Le Steak* (1992; 76 minutes) for which the directors, Pierre Falardeau and Manon Leriche, went to a novella by Jack London about a confrontation between two boxers, one young, the other aging. The film is a loose interpretation of London's story; in it Gaétan Hart is compelled—at the advanced age of 37—to fight for his bread and butter, or to bring home the "steak," which, besides, he needed to have eaten in order to win the fight. He wins it anyway.

Chapter 5. Québec as a Mirror of Society: The Couple; the Family; Encounters with Death; Children

1. For a discussion of this work, see Magessa O'Reilly's "Grignon plurilingue," *Voix et Images* 37 (Autumn 1987): 123–38.

2. See Robert Daudelin's "The Encounter Between Fiction and the Direct Cinema," *Self-Portrait*, Ed., Pierre Véronneau and Piers Handling (Ottawa: Canadian Film Institute, 1980): 94.

3. Noguez, 117.

4. Alain-Napoléon Moffat, "*A Tout Prendre* de Claude Jutra: Le Docu-Drame de la Confession," *Québec Studies* 13 (Spring/Summer 1991): 147–54.

5. Some parts of this discussion were first published in the *AATF Newsletter* (see bibliography, J. L. Pallister, "Observations on Claude Jutra's 'Mon oncle Antoine'"). Acqueline Viswanathan gives us an "Approche pédagogique d'un classique du cinéma québécois: *Mon oncle Antoine*," in *The French Review* 63:5 (April 1990): 849–58. Here Benoît's name is incorrectly written without accent throughout. Information on obtaining the film and the *scénario* are inaccurate and incomplete; an implication remains that the *scénario* was available to the author only in manuscript. Here is the crowning injury: "Par certains côtés, *Mon oncle Antoine* est une comédie légère, un 'film de Noël' qui convient à toute la famille. Mais d'autre part, c'est aussi un film noir . . . ." (856). It is neither a light comedy nor a *film noir*!

The *scénario* of this film was published by Art Global (Montréal, 1979). It can be of considerable use in preparation for the viewing of the picture, or for a reconsideration of the dialogue as an important though not *the* most important quality of *Mon oncle Antoine*. A subtitled video of this film exists and is available for rent or for sale from Polyglot, from Walden (by Mail), Critic's Choice, Vedette Visuals, etc. The film version can be rented from Films Incorporated; but one should request the subtitled and not the dubbed version.

6. See Bill Wine, *Magill's Survey of Cinema* (*Foreign Language Films*) (Englewood Cliffs, N.J.: Salem Press, 1985). He compares the film to Truffaut's *Quatre Cents Coups* of 1959, but finds it lacks Truffaut's unswerving point of view (V, 2094).

7. *Carmen*, still a young teenager, has been placed in Antoine's employ by her father, who comes into the store periodically to collect her pay. This

exploitation, which Antoine wants to soften by trying to convince the father to give the girl some small part of the pay, is of sociological interest, as it underscores the hard life of the rural Québécois adolescent in the early decades of the century. While not a matter of child labor, strictly speaking, several instances substantiate our impression that she and Benoît are definitely expected to do more than their fair share of the work. For example, Benoît is ordered to carry a heavy keg of nails, which everyone is tripping over, upstairs.

8. Jay Cocks [*Time Magazine*] and Andrew Sarris [*The Village Voice*] as quoted on the video jacket of *Mon oncle Antoine*.

9. R. Bruce Elder, "The Cinema We Need," *Canadian Forum* (February 1985): 32.

10. Pratley, "Mon oncle Antoine," *Variety* (9 June 1971) (New York: Garland Publishing Inc., 1983. Vol. 13, n.p.

11. Quoted in Program 4 of *La Revue de la Cinémathèque* (Dec. 1989–Jan. 1990): 20.

12. *Les Bons Débarras*: Best picture, best director, best original screenplay, etc. (Abel, 318.)

13. One of French Canada's greatest actresses, Tifo has appeared as the club-footed telegraph operator in love with François Paradis in *Maria Chapdelaine*, and as Irène in *Les Fous de Bassan*. She is the wife of Pierre Curzi, an equally renowned and highly-gifted actor, who has appeared in *Maria Chapdelaine, Le Déclin de l'empire americain, Les Plouffe*, and many other first-class *québécois* films.

14. Josée Boileau, "Images récentes dans les films à succès," *Femmes et cinéma québécois* (Ed. Carrière), 129.

15. Jean Blouin and Myette, "Réjean Ducharme," *L'Actualité* (July 1982): 48.

16. See Gaylyn Studlar's "Masochism and the Perverse Pleasures of the Cinema," in *Movies and Methods*, ed. Bill Nichols, vol. 2 (Berkeley: University of California Press, 1985): 602–621.

17. France Vézina, *Androgyne* (Montréal: l'Hexagone, 1979), 82. My translation.

18. Brunette and Willis indicate that *Gianni Schicchi* is also the apparent source of Bernard Herrmann's scores for *The Bride Wore Black* and *Marnie*.

19. Charles Baudelaire, *Poèmes* (Paris: Hachette, 1951), 212–13.

20. [J.-P.] Tad[ro]s, "*Le Temps d'une chasse*," *Variety* (18 October 1972) (New York: Garland Publishing Inc., 1983). Vol. 13, n.p.

21. Although some might wish to set *Les Bons Débarras* on a par with Mankiewicz's acclaimed *Temps d'une chasse*, Pratley says of *Le Temps* ... that it "never takes a false step ..." (*TS* 1987, 205). (This has also been said of William Wyler's *Wuthering Heights*.)

22. Blouin and Myette, 49. My translation.

23. The film's introspection and inclination toward dialogue are, as I indicated above (in the text), *québécois* in nature; but they are also Greek. One should, in all fairness, point out that the film was widely viewed in a dubbed version, rather than with subtitles, and the falseness of the speech may explain the film's undervaluation by Americans. (I have only viewed one really successfully dubbed French-Canadian film, and that was *Maria Chapdelaine*.)

24. In the preparation of this discussion of *Les Bons Débarras* (delivered in abbreviated oral form at Heidelberg College in Tiffin, Ohio on 20 October 1989, and at the University of Toledo on 13 November 1989) I used the bilingual libretto of *Gianni Schicchi* published for the Metropolitan Opera by Belwin Mills Publishing Co., Melville, N.Y. [s.d.].

25. Most of this discussion of *Le Déclin de l'empire américain* first appeared in the *Acts* of the conference on Canada/America at Western Michigan University.

My remarks on *Le Déclin* ... as they relate to *The Big Chill* owe nothing to Adrian Van Den Hoven's "*The Decline* ... in a North-American Perspective" (*Essays in Quebec Cinema*, Ed., Donohoe, 145–55). Van Den Hoven's essay appeared long after my observations on the place of *Le Déclin* ... in world cinema were published in the *Acts* of Western Michigan University. (See Pallister, bibliography). But it is worth noting that Van Den Hoven (who teaches at the University of Windsor) concludes that "While *The Big Chill* starts with the death of an illusion, the group's verbal interactions provide just enough empty talk ... for the group to go on with the show. Quebec society, however, is driven by a moral ideology. Whether its members need to believe in God, in the French language, or in survival and the resurrection, it remains a fact that without an intense unifying belief, Quebec ... cannot survive; it simply cannot afford the casualness, aimlessness, individualism, and 'suicidal' anarchism that ultimately surfaces in *The Big Chill*" (155). Would Van Den Hoven be implying, then, that the United States *can* afford such undercuttings to its fabric? That it is *not* driven by a moral ideology? That the group depicted in *The Big Chill* is *not*, like the group in *Le Déclin* ..., a very special cross-section of the larger society?

26. Louis-Guy Lemieux, *Réjeanne Padovani*, *Scope* (April 1987): 3.

27. Renoir, of course, liked to insert gastronomic episodes into his films. As a result we not only have memorable eating scenes in *La Règle* ..., but also additional allusions to *gourmandise* (Charlotte) and to gourmet items and special diets. (Mme de La Bruyère must have *sel marin* [coarse salt]; Mme de la Plante takes no tea, but only coffee; the General takes hot water with lemon; etc.) We might also mention, as a point of comparison, the famous tarragon omelette being consumed in *Une Partie de campagne* (1936).

28. Lemieux, 3.

29. In his preface to the *scénario* of *Le Déclin* ..., Arcand says that this film is closely modeled on his own environment, and imitates conversations he has heard around him. Thinking it might be his last film, or the last but one, he decided to enjoy himself and to "create a film that would go against all the laws commonly recognized as those of cinematographic art: little action, a lot of dialogue many personal references." The success of the film surprised him; he did not know how much he had put there, it seems. But in fact, was he not putting there his lived reality; was he not creating a "documentary" without realizing it? See Denys Arcand, *Le Déclin de l'empire américain* (Montréal: Les Editions du Boréal, 1986).

The reader is also referred to an interview of Denys Arcand in *Journal Français d'Amérique* (5–25 December 1986): 20–21 and 24, where he again states that this film—an *auteur* film—had to do with his own life and that of his friends.

Noteworthy here is the fact that *La Règle* ... also was a personal film, but, unlike *Le Déclin* ..., it was a commercial disaster. An utterly pessimistic film, it was an early exploration of the absurd. When finally this latter came into vogue, the film could be appreciated, and in 1962 it was voted by an international poll of critics as the third greatest film ever made.

30. Though they do not use "comedy" as their mode (any more than do *The Shooting Party* and *La Règle* ...), several other great films of recent times carry the fall of the "aristocracy"—engaged in furious dialogue—as their burden: *The Dead* (John Huston's last work); *Room with a View*; *To the Lighthouse*, and so forth.

31. Véronique Dassas, *CopieZéro* 34–35 (December 1987–March 1988): 56–57.

32. *Film Review Annual* (1987): 297.

33. Perhaps the characters have more in common with those of Woody Allen's *Midsummer Night's Sex Comedy* (1982) than we at first realize.

34. This is the formulation of Louis van Delft, in "La Bruyère a-t-il écrit Les Caractères?", *Le Tricentenaire des* Caractères, Ed., Louis van Delft (Paris, Seattle, Tübingen: [PFSCL] Biblio 17, 1989).

35. The archetypal *Règle du jeu* sets the dizzying pace of the sexual lives of these characters: The Marquis, Robert de La Chesnaye, cheats with Geneviève on his wife Christine, who is loved by the pilot, André Jurieu. (Saint-Aubin figures in this triangle, also.) Among the servants — in a sort of *Upstairs, Downstairs* arrangement that brings about an echo technique — Lisette, married to Schumacher, cheats with Marceau, the *braconnier*, or poacher. Most interesting in this respect is *La Ronde*, which, as its name implies, is like a chain that starts with an episode between the prostitute (played by Simone Signoret) and a soldier, and ends with an episode between her and a different man. Here love is "voltiger," as we see in the use of the quotation from Beaumarchais's *Marriage of Figaro* (Act 4, Scene. 10).

36. *International Dictionary of Films and Filmmakers*, 2nd ed. (Chicago and London: St. James Press, 1991).

37. James E. Page, 33–34.

38. Richard Martineau, "*Une Histoire inventée*," *Séquences* 149 (November 1990): 73.

39. Ibid., 74.

40. See *The Film Center Gazette* (Chicago School of the Art Institute) for November 1990.

41. Ibid.

42. Another film about bar life, one of questionable success, is *Cruising Bar* (1989–90; d. Robert Ménard). In this satire of the singles bar, Michel Côté plays four different characters, each looking to "score." (Côté was shown on Victoria Tennant's Sunday Arts Entertainment (CBC) — mentioned in relation to Forcier — playing these four types of male pickup-artist [bull, lion, worm and snake] in *Cruising Bar*.) The film is also called *The Meet Market*, and stars Louise Marleau opposite Côté. Some of the scenes are quite untasteful.

43. Quoted on the video jacket of *Au clair de la lune*. My translation.

44. Quoted in *La Revue de la Cinémathèque*, program 5 [Feb./Mar./April 1990]: 22.) My translations.

45. Peter Harcourt, *Jean Pierre Lefebvre* (Ottawa: Canadian Film Institute, 1981), 45; stills on 40–44.

46. Marcel Jean in *Essays in Québec Cinema*, ed. Donohoe (1991) 181.

47. Léo Bonneville, "Interview with Jean Beaudry," *Séquences* (September 1990): 23.

48. Janine Marchessault, "*Jacques et Novembre* : Emergence of a New Paradigm," *Dialogue*, Ed., Pierre Véronneau, Michel Dorland, and Seth Feldman (Montréal: Médiatexte: Cinémathèque Québécoise, 1987): 223–9. Quotation is from the abstract of her article. My translation.

49. Quoted in Program 5 of *La Revue de la Cinémathèque* (May/June 1990): 29.

50. *CopieZéro* 31 [March 1987]: 4. (Special issue on Melançon.). My paraphrase and translation.

51. Ibid., 6. My paraphrase and translation.

52. Ibid., 7. My paraphrase and translation.

53. Quotations in this paragraph from *CopieZéro* 30: 4–5.

54. Charles Caouette, "Un cinéaste ...," *CopieZéro* 31 (March 1987): 18.

55. Sylvie Halpern, "André Melançon ...," *L'Actualité* (April 1987): 11–12; 14.

56. Véronneau, "Observation, 1, 2, 3 ...," *CopieZéro* 31 (March 1987): 9.

57. *CopieZéro* 31: 7.

58. Véronneau. "Observation ...." (1987): 11. My translations.

59. Léo Bonneville, "Interview with Michael Rubbo," *Séquences* 150 (January 1991): 62.

60. Sylvie Beaupré, "*Simon les nuages*," *Séquences* 147 (September 1990): 80– 81. My translation.

61. Léo Bonneville, "Interview with Michael Rubbo": 61.

62. *Journal Français d'Amérique* 8 (21 March 1991): 14.

63. Marc Sévigny, "Le Cinéma pour enfants au Québec," *Cinéma/Québec* 58; 6:8 (September/October 1978): 24–32.

64. Ibid., 30.

65. Ibid., 31.

66. Ibid., 31–32.

Chapter 6. Québec Film as a Mirror of Society: Institutions

1. The reader is referred to Louis Balthazar's *French-Canadian Civilization* (Washington, D.C.: ACSUS Paper, 1989) for a succinct presentation of the French-English conflicts as they were lived out through the centuries. The reader of French should also consult Françoise Tétu de Lapsade's *Le Québec: un pays, une culture* (Québec: Boréal; Paris: Seuil, 1990).

2. Lacasse himself, an employee of the ministery of International Affairs, had firsthand knowledge of these troubled times. In the summer of 1968, and exactly on the feast of St. John the Baptist (a traditional holiday in Québec, due to the fact that St. John the Baptist is the patron saint of French Canada), Trudeau — an ardent federalist — was taken apart by nationalist (Québécois) demonstrators, and pressure became more insistent in the general quarter of Rue Bonsecours in Montréal to accelerate the formation of the antiterrorist sector (the SAT). The head of the police asked Lacasse to accept the prospect of breaking with his sector in order to give a hand to this organization. After only a few working sessions, Lacasse, along with the representatives of the Royal Gendarmerie of Canada (GRC), returned. 1970 was a year of election; a year of agitation; a year of crisis. There was nothing spontaneous about these things: disappointing electoral returns for the nationalist militants and demonstrations of a magnitude now forgotten. Was the police corps badly or well prepared? In his novel, Lacasse advances his hypotheses.

3. The films that Weinmann sets, and often forces, into sociopolitical context are: *La Petite Aurore*, *Tit-Coq*, *Les Portes tournantes*, *Un Zoo la nuit*, *Le Déclin de l'empire américain*, and *Jésus de Montréal*.

4. The collected poems of Godin appeared for the first time in English in 1991.

5. This report, completed in January 1839 and presented to the Colonial Office on 4 February 1839, was prepared by John George Lambton, Earl of Durham, who had been appointed by the Governor General to investigate the colonial grievances that had fired the rebellions of 1837. He found that Upper Canada was in the power of a corrupt and insolent Tory clique that was in part responsible for causing the discontent leading to the rebellions. But the more disturbing part of his report claimed that Lower Canada should be brought to a state of harmony and progress by the assimilation of French Canadians, whom he called "a people with no literature and no history." He held that this assimilation could be achieved by a legislative union of the Canadas, in which an English-speaking majority would dominate. It goes without saying that while some welcomed the report, the French Canadians were bitterly opposed to this route to union, and became even more determined to protect their Church and their culture, as expressed through their religion and their language.

6. The Union Nationale was a coalition of the Conservative Party and the Action Libérale Nationale (ALN), formed to contest the 1935 elections in the province of Québec; its leaders were Maurice Duplessis of the Conservative Party and Paul Gouin of the ALN. Under this coalition — which became a single party — Duplessis won the provincial election in 1936. This conservative party lost to the liberals in 1939 due to the liberals' promise that French Canadians would be saved from conscription; but it was reelected in 1944. From this time forward the Union Nationale party had a strong nationalistic emphasis. After Duplessis's death in 1959, the party was led by Paul Sauvé, but lost the 1960 election, and has come to power only once since then (1966–70). In 1970 it was defeated by Robert Bourassa. The party was ultimately supplanted by the Parti Québécois. The Union Nationale is no longer a political force in Québec. It of course had its supporters among farmers, small businessmen, and unorganized labor. It was more successful in Québec City than in Montréal. (Vincent Lemieux in *The Canadian Encyclopedia*, Vol. 4: 2214.)

7. Page (1979–80): 95.

8. Bethune was a physician of Scottish heritage about whom Donald Sutherland and Kate Nelligan made a CBC TV film in 1980 with Eric Till as director, and about whom Sutherland has recently made an excellent full-length fictionalized biographical film aired in early 1992 on CBC. The Chinese have also made a film about him, starring the American actor Gerry Tannenbaum. Only recently, too, paintings made by Bethune during his recovery from tuberculosis have been published in book form.

9. Pierre Vallières, "Brault a manqué son coup: témoignage d'un otage privilégié des 'ordres'," *Cinéma/Québec* 4:1 (December 1974): 18–20. My paraphrases and translation.

10. Michel Brûlé, "Un constat d'impuissance à l'égard des groupes d'opposition," *Cinéma/Québec* 4:1 (December 1974): 14–17. My translation and paraphrases.

11. There is also a fairly recent film entitled, in English, *Paper Marriage*, whose action is situated in Canada, and is on the same subject. It is available only in Chinese, and at that is rather difficult to obtain.

12. Brunette-Willis, 95.

13. Ibid.

14. Pierre Falardeau, "La Liberté n'est pas une marque de yogourt," *Lumières* 21 (Winter 1990): 10–12.

15. Yves Lever, "(Une) Histoire à suivre: Octobre 70 dans le cinéma québécois," *Cinéma/Québec* 4:5 (1974): 14–15.

16. Ron Burnett, *Explorations in Film Theory* (22 essays from *Ciné-Tracts*, edited by Burnett) (Bloomington, Indiana: Indiana University Press, 1991): 111–20.

17. Quoted in Judy Wright and Debbie Magidson, "Making Films for Your Own People," *Canadian Film Reader*, Ed., Seth Feldman and Joyce Nelson (Toronto: Peter Martin Associates, 1977): 219.

18. Burnett: 116.

19. *CopieZéro* 34–35 (December 1987–March 1988); Michel Larouche: 32–34; Gérald Godin: 45.

20. Burnett, 1991: 118.

21. Ibid., 118–9.

22. Ibid., 119.

23. Ibid., 119.

24. Ibid., 119.

25. Véronneau brings together here the appreciations by several critics of several early Québec films, including *La Forteresse*, *Le Curé de Village*, *Séraphin*, *Son Copain*, *La Petite Aurore*, *Tit-Coq*, and others. One may sample a 1952 critique of *Le Rossignol et les cloches* (Véronneau, *Cin . . . .*, 52) by René Lévesque, who was film critic and journalist prior to launching out on his political career.

26. Major, 91. My translation.

27. Ibid., 91–97.

28. *Réjeanne Padovani*, cited in Henry Garrity, "Subversive Discourse . . . ." *Québec Studies* 9 (Fall, 1989–Winter, 1990): 35. (Denys Arcand, *Réjeanne Padovani*, preface: 11.) My translation.

29. [G.] Mosk[owitz], *Variety* (13 June 1973. New York: Garland Publishing Inc., 1983). Vol. 13, n.p. See also *Réjeanne Padovani*, Lever *Hist.* (1988), 287; 350; 357.

30. Richard Gay, "Interview with Jacques Godbout," *Cinéma/Québec* 4:1 (1974): 33–36.

31. Ibid., 36.

32. Garrity "Subversive . . .": 31.

33. Ibid., 29.

34. Paul Warren, "Américanisation . . .," *La Revue de la Cinémathèque* 1 (May/June 1989): 18.

35. My translation. See also Program 5 of *La Revue de la Cinémathèque* (Feb./Mar/April 1990): 26.

36. Maltin, 820.

37. Both quoted on video jacket.

38. Janick Beaulieu and Johanne Larue, "*Léolo*: Pour (et) Contre," *Séquences* 159/160 (September 1992): 52–3.

39. Jacques Rendu, "*Un zoo la nuit*," *Le Journal français d'Amérique* (22 April–5 March 1988): 20; and also Rendu (17–30 June 1988): 16. My translation.

40. Henry Garrity, "The Politics of Subversion in Jean-Claude Lauzon's *Un Zoo la nuit* . . . " In *Film and Society*, ed. by Douglas Radcliff Umstead, 54–60 (Kent, Ohio: Kent State University Press, 1990). (Proceedings of 8th International Film Conference.)

41. Léandre Bergeron, *Dictionnaire de la langue québécoise* (Montréal: VLB Editeur, 1980). (Since Marcel has already ruined one lunch, George, cutting his face, says to him "Maintenant tu me dois un smoked meat.")

42. Jean Charbonneau, "*Un zoo ...*," *CopieZéro* 36 (August 1988): 13–15.

43. Ibid., 14.

44. Source of information in this paragraph: Stanley Gordon, *Canadian Encyclopedia*, Vol. 4, 2136.

45. *Dead Ringers* is important to Canadian film as a document on the social structures that allow for two Toronto-born surgeons — twins played by Jeremy Irons — to become involved with a Québécoise, or at least a French-Canadian, actress, Claire Niveau (a symbolic name, to say the least), a part so well played by Geneviève Bujold.

A recent article by Marcie Frank, herself living and teaching in Montréal, overlooks these factors, but she also seems to force Cronenberg into a Lacanian mold, and to apply feminist theories that run counter to his themes and aims. (Marcie Frank, "The Camera and the Speculum: David Cronenberg's *Dead Ringers*" [*PMLA* 106: 3, May 1991]: 459–470.) He is primarily concerned with the body as it attacks itself, and with how the body plays on the mind; and he focuses — within this concern — both on sociopathic detachment, and, above all, on the failure of his heroes to stop the forces of apocalyptic evil. While Frank insists on themes of misogyny and separation in *Dead Ringers*, on longings in the twins for separation from the mother's womb and from each other, a separation she says they achieve in death, this seems to me quite erroneous. The Mantle twins are like the variations on Siamese twins as depicted in such Renaissance monster books as that of Ambroise Paré (*Des Monstres et prodiges*), whose iconic-like illustrations adorn the credits at the beginning and end of the film. The fact is that in death the Mantles are still tragically united: one lies across the other, giving the final visual impression of a heterotypic heteradelphic deformity, or a thoracopagus epigastricus, that is, a conjoined twin, one parasite attached to the autosite at the thoracoepigastric region. This physical monstrosity is as important a factor to Cronenberg as any psychological ramifications it may bring about: the video inserted into the chief protagonist's belly in *Videodrome* was hardly different. And thus Frank's reproduction of Rueff's portrayal of the womb from his *De Conceptu et generatione hominis* may have more to do with opened guts than with womb separation motifs in *Dead Ringers*. All of Cronenberg's films involve such physical problems, which then bring about weird behaviors. From his earliest films (*Stereo* [1969]; *Crimes of the Future* [1970]), Cronenberg's preoccupation has been the relationship between the body and the mind. (See *La Revue de la Cinémathèque*, program 5 [Feb./March/April 1990]: 26.)

46. Pierre Hébert, "*Les Tisserands du pouvoir*," *Voix et Images* 42 (1989): 510–11.

47. Peter Harcourt, *Jean Pierre Lefebvre* (Ottawa: Canadian Film Institute, 1981), 87–95.

48. Noguez, 126–37.

49. Michel Buriana, "Interview with Jean-Claude Lauzon," *Séquences* 158 (June 1992): 42.

50. James E. Page, *Seeing* ..., 114–12.

51. Ibid., 163.

52. Ibid.

53. In Véronneau's *Le succès; hist. du cin* .. *I* (1979): 84 ff, we see that even in the times of these films the CIF still had a grip on the matter.

54. Most of these films are briefly analyzed by Pratley, and can also be studied in Véronneau, *Le Succès est* ... (1979) and *Cin* .. *duplessiste:Histoire du Cinéma au Québec* (1979) I; II.

55. Quoted in Véronneau, *Cin ... duplessiste*, 45.

56. Quoted in Véronneau, *Cin ... duplessiste*, 51.

57. For a long discussion of the influence of the Catholic clergy and the Holy See on "censorship" of the Québec film, see Véronneau, *Le succès, ...* 79–99.) See also Yves Lever's article "Eglise et Cinéma" (Coulombe 1991), 172–3. Lever has also written a mémoire, published by the University of Montreal in 1977, entitled *L'Eglise et le cinéma au Québec*.

Censorship may, of course, come from lay governments as well, sometimes working with the Church. Yves Lever has written an excellent article on the subject (Coulombe 1991, 88–90). Here one will learn of the nonclerical censorship of such sociocritical films as occurred with *On est au coton*; of amputations and excisions for political reasons, as occurred with *Québec: Duplessis et après* and *Action: the October Crisis of 1970*; and of censorship via delays in or limitation of distribution, as occurred with *Un pays sans bon sens*; *Gens d'Abitibi*, etc.

On a CBC Sunday Afternoon Arts program hosted by V. Tennant (26 May 1991), Catherine Jonasson, curator of film at the Art Gallery of Ontario, spoke on the subject of provincial censorship. Her notion was that sexual representation and violence characterize "The American Experience," and this as such is glorified in its presentation. Her point was already questionable, when one considers the immense violence of any number of early French films, including *Un Chien andalou*, for example, or even the graphic violence of the French-Canadian film *La Petite Aurore*. But she went on to speak of Jesse Helms and the Mapplethorpe incident, and of the cuts in funds that can come from what might be deemed offensive, adding that "censorship is not at present a problem in Canada." (Is this really true, considering the many artful ways in which censorship can find expression, such as tinkering with the film, editing out unwanted scenes, causing delays of its release, etc.—outright banning being only the most direct and obvious?) She added that viewers must assist in indicating what is acceptable material. (That too is fraught with danger when it comes to any art product.)

The Bureau de Surveillance du Cinéma of the provincial government continued to issue its *Cahier des films visés* (approved films) without interruption well into the century, as witnessed by publications of November 1967, 1968, 1970, 1971, 1972, and 1973 to 1975, all to be found in the Université Laval library.

58. *La Presse*, 12 November 1949; quoted in Véronneau's *Cin ....*, 52–3.

59. Found in Véronneau's *Cin ....*, 54; first appeared in *Le Front ouvrier*, 19 November 1949.

60. Quoted in Véronneau's *Cin ....*, 52.

61. Gerald Pratley, "L'Amour humain," *Variety* (9 June 1971): 7.

62. Arcand's *Ville-Marie*. This beautiful film is a must. The singers in the background open on the text *miserere ...* and end on the text *spiritu*; their performance throughout adds to the sacredness and reverence with which the story is told.

Readers should not confuse this work with another piece of editing and directing on Montréal done by Arcand, also in 1965. That film, entitled *Montréal, un jour d'été*, was done for the Office du Film du Québec for the Québec pavillion at Expo 67. It is an original film, emphasizing the geometry of the city and bringing out its noises. It shows the people at leisure, the markets, and the famous clotheslines on pulleys that so impressed me the first time I visited Québec in 1946. It also shows the great vessels in the harbor. Overhead shots outline streams of traffic, cars, and people. Closeups show faces, and night scenes feature lights and fireworks stabbing large black spaces. The photography of this film was done by

Bernard Gosselin and Stéphane Venne; production delegate was Raymond-Marie Léger. And while it does not deal with the profound spirituality at the founding instant, it tells us that Arcand knows every nook and cranny of this city.

In 1990, Vidéo Québec tied two other lesser films to *Montréal, un jour d'été*, to make a package. One was a very old documentary called *La Restauration de l'Ile Sainte Hélène* (a place of family recreation), directed by W. T. Hand, with photography by Jean Arsin, sound by Alphonse Cloutier, commentary by Henri Poitras, and editing by Frank Alexander. The sound track is in poor shape but the film shows how 1600 *chômeurs* (unemployed men) were put to work on the project. Though the film itself is without date, Arsin was a cameraman in the late 10s and early 20s, and Coulombe (1991, 14) gives the date of this film as 1937. The other is a silly touristic piece entitled *Montréal: une ville nommée Marie* (s.d.); it is signed by the director Anton Van de Water; the text is by Jean Laforest and the sound by Pierre Desmarchais. It was made for the Office du Tourisme de la Province du Québec by the Office du Film de la Province du Québec. This film features Mary Robbins, who, while in search of her fiancé Leslie, also tours the city with her friend Jeannine and sees all. If there is one useful thing in this work as it relates to a source of general confusion on the part of natives and visitors alike, it is to point out that the Cathedral of Montreal is Marie, Reine du Monde, modeled on St. Peter's of Rome, and huddled among skyscrapers and modern hotels, whereas the beautiful church in Old Montréal—the one tourists always visit (and which is no longer serving numerous parishioners)—is adjacent to the old Sulpician monastery with the fine clock. This church, Notre Dame, is not far from another famous church, much smaller, Notre Dame de Bonsecours. The film does show many of Montréal's monuments, and speaks to the history of the city, of Maisonneuve, of Marguerite Bourgeois, who "taught the Iroquois," etc. But it is not in a league with Arcand's *Ville-Marie*.

Yet another film about Montréal—made by Vincent Paquette (ONF 1942; 30 min.)—is *La Cité de Notre-Dame*. In Houle (*Dict.* 1978, 56—57) it is linked to the history of the ONF, as it was the "first film in the French language directed by a permanent employee of the ONF." The film gives some history, and relates the festivities and the ceremonies marking the tricentennial of Montréal. A tableau of cultural, financial, and industrial activities is also presented. The touristic and historic sites are shown, as well.

63. See *Terre et Foyer* (May/June 1949): 9, a periodical published by the Québec Ministry of Agriculture, where, as I model a hat, I hold a bouquet of those daisies in my hands.

64. Denys Arcand, *Jésus de Montréal* (Montréal: Les Editions du Boréal, 1989), 8. My translation.

65. Ibid., 169—70.

66. Ibid., 156—57.

67. Ibid., 175.

68. E. Ann Kaplan, *Women & Film: Both Sides of the Camera* (New York: Methuen, 1983), 36.

69. Covered in several issues of *Cinéma/Québec* [q.v., biblio.] in 1971.

70. Gerald Godin, "Un film didactique," *Cinema/Québec* (June/July 1971): 33—34.

71. Chris Braiden, *Canadian Encyclopedia*, 537.

72. John of the Cross (Saint), *Living Flame of Love* (New York: Doubleday [Image], 1962), 262.

73. Henry Garrity: An interpretation of *Jésus* ... set forth in a paper given in November 1990 at the ACQS convention in Chicago.

74. Compare the translation, *The Alley Cat*, 171 ff. If we compare the problems of getting a tooth cared for in that novel with Roger Weisberg's 1990 PBS film "Borderline Medicine," hosted by Walter Cronkite — in which it is claimed that routine care is very accessible in Canada, while expensive state-of-the-art procedures are readily accessible only in the United States — we have a serious gap in perceptions.

75. Again compare *The Alley Cat*, on Monsignor Ignace Bourget, the gourmet bishop, 41–42, and on Father Jeunehomme, the gourmet and bookworm, throughout.

76. Olivier Lefebure du Bus, *Séquences* (March 1991): 55.

77. Vincent Canby, "*Black Robe*," *New York Times* (Sunday, 3 November 1991): Y21.

78. Terrence Rafferty, "*Black Robe*," *The New Yorker* (18 November 1991): 120–23.

79. *The American Video Review* 12: 7 (October 1991): 119.

80. Paul Salmon, "*Jesus of Montreal*," *Magill's Cinema Annual* (1990): 201–2. Salmon also treats us to an excellent synopsis of the story.

81. Marie Naudin, "Denys Arcand: Un Montréal poste-moderne," *Etudes Canadiennes/Canadian Studies* 30 (June 1991): 73–77. (I am quoting from a prepublication typescript.)

82. Arcand is not a pure cut-and-dried moralist; he is also an arbiter of taste. According to Jean Larose, as quoted by Jean Fisette in "Chroniques" *Voix et Images* 39 (Spring 1988): 486, Arcand criticizes "la quétainerie" (bad taste).

83. Craig MacInnis, "Toronto and Montreal go reel to reel," *The Toronto Star* (Sunday, 22 August 1993): C1 — C2. "Even Denys Arcand, a life-long Montrealer, has decided to unveil his new film, *Love and Human Remains*, right here in the hard heart of English-speaking Canada (i.e., Toronto) ... 'The Cannes people saw it and the people (at the Venice film festival) saw it and they didn't take it for competition'" (C — 2).

Chapter 7. Other Voices — Voices of the Other

1. Mordecai Richler, "Inside/Outside" (A Reporter at Large), *The New Yorker* LXVII, 31 (23 September 1991): 40–92.

2. Michel Houle in *Self-Portrait* (Ed., Pierre Véronneau and Piers Handling, 1980) talks of some of these disparate elements in a section he calls "Dissidents, Dispossessed Marginals and Minorities" (174–81), but the treatment is very condensed, and also now rather dated.

3. *Cinéma au féminin*, 44–45.

4. *National Film Board of Canada, International Film and Video Resource Guide* (U.S. Edition) (New York: National Film Board of Canada, 1987), 45.

5. Ibid., 13.

6. Page, 18, 20, 48, 134, 168, and elsewhere.

7. Ibid., 135.

8. Ibid., 18.

9. *L'Arbre qui dort rêve à ses racines* (1992; 81 minutes; d. Michka Saäl) was reviewed by Johanne Larue in *Séquences* 158 (June 1992): 47–48.

10. *The Street* (Caroline Leaf, 1976), is one of the most haunting pieces of animation one could view. Leaf's famous style involves swirling effects coming from the way she handles the paint and sand. Another well-known work of hers is *The Marriage of the Owl* (1974), using "Eskimo" motifs. She is the subject of an article by Louise Carrière in Coulombe (1991, 322–24), and also by Jacqueline Levitin in *Femmes et cinéma québécois* (1983, 237–42).

11. Richler, "Inside Outside," 46.

12. *Séquences* (June 1992): 41.

13. Véronneau, "Mariage à l'italienne" *La Revue de la Cinémathèque* (December 1990/January 1991): 4–8.

14. Reviewed in *Magill's Survey of Cinema, Foreign Language Films*. Vol. 6: 2847–51. See *Film Review Index* for others.

15. Pratley also reviews *It Happened in Canada* (1961; 96 min.; produced, directed, written, photographed, and edited by Luigi Petrucci, with music by Carmine Rizzo) as an "Italian" film from Toronto that has the added luster of being set in Canada. It concerns Rita, a young Italian teacher who comes to Canada to meet Andrea, a forty-five-year-old widower whom her parents have agreed she shall marry. But instead she meets and marries Andrea's nephew, Carlo. He had been a good-for-nothing, fathering an illegitimate child by Carmela; but he reforms under Rita's influence, and becomes the hard-working laborer we will encounter again in *Caffè Italia*. When Carlo is killed, Rita would like to return to Italy, but is unable to do so. Carmela's death sets before her a moral imperative: she, a widow, must now raise Carlo's orphaned child.

Performed in Italian by nonprofessionals (Nello Zordan, Gisela Zdunke, Dedena Morella, and Pino Ubaldo), this film was photographed entirely in Toronto; the music and sound track were prepared in Italy. This film was never released in Canada, but it was released in Italy by Italo-American Films (Pratley *TS* 172).

16. Véronneau, "Mariage …."

17. Denis Bachand, "La Réception des films québécois en France," *Québec Studies* 9 (Fall 1989/Winter 1990): 77.

18. Carlo Mandolini, "Interview with Paul Tana," *Séquences* 158 (June 1992): 17–20.

19. Janick Beaulieu, "*La Sarrasine*," *Séquences* 158 (June 1992): 46–47.

20. A beautiful piece of Canadian (not *québécois*) animation regarding the Inuits, meant for children, but enjoyable to anyone who loves animation and is interested in the Inuit, is *The Woman Who Raised a Bear as Her Son*.
I would point out here the Canadian series on the Inuit boy, Tuktu, which are NFB films prepared for both French-speaking and English-speaking children. Notable is *Tuktu et la Chasse au Caribou*, in the collection *L'Aventure en images*, a two-volume work, the first containing three fiction and documentary films, the second four films, all seven films destined for children. The two volumes are available (without subtitles) from Vedette Visuals.

21. See, e.g., Janick Beaulieu, "*L'Automne sauvage*," *Séquences* 159–60 (September 1992): 60.

22. Carrière, *Femmes* …, 241.

23. Born in Toronto (1935), Owen has collaborated with Québécois filmmakers upon occasion. Notable is his camerawork on *La Lutte* (1961, with Michel Brault, and Claude Jutra); he also did camerawork on another piece of *cinéma direct*, *A Saint-Henri le 5 Septembre* (d. Hubert Aquin, 1962). Above all, he is known

for his directorship of *The Ernie Game* (1967). Ernie (played by Alexis Kanner) is the "American cousin of Pierrot the fool and an unstable drifter who wanders around Montréal" (Marcel Jean in Coulombe 1991, 417). *The Ernie Game* is a *must*, as is also Owens's *Nobody Waved Goodbye*. As Clanfield writes (1987, 89–90), Owen expresses the tensions of the problems of international youth of the 60s. "*Nobody Waved Goodbye* is usually singled out as the groundbreaker," he writes. In this film, the marginal protagonist Peter abandons his pregnant girlfriend in a stolen car. It is to be noted that in 1984 Owen returned to the characters of this film in his *Unfinished Business*. I agree with Clanfield's assessment that it is not on a par with *The Ernie Game*.

24. Thomas Waugh, "Le cinéma anglo-québécois est surtout le fait d'immigrants," *CinémAction: Aujourd'hui le cinéma québécois*, Ed., Louise Carrière, preface by Dominique Noguez (Paris: Cerf-OFQJ, 1986): 66–75.

25. Ibid., 68.

26. The reader should check Janet Edsforth on Paul Almond: she writes at length about this film in her book. Also see Pratley *TS* 100, 101, 189.

27. Michel Euvrard, "'Journey' de Paul Almond: Eurydice deux fois perdue," *Cinéma A Québec* 2; 4 (1972): 9–13.

28. Janet Edsforth, *Paul Almond: The Flame Within* (Ottawa: Canadian Film Institute, 1972), 21.

29. Ibid., 20.

30. Piers Handling, *Canadian Feature Film: 1913–1969* (Ottawa: Canadian Filmography Series No. 10, Canadian Film Institute, 1975), 20.

31. Edsforth, 24.

32. Michel Euvrard, "Le Rôle d'acteur, malheureusement . . . ." *Cinéma/Québec* (March–April 1973): 12. My translation.

33. Denis Bachand, "La Réception . . . ." 77.

Concluding Remarks

1. Noguez, 206–7. My paraphrase and translation.

2. Léo Bonneville, "*Nelligan*," *Séquences* 155 (November 1991): 57–58. My translation.

3. Richard Martineau (with Gilles Carle), "Pour la suite du cinéma québécois," *Séquences* 150 (January 1991): 17.

4. Gilles Carle and Richard Martineau, "Pour la suite du cinéma québécois," *Séquences* 150 (January 1991): 23. (Interview with five young filmmakers.)

5. Ibid., 23–24.

6. Ibid., 24.

7. Francine Laurendeau, "François Girard," *Séquences* 150 (January 1991): 25–27. (Interview.)

8. Richard Martineau, "*Cargo*," *Séquences* 150 (January 1991): 95–96. Review.

9. Léo Bonneville, Review of *La Femme de Pablo Ruiz*, *Séquences* 150 (January 1991): 41–44.

10. Johanne Larue, "*Archangel* et *La Liberté d'une statue:* fictions expérimentales de jeunes cinéastes," *Séquences* 150 (January 1991): 45–46.

11. Martin Girard, "Geneviève Rioux," *Séquences* 150 (January 1991): 29–34. Janick Beaulieu, "Denis Bouchard," same issue of *Séquences*: 35–9. Interviews of authors with these new stars.

12. Léo Bonneville, Interview with Joan Pennefather, *Séquences* 150 (January 1991): 76–80.

13. Pierre Véronneau, "Repères bibliographiques sur le Cinéma québécois des années 80," *Québec Studies* 9 (Fall 1989): 83–84.

14. Bachand, "La Réception ....," 74–5.

15. Seth Feldman, ed, *Take Two: A Tribute to Film in Canada* (Toronto: Irwin Publishing, 1984), 32.

16. André Bazin, *Le Cinéma de la cruauté* (Paris: Flammarion, 1987), 204.

17. Ibid., 206–7.

18. Giles Therrien, "L'Empire et les barbares," *Cinémas: Revue d'études cinématographiques/Journal of Film Studies* 1: 1–2 (1991).

19. Louise Carrière, *Aujourd'hui le cinéma québécois*, 12–16.

21. Ibid., 21.

22. Ibid., 19.

23. Ibid., 19.

24. 1986, ibid., 1–10 (Préface).

Annotated Bibliography of Works Consulted

Publications

Abel, Marie-Christine, André Giguere, and Luc Perrault. *Le Cinéma québécois à l'heure internationale*. Montréal: Les éditions internationales Stanké, 1990.

Alion, Yves. "Entretien avec Denys Arcand." *La Revue du Cinéma. Image et son* 424 (February 1987): 16–17.

Alemany-Galway, Mary. "The contemporary reality of Quebec reflected in two films." *CopieZéro* 28 (June 1986): 8–10. Claims *Joshua Then and Now* (Ted Kotcheff) presents a fable on the death of English power in Québec, and *90 Days* (Giles Walker) presents changes in relations between sexes brought on by the feminist movement.

Andreu, Anne. "Entretien avec Denys Arcand." *L'Evénement du jeudi* (5–11 February 1987): 82–3. Historic and political aspects of *Le Déclin* .... Arcand says: "The Québécois are parasites lodged on the back of the American whale."

Annuaire du cinéma québécois 1989. Montréal: Cinémathèque Québécoise, 1990.

———— *1990*. Montréal: Cinémathèque Québécoise, 1991. These directories contain virtually all information on films one could desire, including complete film credits.

Arcand, Denys. *Le Déclin de l'empire américain* Montréal: Les Editions du Boréal, 1986. *Scénario*.

————. *Duplessis*. Montréal: VLB Editeur, 1978. *Scénario*.

————. Interview with. *Journal Français d'Amérique* (5–25 December 1986): 20–21; 24.

————. *Jésus de Montréal*. Montréal: Les Editions du Boréal, 1989. *Scénario*.

———— (on). See *Cinéma/Québec* and *CopieZéro*, infra.

———— (on). See *Film Review Annual* (1986): 296–306 for abstracts of journal reviews of *Le Déclin*.

Auerbach, Erich. *Mimesis*. Garden City, N.Y.: Doubleday-Anchor, 1957.

Aujourd'hui le cinéma québécois (Dossier). Edited by Louise Carrière; preface by Dominique Noguez. Paris: Cerf: Office Franco-Québécois pour la jeunesse, 1986. Extremely useful publication.

Baby, François. "La Lanterne magique." *Découvrir Québec: Guide culturel*. Sainte-Foye: Les Publications Québec Français, 1987: 79–82. In the 1984 issue, Baby had presented an account of Québec's cinema, stressing its economic difficulties. The 1987 issue asks whether the recent intense activity in *québécois* cinema will continue, and whether the industry will be able to continue its

cinema will continue, and whether the industry will be able to continue its
recent commercial turn without sacrificing quality or becöming complacent.

Bachand, Denis. "La Réception des films québécois en France." *Québec Studies* 9
(Fall 1989/Winter 1990): 69–78.

Backhouse, Charles. *Canadian Government Motion Picture Bureau: 1917–41.*
Ottawa: (Canadian Filmography Series No. 9) Canadian Film Institute, 1974.

Bailey, Cameron. "*I've Heard the Mermaids Singing.*" *Cinéma Canada* (November
1987): 25.

Balthazar, Louis. *French-Canadian Civilization.* An ASCUS paper. Washington,
D.C.: The Association for Canadian Studies in the United States, 1989.

Barthes, Roland. "On the Face of Garbo." In *A Barthes Reader*, edited by Susan
Sontag, 82–84. New York: Hill and Wang, 1982.

Baudelaire, Charles. *Poèmes.* Paris: Hachette, 1951.

Bazin, André. *What Is Cinema?* Edited and translated by Hugh Gray. Vol. 1.
Berkeley: University of California Press, 1987.

_____. *Le Cinéma de la cruauté.* Paris: Flammarion, 1987.

Beattie, Eleanor. *The Handbook of Canadian Film.* Second edition. Toronto:
(PMA/Take One Film Book Series) Peter Martin Assn. Ltd., 1977. Though
dated, gives useful information through 1976–77. Extensive bibliographies
of critiques.

Beauchemin, Yves. *The Alley Cat.* Translated by Sheila Fischman. New York:
(Owl Book Paperback) Henry Holt and Company, 1986.

_____. "Furor over *Cinema Canada's le Matou* review." *CopieZéro* 32 (July
1987): 54. A previous review in *Cinema Canada* (no. 28; March 1986: 6) had
found *Le Matou* (Jean Beaudin) to be antiSemitic.

_____. *Le Matou.* Montréal: Editions Québec-Amérique, 1985. (First copyrighted
in 1981 by Editions Québec/Amérique, Montreal.)

Beaulieu, Janick. "*Agaguk.*" *Séquences* 163 (March 1993): 33–35.

_____. "*Les Amoureuses.*" *Séquences* 164 (May 1993): 48–49.

_____. "*L'Automne sauvage.*" *Séquences* 159–160 (Sept. 1992): 60.

_____. "Denis Bouchard." *Séquences* 150 (January 1991): 35–39. Interview with
Bouchard.

_____. "*La Sarrasine.*" *Séquences* 158 (June 1992): 46–47.

_____ and Johanne Larue. "*Léolo*: Pour (et) Contre." *Séquences* 159/160 (September 1992): 52–53.

Beaupré, Sylvie. "*Simon les nuages.*" *Séquences* 147/148 (September 1990): 80–81.

Bergeron, Léandre. *Dictionnaire de la langue québécoise.* Montréal: VLB Editeur,
1980.

Bersianik, Louky. "L'Empire du statu quo." *Le Devoir* (Saturday, 9 August
1986): C1; C6. Feminist analysis claims *Le Déclin* ... reproduces "clichés de la
politique sexuelle" from beginning to end. [*Le Devoir* ... received many letters
objecting to what was considered a too-limited view as presented in this article.]

Bérubé, Robert-Claude. "*Vincent et Moi.*" *Séquences* 150 (January 1991): 94–95.

Bilodeau, François. "Le Cauchemar d'un fils déçu: *Les Fous de Bassan* d'Yves
Simoneau." *Spirale* 68 (1987): 15.

Bishop, Neil P. "Le personnage français dans quelques romans québécois contemporains." *Voix et Images* 37 (Fall 1987): 90–91.

Blais, Marie-Claire. *Le Sourd dans la ville*. Montréal: Stanké, 1979.

Blouin, Jean, and Jean-Pierre Myette. "Réjean Ducharme." *L'Actualité* (July 1982): 48.

Bluestone, George. *Novels into Films: The Metamorphosis of Fiction into Cinema*. Berkeley: University of California Press, 1957.

Boggs, Joseph M. *The Art of Watching Film*. 2d ed. Mountain View, Calif.: Mayfield Publishing Company, 1985.

Boileau, Josée. "Images récentes dans les films à succès." *Femmes et Cinéma Québécois*, Ed. Louise Carrière. Montréal: Boréal Express, 1983: 113–29.

Bolduc, Denis. "Le 'bébé' d'Yves Simoneau." *Le Journal de Québec* (20 December 1986): 3A. On *Les Fous de Bassan*.

Bonneville, Léo. "A la recherche du *Sexe des étoiles*." *Séquences* 163 (March 1993): 10–12.

———. "André Melançon." *Séquences* 127 (December 1986): 20–26.

———. *Le Cinéma québécois par ceux qui le font*. Montréal: Editions Paulines, 1978. Treats, among others, Paul Almond, Denys Arcand, Jean Beaudin, Michel Brault, Gilles Carle, Jean Chabot, Mireille Dansereau, Georges Dufaux, André Forcier, Jacques Godbout, Gilles Groulx, Claude Jutra, Jean-Claude Labrecque, Arthur Lamothe, Jean-Pierre Lefebvre, Jean-Claude Lord, Francis Mankiewicz, André Melançon, Pierre Perrault, Anne Claire Poirier, and Thomas Vamos.

———. *Dossiers de cinéma*. Montréal et Ottawa: Fides, 1968.

———. "La folle aventure des *Fous de Bassan*." *Séquences* 126 (October 1986): 43–47. Interview with Yves Simenon on the filming of *Les Fous* ....

———. "Jean Beaudry." *Séquences* 147/148 (September 1990): 23–29. Information on *Jacques et Novembre* and on Beaudry's collaboration with Rock Demers (*Les Matins infidèles*; *Pas de répit pour Mélanie*).

———. "Joan Pennefather." *Séquences* 150 (January 1991): 76–80.

———. "*Manuel, le fils emprunté*." *Séquences* 150 (January 1991): 99–100. Finds in his review that *Manuel* is a beautiful film, showing the influence of adults on young people, and also showing that young people should have a purpose in life.

———. "Michael Rubbo." *Séquences* 150 (January 1991): 60–63. Rubbo the painter speaks of his films, especially of his recent film entitled *Vincent et moi*, made on the centennial of Van Gogh's death. Declares that the message is to never give up.

———. "*Nelligan*." *Séquences* 155 (November 1991): 57–58.

———. "Retrouver Nelligan (*l'Ange noir*)." *Séquences* 152 (June 1991): 17–24. Interviews with Favreau and actors of this film; information on the life of Nelligan and on his friends; selected poems.

———. "Une visite chez *La Postière*." *Séquences* 156 (January 1992): 30–34. Interview with Gilles Carle.

Bor, Aaron. "An Interview with Léa Pool." *Québec Studies* 9 (Fall 1989): 63–68.

Bordwell, David. *Making Meaning: Inference and Rhetoric in the Interpretation of Cinema*. Cambridge: Harvard Film Studies, Harvard Univ. Press, 1989. Canada not included.

———. *Narration in the Fiction Film*. Madison: University of Wisconsin Press, 1985.

Bottin professionnel du cinéma. Montréal: Conseil Québécois pour la Diffusion du Cinéma, 1972.

Bouchard, René. *Filmographie d'Albert Tessier*. Montréal: Editions du Boréal Express, 1973.

───. "Un Précuseur du cinéma direct." *Cinéma/Québec* Part 1: 51; Vol. 6 (1977): 19−24. Part 2: 52; Vol. 6 (1977): 27−33. Part 1 studies Mgr. Albert Tessier's photographic and cinematographic work; Tessier (1895−1976) is viewed as "one of the great *précuseurs*" of the *cinéma direct*. Part 2 is an interview between Bouchard and Tessier a few months before his death. Bouchard's "biography" of Tessier (33) is also an essential filmography.

Boyum, Joy Gould. *Double Exposure: Fiction into Film*. New York: Universe Books, 1985.

Brochu, André. *Le singulier pluriel*. Montréal: l'Hexagone, 1992. Contains essays on André Langevin's *Poussière sur la ville* as filmed by Arthur Lamothe (1965−8; 95 min.); on *Les Fous* . . . .

Brûlé, Michel. *Pierre Perrault ou un cinéma national, essai d'analyse socio-cinématographique*. Montréal: Les Presses de l'Université de Montréal, 1974.

───. "Un constat d'impuissance à l'égard des groupes d'opposition." *Cinéma/Québec* 4:1 (December 1974): 14−17.

───. *Vers une politique du cinéma au Québec, document de travail*. Québec: Direction générale du cinéma et de l'audiovisuel, ministère des Communications, 1978.

Brunette, Peter, and David Wills. *Screen/Play: Derrida and Film Theory*. Princeton, N.J.: Princeton University Press, 1989.

Buriana, Michel. "Claude Berri." *Séquences* 152 (June 1991): 31−42. Extensive coverage of this French director, including commentary on his making of *Le Vieil homme et l'enfant*, Gabrielle Roy's novella.

Buriana, Michel. "[Interview with] Jean-Claude Lauzon." *Séquences* 158 (June 1992): 32−34; 41−44. Discusses *Léolo*.

Burnett, Ron. *Explorations in Film Theory*. Bloomington, Indiana: Indiana University Press, 1991. 22 Essays from *Ciné-Tracts*, edited by Burnett.

───. Review by Janis L. Pallister, *Journal of Popular Culture*. 26; 2 (Fall 1992): 168−9.

Canadian Culture at the Crossroads: Film, Television, and the Media in the 1960s. [Wendy Michener Symposium, York Univ., 1989. Participants: Douglas Leiterman, Robert Daudelin, Peter Morris, June Callwood.] ECW Press, 1989.

The Canadian Encyclopedia. Edmonton, Alberta: Hurtig Publishers, Ltd., 1988. Second Edition.

Canby, Vincent. "Saving the Huron Indians: Piety Awry" (*Black Robe*). *The New York Times* (Sunday, 3 November 1991): Y21−2. (Review.) Faults Bluteau as "passive and rather wimpish . . . ."

Caouette, Ch. E. "Un cinéaste qui voit bien . . . avec le coeur!" *CopieZéro* 31 (March 1987): 18.

Carbonneau, Alain. "*Kamouraska*, roman et film." *Revue d'Histoire Littéraire du Québec et du Canada français* 11 (Winter-Spring 1986): 93−100. "Far from being a copy too close to the novel, the film reworks the signs within its stripped down nature . . . ; it thus operates a symbolizing appropriation. From scripting to projection a redistribution of the structures of the imagination is brought about." (My translation.)

Carle, Gilles. "Gilles Carle s'explique." *Cinéma/Québec* 51; vol. 6; 1 (1977). An interview with Carle on his film *L'Ange et la femme*.

———. w/ Richard Martineau. "Pour la suite du cinéma québécois." *Séquences* 150 Janvier 1991: 17–24. (Interview with five young filmmakers.)

Carrière, Louise. "A propos des films faits par des femmes au Québec." *CopieZéro* #11 (1981): 44–51.

———. "Et si on changeait la view?" Excellent article on animation at the ONF, (1968–1984), followed by a brief appreciation of the work of "Pierre Hébert." In Patrick Leboutte's *Cinemas du Québec*: 67–70; 71–72, q.v. infra.

———. See also *CinemAction*, infra; and *Femmes et cinéma* . . . , infra.

Cauchon, Paul. "Simoneau et *Les Fous de Bassan*: 'On a fait un mur contre les vagues." (Interview with Yves Simoneau). *Le Devoir* (26 July 1986): C1 and C4. Simoneau tells of the problems facing him in making the cinematographic adaptation of the novel.

Chaban de Santandreu, Patricia. "*Leolo*." (sic.) *Journal français d'Amérique* 15:10 (30 avril - 13/ mai 1993): 13.

Chabot, Claude; Michel Larouche; Denise Perusse; et Pierre Véronneau, Eds. *Le Cinéma québécois des années 80*. Montréal: Cinémathèque Québécoise/Musée du cinéma, 1989. Reviewed by Jean-Claude Jaubert, *French Review* [December 1990]: 374–5.

Champ-Libre. Montréal: Les Cahiers du Québec, Ed. Hurtubise; 1971 ff.
Periodical on world cinema, incl. Québec. Spring 1973 issue has article by Pierre Véronneau on *débuts* of Québec cinema (59 ff.) and article on Arcand (68 ff.).

Charbonneau, Jean. "Mise au point sur une image du père québécois." *CopieZéro* 36 (August 1988): 13–15. Diabolical image of the "father" in the police and godlike image of same through Marcel's father in *Un Zoo la nuit*.

Chassay, Jean-François. "Outrager le texte: *Mario*, de Jean Beaudin." *Revue d'histoire littéraire du Québec et Canada français* 11 (Winter–Spring 1986): 113–16. In cinematographic adaptations, too great a fidelity to the book leads to monumental failure; too great a respect for the author and his/her text leads to a "confusion of languages." "To intelligently account for a [literary] work on the screen, it must be adapted to filmic language. Jean Beaudin did that with his film *Mario*, drawn from Claude Jasmin's novel, *La Sablière*." (My translation.)

La Châtelaine. Special Issue on Women's Films. (April 1990).

Cherry, Nanciann. "Historical film packs power but forgets soul" (*Black Robe*). *The (Toledo) Blade*. (28 December 1991): P-4. One of the many critics who (erroneously) faults Bluteau's performance.

Ciment, Michel. "Entretien avec Denys Arcand sur *Le Déclin* . . . ." *Positif* 312 (February 1987): 16–20.

"Cinéastes du Québec." Series published by Conseil Québécois pour la Diffusion du Cinéma. Vol. 2. (1975–6) Gilles Carle (reedition); Vol. 3. J. P. Lefebvre; Vol. 4. Claude Jutra; Vol. 5. Perrault; Vol. 6. (1971) Arthur Lamothe; Vol. 7. Labrecque; Vol. 8. (1971) Denys Arcand; Vol. 9. Jacques Godbout; Vol. 10. Fernand Dansereau; Vol. 11. Michel Brault; Vol. 12. (1974) Jacques Leduc.

Cinéma au féminin. Montréal: (Cinéma Libre) Bibliothèque nationale du Québec, 1990.

Cinéma aujourd'hui, Le: Films, théories, nouvelles approches. Edited by Michel Larouche. Montréal: Guernica, 1988. (See Larouche, below.)

Cinéma au Québec: Bilan d'une industrie. Edited by Jean-Pierre Tadros. Montréal: Les éditions Cinéma/Québec, 1975. Technical information, cataloging, addresses, statistics, etc.

(CinémAction:) Aujourd'hui le cinéma québécois. Edited by Louise Carrière, preface by Dominique Noguez. Paris: Cerf-OFQJ, 1986. (164) *CinémAction* is under the general editorship of Guy Hennebelle. See also under *Aujourd'hui*, above.

Cinéma et histoire. Montréal: Yves Lever et AQEC, 1986.

Acts of the Association québécoise des études cinématographiques, 15 november, 1986's colloquy. Notable are "*Le Festin des morts* and the Jesuits" by Marcel Lefebvre (41–88) and "Histoire chez Denys Arcand" by Marcel Jean (49–53).

Cinema/Québec. Special issue on Michel Brault's *Les Ordres* 4:1 (December 1974).

―――――. Special issue on Political Censorship (June–July 1971): 19–37. Censorship by Sydney Newman (Commissioner of the ONF) of Denys Arcand's *On est au coton* (by withdrawal and editing); censorship of Perrault's *Un Pays sans bon sens*, and his *L'Acadie, l'Acadie*. Discussion ("De la notion de pays à la représentation de la nation") held among Michel Brûlé, Fernand Dumont, and Pierre Perrault, largely about Acadia, but also on *Un Pays sans bon sens*. Perrault tells how because of *cinéma direct* he did not have to rely on written history or his memory (in *Pour la suite du monde*, which was a communal enterprise), and how in his films it is the camera that observes. Interview with Arcand, "La genèse du film": 32. Denys Arcand and Gerald Godin converse in "'Un film didactique'": 33–34.

―――――. Special issue on politics in and of the Québec cinéma: "Pour décoloniser le cinéma québécois." 4:4 (1975). Discussion of "*loi-cadre.*" Also of the Institut du Cinéma, whose principal objective was to give the Québec film industry a chance to get established and to develop in such a way as to reflect the cultural specificity of the Québécois. It assured *québécois* cinema its *droit de cité*.

"Cinéma québécois, nouveaux courants, nouvelles critiques." *Dérives* 2 (Montréal, 1986.)

Cinéma québécois: tendances et prolongements, Le. Edited by Renald Bérubé and Yvan Patry. Montréal: Editions Sainte-Marie, 1968. Articles (1) on "Pierre Perrault et la découverte d'un langage," by Maximilien Laroche [25–48]; (2) on J. P. Lefebvre, by André Larsen [49–54]; (3) on the "Trajectoire de Don Owen," by Louise and Yvan Patry [55–82]; and a "Repertoire des cinéastes." Now quite out of date.

Cinémas canadiens et québécois. Montréal: Collège Ahuntsic, August 1977. A history from the silent film to 1977; chiefly a list of titles and dates.

Cinéma: une question de survie et d'excellence, Le. Edition project director, Thérèse Gagné Krieber. Québec: Gouvernement du Québec, 1982. (Rapport de la commision d'étude sur le cinéma et audovisuel.)

50 ans de l'ONF, Les. Montréal: Editions Saint-Martin, 1989. Articles on documentaries (39–50), fictional films (51–64), animation (65–78), English production (79–92), Women at the ONF, esp. Anne Claire Poirier (93–108), technical services (109–24), distribution (125–38), and chronology of the ONF (163–66).

Cixous, Hélène and Catherine Clement. *The Newly Born Woman* . Minneapolis: University of Minnesota Press, 1986.

Clanfield, David. *Canadian Film*. Toronto: Oxford University Press, 1987. Excellent quick reference with many brief analyses included.

Claude, Renée. "Claude Renée rencontre Léa Pool." *Montréal, ce mois-ci*. (June 1986): 12−14. An interview in which L. P. reveals her concept of physical beauty.

Collins, Maynard. *Norman McLaren*. Ottawa: Canadian Film Institute, 1976.

Conley, Tom. *Film Hieroglyphs*. Minneapolis: University of Minnesota Press, 1991.

CopieZéro Annuaire (1985). "Improvisation sur un thème connu." Josée Beaudet speaks about her first solo directing with her *Film d'Ariane*: 8−9.

―――. Special issue on Denys Arcand. 34−35 (December 1987−March 1988). Includes articles by Pierre Véronneau, Marcel Jean, Roger Bourdeau, Michel Larouche, Henri-Paul Chevrier, Gérald Godin, Luce Guilbeault, Denise Pérusse, and others, on the films of Arcand through *Le Déclin* .... Contains a filmography and a bibliography. See also Godin, Gérald below; and Pérusse, Denise below.

―――. Special issue on Michel Brault. 5 (1980).

―――. Special issue on the Documentary. 30 (December 1986). Remarks on: *Quel numéro?* (*What number?*), *Journal inachevé*, *Au rhythme de mon coeur*, *Le Futur intérieur*, and *Albédo*.

―――. Special issue on Georges Dufaux "cinéaste du direct." 1 (1979).

―――. Special issue on André Forcier. 19 (1983). (Synopsis of *Kalamazoo*: 13).

―――. Special issue on Claude Jutra. 33 (September 1987). (Hommages following his death.) Article by Ralph Thomas, "Comment Claude Jutra en vint à travailler au Canada anglais" (34 ff.): Jutra's *Ada*, filmed in Toronto; his *Dreamspeaker*, filmed in Vancouver; and his *Seer Was Here*, the most popular of his English-language films; also discusses his documentary from Cuba, *Arts Cuba*.

―――. Special issue on André Melançon. 31 (March 1987). In an interview Melançon discusses his works, especially *Bach et Bottine*: 4−7. Article by Pierre Véronneau, "Observation 1, 2, 3, ...": 9−11; article by Bernard Emond, "Qui parle?" on *Les Vrais Perdants* and *La Guerre des tuques*: 12−13.

―――. Special issue on Anne Claire Poirier. 23 (February 1985).

Corliss, Richard. "The Art of Childhood." *Time* 141:14 (5 April 1993): 60−61. Refreshingly finds that "Hollywood can still spin a cute kids' fable, but a film from Quebec gets the magic and fear right." The review concentrates on Lauzon's *Léolo*, which "sees childhood as the acid test for maturity."

Coulombe, Michel, and Marcel Jean. *Le Dictionnaire du cinéma québécois*. Montréal: Boréal, 1988; 2d ed. 1991.

Coutu, Angèle. *Le Journal de Montréal* (29 November 1986): 16. In an interview, the actress speaks of her role as Maureen in *Les Fous de Bassan*.

Dandurand, Anne. "Léa Pool et le cinéma du dedans." *La Châtelaine* (February 1986): 40−43.

Dansereau, Fernand. "Le cinéma québécois: un cinéma colonisé." *Cinéma/Québec* 3: 9/10 (August 1973): 81−85. Despite being a colonized cinema and perhaps because of it, "We invented *cinéma direct* in Québec ... The *cinéma direct* came to us from elsewhere ...; but we caused it to flourish and ... we established with our milieu a first living and functional artists' connection in which foreign confirmation played a minimal role" (82). Pierre Perrault's films are plugged into *a cultural milieu that is their own*. Marketing, however, was and has remained a problem. "If *Les Ordres* is not sabotaged when distributed ... [Brault] will perhaps have opened a valid hypothesis for at least a part of *québécois* cinema (83).

[This issue of *Cinéma/Québec* devoted to "the grave state of dependence of *québécois* cinema," and to the "situation" of new young directors.]

Dansereau, Mireille. "*Le Sourd dans la ville.*" *Lumière* 2:7 (May–June 1987): 8.

Dassas, Véronique. "*Le Déclin de l'empire américain.*" *CopieZéro* 34–35 (December 1987–March 1988): 56–57.

Daudelin, Robert. "The Encounter Between Fiction and the Direct Cinema." In *Self-Portrait*, edited by Pierre Véronneau and Piers Handling, 94. Ottawa: Canadian Film Institute, 1980.

———. *Vingt ans de cinéma au Canada français.* Québec: Ministère des Affaires culturelles, 1967.

Delaney, Bill. "*Black Robe.*" *Magill's Cinema Annual.* Englewood Cliffs, N.J.: Salem Press, 1992: 51–54.

De Lauretis, Teresa. *Alice Doesn't (Feminism, Semiotics, Cinema).* Bloomington: Indiana University Press, 1984.

Demers, Pierre. "La Leçon du cinéma 'nature': L'abbé Proulx et le cinématographe." *Cinéma/Québec* 4:6 (1974): 17–33. Informative dossier on Proulx as a "pioneer of the *québécois* documentary." Complete study of Proulx's work, filmography, and quotations from his writings.

———. "*Le Cinéma en question*: Chabot et 'Ti-gars' Vertov." *Cinéma/Québec* 3/8 (October 1974): 37–8. Most Québécois filmmakers turn to the reality of the daily life of Quebeckers for their films. Certain filmmakers (Roger Frappier and Claude Jutra) stress that *québécois* cinema, impregnated with this reality, is directed away from commercial cinema, and is more turned toward the people than toward the bourgeoisie.

Denault, Jocelyne. "Le Cinéma féminin au Québec." *CopieZéro* 11 (1981): 36–43.

Deslandes, Jeanne. "*La Demoiselle Sauvage.*" *Séquences* 155 (November 1991): 56–57.

Dictionnaire du cinéma québécois. Compiled by Michel Houle and Alain Julien. Montréal: Fides, 1978.

Dictionnaire du cinéma québécois, Le. See Coulombe.

Documents in Canadian Film. Edited by Douglas Fetherling. Peterborough, Canada: Broadview Press, Ltd., 1988.
Review: Janis L. Pallister, *Journal of Popular Film and Television.* 17; 4 (Winter 1990): 173.

Donohoe, Joseph I., Jr., ed. *Essays on Quebec Cinema.* East Lansing: (Can. Series #2) Michigan State University Press, 1991.

———. "*Sonatine* in Context: A Neglected Film of Micheline Lanctôt." In *Essays on Quebec Cinema*, edited by Joseph I. Donohoe, Jr., 157–167. East Lansing: (Can. Series #2) Michigan State University Press, 1991.

Dubeau, Alain. "*Robe noire.*" *Séquences* 155 (November 1991): 55−56. Finds the film superficial. ("In spite of all its aesthetic and anthropological qualities, *R. n.* lacks substance.")

Dubuc, Madeleine. "'Les Fous de Bassan' à l'île Bonaventure." *La Presse* (Saturday, 19 July 1986): E1 and E10. Difficulties of production. Concludes that "Anne Hébert est bien servie."

Dumas, François Ribadeau. *Dossiers secrets de la sorcellerie et de la magie noire.* Paris: Editions Pierre Belfond, 1971.

Dussault, Serge. "*Les Fous de Bassan.* Yves Simoneau: un artisan passionné." *La Presse* (Saturday, 20 December 1986): E1 and E16. Interview with Simoneau in which the latter confesses his interest in Orson Welles. Dussault claims Simoneau makes one think of Stanley Kubrick." We learn that the film was made in Gaspésie on the île Bonaventure. However, no one has a *gaspésien* accent; the actors are all French or Québécois. (Also that *Les Fous* ... cost three million dollars; *Pouvoir intime* one million, seven hundred thousand dollars.)

_____. "Jouer le fou du village." *La Presse* (Saturday, 20 December 1986): E16. Short piece on Lothaire Bluteau.

Dwoskin, Stephen. *Film Is the International Free Cinema.* Woodstock, N.Y.: The Overlook Press, 1985.

Edsforth, Janet. *Paul Almond: The Flame Within.* Ottawa: Canadian Film Institute, 1972.

Elder, R. Bruce. "The Cinema We Need." *Canadian Forum* (February 1985): 32−35.

_____. *Image and Identity: Reflections on Canadian Film and Culture.* Waterloo, Ontario: Wilfrid Laurier University Press, 1989. An examination of the unique qualities of Canadian cinema, situating it within the broad spectrum of Canadian culture as a whole. There is little to do with Québec's cinema here.

Élia, Maurice. "*Hotel Chronicles.*" *Séquences* 150 (January 1991): 97−98.

Émond, Bernard. "Qui parle?" *CopieZéro* 31 (March 1987): 12−13. On *Les Vrais Perdants* and *La Guerre des tuques.* (Special issue of *CopieZéro* on André Melançon.)

Essays on Quebec Cinema. Edited by Joseph I. Donohoe, Jr. East Lansing, Mich.: Michigan State University, 1991. Contains contributions by Paul Warren, Philip Reines, Esther Pelletier, Pierre Perrault, Jean Pierre Lefebvre, Lucie Roy, Cedric May, Janis L. Pallister, Richard Vernier, Adrian van den Hoven, Joseph I. Donohoe Jr., and Marcel Jean.

Éthier, Chantal. "'Le Déclin' en France et aux Etats-Unis: coup d'oeil sur une mise en marché−Qui fait quoi?" *CopieZéro* 35 (April−May 1987): 16. Gives a description of the steps and stages in the launching of this film.

Euvrard, Michel. "Le Rôle d'acteur, malheureusement ...." *Cinéma/Québec* (March−April 1973): 11−14. Interview between Euvrard and Geneviève Bujold just prior to release of *Kamouraska.*

_____. "'Journey' de Paul Almond: Eurydice deux fois perdue." *Cinéma/Québec* 2; 4 (1972): 9−13. Euvrard discusses the cold reception this film received from the critics.

Evans, Gary. *In the National Interest: A Chronicle of the National Film Board from 1949–1989.* Toronto: University of Toronto Press, 1991. Insufficient reflection of the French minority in the NFB (ONF). Many portraits, analyses of films.

———. *John Grierson and the National Film Board.* Toronto: University of Toronto Press, 1984.

Falardeau, Pierre. "La Liberté n'est pas une marque de yogourt." *Lumières* 21 (Winter 1990): 10–12.

Faucher, Carol. *La Production française à l'ONF. 25 ans en perspective.* Montréal: (Les Dossiers de la Cinémathèque 14) Cinémathèque Québécoise, 1984.

Feldman, Seth, Ed. *Take Two: A Tribute to Film in Canada.* Toronto: Irwin Publishing, 1984. Synopses. Articles are often slick and glib, but see James Leach's article on Paul Almond's trilogy and, in Part 3, David Clanfield on *cinéma direct.* See also Harcourt on Perrault and Brenda Longfellow's pedantic piece dealing with Mireille Dansereau's *La Vie rêvée* and Paule Baillargeon's "brechtian" *Cuisine rouge.*

Feldman, Seth, and Joyce Nelson. *Canadian Film Reader.* Take One Film Series Toronto: Peter Martin, 1977. Contains articles on Perrault (144–52); Don Owen (160–78); *Mon oncle Antoine* by Bruce Elder (194–8), Gilles Carle by Piers Handling (199–207), interview with Denys Arcand (217–31), interview with Mireille Dansereau on *La Vie rêvée* (250–57).

Femmes et cinéma québécois. Edited by Louise Carrière. Montréal: Boréal Express, 1983. Contributions by Louise Beaudet, Sophie Bissonnette, Danielle Blais, Josée Boileau, Louise Carrière, Monique Caverni, Nicole Hubert (with Diane Poitras), Pascale Laverrière, Marquise Lepage, Jacqueline Levitin, Marilú Mallet, and Christiane Tremblay-Daviault.

Fetherling, Douglas. See *Documents.*

Film Canadiana. Montréal: National Film Board, 1980–82, 1983, and 1985. History of the Canadian film.

The Film Center Gazette [Chicago School of the Art Institute] Vol 18; no. 11 (November 1990). Remarks on André Forcier's "Rabelaisian" films.

Film Quarterly (Winter 1986–7): 13–19.

Fisette, Jean. "Chroniques." *Voix et Images* 39 (printemps 1988): 486.

Fortin, Lucien. "Les expériences de Gilles Carle." *CopieZéro* 37 (October 1988): 35–37.

Fournier-Renaud, Madeleine, and Pierre Véronneau. *Ecrits sur le cinéma (bibliographie québécoise 1911–1981).* Montréal: La Cinémathèque Québécoise, 1982.

Frank, Marcie. "The Camera and the Speculum: David Cronenberg's *Dead Ringers.*" *PMLA* 106, 3 (May 1991): 459–470.

Gagnon, Lysiane. "French Culture in Quebec." *Canada Today/Canada Aujourd'hui.* 20:1 (1989). [Washington: D.C.: Canadian Embassy, 1989]: 6–8.

Garrity, Henry A. "Subversive discourse in Yves Simoneau's *Pouvoir intime.*" *Québec Studies* 9 (Fall 1989): 29–37.

———. "The Politics of Subversion in Jean-Claude Lauzon's *Un Zoo la nuit.*" In *Film and Society*, edited by Douglas Radcliff Umstead, 54–60. Kent, Ohio: Kent State University Press, 1990. Proceedings of 8th International Film Conference.

Gaudreault, Léonce. "Yves Simoneau élargit son horizon de cinéaste." *Le Soleil* (Saturday, 20 December 1986): E1. On *Les Fous de Bassan*, whose village sets were constructed and filmed on l'île Bonaventure.

————. "Une oeuvre poétique étonnante: à voir!" *Le Soleil* (Saturday, 20 December 1986): E2. Review of *Les Fous de Bassan*. "On s'attarde ... sur la beauté frissonnante de ce décor du début du monde ...."

Gaulin, Suzanne. "Pool's Splash." *Cinema Canada* (October 1984): 8. Interview with the Québécoise filmmaker, Léa Pool.

Gay, Richard. "Canada's Young and Diversified Film Industry," in *Canada Today/Canada Aujourdhui*. 20:1 (1989). [Washington: D.C.: Canadian Embassy, 1989]: 19–20.

————. "Jacques Godbout, 'La gammick' ou Comment les gangsters québécois sont aussi victimes de l'impérialisme américain." *Cinéma//Québec* 4:3 (1974): 33–36. Interview with Godbout. Compares *La Gammick* to Cocteau's *Voix humaine*. Says Godbout wanted to show "the manipulation of people that is always done with an open line."

Gélinas, Gratien. *Tit-Coq*. Montréal: Les Editions de l'Homme, 1968. This edition illustrated with photos by Henri Paul.

Girard, Martin. "Geneviève Rioux." *Séquences* 150 (January 1991): 29–34.

Godbout, Jacques. "*Bingo*: Critique de gauche ou critique gauche." *Cinéma/Québec* 3: 6/7 (1973): 34–37.

————. *L'Ecran du bonheur*. Montréal: Boréal, 1990. On the social aspects of Québec television.

Goddard, Peter. "At the Genies." *The Toronto Star* (Wednesday, 21 March 1990): C1. Confirms the contention that only "a tiny fraction of" Canadians appreciate and attend Canadian films.

Godfrey, Stephen. "A ride on a feminist rollercoaster." *Toronto Globe and Mail*. (Friday, 15 June 1990): C8.

Godin, Gérald. "Un film didactique." *Cinéma/Québec* (juin/juillet 1971): 33–34. Interview with Denys Arcand.

————. "Les origines: *On Est au Coton*." *CopieZéro* 34–5 (December 1987–March 1988): 45–9. Draws parallels between *Le Déclin* ... and the earlier *On est au coton*.

Goyette, Louis. "L'Opéra revisité: *Réjeanne Padovani* et *Au Pays de Zom*." *CopieZéro* 37 (October 1988): 27–31.

Graham, Gerald G. *Canadian Film Technology, 1896–1986*. Cranbury, N.J.: University of Delaware Press, 1987.
Review by Janis L. Pallister. *Journal of Popular Film and Television*. 18; 3 (Fall 1990): 131.

Green, Mary Jean. "Filmer Anne Hébert: *Les Fous de Bassan* et le regard masculin." CIEF Annual Meeting. Montréal, 14 April 1988.

————. "Léa Pool's *La Femme de l'hôtel* and Women's Film in Quebec." *Québec Studies* 9 (Fall 1989): 49–62.

Green, Roberta F. "*Strangers in Good Company*." *Magill's Cinema Annual*. Englewood Cliffs, N.J.: Salem Press, 1990: 376–79. Director Scott herself places this film among the new "big thing" of films about elderly people (379).

Guénette, Jean T. *National Film, Television and Sound Archives*. Public Archives of Canada: Minister of Supply and Services, 1983. Archives, according to subject areas.

———— and Jacques Gagné. *Inventory of the Collections of the National Film, Television and Sound Archives*. Public Archives of Canada: Minister of Supply and Services, 1983. Especially useful are a photo of the cast of *Les Plouffe*, the montage of frames for the documentary *Rhapsody in Two Languages*, and stills of *Whispering City*, *Le Rossignol et les cloches*, *A Chairy Tale*, and *Promised Land*.

Haim, Monica. "Le Lecteur fait le film." *CopieZero* (22 July 1987): 6–7. *Le Déclin*'s real subject is history, or the historical experiences the sexes have in common.

Halpern, Sylvie. "André Melançon, le cinéaste aux enfants." *L'Actualité* (April 1987): 11–12, 14.

Hamblet, Edwin. *La Littérature canadienne francophone*. Paris: Hatier, 1987.

Hamelin, Lucien and Lise Walser. *(Petit Guide du) Cinéma québécois*. Montréal: Conseil Québécois pour la Diffusion du Cinéma, 1973.

Handling, Piers. *Canadian Feature Films: 1913–1969*. Canadian Filmography Series No. 10. Ottawa: Canadian Film Institute, 1975.

———. Chapter entitled "Canada." In *World Cinema since 1945*, edited by William Luhr, 86–115. New York: Ungar, 1987. A panoramic view of Canadian cinema, with scattered critical insights. Finds major theme to be study of "victim figures" (103).

———. *Derek May: The Search for Country*. Ottawa: Canadian Film Institute, 1980.

Harcourt, Peter. "*The Cat in the Sack* ..." *Magill's Survey of Cinema (Foreign Language Films)*. Vol. 1 Englewood Cliffs N.J., Salem Press, 1985: 487–91.

———. "*Il ne faut pas mourir pour ça.*" *Magill's Survey of Cinema (Foreign Language Films)*. Vol. 3 Englewood Cliffs, N.J.: Salem Press, 1985: 1450–54.

———. *Jean Pierre Lefebvre*. Ottawa: Canadian Film Institute, 1981.

Hébert, Anne. *La Cage*, suivi de *L'Ile de la demoiselle*. Paris: Ed. du Seuil, 1990.

———. *Les Enfants du sabbat*. Paris: Ed. du Seuil, 1975.

———. *Les Fous de Bassan*. Paris: Ed. du Seuil, 1982.

———. *Héloïse*. Toronto: Newpress Canadian Classics, 1982.

———. *Kamouraksa*. Paris: Ed. du Seuil, 1970; 1982.

———. *Shadows in the Wind*. Toronto: Newpress Canadian Classics, 1983.

Hébert, Pierre. "Cinéma québécois—cinéma d'animation québécois?" In *Cinémas du Québec*, edited by Patrick Leboutte, 73–74. Crisnée [Liège]: Editions Yellow Now, 1986.
Brief history, stressing effects of establishment of NFB in Montréal ("in 1954") on Québec animation; theory that Québec animation shows same tendencies as other types of cinema from Québec, but may have more connection with animation cinema on an international scale than with *québécois* cinematography.

———. "Les fruits de l'hiver." *Voix & Images* 42 (Spring 1989): 508–12. Remarks on *Les Tisserands du pouvoir*.

Heller, Scott. "Once-theoretical Scholarship on Film ...." *Chronicle of Higher Education* (21 March 1990): A6–8, A-12.

Héroux, Justine. Interview with ..., in *Le Journal de Montréal* (13 December 1986): 16. Héroux explains why she decided to produce *Les Fous* ....

Hommage à M. L. Ernest Ouimet. Montréal: La Cinémathèque Canadienne, 1966.

Houle, Michel, and Alain Julien. *Dictionnaire du cinéma québécois*. Montréal: Fides, 1978.

International Index to Film Periodicals. An annual annotated guide to writings on film and films. Many films discussed in my text are entered in this index.

Jacob, Suzanne. *Laura Laur.* Paris: Seuil, 1983.

Jaffe, Chapelle, ed. *Who's Who in Canadian Film and Television.* Toronto: Academy of Canadian Cinema & Television, 1986.

Jasmin, Claude. *Rimbaud, mon beau salaud.* Montréal: Editions du Jour, 1969.

──────. *La Sablière (Mario).* Ottawa: Leméac/Poche-Québec, 1986. (First pub. in 1979.)

Jaubert, Jean-Claude. "La Représentation du pouvoir dans le cinéma québécois." *Cinéma/Québec* 54, 6, 4 (1978): 18–23. Analyzes images of power in films from three periods of Québec history: (1) the Duplessist era (*La Petite Aurore* ...; *Les Brûlés*); (2) la Révolution tranquille (*Le Chat dans le sac, Poussière sur la ville, Il ne faut pas mourir pour ça*); (3) the October 1970 crisis and the resumption of power under Robert Bourassa in the 1973 elections (*Réjeanne Padovani, Les Ordres,* followed by *La Vraie Nature de Bernadette, Isis au 8, La Piastre, Les Mâles, Le Bonhomme; Tu brûles, tu brûles; Noël et Juliette; Bulldozer*).

Jean Pierre Lefebvre: The Québec Connection. Edited by Susan Barrowclough. London: British Film Institute, 1982.

John of the Cross, Saint. *Living Flame of Love.* N.Y.: [Image] Doubleday, 1962.

Johnston, Claire. *"Women's Cinema as Counter-Cinema."* In *Movies and Methods.* Edited by Bill Nichols. Berkeley: University of California Press, 1976: I, 208–17.

Journal Français d'Amérique. Supplément spécial [sur le] Québec. "Les Québécois, qui sont-ils?" *Journal Français d'Amerique* (5–18 'April 1991): 1–24.

Jutra, Claude. *Mon oncle Antoine.* Montréal: Art Global, 1979.

Kaplan, E. Ann. *Women & Film: Both Sides of the Camera.* New York: Methuen, 1983.

Katz, Ephraim. *The Film Encyclopedia.* New York: (Perigree) Putnam, 1979.

Lacasse, Germain. *L'Historiographe (Les débuts du spectacle cinématographique au Québec).* Montréal: (*Les Dossiers de la cinémathèque* 15) Cinémathèque Québécoise, 1985: 48–9.

Lafrance, André A., and Gilles Marsolais. *Cinéma d'ici.* Montréal; Ottawa: Leméac, 1975. Now dated study; gives history of the ONF, discussion of direct cinema (77–130); the feature length film (131–82), and commercial successes.

Lamartine, Thérèse. *Elles cinéastes ad lib 1895–1981.* Montréal: Ed. du Remue-ménage, 1985.

Lamonde, Yvan. "Indirectement le cinéma direct: réflexions autour d'un cinéma." *Cinéma/Québec* 4:1 (December 1974): 22–24.

──────, and Pierre-François Hébert, eds. *Le Cinéma au Québec: Essai de statistique historique (1896 à nos jours).* Québec: Institut Québécois de Recherche sur la Culture, 1981. A sociological, statistical study; not useful for general reference, history, or aesthetics of *québécois* cinema.

──────, and Raymond Montpetit. *Le Parc Sohmer de Montréal, 1889–1919.* Québec: Institut Québécois de Recherche sur la Culture, 1986.
Review: Janis L. Pallister, *Journal of Popular Culture* 23:2 (Fall 1989): 169–70.

Lamy, Suzanne. Commentary on *Anne Trister. Spirales* (Summer 1987): 8.

_____. "Le roman de l'irresponsabilité." *Spirales* (November 1982−83):3. Harsh criticism of *Les Fous de Bassan*.

Langevin, André. *Poussière sur la ville*. Montréal: Edition Cercle du Livre de France, 1953.

Larose, Jean. "Le Cheval du Réel." *Québec Studies* 9 (Fall 1989−Winter 1990): 38−47. (On *Alias Will James*.)

Larouche, Michel, ed. *Le Cinéma aujourd'hui − Films, théories, nouvelles approches*. Montréal: Les éditions Guérnica, 1988. Valuable chapter on the "mise en espace-temps" of women in Québec cinema, with Poirier's *Mourir à tue-tête* as focal. (See Pérusse below.)

Larue, Johanne. "*L'Arbre qui dort rêve à ses racines*." *Séquences* 158 (June 1992): 47−8.

_____. "Comment faire l'amour ..." *Séquences* 140 (June 1989): 161−62.

_____. "*Archangel* et *La Liberté d'une statue:* fictions expérimentales de jeunes cinéastes." *Séquences* 150 (janvier 1991): 45−46.

_____, with Janick Beaulieu. *Léolo*: Pour (et) Contre." *Séquences* 159/160 (September 1992): 52−53.

Latour, Pierre. *Bar Salon*. Montréal: VLB éditeur, 1978.

_____. *Gina*. Montréal: Editions de l'Aurore, 1976. Study of the 1975 film about the rape of a stripteaser, directed by Denys Arcand.

Laurendeau, Francine. "François Girard." *Séquences* 150 (January 1991): 25−27. (Interview).

Leboutte, Patrick, ed. *Cinémas du Québec au fil du direct*. Crisnée [Liège]: Editions Yellow Now, 1986. Some say direct cinema still has influence, while others maintain there is a return to the chattier classic documentary (Leboutte, 51ff). Interview with Léa Pool (54−6). (Other articles by Jacques Kermabon [53], Louise Carrière [on animation], 67−70 et al.) See also *CopieZéro* 32 : 6 (1987).

Leduc, Jean. "Sweet Cinema/Sweet Movie." *Cinéma/Québec* 3:8 (October 1974): 15−20. Article on this cult film starring Carole Laure.

Lefebure du Bus, Olivier. "Bilan: le cinéma québécois en France." *Séquences* 151 (March 1991): 55. Reception of French films in France: triumph of *Le Déclin*, failure of *Un Zoo la nuit*, low attendance at *Jésus de Montréal*, few viewers for Carle's *La Guêpe*, no excitement over Brault's *Noces de papier* (despite Geneviève Bujold's participation, and her beauty as a bride!), and better reception of Rubbo's *Tommy Tricker* ... (though films for children have never been popular in France).

Lefebvre, Jean Pierre. "La cohérence dans le cinéma québécois." *Cinéma/Québec* 4:9/10 (1974): 42.

_____. "Le concept de cinéma national." In *Dialogue*, edited by Pierre Véronneau, Michael Dorland, and Seth Feldman, 84−95. Montréal: Mediatexte Publications Inc. & La Cinémathèque Québécoise, 1987. There has been a political will to make *québécois* national cinema international. Article rambles.

_____. "Pourquoi?" *Cinéma/Québec* 49; 5−9 (1975−1977): 13−29. Interview after making of *Le Vieux Pays où Rimbaud est mort*.

_____. "*Une Nuit en Amérique*, ou last call pour un cinéma de la conscience." *Cinéma/Québec* 3:8 (October 1974): 33−36. Chabot's *Une Nuit* ... expresses the absurdist concept that we will never get where we never go, while showing imaginary but believable people, slowly dying of despair and pain. Film is work of a poet who says poetry is dead and film of a filmmaker who wants to persuade us of the uselessness of a certain kind of cinema made for a certain type of society.

Lefebvre, Marcel (and Yves Gélinas). *"Mustang." Cinéma/Québec* 4:7 (1974): 20–21. "I made a baroque film . . . and yet it resembles us . . . ." *Mustang* is discussed again in *Cinéma/Québec* 4:8 (1974): 24–25.

Lemelin, Roger. *Au pied de la pente douce.* 3d ed. Montréal: Le Cercle du Livre de France, 1967. [In English, *The Town Below.* Toronto: McClelland and Stewart, 1961.]

―――. *Le Crime d'Ovide Plouffe.* Québec: ETR, 1982. [In English, *The Crime of Ovide Plouffe.* Alan Brown, trans. Toronto: McClelland and Stewart, 1984.].

―――. *Les Plouffe.* Paris: (Ed. J'ai Lu) Flammarion, 1985). [In English, *The Plouffe Family.* Toronto: McClelland and Stewart, 1961.]

Lemieux, Louis-Guy. "Filmer la vie en trompe-l'oeil: l'art de Léa Pool." (Entretien avec Léa Pool). *Le Soleil* (8 March, 1986): C and C3.

―――. *Réjeanne Padovani. Scope.* (April 1987): 3.

Lever, Yves. *Cinéma et Sociéte Québécoise.* Montréal: Editions du Jour, 1972. Essays entitled "Pierre Perrault et la construction du Québec libre" (21) and "Appréciation morale des films; position officielle des catholiques" (57 ff.); plus critiques of *Valérie*; *Chambre blanche*; *Q-Bec, my love*; *Red*; *Deux Femmes . . . en or?*; *Acte du coeur*; *Un Pays sans bon sens*, and others.

―――. "(Un) Cinéma pour imaginer le pays." In *Le Québécois et sa littérature*, edited by René Dionne. Sherbrooke, Québec: Editions Naaman, 1984: 380–96.

―――. "(Une) Histoire à suivre: Octobre 70 dans le cinéma québécois." *Cinéma/Québec* 4:5 (1974): 10–15.

―――. *Histoire du cinéma au Québec.* Montréal: Boréal, 1988. Indispensable and monumental history.

―――. "Pour saluer . . . ." *Cinéma/Québec* 4: 8 (1975): 22–23. Discusses Clément Perron's *Partis pour la gloire*, concerned with the 1942 Ottawa draft of the Beaucerons, as a portrait of two worlds colliding. Calls reconstruction of La Beauce of 1942 "une petite merveille."

―――. "Pour une mémoire de fête." *Cinéma/Québec* 48; 5: 8 (1975–1977): 14–16. Discussion of Jean Beaudin's *J. A. Martin photographe*.

"Littérature québécoise et cinéma." *Revue d'histoire littéraire du Québec et du Canada français* 11 (Winter/Spring 1986). This issue concerns adaptations; article by Paul Warren.

Lloyd. (See Robinson.)

Longfellow, Brenda. "From Didactics to Desire." *Canadian Forum* (February 1985): 28–32. On women's films, especially those of Léa Pool.

Luhr, William. *World Cinema since 1945.* See Handling, Piers.

Lyon, Nancy. "Quebec's Cuisine Has a New Flavor." *The New York Times* (Sunday 8 December 1991): 6 xx. Reference to *Le Matou*'s Binerie.

Magill's Survey of Cinema (Foreign Language Films). English-speaking reader's reference for all important Québec films. Articles on *The Cat in the Sack* (I–487), *Il ne faut pas mourir pour ça* (III-1450), *Mon oncle Antoine* (V-2091), *The Old*

Country Where Rimbaud Died (V-2260), and *Mourir à tue-tête* (V-2461). See also *Magill's Cinema Annual* (1992): *Jesus of Montreal, Black Robe*, and many other films.

Major, Ginette. *Le Cinéma québécois à la recherche d'un public. Bilan d'une décennie: 1970–1980*. Montréal: Presses de l'Université de Montréal, 1982. Gives plots and themes.

Malcolm, Andrew H. *The Canadians*. New York: Bantam Books, 1985. General history and culture of the people.

Maltin, Leonard. *TV Movies and Video Guide*. New York: (Penguin Books) Signet, 1989; 1990; 1991; 1993; 1994.

Mandolini, Carlo. "[Interview with] Paul Tana." *Séquences* 158 (June 1992): 17–20. Tana discusses his life as an immigrant (since arriving in Canada, 1958) and his recent film, which deals with the "wounds of the immigrant."

Marchessault, Janine. "*Jacques et Novembre*: Emergence of a New Paradigm." In *Dialogue*, edited by Pierre Véronneau, Michel Dorland, and Seth Feldman . Montréal: Médiatexte: Cinémathèque Québécoise, 1987: 223–29.

Marsolais, Gilles. *Le Cinéma canadien*. Montréal: Les Editions du Jour, Inc., 1968.

_____. *Les Dernières Fiançailles*. Montréal: Editions le cinématographe et VLB éditeur, 1977.

_____. *Les Ordres*. Montréal: Editions de l'Aurore, 1975.

Martin (-Thériault), Agathe. "*Le Temps d'avant* (Anne Claire Poirier)." *Cinéma/ Québec* 42; 5: 2 (1975): 32 ff. Discusses this early work on abortion.

Martineau, Jocelyne. *Cinémas*. Montréal; Ville de Montréal/Québec: Ministère des affaires culturelles, 1988. On architecture.

Martineau, Richard. "*Cargo*." *Séquences* 150 (January 1991): 95–96. Review.

_____. "*Une Histoire inventée*." *Séquences* 149 (November 1990): 73–74.

_____. "*Maria Chapdelaine* versus Louis Hémon." *Cinema Canada* 97 (June 1983): 17–19.

_____. (with Gilles Carle). "Pour la suite du cinéma québécois." *Séquences* 150 (January 1991): 17–24.

Martin-Thériault, Agathe. "Jeunes femmes en proie aux images." *Cinéma/Québec* 2: 3 (November 1972): 30–31. A review of Mireille Dansereau's *La Vie rêvée*.

Mayne, Judith. "Feminist Film Theory and Women at the Movies." *Profession 87* (MLA publication, 1987): 14–19. Main subject is voyeurism and female spectatorship in the Hollywood cinema. (Mayne has as similar article in *Signs* 11: 1 [1985].)

Macinnis, Craig. "Toronto and Montreal go reel to reel." *The Toronto Star*. Sunday 22 August 1993: C1– C2.

_____. *Private Novels, Public Films*. Athens: University of Georgia, 1989.

Melançon, André. "Le plaisir de raconter une histoire." *CopieZéro* 31 (March 1987): 4–11. Entretien with Pierre Véronneau, in special issue on Melançon.

Mémoire du Comité de Civisme et de Moralité Publique au Gouvernement de la Province de Québec (proposant "La Régie du Cinéma du Québec"). Diocese of Québec City. 20 February 1964. (Found in mimeographed form in Laval University library.)

Miller, Lynn Fieldman, ed. *The Hand that Holds the Camera.* N.Y: Garland, 1980.

Moffat, Alain-Napoléon. "*A Tout Prendre* de Claude Jutra: Le Docu-Drame de la Confession." *Québec Studies* 13 (Spring/Summer 1991): 147–54.

Morris, Peter. *Canadian Feature Films: 1913–1963*, Part 2. 1941–63. Ottawa: (Canadian Filmography Series, No. 7) Canadian Film Institute, s.d. [after 1969].

———. *Embattled Shadows: A History of the Canadian Cinema, 1895–1939.* Montréal: McGill-Queen's University Press, 1978; reprinted 1992. Scant information on early *québécois* cinema; short treatments of *Evangeline* (48–49), *The Battle of Long Sault* (48), *Madeleine de Vercours* (48), Ouimet (23–25; 85; 88–90), Proulx and Tessier (221–2). Tessier's "lyric reportage [is] . . . not far removed from that of Pierre Perrault and Michel Brault in a later generation" (222).

———. *The National Film Board of Canada: The War Years.* Ottawa: (Canadian Filmography Series, No. 3) Canadian Film Institute, 1965; repr. 1972.

Morrissette, Bruce. *Novel and Film.* Chicago: University of Chicago Press, 1985.

Morton, Desmond. *A Short History of Canada.* Edmonton: Hurtig Publishers Ltd., 1983.

Moskowitz, G. "*Kamouraska.*" *Variety* (23 May 1973). N.Y.: Garland Publishing, Inc., Vol. 13, 1983: n.p.

———. "*Réjeanne Padovanni.*" *Variety* (13 June 1973). N.Y.: Garland Publishing, Inc., Vol. 13, 1983: n.p.

National Film, Television and Sound Archives. See Guénette.

National Film Board of Canada, International Film and Video Resource Guide (U.S. Edition). New York: National Film Board of Canada, 1987.

Naudin, Marie. "Denys Arcand: Un Montréal poste-moderne." *Etudes Canadiennes/Canadian Studies* 30 (June 1991): 73–77.

Noguez, Dominique. *Essais sur le cinéma québécois.* Montréal: Editions du Jour, 1971. René Jodoin—in his 1966 *Notes sur un triangle*—follows the lessons of McLaren [35]; the ONF is both the weakness and the strength of the *québécois* cinema [36–37]; Jutra is the most literary and the most French of the Québécois filmmakers [105]. Studies Jutra's *A tout prendre* [103–10]; Owen's *Ernie Game* [114–17]; Carle's "very québécois" *Le Viol d'une jeune fille douce* [117–19]; Jean Pierre Lefebvre's *Jusqu'au coeur* [122–25]; Jutra's *Wow* [126–39]; Norm McClaren [139–51]; film and painting, especially, Jean-Paul Lemieux and Gilles Gascon's *Québec in silence*, which is "une autre vision du même Québec que celle de Lemieux" [151–61]; films of Pierre Perrault [200–207]. Chapter on the teaching of film.

Nunes, Julia. "Researching the ratings." *Comment faire l'amour . . . The (Toronto) Globe and Mail* (Friday, 15 June, 1990): A12[N].

Office national du film: Répertoire (Vidéo). Textes by Louise Dugas; *Révision* by Jacqueline Généreux. Montréal: Office national du film du Canada, 1988; 1989. Catalogue of most films in French available from the ONF.

O'Reilly, Magessa. "Grignon plurilingue." *Voix et Images* 37 [Autumn 1987]: 123–38.

Page, James E. *Seeing Ourselves: Films for Canadian Studies.* Montréal: National

Film Board of Canada, 1979–80. Designed as a guide to the use of film as a teaching tool. Mostly shorts. Arranged by themes.

Pageau, Pierre. "Colin Low et Pierre Perrault: Points de convergence." In *Dialogue*. Edited by Pierre Véronneau, Michel Dorland, and Seth Feldman. Montréal: Médiatexte: Cinémathèque Québécoise, 1987: 139 ff.

Pageau, Pierre and Yves Lever. *Cinémas canadien et québécois. Notes historiques.* Montréal: Collège Ahuntsic, 1977. See also Lever.

Pallister, Janis L. "The 'Esguillette nouée': Renaissance Forebears of Anne Hébert's *Enfants du Sabbat.*" In *Il tema della fortuna nella letteratura francese e italiana del rinascimento.* Firenze: Leo S. Olschki Editore, 1990.

_____. "Eros and Thanatos in Anne Hébert and Marguerite Duras: *Kamouraska* and *Hiroshima mon amour.*" *Dalhousie French Studies* 10 (Spring–Summer 1986): 56–71.

_____. "Léa Pool's Gynefilms." In *Essays on Quebec Cinema.*, edited by Joseph I. Donohoe, Jr., 111–34. East Lansing: Michigan State University, 1991.

_____. "Observations on Claude Jutra's *Mon oncle Antoine.*" *AATF National Bulletin.* Vol. 14: No. 1 (September 1988): 23.

_____. "The Place of *Le Déclin* ... in World Cinema." In *Acts.* Kalamazoo: Western Michigan University, 1990.

_____. "Satanism, Jansenism and Greek Myth in *Les Fous de Bassan.*" In *Carrefour de Cultures*, edited by Régis Antoine, 541–54. Tùbingen Germany: Gunter Narr Verlag, 1993.

Pelletier, Esther. "Texte littéraire et adaptation cinématographique: la rencontre de deux systèmes." In *Les Dossiers de la Cinémathèque* 12 (1983): 37–42. The film of adaptation, based on a *scénario d'adaptation*, is different from an "original" film and should be considered as a rewriting in cinematographic form of a previous literary form. But once the process of adaptation is completed, the film is an autonomous production that should be considered as a "new discourse," with its own value. Moreover, the "original" film, built on a *scénario de création*, is also a form of adaptation, proceeding from the transcription of systems of representations produced by the society. Guy Fournier's and Gilles Carle's recent adaptation of *Maria Chapdelaine* is studied in terms of borrowing and omissions from Hémon's novel.

Pendakur, Manjunath. *Canadian Dreams & American Control.* Detroit: Wayne State University Press, 1990. Studies the industry from the perspective announced in the title. Political and financial problems of distribution in Québec, role of Parti Québécois, introduction of Québec's Cinema Act (Bill 109), reactions and actions of Motion Picture Export Association of America, etc., treated with sobriety (259–61). These and section on Disney (Buena Vista) in Canada (267–69) of importance to history of Québec cinema as regards distribution problems and American film domination in Québec (and/or Canada).

Penley, Constance. *Feminism and Film Theory.* New York.: Routledge, 1988.

_____. *The Future of an Illusion: Film, Feminism and Psychoanalysis.* Minneapolis: (Media and Society) University of Minnesota Press, 1989.

Perrault, Pierre. *Au coeur de la rose.* Montréal: éditions Lidec, 1964. Theater.

_____. *Ballades du temps précieux.* Montréal: éditions d'Essai: 1963. Poems.

_____. *La Bête lumineuse.* Montréal: Nouvelle Optique, 1982.

_____. *Caméramages*. Montréal: éditions de l'Hexagone, 1983. Also published in Paris (Edilig, 1983). All his cycles.

_____. *Chouennes*. Montréal: l'Hexagone, 1975. Poems.

_____. *De la parole aux actes*. Montréal: éditions de l'Hexagone, 1985. Essays.

_____. *Discours sur la condition sauvage et québécoise*. Montréal: éditions Lidec, 1977. Album of photos and *témoignages*.

_____. *Ecritures de ...*. Montréal: Cinémathèque Québécoise, 1983.

_____. *En Désespoir de Cause*. Montréal: éditions Parti Pris, 1971.

_____. *La Grande Allure*. Montréal: L'Hexagone, 1989.

_____. *Portulan*. Montréal: éditions Beauchemin, 1961. Poems.

_____. *Le Règne du jour*. Montréal: éditions Lidec, 1968.

_____. *Le Saint-Laurent*. Montréal: Libre Expression, 1984.

_____. *Toutes Isles*. Montréal: éditions Fides, 1963. Récits (Tales).

_____. *Un Pays sans bon sens*. Montréal: éditions Lidec, 1972.

_____. with Bernard Gosselin and Monique Fortier. *Les Voitures d'eau*. Montréal: éditions Lidec & Ici-Radio-Canada, 1969.

Perreault, Luc. "*Anne Trister*: L'artiste et sa quête." *La Presse* (Saturday, 8 February 1986): E19.

_____. "Le cinéma selon Léa Pool: Une exigence intérieure." *La Presse* (Saturday, 8 February 1986). E1 and E16. (An interview.)

_____. "*Les Fous de Bassan*: Les hauts (et les bas) de Hurlevent." *La Presse* (Saturday, 20 December 1986): E16. "Le fait que cette communauté s'exprime en français et, qui plus est, dans un français plus ou moins international vient renforcer l'illusion qu'il s'agit là d'un drame situé hors du temps et de l'espace." (The international French spoken in the film adds to the illusion of a drama occurring outside time and space.)

Pérusse, Denise. "*Le Déclin ...*: une stratégie filmique oscillant entre le cliché et l'ironie." *CopieZéro* 34–35 (December 1987–March 1988): 49–51. Finds that cliché and irony are two entirely different universes, and that "it is in the process of reading all the words and speeches of the two camps that the ironic relationship of the two antinomic poles is realized."

_____. "*Mourir à tue-tête.*" In *Le Cinéma aujourd'hui*, edited by Michel Larouche. Montréal: Les Éditions Guérnica, 1988: 81–96.

Picard, Yves. "Les succès du cinéma québécois des 10 dernières années: des rendez-vous réussis avec l'imaginaire instituant d'ici." In *Dialogue*, edited by Pierre Véronneau, Michael Dorland and Seth Feldman. Montréal: Médiatexte Publications Inc. et La Cinémathèque Québécoise, 1987: 97–107. Tendencies of *québécois* fictional cinema from 1975–85 are *passéiste* (digging up the past, especially through literary patrimony), or else *misérabiliste* (concentrating on poverty, as *L'Eau chaude l'eau frette*; *Les Bons Débarras*; *Lucien Brouillard*; *Sonatine*). Kafkaesque and morose depictions of the Other, and of the State Bureaucracy. Strong matriarch of the past (*Gina, Maria Chapdelaine*) contrasts with glorification of State-as-Mother, as protector (*J. A. Martin photographe*) —which in turn contrasts with recent male depictions (*Lucien Brouillard*, *Mario, Jacques et Novembre, Le Crime d'Ovide Plouffe*), male becoming finally the Entrepreneur of the expansionist State (*Le Matou*).

Pielmeier, John. *Agnes of God* (1978). N.Y.: (Plume) New American Library, 1985.

Pierre Perrault. Special issue, collective (of) *La Revue du Cinéma, Image et Son* 256 (Paris; January 1972).

Pleau, Marcel. "La sagesse du nihilisme." *CopieZero* 32 (July 1987): 4–5. *Le Déclin* ..., a nihilistic film, excludes suicide from its cadre, perhaps because nihilism requires one to be resigned to surviving within the limits of the experience imposed by the present state of civilization. Nihilism provides the how (if not the why) to survive when one senses one is the last man on the planet.

Pratley, Gerald. Canadian section in *International Film Guide*. London: Tantivy Press, 1987.

_____. *Torn Sprockets: The Uncertain Projection of the Canadian Film*. Newark: University of Delaware Press; Toronto: Associated University Presses, 1987. One of the best references in English to pan-Canadian film. Many stills. Review by Janis L. Pallister: *Journal of Popular Film and Television* 13:3 (Fall 1988): 134–35.

Prat[ley], [Gerald]. "*L'Acadie, l'Acadie*." *Variety* (9 June 1971). N.Y.: Garland Publishing, Inc., Vol. 13, 1983: n.p.

_____. "*L'Amour humain*." *Variety* (9 June 1971). New York: Garland Publishing, Inc., Vol. 13, 1983: n.p.

_____. "*Laura Laur*." *Variety* 335/7 (31 May–7 June 1989): 34. "The pace is slow, the camerawork unimaginative, the acting uneven."

_____. "*Le Martien de Noël*." *Variety* (9 June 1971) New York: Garland Publishing, Inc., 1983: Vol. 13, n.p.

_____. "*Les Matins infidèles*." *Variety* 335/7 (31 May–7 June 1989): 34. "... audiences who attempt to cope with it are in for a punishing time."

_____. "*Les Maudits Sauvages*." *Variety* (9 June 1971) New York: Garland Publishing, Inc,. 1983: Vol. 13, n.p.

_____. "*Mon oncle Antoine*." *Variety* (9 June 1971) New York: Garland Publishing, Inc., 1983: Vol. 13, n.p.

_____. "*Stop*." *Variety* (9 June 1971) New York: Garland Publishing, Inc., 1983: Vol. 13, n.p.

_____. "*Wow*." *Variety* (21 April 1971) New York: Garland Publishing, Inc., 1983: Vol. 13, 1983: Vol. 13, n.p.

Quart, Barbara K. *Women Directors*. New York.: Praeger Pub., 1988.

Québec Studies 9. (Fall 1989–Winter 1990). Special issue on film. Articles separately listed here by authors.

Rafferty, Terrence. "True Believers": Current Cinema. *The New Yorker* (18 November 1991): 120–23. Review article of *Black Robe*.

Randall, Marilyn. "Les énigmes des *Fous de Bassan*: féminisme, narration et clôture," *Voix et Images* 43 (Fall 1989): 66–82.

Reid, Alison. *Canadian Women Film Makers, an Interim Filmography*. Ottawa: Canadian Film Institute, 1972.

_____. and P. M. Evanchuck. *Richard Leiterman*. Ottawa: The Canadian Film Institute, 1978.

Rendu, Jacques. "*Un Zoo la nuit*." *Le Journal Français d'Amérique* (22 April–5 March 1988): 20; also (17–30 June, 1988): 16.

Répertoire Vidéo. Textes, Louise Dugas. Montréal: Office National du Film du Canada, 1988.

Rétrospective Albert Tessier (Collective). Québec: Ministère des Communications, DGCA, 1977.

Richler, Mordecai. "Inside/Outside" (A Reporter at Large). *The New Yorker* LXVII, 31 (23 September 1991): 40−92.

―――. "The October Crisis, or Issue-Envy in Canada." *Home Sweet Home*. Markham, Ontario, Canada: Penguin Books Canada, Ltd., 1985: 142−55.

―――. *Oh Canada! Oh Quebec! Requiem for a Divided Country*. New York: Knopf, 1992. Richler's sardonic wit is focussed on Bill 178, which disallows exterior signs in any other language but French. Richler indicts those Canadians (anglophone and francophone alike) who would destroy the cultural traits that make Canada different from the U.S.A.

Rist, Peter. "*Primal Fear*." *Magill's Survey of Cinema (Foreign Language Films)*. Englewood Cliffs, N.J.: Salem Press, 1985: V, 2461−66. *Primal Fear* is the alternate English title of *Mourir à tue-tête*.

―――. "*The Old Country Where Rimbaud Died*." *Magill's Survey of Cinema (Foreign Language Films)*. Englewood Cliffs, N.J: Salem Press, 1985: V, 2260−65.

Robinson, David, and Ann Lloyd, editors. *The Illustrated History of the Cinema*. New York: Macmillan, 1986. Section on Canadian Film.

Roy, Gabrielle. *Bonheur d'occasion*. Montréal: Stanké, 1977. [English translation: *The Tin Flute*. Toronto: McClelland and Stewart's New Canadian Library, 1980; 1982.]

―――. *Un Jardin au bout du monde*. Montréal: Beauchemin, 1975.

―――. *La Route d'Altamont*. Montréal: (Collection l'Arbre V10) Editions HMH, 1966; 1969.

Sadoul, Georges and Emile Breton. *Dictionnaire (microcosme) des cinéastes*. 4e ed. mise à jour, octobre 1989. Paris: Collection de Poche, 1989.

―――― *Dictionnaire (microcosme) des films*. 4e ed. mise à jour, mai 1989. Paris: Collection de Poche, 1989.

Salmon, Paul. "*Jésus de Montréal*." *Magill's Cinema Annual 1990−A Survey of the Films of 1988*. Englewood Cliffs N.J.: Salem Press, 1989 : 201−4.

Saouter, Catherine. "*Le Matou*." *Voix et Images* 36 (1987): 397−98.

Scheuer, Steven H., Ed.. *Movies on TV, 1986−7*. New York: Bantam Books, c. 1985.

Schwartzwald, Robert. "Du ressentiment à la cession altruiste: Une trilogie filmique de Denys Arcand." *Revue de l'institut de sociologie* [spec. issue: "Situations de l'écrivain francophone."] Bruxelles: Université Libre de Bruxelles, 1990−91: 221−35. Brilliant syncretic study of Arcand's "trilogy"− *Le Confort et l'indifférence, Le Déclin* ..., and *Jésus* ... − in relation to the defeat of the May 1980 referendum.

Self-Portrait: Essays on the Canadian and Quebec Cinemas, edited by Pierre Véronneau and Piers Handling. Ottawa: Canadian Film Institute, 1980. Useful reference, with short histories and some criticism; but only goes to 1980.

Sévigny, Marc. "Le Cinéma pour enfants au Québec." *Cinéma/Québec* 58; 6:8 (September−October 1978): 24−32. Dossier on cinema for children, including treatment of André Melançon (*Tou'l monde parle français*; Richard Lavoie

(*Guitare; Cabane*); and François Labonté (*Babiole*). Financial problems; role of television; freedom of children away from adults and their traps.

Shek, Ben-Z. "History as a Unifying Structure in *Le Déclin de l'empire américain*." *Québec Studies* 9 (Fall 1989): 9 −15.

Simoneau, Yves. "Les Fous de Bassan." *Le Journal de Montréal* (18 December 1986): 58. The director claims emotion takes precedence over physical action; that passion drives the film; that he considers the film his best.

Sinyard, Neil. *Silent Movies*. New York: (Gallery Books) W. H. Smith Publishers, Inc., 1990.

Slott, Kathryn. "From Agent of Destruction to Object of Desire: The Cinematic Transformation of Stevens Brown in *Les Fous de Bassan*." *Québec Studies* 9 (Fall 1989): 17−28.

Smith, Martin. "Léa Pool: les belles images d'un voyage intérieur." *Le Journal de Montréal* (15 February 1986): 15. (An interview.)

Solomon, Charles. *The History of Animation: Enchanted Drawings*. New York: Alfred A. Knopf, 1989. The long history of this genre through the magic lantern and the comic strip into modern film forms; seriously flawed by almost complete disregard of the Canadian contribution to the eighth art.

Stam, Robert. *Subversive Pleasures: Bakhtin, Cultural Criticism and Film*. Baltimore, Maryland: Johns Hopkins University Press, 1989.

Sterritt, David. "Behind the Scenes at a Canadian Passion Play." *The Christian Science Monitor* (5/24/90): 10.

Straram (Le Bison Ravi), Patrick. "Blues clair Salut l'anar." *Les Dossiers de la Cinémathèque* #12 (1983): 17−20. Disjointed, "avant-garde" critique; more subjective than most, as are all of Straram's writings on film. Straram (b. Paris 1934; d. 1988), who took the additional name of "le Bison Ravi" to reflect his Amerindian ties, was also a well-known Québécois poet. He speaks of films (and of his *Blues clair*) in his *poème-blason*, "The Blues Is a Feeling Blues Clair." (See also Lever, 422; 425; 497: Straram, a frequent contributor to Tadros's *Cinéma/Québec* and to Université Laval's short-lived *Cinécrits*, puts commas where he wants, and so his text floats.)

―――. "Le cinéma, bien, mais plus que le cinéma." *Presqu'Amérique* (1972): 37−40.

Studlar, Gaylyn. "Masochism and the Perverse Pleasures of the Cinema." In *Movies and Methods*, edited by Bill Nichols, Vol. 2: 602−21. Berkeley: University of California Press, 1985.

"Study Thy Neighbor." *Detroit Free Press* (31 May 1990): 1F:2F.

Suchet, Simone. "Anne Hébert et *Les Fous de Bassan*." *Séquences* 129 (April 1987): 54. Hébert claims that in her own (unused) screenplay she privileged Olivia's point of view.

Sullivan, Kaye. *Films for by and about Women*. Metuchen, N.J.: Scarecrow Press, 1980; 1985.

Sultanik, Aaron. *Film: A Modern Art*. New York: Cornwall Books, 1986.

Sylvestre, Guy. *Anthologie de la poésie québécoise*. Montréal: Librairie Beauchemin, Ltée., 1974.

Tadros, Jean-Pierre. *En première #3*. Montréal: Editions Cinéma/Québec, 1977. On Lefebvre's *Vieux pays où Rimbaud est mort*. Interview. Also found in *Cinéma/Québec* 49; 5:9 (1976): 13−29.

————. "Etre cinéaste anglophone à Montréal." *Cinéma/Québec* 49; 5:9 (1976): 35 ff. Robin Spry and his *One Man.* Spry expresses the difficulty of being an anglophone *cinéaste* in Montréal, where he is far from writers, actors, and other directors (36).

————. "*Grand Remue-ménage* pour une fondamentale remise en question." *Cinéma/Québec* 58; 6/8 (September/October 1978): 15–17. Article on the film, directed by Sylvie Groulx/Francine Allaire.

————. "Denys Arcand: *La Maudite Galette.*" *Cinéma/Québec* 1:9 (May–June 1972): 26–9. Interview. Arcand sees *La Maudite* ... as part of a triptych, along with *On est au coton* and *Duplessis.* Fiction permits one to do many more things than documentary. Says *La Maudite* ... is most political film he has made, yet is not about politics; in it he made a great effort to show physical and moral poverty (*misère*). It is a *fait divers*; about gangsters but not a gangster film: a subversion of the gangster film.

————. "Denys Arcand: *Réjeanne Padovani.*" *Cinéma/Québec* 3:1 (September 1973): 17–24. Interview.

————. "J. P. Lefebvre: *L'Amour blessé.*" *Cinéma/Québec* #46; 5:6 (1975–77): 16–21.

————. "Luce Guilbeault, Cinéaste et Ménagère." *Cinéma/Québec* 57; 6:7 (July–August 1978): 14–6; 54. Interview in which Guilbeault explains that she has chosen to do a film on housewives because of a "hereditary" problem, her own, and that of all Québécoises, who are plagued with a double task: the need to make everything in the house Spic and Span; to run the house and do one's job. She prefers to make films about women, because "it is less frightening." Guilbeault also speaks of her transformation from housewife (*ménagère*) to actress to director.

————. "Monique Mercure: l'apprentissage de la gloire." *Cinéma/Québec* 51; 6:1 (1977): 5–13. An interview with this Québécoise star.

————. "Paule Baillargeon, au rouge." *Cinéma/Québec* 57; 6:7 (July, August 1978): 12–16; 54. Deals with the ONF program committee's decision not to finance projects that are submitted by filmmakers "de l'extérieur"—that is, *cinéastes-pigistes.* Baillargeon's *La Cuisine rouge* fell victim to this policy after much of the work was already in place, so that she had to launch a subscription campaign. (See also Feldman.)

————. "Un[e] Espèce de joie dans la création." *Cinéma/Québec* 3: 4–5 (March–April 1973): 15–9. Interview between Tadros and Claude Jutra on the making of *Kamouraska.*

———— with Marcia Couelle and Connie Tadros. *Le Cinéma au Québec: bilan d'une industrie.* Montréal: Cinéma/Québec, 1975.

Tad[ro]s, J[ean].-P[ierre]. "*Et du fils* ..." *Variety* (1 November 1972). New York: Garland Publishing, Inc., 1983: Vol. 13, n.p.

————. "*Quelques arpents de neige.*" *Variety* (7 March 1973). New York: Garland Publishing, Inc., 1983: Vol. 13, n.p.

————. "*La Vie rêvée.*" *Variety* (16 October 1972). New York: Garland Publishing, Inc., 1983: Vol. 13, n.p.

Tamarelle's Catalogue of Foreign Films. 1990: 3 and 10.

Testa, Bart. "Denys Arcand's Sarcasm: A Reading of *Gina.*" In *Dialogue*, edited by Pierre Véronneau, Michel Dorland, and Seth Feldman, 204–22. Montréal:

Médiatexte: Cinémathèque Québécoise, 1987. Arcand's films are neither pessimistic nor cynical, but sarcastic. Arcand can combine commercial success with political meaning, *Gina* being a good example, with the narrative structure Arcand is fond of: parallel *montage*. In its autobiographical dimension, its reflection of documentary ethic, its fictional aspect, *Gina* shows Arcand's sarcasm very well.

Tétu de Lapsade, Françoise. *Le Québec: un pays, une culture*. Québec: Boréal; Paris: Seuil, 1990. Historical, geopolitical, and cultural study of Québec, sustaining a neutral tone.
"Does not come out with all ideological flags flying" says Marjorie A. Fitzpatirck in *The French Review* 66:4 (March 1993): 708–9.

Thériault, Yves. *Agaguk*. Montréal: L'Actuelle, 1971. Illustrated by Siasi Irgumia. The first edition of this novel, on which *Shadow of the Wolf* is based, was published in 1958.

Thérien, Gilles. "L'Empire et les barbares." *Cinémas: Revue d'études cinématographiques/Journal of Film Studies* (1991) 1: 1–2.

Tremblay-Daviault, Christine. *Structures mentales et sociales du cinéma québécois (1942–1953): Un cinéma orphelin*. Montréal: Québec/Amérique, 1981. Part 2 analyzes: *A la croisée des chemins, Le Père Chopin, La Forteresse, Un Homme et son péché, Séraphin, Le Gros Bill, Les Lumières de ma ville, La Petite Aurore* (La morale de l'histoire, une vie de misère, aliénation des référants traditionnels, rétrécissement des forces vives, la parole interdite, structures mentales et sociales épuisées), *Le Rossignol et les cloches, Tit-coq, Coeur de maman*. Appendices and some additions follow.

Turner, D. J[ohn]. *Canadian Feature Film Index* or *Index des films canadiens de long métrage: 1913–1985*. Canada [Ottawa]: National Film TV and Sound Archives [Archives publiques], 1987–88.
Feature length films from *Evangeline* (Nova Scotia and Québec, 1913) to *Le Million tout-puissant* (1985); includes 1, 222 productions. Indexes of films by title, by actors, and by technicians, with filmographies under each name. Index of coproductions with foreign countries.

Vallières, Pierre. "Brault a manqué son coup: témoignage d'un otage privilégié des 'ordres'." *Cinéma/Québec* 4:1 (December 1974): 18–20.
_____. *Nègres blancs d'Amérique*. 3d ed. Paris: Maspéro, 1968, 1969. Written during the author's four-year prison term (1967–71) for his alleged terrorist activities during the Revolution. Translated into English as *White Niggers of America*, 1971.

Van Den Hoven, Adrian. "*The Decline* . . . in a North-American Perspective." In *Essays in Quebec Cinema*, edited by Joseph I. Donohoe Jr., 145–55. East Lansing: Michigan State University, 1991.

Véronneau, Pierre. *André Melançon*. Montréal: Cinémathèque Québécoise, 1987.
_____. "Observation 1, 2, 3, . . ." *Copie/Zéro* 31 (March 1987): 9–11. Special issue on André Melançon.
_____ with Pierre Jutras et al. *Anne Claire Poirier*. Montréal: Cinémathèque Québécoise, 1985.
_____. "Les Années 80: Le Sextant défaille." *Québec Studies* 9 (Fall 1989): 1–8.
_____. *Le Cinéma: théorie et discours*. (Montréal?: Actes du colloque de l'Association québécoise des études cinématographiques, 1983. Pub. 1984).

———. *Les Cinémas canadiens*. Montréal: La Cinémathèque Québécoise [co-edited Paris: Pierre Lherminier], 1978). General overview. Chapter 7 on *Le cinéma direct* (87–106); Ch. 10 on *Le cinéma québécois* (137–64). Several appendices.

——— with Michel Dorland & Seth Feldman, eds. *Dialogue: Cinéma canadien et québécois/Canadian and Quebec Cinema*. Canadian Film Series 3. Montréal: Médiatexte Publications/Cinémathèque Québécoise, 1987.

———. *Ecritures de Pierre Perrault*. Actes du colloque 'Gens de paroles' à La Rochelle, France, 1982. (Pub. 1983).

———. "Les Evénements d'octobre au cinéma," *Québec Studies* 11 (Fall 1990/1991): 29–36.

———. *L'Histoire du cinéma au Québec, I et II*. In *Les Dossiers de la Cinémathèque*, Vol. 3 (*Le Succès est au film parlant français*); Vol. 5 (*L'Office National du Film, l'enfant martyr*, 1979); and Vol. 7 (*Cinéma de l'époque duplessiste*). Montreal: Le Musée du Cinéma, 1979.

———. *L'Histoire du cinéma au Québec, III. Résistance et affirmation: la production francophone à l'ONF–1939–1964*. Montréal: Cinémathèque Québécoise, 1987.

———. *L'Histoire du cinéma au Québec*. 3 vols. Montréal: Cinémathèque Québécoise, 1969–88.

———. *Kamouraska: Etude du roman et de son adaptation cinématographique*. Montréal: Université du Québec, mémoire de maîtrise ès arts, 1977.

———. "Mariage à l'italienne." *La Revue de la Cinémathèque*. (Programme.) 4e trimestre (December 1990–January 1991): 4–8. Collaboration of Québec and Italian directors since the 1960s.

———, ed. *A la recherche d'une identité: Renaissance du cinéma d'auteur canadien-anglais*. Montréal: Cinémathèque Québécoise, 1991. Deals with former Canadian greats filming in English, including Paul Almond, Allan King, Don Owen, and Don Shebib, and also with new directors Patricia Rozema, Atom Egoyan, William D. McGillivray, and Anne Wheeler.

———, ed. *Montréal, Ville de Cinéma*. Montréal: Cinémathèque Québécoise, 1992. Heavily illustrated (black and white).

———. "Repères bibliographiques sur le Cinéma québécois des années 80." *Québec Studies* 9 (Fall 1989): 79–84. Updated bibliography.

———, Michel Dorland and Piers Handling, eds. *Self-Portrait: Essays on the Canadian and Quebec Cinemas*. Ottawa: Canadian Film Institute, 1980. Essays include "The First Wave of Quebec Feature Films: 1944–1953," by Pierre Véronneau," [54]; "Direct Cinema," by Michel Euvrard and Pierre Véronneau [77 ff.]; "Animation," by Louise Beaudet [107 ff. "Some Ideological and Thematic Aspects of the Quebec Cinema: 1963–1977," by Michel Houle [159 ff]; and lists of 75 filmmakers and 125 films. Many stills.

Vers une politique du cinéma au Québec. Project director, Michel Brûlé. Québec: Ministère des Communications, 1978. Largely a politicolegal proposal.

Vézina, France. *Androgyne*. Montréal: l'Hexagone, 1979: 82.

Viswanathan, Acqueline. "Approche pédagogique d'un classique du cinéma québécois: *Mon oncle Antoine*." *The French Review* 63:5 (April 1990): 849–58.

Walser, Lise. *Répertoire des longs métrages produits au Québec 1960–1970*. Montréal: CQDC, 1971.

Warren, Denise. "Beauvoir on Bardot: The Ambiguity Syndrome." *Simone de Beauvoir et les féminismes contemporains*. Vol. 13 (Fall—Winter 1987): 39—50.

Warren, Paul. "Américanisation." *La Revue de la Cinémathèque* 1 (May—June 1989): 18.

_____. "Pierre Perrault, cinéaste." In *Dialogue*, edited by Pierre Véronneau, Michel Dorland, and Seth Feldman, 123—38. Montréal: Médiatexte: Cinémathèque Québécoise, 1987. Influence of the oral tradition in Perrault's films. Storytellers-characters take charge of the construction of the tale, and the tale itself takes over. Continuity and time give Perrault's films their symbolic meaning: "continuation of the world."

_____. "Les Québécois et le cinéma: un mode spécifique d'exhibition." In *Dialogue*, edited by Pierre Véronneau et al, 109—20. Montréal: Médiatexte: Cinémathèque Québécoise, 1987. Studies Pierre Perrault, whose films are "the fullest expression of Québec cinema and the clearest line of demarcation from cinema of English Canada." Even features like *La Quarantaine* and *Laure Gaudreault*, by their documentary configuration, follow in Perrault's trajectory (116—19). However, *Le Déclin* ... may mark the decline of cinematographic Quebecitude (120).

_____. "Le refus du jeu." *Revue d'histoire littéraire du Québec et du Canada Français*. 11 (1986): 123—8. "The Québec cinema has an undeniable documentary approach. The analysis of two films—*La Quarantaine* of Anne Poirier and *Rencontre avec une femme remarquable, Laure Gaudreault* of Iolande Cadrin-Rossignol—illustrates this approach to cinema."

_____. *Le Secret du "Star System" américain*. Montréal: l'Hexagone, 1989.

_____. "La Technique n'est pas innocente." *Cinémas et Réalités*. St. Etienne: Université de St. Etienne, 1984: 59—64.

Waugh, Thomas. "The sexual anxiety of the boy's club." *CopieZéro* 24 (June 1985): 7—9. Sexual anxiety and homosexuality in *Bay Boy*.

_____. "Le cinéma anglo-québécois est surtout le fait d'immigrants." *CinémAction: Aujourd'hui le cinéma québécois*, edited by Louise Carrière, preface by Dominique Noguez. Paris: Cerf-OFQJ, 1986: 66—75.

Weinmann, Heinz. *Cinéma de l'imaginaire québécois, de La petite Aurore à Jésus de Montréal*. Saint-Laurent, Québec: l'Hexagone, 1990. Strong biases in theses of Québec as orphaned by France, martyred by English; and of Québec as a closed society. Errors regarding Catholicism. Lack of index is serious shortcoming.
Review: Janick Beaulieu. *Séquences* 147 (September 1990): 17.
Review: Janis L. Pallister. *Québec Studies* 12 (Spring/Summer 1991): 187—88.

Weiss, Jonathan. *French-Canadian Literature*. Washington, D.C.: ACSUS Papers, 1989.

Wine, Bill. "Mon oncle Antoine." *Magill's Survey of Cinema* (*Foreign Language Films*). Englewood Cliffs, N.J.: Salem Press, 1985: V, 2091—94.

Women Make Movies Film and Video Catalogue. (New York: Women Make Movies, Inc., 1992—1993): 16; 40.

Wright, Judy and Debbie Magidson, "Making Films for Your Own People." *Canadian Film Reader*, edited by Seth Feldman and Joyce Nelson. Toronto: Peter Martin Associates, 1977.

Zoom sur elles. Montréal: Office National du Film du Canada, (Winter) 1990. Information on women directors, actresses, etc.

Zucker, Carole. "Les oeuvres récentes d'Anne Claire Poirier et Paule Baillargeon." *CopieZéro* 11 (Special feature on *Vues sur le cinéma québécois*, 1982): 52–54.

Films and Films about Films

Cinéma d'ici (1972; 11 parts; Radio Canada). A documentary history of Québec cinema, including interviews and excerpts.

Co Hoedeman, Animator (1981; Nico Crama, NFB).

Creative Process: Norm McLaren (1990; directed, written, and edited by Donald McWilliams). A National Film Board documentary, aired on CBC, Fall, 1991.

Dreamland: A History of Early Canadian Movies, 1895–1939. (1974; Donald Brittain, NFB). A documentary with extracts from films of the period.

Eve Lambart (1978; Margaret Wescott, NFB).

Every Child. Released by Smarty Pants, 1990. NFB Animation. (*Every Child; Catour, The Magic Flute; Log Driver's Waltz; The Town Mouse and the Country Mouse.*) Available from Walden by Mail (Dept. 009, P.O. Box 305188, Nashville Tenn. 37230–5188); or the Video Catalogue (1000 Westgate Drive, St. Paul, MN, 55114).

Fantasmagorie (1974; Glover/Patenaude, NFB). History of animation at the ONF since 1941; in English called *The Light Fantastick.*

Grierson (1973; Roger Blais & James Beveridge, NFB).

Has Anybody Here Seen Canada? A History of Canadian Movies. 1939–53 (1978; Kramer, NFB). A documentary with clips from films of the period.

NFB Thursday Night Movie (Animation). Hosted by Gordon Pinset. (CBC-NFB Co-production, 1989).

The Sand Castle. Released by Smarty Pants, 1991. NFB animation. Includes *The Sand Castle, The North Wind and the Sun, Alphabet,* and *The Owl and the Lemming.* [VHS 3066 at Walden.]

Sea Dream. Released by Smarty Pants, 1990. NFB animation. Includes *Sea Dream, Nébule,* and *The Sound Collector.* [Walden by Mail.]

The Sweater. Released by Smarty Pants, 1991. NFB animation. Includes *The Sweater, The Ride,* and *Getting Started.* [VHS 4249 – Walden by Mail. Also at SUNY.]
    The Sweater is based on Roch Carrier's *Le Chandail,* published in English as *The Hockey Sweater* (Tundra Books).

The Tender Tale of Cinderella Penguin. Released by Smarty Pants, 1990. NFB Animation. Includes *Cinderella Penguin, Metamorphoses, Mr. Frog Went a-Courtin', The Sky Is Blue, The Owl and the Raven.* (Walden by Mail.)

Le Fleuve aux grandes eaux. (1993, Back). Periodica Videos.

[Facet's Video (Chicago) makes available several of these animated films from NFB. *Masters of Animation,* Vol. 1(SO7613), gives Disney, McLaren, and Back. *A Christmas Gift* (S13342) contains eight shorts: *The Great Toy Robbery, The Story of Christmas, The Sweater, December Lights, The Energy Carol, An Old Box, The Magic Flute,* and *The Christmas Cracker. Hollywood Salutes Canadian Animation* (S13340) presents Seven National Film Board productions that have won Oscars: *Every Child*, *The Sand Castle*, *The House That Jack Built*, *Special Delivery*, *The Street* and *Neighbours*. (There is also a tape of *Manitoba Animation*, containing famous NFB films, as well as one called *A Short Film Festival*, containing seven films from the NFB.)]

Additional Videos and Films about Canadian Film (not viewed)

Cinéma, cinéma (1985; Gilles Carle/Werner Nold, NFB). Documentary that deals with the NFB francophone films over period of 25 yrs.)
Self-Portrait (1961; 5 parts; Guy Glover)
"How They Saw Us" (1977; 8 parts; Ann Pearson, NFB)
The Image Makers (1980; Albert Kish, NFB)
The Working Class on Film (1975; NFB). On the Griersonian documentary.
Hors d'Oeuvre (1960; Potterton/Verrall/Lipsett; NFB). Animation.
Pot-Pourri (1962; NFB). Animation.
Backlot Canadiana (1975; Peter Rowe). On the Canadian Co-operative Project.
Chambers: Tracks and Gestures (1982; John Walker/Christopher Lowry).

Other Videos Used

Joseph Campbell (with Bill Moyers). *The Power of Myth*, Program Five: *Love and the Goddess*. Mystic Fire Video (Parabola), 1988.
_____. *The World of Joseph Campbell*. Vol. 1, tape 1: *Transformations of Myth through Time*. Public Media Video. 1989.
Home of the Birds. Directed by Blad Hansen.CBC, 1986. (Featured on *The Nature of Things*, David Suzuki). This video shows the ways of gannets.

Selected Periodicals

Cinéaste.
Ciné-Bulles. Review, published since 1980, devoted in large part to cinéma québécois. It is published by L'Association des cinémas parallèles.
Cinefan. Review.
Cinema Canada. Published since 1972. This review is in English.
Cinema/Québec. Periodical (Laval: 1971 forward). Articles cited by authors.
Cinémas: Revue d'études cinématographiques/Journal of Film Studies
CopieZéro. Important review, published since 1979. Also provides bibliographies and abstracts of articles from other journals and of books on films. Published by Cinémathèque Québécoise.
Lumières. Published since 1986. An organ of the Association des réalisateurs et réalisatrices de films du Québec.

Revue de la Cinémathèque, La.

Séquences: Revue de Cinéma. Has Catholic origins, was founded in 1855. Gives reviews of French Canadian films, and films from all parts of the world, for that matter. 4005 Bellechasse; Montréal (Québec) CANADA H1X 2H8.

Spirales. All issues of this review are of importance for the feminist slant the essays and interviews will provide.

24 Images. Review published since 1979; international with focus on cinema from Québec.

Information and Film Sources

Regarding rental of Québec films contact Edu-Québec, Québec Gvt House; 17 West 50th Street; N.Y., NY 10020–2201

CBC WINDSOR

Center for the Study of Canada (SUNY Plattsburgh)

Cinémathèque Québécoise; 335 Blvd de Maisonneuve (East); Montréal PQ H2X 1K1; Tel. 514–842–9763

Ciné-Video (Québec City)

Critic's Choice

Evergreen

Facets

Information re Québec ... Tel. 1–800–363–7777

National Archives of Canada

National Film Board of Canada (N.Y; Montréal)

Periodica Video. Journals, videos, compact discs. C.P. 444; Outremont, Québec CANADA H2V 4R6

Polyglot

Tamarelle's — now not in business

Vedette Visuals. 4520 58th Ave. W., Tacoma, Washington 98466

Vidéoclub (Québec City)

Walden by Mail (La Vergne, TN)

Women Make Movies. 462 Broadway, Suite 501, NY NY 10013

Index

571